Doing Empirical
Political Research

Doing Empirical Political Research

James M. Carlson
Providence College

Mark S. Hyde
Providence College

Houghton Mifflin Company   Boston   New York

From Jim—
To my wife, Harriet, and my daughter, Erica.

From Mark—
To my wife, Patricia, and my daughter, Jennifer.

Editor in Chief: Jean L. Woy
Sponsoring Editor: Katherine Meisenheimer
Assistant Editor: Michael Kerns
Editorial Assistant: Sabrina Abhyankar
Senior Project Editor: Tracy Patruno
Senior Manufacturing Coordinator: Priscilla Bailey
Internet Producer: Scott Diggins
Marketing Manager: Nicola Poser
Marketing Assistant: Laura McGinn

Cover image: © John Still/Photonica

Printed in the U.S.A.

Library of Congress Control Number: 2001133237
ISBN: 0-618-11672-9

1 2 3 4 5 6 7 8 9–EB–06 05 04 03 02

Contents

Part 4   Analyzing and Reporting Results   303

Preface

Not too long ago, during an online discussion about teaching social science research methods, there was a rather lengthy exchange concerning the impact of teaching a "methods" course on the evaluation of faculty. The prevailing view was that student dislike for methods courses was often reflected in negative evaluations of the faculty who taught them. We have been teaching research methods to political science undergraduates for a combined fifty years and appreciate the challenge inherent in that task. We know all too well, as do all our colleagues who teach in this area, that students approach our courses with some trepidation. The anxiety of the students is understandable. Research methods courses, compared to other political science offerings, emphasize conceptual reasoning, skill development, and quantitative analysis more than the mastery of substantive material.

We wrote this book for undergraduate political science majors. Most of our students do not plan to become social scientists, however, so we must work hard to communicate the relevance of a methods course for them. We believe that scholarly research is exciting and that the enthusiasm we feel for the research process can be conveyed to students. In our courses, we have been able to engage students by emphasizing the practicality of the techniques they learn from us and encouraging them to use those techniques to answer questions of interest to them. From surveys of former students, our department has found that many who were initially resistant to learning research methods say the course was the most useful and relevant of their undergraduate careers.

Both our experience and the research on learning tell us that students better understand material and more effectively master skills when they are actively engaged in the learning process. As a result, *Doing Empirical Political Research* reflects the pedagogy we have employed successfully in our classrooms, especially the emphasis on an active learning approach. The book continually gives students the opportunity to practice themselves what the text is preaching, actually doing empirical analysis. It encourages and provides guidance for students to develop their own research questions so they too can experience the excitement of undertaking original research. Along with its varied exercises and activities, the book is intended to build a conceptual understanding and foster basic research skills that are transferable to other courses and an assortment of careers.

Organization

We selected content for the text and Web site based on the students in our classes needing it, using it, and appreciating its relevance for later courses. The text is organized chronologically into four parts in a way that is consistent with the steps in the research process, from problem formation to report writing. However, in Part 1, "Science and Behavior," we give a lot of consideration to the issues of philosophy of science and building blocks of research. Students need to understand that the scientific approach comes with some debatable assumptions and learn that the early stages of research, especially the transition from developing a research question to developing testable hypotheses, are critical to acceptable results.

Within the context of Part 2, "Preparing for Research," we dedicate a chapter (Chapter 4) to building bibliographies and reviewing relevant literature. Much of the important background research that used to take place in the library can now at least be initiated at a computer, since most library catalogs and indexes can be accessed from remote locations, and many journals now provide full text articles online. Students should become familiar with electronic searches for material, be able to evaluate the utility of Web sites, and learn to distinguish academic journals from publications that emphasize news and opinion. In addition, Chapter 5 presents a systematic analysis of reports of social science research alongside a full research paper from the *American Journal of Political Science*. Students need to have at least a preliminary understanding of previous research before beginning a process of hypothesis development.

Part 3, "Data Collection," guides students through the steps of gathering and managing data in their research process. In Chapter 8 we introduce students to SPSS, one of the most widely used statistical programs. This early introduction frames the discussion of data organization and analysis in a way that students with access to SPSS are likely to find most useful. At the same time, instructors using other software can easily adapt our SPSS-related examples and exercises to their statistical packages. In addition to the data-collection techniques usually included in research methods texts, such as survey research, aggregate data, and content analysis, we also include a chapter (Chapter 12) on experimentation and intensive techniques.

Part 4, "Analyzing and Reporting Results," introduces students to some basic approaches to data analysis and acceptable practices for reporting the findings of an empirical political research project. While more sophisticated techniques should wait for a course specifically on statistics or data analysis, students should understand how to communicate large amounts of information in the most efficient way. Finally, the book closes with several appendixes to serve as additional resources: a short guide to avoiding plagiarism, and tables of random numbers and the critical values of chi square, t and F.

Features

There are many ways this text and the accompanying Web site facilitate learning and make the development of research skills more pertinent to students. We have designed the pedagogy in *Doing Empirical Political Research* to reflect our teaching practices—emphasizing active learning and engaging students by showing them the usefulness of social science skills. This dynamic approach takes form in a wide variety of interactive exercises for use both inside and outside the context of the classroom. For example, as early as the second chapter, we employ an exercise in which students actually engage in data analysis. Throughout the book, we encourage the use of the Internet for accessing materials relevant to research (from libraries, data archives, and so on) and for communicating with instructors and fellow students. In keeping with that goal, every chapter has at least one "To the Web" box tied to specific in-text discussions. This feature sends students to the textbook Web site (**politicalscience.college.hmco.com/students** and then click Carlson/Hyde), where they can either complete exercises—many using SPSS—that reinforce skills outlined in the chapter or link with supplementary material on the Web.

Each chapter is tailored to well-known principles of learning that help students comprehend and review the material, beginning with a clear statement of learning objectives and ending with a conclusion and a summary of the main points. In addition to the "To the Web" boxes, each chapter has two additional types of text boxes keyed specifically to content. "Questions for Thought and Discussion" boxes provide a starting point for students to study alone or discuss with others in the context of a small group, the entire class, or an online forum facilitated by a course management system such as Blackboard, WEBCT, or Angel. "Key Points" boxes highlight important material within individual chapters, providing an easy way for students to summarize what they have just read. New terms introduced and boldfaced in the text are listed at the end of chapters and compiled in the Glossary. We have also provided a selection of readings appropriate for expanding on each chapter's material. At the end of each chapter we further emphasize an active approach through activities to be completed outside of class, designed to help with evaluating how well students have met the chapter learning objectives. After Chapter 8, where we introduce data organization, many of these activities send students to SPSS to complete the assignment.

The student Web page accompanying this text is not an afterthought but an integral part of our approach. The site has interactive exercises and numerous links to sites that facilitate learning, both tied to specific chapter discussions through the "To the Web" boxes. To access the Web site, go to **politicalscience.college.hmco.com/students** and click Carlson/Hyde. Many of the exercises and chapter activities make use of the five downloadable data sets that we have compiled. "GSS2000depr" has 342 variables from the 2000 General Social Survey, while "NES2000depr" has 154 variables from the 2000 National Election Study. "HOUSE106depr" has information on 39 variables for all 435 members of the U.S. House of Representatives elected in 1998. "STATESdepr" has information on 153 variables for the American states, and "COUNTRIESdepr" has information on 79 variables for 208 countries.

A further resource available on the Web site for students is a series of Java-based modules designed to help students visualize the concepts behind basic statistical analysis.

Topics covered in this section include sampling, distribution curves, percentage tables, regression lines, and t-tests. In addition, the student Web site has the learning objectives for each chapter, practice quizzes, chapter outlines, and all of the end-of-chapter activities in a format that allows students to e-mail their completed assignments to their instructors. The instructor Web site (**politicalscience.college.hmco.com/instructors**) includes answers for activities and exercises where appropriate.

Acknowledgments

Many people have helped with this text and deserve recognition and thanks. At Houghton Mifflin, Melissa Mashburn, who has moved on to another job, initially saw the potential of this undertaking. Michael Kerns, Assistant Editor, and Katherine Meisenheimer, now Sponsoring Editor, were responsible for overseeing the project at different times and both provided us with direction and encouragement. Thanks to Tracy Patruno, Production Project Editor, and Nicola Poser, the Political Science Marketing Manager, for their help. Debbie Prato served as our copy editor and Nancy Benjamin of Books By Design oversaw the actual production; we appreciate their assistance. In addition, Mary Dougherty and Jean Woy at Houghton Mifflin have both been supportive. At Providence College, four of our faculty colleagues provided assistance. Michael Spiegler advised us generally on publishing a college text; Joe Cammarano provided some useful suggestions for Web page content and student exercises; Rick Lavoie read early drafts of the quantitative chapters; and Bob Trudeau, our department chair and former director of the college's Center for Teaching Excellence, read the entire manuscript and provided many constructive comments on pedagogy.

The reviews of political science colleagues commissioned by Houghton Mifflin also made this a better text. They included Steven J. Balla, George Washington University; Lorraine Bernotsky, West Chester University; Rebecca E. Deen, University of Texas at Arlington; Michelle Anne Fistek, Plymouth State College; Christopher Gilbert, Gustavus Adolphus College; Rodger M. Govea, Cleveland State University; Mark R. Joslyn, University of Kansas; Richard LeGates, San Francisco State University; Melissa J. Marschall, University of Illinois at Chicago; Barbara Norrander, University of Arizona; J. Michael Thomson, Northern Kentucky University; Ming Wan, George Mason University; Peter W. Wielhouwer, Regent University; and J. Oliver Williams, North Carolina State University. Thanks to Providence College students Amber Sarno, Kelly Elam, and Katie Buckley, who worked at various times as our research assistants. We extend a very special thanks to Providence College student Brianne Brady, who did a lot of the hard work creating the data sets, as well as helping set up many of the tables and figures in the text. She also worked as our research assistant for an entire summer. And we must recognize all those Providence students who enrolled in our research methods course over the years. They are the ones who helped us learn how to teach research methods to undergraduates. Finally, we would like to acknowledge some of our mentors who stimulated our interest both in teaching and in empirical political science: Dickinson McGaw and George Watson of Arizona State University, John Gargan and Steven Brown of Kent State University, the late Robert Gaudino of Williams College, and Richard Hofferbert, formerly of Williams College and now at SUNY–Binghamton.

James M. Carlson
Mark S. Hyde

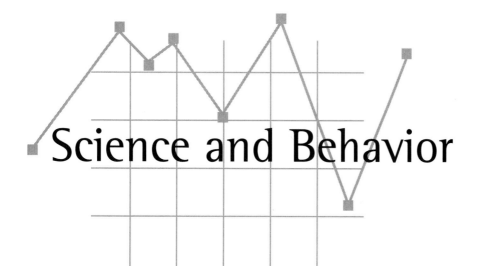

Science and Behavior

Chapter 1

How Do We Know What's True?

Learning Objectives

After completion of this chapter, students should be able to do the following:

Distinguish among different methods of knowing about the world: investment, authority, logic, faith, and science.

Understand the rationale for using science as the basis for learning about political behavior.

Understand that, in scientific terms, truth is tentative.

Recognize the boundaries and limits of science for knowing about the world in general and for studying human behavior in particular.

Asking and Answering Questions About Politics

This book helps you learn how to ask and answer questions about political behavior. More specifically, after reading this book, you should be able to develop your own questions about politics and learn how to answer them, guided by the scientific method. This type of inquiry is called **empirical political analysis.** *Empirical* refers to information received through the senses—observed evidence—so empirical political research consists of using the scientific method to test one's ideas about politics by collecting and analyzing information. This process involves understanding the nature of scientific inquiry, mastering how to apply the scientific method to the study of human behavior, and grasping how to analyze and interpret data about politics.

We are applying the scientific method to the study of political behavior because we believe this method provides the most reliable and valid knowledge about politics and political behavior—of people, groups, institutions, governments, or nations. By carefully gathering and analyzing data about political behavior, we can produce knowledge about politics that will be accepted by all impartial observers. The scientific method, however, does have boundaries and limits, and it is not the basis for answering all questions about politics. Questions are limited to those that can be answered by gathering information and not, for example, those that are based on values. We will discuss the boundaries and limits of the scientific method, including the differences between fact-based and value-based questions, later in this chapter.

To fully understand why we choose to be empiricists, why we employ the scientific method to study political behavior, we must consider the more general questions: "How do people know what they know?" and "How do we know what's true?" There are several answers to these questions, but only one is "Through science." Let's consider some of the alternative answers to this question so that you can begin to understand what the process of the scientific study of political behavior is all about. Specifically, to the question "How do we know what we know?" we will consider five alternative responses: **investment, authority, logic, faith,** and **science.** [1] While each is a separate way of knowing about the world around us, they ultimately all play a role in the scientific method.

▓ Investment

This method of knowing has to do with people believing something simply because they have *always,* without question, accepted it as true or, alternatively, because they have invested a lot of time, money, or other resources in that particular belief. For many years people accepted the notion that the earth was flat and that the sun revolved around the earth, and it is easy to understand why. Both of these convictions were consistent with what people observed, and they posed no problems for individuals in their daily lives. While the land on which they walked might have hills and valleys, or even mountains and deep ravines, these were perceived to be small discrepancies upon an otherwise flat plane. And does it not still seem to the human eye that the sun revolves around the earth and not vice versa? When you spend a day at the beach, you see the sun move slowly across the sky, while the sand beneath you, your beach chairs, and you all stay in the same place. And at the end of the day, you observe a colorful "sunset." The sun is not setting, or moving at all; the earth is turning. People speak to one another, however, as if what we see is actually true. In this case, rather than describing the beautiful "earth-turn" at the end of a day at the beach, they use the less descriptive but certainly more accepted term of *sunset.* When Copernicus first suggested that the earth revolved around the sun, people were understandably resistant to this new idea because it ran counter to longheld beliefs and defied what people could see with their own eyes. While most people now accept that the earth moves around the sun, there are other ideas to which people cling tenaciously because they are central to how individuals think about themselves and the (sometimes small) world in which they spend their days.

Social psychologist Leon Festinger and his colleagues were some of the first people to consider systematically that people held certain beliefs because they had so much invested in them. [2] In the 1950s, they and their graduate students studied a California cult that was predicting the end of the world. The members of the cult believed that only they would survive the apocalypse because a spaceship was going to whisk them away just before the world ended. The cult members spoke publicly about their predictions and arranged their lives in preparation for the coming disaster. Of course, the world did not end, but Festinger found that the failed prophecy did not dissuade cult members from their basic beliefs and commitment to the group. In fact, members initially believed even *more strongly* in the cult after the prediction of doom was factually determined to be incorrect. Festinger reasoned that the cult members' strong personal investment in the group and public commitment to the group's belief system overrode their directly experiencing the fallibility of the group's views. They could not bring themselves to believe the group was wrong. They had invested so much of themselves in the cult's belief system that they even rejected "facts."

Probably not many college students who study empirical analysis, or professors who teach it, are members of a cult, so how do these research findings apply to you? Let's consider as an example your political beliefs or attitudes and the candidates you support. Most people assume that their support for one political candidate or another is based on the similarity of the candidate's political views and policy positions to their own. An individual citizen may share the same general political ideology as the candidate or the same positions on issues such as health care or national defense. Agreement with the candidate on political views leads the citizen to support that candidate by casting a vote for him or her, making a monetary contribution to the candidate's campaign, or providing some other desired resource. But there is another compelling explanation for why these citizens, and you, might support one candidate over another.

These people may have voted for the candidate in the past and told friends and coworkers about it. In addition, they may have urged acquaintances to vote for the candidate, contributed money to a past campaign, organized a fundraiser, or worked for the campaign as a volunteer. All of these behaviors constitute a personal investment in that candidate on the part of the citizen. After the citizen invests that time, effort, or money, and recognizing that he or she has publicly identified with the candidate, the citizen may adjust his or her beliefs on any newly developing or changing issues to the candidate's beliefs to confirm that commitment of resources. Disagreeing with the candidate one has supported in the past on an important issue is tantamount to admitting that the time, money, and effort invested was misdirected. Prior support cannot be taken back—that is, past behavior cannot be changed—so the voter changes his or her attitude to agree with that of the candidate.

Any situation that is difficult or impossible to change is generally accompanied by an attitude adjustment designed to make the individual more comfortable. So you must be careful in these situations. When you accept something as "true" or "known," you must be sure that you are not just convincing yourself that it is so, for whatever reason, because you *want* to believe it. When it comes to doing empirical political research, you must guard against commitment to a particular approach just because it always has been done that way or believing too strongly in your own findings due to the considerable time and effort required for completing your research.

■ Authority

By the way, after a day on the beach, how do you know that the sun does not revolve around the earth as it certainly appears to? You probably know because someone told you—someone you considered an authority on the subject, like one of your elementary school teachers. That teacher probably showed you a diagram of the solar system and explained that because the earth spins on an axis, the sun only *appears* to go around the earth. Knowledge from an authoritative source is the most common method by which people know things, and much information is effectively passed from one individual to another by the method of authority.

By reading this book, you are participating in the process of knowing through authority. You will likely accept most of what you read here because your instructor (an authority) has chosen the book, a reputable company has published it, and the qualifications and backgrounds of the authors who wrote it are available for perusal—all indicating that the book is a credible source of information. Your college library is full of books and articles written by authorities in a wide variety of areas, and you likely rely on them for many of your term papers. These secondary sources in the library provide information and analysis that you can summarize and blend into your own thinking for constructing your term papers.

Parents, other family members, and friends were likely your first authoritative sources, followed by teachers. And while the information and advice provided by your parents was surely helpful and usually correct, that wisdom offered by your older siblings, cousins, or friends may have turned out to be a bit shaky. (Of course, your teachers—especially your college instructors—are *always* right!) Eventually, secondary sources such as books, newspapers, television, and, more recently, the Internet become sources of information for both adults and youngsters. But you need to ask how authoritative these sources, both primary and secondary, actually are. Where did these sources get their information? Only when you can be assured that the knowledge was developed or gathered in a reliable way will you be confident about accepting authoritative sources as "true." That is why, as we will see, the results of empirical studies include the methods used as well as the conclusions reached so the reader can decide for him- or herself if the results are valid.

▓ Logic

A third way of "knowing" is logic, and one of the criteria to apply to knowledge from authoritative sources is whether it meets the test of logic. When information is put forward based on a presentation that is "agreeable to reason," it generally means that the argument is internally coherent and violates no logical premise. Under those conditions, you tend to accept the knowledge because it "stands to reason" that the information is correct. But methods of knowing that "agree with reason"—that is, logic—may not necessarily agree with experience—that is, empirical evidence.

For example, economist Kenneth Arrow points out that a logical prediction of how a group of people will make a collective decision about alternatives presented to them may be different from how the group actually behaves. [3] Assume that there are three people who are voting on some issue, perhaps which health care plan their small, three-person company will join. The group must choose one of three health plans. Majority rule will prevail, and each voter has the following preferences.

- Person #1 ranks plan A first, B second, and C third.
- Person #2 ranks B first, C second, and A third.
- Person #3 ranks C first, A second, and B third.

The only rule we impose on the situation is that if any person prefers, for example, A to B and B to C, they will logically prefer A to C. It only stands to reason that if a person prefers, for example, chocolate ice cream to vanilla and prefers vanilla to strawberry, she will prefer chocolate to strawberry ice cream.

A call for a simple majority vote will produce a tie on which health care plan to choose. Each plan will get one vote: plan A from Person #1, plan B from Person #2, and plan C from Person #3. To avoid this conundrum, let's figure out logically which plan the group prefers by choosing between two alternatives at a time rather than all three at once, remembering our commitment to majority rule. Let's start by figuring out logically whether the group prefers plan A or plan C. A majority of the group, persons #1 and #3, prefer plan A to plan B. And a majority of the group, persons #1 and #2, prefer plan B to Plan C. It is now clear that we have a majority of the group that prefers A to B and a majority that prefers B to C, so consistent with the logical rule stated above, a majority of the group must then prefer A to C. Among these two alternatives, A or C, the group would logically choose A (see Figure 1.1).

Figure 1.1
Arrow's Paradox: A Discrepancy Between Logic and Behavior

Group of Three Must Use Majority Rule to Choose Between Alternative A and Alternative C

Individual Preferences for Alternatives A, B, or C
- Person #1   A preferred to B preferred to C
- Person #2   B preferred to C preferred to A
- Person #3   C preferred to A preferred to B

Logical Choice of Alternative A Versus Alternative C
- A majority prefers A to B (Person #1 and Person #3).
- A majority prefers B to C (Person #1 and Person #2).

Logically, if a majority prefers A to B and B to C, then **a majority prefers A to C.**

Behavioral Choice of Alternative A Versus Alternative C
- Person #1 votes for A rather than C.
- Person #2 votes for C rather than A.
- Person #3 votes for C rather than A.

Behaviorally, two persons (Person #2 and Person #3) choose C, one person (#1) chooses A, and so **a majority prefers C to A.**

Logic indicates a majority prefers A to C. Behavior indicates a majority prefers C to A.

However, let's see what would happen if the members of the group were allowed to vote on the choice between A and C. Given their stated preferences, Person #1 would vote for plan A, but both Persons #2 and #3 would vote for plan C, thus giving plan C a 2-1 victory—just the *opposite* of our logical deduction. The result of the group vote between alternatives A and C is the exact reverse of what was logically predicted. While the discussion of what is called "Arrow's Paradox" could continue for some time, the basic point has been made: Logic will not always lead you to knowledge that stands up to experience.

Another problem with knowing things by the method of logic occurs when people present conclusions that seem equally logical or acceptable. One might ask, "Why do some people vote in elections and others do not?" At least two reasonable, but conflicting, explanations of why people do not vote in elections can be presented. One rationale argues that people who do not vote, compared to those who do, are more content with the political system. Feeling things are going well and content with their circumstances, they do not bother to vote. The other explanation says that people who do not vote are *less* satisfied with the political system than those who do vote. The nonvoting citizens may be unhappy with the candidates running, sick of politics as usual, or completely alienated from the political system—resulting in a boycott of the electoral process. A reasonably logical case could be made for each of these two contradictory explanations, and the only way to determine which logical explanation is more correct is to collect information about people's attitudes toward the political system—that is, carry out an empirical study. You will find lots of empirical research in political science that attempts to sort out competing explanations for the same observed behavior, such as voting. So from the empiricist's point of view, logic is a good starting point from which to generate questions. Clearly you do not want to base a study on obviously illogical premises, but logic is not enough. You need to test your logic against experience.

▪ Faith

Faith is yet another method of knowing. In one sense, faith is similar to the method of authority, in that people are willing to accept at face value what someone tells them. But in another sense, faith is about knowing things outside of logic, experience, or other traditional methods of knowing. Most religions are faith-based—that is, members accept the principles of the religious doctrine without expectation of outside verification. Among Christians, for example, the divinity of Jesus Christ is accepted as a matter of faith. It is a basic belief of the religion, and Christians do not seek to verify this belief beyond the boundaries of this system of thought. While the New Testament of the Bible, which outlines the basic doctrine of Christian beliefs, reports the working of miracles to verify the contention of Christ's divinity, practicing Christians generally reject the idea that some type of experiential "proof" is necessary to accept as true the divinity of Christ. While knowing something through faith may seem at first thought to be a long way from knowing things through science, we will argue later that science, as well, has an element of faith to it.

Questions for Thought and Discussion

Sometimes faith-based and science-based knowledge conflict in the public arena. Some school districts in the United States, for example, have tried to include in their science curriculum both creationism, the idea that a deity created humans uniquely, and evolution, the theory that humans evolved from other life forms, resulting in political clashes between groups holding these two views. Do you believe that some faith-based beliefs and scientific findings are incompatible? If so, why? If not, why not?

Science

Science is an activity, something that people do, a way by which people learn about the world. From our perspective, science is *not* a set of facts that individuals rely on to know about the world. The body of knowledge produced by scientists is important in and of itself, of course, but it is more interesting to us as the basis for further scientific inquiry. [4] It is the activity of inquiry, a specific type of inquiry, that we label science. It is a method that involves developing theories, conjecturing about relations among variables based on those theories, and collecting empirical data to confirm or reject our hypothetical statements about the world around us. The purpose is to describe, explain, and predict natural phenomena; as social scientists, the phenomenon about which we inquire is human behavior. The goal of this book is to help you learn how to carry out that activity we call science in order to describe and explain political behavior. The description of exactly how one carries out this process begins in Chapter 2.

Interestingly enough, the activity called science involves elements from several different methods of knowing about the world. The existing body of scientific knowledge—the scientific literature that reports the knowledge in a field—is accepted as an *authoritative* source and provides one of the springboards from which new research is developed. The other springboard for research is theory, from which one can *logically* derive the ideas about politics that are tested with empirical evidence. And scientists do have *faith* in the scientific method itself.

Yet, science does have some advantages over other ways of knowing about the world and does not succumb to the obvious pitfalls previously discussed. It is more self-correcting: There are built-in checks throughout the inquiry with the goal of attaining dependable knowledge outside of the individual person who generated it. For example, any procedures employed during a scientific inquiry must be fully revealed and open to public inspection by other researchers, and, as we will point out in Chapter 6, alternative explanations for the findings must be considered before coming to any conclusions. Science will accept the statements of authorities, including other scientists, only if the methods employed in the search for knowledge are subject to scrutiny by scientific peers. And scientific work is reviewed from the perspective of safeguarding against researchers being, albeit unintentionally, too committed to their own approaches or too anxious to conform to anticipated findings—the *investment* problem we just discussed. Science accepts the principles of logic and tries not to violate any of its basic precepts, but science also

To the Web

Exercise 1.1   Distinguishing Sources of Knowledge

This exercise asks you to think about how you look at and have come to know about the world. Using concepts introduced in this chapter and supplying your own examples will help you more fully understand new ideas that we have discussed. Go to the **DEPR Web Page,*** click on **Web Exercises, Chapter 1,** then on **Distinguishing Sources of Knowledge.**

*The Web page for this text can be found by going to *www.politicalscience.college.hmco.com/students* and selecting Carlson/Hyde. The site contains all of the Web links and exercises from the "To the Web" boxes as well as numerous other learning resources.

demands that ideas about how the world works, including how people behave, be tested against experience with empirical evidence as well.

Key Points

Knowledge achieved by differing methods:

- Investment—knowledge based on personal stake in an idea
- Authority—knowledge provided by a trustworthy or convincing source
- Logic—knowledge derived from an internally coherent, rational argument
- Faith—knowledge accepted without expectation of outside verification
- Science—knowledge arising from a self-correcting method of inquiry and empirical evidence

The Boundaries and Limits of Science

Science has great value as a method for learning about politics and political behavior, and it has advantages over the other methods of knowing that we have discussed. But science has its limitations as well. If you are to more fully understand the basis of empirical political research, you should be familiar with the limitations of science as well as its strengths.

Tentative Truth

First, even at its best, science does not produce knowledge that is universally accepted as "true," even among scientists. What is scientifically "true" at one point—for example, the smallest particle of matter in the physical universe—may not be so at another time. The best description and explanation of a physical phenomenon that science can produce may later be replaced by a better description made possible by improved technology (in the case of physics, a new particle collider) or a different explanation based on a new theory (for physics, string theory). In the social sciences, the development of survey research based on scientific sampling procedures (improved technology) led political scientists to a new understanding of the nature of public opinion.

In a sense, science does not even try to label findings as "true." Individual scientists publicly report the results of their inquiries, accompanied by the theory and methods on which the work was based, for others to consider and hopefully improve upon. As long as the findings are not successfully challenged by new research, they are accepted as the best explanation of how the world works that is consistent with experience. New research may ultimately produce more accurate descriptions and fuller or better explanations, which then become the new standard for understanding how the world works. Scientists offer their conclusions as the best description and explanation of some phenomenon in which they are interested, but rarely do they claim that they have discovered "the truth."

▥ Fact-Based Versus Value-Based Questions

Second, science answers only fact-based, not value-based, questions. Empirical political analysts limit their inquiries to matters of *description* and *explanation,* avoiding statements that recommend or prescribe one behavior over another. Because empiricism rests on gathering data based on the senses, it is indeed fact, rather than value, based. For example, the **descriptive question** "Who votes in elections?" is an **empirical question** within the boundaries of scientific inquiry. The question can be answered by gathering information and summarizing the results. Other examples of descriptive questions, those that can be answered by collecting data, include "How many countries belong to the North Atlantic Treaty Organization?," "Which states have the death penalty?," and "What proportion of their budgets do cities spend on education?"

Explanatory questions are more common than descriptive inquiries in political science because ultimately political scientists are more interested in explaining political behavior through testing theories than simply describing events. When discussing logic as a method of knowing, we asked the question "Why do some people vote in elections and others do not?" and suggested that there was more than one logical answer. This is an example of an *explanatory* question, asking *why* people behave the way they do, and it follows reasonably from the prior descriptive question "Who votes?" Similarly, after answering the descriptive question about which states have the death penalty, an empirical political analyst would quickly move to ask why those states with the death penalty had adopted it, whereas those without it had not. To answer this explanatory question, one might start by gathering information to determine how the states with and without the death penalty are different from each other. This topic of descriptive and explanatory questions will be examined in more detail in Chapter 2.

On the other hand, those questions involving values—for example, "*Should* people vote in an election?" or "*Should* the death penalty be abolished in the United States?"—are considered outside the boundaries of empirical political analysis because they cannot be satisfactorily answered by gathering information. Such value questions, also called **normative questions,** are extremely important in the discussion of politics and often underlie empirical research, but they are not the direct focus of empirical work. People often hold strong views on matters of right and wrong, and these views become the basis for positions on public policy. For example, people certainly differ on whether the death penalty *should* be used as punishment for certain types of crimes. This is a normative debate, with various positions on the issue reflecting the values of individuals involved in the discussion. Normative and empirical questions are often closely intertwined, and empirical political analysts frequently play an important role in such debates by conducting studies about fact-based questions surrounding the issue.

To continue with this example, some proponents of the death penalty base their decision, in part, on its deterrent effect. Severe punishment, they argue, will dissuade others from committing those crimes for which violators have been executed. An empiricist could design a study that compared rates of particular types of crimes in states with and without the death penalty to try to determine if capital punishment is in fact a deterrent. The results of this empirical inquiry would have important consequences for the normative discussion and public policy question of whether states should employ the death penalty. In Chapter 3, you will learn more about the intersection of normative and empirical questions and how they can be untangled from one another.

Recursive Behavior

Social, as opposed to physical, scientists have additional problems in using the scientific method to determine what is true. Earl Babbie states, "Society is a recursive phenomenon: We engage in the same business over and over, day in and day out." [5] What people do today is affected by what they did yesterday, and what they will do tomorrow is affected by what they are doing today *and* did yesterday, and so on. For example, in order to determine citizens' preferences for presidential candidates, political scientists might conduct a poll and report what percentage of the electorate supports each candidate. But the results of that poll may influence the preferences of citizens when the next poll is conducted or when the election is held—the so-called bandwagon effect. Candidates who do well in the poll will be more attractive to undecided voters or to those who have only a weak commitment to another candidate. At the same time, candidates who do *not* show well in the poll may be perceived as having no chance of being elected and may well lose what few supporters they had. So our attempts to describe and explain voting behavior may in fact change the very behavior we are trying to study. This is a constant challenge to those who attempt empirical political research by applying the scientific method to the study of human behavior.

◼ Assessing Objective Reality

A fourth, and even more fundamental, problem for empirical political science in determining the "truth" revolves around the question of whether an individual can ever really assess an objective reality. As we discussed previously, science is based on empiricism, evidence obtained through the senses. But does a person's sensory observations actually reflect a physical or social reality that exists independent of and apart from the individual making the observations? The short answer is "We don't know." This is a problem of objectivity/subjectivity.

People generally assume that their senses are relaying a fairly accurate representation of the world around us—that is, they can objectively perceive their surroundings. A second interpretation is that everything experienced by individuals may simply be all in their minds, for there is no way to determine independently if their senses are reflecting something outside of them. Reality is solely a subjective experience. A third alternative suggests that reality is a function of the interaction of the subject and the object, meaning that sensory observations do indeed reflect a social and physical world around individuals but that each person's reality, depending on his or her orientation to the world, may be unique. The latter two options are a problem for social science because all impartial observers must agree on the findings of empirical research.

The solution to this dilemma is for social scientists to limit their work to phenomena observable through the senses and to take great care that agreement exists among observers as to what they are perceiving. This does not mean agreement on the existence of an objective world—only that empirical political scientists have accepted an **intersubjective agreement** (an agreement among observers) about what constitutes reality. In the actual practice of empirical political research, this agreement becomes crucial when one begins to collect political information from "the real world." How one moves from the abstract level of thinking about the world around him or her to actually collecting data is covered in general terms in Chapter 2 and more specifically in Chapter 7.

If empirical political scientists accept reality as an intersubjective agreement among themselves, does that mean individual personal values are somehow injected into the research process? If so, how does that square with science being "value free"? Personal values *do* enter the research process, but they are largely confined to the front end, to one's choice of substantive topic. What an individual researcher ultimately chooses to study, whether it be the U.S. Congress, international relations in the Middle East, political communication, is a personal choice reflecting the values of that person.

There is no way to avoid this intrusion of values into the research process. Once the topic has been chosen and the research begins, however, every caution is taken, every safeguard is put in place, so that the conclusions drawn from the work are independent of the person conducting the research and replicable by anyone following the same set of scientific procedures.

■ Free Will Versus Determinism

Another matter of more concern for social rather than physical scientists is the question of free will versus determinism. Do individuals make free choices about their behavior, or is their behavioral pattern determined by their previous social experiences? As you try to explain political behavior, the answer to the question will have important ramifications about how you conduct your work. Most empirical political scientists accept that individuals do have a free will and choose the behavior in which they will engage but that their life experiences make some choices much more likely than others. That is, social scientists assume individuals live in a probabilistic world. At any moment, a person has virtually an infinite number of alternative behaviors from which to choose, and the social scientist's job is to determine the probability of choosing each alternative based on that individual's background and present situation. As you read this book, for example, you have a whole host of choices: You can sing "Happy Birthday," ask the person next to you about the weather, call your parents, fall asleep, scratch your head, and so on, but the choice is yours. Most likely (a probabilistic statement), you will continue to read for a while longer, at least until you finish this sentence. Our prediction is based on the premise that people are unlikely, because of past experiences, to stop reading in the middle of a sentence. Everyone *could* stop reading in midsentence, and some *might* do that, but most *probably* will not.

Some empiricists believe that behavior is completely deterministic: One specific behavior will always occur. They believe that if social scientists know enough about the individual and the immediate situation, they could predict a person's behavior correctly every time. However, either because people really do choose or because the data or methods for studying behavior are incomplete, empirical political scientists are limited to assigning greater or lesser probabilities to the person's choices rather than predicting exact outcomes. But that does not change the goal of trying to explain all behavior, even if those efforts are rarely 100 percent successful.

To the Web

Epistemology and Philosophy of Social Science

The area of philosophy concerned with how individuals come to know what they know is called *epistemology*. Political scientists and, more generally, social scientists raise epistemological issues in the context of what is called the philosophy of social science. Go to the **DEPR Web Page**, click on **Web Links, Chapter 1**, then on **Epistemology, the Theory of Knowledge** and **Philosophy of Social Science**.

Key Points

Concerns when employing the scientific method to study behavior:

- Tentative nature of scientific truth
- Inquiry limited to empirical questions
- Recursive nature of human behavior
- The intrusion of personal values into empirical research
- Disagreement about the existence and nature of objective reality

Conclusion

Ultimately, you don't have to worry so much about finding the truth as simply trying to explain political behavior as best you can, which means employing the approach, methods, and tools of science. And while the tools of science are not appropriate for answering *all* the questions you might pose about politics, we have tried to make the case that this approach is at least more satisfactory than other available alternatives for describing and explaining political behavior. As Earl Babbie says, researchers would do better "to settle for the thrill of discovery than to worry about whether what we've discovered is the ultimate truth or simply a new and currently useful way of viewing things." [6] As a scientist, you will always be open to research that offers competing explanations or to fresh findings that may reveal yet another way of viewing things.

This book is our attempt to help you learn how to apply the scientific method to the study of political behavior, with an emphasis on having you actually doing hands-on empirical research. Chapter 2 is an explicit description of the scientific approach to understanding politics. In Chapters 3 through 5 you will learn how to find and review previous research in political science as the basis for generating your own research topic. Chapter 6 focuses on questions of causality in trying to explain behavior. Chapter 7 explains how empiricists move from the environment of abstraction, generating theories and ideas, to the domain of observation, gathering empirical information. Data collection and management are covered in Chapters 8 through 12, with data analysis found in Chapters 13 through 17. Chapter 18 explains how to best communicate your research findings to others.

Summary of the Main Points

- Investment, authority, logic, faith, and science are the different methods that people use to know about the world.
- Empirical political scientists rely primarily upon science to describe and explain human behavior.
- Knowledge obtained by use of the scientific method is fact rather than value based and not absolutely but, instead, tentatively true.
- Special difficulties associated with studying human behavior scientifically are the recursive nature of that behavior, agreement on an objective reality, and the intrusion of personal values into empirical research.

Terms Introduced

authority
descriptive question
empirical (fact-based) question
empirical political analysis
explanatory question
faith

intersubjective agreement
investment
logic
normative (value-based) question
science

Selected Readings

Brown, Harold I. *Observation and Objectivity.* New York: Oxford University Press, 1987.
Cole, Stephen. *Making Science: Between Nature and Society.* Cambridge, MA: Harvard University Press, 1992.
Faust, David. *The Limits of Scientific Reasoning.* Minneapolis: University of Minnesota Press, 1984.
Newton-Smith, W. H. *The Rationality of Science.* Boston: Routledge and Kegan Paul, 1981.
Pirsig, Robert. *Zen and the Art of Motorcycle Maintenance.* New York: Bantam Books, 1974.
Skinner, B. F. *Beyond Freedom and Dignity.* New York: Alfred A. Knopf, 1971.

Activities

Activity 1.1
Knowledge and Attitudes

The *Atlanta Journal-Constitution* newspaper reported some research about the death penalty in March 2002. [7] Researchers from the Emory University School of Law, based on an analysis of every county in the United States from 1977 to 1996, concluded that executions were a deterrent to the crime of murder. Their conservative estimate was that every execution deterred an average of eighteen murders.

Find five people you know who oppose the death penalty, and tell them about these research findings. Ask them how and why this information affects their opposition, and write down a description of their reactions. Do they hold fast to the attitude, regardless of this information? If so, why? If not, why not?

Activity 1.2
Empirically Based Scientific Knowledge

Answer each question with a short essay based on material in this chapter.

1. What was considered true 100 years ago that is not true now? What do you think is considered true now that will not be in another 100 years, and why do you think that?
2. Do you believe in ghosts? Why or why not? Could the scientific method be employed to determine if ghosts exist? Why or why not?
3. The issue of subjectivity/objectivity leads to interesting questions about how people perceive the world. Can you be sure all people see the world in identical terms? For example, is it possible that people actually see colors differently? Can you determine that what another person sees and calls red is in fact the same color you see and call red? Perhaps the other person is seeing what you call blue, but because it was always labeled by his or her parents (who see the world as you do) as red, he or she is seeing blue but calling it red. Are differences in perceptions of the world, such as this color example, possible?

Chapter 2

Using the Scientific Method in Political Science

Learning Objectives

After completion of this chapter, students should be able to do the following:

Describe the characteristics of scientific knowledge.

Describe some errors that often result from personal human inquiry.

Distinguish between description and explanation.

Summarize the basic assumptions of social science.

Describe the general steps in the process of conducting a social scientific study.

We Are All Scientists

We often think of science as a body of knowledge about a particular topic, but more correctly it is an activity; science is something we do. More specifically, science is a method of acquiring knowledge in which reason is applied to careful observations. We all are naive scientists but are generally unaware of it. We engage in the activity of gathering information with our senses (empiricism) and making reasoned inferences (rationalism) regarding that information.

Acquiring knowledge scientifically may, indeed, be a natural process. For example, young children are probably not born with the knowledge of how to open doors by first turning a doorknob, but they use their sense of sight to observe others opening doors and eventually try it for themselves. When they see a door they have never seen before, they can make the logical inference that it is similar to the other doors they have encountered that opened by using a doorknob. Over time, a series of generalizations about objects in the world, such as doors, and useful behaviors regarding those objects, such as opening doors, are developed. None of us could function in the world without a storehouse of such generalizations about how the world works, and ultimately, science is a process with the goal of building a set of useful generalizations.

Adults, and sometimes children, use a naive scientific approach to gather information about politics. A citizen may learn by viewing television news, for example, that one candidate for the U.S. Senate is a conservative and another is a liberal. Using generalizations developed earlier in life, the citizen may infer that the liberal candidate is a Democrat and the conservative a Republican. Other inferences can be made using the cue of candidate ideology. Given the knowledge that a candidate is a conservative, a citizen may infer that he or she is pro-life, pro-military, and supports economic growth over protecting the environment. The child and the prospective voter may end up arriving at incorrect generalizations; not all doors are opened by using doorknobs, not all liberals are Democrats, and not all conservatives are Republicans. Not all conservatives are pro-life or uncritical of the military.

That we all are capable of observing phenomena and reasoning about what we perceive does not make us scientists in the formal sense of the term. Sociologist Earl Babbie calls this naive scientific approach to the world "personal human inquiry" and points to the many errors that can result. [1] First, our senses may not be perfectly reliable, resulting in *inaccurate observations.* As observers, most people are not very careful. It is common in politics for citizens to misperceive ideological positions of candidates. These mistakes are easily made, given the ambiguity and quantity of political information, as well as other "noise." Care and attentiveness are necessary for obtaining accurate information.

Second, people also have a tendency to *overgeneralize,* a problem of accurate rational inference. As one example, people who watch television cannot help but notice that a very large amount of news time is given to reporting violent crime. [2] It would seem reasonable to conclude that the violent crime rate in the country is very high and increasing, but this is an instance of overgeneralizing as a result of a lack of representativeness of information. The fact is that the amount of time given to crime on television news has been increasing despite the fact that the rate of violent crimes has been decreasing in the United States. This overgeneralization from the news would be remedied by increased attention to the representativeness of observations. A third illustration of error in personal human inquiry related to overgeneralization is *selective observation.* Once an individual arrives at a generalization about a pattern of events, he or she may choose to observe only those events that are consistent with current understanding. If a political observer believes that all conservatives are Republicans, then there may be a tendency to ignore examples of conservatives who are Democrats.

We could list many other instances of errors that everyone makes in the process of acting as naive scientists, but the important point is that the scientific approach to understanding politics involves a formal system of acquiring knowledge that is guided by a set of rules and procedures. The methodology of science emphasizes a consistent approach to understanding that is aimed at minimizing errors in observation and logical inference. For political scientists, the general goal is to develop broad generalizations that can be applied consistently to understand and explain the political world.

Q Questions for Thought and Discussion

Are news media biased? Many citizens believe that they present a distorted view of the political world, perhaps because journalists and pundits often engage in what Earl Babbie calls "personal human inquiry." Can you describe some recent examples of news reports or assertions made by political pundits that illustrate misperception of public affairs, overgeneralization due to a lack of representative information, and selective observation?

Characteristics and Assumptions of the Scientific Approach to Understanding Politics

We noted in Chapter 1 that there are a variety of sources of knowledge, and, consistent with that, there are a number of ways to obtain knowledge about politics. We believe, however, that a rigorous social scientific approach is preferable to relying on common sense or faith in authorities, and it is now time to specify what we mean by goals of a scientific approach and scientific knowledge of politics. You will see that scientific knowledge is based on careful observation of the political world and the use of reason to arrive at generalizations about how that world works. You will also see that faith does play a role in that process, inasmuch as we have faith in science as a means of acquiring knowledge and in our ability to engage in objective scientific research.

Characteristics of a Useful Social Science

The scientific process is first and foremost an *empirical* process, which means knowledge of the social and political world is grounded in observations using the senses and experience. Social scientists either observe phenomena directly using their senses or employ indirect extensions of their senses, such as surveys. In addition, they accept as facts information gathered empirically by others, such as facts and figures from the U.S. Census. Social scientists also assume that the knowledge collected using the senses (sense-data) can be *verified* empirically by others at some future date.

Scientific knowledge is *transmissible*. Arnold Brecht emphasized this point when he stated that scientific knowledge "can be transmitted from any person who does not have it but can grasp the meaning of the symbols (words, signs) used in communication and perform the operations, if any, described in these communications." [3] In other words, the precise methodology that is used to obtain knowledge must be made explicit so that researchers can replicate studies undertaken by others. Only through replication is it possible to gain confidence in the reliability of knowledge. If a political scientist undertakes a survey and determines that people with more education are more likely to participate in politics than those with less education, then it is important that the author of the survey inform readers of the precise questions asked. If a later researcher were to ask about education and political participation using different questions, and that researcher obtained different results, no one could be certain whether the knowledge gained by the original study was disconfirmed or the differing results were due to alternative ways of asking questions. The idea that knowledge is transmissible assumes *objectivity*—that different competent people can use identical methods to answer a question and produce the same answer.

Scientific knowledge should be *general* rather than narrowly specific. [4] Knowledge obtained scientifically should describe and explain a wide range of phenomena extending over time and space. For example, a generalization that school districts that spend more on education have students who score higher on standardized tests is more useful if it applies to all of the states in the United States rather than only California. Similarly, in trying to explain the outcome of elections, it is of less value to learn that John Smith from Portland, Oregon, has an income that exceeds $100,000 per year and is a Republican than the scientifically verified generalization that adults with higher incomes are more likely to be Republicans. Scientific methodology is used to obtain knowledge that is applicable in a wide variety of situations, contributing to the extension of knowledge.

Furthermore, scientific knowledge is most useful when it is *explanatory*. A great deal of social scientific research attempts only to *describe* the way things are. **Descriptions** usually involve information about such phenomena as a single vote in Congress or a delineation of patterns, such as how many members of the House of Representatives are Republicans or Democrats. Descriptions tell us *what* happened or the current state of affairs. **Explanations** move beyond descriptions to focus on *why* events occur or why patterns are present in social behavior. Descriptions are necessary to develop explanations, but the ultimate goal of social scientific research is to build generalizations that *explain* a wide range of social and political phenomena.

The process of description begins with collecting information or making observations. Table 2.1 provides a number of observations about some members of the U.S. Senate. The table lists for each senator party affiliation, number of terms in office, state represented, and vote on roll calls dealing with the minimum wage and aid to Vietnam. By just looking at the table, it may be difficult to perceive patterns of individual characteristics or voting behavior, but description can be aided by a process of *classification*—that is, rearranging the list by characteristics or behavior. For example, senators could be classified in terms of their support for or opposition to increases in the minimum wage.

Table 2.1
Characteristics and Roll Call Votes of Twenty U.S. Senators

| Senator (State) | Party | Term | ROLL CALL VOTE | |
			Increase Minimum Wage	Aid to Vietnam
Akaka (HI)	D	2nd	Yes	Yes
Bennett (UT)	R	2nd	No	Yes
Bingaman (NM)	D	3rd	No	Yes
Dewine (OH)	R	1st	Yes	Yes
Dorgan (ND)	D	2nd	Yes	No
Feinstein (CA)	D	2nd	Yes	Yes
Gorton (WA)	R	2nd	No	Yes
Graham (FL)	D	3rd	Yes	Yes
Helms (NC)	R	5th	No	No
Hollings (SC)	D	6th	Yes	Yes
Kennedy (MA)	D	7th	Yes	Yes
Leahy (VT)	D	5th	Yes	Yes
Mack (FL)	R	2nd	No	Yes
McCain (AZ)	R	3rd	No	Yes
Sarbanes (MD)	D	4th	Yes	Yes
Smith (NH)	R	2nd	No	No
Spector (PA)	R	4th	Yes	Yes
Stevens (AL)	R	6th	Yes	Yes
Thomas (WY)	R	1st	No	No
Wyden (OR)	D	1st	Yes	No

Source: Michael Barone and Grant Ujifusa, *The Almanac of American Politics, 1998* (Washington, DC: National Journal, Inc., 1998).

Supports Increases	Opposes Increases
Akaka	Bennett
Dewine	Bingaman
Dorgan	Gorton
Feinstein	Helms
Graham	Mack
Hollings	McCain
Kennedy	Smith
Leahy	Thomas
Sarbanes	
Spector	
Stevens	
Wyden	

Once the senators are classified this way, you can easily determine that more senators voted in favor of increasing the minimum wage than voted against. Senators could also be classified by the region of the country they represent, their party, number of terms in office, or their vote on aid for Vietnam. All of these classifications can be used to describe this sample of members of the U.S. Senate. Classification is an exercise in description, but it is also an important first step toward developing explanations of events and patterns of behavior.

As we just noted, social scientists are usually interested in moving beyond descriptions of behavior and events to developing explanations, such as *why* some senators support minimum wage increases and others do not. One hunch might be that the party affiliation of senators has something to do with their support for increases in the minimum wage. Classification is a first step in testing this possible explanation that is based on party affiliation. In this instance, the senators are classified by political party with their vote on increasing the minimum wage indicated by a Y (yes) or N (no).

Democrats	**Republicans**
Akaka—Y	Bennett—N
Bingaman—N	Dewine—Y
Dorgan—Y	Gorton—N
Feinstein—Y	Helms—N
Graham—Y	Mack—N
Hollings—Y	McCain—N
Kennedy—Y	Smith—N
Leahy—Y	Spector—Y
Sarbanes—Y	Stevens—Y
Wyden—Y	Thomas—N

By counting, respectively, the Democratic and Republican senators who supported increasing the minimum wage and comparing the totals, you can see that most Democrats (nine out of ten) voted for the increase, while most Republicans (seven out of ten) opposed it. These figures support a possible explanation for the reason some senators support increasing the minimum wage and others do not: The philosophies of members of the two political parties differ on the issue. We have moved past the simple descriptive question of how many senators voted to support increases in the minimum wage toward answering the "why" question that will provide an explanation of senatorial behavior.

In addition to explaining events and political behavior, a goal of social science research is to be *predictive*. Scientific "truths" in the physical sciences are

To the Web

Exercise 2.1   Classifying Senators to Explain Votes

You can use the information in Table 2.1 to classify the senators in such a way to develop alternative explanations for their roll call votes. To access Exercise 2.1, go to the **DEPR Web Page** and click on **Web Exercises, Chapter 2**, then on **Classifying Senators to Explain Votes**.

often perfectly predictive and indicate deterministic relationships. For example, when the temperature of water is lowered to 0° C at sea level, it becomes solid. This phenomenon occurs under these conditions virtually without exception. In the social sciences, however, "truths," and therefore **predictions** about behavior, are *probabilistic*. That is, "truths" are expressed by statements of tendencies or the likelihood of predicting an event or behavior given other explanatory information. For example, one probably could not predict with certainty that all Democrats would vote for the Democratic candidate in an election. But one may be able to attach a likelihood, such as a 75 percent probability, of consistent partisanship in voting. Likewise, given a large number of observations of votes in the U.S. Senate, we may be able to estimate a probability that Democratic senators will support foreign aid programs. Probabilistic statements are useful to analysts and are common in other fields, such as medicine. Medical researchers studying cancer, for example, have been able to establish that smokers have a greater probability than nonsmokers of contracting lung cancer, but they cannot say with certainty that everyone who smokes will get lung cancer.

In sum, social science seeks to move beyond simple description, trying to explain and predict a wide variety of phenomena. The focus is on obtaining general knowledge, not on examining individual countries, people, or events. Two questions that display these properties are (1) Why do some countries embrace capital punishment, whereas others do not? and (2) Why does presidential popularity increase during times of national crisis? The emphasis of these questions is on the *explanation* of behavior of an array of people or countries.

Key Points

Scientific knowledge has the following characteristics:

- Empirical—grounded in observations using the senses and experience.
- Transmissible—methodology is explicitly communicated so results can be replicated.
- General—explains a wide range of behaviors or phenomena extending over time and space.
- Explanatory—focuses on why events and behaviors occur and is not simply descriptive.
- Predictive—describes deterministic or probabilistic relationships between phenomena.

Assumptions of Social Science

There are many basic assumptions behind social science. You need to think about these as part of your own approach to knowledge. In a sense, the assumptions represent the intrusion of "faith" in a process supposedly based on only sense-experience and reasoning. Scientists take these basic assumptions as axiomatic; that is, they accept them as true without scientific justification. We believe that these assumptions need to be made explicit. It is important for you to know that they are contested and controversial, and as a result, they deserve careful consideration and discussion. Methodologists differ on the number of assumptions and their importance, but for our purposes we will discuss the ten that seem to form the basis of social scientific research. [5] Remember, these are assumptions: statements that cannot be determined scientifically to be incorrect or correct but are accepted on "faith."

Every event has a natural cause. Social science assumes determinism; forces outside of nature cannot cause events and behaviors. Explanations for events that rely on the spiritual and supernatural are rejected because they are considered beyond the scope of scientific investigation. The assumption of determinism makes many of us uncomfortable because we have learned to believe that we exercise "free will" and are responsible for our own behavior and fate. This assumption says that while a person does make decisions about his or her own behavior, there are causes for that particular behavior that make it much more likely than other possible behaviors available for that person to choose.

To the Web

Free Will Versus Determinism

The issue of whether human behavior is socially determined or if humans *choose* to behave as they do has been a subject of debate among philosophers, theologians, and social scientists for centuries. To get a sense of the nature of the debate, go to the **DEPR Web Page**, click on **Web Links, Chapter 2**, then on **Free Will Versus Determinism**.

The assumption of determinism also has implications for public policies. For example, the criminal justice system holds that those who commit crimes do so of their own free will and are therefore appropriately held responsible. If we assume that individuals commit crimes due to prior circumstances beyond their control, punishment or retribution for crime would seem to make little sense. Still, a methodology that emphasizes patterns of events and their ultimate prediction must assume that those events have external causes, and probabilities can be assigned showing some events to be more likely than others. And if the causes of events are natural, then they can be determined empirically through observation and reason.

Questions for Thought and Discussion

B. F. Skinner, in *Beyond Freedom and Dignity,* argues that people's behaviors are the result of the sum of the environmental forces that have acted on them over the course of a lifetime.

Consider the hypothetical situation in which two legislators are each secretly offered bribes in a videotaped "sting" operation. One accepts the bribe, but the other refuses. Skinner's analysis would suggest the bribe taker cannot be labeled a scoundrel nor the one who refused the bribe a saint because neither of them made a decision based on free will. The behavior of each was simply an inevitable result of all that happened to them up to that point in their lives. Do you agree with this analysis? Why or why not?

Humans are part of the natural world. The same methods that are used in the physical sciences and biological sciences can be used to study human behavior. Human beings are just as much a part of nature as are other animals, plants, minerals, and physical phenomena such as weather patterns. The same general methodology can be used to acquire knowledge about why revolutions occur and about why the number of salmon is decreasing in the waters off Alaska. Many would argue that human beings are unique and stand apart from nature, and this assumption, like the one concerning determinism, would seem to clash with some fundamental religious beliefs that a deity is the creator of human beings and the determinant of events in the world. Both philosophers and scientists have struggled for years to reconcile these assumptions and religious beliefs, with some arguing that religion and science are not necessarily incompatible.

To the Web

Human Nature

A Web site with an online publication called *Human Nature Daily Review* is devoted entirely to the understanding of human nature. Contributors include scientists, philosophers, and theologians. You can reach the site from the Web page. Go to the **DEPR Web Page**, click on **Web Links**, **Chapter 2**, then on **Human Nature**.

Nature is orderly and regular. To conduct social scientific research, it must be assumed that the world is an orderly place. Sociologist Ernest Gellner says, "Assume the regularity of nature, the systematic nature of the world, not because it is demonstrable, but because anything that eludes such a principle also eludes real knowledge: if cumulative and communicable knowledge is to be possible at all, then the principle of orderliness must apply to it." [7] We assume that events do not happen completely by chance and are not completely unique. Some may argue that events such as the American Revolution or World War I were unique events and that their occurrence was based on some elements that could be characterized as chance. Examined in the context of other revolutions and wars, however, both may be explicable in terms of historical patterns and regularities. Regularities and patterns underlying seemingly unique events, once discovered, can lead to generalizations and predictions.

Nature changes slowly. It must be assumed that nature changes slowly, or it would make no sense to attempt to develop a reliable set of generalizations about social phenomena. There are events, such as a terrorist bombing, that occur quickly and produce rapid change. It may seem nearly impossible to learn about an event that happens so quickly, but if the event is examined in the context of other similar events, then some generalizations can be made about it and how it fits into previously discovered patterns.

All observable phenomena are eventually knowable. This assumption indicates the belief that human beings can eventually come to understand anything that they can observe. What it means is that there should be no mysteries and that social science is optimistic about the abilities of human beings to understand their universe. It also means that anything that can be observed is a legitimate subject for social scientific study. The objects of some inquiries may be unpopular and, in the eyes of some, inappropriate for study. Just because some think a topic is inappropriate, however, does not mean it is not eventually knowable through empirical study.

Nothing is self-evident. Social scientists are skeptical. They take nothing for granted and are reluctant to accept common sense notions of the truth or statements of authorities concerning what is true. Truth must be demonstrated with the use of methods that are acceptable and understood by social scientists. All scientists know that scientific truths have often been found to be different from the truths generally accepted as common sense or asserted by some type of authority. For example, both common sense, as well as the assertions of religious and political authorities, once indicated that the sun revolved around the earth. Skeptical scientists refused to accept that "truth," and eventually persuaded most of us that the earth revolves around the sun. In this instance, a scientific truth replaced one that seemed to be self-evident.

Questions for Thought and Discussion

Can you think of examples of some truths that appeared to be common sense but on closer examination turned out not to be true? We often accept things as true because some trusted authority tells us they are true. What are some examples of some truths articulated by authorities that later proved to be not true after scientific investigation?

Truth is tentative. We noted earlier that truth is dynamic and constantly changing. What is true at one point in time may not be true in the future. Truth is always relative to the existing state of knowledge. As scientific methodology is applied to increasing numbers of observations, what most thought was once true may be modified. Truth, often expressed as a generalization, most often changes when scientific observations are made that simply do not fit. From the social scientific point of view there are no eternal truths. What is true is always open to modification as new observations and events occur over time and space.

The world is perceived through our senses. This is the empirical assumption. It relates to all of the sources of knowledge discussed in Chapter 1 and indicates that our observations of the world make for the most useful and reliable sources of truth. As social scientists, we assume that what is perceived is more likely to be true than knowledge acquired by other means.

Our perceptions, memory, and reasoning can be trusted. Social science depends on the ability of human beings to make accurate observations and reason logically about them. Social scientists assume that their senses are reliable instruments for acquiring knowledge. To be sure, there are optical illusions, such as mirages that are seen in the desert, and there are instances where individuals seem to see different things. Empirical reliability is established when there is agreement among a number of individuals that they perceive the same things. One can raise interesting questions about whether perception is influenced by language and culture. Does someone who speaks Chinese "see" the same thing when viewing a common object such as a table as someone who speaks English? The issue of the reliability of sense perception becomes even more contestable when, for example, eyewitness evidence of a crime given by two or more individuals is closely examined and found to be markedly different.

Truth should be established objectively. Social scientific conclusions should not be influenced by personal value systems. Ideally, social scientific observations made by individuals with a variety of personal values should be identical. Furthermore, given agreement on a set of facts, social scientists who disagree about values should draw the same conclusions. Many argue that objectivity is impossible and that individuals can never be expected to agree in all instances on what they see or conclude. Most social scientists would agree and point to the importance of carefully and consistently applying the scientific rules of observation and logical inference in order to maximize agreement among people with different value positions.

Questions for Thought and Discussion

Many people would find some of the assumptions of social science difficult to accept and, at the very least, controversial. Which of the assumptions do you find most difficult to accept? Which assumptions do you think most people would find to be controversial? Why?

The Wheel of Science Describes the Stages in the Research Process

The Wheel of Science

Scientific inquiry is a process that takes us through a number of steps. The steps are pretty much the same whether you are interested in answering questions that usually concern the physical sciences—such as why some volcanoes erupt and some do not—or the social sciences—such as why some people exhibit prejudice against racial groups

Figure 2.1
The Wheel of Science

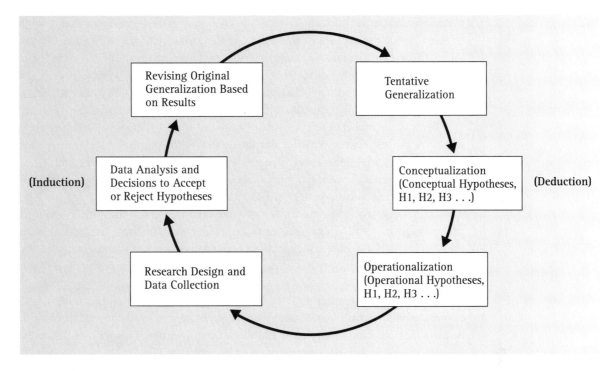

other than their own. The process of scientific inquiry has often been termed the **hypothetical-deductive system,** or the "wheel of science." The hypothetical-deductive system describes the logic and procedures of scientific investigation and the ways in which observation and the application of reasoning result in generalizations about the nature of the world. Within the system are steps in the scientific process that involve both empirical observations and logical inferences about the nature of reality. Although the wheel of science is often called "hypothetical-deductive," we will see that both deductive and inductive forms of reasoning are critical to the process. Figure 2.1 provides an illustration of the Hypothetical-Deductive System.

We have already noted that a goal of social science is to develop generalizations that explain aspects of social life. The more ambitious goal is to develop theories that explain a broad range of social behaviors. **Theories** are tentative sets of generalizations that are systematically and logically related to each other that serve to explain and predict some aspect of social life. As we have noted before, truth is tentative, so theories are always taken to be tentative and subject to empirical tests. The process of theory construction is described by the hypothetical-deductive system and is an activity that results in the elaboration, modification, extension, and sometimes rejection of explanations of social life. The ideal social theory would be broad based—in the sense that it would explain a wide variety of social behaviors—and deterministic—in the sense that it would be able to predict social behaviors perfectly. In the social sciences what we usually strive for are **theories of the middle range** that offer reasonably accurate explanations of aspects of a limited number of social behaviors. [8] While there are general theories that purport to explain all human behavior, as political scientists we hope to develop sets of generalizations that might explain, for example, the behavior of voters.

Because the model of science is described as a "wheel," there is some debate about where the process begins. We will enter the process at the point of deduction: the formation of a tentative generalization. Most social scientists begin their research with a very tentative generalization or prehypothesis about the social and political world. Initially, this generalization may be posed as a question such as "Why are some people politically conservative?" There may be many possible answers to the question, but the process must start with only one. For this example, we choose the tentative generalization that "people with higher social status are most likely to express conservative views." The goal of the scientific process, then, is to determine the truth or falsity of the tentative generalization.

After such a generalization is developed, the next step is concept definition. Both of our concepts in this generalization—social status and political conservatism—must be defined. Definition often takes a number of steps, with precision increasing as the process moves forward. For example, social status might be defined in a number of ways. Two common approaches are to say that people with higher family income have higher social status than those with lower income, or alternatively, those who have achieved a higher level of education have higher social status compared with those with lower levels of education. Political conservatism, our other concept, may be even more difficult to define. But let's start by saying that, in the contemporary context, conservatives, as compared to liberals, are more supportive of traditional family values and oppose the expansion of the federal government.

Many complex concepts such as social status and political conservatism are multidimensional and can be defined in a number of alternative ways. The process of concept definition may result in a number of conceptual hypotheses that are directly related to the generalization to be tested. A **hypothesis** is a conjectural statement of a relationship, association, or connection between two concepts. It is conjectural because we do not know whether it is correct until we have collected information to test it. The process of conceptual definition (making more precise the meanings of the concepts in the original generalization) results in conceptual hypotheses directly related to the original generalization. In the case of our example of social status and political conservatism, these hypotheses include the following.

1. People with higher incomes are more supportive of traditional family values than those with lower incomes.
2. People with more education are more supportive of traditional family values than those with lower levels of education.
3. People with higher incomes are more likely to oppose the expansion of the federal government than those with lower incomes.
4. People with more education are more likely to oppose the expansion of the federal government than those with less education.

Note that the four conceptual hypotheses are more specific expressions of the original generalization that "higher-status people tend to be more conservative." What has taken place in the process of developing conceptual definitions is **deductive reasoning,** a process in which generalizations about the world are used to generate specific statements about specific events or behaviors. Deduction moves from the general to the particular. For example, one political science generalization (theory) states that candidates who find themselves involved in divisive primary elections have difficulty winning their subsequent general elections. We could easily *deduce* from this generalization that candidates for the state legislature in Oregon with smaller margins of victory in their primary elections are more likely to have smaller margins of victory, or will lose their general election contests, than those candidates with larger primary victory margins.

To the Web

Exercise 2.2   Thinking Deductively and Inductively

The process of deductive and inductive reasoning concerning politics requires some practice. Exercise 2.2 concerns reasoning from the general to the specific and developing generalizations from specific statements. To access this exercise, go to the **DEPR Web Page,** click on **Web Exercises, Chapter 2,** then on **Thinking Deductively and Inductively.**

The process of deductive inference continues as concepts are defined more precisely. After conceptual definitions and conceptual hypotheses are developed, the concepts must be *operationalized* in ways that facilitate the gathering of evidence through observations. Operationalization requires even further specification of concepts. The process is best illustrated by example. In our previous theory linking social status and political conservatism, we indicated that a common definition of social status is annual family income. An operationalization of high family income might be those whose family income was greater than $75,000 in the most recent tax year. An operational definition of political conservatism could be agreement with the following statement on a survey: "Spending on federal government programs should be reduced." These operational definitions would lead us to the following *operational hypothesis:* "People with incomes of more than $75,000 per year, compared to those with lower incomes, are more likely to agree that spending on federal welfare programs should be reduced." It is easy to see the logic of deduction here as our statements have developed from the most general to the most specific.

If "People with higher social status are more likely to express conservative views."

Then it follows that

"People with higher incomes are more likely to oppose the expansion of federal government than those with lower incomes."

Then it follows that

"People with incomes of more than $75,000 per year, compared to those with lower incomes, are more likely to agree that spending on federal welfare programs should be reduced."

In fact, through deductive inference, it is possible to arrive at a surprising number of implications of our original generalizations. Here are a few other possibilities.

"People with incomes of more than $75,000 per year, compared with lower incomes, are more likely to disagree with increased federal aid for education."
"People with at least a college degree, compared to those with less than a college education, are more likely to agree that spending on federal welfare programs should be reduced."

After operational hypotheses or implications of the theory have been developed, *observations* are made to determine their truth or falsity. You should develop methods of observation that will minimize the errors discussed earlier, such as misperception and overgeneralization, that are often present when individuals engage in personal inquiry. Later chapters will cover a wide variety of research designs and means of data collection, but the goal is always to minimize error. Most likely, you would test the operational hypotheses we generated to examine the link between social status and political conservatism by using a survey to collect information from people.

After you have made your observations—that is, you have systematically collected the necessary data—you must analyze and summarize the results. You will have a choice of statistical tests to analyze the data in order to estimate whether observations collected correspond with the statements developed in the form of operational hypotheses. These statistical results will be displayed in such a way that you can make judgments about the likely truth or falsity of each operational hypothesis.

Figure 2.2
Inductive and Deductive Reasoning

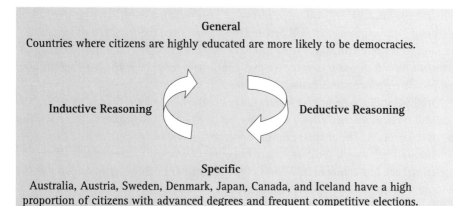

General
Countries where citizens are highly educated are more likely to be democracies.

Inductive Reasoning   Deductive Reasoning

Specific
Australia, Austria, Sweden, Denmark, Japan, Canada, and Iceland have a high proportion of citizens with advanced degrees and frequent competitive elections.

To close the circle of the scientific process, you must return to the original generalization to decide whether the tests of your operational hypotheses support, falsify, or somehow modify that generalization. This pattern of moving from specific observations or data to generalization is the opposite of deductive reasoning and is called **inductive reasoning.** Both deduction and induction are critical to the process of building theory through science. Based on many empirical observations or facts, social scientists arrive at generalizations by seeking patterns that may apply to previously unobserved events (see Figure 2.2).

Returning to our example of social status and conservatism, tests of operational hypotheses may have a variety of impacts on the original generalization. Some operational hypotheses that we deduced from the original generalization may be falsified, meaning the generalization would need to be modified to take into account such exceptions. For example, you may find that people with higher levels of income do not oppose new government programs as long as the programs benefit big business. In fact, it is unusual for generalizations to gain complete support from a testing of a large number of operational hypotheses, and likewise, it is unusual for a single research project to result in a complete rejection of a generalization.

We have described the hypothetical-deductive system as deductive and circular, but actually it is neither. The system of scientific development of generalizations is not closed but is instead a process where the truth of generalizations and theory are tested and retested. Each time you undertake a test, you either gain confidence in the truth or utility of the theory or the theory is modified and tested again. On the other hand, if, based on evidence, you reject the theory, new theories will be developed and tested. As you have seen, the process involves both induction and deduction. The system can begin with observations and proceed inductively or begin with theory and proceed deductively. When a theory is falsified, you must return to observations in an attempt to discern patterns and explanations that will become the basis of new theories to test. In our earlier example, if no relationships were found between social status and political conservatism, we would develop alternative explanations—new theories—to explain why some people are more conservative than others.

This hypothetical-deductive system describes the basic methodology of all the sciences, and social scientists' efforts to answer research questions sequentially follow the steps of the process. The chapters in this book are loosely organized around the wheel of science, and as you will see later, research reports of empirical investigations found in professional academic journals follow the same familiar outline. Since our goal is for you to develop the knowledge and skills needed to conduct a research project, we will quickly summarize the specific, basic steps students must follow in doing empirical political research. Each of the steps, or stages, is covered more completely in later chapters.

■ Stages in the Research Process

Research projects must be carefully planned to avoid the kinds of errors that can emerge from personal human inquiry. Social scientists are obligated to record and describe what was done at each stage of the project so that others can both understand and replicate the original research. Advanced planning is crucial because the decisions made at one stage affect those to be made at later stages. Building a research project and resulting report is like building a house: If the foundation is poorly prepared, or construction does not proceed in the proper order, the result will be less than satisfactory and impossible to repair without great cost. Many experienced researchers argue that the initial stages are the most critical because they set the standard for the entire project. These are the stages of social science research (see Figure 2.3).

Formulating a research idea. The first stage in the process of social scientific research is to choose and define a topic. Research ideas can come from a number of sources. We noted previously that some social scientists begin inductively by observing patterns in social and political behavior that they find interesting and would like to explain. In fact, many researchers argue that all research topics should be grounded in empirical observations. Others proceed deductively, starting with either a well-developed theory or research findings presented by others. An interesting theory in political science, for example, is that the increase in the prominence of television in America has contributed to a decline in a sense of political community. [9] You could formulate a topic to determine if

Figure 2.3
Steps in the Research Process

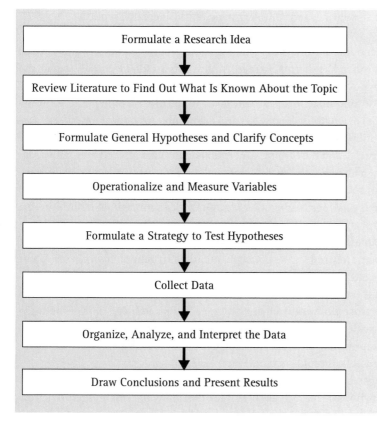

heavy television viewers spend less time discussing politics with others. Chapter 3 covers the choice and definition of research ideas.

Reviewing literature to find out what is known about the topic. Social scientists must immerse themselves in material relevant to the topic. Many others may have already researched the topic to be studied, and most of the questions you have posed have probably been thoroughly answered by previous researchers. More likely, you will find that previous research on the topic opens more questions than originally considered and will contribute to your more carefully specifying how you want to proceed. Reviewing previous research can also help avoid the pitfalls of others, as well as link a topic to more general theories.

The actual process of reviewing previous literature proceeds in two steps: (1) identifying relevant literature and building a bibliography and (2) systematically reading and summarizing previous studies relevant to the research topic. Chapter 4 is dedicated to conducting literature searches using the library and the World Wide Web. Chapter 5 focuses on reading, reviewing, and summarizing empirical research reports.

Formulating general hypotheses and clarifying concepts. After developing a clear picture of the research question, you must generate some general hypotheses and develop conceptual definitions of key terms. Research questions are often initially vague and ambiguous, but hypotheses must be clear statements that are amenable to empirical tests. A great deal of time and effort is usually given to the process of hypothesis formation. We will discuss at length in Chapters 3 and 6 a number of important criteria used to determine the utility of hypotheses. A clear understanding of the concepts included in hypotheses is crucial, and developing conceptual definitions is aided by a knowledge of previous research and sources, such as political dictionaries. Conceptualizing variables will be part of the focus of Chapter 7.

Operationalizing and measuring variables. Once clear conceptual definitions are formulated, the researcher must devise precise operational definitions and measurements of the variables. The concern at this stage is with the extent to which empirical measurements accurately reflect the concepts included in general hypotheses. There will often be many alternative operationalizations and measurements of the same concept, and the goal is a set of operational hypotheses that are accurate deductions from the concepts. The process of measurement is often a "nuts and bolts" part of the study, where questions are designed for inclusion on a survey or government-supplied statistics are chosen to represent a particular concept. Chapter 7 is dedicated to facilitating the transition from general concept to accurate empirical measurement.

Research design: formulating a strategy to test hypotheses. You must develop an overall strategy to test hypotheses in such a way that the possibility of error and resulting contamination of the findings is minimized. In general, the researcher must decide whether to employ the controlled environment of a laboratory experiment or a more general field study to test hypotheses and understand the implications of these choices. We will give careful attention to various types and sources of error and the means of controlling their effects when we discuss research design.

Collecting data. There are many different means of collecting data to test hypotheses—so many that four chapters of this book are dedicated to data collection. We will discuss the use of surveys and questionnaires (Chapters 9 and 10), data obtained from published sources, including the messages from mass media (Chapter 11), as well as experimentation and other intensive approaches (Chapter 12). Often data already exist that can be used to test hypotheses—five sets of existing data are available to those who use this book—and secondary analysis of others' data is a very common practice in testing social science hypotheses.

Organizing, analyzing, and interpreting data. Once you have collected the required data, you must organize them in order to facilitate analysis. We will introduce you to the most widely used computer program for organizing and analyzing social science data: SPSS (Statistical Package for the Social Sciences). You will learn how to code and organize data into a data matrix (Chapter 8) so that analysis can be easily undertaken. There are three goals of data analysis: (1) describing results, (2) revealing relationships between variables, and (3) determining the risk of accepting a conclusion regarding support for a hypothesis. The data have to be statistically summarized and analyzed before it is possible to draw conclusions about hypotheses. Chapters 13 through 17 concentrate on the analysis of data.

Drawing conclusions and presenting results. The final stage of the research process entails deciding whether data collection and analysis support the operational hypotheses and, ultimately, answer the question that was the impetus for the research. Using an inductive process, you must draw conclusions regarding broad theoretical generalizations. Research reports follow a familiar format in the social sciences. While students should be familiar with the format from reading Chapter 5 and examining actual social science articles from professional journals, in Chapter 18 we outline the structure of research reports and suggest some useful ways to present statistical results.

Conclusion

We have argued in this chapter that science, a process of acquiring knowledge where reason is applied to observations, is a useful method for developing generalizations about politics. Scientific knowledge systematically acquired is empirical, transmissible, general, explanatory, and predictive. The scientific process, while characterized by the analysis of sense-data and the application of rational inference, is based on a set of assumptions or axioms that are accepted as true without justification. Many of the assumptions of social science, such as determinism, are controversial but essential to the process of developing social scientific knowledge.

Social scientific knowledge is acquired through an orderly process that proceeds along a series of well-defined steps. This process is described by the hypothetical-deductive system within which you develop tentative generalizations, define and operationalize the concepts in the generalization, deduce implications in the form of hypotheses, collect and analyze data to determine if hypotheses are supported, and finally, through a process of induction, evaluate the utility of the original generalization. The hypothetical-deductive system describes the steps in the research process that define the outline of the research design you are employing and ultimately sets the outline for the written report of your research results. The next chapter shows you how to formulate specific research questions within the context of this hypothetical-deductive system and gives you plenty of opportunity to practice this new skill.

Summary of the Main Points

- Science is a process of acquiring knowledge where reason is applied to careful observations.
- Everyone engages in science as a form of personal human inquiry in which we collect information with our senses and reason about it. A scientific approach to acquiring knowledge, however, involves the application of rigorous rules to reduce errors.
- Scientific knowledge is empirical, transmissible, general, explanatory, and predictive.
- Social science proceeds from a set of assumptions, some of which are controversial and contested.
- All scientific endeavors proceed through a series of steps in what has been called the hypothetical-deductive system, an interaction between the collection and analysis of observations and the logical processes of deduction and induction.
- The stages of a social science research project are consistent with the hypothetical-deductive system, beginning with the development of a research question and concluding with a written report.

Terms Introduced

deductive reasoning   inductive reasoning
description   prediction
explanation   theories of the middle range
hypothesis   theory
hypothetical-deductive system

Selected Readings

Agnew, Neil McK., and Sandra W. Pyke. *The Science Game: An Introduction to Research in the Social Sciences,* 6th Ed. Englewood Cliffs, NJ: Prentice-Hall, 1994.
Hempel, Carl G. *Aspects of Scientific Explanation.* New York: Free Press, 1965.
Homans, George. *The Nature of Social Science.* New York: Harcourt, Brace & World, 1968.
Kaplan, Abraham. *The Conduct of Inquiry: Methodology for Behavioral Science.* New York: Chandler, 1974.

Activities

Activity 2.1
Identifying Distortions in News Reports and Commentaries

Many citizens believe that the news media are biased and present a distorted view of the political world. Journalists and pundits, like the rest of us, may fall victim to (or in some cases purposely engage in) personal human inquiry when formulating statements about current events and issues. In this activity you will examine some news reports and editorials to identify instances of misperception, overgeneralization, and selective observation. You can access Web sites for newspapers, magazines, and television stations at a Web site called **NewsLink** at http://www.newslink.org/news.html. Identify stories or commentaries that illustrate each of the three errors that can result from personal human inquiry. Among the six illustrations you select there should be at least one each from a magazine, newspaper, and television station. There should also be at least one example from a news story and one from a commentary or editorial. Provide the source of each illustration and describe why you think that is a good example of one of the three human errors committed by naive scientists.

Activity 2.2
Description and Explanation

Consider Table 2.2, which describes characteristics of fourteen states in terms of the number of executions in 1995, the vote received by the Republican candidate for governor in the last election, and the murder rate. Three descriptions of the states are given explicitly in the table. The task of this activity is to organize the descriptive information for purposes of explanation.

Table 2.2
Selected Characteristics of Fourteen States

State	Executions, 1995	% Vote for Republican Candidate for Governor	Murder Rate per 100,000
Arizona	1	52.5%	10.4
Arkansas	2	40.2%	10.4
California	0	55.2%	11.2
Florida	3	49.2%	7.3
Georgia	2	48.9%	9.5
Indiana	0	48.5%	8.0
Maryland	0	50.2%	11.8
Missouri	6	57.2%	8.8
New Hampshire	0	42.8%	1.8
New York	0	51.2%	8.5
North Carolina	2	44.0%	9.4
Ohio	0	71.8%	5.4
Texas	19	54.3%	9.0
Washington	0	42.0%	5.1

Source: Bureau of the Census, *State and Metropolitan Data Book, 1997–1998.*

A. Fill in Table 2.3 by using the information in Table 2.2 so that it can be used to explain why some states have more executions than others.

Table 2.3
Executions in Fourteen States by Vote for Republican Candidates for Governor

PERCENTAGE VOTE FOR REPUBLICAN CANDIDATE	
Less Than 50%	More Than 50%
Arkansas 2	Arizona 1

Does knowing the support Republican candidates receive in a state help explain the number of executions? Write a brief essay of explanation.

B. Divide the states by location (North versus South) to see if region helps explain the execution rate by filling in Table 2.4.

Table 2.4
Executions in Fourteen States by Region

REGION	
South	Outside of the South

Does knowing the location of a state help explain the execution rate? Write a brief essay of explanation.

C. Construct your own table to determine if a state's murder rate helps explain executions. (*Hint:* Divide the states into low [seven lowest] and high [seven highest], based on their murder rates.)

Activity 2.3
Deductive and Inductive Inference

A. The following is a series of generalizations about politics. Deduce three specific expectations that should follow from each of them.

1. Civil violence tends to occur in countries with populations with great social differences.
2. Candidates who are successful in their elections are the ones who express views on issues similar to those of the electorate.
3. People who live in political systems with monarchs (kings and/or queens) are more satisfied with their government than those who live in countries without monarchs.
4. The quality of life is higher in democratic countries than in authoritarian countries.
5. Political groups that are organized along democratic lines are more effective than those with strong leaders who make most decisions.

B. The following are some descriptions of specific facts. Develop some generalizations that might apply to other facts or events.

1. Political corruption has been common in Boston, New York, and Philadelphia. It has been uncommon in Seattle, Minneapolis, and San Diego.
2. The following countries have relatively high rates of suicide: Sweden, Finland, Russia, Hungary. The same countries experience very few murders with handguns.
3. People who frequently attend religious services, pray often, and are active in religious organizations oppose abortion rights, support prayer in schools, and oppose laws that protect homosexuals from discrimination.
4. In the past fifty years the Democrats and the Republicans have successfully elected candidates to all levels of office in the United States. In the past fifty years the Constitution party, the Libertarian party, the Natural Law party, the Reform party, and the Communist party USA have not been successful in electing candidates.
5. Members of the U.S. Senate from the following states oppose proposals for campaign finance reform: Alabama, Texas, Kansas, Mississippi, Wyoming, and Utah. Members of the U.S. Senate from the following states support proposals for campaign finance reform: Washington, Rhode Island, Massachusetts, California, and Vermont.

Preparing for Research

Chapter 3

Formulating Problems and Hypotheses

Learning Objectives

After completion of this chapter, students should be able to do the following:

Describe a set of criteria that can be used for evaluating potential research topics.

Discuss ethical issues concerning the treatment of human subjects.

Transform a general question about politics into testable hypotheses.

Describe the characteristics of a useful hypothesis.

Reformulate questions and statements about politics into useful hypotheses.

Identify the elements of a hypothesis, including variables, their values, and the units of analysis they describe.

How to Develop a Political Research Question

The early stages of a research project are the most critical. Dickinson McGaw and George Watson describe the original research question as the "foundation of the house of inquiry" and point out that a poorly constructed, weak, or crooked foundation will produce a multiplicity of errors as a project proceeds. [1] The choice of general topic and subsequent development of research questions are intimately related to the confidence you and others will have in the results of the research effort. This chapter is devoted to the progression of a project from the choice of a general topic to the development of useful hypotheses. Like McGaw and Watson, we believe that the choice of research topic and the development of questions and hypotheses set the tone and frame a project. This chapter is dedicated to ensuring that the foundation of your political research project will be straight and strong.

When selecting a topic the first step is to choose a general area of interest. The fact that you are reading this book indicates you have chosen to study political science or a related social science, narrowing the field of likely topics considerably. Narrowing down the choices and formulating a clearly defined political question are the most difficult and critical steps that you, as an investigator, will make. Unfortunately, choosing a topic is also the most difficult stage in the research process to teach. To help, we can suggest some sources of topics about politics, provide a set of criteria to evaluate topics, and guide you in turning a topic into a researchable question.

Sources of Research Topics

The process of choosing a research topic is highly personal, and the first step is to determine what is interesting and important to you. Sociologist C. Wright Mills urged social scientists to use their imaginations and choose topics that are related to what is going on in their world and in their lives. [2] In other words, drawing on your own experience to choose a topic will help you find research that has a personal relevance, sustaining your interest and enthusiasm through what is often a long and sometimes tedious process. A fine example of how personal experience converged with professional interest to produce an interesting and important political research project is S. M. Lipset's decision to study the International Typographical Union (ITU). Because his father was a member of that group, Lipset was familiar with the union's decision-making processes, which he noted were surprisingly democratic and therefore inconsistent with an important generalization about politics called the "iron law of oligarchy." That "law" predicts large organizations may be democratic early in their development, but that over time their decisions increasingly are made by a few organizational elites. This inconsistency between the "iron law of oligarchy" and the ITU's democratic practices sparked Lipset's curiosity and led him to develop a study that produced some modifications of prevailing theory about organizational structure and decision making. [3]

Another good example of how a topic of personal relevance evolved into an important research report is provided by political scientist John Sullivan. Professor Sullivan was teaching a course on research methods at Indiana University in the early 1970s. One of the activities of the course was to be a survey of student opinion. At the time, there was conflict on the campus between older students who were "children of the 1960s," part of the New Left counterculture, and younger students who were more conservative. As a result, the older students decided the survey should focus on tolerance of "hippies" and radicals. The project developed into a more general study of political tolerance, and the results were ultimately reported in a widely cited article published in the *American Political Science Review*. [4] Professor Sullivan's experience is a classic example of the choice of a research topic being influenced by student personal interest and what was going on in the world at the time. It is also a fine example of how student interest in a topic can engage an instructor.

We had a similar experience a few years ago with a seminar we conducted on advanced research methods for undergraduates. Our group was brainstorming ideas for a class project, using experimental methods. At the time, President Clinton's alleged sexual harassment of a former Arkansas state employee while he was governor was in the news. (This was before the Monica Lewinsky affair was exposed.) The students thought it would be interesting and worthwhile to study the effects of sexual and financial scandals on the images of political candidates. A discussion ensued about whether the images of male or female candidates would suffer more from scandal. We searched the professional literature and found just a few earlier studies, developed an experimental design, and completed the project. The results showed some interesting interactions between candidate sex and the effects of scandals, and a paper based on that research that we coauthored with one of the seminar students was published in a political science journal. [5]

Social scientists often are influenced by both personal and professional factors when choosing a research topic. As scholars they usually have well-developed interests in a number of subjects and are aware of the state of research and theory development. For example, political scientists have debated over many years the causes and consequences of low levels of political sophistication (lack of political knowledge, interest, and participation) in the American public. Many scholars have dedicated their careers to seeking to understand this phenomenon because they are familiar with the literature (research by others) and have confidence in a particular theory they believe contributes to an explanation. They are content to generate questions and seek answers related to a relatively narrow, but important, topic.

But more than just substantive interests guide choices of research topics. As we noted in Chapter 2, social scientific knowledge advances by posing questions and developing the means to answer them, but as a practical matter, some social scientists believe that particular forms of data collection and analysis are more appropriate than others for acquiring knowledge. In effect, they let their preferred technique guide their choice of research topic. Political viewpoints also play a role because political scientists usually care a great deal about what is going on in the political arena and often have strong opinions on political issues. To assume that many political scientists are not influenced by their personal political ideologies when they decide what they want to study would be foolish, as was mentioned in Chapter 1.

Regardless of their theoretical, methodological, or political perspectives, scholars seek to answer research questions that are interesting to others and will advance knowledge in their field. The cumulative knowledge in an academic subject is found in articles in scholarly journals, books, and papers presented at professional meetings, so a formal source of research topics is the writing of others. Scholars are motivated to choose topics that raise questions inadequately answered or that produce inconsistent answers. Reviews of the literature on a topic will often reveal inconsistent explanations for phenomena or information (data) that is at odds with commonly accepted theories. A good strategy for students who are searching for topics is to examine tables of contents of major political science and social science journals, where titles of articles will give you a general idea of what topics are perceived to be most important and deserving of attention. Since academic journals usually specialize in particular substantive fields, you should consult a wide variety of these academic journals. Books and their tables of contents may also be a source of interesting topics, but the most recent research is usually found in academic journals or in papers presented at professional meetings. In Chapter 4 we will focus on ways in which topics can be explored, using library resources and the World Wide Web.

Finally, the choice of a research topic may be influenced by interpersonal and practical concerns. Graduate students often choose a research topic of interest to one of their professors, and PhD candidates will often conduct research seeking answers to questions related to their faculty adviser's larger project. This makes sense because advisers will likely be enthusiastic and supportive of the research, and they can be a source of expertise and data as well. Scholars are often guided in their choice of research topics by such practical concerns as career advancement, funding by grant agencies, the availability of data, and the support of their faculty colleagues (some of whom may be collaborators in a research project).

Criteria for Evaluating Potential Political Research Topics

We must reiterate the point that the choice of research topic is highly personal—a value judgment. To aid you in your choice, we summarize the criteria that are used to evaluate research topics, but like the choice itself, *you* must decide which of these criteria are most important to you.

Research should make a contribution to knowledge and development of theory. A major goal of research should be to increase knowledge about political phenomena. Ideally, research questions should aim at providing explanations and developing generalizations while answering questions of interest to you and others. In fact, research should contribute to a change in the way others think about the topic. Even undergraduate student projects that are completed within a single term should be related to existing theory and to the literature found in academic publications. Expecting students to contribute to knowledge and theory may seem ambitious, but a surprising number of student research projects have ultimately led to PhD dissertations or contributed to collaborative research with professors.

There should be general interest in the topic. Topics should be of interest to you and scholars who are specialists, but ideally the question you seek to answer should also interest the community of scholars and the public at large. A topic should be limited in scope but broad in implications. You may, for example, be interested in explaining why a seemingly large number of public officials in your state have been convicted of bribery. In developing such a topic, try to place it in the context of explaining bribery of government officials *in general* and relate acts of bribery to other acts of public corruption. Your initial motivation may be only to understand the behavior of officials in your own state, but other social scientists will be interested in your contribution to an explanation of public corruption relevant to other states or countries and to similar behaviors. Topics such as bribery also are of relevance and interest to the public who suffer the consequences of such behavior on the part of their representatives.

The topic should focus on some aspect of politics. Politics is a contested concept, with scholars offering a variety of sometimes inconsistent definitions. A common perspective is that *politics* is a process by which scarce resources are authoritatively allocated for society. [6] Most definitions focus on the use of power and authority and implications for large social units such as organizations, nations, or society. Regardless of the definition used, politics clearly does not include all human behaviors. For example, a study comparing the reading habits of Californians and New Yorkers would be unlikely to advance understanding of politics as it is defined by most political scientists.

The subject of the research should have some relevance for public policy. The debate over the importance of "pure" versus "applied" research is an old one. Many argue that political scientists should not pursue knowledge for its own sake but should instead choose topics that are related to either the improvement of society and the political system or to the solution of a particular problem. Obviously, scholars will disagree about what is a "social problem," but it seems clear that many research projects could advance theoretical knowledge and at the same time contribute to solutions of problems. For example, research on the effect of campaign spending on election outcomes has important theoretical elements but also may ultimately influence policy on campaign finance reform. Since topic choices are personal choices, research agendas should appropriately be influenced by, and evaluated in terms of, citizenship values.

Research should be original. We previously indicated that topics should be evaluated, in part, by the possible contribution to new knowledge. Originality of a research idea can only be evaluated with reference to previous studies. If a literature search reveals few previous studies on a topic, there may be a couple of implications. Perhaps the question is truly original and ripe for research, or others may have investigated the question and found no interesting or useful explanations. In the latter case, it may not be fruitful to travel a road that others found leads nowhere. Pursuing general topics that have received attention from others is a good choice, but such an effort should involve developing new approaches, finding new sources of information, and/or providing alternative explanations. Knowledge is built and modified through a process of **replication** and confirmation of previous research, but replication does not necessarily mean exactly duplicating that previous work. Replication of earlier work routinely involves examining similar questions, but it also requires collecting data from different locations at different points in time, using fresh methods, and/or trying alternative measurements of variables. A number of interesting studies, for example, have found religious affiliation related to opinions on issues of morality. A common replication of previous studies of this topic involves classifying religious groups in different ways and examining alternative morality issues. By replicating earlier studies under different circumstances, researchers have both confirmed and modified answers to the general question: "Does religious affiliation influence opinion on social issues?" [7] The general topic is obviously not original, but research that has replicated earlier studies is original and makes a contribution to knowledge. [8]

The proposed research should be feasible and manageable. If you cannot complete the research or answer the question you have chosen, then you have obviously made the wrong choice. Some research is not possible for practical reasons, such as inability to collect the data necessary to answer the research question. Many political scientists would like to administer psychological tests to the world's leaders to determine what motivates them, but, of course, no leader would consent to such an intrusive and revealing procedure. The paucity of certain resources can also make a project unfeasible. Surveys that involve face-to-face interviews, rather than over the telephone, are very expensive and time consuming and therefore rarely used. Also, few researchers can obtain grant money to administer large-scale surveys of any kind and must be content to use survey data collected by others to answer their research questions. Students must be especially careful to choose a manageable question that can be answered through research conducted during an academic term—time is a pivotal factor in evaluating topics. The key to evaluating the feasibility of a research topic is foresight. You should have enough knowledge about the process of research to envision the work and skills involved in completing a project. Manageability is maintained by narrowing the topic and making sure you have the expertise and resources to complete the proposed task. Your professor is probably the best source of information concerning the level of expertise you can expect to acquire.

The project should avoid ethical problems. Ethical questions and how they can be resolved should be thoroughly considered at the stage of problem selection and formulation. There are two broad ethical questions to consider: (1) Will the people being studied be adversely affected? and (2) Will the reported results of the study have unfavorable effects on society or groups? Ethical considerations in formulating research projects are so important that we will give them special attention. In the next section of this chapter, we will focus on treatment of the people we study. In Chapter 18 we will discuss ethical considerations in the reporting of results.

We have just outlined in some detail criteria that should be used to evaluate a possible research topic, but we want to reemphasize the importance of choosing a topic that interests *you*. The topic may be something about which you are curious, that holds an intellectual appeal for you, or relates to a policy problem that concerns you. Conducting research on a subject that does not engage you is pointless. So consider the preceding criteria, but do not dwell on them. If you have found a topic that excites you and you think you can do a satisfactory job of research in the time available, move forward.

Key Points

When evaluating potential research projects, consider the following:

- Potential for a contribution to knowledge and development of theory
- Level of interest in the topic
- Political aspects of the topic
- Relevance of the topic for public policy
- Originality of at least some aspects of the research (but not necessarily the topic)
- Feasibility and manageability of the proposed research
- Potential ethical problems

Ethical Issues in Political Science Research

Ethical implications of research and how they might be handled should be thoroughly considered at the stage of problem formulation and the construction of a research design. The most important ethical considerations are the people who will be the subjects of your study, those from whom you will collect information. The concern with the ethical treatment of research subjects grew out of revelations following World War II of atrocities inflicted on Jews and others who were subjects of medical experiments conducted in Nazi Germany. [9] Several other cases of extreme abuse of subjects in medical experiments that occurred during the post–World War II years culminated in the National Research Act of 1974 that created the National Commission for the Protection of Human Subjects of Biomedical and Behavioral Research. In 1979, the Commission issued the *Belmont Report* that outlined basic ethical principles that must underlie research using human subjects. [10] Three basic ethical principles, outlined by the Commission, must guide research on human subjects: *respect for persons, beneficence,* and *justice.* All three principles are relevant to research concerning political behavior. By *respect for per-*

sons the Commission meant that individuals should be treated as autonomous, and those whose autonomy is diminished for some reason should be protected. *Beneficence* alludes to the importance of protecting subjects from harm and maintaining their well-being. *Justice* refers to the "fairness of distribution" among subjects and potential subjects of the burdens and benefits of research. [11] Research projects proposed by political scientists and political science students are less likely than those proposed by those engaged in medical research to conflict seriously with these broad ethical principles. However, ethical issues are encountered frequently by practitioners of social research, so we must discuss some of the more common ones. In the sections that follow we will describe some situations that can give rise to ethical concerns and some means that have been developed to protect human subjects.

■ Some Specific Ethical Dilemmas

The treatment of subjects in social research should be determined by weighing the potential value of the research against the possible harm or inconvenience that may come to them. That might seem to be a clear-cut approach for making ethical decisions, but as we shall see, the stakeholders in the research process, subjects and social scientists, might have vastly different views of what constitutes potential harm and how much harm or inconvenience should be tolerated in the interest of increasing knowledge.

Risk of Harm to Subjects. Of course, all research should seek to avoid harming subjects in any way. In extreme cases, usually involving medical research, studies using experimental methods have caused physical harm to subjects, including injury and death. As recently as thirty or forty years ago medical researchers conducted experiments that involved injecting subjects, who were not aware of the dangers, with cancer cells. Other research during the same time period involved administering LSD to subjects to examine its effects. [12] Social scientists are unlikely to propose research that poses a direct threat of physical injury, but other, more subtle forms of injury can result from studies of social and political behavior. There are infamous, and politically relevant, studies where subjects were exposed to psychological stress and loss of self-esteem. One such study, conducted by psychologist Philip Zimbardo, was a prison simulation experiment designed to study the effects of status on behavior. Students were randomly assigned to take on the roles of prisoners or guards for a period of two weeks in a mockup "prison" in the basement of a building at Stanford University. "Prisoners" were dressed in prison garb, placed under constant surveillance, and assigned numbers to replace their names. "Guards" wore military-style uniforms, carried nightsticks, and maintained order among the prisoners. In the end, Zimbardo had to stop the experiment because the subjects got so caught up in their respective roles that guards became aggressive and verbally abusive, whereas the prisoners became passive. Some of the "prisoners" cried uncontrollably, and the "guards" exhibited fits of rage. Clearly, there was an immediate risk of psychological and possibly physical harm to subjects. [13]

Research that exposes aspects of subjects' selves that they would rather conceal or that encourages reflection on past events they would rather forget can diminish self-esteem or produce anxiety. Survey questions, for example, might reveal a respondent's underlying prejudice toward some group, an attitude that may be inconsistent with self-respect. Likewise, a respondent who fears revealing ignorance and is asked a set of questions measuring knowledge of current events might experience stress and anxiety. The latter two examples of harm are not extreme, but they need to be considered in evaluating prospective research projects.

Research could pose a threat to subjects' reputations or even cause legal harm. Political elites, perhaps justifiably, are often reluctant to consent to interviews or complete questionnaires because of a concern with how their responses might be reported or perhaps incorrectly characterized. It is easy to see how information that a researcher might obtain could be damaging to a politician's reputation or do harm to the relationship between a government employee and his or her superior. Political scientists rarely find themselves in a situation where they are collecting information that might lead to an arrest or place a respondent in legal jeopardy, but it is conceivable.

Voluntary Participation, New Inequalities, and Coercion. Have you ever filled out a survey questionnaire or been asked to participate in an experiment? Did you feel free to refuse to participate, or did you feel some pressure to cooperate? People should not be coerced into participating as research subjects or respondents. Even if they agree to participate, they should feel free to decline answering survey questions found personally objectionable and to refuse engaging in acts they feel will threaten their well-being or that of others. This point is important because a surprising amount of social and political research is conducted using "captive audiences." For example, professors commonly ask their students to fill out questionnaires in the classroom or to participate in experiments. Do students really feel they can refuse such a request when they believe that their grade might be affected? If they volunteer for an experiment, do they feel free to refuse to engage in an activity requested by the people conducting the experiment? Other captive audiences include prisoners who are commonly offered incentives for participation in research studies. How voluntary participation actually is can be a sticky issue. When requests for participation in surveys and experiments are closely examined, social situations and forces of conformity are often seen to play a role.

The issues of "new inequalities" and a "right to service" also arise with participation in research studies. Some subjects in experiments receive no benefits from participation, whereas in others the benefits and burdens of the experimental process differentially impact subjects. For example, when a new drug is tested experimentally to determine its effects on a disease or disorder, one group may receive the drug and others may receive a placebo (perhaps a sugar pill). If the drug turns out to have positive effects, those people in the group who got the placebo were denied the benefits of the drug. You probably already know of some instances of inequalities in social and political research. In a well-known study to determine the effects of police patrols on crime rates, some precincts were assigned the normal number of patrols, some were saturated with patrols, and others were allocated no patrols at all. Those citizens who lived in precincts with more than the usual number of police patrols potentially enjoyed greater protection from crime than citizens whose neighborhoods were left unpatrolled. [14]

Covert Research, Invasion of Privacy, and Deception. Would you feel uncomfortable or somehow "violated" if you learned that your behavior had been observed without your knowledge as part of someone's research project? Many social science research projects involve observing individuals and recording their behaviors. Political scientists regularly observe citizens in public forums, such as a city council meeting, and record their comments or behavior. Those being observed may not be aware that their behaviors are being recorded. Even more problematic are observations of people who have every reason to believe their actions are private. Such covert research, by its very nature, violates individual privacy.

Some of the most interesting and theoretically useful studies of groups that embrace secrecy, however, have by necessity relied on covert observation. Sociologist Scott McNall posed as a recruiter for a right-wing, extremist political group in an attempt to understand the members' political views and the nature of the organization. His findings advanced our understanding of what motivates extremist activity, but his research could not have been accomplished if the members of the organization knew they were being observed. [15]

Just about every research project that involves the direct collection of information from respondents through questioning involves an invasion of their private lives. Respondents answering survey questions about their background characteristics (for example, family income), political views (for example, opinions on affirmative action), or social behavior (for example, frequency of church attendance) may be revealing sensitive private details about their lives. Privacy has to do with the extent to which individuals have control over who has access to information about them. Because none of us lead completely private lives, privacy is to some extent the result of compromise and negotiation. What constitutes "sensitive" information will vary with each respondent, so the ethical issue regarding what is revealed revolves around autonomy, control, and consent.

Almost all social and political research involving direct contact or observation of people results in some deception. Researchers are always concerned that if subjects know the purpose of the research, they will somehow modify their behavior and in some way distort key information. A common form of deception is misrepresentation. Researchers, like Scott McNall in his study of right-wing extremists, have misrepresented their identification and hid the fact that they are conducting research in order to gain access to reluctant respondents. More common is the misrepresentation of the purpose of a research project. Many pollsters tell respondents they are interested in their views "on a variety of political issues," when their focus is exclusively on a more sensitive issue, such as abortion rights. In fact, researchers commonly include irrelevant questions on a survey to deflect attention from the actual purpose of the study.

Deception is most common in experiments where the purpose of the study must be concealed. Experimentation by its very nature (as we shall see in Chapter 12) requires researcher control and manipulation. A straightforward example is the experiment mentioned earlier in which we examined the effects of scandal on the images of candidates. In conducting this experiment, we informed our subjects that the study dealt with learning how people form images of candidates. We did not tell them the study was an experiment during which some subjects would be evaluating candidates involved in financial scandals, while others would be appraising candidates caught in sexual scandals. [16] The purpose of the deception, which was absolutely necessary for the study, was to control the information available to subjects so valid comparisons could be made.

There are some social scientists who argue that covert observation and deception violate the autonomy of individuals and are unethical under all circumstances. Sociologist Kai Erikson argues "it is unethical for a sociologist to deliberately misrepresent his identity for the purpose of entering a private domain to which he is not eligible; and second, . . . it is unethical for a sociologist to deliberately misrepresent the character of the research in which he is engaged." [17] Humanist psychologist Herbert Kelman and others see the deception and manipulation common in experiments as dehumanizing because subjects are treated as objects. [18]

Protecting the People We Study

Formal and informal procedures have been developed to protect the rights of the people we study. The U.S. Department of Health and Human Services in particular has insisted, by establishing regulations, that ethical issues be considered before beginning a research project with human subjects. Professional associations and institutions of higher learning have set out additional requirements that must be considered during the problem formulation and proposal stage of research. In this section we briefly discuss some of the means of protecting human subjects and point you to some useful sources of information on the Web.

Institutional Review Boards. Any organization (such as a university, hospital, or research institute) where researchers seek federal funds to conduct studies using human subjects has to establish an **institutional review board (IRB).** Researchers must submit their proposals to their organization's IRB for approval before proceeding with the project. Institutional review boards follow strict guidelines set out by the government to ensure that human subjects are protected from harm. Most colleges and universities require that all research on human subjects be submitted for review, even if federal sponsorship is not requested. It is the function of institutional review boards to ensure that the risks to subjects are minimized, that there is a reasonable balance of risk to subjects and benefits of the research, that selection of subjects is consistent with the principle of justice, and that subjects will be required to provide their informed consent before they participate in the project. The rules for reviewing proposals make provisions for exempting some types of research from review and provide for expedited review for others. IRBs decide which projects receive exemptions or expedited reviews.

To the Web

The Federal Government and Protection of Human Subjects

Since the 1970s the federal government has been active in establishing ethical guidelines and developing regulations aimed at protecting human subjects from harm and abuse. You can easily access the *Belmont Report* and explicit descriptions of how IRBs operate from Web pages associated with the U.S. Department of Health and Human Services. Go to the **DEPR Web Page,** click on **Web Links, Chapter 3,** then on **The Federal Government and Protection of Human Subjects.**

Informed Consent and Debriefing. One established standard important for protecting subjects from harm, as well as their privacy, is **informed consent.** Loosely, informed consent is achieved when subjects, before agreeing to participate, clearly understand the purpose of the study, who is conducting the study, the type of information that will be requested, and the risks involved. In some, but not every, case IRBs will require researchers to provide a written description of the project to prospective subjects and receive written consent for participation. Written consent statements usually emphasize the voluntary nature of participation, the maintenance of anonymity or confidentiality (see following), an offer to provide a summary of findings when the research is complete, as well as the general points of informed consent previously mentioned.

We pointed out earlier that deception is common in experimental research, which may not even be possible if subjects are fully aware of the purpose of a study before participation. **Debriefing** helps mitigate the problem of deception. Debriefing is simply providing an explanation to subjects about the nature of the experiment after the participants' activities are completed.

Anonymity and Confidentiality. Revelation of a subject's personal characteristics, opinions, or behaviors, as noted earlier, is a violation of privacy and could cause embarrassment or damage to a reputation. Social science researchers generally are not concerned with the particular information provided by a particular subject or respondent. Instead, the goal is to develop generalizations about groups of people. Subjects are usually guaranteed, sometimes in a consent statement, anonymity or confidentiality.

Anonymity means that the researcher cannot link information provided with the person who provides it. For example, questionnaires might be distributed to a large group of people for completion. If no identifying information is requested, the researcher will have no way of knowing who filled out each questionnaire that is returned. You are probably familiar with this procedure because it is often followed when college students are asked to complete written evaluations of their instructors. This guarantee of anonymity protects students from retribution by instructors in the form of lowered grades. **Confidentiality** exists when information can be associated with the person who provided it, but the researcher promises to hold that information in confidence and not reveal it. By identifying subjects or survey respondents with code numbers rather than names, the researcher can maintain confidentiality while still being able to associate specific information with an individual.

To the Web

Ethical Codes of Professional Associations

The major social science professional organizations provide their codes of ethics, including guidelines concerning the treatment of human subjects, on their Web pages. To access the ethical guidelines set forth by the American Political Science Association, American Sociological Association, and the American Psychological Association, go to the **DEPR Web Page**, click on **Web Links**, **Chapter 3**, then on **Ethical Codes of Professional Associations**.

Ethical Guidelines Set Forth by Professional Organizations. Important sources of protection for human subjects are ethical codes developed by professional associations. These ethical codes are usually comprehensive. Not only do they set guidelines for the treatment of human subjects, but they also seek to govern relationships among researchers, to establish procedures for disseminating research results, and to monitor professional behavior in general. Colleges and universities also have developed separate guidelines for ensuring that human subjects are protected.

The Freedom to Conduct Research and the Rights of People Under Study

We have described some abuses that subjects of political and social research have endured in the past and suggested some principles and procedures that have been developed to avoid future harm to the people we study. While human subjects of research must certainly be protected, scholars in a free society have the right to seek new knowledge that requires the intellectual freedom to explore new ideas and theories. Some of the preventive measures aimed at protecting subjects may make it more difficult, and in some cases impossible, to conduct research that will produce useful generalizations. For example, the requirement of informed consent may limit generalizations about political behavior to those who are willing to take part in studies. If people who give their consent to participate in research projects are substantially different from those who withhold their consent, those generalizations may be faulty. Additionally, some hypotheses may be untestable without deceiving subjects, and development of theories in some areas may require covert observation.

The key, it seems to us, is to balance the interests of the people who are studied with the rights of social scientists to pursue knowledge. The mechanisms designed to protect subjects are reasonable and necessary to maintain high ethical standards in research. However, social scientists should be allowed to argue their case for research projects requiring deception or covert observation to an independent group of evaluators, such as an institutional review board. Such boards can find an appropriate balance between the potential value of proposed research and the possible inconvenience or harm that befalls subjects.

Questions for Thought and Discussion

A political scientist is interested in explaining why some people are truthful and others are not in reporting their participation in politics. He proposes the following study. Researchers will attend the town meeting in a New England town to record the names and comments of those who ask questions or argue for motions. A week after the meeting, a mail survey (with a stamped, return envelope) will be sent to a sample of registered voters that includes some who attended the meeting and some who did not. Respondents will be asked about their social background, whether they attended the town meeting, and if so, whether they spoke. No identifying marks will be placed on the questionnaires, and potential respondents will be told that answers will be held in the "strictest confidence." However, because researchers will need to identify those who attended the meeting, as well as those who asked questions or argued for motions at the meeting, code numbers revealing the identity of the respondent will be written inside the return envelopes where respondents are unlikely to detect them. The researchers will compare the social background characteristics of those who were truthful about their participation at the town meeting (both attendance and oral participation) with those who were not truthful. Discuss potential ethical problems, and their possible solutions, posed by this research.

Transforming Research Topics into Researchable Questions: Narrowing the Focus

Once you have chosen a general topic for research, you must narrow the focus and develop specific research questions. The process of transforming topics into researchable questions ordinarily proceeds through a number of steps. Very general topics sometimes have subfields or categories, and in that case you can identify those subfields as one way to break down the topic. If you have a general interest in social welfare policy, for example, through library research and brainstorming you might narrow the focus by identifying specific policies aimed at differing substantive areas such as housing, children, income maintenance, or health. Once you have broken down a topic, you must choose the subarea that will become the focus of your research. The criteria for choosing and evaluating research questions outlined previously can be used to structure decisions about subareas.

A researchable problem must then be singled out within your chosen subarea. We suggest that you engage in a brainstorming session, perhaps involving others, to develop a series of questions. List as many questions as possible. If, for example, you have an interest in international politics and have narrowed your focus to the subject of war, what would you want to know about this subject? Here are some possible questions:

- What are the causes of war?
- What are some consequences of war for the warring nations?
- What are some consequences of war for the international economy?
- What are the characteristics of countries that are most likely to engage in wars?
- What are the characteristics of countries that are most likely to win or lose wars?

We are sure that you can think of many other interesting questions about the subject of war. The point to remember is that narrowing the focus of potential research projects is an evolutionary, creative process that leads to increasingly specific questions.

Once you have chosen a narrowly focused question, it is time to develop some possible answers—also a creative process that takes advantage of previous research. (Although we strive for originality, others have probably asked and developed tentative answers to the same question that interests you.) Look at the preceding questions, and develop some possible answers for each one. Each answer that you generate (and we are sure that you can think of more than one answer for each question) has the potential to be the focus of a research project. This potential is realized by reformulating and restating answers into hypotheses that will facilitate the collection and analysis of information to determine whether your answers are correct or incorrect.

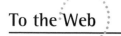

To the Web

Computer-Assisted Brainstorming

Computer software is available to assist with narrowing the focus of problems and thinking through possible implications. Most of the programs have been developed to help planners in the public or private sector "brainstorm" ideas, but some have been developed specifically for educational purposes. To access linkages that describe some of these software programs, go to the **DEPR Web Page**, click on **Web Links, Chapter 3**, then on **Computer-Assisted Brainstorming**.

To the Web

Exercise 3.1   Developing Research Questions and Answers

Developing research questions and potential answers requires creativity and patience. Questions and tentative answers can come from a knowledge of prior research on the subject, but some of the more interesting responses result from brainstorming. To practice this intermediate step in narrowing research topics, access Exercise 3.1 on the DEPR Web Page. Click on **Web Exercises, Chapter 3**, then on **Developing Research Questions and Answers**.

Useful Hypotheses: Definition and Functions

Thus far we have described two stages in the research process: identifying a general topic and developing a specific research question. Recall from the stages of a research project described in Chapter 2 that after a research idea is formulated, a researcher first reviews the literature to find out what is known about the topic (Chapters 4 and 5 will focus on locating and reviewing previous research) and then formulates general hypotheses. A *hypothesis* is an affirmative statement of a testable relationship between two concepts. Hypotheses can vary a great deal with regard to generality and abstraction. Initially, hypothesis construction focuses on developing clear concepts, but with further definition, hypotheses are transformed into more specific operational statements about reality. Because they are the basis of every social science research project, and the second layer of bricks in the "foundation of the house of inquiry," hypotheses development requires a considerable amount of time and effort.

Hypotheses are necessary to foster systematic social science research. Science proceeds though the continuous verification of specific statements that have been deduced from a theory or generalization. More precisely, social science advances through a process of falsification. Researchers never have enough evidence to be sure that a hypothesis is true; they only know when it is false. [19] You will recall that in Chapter 1 we argued that all knowledge is tentative, and it is the temporary nature of truth that requires the continuous testing of hypotheses. Hypothesis testing is the only way that theories can be evaluated. Ernest Gellner clearly makes the point: "Our theories can touch the world only at those points at which they risk falsification though non-congruence of facts." [20]

The formulation of hypotheses guides research and provides focus. Carefully and dispassionately constructed hypotheses enhance the objectivity of a study. They are, according to Kerlinger, "particularly potent means of objectively bridging the gap between one's beliefs and empirical reality." [21] A well-constructed hypothesis provides guidance for data collection and analysis. Ultimately, the quality of the hypothesis influences the ease with which research is conducted and the inferences that can be made about the predictability and accuracy of theory.

Characteristics of Useful Hypotheses

A hypothesis should be evaluated in terms of its usefulness, as noted previously, determined by the extent to which it provides direction for research. Poorly constructed hypotheses will lead to uncertainty regarding the nature of relationships between concepts, confusion about what the generalization describes, and hesitation about how to proceed with the collection and analysis of data. You must understand the characteristics of useful hypotheses and how to reformulate poorly constructed hypotheses to make them more useful. We begin by describing the characteristics of useful hypotheses.

A hypothesis should be stated affirmatively, not in the form of a question. The logic of social science focuses on the confirmation or falsification of affirmative statements, so hypotheses should be affirmative statements, not questions. Reformulation of questions into affirmative statements is easily done.

> **The question:** "Do candidates who spend the most money on their campaigns usually win?"

can easily be reformulated into

> **the hypothesis:** "Candidates who spend more money on their campaigns than their opponents usually win."

> **The question:** "Do democratic nations provoke wars?"

can be reformulated into

> **the hypothesis:** "Democracies are less likely to provoke wars with other nations than dictatorships."

A hypothesis must be testable with empirical evidence. Hypotheses are statements that may be true or false, but most important, they must be testable and verifiable with empirical evidence. If the truth or falsity of a statement cannot be determined with empirical evidence (sense-data), then the statement is not a hypothesis. Distinguishing between factual statements, such as hypotheses, and value statements that express a personal preference is critical because the truth or falsity of value statements cannot be determined by empirical evidence. There are three types of value statements, also called normative statements, and all of them can be reformulated into testable, factual statements. [22] First, an **evaluative statement** usually involves the expression of a judgment about an object or idea. In this type, value-laden terms such as "good" or "beautiful" are used for description. The following are examples of evaluative statements.

> "Democracy is the best form of government." (The term "best" is a matter of opinion.)
> "Corruption in government is bad." (The term "bad" is a matter of opinion.)
> "The House of Representatives was right to impeach President Clinton." (Determinations of "right" and "wrong" are based on values.)

A second type of value statement is called a **comparative value statement,** and it compares the relative worth of objects or ideas in terms of an individual's principles.

Often comparative value statements are difficult to identify because useful hypotheses also involve a comparison. Here are some examples of comparative value statements.

"Swedes are less moral than Americans." (Morality is a value; Swedes and Americans are comparatively evaluated.)

"Republicans are better than Democrats." (What is "better" is a matter of personal opinion; Republicans and Democrats are comparatively evaluated.)

"Fair judgments are more likely to occur in federal than in state courts." (What is "fair" or "just" is a matter of personal opinion; federal courts and state courts are comparatively evaluated.)

A third type of normative statement is called a **prescriptive value statement,** characterized by imperative terms such as "should" or "ought." They express an opinion based on personal values about some type of action or behavior. Here are some examples of prescriptive value statements.

"The campaign finance laws should be changed." (The term "should" indicates a preferred change reflecting a personal preference.)

"America would do well to reform the national health care system." (The term "would do well" indicates an imperative based on personal opinion.)

"Americans have an obligation to help the poor in Third World nations." (The term "obligation" is prescriptive and indicates a value-based preference.)

There are several methods for reformulating value statements into testable, factual statements, the easiest of which is to change the frame of reference from the implicit "*I* believe" to what a group of people think. A reformulation that changes the frame of reference does not retain the intent and relevance of the original value statement (a description of reality is changed instead to what people think about that reality), but oftentimes that is the only change possible. Following are examples of how all three types of value statements can be reformulated by changing the frame of reference. Note that the reformulated statements can be determined to be correct or incorrect by gathering information—that is, asking a group of people what they believe about a topic.

Evaluative Statement: "Democracy is the best form of government."

Reformulation: "Most political scientists believe that democracy is the best form of government."

Comparative Value Statement: "Swedes are less moral than Americans."

Reformulation: "Most Americans believe that Swedes are less moral than Americans."

Prescriptive Value Statement: "The campaign finance laws should be changed."
Reformulation: "Liberals believe that campaign finance laws should be changed."

A more useful way to retain the relevance of normative statements is to reformulate them by redefining the value terms into more fact-based terms. The following are examples of how statements with value terms can be reformulated by replacing them with fact-based terms.

Evaluative Statement: "Corruption in government is bad."
Reformulation: "Corruption in government is costly to taxpayers."
Comparative Value Statement: "Republicans are better than Democrats."
Reformulation: "The economy grows at a faster rate when Republicans control Congress."

A third method of reformulation is most appropriate for prescriptive value statements. Implicit in prescriptive statements is a causal connection between concepts, and a way to reformulate them is to make that logic explicit in the form of "if-then" statements. The following are some examples of how this can be accomplished.

Prescriptive Value Statement: "Campaign finance laws should be changed."
Reformulation: "If campaign finance laws were changed, then members of Congress would spend more time working on public policy."
Prescriptive Value Statement: "America would do well to reform the national health care system."
Reformulation: "If America reformed the health care system, then the cost of health care would be greatly reduced."

As we have seen, the truth or falsity of value statements cannot be determined with empirical evidence, and in a similar sense, a hypothesis that has been reformulated from a value statement is not useful if the data necessary to test it are unattainable. There is no point to developing statements about the way you think the world works if, as Kerlinger implied, the means for determining the gap between your belief and reality are unavailable to you.

A hypothesis states how two concepts (variables) are related. Hypotheses are most useful when they clearly indicate how two concepts are related. In Chapter 2, we distinguished between description and explanation as goals for social science and demonstrated that explanations make larger contributions to knowledge. Technically, a descriptive statement such as the following is a testable hypothesis: "Senators Kennedy, Graham, and Hollings support increases in the minimum wage." But an explanatory statement such as the following is a more useful hypothesis: "Democratic Senators are more likely to support increases in the minimum wage than Republicans." The explanatory statement is more useful because it contains two concepts: party affiliation of senators and support or nonsupport of increases in the minimum wage. One concept—party affiliation—is used to *explain* another—support for increases in the minimum wage. Explanatory hypotheses, the most useful type, always contain at least two concepts, but sometimes hypotheses are constructed using more than two concepts. These are called **compound hypotheses,** and while they can satisfy the conditions of a useful hypothesis, they are often confusing. One goal is to simplify, so a good approach to compound hypotheses is to split them into two variable hypotheses.

Compound Hypothesis:	The poor and alienated are unlikely to vote.
Reformulations:	Poor people are less likely to vote than wealthy people.
	More alienated people are less likely to vote than those less alienated.

The original hypothesis contained three concepts: degree of wealth, degree of alienation, and voting participation. In the first reformulation, wealth is hypothesized to explain voting participation, while in the second, alienation is hypothesized to explain voting participation.

Relating two concepts in a hypothesis always implies a comparison. The hypothesis "Democratic senators are more likely to support increases in the minimum wage than Republicans" implies that Democratic and Republican senators will be compared to explain differences in support for increases in the minimum wage. The hypothesis "Poor people are less likely to vote than wealthy people" implies that poor people and wealthy people will be compared to explain differences in voting participation. Comparisons should be made explicit when writing hypotheses, even if they seem obvious.

Useful hypotheses state relationships between concepts, but they should also specify the nature of the connections. The simplest, and least useful, statement of a relationship emphasizes an *association* between concepts, such as "Religious affiliation is related to opinions on capital punishment." Associational hypotheses indicate the existence of a relationship, but they do not tell us in what manner the concepts are related. A more useful **directional hypothesis** indicates in what sense concepts are related: "Catholics compared to Protestants oppose capital punishment." Most hypotheses in political science are directional. Less common are **causal hypotheses** that state that one concept causes another without exception. An example of a causal hypothesis is "Compared to all other religious groups, Quakers always oppose capital punishment." Causal hypotheses are the most difficult to confirm. In fact, most social scientists argue that causality can only be logically inferred and not determined empirically. The criteria necessary to infer causality are discussed in Chapter 6.

A hypothesis is meaningful and conceptually clear. A useful hypothesis communicates clearly how a researcher believes the relationship between two concepts appears. Clarity, especially conceptual clarity, is extremely important because only clearly written hypotheses can be convincingly verified or falsified. A hypothesis that is tautological (states a relationship that is true by definition) cannot be verified or falsified, so you must be sure that the concepts under study are conceptually distinct. The following statement is a **tautology** and does not offer a meaningful explanation: "Liberal members of the House of Representatives receive high ratings from liberal interest groups." The term "liberal" used to describe members of the House is not conceptually distinct from ratings by liberal groups—the distinction between the two is neither clear nor meaningful. We will return to how meaningful concepts are defined in Chapter 7.

We believe that hypotheses should be stated with as much precision as possible. The concept that is expected to influence another concept, and be the basis of comparison, should be mentioned first in the hypothesis. The concept or variable that is being explained should be mentioned second. The nature of the relationship should also be specified as precisely as possible. The hypothesis "Voting participation is greatest among the highly educated" is less clear and precise than "College-educated adults, compared to those without a college education, are likely to vote in presidential elections." In this example, the intent to use the concept of education to explain voting participation is clearly stipulated. Since the hypothesized direction of influence is from education to voting participation, the second hypothesis is also more accurately stated. The second hypothesis is also more specific by inviting a comparison between college-educated adults and those with less than a college education; that is, distinct characteristics of education are linked to particular characteristics of the voting participation.

Hypotheses are also more useful, since they more definitively suggest the information necessary to confirm or falsify them. The reformulation of hypotheses from an abstract, conceptual level to a more concrete, operational level takes place as concepts are defined more narrowly. Concepts in hypotheses should be clearly defined and unambiguous. The hypothesis "Developed countries are less likely than undeveloped countries to restrict freedom" would be usefully reformulated as "Countries with a high literacy rate are less likely than those with a low literacy rate to censor the press." When we focus on defining and measuring concepts and variables in Chapter 7, we will give additional attention to making sure hypotheses are specific.

Hypotheses should be general and related to a body of knowledge. The purpose of social scientific research is to develop generalizations, so it is important to avoid hypotheses that focus on single events or individuals. A hypothesis might state, "The infant mortality rate is lower in Sweden than in the United States," and if information were collected that confirmed this hypothesis, the result would be knowledge about only two countries and not generalizable beyond Sweden and the United States. A wider perspective would expand the focus to many countries: "The more countries spend on health care per capita, the lower the infant mortality rate." The confirmation of this hypothesis would contribute to general knowledge about the influence of government spending on health care while also telling us about the infant mortality rates in the United States and Sweden.

The emphasis should be on explaining general phenomena rather than single events such as elections or individual behaviors of government officials. It is possible to reformulate hypotheses that are too specific and narrow to ones that contribute to more general knowledge.

Narrow Hypothesis: Northern Ireland has experienced conflict because of religious differences.
Reformulation: Countries with populations characterized by religious diversity are more likely to experience civil strife than more religiously homogeneous countries.

Narrow Hypothesis: Senator Ted Kennedy won his election because he spent more on his campaign than his opponent.
Reformulation: Candidates who spend more money than their opponents on their campaigns usually win.

A hypothesis should be related to an existing body of knowledge and have the potential to add to that knowledge. Remember that hypotheses are deduced from theories; they should be testable implications of very general theoretical statements. Hypotheses are most useful when they are explicitly linked to a theory and, through that theory, to many other hypotheses. The test of a hypothesis has implications for more general explanations, broad-based theory, and a body of knowledge. As an illustration, one theory of democratization generalizes that the socioeconomic development of nations contributes to the development of democratic institutions. [23] An implication of this broad generalization, stated in hypothesis form, is that nations with more-developed mass media will exhibit higher rates of political participation than nations with less-developed mass media. The verification or falsification of the hypothesis will help determine the accuracy and utility of the general explanation for democratic development. It should always be possible to trace back a hypothesis to a more general statement or theory.

Hypotheses should be plausible and make sense. Finally, a hypothesis is of no worth without a good reason to believe that it will be verified: It must make sense. Many hypotheses might be tested, but few are worth your time and effort. For example, you may put forward the following hypothesis: "The greater the amount of air pollution in a city, the higher its crime rate." No theory or logic underlies the hypothesis, and there is no reason to expect its verification. Even if it were tested and confirmed, most researchers would respond with the question "So what?" because any relationship found would likely be circumstantial or explained away by other factors. The justification for hypotheses should flow logically from a general theory (deductively) or from repeated observations (inductively). Hypotheses are most plausible and make the most sense if they reflect the logic of what is tentatively known.

Key Points

Useful hypotheses have the following features:

- They are stated affirmatively, not in the form of a question.
- They are testable with empirical evidence.
- They state how two concepts (variables) are related.
- They are meaningful and conceptually clear.
- They are general and related to a body of knowledge.
- They are plausible and make sense.

To the Web

Exercise 3.2   Reformulating Hypotheses

A crucial step in any research project is developing a useful hypothesis. Research often starts with a vague question or statement but must end up as a testable hypothesis providing a direction for the research. For some exercises in reformulating hypotheses, go to the **DEPR Web Page,** click on **Web Exercises, Chapter 3,** then on **Reformulating Hypotheses.**

We cannot overemphasize the importance of constructing useful hypotheses. Their development further specifies the key aspects of a research problem to be investigated. They form the basis of every social science research project because they provide direction, specificity, and focus. A well-structured hypothesis will tell you what concepts must be defined and measured, what is to be explained, and what information must be collected for its confirmation or falsification. As we noted earlier they constitute key components of the "foundation of the house of inquiry," and their development requires care and considerable effort. We now turn to the basic elements in hypotheses.

Elements in Hypotheses: Concepts, Variables, and Units of Analysis

Earlier we defined a hypothesis as an affirmative statement of relationship between two concepts. **Concepts** are abstract terms that we all employ to make sense of what we experience. They are nothing more than the words we give to attributes of objects, phenomena, and ideas. We use concepts every day to describe objects (such as "dogs"), phenomena (such as "thunderstorms"), and ideas (such as "fairness"). As first mentioned during our discussion of the search for "truth" in Chapter 1, concepts are culturally developed through a process in which implicit agreement is reached to give specific names to objects, phenomena, and ideas. Because they are mental images, there will not always be agreement on meanings. The meaning of any concept is determined in part as a result of individual perception, so great differences from person to person may appear. There will be widespread agreement on the meaning of some concrete objects such as "table" but likely a great deal of disagreement on such contested concepts as "love." Unfortunately, the meaning of many concepts of interest to political scientists—such as justice, power, democracy, and equality—are contested and the source of substantial disagreement. Concepts are never seen as true or false but evaluated only to the extent that they isolate distinct segments of reality and facilitate communication about them. Lack of widespread agreement on the meaning of a concept will certainly lessen its usefulness for advancing knowledge.

As we noted, concepts are terms that can be used to describe objects, phenomena, and ideas. When we see or hear a word that denotes a concept, we usually think of a set of *properties*. The word "table" triggers an image of an object with a flat surface with three or four supports (legs). "Democracy" evokes a variety of images, perhaps a voting machine, the U.S. Capitol Building, or a number of additional unobservable concepts such as freedom of the press or majority rule. Hypotheses are constructed with concepts that can take on a number of values, and these special types of concepts are called **variables.** Defining a variable without being redundant is troublesome. A typical definition is provided by Fred Kerlinger: "A variable is a property that takes on different **values.** Putting it redundantly, a variable is something that varies. . . ." [24] Almost any concept can be a variable. Undergraduate class is a variable that describes college students and classifies them into categories or values: Freshman, Sophomore, Junior, Senior. As in this example, the categories of the concept are the values that the variable can take on, and often these values also indicate an amount of the characteristic. The variable annual income, for example, can take on any dollar amount.

As we know, hypotheses are statements of relationship between variables. Sometimes the values of a variable, rather than the variable name itself, are used when stating hypotheses, causing confusion for inexperienced researchers. Consider this hypothesis: "Democrats in the U.S. Senate are likely to favor increases in the minimum wage." "Democrat" is a *value* of the variable "party affiliation" and "favor increases in the minimum wage" is a value of the variable "attitude toward increasing the minimum wage." The other values for the two variables are likely "Republican" and "oppose increases in the minimum wage." Careful examination of the values of the variables will usually allow you to infer the variables related in the hypothesis, and conversely, in most cases a variable name should give you an idea of what the values will be.

Well-fashioned hypotheses are also clear about to whom or what the explanation is intended to apply.

To the Web

> **Exercise 3.3   Variables and Values**
>
> Given the name of a variable, you should be able to infer some of its values. Alternatively, given several values that a variable might take on, you should be able to supply a variable name. Exercise 3.3 will help you develop these skills and understand how variables vary. Practice at matching variables and values should also help you to identify variables in hypotheses when only their values are stated explicitly.
> To access Exercise 3.3, go to the **DEPR Web Page,** click on **Web Exercises, Chapter 3,** then on **Variables and Values.**

The **unit of analysis** is what the hypothesis describes, and political scientists hypothesize about a wide variety of units of analysis, including people, political groups such as political parties or interest groups, cities, counties, countries of the world, legislatures, and government agencies. The following hypothesis describes the fifty United States: "Southern states exhibit less competition between parties than states outside of the South." Usually, knowledge of the variables included in hypotheses makes it possible to surmise the units of analysis they describe. Age in years customarily describes people and "democracy versus dictatorship" usually describes the form of government in countries.

Sometimes the units of analysis described by variables and hypotheses are not so clear. For example, "voting participation" could describe individual participation in elections or the proportion of people who voted in a recent election in cities, counties, states, or countries. The most useful hypotheses explicitly state the units of analysis they describe. When we discuss data collection in later chapters, we will see that a lack of specificity about units of analysis can lead to some confusion and error concerning what hypotheses actually describe.

To the Web

Exercise 3.4   Identifying Units of Analysis

Since units of analysis are sometimes not explicit in hypotheses, it is useful to develop the ability to infer them, given names and descriptions of variables. Exercise 3.4 concerns identification of units of analysis. To access the exercise, go to the **DEPR Web Page,** click on **Web Exercises, Chapter 3,** then on **Identifying Units of Analysis.**

Conclusion

We said earlier in this chapter that hypotheses are the "second layer of bricks in the house of inquiry" and that particular care must be taken in their construction. In fact, the hypothesis is the basis of political and social inquiry. Properly constructed hypotheses clearly identify the variables related, the values those variables take on, and the nature of the relationship between the variables. Furthermore, the unit of analysis should be obvious. A carefully chosen topic and a clearly written, useful hypothesis will allow you to proceed with confidence to the next steps in a research project: identifying and reviewing previous studies, defining and measuring variables, and devising means for collecting and analyzing data. If care has been taken in the original formulation of the research problem, each step in the process should lead logically to the next.

In the next two chapters you will learn how to find what others know about the substantive topic you have chosen for research. Chapter 4 explains that original research starts in the library with building a bibliography, and Chapter 5 helps you understand how to read and interpret previously completed empirical studies.

Summary of the Main Points

- The choice of a political research topic is highly personal. Beginning with your own experiences and what is going on in the world is generally the best alternative.
- A set of criteria can be systematically applied to determine the value of potential research topics.
- Ethical issues should be considered at the time of problem formulation.

■ Narrowing a topic to a number of possible research questions and then to possible answers to questions is evolutionary and taken through a number of steps.

■ Hypotheses provide studies with focus, guide research, and are evaluated in terms of their usefulness.

■ A well-developed and well-written hypothesis clearly indicates the variables related, the nature of the relationship, the values the variables will take on, and the unit of analysis.

Terms Introduced

anonymity

causal hypothesis

comparative value statement

compound hypothesis

concept

confidentiality

debriefing

directional hypothesis

evaluative statement

informed consent

institutional review board (IRB)

prescriptive value statement

replication

tautology

unit of analysis

value

variable

Selected Readings

Barnes, J. A. *Who Should Know What? Social Science, Privacy and Ethics.* New York: Cambridge University Press, 1979.

Jacob, Herbert, and Robert Weissberg. *Elementary Political Analysis.* New York: McGraw-Hill, 1975.

Kimmel, Allen J. *Ethics and Values in Applied Social Research.* Newbury Park, CA: Sage Publications, 1988.

Mills, C. Wright. *The Sociological Imagination.* London: Oxford University Press, 1959.

Shively, W. Phillips (Ed). *The Research Process in Political Science.* Itasca, IL: F. E. Peacock Publishers, 1984.

Sieber, Joan E. *Planning Ethically Responsible Research: A Guide for Social Science Students.* Newbury Park, CA: Sage Publications, 1992.

Activities

Activity 3.1
Identifying Examples of Ethics Violations in Social and Political Research

Early in this chapter we discussed a number of ethical dilemmas facing social science researchers. They included risk of harm to subjects, lack of voluntariness in participation, coercion of subjects, covert research, invasion of privacy, and deception. In this activity you will search the Web for examples of alleged unethical treatment of research subjects. Enter search terms such as "ethical violations in social research" or "deception in social research" (we are sure that you can think of many others) in a search engine such as *Google* or *AltaVista*. Locate and describe three examples of alleged ethical violations and relate them to the dilemmas mentioned above. Be sure to provide the URLs (Web addresses) of your sources.

Activity 3.2
Converting a General Topic to Hypotheses

How might you turn the topic of "characteristics that influence the electoral prospects of female candidates" into a research project?

1. Brainstorm and develop six research questions related to the general topic.
2. Choose four of the research questions from question 1 and convert them into useful hypotheses.

Activity 3.3
Identifying Hypotheses

There are numerous sources of hypotheses. Expressions of political opinion found on editorial pages (and op-ed pages) in newspapers often contain testable propositions, stated as fact, that are used to support arguments. The authors of these editorials want readers to assume these "statements of fact" are true in order to support the opinions in the article, but often these "facts" have not been systematically confirmed using appropriate research methods. Carefully read the following editorial taken from a daily newspaper.

1. Extract and write at least four statements from the editorial or column that might be considered "hypothetical."
2. Rewrite the four statements as useful hypotheses.

Democracy Withers in R.I.

Citizens get back what they put into representative democracy. That is the system's greatest strength, and its greatest weakness.

If citizens care enough to get out and vote, if they arm themselves with information, learn how to see through propaganda, find the courage to speak out against corruption, and even run for office, they get a responsive and reasonably honest government. If they fail in large numbers to do any of those things, they get the kind of government Rhode Island (too often) has.

The headline of a July 9 story by Scott MacKay says it all: "It's no contest: Democracy is withering in Rhode Island." Voter apathy is rampant. More than 40 percent of those now in the General Assembly are running unopposed, more than at any time during the last 50 years. (How much do you think *those* members worry about what the public wants?) And the opposition party—which might challenge and expose those in power—is moribund, unable to field candidates for key positions.

Does all that matter? It does. An apathetic democracy is a breeding ground for special-interest legislation, rank corruption, abuse of power, arrogant indifference to the public good, and other forms of political rot.

Ever wonder why politicians are perpetually falling over each other to expand benefits to senior citizens, often by dumping the cost on the backs of even less well-off taxpayers? It is because senior citizens vote, contribute to candidates and form lobby groups. In a democracy, those are the people with clout.

There are various theories for Rhode Island's shocking decline in civic culture. Good times, of course, breed apathy. So does a society that links status almost entirely to wealth, and scorns service to others. So does a public education system that no longer places a high priority on teaching children the rudiments of civics and American history, leaving them without essential tools of political power, easy prey for politicians who capitalize on their ignorance and indifference by selling an image instead of serving the public.

Rhode Island desperately needs to restore its civic culture. But it can't do that from the top down. Citizens themselves must start to care enough to vote, read, question, run.

Ultimately, in a representative democracy, we get the kind of government we deserve. That's just the way it's set up.

"Democracy Withers in R.I.," from
The Providence Journal, July 16, 2000, p. B6.
Reprinted by permission of *The Providence Journal.*

Activity 3.4
Reformulating Value Statements

Each of the following are value statements. Indicate why they are value statements and reformulate them into factual statements.

1. "There should be a Constitutional Amendment mandating a morning prayer in American schools."
2. "Cities are better places to live than the suburbs."
3. "The Republicans have presented a good plan to reform Social Security."
4. "Other states would do well to adopt California's tough auto emission laws."
5. "You can usually trust the Supreme Court to do the right thing."
6. "The movies produced in Hollywood threaten the morality of the American people."
7. "Something should be done to reduce the amount of pornography on the Internet."
8. "The Canadian approach to national health care is superior to the American approach."

Activity 3.5
Reformulating Hypotheses

Indicate why each of the following statements needs reformulating and then offer a reformulation.

1. "Ronald Reagan was a stronger president than Jimmy Carter."
2. "The number of convicts on death row is greater in Texas than in Utah."
3. "Republican electoral success is related to how the economy is doing."
4. "Americans are generally satisfied with their congressional representative."
5. "People who are dissatisfied with the government tend to exhibit political cynicism."
6. "More legislation was passed by Congress in 1934 than in 1954."
7. "Corruption among world leaders is related to average annual rainfall in their country's capital."
8. "Political participation is high among residents of affluent suburbs."

Activity 3.6
Identifying Components in Hypotheses

For each of the following hypotheses identify the variables, units of analysis, and the nature of the relationship.

1. "The greater the inequality in the ownership of land in countries, the greater the civil strife."
2. "Women are more likely to oppose capital punishment than men."
3. "Local television news stories are more likely to be about crime than network news stories."
4. "The proportion of the vote a party receives determines the proportion of seats it receives in the legislature."
5. "Daughters tend to acquire their interest in politics from their mothers."
6. "The greater the number of highway patrol officers per capita in a state, the fewer the number of highway fatalities."
7. "Interest groups that spend the most on professional lobbyists receive the greatest financial rewards from government programs."
8. "The size of a government agency influences the decision-making authority of its director."
9. "Lawyers who attended highly rated law schools are less likely to run for elective office than those who attended less prestigious law schools."
10. "State judges who are elected, as opposed to appointed, to their positions assign harsher sentences to those who are convicted of crimes."

Chapter 4

Determining What Is Known: Building a Bibliography

Learning Objectives

After completion of this chapter, students should be able to do the following:

Develop a strategy for library and World Wide Web searches.

Demonstrate familiarity with specialized dictionaries, encyclopedias, and yearbooks.

Locate books and articles published in professional periodicals relevant to a particular question about politics.

Locate scholarly papers that have been presented at professional meetings.

Distinguish between articles in professional periodicals that test empirical hypotheses about politics from articles that only describe or offer opinions.

Locate and evaluate information on the World Wide Web.

Serious Political Science Research Begins (But Does Not End) with the Library

After first developing a tentative idea for a research topic and perhaps a general hypothesis, the next step is to become informed about that area of research. The process begins with building a bibliography of resources, the initial step toward reviewing the relevant literature about the area of research. Students often make a distinction between an empirical research project and "library research." Most traditional term papers involve integrating and summarizing a variety of material found in library books and periodicals; the emphasis is on research produced by others. Empirical research projects, which emphasize the production of new knowledge, is equally dependent on the resources found in libraries. Libraries are storehouses of knowledge and are therefore places we must visit to learn about a topic and how others have answered questions that interest us.

There are several important reasons for building a bibliography and reviewing research related to your topic.

To discover what is known about the topic. There are thousands of political scientists in the United States and many thousands more in the rest of the world. The question of interest to you is likely to have been of interest to others who have already produced a body of existing knowledge. The two questions that must be answered are "What is known about this topic?" and "How can I contribute to knowledge about this topic?" If your topic has been thoroughly researched by others, and generalizations have been well established, it may make little sense for you to pursue the topic unless you are aware of some information that runs counter to the prevailing view. If, on the other hand, there have been only a few studies that have addressed your question, and they have produced inconsistent results, you probably have found an area of research where you can make a contribution.

As we pointed out in Chapter 3, social scientific knowledge grows through a process of replication during which analyses are repeated under different conditions or take into account different factors. It is well established, for example, that in the United States people with higher levels of education are more likely to participate in politics than those with lower levels of education. Further research with a narrow focus on this topic in the context of U.S. politics would be unlikely to make a contribution. However, an examination of factors, such as race, that mitigate the effects of education on participation might deserve attention. Likewise, if the effects of education on participation in several other countries were examined, the results might strengthen or modify current knowledge. In short, by learning what is known, it is possible to learn what might be contributed.

If no studies are reported on a particular topic, there may be a good reason not to pursue it any further. A lack of interest by others might indicate that no interesting generalizations have been developed or that data are not available to conduct empirical research. This does not mean that it is impossible to develop new questions or new answers, but it is simply unusual to find topics that have not received attention by others. The only way to find out if a topic is worth your consideration is to determine what others have found.

To acquire general knowledge of a topic. In beginning a new piece of research, you must read widely to broaden your knowledge. General knowledge is built from the answers to narrow questions; bits of knowledge fit together to form broad generalizations. For example, your research question may have to do with the impact of divisive election primaries on party solidarity. To gain a fuller understanding of your question, you must learn how political party organizations function and how they relate with individual candidates. Political science has increasingly taken an interdisciplinary perspective in seeking answers to questions, so to answer a question about primary divisiveness, group behavior literature in sociology or literature on interpersonal conflict found in psychology might have to be reviewed. Political scientists often begin the research process with broad knowledge of their subfield, but many scholars have to read to "get up to speed" in areas that are related to their primary concerns. Generally, the more knowledge that is acquired, the more scholars realize there is even more to know.

To increase focus and clarity in framing the political research question. As you read broadly about your research question, you should begin to clarify and narrow your focus. Concepts will be defined more clearly; the research question will be placed into a theoretical context and achieve a certain "fit" with other, similar questions. As you become more aware of previous studies, you should be able to narrow your research in such a way that it is not only manageable but also will contribute to a subset of knowledge in the discipline.

To determine what methodology has been used by others. A review of earlier research will help you learn how others have defined the concepts that are of interest to you, designed research, collected data, and undertaken analysis. How others have sought answers to questions similar to yours is important so you can replicate their findings, or take advantage of what has worked well for them, or learn from their mistakes. There is often disagreement about methodological approaches because different approaches may produce conflicting results. Consequently, awareness of criticisms of research procedures, as well as the research results themselves, is vital. In the end, a review of literature that focuses on methodology as well as substance will leave the researcher in a better position to make choices from among a number of possible approaches to answering a research question.

Key Points

Building a bibliography of previous research helps you accomplish the following:

- Discover what is known about the topic.
- Acquire a general knowledge of a topic.
- Increase focus and clarity in framing the political research question.
- Determine what methodology has been used by others.

In the rest of this chapter, we will focus on gathering resources that will contribute to a thorough review of current research. We will concentrate on finding resources, evaluating their utility, organizing them in a proper form, and compiling all this in a preliminary form. As noted in the title of this section, research starts in the library, but the concept of a library has changed dramatically in recent years. Libraries are accessible not only by entering the actual building but also by using a computer to do library searches from a remote location. It is also possible to download library materials to a remote computer. But while it may not be necessary to physically visit a library to develop a bibliography, we are not yet to the point where it is possible to obtain all needed library materials without a visit. The concept of a "library" has also been expanded with the development of electronic databases and the World Wide Web. Almost all libraries now have their catalogs on their Web pages, so it is possible to make a virtual "visit" to libraries from all over the world.

To the Web

Exercise 4.1   Getting to Know Your Way Around the Library

You need to become familiar with the resources made available by libraries. This exercise requires you to visit and familiarize yourself with the library at your college or university. Additionally, you will access your library's Web page, as well as one of a library at a college or university other than your own. To access the exercise go to the **DEPR Web Page,** click on **Web Exercises, Chapter 4,** then on **Getting to Know Your Way Around the Library.**

In addition to library resources, there is a huge amount of information available from an uncountable number of sites on the World Wide Web. The absolute amount of information is overwhelming, and the problem for researchers is not only finding useful information, but also evaluating its credibility. Evaluating information found within the walls of libraries can be challenging, but today nearly anyone can create a Web site and "publish" information, making evaluation of this type of material many times more difficult. There is a great deal of material in libraries and on the Web that is not useful, and there is some that is deceiving. All researchers must develop strategies for evaluating the quality of publications, so we direct attention to evaluating periodical literature and Web sites in this chapter.

Developing a Strategy for Finding Sources and Keeping a Record

Careful planning of time and labor is basic in searching for library and Internet sources. As you will see, the development of a bibliography of resources is a creative process that often leads in unexpected directions, but the sheer volume of material will lead to nothing but confusion without a plan for focusing research and keeping track of sources. For example, if you were to begin a literature search for research on the influence of interest groups on legislation by typing the term "interest groups" in the Internet search engine *AltaVista,* the result would be more than 100,000 Web pages for you to investigate. If you were to type "interest groups" into the subject search of a university library catalog (we used Brown University for this example), you would get a listing of more than 300 books on "pressure groups." If you type "interest groups" into the subject search in the *Social Science Index* you would get more than 1,200 entries! It is almost impossible to examine this many Web pages and read all these books and articles, let alone keep an efficient and useful record of what they contain.

Because of this avalanche of information, you should have a clear, if tentative, idea of your research topic before you touch a computer or go to the library. Almost all avenues of access to books, periodicals, and Internet sources use title or subject **keywords** or **phrases,** so the first step in a library or Internet search is to develop your own list of these keywords and phrases. Some keywords may be obvious, but it is important to think of related words and terms. If you were interested in the relationship between political ideology and political alienation, for example, you would likely search using the phrases *political ideology* and *political alienation,* but you would probably want to try synonyms such as *political philosophy, political viewpoints, political attitudes, cynicism, anomie,* and *distrust.* Your library and Internet searches would lead you, inevitably, to even more keywords and phrases. Some Internet search engines, such as *Google* and *Ask Jeeves,* and online encyclopedias, such as the *Encyclopedia Britannica,* let users enter questions as well as keywords.

There are a wide variety of catalogs, electronic databases, indexes, and search engines that can be used to find material related to an empirical political question, so in addition to developing a list of keywords and phrases, you must formulate a search strategy. We offer advice regarding the usefulness of specific resources for building a bibliography of materials relevant to political science, but the most important resource is probably the reference librarian. Smaller libraries may have reference librarians who are generalists, whereas large research libraries often have specialists in the social sciences. Regardless of library size, do not be reluctant to ask for assistance; reference librarians are employed to help researchers such as yourself.

Keep a record of materials as your search is conducted. For many years, scholars and students have used index cards to record full citations of articles and books. In addition to noting citations that can be transferred to a typed bibliography, researchers write summaries on the cards, which can then be ordered alphabetically by the last names of authors, just as they will appear in the bibliography. It is best to use a consistent style for bibliographical references, beginning with the first source recorded. In Chapter 18, where we discuss writing research reports, we will point you to some style manuals that are commonly used by social scientists. If you settle on a bibliographic style when you begin building your bibliography and recording citations, you may be able to avoid editing your reference section later when you write your report.

These days many researchers use laptop computers for bibliographical research and recording of sources. If a laptop is used, then an annotated bibliography can be maintained in a single file. If the laptop can be connected by modem to library catalogs or to databases such as *LEXIS/NEXIS* and the World Wide Web, it may be possible to cut and paste citations directly from sources to the annotated bibliography. Some electronic library catalogs and indexes facilitate sending citations as e-mail messages. If that is the case, researchers can send citations to their own e-mail addresses and later cut and paste them into bibliographies. Technology creates opportunities for finding and recording information more easily, but it also necessitates the development of skills in evaluating, recording, and organizing sources.

An element of a strategy that is not often discussed is based on the old saying "Don't reinvent the wheel." Since it is likely that other researchers have been interested in your topic, the probability is high that others have constructed bibliographies. As you find sources, especially scholarly articles, closely examine the references and add those that seem relevant to your own bibliography. A useful approach is to try to find the most recent article on your topic that has been published in a professional journal and record items from the bibliography. Of course, you cannot count on other scholars to find every useful source, but building on the work of others will save a great deal of effort. Catalogues and indexes are still indispensable for finding the most recent studies because professional journals often do not publish articles until as long as two years after receiving them.

Questions for Thought and Discussion

Imagine that you are beginning a research project on the influence of religious affiliation on political party membership in Europe and Asia. You need to build a bibliography on the subject. What keywords and phrases would you use for your library and Internet searches?

Finding Resources

The changing nature of the very concept of a "library" makes it troublesome to develop categories of resources. Many articles that appear in professional periodicals are indexed and published in both hard copy and electronic format. Scholarly papers read at professional conferences, which used to be difficult to obtain, are now available online from archives. Other important pieces of information may be published only on a Web page located on a server at a remote location. In the discussion of resources that follows, we will use the conventional distinctions between books and periodicals but note that these resources may be available in hard copy, online, or both. We will list some of the more important reference works and indexes and provide links to them from the

DEPR Web page if versions are available online. Web pages are a new format for publishing research, and they deserve a category of their own.

Before moving on to a discussion of how to locate sources for a bibliography, we want to emphasize the increasing ease of obtaining research material and the importance of specialists. While some of you attend large universities with libraries that have extensive collections necessary for faculty and graduate student research, many of you are probably at colleges with smaller libraries. If your library's on-site collection is relatively small and geared to undergraduate studies, the good news is that it is increasingly easier to access the type of materials available in large research libraries. Many college libraries are members of consortia with other libraries and participate in interlibrary loan programs. If you find that a book you need is not available in your library, you can likely order it from another library through the online catalog. If your library does not subscribe to the hard-copy version of a professional journal that contains an article you need, it is likely that you will be able to download a full-text version from an electronic database linked to your library's Web page. As we mentioned earlier, a very important resource is the reference librarian. Reference librarians are specialists who can help you locate the resources you need, whether they are located in your library or elsewhere, and can teach you how to conduct effective searches. Take advantage of their expertise and willingness to assist you.

▣ Using the Library Catalog to Identify Books

The online catalog contains a listing of all of the books in a library's holdings. In most cases, access to the catalog is from a computer terminal within the library or from a remote computer through the library Web page. Most academic libraries participate in interlibrary loan programs, so it is often useful to search more than one library, especially if the holdings on your topic are not extensive in your "home" library. Library catalogs allow searches by author, title, and subject. Initial searches often focus on subjects, but it is also useful to search by title. Electronic catalogs will retrieve lists of books that have as few as one requested word in a title. Keywords can be connected with **Boolean connectors** like *and, or,* and *not,* helping to limit searches. A request for subjects that link states *and* legislatures, for example, would eliminate titles concerning Congress. Like the paper cards that used to appear in library catalogs, electronic cards will provide all the information necessary to find specific books and add them to a bibliography. Subject searches usually produce a list of books and suggestions for ways to extend a search, with alternative keywords or phrases often suggested. Once a potentially useful book is located, many catalogs will offer to show a list of books that are nearby on the library shelf.

If you identify a book through a subject search, the citation will contain a subject heading, author's name (last name, first name), title of the book, publisher, date of publication, the number of pages in the book, and a **call number.** The call number is needed to locate the book in the library. Most libraries use a subject matter classification system developed by the Library of Congress. The following is an abbreviated list of Library of Congress subject matter categories.

A	General Works
B	Philosophy, Psychology, Religion
C	History–Auxiliary Sciences
D	History (except America)
E–F	History America
G	Geography and Anthropology
H	Social Sciences
HB–HJ	Economics and Business
HM–HX	Sociology
J	Political Science
J	Official Documents
JA	General Works
JC	Political Theory
JF	Constitution and Administration
JK	United States
JL	British America, Latin America
JN	Europe
JQ	Asia, Africa, Australia, Pacific Islands
JS	Local Government
JV	Colonies and Colonization
JX	International Law and International Relations
K	Law
L	Education
M	Music
N	Fine Arts
P	Language and Literature
Q	Science
R	Medicine
S	Agriculture
T	Technology
U	Military Science
V	Naval Science
Z	Bibliography and Library Science

Note that works dealing with political science are categorized under "J," but that it would not be unusual to find politically relevant material under most of the classifications. Libraries often use the Library of Congress classification system to identify and shelve periodicals as well as books, but alternatively, periodicals may be found in the shelves classified by subject matter (for example, Sciences and Humanities) and then alphabetically by title. Government publications have a separate classification system.

> **To the Web**
>
> **Locating Government Publications Online**
>
> Publications of the U.S. government are usually stored separately from books and periodicals in libraries and are not cataloged using the Library of Congress system. Fortunately, the U.S. Government Printing Office has a useful online catalog that provides an easy-to-use search engine. Publications by other governments can also be searched online. To access the Catalog of U.S. Publications and other government publications, go to the **DEPR Web Page**, click on **Web Links, Chapter 4**, then on **Locating Government Publications Online.**

Reference Works: Dictionaries, Encyclopedias, Almanacs, and Yearbooks

A good place to start a search for resources concerning a political topic is the huge selection of reference works in the library, now also found online. Reference works often provide a general overview of subjects, a bibliography, and in the case of online sources, relevant Web links. Reference sources can also be used to clarify key concepts and ultimately help to specify and frame a research topic. In this section, we will discuss a number of prominent and useful examples of sources of background information, but it is imperative for you to understand that there may be many additional sources and that reference librarians should be consulted for assistance. Except for the online references discussed below, most reference works are found in the reference section of the library and do not circulate.

Specialized Dictionaries. We are all familiar with general use dictionaries, but as researchers we must become familiar with specialized dictionaries, which usually contain very short entries about specific concepts or processes. They are especially useful for concept definition and specification. The following are just a few of the most useful dictionaries about politics.

> Bealey, Frank. *The Blackwell Dictionary of Political Science: A User's Guide to Its Terms.* Malden, MA: Blackwell Publishers, 1999.
> Chandler, R. C., and J. C. Plano. *Public Administration Dictionary,* 2nd Ed. Santa Barbara, CA: ABC-CLIO, 1988.
> Collin, P. H. *Dictionary of Government and Politics,* 2nd Ed. Teddington [U.K.]: Collin, 1997.
> Elliot, J. M., and R. Reginald. *The Arms Control, Disarmament, and Military Security Dictionary.* Santa Barbara, CA: ABC-CLIO, 1989.

Plano, J. C., and M. Greenberg. *The American Political Dictionary,* 11th Ed. Fort Worth: Harcourt Brace College Publishers, 2002.

Plano, J. C., R. E. Riggs, and H. S. Robin. *The Dictionary of Political Analysis,* 2nd Ed. Santa Barbara, CA: ABC-CLIO, 1982.

Riff, M. A. *Dictionary of Modern Political Ideologies.* New York: St. Martin's Press, 1987.

Encyclopedias. Encyclopedias usually contain articles (look for the author's name at the end of the article) that contain very useful background material on general subjects. They almost always include a bibliography and a list of other related articles that are contained in the same volume. Here are some examples of hard-copy encyclopedias we and our colleagues have found most useful.

Goodin, R. E., and H. D. Klingemann. *A New Handbook of Political Science.* New York: Oxford University Press, 1996.

Greenstein, F. I., and N. W. Polsby. *Handbook of Political Science.* Reading, MA: Addison-Wesley, 1975.

International Encyclopedia of the Social and Behavioral Sciences. New York: Pergamon Press, 2001.

Kurtz, L. *Encyclopedia of Violence, Peace, & Conflict.* San Diego: Academic Press, 1999.

Levy, L. W., and L. Fisher. *Encyclopedia of the American Presidency.* New York: Simon & Schuster, 1994.

Sills, D. L. *International Encyclopedia of the Social Sciences.* New York: Macmillan, 1986.

Several encyclopedias are now available online, and a number of them provide a surprising amount of sophisticated and detailed information about political topics. We think the most useful of these encyclopedias is the *Encyclopedia Britannica On-Line.* When we put the term "alienation" in *Britannica*'s search engine, we received a brief definition of the term, an article that offered a detailed discussion of the concept, a list of ten related books, a list of potentially useful Web sites, and a list of related keywords. Also online are the *Encyclopedia Americana* and the *Grolier Multi-media Encyclopedia.* Encyclopedias are, of course, useful as a first step in a search process. The information they provide is usually too general for focused research projects and should be used only for background information.

Almanacs and Yearbooks. These reference works provide both background information and, in some cases, data that may be used to test empirical hypotheses. There are a wide variety of almanacs and yearbooks, and the type of information they provide varies a great deal. Unlike encyclopedias, they are published frequently (usually yearly) and provide very current information.

Almanacs usually provide some statistical information, but often they also contain biographies and news summaries of the past year. This is a widely used almanac that deals with a range of political subjects.

Quain, Anthony J. *The Political Reference Almanac, 2001–2002,* 2nd Ed. Arlington, VA: Polisci Books, 2001.

An abbreviated version of *The Political Reference Almanac* is available online and Anthony Quain also supports a "political reference desk" where you can access information about politics if you pay a subscription fee or if your college or university is a subscriber. Both scholars and journalists make extensive use of the following almanacs that focus on contemporary American politics.

Barone, M., G. Ujifusa, and D. Matthews. *The Almanac of American Politics.* Washington, DC: Barone & Co., 2001.
Congressional Quarterly Almanac. Washington, DC: CQ Press, 2000.
Congressional Quarterly's Politics in America. Washington, DC: CQ Press, 1999.

All three of these almanacs provide biographical information about the members of Congress, demographic characteristics of states and congressional districts, and votes on key roll calls. The *Congressional Quarterly Almanac* provides a review of elections and legislation for the previous year.

There are a number of useful yearbooks that provide recent statistics and developments, as well as background information about American states, U.S. municipalities, and the countries of the world.

The Book of the States. Lexington, KY: Council of State Governments, 2000–2001.
The Europa World Yearbook. London: Europa Publications Limited, 2000.
The Municipal Year Book. Washington, DC: International City Management Association, 2001.
Political Handbook of the World. New York: McGraw-Hill, 1999.
The Times Yearbook of World Affairs. London: Times Books, 1999.

To the Web

Yearbooks and almanacs provide some background and a great deal of detailed information. They are less useful than encyclopedias early in a research project but can be extremely useful when statistical information or accounts of actual events are needed once a project is well formulated.

Online Reference Sources

Specialized dictionaries, encyclopedias, and yearbooks are increasingly available online. Most online dictionaries have abbreviated citations and are useful only for quick references, but online encyclopedias often provide extensive links to other sources. Go to the **DEPR Web Page,** click on **Web Links, Chapter 4,** then on **Online Reference Sources.**

Finding Articles in Periodicals

Books and reference works are useful, but most contemporary social science research is found in professional journals, most of which are published quarterly. Scholarly journal articles and those in news and opinion magazines are indexed in a variety of paper and online periodical indexes that can be searched by subject, author, or title. You should check your library's Web page or consult a reference or periodical librarian to learn which bibliographical indexes and databases are available to you. We think that a search for scholarly journals in political science should begin with the *Social Sciences Index,* available in both hard copy and electronic format. Most of the journals indexed in the *Social Science Index* are quarterlies, such as the *American Political Science Review,* that contain scholarly articles. However, some news magazines, such as *The Economist,* and opinion magazines like the *American Prospect,* are also indexed. If a search is conducted using keywords, articles relevant to those words are retrieved electronically or found alphabetically in printed indexes, and a "see also" list of related keywords and phrases is also provided. Limits can be placed on an electronic search, such as a restriction to certain years of publication.

A second important index for political science and the social sciences is the *Public Affairs Information Service Bulletin* (*P.A.I.S.*), which, as the *Social Science Index,* is available in print and electronic format. Unlike the *Social Science Index,* however, it can be used to find monographs, books, some government publications, reports, and scholarly articles. Searches can be conducted by author, title, and subject. Limits can be placed on searches based on years of publication, publication type (articles, monographs, government documents), and language. Most scholarly articles of interest to political scientists can be located in the *Social Sciences Index,* but *P.A.I.S.* is certainly worth using because it indexes some obscure sources listed nowhere else. Electronic versions of periodical indexes generally list only publications that appeared within the past twenty or thirty years. Paper copies of an index may have to be consulted for earlier publications.

The *Readers' Guide to Periodical Literature* is an index most students have used by the time they come to college. This index is the one to use for locating news articles in magazines like *Time* and opinion articles in magazines like the *New Republic* or *National Review.* For the most part, scholarly periodicals are not indexed in this guide. Like the other indexes, it is available in hard copy and online. The online version of the index provides not only citations but also abstracts that can be read to determine the substance of articles. There are also indexes available for searching newspapers; perhaps the most

To the Web

Accessing Media Web Sites and Their Search Engines

Most media outlets (newspapers, magazines, radio and television stations, television networks) maintain Web sites and provide search engines to access archives of articles or reports, sometimes in full text. Several gateway sites have consolidated the links of these media Web sites. To access these links, go to the **DEPR Web Page,** click on **Web Links, Chapter 4,** then on **Accessing Media Web Sites and Their Search Engines.**

prominent of these is the *New York Times Index*. Many daily newspapers have search engines on their Web pages that can be used to search back issues by subject.

Many other indexes are useful for searches for periodicals of scholarly interest. Numerous libraries subscribe to a service such as the On-line Computer Library Center (OCLC) that consolidates myriad indexes onto a single Web page. Providers like Silver Platter Products offer subscriptions to libraries that allow users to search several indexes, such as the *Social Science Index, P.A.I.S., ERIC,* and *EconLit,* simultaneously. A thorough search for periodical articles would likely involve the use of a number of indexes, but for most purposes, the *Social Science Index* and *P.A.I.S.* will be enough to locate what is needed to proceed with a political science research project.

Online Databases

The most exciting recent development in "library research" has been the increased availability of full-text material online. *Uncover* and *EBSCO* are two examples of bibliographic databases that facilitate searches and provide full-text copies of publications. Many professional journals, through services such as JSTOR (Journal Storage) and *Project Muse,* now also make the full content of articles available online to subscribers. Another widely used full-text database is *LEXIS/NEXIS Academic Universe,* designed for legal research with the goal of targeting large law firms and libraries. While *LEXIS/NEXIS* emphasizes legal documents, it also includes the most recent issues of newspapers and magazines, as well as television and radio transcripts from all over the world. Check your school's library Web page to see what full-text services are provided.

Locating Unpublished Professional Papers

The most current research in political science is usually not published in books or academic journals. Research reports usually first appear in the form of unpublished papers that are presented by scholars at professional meetings. The listing of papers is printed in meeting programs available to participants, but these days those programs are published online by the professional organizations themselves. It is possible to locate papers of interest (they are usually not indexed but instead organized by substantive area) and write to the authors requesting copies. The following are some professional political science organizations that routinely have their most recent, and sometimes past, meeting programs on their Web pages.

American Political Science Association
International Society of Political Psychology
International Studies Association

Latin American Studies Association
Midwest Political Science Association
Southern Political Science Association
Western Political Science Association

Increasingly, professional organizations are archiving full-text versions of papers presented at professional meetings. Papers presented at the most recent meeting of the American Political Science Association are archived and available for downloading from the Harvard University Library at a Web site called *PROceedings (Political Research On-line)*.

■ Locating Material on the World Wide Web

The World Wide Web is an unimaginably large array of information (and misinformation) stored on computers (servers) around the world by educational institutions, governments, interest groups, businesses, and individuals. With a few hours of training and a small amount of money, just about anyone can set up a Web page complete with text, images, video, and sound. A search for information relevant to a specific political research question can be overwhelming. We suggest two possible means for beginning a search, but we must caution you that you will likely find more useless than useful information related to a research project. The two approaches involve the use of *search engines* and established *gateways*. We leave the evaluation of information sources to later in this chapter.

There are hundreds of **search engines** that can be accessed using a Web browser—in most cases Netscape or Microsoft Internet Explorer. All search engines require the use of keywords and phrases, but some allow the entry of questions, and others will provide links through a series of subject categories. Each search engine is structured a bit differently from the others, and it pays to read the instructions that are offered in order to conduct an effective search. There are many search engines, with new ones developed frequently and others consolidated over time.

Everyone has his or her favorite search engine, and we want to pass on *our* preferences to you. Over time we have found that *AltaVista* produces more pages relevant to our search for social science information than most others. *Yahoo!* is a good page to begin a search because it allows searchers to work their way through categories

To the Web

About Search Engines and Their Use

Without search engines it would be impossible to navigate the Web. They have become so numerous, however, that you need to pay attention to how they operate. Search engines vary in size and produce different results. They have different search procedures and different means for prioritizing results. Some Web sites are devoted to providing instructions on the general use of search engines, and others offer comparisons and reviews. While you should always use several sites for your searches, with experience you will learn which search engines work best for your purposes. Be sure to bookmark your favorite sites for future access. We have linked the most prominent and useful search engines to the Web page along with some sites that provide instructions for their use. To learn about search engines, go to the **DEPR Web Page,** click on Web Links, Chapter 4, then on About Search Engines and Their Use.

including "Social Sciences" and "Government." *Ask Jeeves* takes an interesting approach in that it encourages users to phrase a question and not simply use keywords and phrases. At the present time we prefer *Google* and *Teoma* because they use state-of-the-art technology to rank-order the relevant Web sites, and it locates their order of relevance, saving searchers the time and effort of looking at long lists of irrelevant pages.

Almost every political science department now has its own Web site and many individual faculty members have personal pages that colleagues and students can use. Many of the designers of these sites have provided the service of establishing linkages to sources that are useful for political science research. Likewise, research libraries have established gateways designed specifically for accessing sites relevant to politics. These sites have links to government agencies, professional organizations, data repositories, news organizations, professional publications, and other gateways to political science materials. It may be useful to take advantage of the expertise of their creators before attempting to use search engines to find useful material. There are hundreds of **World Wide Web gateways** that have been established by social scientists and libraries. We have linked to the DEPR Web site the ones that we believe are the most useful and convenient to use.

To the Web

Gateways to Political Science Resources on the Web

Gateways designed by social scientists and librarians can save a lot of time and effort when conducting searches of the Web. We have linked to the DEPR Web site some very useful gateways that lead to governments, professional academic organizations, sources of data, news media, professional publications, college and university sites, political scientists' personal home pages, and other political science materials. To access these gateways, go the **DEPR Web Page**, click on **Web Links, Chapter 4**, then on **Gateways to Political Science Resources on the Web**.

Letting Others Help with the Work: Bibliographical References

Librarians, social scientists, and professional organizations compile and publish bibliographies on a wide variety of subjects, with some very focused on specific subjects and others aimed more broadly. Published bibliographies vary a great deal in their ease of use and completeness. Students should be aware that bibliographies are available and that reference librarians are probably the best source of information about them. Our goal here is to provide some examples of bibliographies that are available in printed form in libraries and online from several Web sites. General political science bibliographies, updated annually, include the following.

Englefield, D., and G. Drewry. (Eds.) *Information Sources in Politics and Political Science: A Survey Worldwide.* London: Butterworths, 1984.

International Bibliography of Political Science. International Political Science Association, in cooperation with the International Committee for Social Sciences Documentation. Paris: UNESCO.

More focused bibliographies are generally more useful for research on a particular research problem. Here are some examples.

Foreign Affairs Bibliography. New York: Council on Foreign Relations, 1933.
Ontiveros, S. R. *Global Terrorism: A Historical Bibliography.* Santa Barbara, CA: ABC-CLIO, 1986.
Radelet, M. L., and M. Vandivet. *Capital Punishment in America: An Annotated Bibliography.* New York: Garland, 1988.

There are numerous bibliographies available online from library Web sites, professional organizations, and scholars, some of which are searchable. A good place to start searching for online bibliographies are political science gateways, such as those linked to the DEPR Web page.

Determining Whether Sources Are Relevant

Building a very extensive bibliography of titles does not guarantee the relevance of the entries. Anyone who has done extensive library and Internet research knows there are a lot of dead ends and irrelevant information. The key to a focused bibliography is to learn to sort out the useful from the less than useful. Fortunately, there are means to determine the relevance of books, academic articles, and Web sites without doing a complete reading of every reference on a tentative bibliography.

Books

It is unnecessary to read an entire book to determine if it contains material that is relevant to your political research question. Many professional journals publish reviews of books within the journal's field. *Perspectives on Political Science* and the *Political Science Reviewer* publish nothing but highly focused reviews of books on politics. Additionally, reviews of books that deal with politics appear in magazines such as the *New York Review of Books, Atlantic Monthly, Harper's,* the *New York Times Book Review,* and numerous other periodicals that emphasize political opinion and analysis. Book reviews are indexed in the *Social Science Index, P.A.I.S.,* and the *Readers' Guide to Periodical Literature,* while the *Book Review Digest* and *Book Review Index* will also help you find reviews of books that you think might be relevant to your research project. In one further step, the *Book Review Digest* provides brief abstracts of reviews.

Commercial booksellers with Web pages (including *amazon.com, barnesandnoble. com,* and *powells.com*) have search engines that can be used to locate books, and their inventories are larger than most libraries. Each book listed is accompanied by a description of contents, table of contents, brief editorial book reviews, customer reviews, and, in some cases, links to reviews published in periodicals. Book reviews can be used efficiently to sort out the books that belong on a bibliography from those that will not contribute to the development of answers to research questions.

Scholarly Articles

Articles published in professional periodicals are probably the most important elements in a research bibliography. Students often have some difficulty distinguishing scholarly articles and journals from articles reporting news or offering opinion because the *Social Sciences Index* and *P.A.I.S.* list articles with scholarly sounding titles that appear in popular magazines. The titles of scholarly journals in political science and the social sciences are too numerous to list here, but we recommend that students examine the current issues of *American Politics Research, Comparative Political Studies,* and *World Politics* and compare them to these magazines of news and opinion: *Time, The Economist, Congressional Quarterly Weekly Report, New Republic,* and *National Review.* These last five look like magazines and are published weekly or monthly, whereas scholarly journals are usually published quarterly and are bound like books. Magazines of news and opinion may be useful for purposes of background, but they seldom report the results of empirical political research. Professional journals that report empirical research usually contain articles with content that is organized much like the flow of research characterized by the steps in the research process outlined in Chapter 2. There will usually be a discussion of the problem, explicitly stated hypotheses, description of data collection, and tables that report statistical analysis of data. Researchers should read and review these reports of empirical political research in advance of undertaking a research project.

There are shortcuts that can help determine the usefulness of scholarly articles. The first, of course, is to determine if the article is published in a scholarly journal. The second is to read *abstracts* of articles that may be relevant to a research project. Many scholarly journals require authors to write abstracts of their articles, which appear under the title of the publication. When an article is found in a journal such as the *American Political Science Review,* you can scan the abstract to determine if you should read the article. Abstracts are also available from other sources; *International Political Science Abstracts,* a publication of the International Political Science Association, provides abstracts of more than 5,000 articles each year. This particular abstract can be a bit difficult to use, but it is worth the time to become familiar with its system of cataloging. Other disciplines, such as sociology, have their own abstracts (*Sociological Abstracts,* available in paper and electronic form) that are very useful for political research, and there are abstracts ranging across more narrowly focused areas such as public administration, urban studies, environmental studies, and criminal justice.

Web Sites

To the Web

Books and scholarly articles are usually subject to review by experts in the field before a decision is made to publish them. This is not the case with Web sites. Anyone with a few hours' training in Web page design and access to a server can "publish" a Web site. The ease of publication on the World Wide Web raises some important issues of credibility and academic quality. You must take extreme care in evaluating the utility and reliability of information obtained from the Web. Librarians have been at the forefront of developing criteria for evaluating Web sources, and many libraries have posted a set of criteria on their Web pages for use by students and scholars. We believe that a set of criteria developed by Susan E. Beck from New Mexico State University is worthwhile. Her Web site is titled *The Good, The Bad and The Ugly, or Why It's a Good Idea to Evaluate Web Sources.* She sets

Criteria Used for Evaluating the Usefulness of Web Sites

There are some helpful Web sites suggesting ways that Web material can be evaluated. The best contain tutorials using actual Web sites to illustrate the criteria that should be considered before accepting information as accurate or credible. To access some sites containing tutorials, including Susan E. Beck's, go the **DEPR** Web site, click on **Web Links, Chapter 4,** then on **Criteria Used for Evaluating the Usefulness of Web Sites.**

out five criteria for evaluating information found on the Web: (1) accuracy, (2) authority—is the site signed by a reputable author or sponsor?, (3) objectivity—does the information show a minimum of bias?, (4) currency—is the date of the page given along with last update?, and (5) coverage—does the site provide a wide range of topics that are not covered elsewhere in depth?

To the Web

There is an awesome amount of information on the World Wide Web, which makes it a tempting and easy first source when developing resources for a bibliography. Take extreme care in evaluating Web sources. There is much of value on the Web, but there is also misinformation that can lead to mistakes in the conduct of political research. We suggest that you use the library as your first source of information and then search the Web for supplementary material or sources not available elsewhere.

Exercise 4.2   Evaluating Web Sites

Let us say it again: You must be very careful to evaluate information found on Web sites. A great deal of political material can be found on the Web—scholarly sites that include academic papers, sites designed to advocate a particular point of view on an issue, media reports, and teaching materials that include lectures and outlines. This exercise is designed to help you think critically about such information found on the Web. To access the exercise, go to the **DEPR** Web Page, click on **Web Exercises, Chapter 4,** then on **Evaluating Web Sites.**

Creating a Bibliography: A Matter of Form

The final step in the creation of a bibliography is to compile it in a proper form. A number of different documentation style sheets are widely used, including those published by the American Psychological Association (APA), Modern Language Association (MLA), and the *Chicago Manual of Style.* The *American Political Science Review* gener-

Table 4.1
Different Bibliographic Styles for a Scholarly Book and Article

Here are several ways to cite scholarly articles and books. We include the styles recommended by the *Chicago Manual of Style* (used by the *American Political Science Review*), the *Publication Manual of the American Psychological Association* (used by *Comparative Political Studies, Political Psychology, Political Communication, Public Opinion Quarterly,* and all journals published by Sage Publications), and the *MLA Style Manual and Guide to Scholarly Publishing.*

AMERICAN POLITICAL SCIENCE REVIEW

Book

Risse-Kappen, Thomas. *Cooperation Among Democracies: The European Influence on U.S. Foreign Policy.* Princeton, NJ: Princeton University Press, 1995.

Article

Dixon, William J. "Democracy and the Management of International Conflict." *Journal of Conflict Resolution* 37 (1993, March): 42–68.

COMPARATIVE POLITICAL STUDIES

Book

Risse-Kappen, T. (1995). *Cooperation among democracies: The European influence on U.S. foreign policy.* Princeton, NJ: Princeton University Press.

Article

Dixon, W. J. (1993). Democracy and the management of international conflict. *Journal of Conflict Resolution, 37,* 42–68.

MODERN LANGUAGE ASSOCIATION (MLA)

Book

Risse-Kappen, Thomas. Cooperation Among Democracies: The European Influence on U.S. Foreign Policy. Princeton, NJ: Princeton University Press, 1995.

Article

Dixon, William J. "Democracy and the Management of International Conflict." Journal of Conflict Resolution 37 (1993): 42–68.

ally follows the *Chicago Manual of Style,* but many social science journals adhere to a variation of the APA format. In Chapter 18, where we discuss writing final research reports, we will point you to a selection of style manuals that outline bibliographical style. As noted earlier, however, you can save time on editing your final report if a consistent style is used as sources are collected. The assorted bibliographic styles agree on what information needs to be provided but vary regarding the order of presentation and format of that material. Table 4.1 provides some comparative examples of the most important formats used for citations of books, articles in academic journals, and Web sites. For a more comprehensive set of examples, consult one of the style manuals listed at the end of Chapter 18.

Conclusion

Once a tentative research problem is identified, a search of the professional research literature must be undertaken to determine what is known about the topic and how earlier studies were conducted. Most of the information needed for a thorough literature search is available from academic libraries. However, useful information can increasingly be found online. In this chapter we have suggested some guidelines and sources that will aid the development of a bibliography. We have also stressed the importance of critically evaluating the credibility and usefulness of sources of information. Searching for relevant literature requires practice. As you become familiar with library indexes and resources, as well as the use of search engines to explore the Web, your efficiency in finding information will increase.

When you find existing empirical research on a substantive topic relevant to your work, especially in professional journals, the work may be difficult to decipher. The next chapter takes you through an article reporting empirical research in one of the leading journals in political science, showing you how to dissect and summarize the important material found there.

Summary of the Main Points

- Bibliographies are developed to determine what is known about a topic, gain general knowledge, help frame a research question, and learn what methodologies have been used in the past.
- Before beginning a search for resources, develop a strategy concerning uses of keywords, places to search, and record keeping.
- An exhaustive search for bibliographical resources includes books, periodicals, online databases, and information from Web sites.
- Books, periodical articles, and material from Web sites must be systematically evaluated to determine their relevance to the research topic as well as their credibility.
- Bibliographies should be organized based on the format suggested by such organizations as the American Psychological Association, the Modern Language Association, or a prominent scholarly journal in the discipline, such as the *American Political Science Review*.

Terms Introduced

Boolean connectors
call number
keywords and phrases

search engines
World Wide Web gateways

Selected Readings

Bolner, Myrtle S., and Gayle A. Poirier. *The Research Process: Books and Beyond*. Dubuque, IA: Kendall/Hunt, 1997.

Bradley, Phil. *Internet Power Searching: The Advanced Manual*. New York: Neal-Schuman Publishers, 1999.

Englefield, Dermot, and Gavin Drewry. *Information Sources in Politics and Political Science: A Survey Worldwide.* London: Butterworths, 1984.

Holler, Frederick L. *Information Sources of Political Science,* 4th Ed. Santa Barbara, CA: ABC-CLIO, 1986.

Knapp, Sara D. *The Contemporary Thesaurus of Search Terms and Synonyms: A Guide for Natural Language Computer Searching.* Phoenix, AZ: Oryx Press, 2000.

Werner, Brian. *Untangling the Web: A Beginner's Guide to Politics on the World Wide Web.* New York: St. Martin's Press, 1997.

Activity 4.1
Using Search Engines

Activities

To complete this activity about search engines, you need to familiarize yourself with a Web browser, either Netscape or Microsoft Internet Explorer. To locate search engines from Netscape, click on Net Search. Alternatively, go to the **DEPR Web Page,** click on **Web Links, Chapter 4,** then on **About Search Engines and Their Use.** If you use Netscape, a search engine will come up, but you can choose alternatives by simply clicking on those listed on the left-hand side of the page. Usually, they display an empty search box. Place the pointer in the box, click, and type in keywords related to your subject. Click on Search or simply touch the Enter key, and a list of sites will appear. Be sure to try a variety of search engines while completing this assignment, and be sure to note the procedures for entering keywords and phrases because they differ in some cases.

A. Use a search engine to find a Web site for an interest group. (You might start by searching for a topic or issue that interests you to see if you find sites for groups concerned with that topic.) Answer the following questions with information from the Web site.
1. What is the name of the interest group?
2. What is the Web address (URL)?
3. With what issues is the group concerned?
4. What information does the Web site provide on how to join the organization?
5. How is the interest group using the Web site to employ a grass-roots or information strategy?
B. Use a search engine to find a site that gives information about a state government agency.
1. Describe how you found the site.
2. What is the Web address (URL)?
3. Describe one piece of interesting or useful information found on the site.
4. Provide a general description of information on the page.

C. Where in cyberspace would you find information about the following? (Give specific addresses, and be prepared to discuss the steps you took to find the address.)
1. The United States Constitution
2. The Federalist Papers
3. The United Nations Charter
4. The text of the War Powers Act passed by the U.S. Congress
5. Information on the People's Republic of China
6. The U.S. president's daily schedule
7. Where to buy CDs over the Internet
8. The cheapest airline fares between Boston and San Diego
9. Your favorite news magazine
10. News about your favorite musical group

Activity 4.2
Comparing Resources Revealed by Academic and Nonacademic Databases

In this chapter we emphasized that in building a bibliography you must take into consideration the quality (reputation) and the credibility of sources. In this exercise you will compare the results of electronic searches of academic and nonacademic databases. Use the keywords "political alienation." Conduct a search using an academic database linked to your library's Web page such as EBSCO HOST (Academic Elite), Cambridge Scientific Abstracts (Social Science Abstract or P.A.I.S. International), or JSTOR. Record the first five resources that are revealed. Repeat the process, using an Internet browser (Netscape or Internet Explorer) and the search engine *Google*. Write a brief essay comparing the resources revealed by each search.

Activity 4.3
Building a Bibliography

In this activity you will build a twelve-entry bibliography for a research project on democracy. The homework consists of two parts: (1) a bibliography that has as its title the research question you wish to answer and (2) evidence that you have explored the resources offered by the library and the Internet.

Part One: Your Bibliography
1. Your bibliography should include the following.
   a. A citation from a specialized dictionary
   b. A citation from a specialized encyclopedia
   c. Four articles from professional/scholarly journals
   d. At least two books
   e. At least two sources from the World Wide Web
2. The bibliography should include references listed alphabetically by authors' last names, using the format of the *American Political Science Review* or one specified by your professor.

Part Two: Evidence of Use of the Library and Internet
1. The citation of one of your articles exactly as it appears in the *P.A.I.S. Index*
2. The citation of one of your articles exactly as it appears in the *Social Sciences Index*
3. The first two sentences of the encyclopedia article included in your bibliography
4. The first two sentences from your specialized dictionary definition
5. The abstract and first paragraph of one of the articles cited in your bibliography
6. A description of how you located one of your Internet sources
7. The citation of a book review of one of the books used in your bibliography

Chapter 5

Reviewing Previous Research

Learning Objectives

After completion of this chapter, students should be able to do the following:

Identify the components of an article reporting the results of empirical political research.

Dissect an article from a professional political science journal—describe and critically analyze in their own words the research question, conceptual hypotheses, operational hypotheses, method of observation or data collection, method of data analysis and presentation, and conclusions.

Summarize in just a few paragraphs the findings of an article reporting empirical research.

Write a focused literature review of research on a specific topic.

Reading and Evaluating Empirical Political Research

An important part of all empirical political research projects is a literature review. In Chapter 4 we outlined the reasons why it is imperative to determine what is known about a particular topic before beginning the development of a research design. We noted that two important reasons for reviewing the literature are to help clarify and frame research questions and to determine the suitability of different methodologies that have been employed by previous researchers. These aspects of a literature review are consequential for early stages of research that develop hypotheses and construct a plan to test them. Once a research project is completed, the review of literature becomes an important part of the resulting report. All research needs to be justified by being placed in the context of earlier work. Early in a research report authors review the literature in order to show that the key questions they are seeking to answer with their research need attention. Social science research should be cumulative, and in reviewing the literature, authors demonstrate how their research makes a contribution to knowledge. Finally, authors commonly return to a discussion of earlier research in the conclusion of their article in order to compare their findings with those produced by other researchers.

In this chapter you will read and analyze a recent article published in a prominent political science journal. Introducing you to research reported in professional political science journals early in this book on research methods creates a bit of a dilemma. You will have acquired the sophisticated skills necessary to critically evaluate empirical research only after you have completed the chapters, exercises, and activities that follow. However, the format of this book is consistent with the flow of the hypothetical-deductive system and the steps in the research process, and the review of relevant literature starts soon after a tentative research question is developed. In other words, the decision to introduce you to empirical research and to encourage you to practice critically reading political science literature at this point is consistent with the chronological development of the research process. You have to start somewhere, and early exposure to high-quality empirical research will facilitate the development of critical skills that are emphasized in later chapters.

A review of research literature on a particular topic or question should be the following.

- *Comprehensive.* All previous work that is directly relevant to your research question should be read and discussed. We know that even very exhaustive bibliographic searches do not turn up every pertinent research report. Often researchers have completed their research and are writing up their findings when they discover that they have "missed" a publication related to the matter at hand. Still, making a "good faith" effort to locate all relevant earlier studies is required.
- *Focused.* In searching the literature related to your topic, you will encounter studies that are only remotely related to your concerns. Although it is important to be comprehensive, it is just as important to limit your literature review to the relevant research reports.
- *Accurate.* Previous research should be read carefully and described accurately. The credibility of your own research depends on how completely you understand the research of others and how well you are able to connect their work with your own project. You also have an ethical obligation to report the research of other scholars accurately.
- *Evaluative and Critical.* Literature reviews attempt to point to questions not adequately answered by earlier researchers. Perhaps the literature simply has not addressed key questions, or earlier studies may contain important limitations and errors. Skepticism is an accepted norm in the social sciences.
- *Comparative.* Literature reviews make comparisons among the results of earlier studies and render a judgment about the state of the knowledge concerning important

research questions. Conclusions of research reports should relate similarities and differences of the current findings with those reviewed earlier.

- *Concise.* Literature reviews often contain references to a large number of relevant books, articles, and professional papers. The article we will analyze in this chapter has more than fifty citations in the bibliography. The best way to handle voluminous material is to summarize and discuss key studies very briefly and simply reference other studies that support a set of findings.

Reading and Dissecting an Article Reporting Research

All literature reviews begin with reading a single article, professional paper, book, or perhaps a bibliographical essay. The initial focus in this chapter is showing you how to dissect and summarize articles found in professional political science journals. Reports of empirical political research in academic journals generally follow a standard format that corresponds with the steps in political research. Once you become familiar with the format, you will find it easier to read articles quickly in order to identify the hypotheses that were tested, how data were collected, and the conclusions resulting from the data analysis employed to test those hypotheses. While the headings and subheadings may differ a bit from article to article, most follow this general format.

- *Abstracts* usually appear at the very beginning of articles in fine print just below the title. Abstracts provide a very brief overview and summary of the research.
- The *Introduction,* although often not labeled as such, is where the research question is stated and the relevance of the problem, such as unresolved theoretical issues and/or policy importance, is discussed.
- The *Review of Previous Research* is the author's critical review and discussion of the findings of earlier research, as well as the methods used to arrive at findings. This section often includes discussions of theories and generalizations relating to a political question. Sometimes the review of literature is part of the introduction to the article.
- An *Explicit Statement of Hypotheses* tested. The author states the conceptual hypotheses to be tested. Often these hypotheses appear at the end of the review of literature.
- *Methodology* used to test the hypotheses. Authors provide detailed information about how the study was conducted, many times divided into subsections (for example, variables, respondents, data collection, procedures). Concepts are defined and operationalized.
- There is customarily a discussion of the measurement of variables. Attention is given to the sources of data and how those data were collected. Sometimes tables are presented that describe the data that will be used to test hypotheses.
- The *Findings* or *Results* section is where the summarized results of the research are placed. When a large number of alternative operational definitions of variables are

employed or several different hypotheses are tested, findings are frequently broken down into subsections. Tables that summarize data are located in this section. You will frequently encounter in this section technical statistical language and elaboration of specific points or additional data in substantive footnotes. Sometimes a *Discussion* section follows, in which an author offers alternative explanations and relates his or her findings to those of earlier studies.

■ The *Summary and Conclusions* is where a brief overview of the reported findings are presented, the major conclusions are reviewed, and suggestions for future research usually offered. Sometimes the discussion of how the research findings relate to earlier research appears in the conclusion section.

> **To the Web**
>
> **Writing Effective Literature Reviews**
>
> Research reports prepared in every scientific discipline begin with a review of previous research. Libraries and professional organizations have developed guidelines and examples to help students and professionals organize and write effective reviews of previous research. You can extend your knowledge of how to write a review by accessing several useful sites from the Web page. Go to the **DEPR Web Page,** click on **Web Links, Chapter 5,** then on **Writing Effective Literature Reviews.**

You are now almost ready to read and evaluate an article that closely follows the format just described. But first we want to offer some advice on how to read an article and record the information you will need to construct a literature review. Begin by reading the abstract and the conclusions to obtain a good overview of the research question, methods employed, results, and conclusions. A reading of the abstract and conclusion is sometimes adequate to conclude that the article is not relevant to your research question. In that case, the effort of reading an irrelevant article will be spared. If the article is relevant, start by quickly going over the headings, tables, and figures. Once you have figured out the organization of the article, read it by focusing on each section in turn. Read with a purpose and evaluate as you read.

Everyone has a favorite approach for making notes to summarize information. Some prefer to read an entire article and then write down the key information during a reread. Others take notes as they read an article for the first time. The approaches are a matter of individual choice, but we have some suggestions that should be helpful. First, develop a system for recording your notes. Since a literature review involves comparison of studies that seek to answer the same or similar questions, it is crucial to record parallel information. We find an efficient addition to be a form that is consistent with the organization of articles and the flow of the research process. You can develop your own form, but it should contain the information outlined in Table 5.1. By recording the types of information laid out in Table 5.1, we believe it will be easier to quickly compare articles as you write your research review.

Notes can be written by hand on a printed form, notebook paper, or index cards, but we recommend using a computer if possible. Notes written using a computer can be easily accessed while writing your literature review. By keeping the citation of articles and books in proper format (see the list of style manuals at the end of Chapter 18), you can cut and paste your notes directly into the bibliography of your research report. Using

Table 5.1
Recording and Summarizing Reports of Empirical Political Research

(1) Full citation of the article, book, or report; author(s), title, publication, and all other bibliographical information)
(2) Hypotheses tested (list all of them at the conceptual and operational levels)
(3) Variables (list all of the independent and dependent variables and how they were operationalized)
(4) Method and data collection (describe the process of collection of data, the units of analysis, and the research design)
(5) Findings (describe the findings regarding the main hypotheses and alternative hypotheses)
(6) Describe the author(s) conclusions
(7) Your comments (criticisms of theory, methods used, and comparisons with the findings of other researchers)

a word processing program also makes it easier to cut and paste quotations from notes to your research report.

Now it is time for you to read an article that reports the results of empirical political science research. The article we have chosen was published in one of the major journals in political science, the *American Journal of Political Science.* We chose the article for a number of reasons. First, it is outlined and structured in a way that is consistent with the steps in the research process. Second, we think that the topic of the article is interesting and focuses on an important theoretical issue. Third, the authors are well known for their high-quality research, and one of them (Sidney Verba) is a former president of the American Political Science Association. Fourth, the article is relatively easy to follow, and the statistics that are presented in the graphs and tables are not, in general, overly sophisticated or complicated. Since the article is representative of recent research in political science, some sophisticated statistics are used in one of the tables. However, the authors of the article write so clearly that we believe you will have little difficulty understanding the nature of the findings. Don't worry if you have difficulty interpreting the statistical tables and graphs. By the time you complete this book and your course, you should be able to interpret most of the figures found in the tables in this article.

We have annotated the article to identify its parts and have inserted *Questions for Thought and Discussion* boxes where we expect you to pause, summarize, interpret, and evaluate what you have read. You should also, for practice, collect the information outlined in Table 5.1, either as you read the article or after you have completed it. Remember that reading, understanding, and critically evaluating empirical political research takes practice, and a close examination of the following article is a good place to start.

Gender and Citizen Participation:
Is There a Different Voice?

Kay Lehman Schlozman, *Boston College*
Nancy Burns, *University of Michigan*
Sidney Verba, *Harvard University*
Jesse Donahue, *Boston College*

Theory: Gender differences are considered in relation to citizen participation, an aspect of politics subject to more speculation than data when it comes to what Carol Gilligan so aptly termed "a different voice."
Hypotheses: Male and female activists specialize in different forms of activity, derive different gratifications from taking part, and bring different policy concerns to their participation.
Methods: Tabular and logit analysis of survey data from the Citizen Participation Study.
Results: We find, overall, more similarity than difference between women and men. Gender differences are not necessarily what we might have expected. Although women are slightly less active than men, there is substantial similarity in the overall pattern of the participatory acts they undertake. With respect to the gratifications attendant to participation, women and men are similar in terms of how they recalled the reasons for their activity. Men and women address similar issues; when it comes to the content of participation, however, men and women do speak with different voices, with educational issues and abortion weighing especially heavily in the policy agendas of female activists.

[Abstract]

[Introduction]

In investigating the nature and extent of gender differences in ways of thinking and in behavior, scholars often ask whether, in Carol Gilligan's resonant phrase, men and women speak "in a different voice."[1] Because issues of representation among citizens are so fundamental in a democracy, whether men and women speak with different voices is a particularly important question when it comes to politics. In this paper we use data from an unusual national survey to ask whether women and men differ as citizen activists—in the forms of their participation, in the rewards they seek, and in their issue-concerns.

Little systematic information has been available that bears directly on whether men and women differ in the kinds of activity they undertake, their motivations for taking part, or the policy concerns behind their participation. However, several bodies of literature—feminist theory, historical accounts of women's organizational and political involvements, and analyses in political science of citizen and elite political behavior—are helpful in developing expectations about men's and women's voices as political activists. We do have systematic evidence in political science about gender differences with respect to

Questions for Thought and Discussion

Did the authors clearly articulate the general research question? Restate the question in your own words. What justifications did the authors offer for undertaking the project? Did you find their reasons convincing?

---

[1] We appropriate the phrase from the title of Gilligan's (1982) book, not because we seek to consider gender differences in moral choices or moral reasoning or because we wish to enter into the scholarly debate that has surrounded Gilligan's work, but because her metaphor captures so aptly the question of gender difference.

many aspects of political behavior—for example, public opinion or the priorities of state legislators. With certain leaps, these studies can provide the basis for hypothesizing about gender differences among activists. With respect to the issues considered here, however, the literature does not provide direct evidence based on systematic samples. We provide that evidence here.

Gender and Participatory Voice: Expectations from the Literature

Let us review what these various bodies of inquiry suggest about the possibilities for gender differences in citizen voice. Feminist theory provides important background for consideration of these matters.

Many feminist theorists emphasize that, compared to men, women speak and act in ways that are more altruistic, more communal, more peaceful, and more nurturing.[2] Particularly relevant is Ruddick's (1989) influential discussion of maternal thinking, thinking that emerges from protecting and nurturing children (see also Bassin, Honey, and Maher 1994). If these orientations are brought to politics, then we would expect women activists to be more likely than men to anchor their participation in concern for the good of the community; to be active on behalf of issues involving children and families, human welfare, broadly shared interests such as consumer or environmental concerns, and international peace; and to derive civic gratifications from their participation.

Historical inquiries generate complementary expectations. The literature on social feminism and women's involvements in the period just before the granting of suffrage emphasizes the extent to which that work was charitably oriented and motivated by communal orientations (Flexner 1975; Baker 1984; Kraditor 1968; Stoper and Johnson 1977). Historians have also alerted us to the important role of women's involvement in organizations both as an incubator for other forms of political participation and as a form of community participation in its own right (Lerner 1979; Scott 1984, 1991; Baker 1984; Giddings 1984; and Cott 1990). In this vein, feminist scholars among political scientists have frequently argued that, in concentrating upon voting and other forms of electoral involvement, political scientists have neglected forms of participation that are especially congenial to women.[3] According to this view, which is supported by case studies of women's grassroots organizations (for example, Acklesberg 1984), women's participation is centered in political organizations, in grassroots and local activities, and in ad hoc rather than formal involvements. In short, we expect women and men to bring distinctive concerns to citizen participation and to specialize in different kinds of activity.

In political science, the most relevant systematic analyses of citizen participation have focused on gender differences in the amount rather than the nature of participation—finding that women now equal or surpass men in voter turnout (for example, Wirls 1986; and Beckwith 1986) and that the disparity between men and women in terms of citizen

---

[2]See, for example, Elshtain (1981), Sapiro (1981), and Eisler (1990). For a cautionary note, see Dietz (1985) and Tronto (1987).

[3]For excellent examples of this point of view, see the discussion in Randall (1987, 55 ff.) and Acklesberg (1994). Some critics (for example, Boals 1975, 171–175; and Baker 1984, 646–647) take this point even further, arguing that our definition of politics should be extended to include all activities undertaken to benefit the community—regardless of whether they involve public authority.

Mainstream political science has developed a reputation for slighting nonelectoral forms of citizen participation because the single best source of continuing survey data is the biennial National Election Study. Because it is anchored in national elections, the NES naturally emphasizes voting and other forms of electoral participation.

activity is quite narrow (Andersen 1975; Welch 1977; Clark and Clark 1986; and Schloz-man, Burns, and Verba 1994). These studies are somewhat less helpful in determining whether men and women differ in national or local focus of their activity and the partic-ular acts in which they specialize. Work using data from the biennial National Election Studies—which focus on national politics and electorally based participation—suggest small and inconsistent gender differences in particular forms of citizen activity. (See, among others, Beckwith 1986; and Rosenstone and Hansen 1993, 141). Using data more appropriate for investigating some of these distinctions, Verba and Nie find that, com-pared to men, women are slightly less likely to be affiliated with an organization (1972, 181) and slightly more likely to be completely inactive (1972, 97). Unfortunately, they do not differentiate local from nationally focused activity. Extending these findings, Verba, Nie, Kim, and Shabad (1978, 235) observe in an important footnote, "We had expected to find a different sex-related participatory pattern for campaign and communal activity. We found, however, no systematic differences between the acts." In short, existing studies based on sys-tematic samples find little evidence for gender specialization in particular forms of activity.

When it comes to the policy concerns animating citizens' activity and the rewards atten-dant to it, studies based on systematic samples are suggestive but less directly relevant. Al-though this literature only rarely connects political orientations to political participation, assessments of the gender gap in political attitudes, partisan identification, and vote choices find evidence for distinctive gender voices (Frankovic 1982; Goertzel 1983; Klein 1985; Shapiro and Mahajan 1986; Wirls 1986; Conover 1988; Kenski 1988; Miller 1988; Mueller 1988; Welch and Sigelman 1989; Conover and Sapiro 1993; and Bendyna and Lake 1994). Over the past 15 years, men have consistently been somewhat more Republican than women in both their electoral choices and their party leanings. Gender differences, some of them long documented in opinion polls, also exist in regard to attitudes on issues. The issues on which women's and men's opinions differ most consistently and most markedly are not women's issues—issues that affect men and women differently, for example, women's rights, abortion, or during the 1970s, the Equal Rights Amendment. Instead, consistent with the expectations derived from feminist theory, the disparities in opinion appear with respect to international aggression, the use of violence, and government welfare policies. We must be somewhat cautious in making inferences to citizen activity from these studies, however, for this literature does not connect these gender differences in opinions to political action.[4]

For systematic studies that link policy preferences to the content of involvement, we must move from the level of the mass public to the level of political elites. Unlike respondents in public-opinion surveys, who are presented a preselected agenda of policy concerns, citizen activists retain considerable control over whether, and about what, to be active. Analo-gously, public officials have discretion over the translation of their policy opinions into political action. Their choices about the committees on which they sit, the bills they co-sponsor, and the subjects they speak on manifest their issue priorities.

Recent studies of public officials—especially legislators in both the state houses and the U.S. Congress—find gender differences.[5] Compared to their male fellow partisans, female representatives tend to have distinctive attitudes; and their attitudes are reflected in their

---

[4]Exceptions include Klein (1984) as well as Welch and Hibbing (1992, 197), who show that men are more likely than women to "cast ego-centric economic votes."

[5]The literature is substantial, much of it recent. Complementary perspectives and extensive bibliographic references can be found in, among others, Kelly, Saint-Germain, and Horn (1991); Welch and Thomas (1991); Mandel and Dodson (1992); Mezey (1994); Tamerius (1993); and Thomas (1994).

behavior and legislative priorities. Most notably, consistent with feminist theory, women legislators are more likely to champion measures concerning women, children and families.

Studies of political elites also suggest that men and women differ in the rewards that they derive from political participation, with women more likely than men to cite civic concerns and men more likely to cite material rewards. For example, in her study of delegates to the 1972 presidential nominating conventions, Kirkpatrick (1976, chap. 12) found women delegates in both parties to be less ambitious for elected office than their male counterparts. In her study of state legislators, Kirkpatrick (1974, 143–145) found women in the state houses to be more comfortable with a conception of politics as an arena characterized by problem solving in search of the common good rather than by self-interested conflict. We must once again urge caution in making inferences, however, for these are data about political elites, and we are asking questions about citizens.

With certain important exceptions, the theoretical and critical literature and studies based on systematic samples converge in suggesting that, if there are differences between women and men in the nature of their political activity, they would conform to the following patterns:

Q *[Conceptual Hypotheses]*

1. Men and women activists specialize in different forms of participation with women more likely to engage in informal, grassroots, and organizationally based activities and to focus their energies at the local level.

2. Men and women derive different gratifications from taking part—with men more likely to emphasize material, as opposed to civic, rewards.

3. Men and women bring different clusters of policy concerns to their participation with women's activity more likely than men's to be inspired by issues involving children and families; broad public interests such as consumer or environmental concerns; the use of violence in the home, the streets, or the international arena; and the protection of human rights and the fulfillment of basic human needs.

Questions for Thought and Discussion

Was the review of earlier research focused and comparative? Are the authors critical of previous studies? Are the conceptual hypotheses that are developed for testing consistent with the findings of earlier studies? Can the hypotheses be easily traced to explanations derived from broader theories? Which hypotheses are most strongly suggested by earlier research? Are the conceptual hypotheses stated clearly?

[Methods]

The Citizen Participation Study

We employ data from the Citizen Participation Study, a large-scale, two-stage survey of the voluntary activity of the American public. The first stage consisted of over 15,000 telephone interviews of a random sample of the American public conducted during the last six months of 1989. These 20-minute screener interviews provided a profile of political and nonpolitical activity as well as basic demographic information. In the spring of 1990, we conducted longer, in-person interviews with a stratified sample of 2,517 of the original 15,000 respondents chosen so as to produce a disproportionate number of both activists as well as African-American and Latinos. The data in this paper are drawn from the 2,517 respondents in the follow-up survey. The data are weighted to create an effective random sample. We use the weighted sample throughout. All data can, therefore, be interpreted as if the sample were a random sample.[6]

---

[6]A more detailed description of the sample, the weighting scheme that creates an effective random sample, a listing of the relevant measures, and data on the effective numbers of cases can be found in Verba, Schlozman, Brady and Nie (1993).

For several reasons, this study is unusually well suited for probing the questions we have posed here. First, the Citizen Participation Study is based on a very broad construction of what constitutes participation allowing, for the first time, empirical testing of the contention that women and men specialize in different kinds of voluntary activity. With respect to politics, the survey asked about an array of citizen activities: modes of participation that require money as well as those that demand inputs of time; unconventional as well as conventional activity; electoral activities as well as more direct forms of the communication of messages to public officials; and activities done alone as well as those undertaken jointly. Furthermore, the survey was particularly unusual in including voluntary activity outside of politics in churches, secular charities, and nonpolitical organizations.

Whenever a respondent indicated having been active in a particular way, we asked a series of questions designed to measure the relative importance of a range of possible rewards in animating the activity. We also inquired whether there was any issue or problem, "ranging from public policy issues to community, family, and personal concerns" that led to the activity. We later coded the verbatim answers into categories of issue concerns. These data permit us to investigate in a way that has never before been possible the roots of citizen activity and to make systematic comparisons between women and men in terms of the gratifications attendant to their participation and the issue concerns behind it.

Questions for Thought and Discussion

Is the process of data collection adequately described? Is there additional information that might have been provided to assist you in evaluating the research?

Gender Differences in Participation

Do women and men specialize in different modes of voluntary involvement? Figure 1 presents data on the proportion of women and men who engage in a range of political acts. What is striking about Figure 1 is how little gender specialization there is in types of political activity. Indeed, rank-ordering the activities by frequency yields identical lists. In terms of the amount of activity for several of the activities including voting,[7] the gender differences in participation are neither substantively nor statistically significant. There are statistically significant disparities for four activities—working informally to deal with a community problem, making campaign contributions,[8] contacting public officials, and affiliation with (membership in or contributions to) organizations that take stands in politics. In each of these cases, men are somewhat more active than women.

In terms of specific acts, the differences in participation do not suggest that women will specialize in ad hoc, informal, local, grassroots activity. Although there is gender parity with respect to attendance at demonstrations, marches, or protests, the gap is larger for informal

[Initial Findings]

---

[7]As in all surveys, the figures for voter turnout are exaggerated. Data from polls taken just after the election, for example, show the opposite result with respect to gender: for example, the 1990 *Statistical Abstract* gives figures from a large government-sponsored survey that 56.4% of men and 58.3% of women reported going to the polls in 1988. With respect to level of turnout, these figures are still inflated, but are closer to the actual turnout than the figures from our survey. With respect to gender difference, there is evidence from vote validation studies (Traugott and Katosh 1979) that men are slightly more likely to misrepresent having gone to the polls than women are. Unfortunately, we have no analogous method of ascertaining the extent of, or gender bias in, overreporting for other activities.

[8]Men are more likely than women to make campaign donations, and to give larger amounts. In Schlozman, Burns, and Verba (1994) we discuss the significance of this disparity, as well as other differences in levels of activity, and the extent to which they can be explained by access to politically relevant resources.

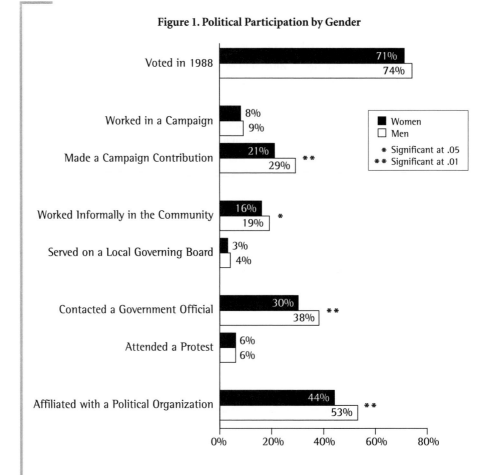

Figure 1. Political Participation by Gender

community activity than for working in electoral campaigns or community activity in the more formal setting of a local governing board. Women are also slightly less likely than men to be affiliated with any organization, political or non-political: 82% of male and 77% of female respondents indicated involvement in an organization. For organizations that take stands in politics, the gap is wider.

Additional data not included on Figure 1 question the notion that women are local specialists. Each time a respondent indicated having engaged in a political act, we asked a series of follow-up questions about the activity including whether it was national, state, or local. Women were only slightly more likely than men to confine their political activity to sub-national politics. Among those who engaged in some political activity beyond voting, 53% of the women, as opposed to 49% of the men, had no activity at the national level.

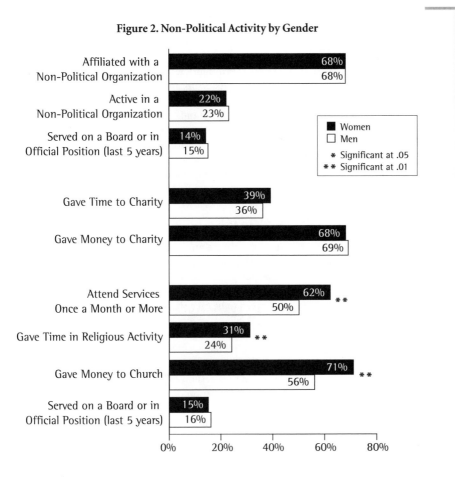

Figure 2. Non-Political Activity by Gender

Voluntary Activity Outside Politics

Figure 2 embellishes these findings by presenting data about voluntary activity in realms outside of politics—nonpolitical organizations and charities as well as religious institutions. Figure 2 suggests, for voluntary participation in the secular domain in nonpolitical organizations and charities, no real gender specialization. What is striking, however, is that women are clearly more active than men in an arena that is rarely mentioned in discussions of gender differences in participation—religious institutions.[9] Not only are women more

---

[9]Luker (1984) and Mansbridge (1986) make the point that advocates of a conservative social agenda have been successful by using Catholic and conservative Protestant churches as a base for recruiting women issue activists. However, none of those who advocate a broadened definition of what constitutes politics mention religious activity as a domain in which women predominate.

Q

Questions for Thought and Discussion

Are the alternative dimensions of political participation (the variable the authors seek to explain) adequately defined and distinguished? Do the authors make a convincing case that their findings contrast with expectations based on earlier research?

[Findings]

likely than men to attend services regularly, they are more likely to give time to educational, charitable, or social activities associated with their church or synagogue and to contribute money to their religion.

In short, for voluntary activity both inside and outside politics, the similarity between women and men in the patterns and levels of their involvement stands out. Where there are differences, they do not support the expectations developed in the literature. Women's activities—at least in 1990—were not more locally based, more ad hoc, more grassroots, or more organizationally focused than men's activities. In many instances, they were less so.

The Rewards of Participation

Although men and women do not undertake significantly different civic activities, they might take part in politics for different reasons and thereby create a different citizen voice. We looked at this question from the perspective of the activists by asking them how *they* interpret their participation, in particular, their recollections of reasons for their activity.[10] As we indicated, we might expect women to be more likely than men to cite civic concerns and less likely than men to indicate seeking material rewards.

In order to capture the broad range of possible gratifications that can flow from voluntary activity, we presented respondents who indicated having participated with a long list of possible motivations for that activity. We asked them to recall whether each reason was very, somewhat, or not too important in the decision to become active—or, in the case of ongoing participation like organizational affiliation or membership on a local governing board, in keeping them active. The theoretical underpinnings of the lists derive from James Q. Wilson's (1973, especially chaps. 2–3) typology of the incentives provided by political organizations,[11] modified to reflect pretest experience about the language and categories that citizen activists actually use in explaining and interpreting their activity. In asking respondents to recollect their motivations for getting involved, we attempted, insofar as possible, to make a complete matrix—that is, to ask each reason-item for each voluntary act, but we were not always able to do so. In assigning items to categories of analysis, we attempted to use items germane to many kinds of participation and to include only items that were unambiguous as indicators of the theoretical dimension in question.

We consider selective benefits of three types—material benefits, social gratifications, and civic gratifications—as well as the desire to influence a collective policy. *Selective gratifications* may be material or intangible. *Material benefits,* such as jobs, career advancement, or help with a personal or family problem, were the lubricant of the classic urban machine. They continue to figure importantly in contemporary discussions of congressional constituency service and incentives for joining organizations. *Social gratifications,* such as the enjoyment of working with others or the excitement of politics, cannot be enjoyed apart

[10]For a detailed analysis of the issue including a discussion of the methodological issues associated with asking respondents to reconstruct their reasons for activity and extensive bibliographic references, see Schlozman, Verba, and Brady (1994).

[11]Other typologies of the gratifications attendant to organizational support have many elements in common with Wilson's. See for example, Salisbury (1969); or Knoke (1991).

Table 1. Gratifications from Political Participation
Percentage Mentioning as "Very Important"[a]

	Material		Social		Civic		Policy	
	Women	Men	Women	Men	Women	Men	Women	Men
Vote	7	6	21	19	95	91**	60	62
Work in a campaign	25	24	47	50	85	84	44	52
Campaign contribution	17	20	28	18	79	80	46	47
Particularized contact	86	67**	26	22	43	38	17	21
Contact on a national issue	16	32**	10	13	87	88	80	79
Informal community activity	17	17	36	34	89	82*	38	39

[a]Items included in scales are listed in the Appendix.

*$p < .05$; **$p < .01$; ***$p < .001$.

from the activity itself. Without taking part, there is no way to partake of the fun, gain the recognition or enjoy other social benefits. Similarly, *civic gratifications,* such as satisfying a sense of duty or a desire to contribute to the welfare of the community also derive from the act itself. *Collective outcomes* are the enactment or implementation of desired public policies or the election of a favored candidate.

> ## Questions for Thought and Discussion
>
> Are the conceptual definitions of the benefits and outcomes of political participation clear and unambiguous? Do the indicators of gratifications derived from participation adequately reflect the definitions? (See also the appendix of the article.)

Table 1 reports the proportion of activists who say that a gratification in one of the four categories was very important in their decisions to undertake six kinds of activity: vote, work in a campaign, make a campaign contribution, contact an official on a matter affecting themselves or their families, contact an official about an issue affecting the nation, and become active with others in an informal community effort. Some gender differences in Table 1 reach statistical significance, but the differences are neither very substantial in magnitude nor consistent across gratifications or political acts. In fact, what is most apparent about Table 1 is how little difference there is between men and women in the gratifications cited.

Much more striking are the differences across political acts. In discussing voting, respondents—whether male or female—referred frequently to civic rewards and only rarely to material ones.[12] With respect to the gratifications attendant to working in a campaign, social gratifications assume greater prominence—again for both women and men. This suggests that the nature of the act rather than the sex of the participant determines the rewards associated with it. Since men and women choose to engage in the same kinds of participatory acts, the consequent rewards accruing to them are necessarily similar.

The Issue-Agenda of Participation

Women and men might speak in different voices as citizen activists by bringing different sets of issue concerns to their participation. Women and men would thereby offer different agendas for politics.

---

[12]This is consistent with the findings of those who study turnout as a rational process. For discussion and extensive bibliography, see Schlozman, Verba, and Brady (1994).

The Scope of the Agenda

We first investigate the scope of the issues behind women's and men's political activity—probing whether men are less likely than women to bring to politics concerns related narrowly to themselves or their families. Each time a respondent indicated having engaged in a particular activity, we asked whether there was any particular issue or problem—"ranging from public-policy issues to community, family, and personal concerns"—that led to the activity. Across all 3,600 political acts discussed, respondents in 63% of cases provided a comprehensible, codeable answer about the policy concerns that animated the activity.[13] Analyzing the substantive concerns behind this issue-based activity allows us to characterize the participatory input from women and men.

Since we wish to assess whether women and men differ in the likelihood of mentioning a concern limited to the individual and the family rather than issues with a broader referent, we focus on contacts with public officials, the only activity for which sizable numbers of respondents said that their concern was narrowly personal. (With regard to all other participatory acts, for the overwhelming majority of participants, the referent was broader.) There is virtually no difference between men and women who contact public officials in terms of whether the matter raised is germane only to themselves or their families, or a policy issue of more general concern. Discussing their most recent contact, 22% of the men and 21% of the women indicated that the subject was a matter of particularized concern. Of the female contactors, 35% indicated that the issue affects the whole community and 25% that it affects the entire nation (or world); the analogous figures for male contactors are 38% and 22% respectively.

The Content of the Agenda

More important to the assessment of the earlier claims than the scope of the policy concerns behind political activity is their subject matter. Table 2 compares women and men respondents with respect to the issue concerns that animate their participation. The issue-based political act is the unit of analysis, and the figures represent the proportion of all issue-based activity for which the respondent mentioned, among other things, a particular set of policy concerns.[14]

---

[13]Only 47% of voters—in contrast to 84% of those active in their communities, 87% of contactors, and 95% of protesters—cited at least one identifiable public policy issue as the basis of their activity.

[14]In coding the open-ended responses we created over 60 relatively narrow categories. In analyzing the data, we have combined these narrow categories in various ways. The components of the categories in Table 2 are as follows:

Basic human needs: various government benefits (welfare, AFDC, food stamps, housing subsidies, Social Security, Medicare, and Medicaid); unemployment (either as an economic issue or in terms of the respondent's own circumstances); housing or homelessness; health or health care; poverty or hunger; aid to the handicapped or handicapped rights.

Taxes: all references to taxes at any governmental level.

Economic issues: local or national economic performance; inflation; budget issues or the budget deficit; government spending; other economic issues.

Abortion: all references to abortion whether pro-life, pro-choice, or ambiguous.

Social issues: traditional morality; pornography; family planning, teenage pregnancy, sex education, or contraception; school prayer; gay rights or homosexuality.

Education: educational issues (school reform, school voucher plans, etc.); problems or issues related to schooling of family members; guaranteed student loans.

Children or youth: recreation for children or youth; day care; other issues affecting young.

Table 2. Percentage of Issue-Based Participation Motivated by Concern about Particular Issues

	Women	Men
Basic human needs	10	9
Taxes	12	15*
Economic issues (except taxes)	9	11
Abortion	14	7***
Social issues (except abortion)	2	2
Education	20	13***
Children or youth (except education)	5	4
Crime or drugs	9	7
Environment	8	10
Foreign policy	5	8**
Women	1	a
Number of respondents	1,327	1,191
Number of issue-based acts	1,162	1,235

[a]Less than 1%.

*$p < .05$; **$p < .01$; ***$p < .001$

The actual issues associated with activity reveal more similarity than difference between women and men. Both groups bring a diverse set of issues to participation. Moreover, their issue agendas are similar, though not identical.[15] Contrary to expectation, we find no statistically significant gender difference in how importantly issues involving basic human needs, children or youth (except for education), the environment, or crime or drugs figure in issue-based participation. Where there are disparities, they do not always conform to the expectations

Questions for Thought and Discussion

Does the list of policy concerns in Table 2 represent all of those that might differentiate the political participation of men and women? Can you suggest some others that should have been included?

Crime or drugs: crime; gangs; safety in the streets; drugs.

Environment: specific environmental issues (e.g., clean air, toxic wastes) or environmental concerns in general; wildlife preservation; animal rights.

Foreign policy: relations with particular nations or to foreign policy in general; defense policy or defense spending; peace, arms control, or international human rights issues.

Women's issues: women's rights; domestic violence; rape; women's health and reproductive issues (excluding abortion).

Note that the categories vary in the extent to which they encompass respondents with quite different issue-positions. For example, activists on the abortion issue are polarized in their opinions. In contrast, activists who cited concerns about the environment tend to be in overall agreement with one another. These activists' opponents might be, for example, activists with concerns about economic development and performance.

It should also be noted that the categories in Table 2 are not exhaustive. Issue concerns ranging from gun control to drunk driving have been omitted from the table. If the universe of issue concerns had been included, the figures in each column would add to more than 100%. A single political act is often inspired by more than one issue concern. The contactor who expressed concern about "public housing, teenage pregnancy, and the child care bill" would have been coded as mentioning three separate issues.

[15]Hansen (1994) finds a similar result when men and women are asked what they consider to be the most important issue facing the country.

generated by the literature discussed earlier. Men are slightly more likely to mention taxes and foreign policy or international issues. When we looked more carefully at the exact content of the foreign policy concerns, we found that, contrary to expectation, there is no gender difference in the likelihood that issue-based activity is inspired by concerns about international peace and cooperation, arms control, or international human rights. A mere 1% of women's and men's issue-based activity is animated by these concerns.

With respect to education and abortion, the gender differences are more substantial. Concern about education animates at least in part 20% of women's issue-based activity, in contrast to 13% of men's. For abortion, the analogous figures are 14% and 8% respectively. Neither of these is an issue like gun control for which men and women have traditionally held differing opinions. Education, however, falls into the domain of issues of care that were the traditional bailiwick of the social feminists and that have traditionally taken precedence among the priorities of women legislators.

Because the availability of abortion is germane to women's lives in a way that it is not relevant to men's, it is the sole item on the list that qualifies as a "women's issue." In interpreting these figures we must recall that they conflate activists who are pro-choice with those who are pro-life. Elsewhere in our questionnaire we asked a standard survey question about attitudes towards abortion. The center of gravity on this issue leans decidedly in the direction of support for the availability of abortion—with men somewhat more pro-choice than women.[16] For both women and men, however, activity on abortion comes disproportionately from the pro-life side.[17] In response to the survey question 35% of women expressed pro-life views; yet 53% of their political activity motivated by concern about the abortion issue emanated from respondents who reported pro-life attitudes. For men the figures are 26% and 43% respectively.[18]

In contrast to the circumstance with respect to abortion, there is no division of opinion among those who mentioned women's issues. All the messages on women's issues indicated support for women's rights or greater attention to such problems as rape or domestic violence. (Interestingly, not one respondent mentioned sexual harassment in these 1990

[16]The data are as follows:

(1) A woman should always be able to obtain an abortion as a matter of choice.

(7) By law abortion should never be permitted.

	1	2	3	4	5	6	7
Men	40%	11%	9%	13%	6%	10%	10%
Women	36%	9%	8%	12%	7%	9%	19%

Women in legislatures—who, unlike women activists, place women's rights issues among their policy priorities—are not as divided in their attitudes about as are women in the mass public and are distinctly less pro-life in their opinions than their fellow legislators who are male (Thomas 1994, 65).

[17]In order to ensure that the direction of opinion on abortion expressed in the survey item could be used as a guide to the direction of opinion expressed through activity on abortion, we conducted the following experiment. We coded the actual verbatims for abortion activists as to whether the activity was pro-life, pro-choice, or ambiguous in direction. In no case that a direction was specified in connection with abortion-related activity did that direction contradict the opinion elicited by the survey item.

[18]Abortion figures more importantly in the activity of those who are pro-life than of those who are pro-choice: abortion was mentioned in connection with 24% of the issue-based activity of pro-life women and 12% of the activity of pro-life men; in contrast, abortion was discussed in relation to 11% of the activity of pro-choice women and 6% of the activity of pro-choice men.

Table 3. Percentage of Issue-Based Political Activity Motivated by Concern about Particular Issues

	White		Black		Latino	
	Women	Men	Women	Men	Women	Men
Basic human needs	9	8	19	21	20	13
Taxes	12	16**	9	8	5	9
Economic issues (except taxes)	9	12*	5	7	1	6
Abortion	15	8***	6	3	6	3
Social issues (except abortion)	2	1	2	2	1	2
Education	20	13***	19	14	24	16
Children or youth (except education)	4	3	8	10	15	2
Crime or drugs	7	5	27	23	16	18
Environment	9	11	1	2	6	10
Foreign policy	6	8	1	7*	6	8
Women	1	*a*	1	1	0	0
Civil rights or minorities	1	1	5	7	3	8
Number of respondents	1,068	1,006	141	92	85	56
Number of issue-based acts	1,009	1,076	103	90	31	41

*a*Less than 1%.

*$p < .05$; **$p < .01$; ***$p < .001$.

interviews.) What is most noteworthy, however, is just how rarely these issues were raised in connection with activity. Women discussed these issues in connection with 1% of their issue-based activity, and men barely mentioned them at all. In short, what is most apparent is not that the government hears more from women than from men about women's issues or that the content of the messages is uniformly in support of equality between the sexes, but rather that public officials hear so little on the subject.

These findings hold up when we compare men and women within groups defined by their race or ethnicity. As shown in Table 3, education figures prominently among the issue concerns of women and men—whether they are Latino, African-American, or white. In each case, however, it weighs even more heavily in the issue-based activity of women than men. Analogously, abortion figures more importantly in the issue priorities of women than men, regardless of race or ethnicity. There are, however, important differences across groups defined by their race or ethnicity. Abortion occupies more space in the political agendas of white activists than of African-Americans or Latinos. In contrast, issues of basic human need as well as crime or drugs weigh more heavily among the issue concerns of Latinos or African-Americans than of whites. When it comes to issues involving civil rights or minorities, there are differences between, on one hand, Anglo-Whites and, on the other, African-Americans or Latinos, for whom these issues figure more importantly in issue-based activity. There is a gender difference as well: issues connected to civil rights or minorities are higher among the issue priorities of African-American and Latino men than women.

For policy issues expressed through activity by men and women differentiated by socio-economic advantage, the findings are more complex. In Table 4 we compare men and

Table 4. Percentage of Issue-Based Political Activity Motivated by Concern about Particular Issues

	Advantaged[a]		Disadvantaged[b]	
	Women	Men	Women	Men
Basic human needs	9	9	27	12**
Taxes	8	16**	13	15
Economic issues (except taxes)	14	15	4	5
Abortion	13	12	6	0**
Social issues (except abortion)	1	1	6	0**
Education	24	14***	17	8
Children or youth (except education)	5	3	9	5
Crime or drugs	8	5	15	6*
Environment	5	10*	0	4
Foreign policy	7	9	2	4
Women's issues	2	c	c	0
Number of respondents	197	228	297	182
Number of issue-based acts	326	338	113	72

[a]Advantaged: At least one year of college and family income at least $50,000.

[b]Disadvantaged: No college education and family income less than $20,000.

[c]Less than 1%.

*$p < .05$; **$p < .01$; ***$p < .001$.

women who are relatively advantaged (who have had at least a year of college education and whose family incomes were $50,000 or more) with those who are much less advantaged (who have no more than a high school education and whose family incomes were no more than $20,000). Educational concerns figure importantly in the issue-based activity of both advantaged and disadvantaged respondents. Once again, however, they occupy greater space in women's activity than in men's. Abortion weighs more heavily in the issue-based activity of the advantaged, for whom there is no gender gap, than in the activity of the disadvantaged, for whom there is a gender disparity in abortion-related activity. Disadvantaged respondents, both female and male, are more concerned with issues of basic human need. Among the advantaged, however, there is no difference between women and men in the extent to which these issues figure in issue-based activity. In contrast, among the disadvantaged issues of basic human need occupy much more space in the issue concerns for women than for men. A similar pattern obtains for issues associated with drugs and crime. Concern about crime and drugs figures much more importantly on the agenda of issues that inspire activity for disadvantaged women than for disadvantaged men or for the advantaged of either sex. In summary, among more advantaged citizens, the

Q

Questions for Thought and Discussion

The authors repeat their tests of hypotheses to take into account race/ethnicity and social status. Do you think that there are other factors that should have been examined to see if they influenced the relationship between gender and participation? What other factors?

**Table 5. Logit Analysis of the Sources of
Participation in Children's Issues**

		Coefficient	Standard Error
Constant		−3.02	(0.21)
Woman		0.36***	(0.12)
Preschool children		−0.05	(0.18)
School-aged children		0.75***	(0.14)
Education		0.36***	(0.04)
Income		−0.01	(0.02)
Free time		−0.03	(0.02)
N		2,278	
2 * Log-likelihood	Pre	−1,957	
	Post	−1,822	

*$p < .05$; **$p < .01$; ***$p < .001$.

Predicted Values from the Logit Analysis

Probability of Participating on Children's Issues

A woman with no children	0.12
A man with no children	0.10
A woman with preschool children	0.12
A man with preschool children	0.09
A woman with school-aged children	0.23
A man with school-aged children	0.19
A woman with preschool and school-aged children	0.22
A man with preschool and school-aged children	0.18

gender differences are relatively muted[19]; among those less well off, there is a decided focus of attention among women on issues associated with poverty and poor living conditions.

Putting Children First: Further Analysis

Across all the groups and all the aspects of citizen involvement we have considered, the most notable manifestation of a different citizen voice is the relative space occupied by issues surrounding education in the bundle of issue concerns of women. Feminist theory alerts us to the potential implications for politics of the fact that women bear a disproportionate share of the responsibility for raising children. Following this line of inquiry, we can investigate whether women's special concern with children's issues is the exclusive bailiwick of mothers or whether women activists pay greater attention to these issues regardless of whether they have children.

In Table 5, we present the results of a logit analysis in which the dependent variable combines two categories that were separate on Table 3 to Table 5: activity involving education or other concerns about the young such as day care or recreational opportunities. We include among the independent variables not only gender and the presence of preschool and schoolage children in the household but also three variables related to the propensity to participate—

[19]One exception is the fact that advantaged men are twice as likely to be concerned with taxes than advantaged women.

education, income, and free time.[20] We report the interpretation of the coefficients at the bottom of Table 5.

The results suggest that there is always a small difference between men and women when it comes to participating about children and education, a difference that is larger for respondents with children than for those without. The largest effect, however, is not a gender-based effect indicating something about a differential propensity to take on—or to be assigned—responsibility for being caring and active when it comes to children. Instead, the most substantial effect comes from the fact of having school-aged children in the first place. Note that what matters is not simply having children, but having *school-aged* children. In our data, women are more likely to have school-aged children living at home with them than are men; that difference is the source of most of the gender difference in activism about children and education that we report in our tables.

[Conclusion]

Conclusion

Across disciplines scholars have been probing the extent, nature, and roots of differences between women and men, an enterprise that is often described—as we have done here—by reference to Carol Gilligan's apt metaphor, the search for "a different voice." Greater headway is possible, however, if instead of asking flatly whether men and women differ, we qualify the question in several ways. First we must recognize the significance of the cleavages of race, class, family status, employment status, that differentiate the experiences of both men and women (Moraga and Anzaldua 1983; hooks 1984; Aptheker 1989). What is characteristic of gender differences among African-Americans may not obtain for whites. Similarly, what we found for the poor may not apply to the affluent, and so on. Hence, we must ask, "Which men? Which women?"

Surely, the extent and nature of gender differences will also vary across domains of endeavor. There is no reason to expect that we can generalize from the committee hearing room to the board room, school room, locker room, operating room, and living room. Gender differences in moral reasoning or rates of violent crime do not necessarily tell us much about the realm of politics. Finally, even within a particular realm of activity, there may be no uniformity across different aspects of behavior. For example, patterns of gender similarity or difference characteristic of congressional roll call voting may not be relevant when it comes to paths of political recruitment or styles of campaigning for the House. In short, ask not "Is there a different voice?" but "With respect to what is there a different voice?"

Armed with inferences drawn from several bodies of theoretical and empirical literature and unusually rich data, we began this enterprise expecting to find gender differences among activists in terms of the activities in which they specialize, the gratifications they reap from taking part, and the issues that animate their participation. Probe as we might, we were surprised to find much more *similarity* than difference between men and women on all these dimensions. Across a wide variety of participatory acts, we found few significant disparities in

---

[20]On the definitions of these variables and the predictors of political participation, see Brady, Verba, and Schlozman (1995); and Schlozman, Burns, and Verba (1994).

We use a logit model because the dependent variable is dichotomous and because we believe that the assumptions of a logit model are more appropriate here. Note that, unlike ordinary least squares, the coefficients cannot be interpreted simply as the effect on the dependent variable of a one-unit change in one of the explanatory variables. A logit model includes the assumption that all of the variables work interactively—that the effects of each explanatory variable depend on the values of the others. Thus, we cannot know about the effects of having preschool children in the house, for example, without knowing whether the person has school-aged children at home.

men's and women's levels of participation. Where differences existed, they confounded the expectations generated by the literature: women do not participate disproportionately in grassroots, organizational, local, ad hoc political activities. In terms of the rewards of participation, men have no monopoly on material benefits, and both men and women are likely to cite altruistic and civic gratifications. Furthermore, the contours of women's and men's participatory agendas bear striking similarity. When we considered the issue priorities expressed through participation for subgroups defined by their race or ethnicity or their condition of socio-economic disadvantage, however, we found some notable group differences. This reinforces a point made earlier, that we must be sensitive to the differences among women and among men as well as to the aggregate differences between women and men.

By and large, gender differences in issue priorities that arise among citizen activists do not appear with respect either to women's rights or to the issues on which women and men have traditionally expressed different opinions in surveys. We found differences in relative issue emphasis with respect to abortion, education and, among the disadvantaged, basic human needs and, to a lesser extent, crime or drugs. We were led to inquire how to interpret these distinctive issue emphases—as the result of particular life circumstances that men or women are disproportionately likely to experience, or the result of distinctively masculine or feminine responses to those circumstances. Our results suggest that both are important.

In the aggregate, the conditions of men's and women's lives differ: women assume a disproportionate share of the child-rearing responsibilities in almost all households and are much more likely than men to raise children on their own; furthermore, women are substantially more likely than men to be poor. Analysis showed that, when it comes to being active on issues related to education, what really matters is having school-aged children; however, gender retains a significant, though smaller, effect. With respect to emphasis upon issues of basic human need, it is not, by and large, simply being poor that has an effect but being poor and female. In comparison with disadvantaged men, disadvantaged women—who our data show to be much more likely to have responsibility for children and to depend on government benefits for support—place a much higher priority on basic human need in their issue-based activity. Given the special impact that abortion policies have on women's lives, it would seem logical to root the relative importance women participants place on abortion in their life circumstances. As we have seen, however, women's (and men's) activity on abortion emanates disproportionately from those who are pro-life.

Making progress in understanding big questions requires both bold theorizing and systematic evidence. With results that are often surprising, this paper has presented significant new data about gender differences in an aspect of politics about which the evidence has not kept pace with the theorizing. Our data tell only part of the story of whether women and men activists speak with different voices, however. Long, in-depth interviews might reveal gender differences that do not emerge from survey data—for example, in the nature of the discourse used to discuss political participation or in the propensity to engage in conflictual rather than co-operative endeavors. Just as we have built on the findings of previous scholars, we invite others to use other methods to elaborate upon our results.

Questions for Thought and Discussion

Did the authors provide adequate tests of their hypotheses, or is more research necessary? Are the conclusions discussed by the authors consistent with their findings? Do the authors relate their findings to earlier research? Did the reported research make a significant contribution to knowledge concerning gender differences in political participation?

[Appendix]

APPENDIX
Indicators of Gratifications Derived from Participation

Material benefits
The chance to further my job or career.
I might want to get help from an official on a personal or family problem.
I might want to run for office someday.
I might want to get a job with the government some day.

Social gratifications
I find it exciting.
The chance to be with people I enjoy.
The chance to meet important and influential people.
The chance for recognition from people I respect.
I did not want to say no to someone who asked.

Civic gratifications
My duty as a citizen.
I am the kind of person who does my share.
The chance to make the community or nation a better place to live.

Collective outcomes
The chance to influence government policy.

[References]

REFERENCES

Acklesbert, Martha A. 1994. "Broadening the Study of Women's Participation." Paper presented at the CAWP Conference.

———. 1984. "Women's Collaborative Activities and City Life: Politics and Policy." In *Political Women: Current Roles in State and Local Government,* ed. Janet A. Flammang. Beverly Hills: Sage.

Andersen, Kristi. 1975. "Working Women and Political Participation, 1952–1972." *American Journal of Political Science* 10:439–55.

Aptheker, Bettina. 1989. *Tapestries of Life: Women's Work, Women's Consciousness, and the Meaning of Daily Life.* Amherst: University of Massachusetts Press.

Baker, Paula. 1984. "The Domestication of Politics: Women and American Political Society, 1780–1920." *American Historical Review* 89:620–47.

Bassin, Donna, Margaret Honey, and Meryle Maher Kaplan, eds. 1994. *Representations of Motherhood.* New Haven: Yale University Press.

Beckwith, Karen. 1986. *American Women and Political Participation: The Impacts of Work, Generation, and Feminism.* New York: Greenwood Press.

Bendyna, Mary E., and Celinda C. Lake. 1994. "Gender and Voting in the 1992 Presidential Election." In *The Year of the Woman: Myths and Realities,* ed. Elizabeth Adell Cook, Sue Thomas, and Clyde Wilcox. Boulder: Westview Press.

Boals, Kay. 1975. "The Politics of Male-Female Relations: The Functions of Feminist Scholarship." *Signs* 1:161–74.

Brady, Henry, Sidney Verba, and Kay Lehman Schlozman. 1995. "Beyond SES: A Resource Model of Political Participation." *American Political Science Review.* Forthcoming.

Clark, Cal, and Janet Clark. 1986. "Models of Gender and Political Participation in the United States." *Women and Politics* 6:5–25.

Conover, Pamela Johnston. 1988. "Feminists and the Gender Gap." *Journal of Politics* 50: 985–1010.

Conover, Pamela Johnston, and Virginia Sapiro. 1993. "Gender, Feminist Consciousness, and War." *American Journal of Political Science* 37:1079–99.

Cott, Nancy F. 1990. "Across the Great Divide: Women in Politics Before and After 1920." In *Women and Political Change,* ed. Patricia Gurin and Louise A. Tilly. New York: Russell Sage.

Dietz, Mary G. 1985. "Citizenship with a Feminist Face." *Political Theory* 13:19–37.

Eisler, Riane. 1990. "The Gaia Tradition and the Partnership Future: An Ecofeminist Manifesto." In *Reweaving the World,* ed. Irene Diamond and Gloria Feman Orenstein. San Francisco: Sierra Club Books.

Elshtain, Jean Bethke. 1981. *Public Man, Private Woman.* Princeton, NJ: Princeton University Press.

Flexner, Eleanor. 1975. *Century of Struggle: The Women's Rights Movement in the United States.* Cambridge: Harvard University Press.

Frankovic, Kathleen A. 1982. "Sex and Politics—New Alignments, Old Issues." *PS* 15: 439–48.

Giddings, Paula. 1984. *When and Where I Enter: The Impact of Black Women on Race and Sex in America.* New York: Morrow.

Gilligan, Carol. 1982. *In a Different Voice.* Cambridge: Harvard University Press.

Goertzel, Ted. 1983. "The Gender Gap: Sex, Family Income, and Political Opinions in the 1980s." *Journal of Political and Military Sociology* 11:209–22.

Hansen, Susan B. 1994. "Talking about Politics: Gender and Contextual Effects on Political Discourse." University of Pittsburgh. Unpublished manuscript.

hooks, bell. 1984. *Feminist Theory: From Margin to Center.* Boston: South End.

Kelly, Rita Mae, Michelle A. Saint-Germain, and Jody D. Horn. 1991. "Female Public Officials: A Different Voice?" In *American Feminism: New Issues for a Mature Movement,* ed. Janet K. Boles. Newbury Park, CA: Sage Publications.

Kenski, Henry C. 1988. "The Gender Factor in a Changing Electorate." In *The Politics of the Gender Gap,* ed. Carol M. Mueller. Newbury Park, CA: Sage Publications.

Kirkpatrick, Jeane J. 1974. *Political Woman.* New York: Basic Books.

———. 1976. *The New Presidential Elite.* New York: Russell Sage Foundation and Twentieth Century Fund.

Klein, Ethel. 1984. *Gender Politics.* Cambridge: Harvard University Press.

———. 1985. "The Gender Gap: Different Issues. Different Answers." *Brookings Review* 3:33–37.

Knoke, David. 1990. *Organizing for Collective Action.* Hawthorne, NY: Aldine deGruyter.

Kraditor, Aileen S. 1965. *The Ideas of the Women's Suffrage Movement.* New York: W. W. Norton.

Lerner, Gerda. 1979. *The Majority Finds Its Past: Placing Women in History.* New York: Oxford University Press.

Luker, Kristin. 1984. *Abortion and the Politics of Motherhood.* Berkeley: University of California Press.

Mandel, Ruth B., and Debra L. Dodson. 1992. "Do Women Officeholders Make a Difference?" In *The American Woman 1992–93: A Status Report,* ed. Paula Ries and Anne J. Stone. New York: W. W. Norton.

Mansbridge, Jane J. 1986. *Why We Lost the ERA.* Chicago: University of Chicago Press.

Mezey, Susan Gluck. 1994. "Increasing the Number of Women in Office: Does It Matter?" In *The Year of the Woman: Myths and Realities,* ed. Elizabeth Adell Cook, Sue Thomas, and Clyde Wilcox. Boulder: Westview Press.

Miller, Arthur. 1988. "Gender and the Vote: 1984." In *The Politics of the Gender Gap,* ed. Carol M. Mueller. Newbury Park, CA: Sage Publications.

Moraga, Cherrie, and Gloria Anzaldua, eds. 1983: *This Bridge Is Called My Back: Writings by Radical Women of Color.* New York: Kitchen Table.

Mueller, Carol M., ed. 1988. *The Politics of the Gender Gap.* Newbury Park, CA: Sage Publications.

Randall, Vicky. 1987. *Women and Politics: An International Perspective.* Chicago: University of Chicago Press.

Rosenstone, Steven J., and John Mark Hansen. 1993. *Mobilization, Participation, and Democracy in America.* New York: Macmillan.

Ruddick, Sara. 1989. *Maternal Thinking.* Boston: Beacon Press.

Salisbury, Robert. 1969. "An Exchange Theory of Interest Groups." *Midwest Journal of Political Science* 13:1–32.

Sapiro, Virginia. 1981. "When Are Interests Interesting?: The Problem of Political Representation of Women." *American Political Science Review* 75:701–16.

Schlozman, Kay Lehman, Nancy E. Burns, and Sidney Verba. 1994. "Gender and Political Participation: The Role of Resources." *Journal of Politics* 56:963–90.

Schlozman, Kay Lehman, Sidney Verba, and Henry Brady. 1994. "Participation's Not a Paradox: The View from American Activists." *British Journal of Political Science.* Forthcoming.

Scott, Anne Firor. 1984. *Making the Invisible Woman Visible.* Urbana: University of Illinois Press.

———. 1991. *Natural Allies: Women's Associations in American History.* Urbana: University of Illinois Press.

Shapiro, Robert Y., and Harpreet Mahajan. 1986. "Gender Differences in Policy Preferences: A Summary of Trends from the 1960s to the 1980s." *Public Opinion Quarterly* 50:42–61.

Stoper, Emily, and Roberta Ann Johnston. 1977. "The Weaker Sex and the Better Half: The Idea of Women's Moral Superiority in the American Feminist Movement." *Polity* 10: 192–217.

Tamerius, Karin L. 1993. "Does Sex Matter?: Women Representing Women's Interests in Congress." Paper delivered at the annual meeting of the Midwest Political Science Association, Chicago.

Thomas, Sue. 1994. *How Women Legislate.* New York: Oxford University Press.

Traugott, Michael W., and John P. Katosh. 1979. "Response Validity in Surveys of Voting Behavior." *Public Opinion Quarterly* 43:359–77.

Tronto, Joan C. 1987. "Beyond Gender Difference to a Theory of Care." *Signs* 12:644–63.

Verba, Sidney, and Norman H. Nie. 1972. *Participation in America.* New York: Harper and Row.

Verba, Sidney, Norman H. Nie, Jae-on Kim, and Goldie Shabad. 1978. "Men and Women: Sex-Related Differences in Political Activity." In *Participation and Political Equity,* ed. Sidney Verba, Norman H. Nie, and Jae-on Kim. Cambridge: Cambridge University Press.

Verba, Sidney, Kay Lehman Schlozman, Henry Brady, and Norman Nie. 1993. "Citizen Activity: Who Participates? What Do They Say?" *American Political Science Review* 87: 303–18.

Welch, Susan. 1977. "Women as Political Animals? A Test of Some Explanations for Male-Female Political Participation Differences." *American Journal of Political Science* 21: 711–30.

Welch, Susan, and John Hibbing. 1992. "Financial Conditions, Gender, and Voting in American National Elections." *American Journal of Political Science* 36:197–213.

Welch, Susan, and Lee Sigelman. 1989. "A Black Gender Gap?" *Social Science Quarterly* 70: 120–33.

Welch, Susan, and Sue Thomas. 1991. "Do Women in Public Office Make a Difference?" In *Gender and Policymaking,* ed. Susan J. Carroll, Debra Dodson, and Ruth B. Mandel. New Brunswick, NJ: Center for the American Woman and Politics, Eagleton Institute of Politics, Rutgers University.

Wilson, James Q. 1973. *Political Organizations.* New York: Basic Books.

Wirls, Daniel. 1986. "Reinterpreting the Gender Gap." *Public Opinion Quarterly* 50:316–30.

Writing a Review Comparing Research Reports

You have now summarized and evaluated one study that tested some hypotheses concerning gender differences in political participation. You should have noted that the authors strived to put their findings in the context of earlier studies. A major reason why we need to summarize and evaluate a group of studies is that generalizations in the social sciences are often not supported over a wide range of respondents and situations. No two studies—since they are conducted at different times, in different places, using at least slightly different methodologies—produce identical results. A determination of the weight of evidence supporting or refuting social science generalizations can only be accomplished by taking a comparative, comprehensive approach to reviewing the literature.

Organizing and writing a literature review presents a number of challenges. The most efficient approach is to consider how your review will be organized before you begin reading and recording information about each relevant report. We recommend that you keep in mind the purpose of your review as you read. You should be concerned with telling readers about previous research but also with convincing them that your research is a worthy undertaking. If the information you collect about each report is categorized and recorded in a form similar to that shown in Table 5.1, you will have several options for organizing your review.

There are a diversity of ways to organize a literature review. One approach is to discuss research reports in chronological order according to their date of publication. This approach would seem to make sense because of the social scientific goal of developing knowledge cumulatively, but it usually is not effective unless there have been new approaches developed over time. Unfortunately, it is often difficult to discern a linear connection among substantive findings, the development of knowledge, and time. In other words, there is no reason to believe that the most recent study represents an advance over previous research. Another approach is to compare methodological approaches that have been taken to answer a research question. It is important to consider methodology because variations in approaches produce different results. However, when the focus is on methodology the approach itself becomes a type of potential variable that must be considered in evaluating results.

We believe that the focus of a literature review should be on the substantive findings and resulting explanations of them that are described in a research report. This involves an integrative approach in which studies are compared in terms of the similarities and differences in findings and the explanations provided for those results. Similarities and differences between studies might rest on factors such as different research loca-

Key Points

An effective, well-written literature review should do the following:

- Group the discussion of research reports according to a common theme related to a specific research question.
- Critically analyze each report reviewed (remember that one assumption of social science is scientific skepticism).
- Provide as much information about each study as is warranted by its contribution to the literature.
- Synthesize and evaluate research reports showing the relationship of findings to current knowledge.
- Identify findings in the literature that are inconsistent.
- Make a case for further research.

tions, methodologies, or the variety of factors (variables) taken into account. Organizing and writing a literature review is a skill that takes time and effort to develop. The best way to learn how to write an effective review is to read reviews written by professionals and published in academic journals.

Conclusion

A literature review is an integral part of a research report in which an author summarizes and evaluates previous research. It lets the reader know the reviewer's familiarity with a body of knowledge, places the study to be reported in context, and offers a convincing justification for pursuing the topic. In this chapter we focused primarily on reading, understanding, summarizing, and evaluating a research report. This is the first step toward writing a review of previous research. We also discussed several ways in which reviews can be organized. We concluded that an effective review is one that is integrative and clearly focused. Writing an effective review requires skills that can only be acquired over time with practice.

The next chapter introduces you to some considerations about a testable hypothesis—its independent and dependent variables, the direction of the relationship between those variables and, most important, the question of whether they are causally related.

Summary of the Main Points

- Reviews of previous research should be comprehensive, focused, accurate, critical, comparative, and concise
- Social science research reports generally follow the familiar format that corresponds to the steps in the research process
- As you read research reports, you should systematically record information needed to construct a literature review and facilitate comparisons.
- Literature reviews are most effective if organized so that findings (and sometimes the methodologies) of studies are compared and evaluated.

Selected Readings

Birley, Graham, and Neil Moreland. *A Practical Guide to Academic Research.* London: Kogan Page, 1998.

Black, Thomas R. *Evaluating Social Science Research: An Introduction.* Thousand Oaks, CA: Sage Publications, 1993.

Katzer, Jeffrey, Kenneth H. Cook, and Wayne W. Crouch. *Evaluating Information: A Guide for Users of Social Science Research,* 3rd Ed. New York: McGraw-Hill, 1991.

Knop, Edward. "Suggestions to Aid the Student in Systematic Interpretation and Analysis of Empirical Sociological Journal Presentations." *The American Sociologist* (May 1967), 90–92.

Light, Richard J., and David B. Pillemer. *Summing Up: The Science of Reviewing Research.* Cambridge, MA: Harvard University Press, 1984.

Stern, Paul C., and Linda Kalof. *Evaluating Social Science Research,* 2nd Ed. New York: Oxford University Press, 1996.

Activities

Activity 5.1
Writing a Summary of an Article
That Reports Empirical Political Research

If you have not already done so, write down the information outlined in Table 5.1 as it pertains to "Gender and Citizen Participation: Is There a Different Voice?" Using the information you have recorded, write a summary of not more than 100 words describing the findings of the article.

Activity 5.2
Identifying Parts of an Article
Published in a Social Science Journal

Choose and make a copy of an article that reports the results of an empirical study of politics from a recent issue of one of the following journals: *American Politics Research, Comparative Political Studies, Social Science Quarterly, Journal of Politics* or *Political Research Quarterly.* Referring to the elements included in research reports that we have outlined in this chapter, identify the parts of the article by creating an outline of its contents.

Activity 5.3
Writing a Comparative Literature Review

Considerable controversy exists about whether candidates who face stiff competition in primary elections are at a disadvantage in their general election races. Look up and read the following three articles that seek to answer the question "Does a divisive primary hurt a candidate's general election chances?"

> Atkeson, Lonna Rae. "Divisive Primaries and General Election Outcomes: Another Look at Presidential Campaigns." *American Journal of Political Science* 42 (January 1998): 256–71.
>
> Kenney, Patrick J., and Tom W. Rice. "The Effect of Primary Divisiveness in Gubernatorial and Senatorial Elections." *Journal of Politics* 46 (August 1984): 904–15.
>
> ———. "The Relationship Between Divisive Primaries and General Election Outcomes." *American Journal of Political Science* 31 (February 1987): 31–44.

Use the format provided in Table 5.1 to take notes on each article. Using the information you have recorded, write a brief (200 words or fewer) comparative review of the three articles.

Chapter 6

Assessing Relationships: Association or Causality?

Learning Objectives

After completion of this chapter, students should be able to do the following:

Distinguish between independent and dependent variables in a hypothesis and identify the direction of the relationship between them.

Differentiate between association and causation in the relationship between two variables and know the four conditions required for establishing a causal relationship.

Grasp the meaning of and write a null hypothesis.

Explain the use of control variables in establishing causal relationships.

Recognize and understand the difference between antecedent and intervening variables.

Understand the process of elaborating a hypothesis.

Looking for Explanations

Now that you have been introduced to the basic building blocks of science—hypotheses and variables—we will consider how to use these instruments to achieve the objective of describing and explaining political behavior. While description is necessary and important, it is explanation that drives empirical political analysis. The ultimate goal of empirical political analysis is to explain political behavior. In this chapter, we begin the task of setting out how to assess cause-and-effect relationships.

Explanation involves looking for causal relationships between variables—that is, trying to determine the cause of some behavior by finding the conditions necessarily present for that behavior to occur. The problem is that some variables that occur together *seem* to be causally related but on closer examination turn out not to be. For example, a child who is building a sand castle on an ocean beach and sees threatening waves approaching her masterpiece may order the water to move away from her construction efforts and then observe that it actually happens. And while the child may think she has imposed her will on the movement of the ocean, the better explanation is that she made her demands as the tide turned from incoming to outgoing. When a farmer in Indiana performs a chant on the perimeter of his property to keep the wild tigers away from his livestock, and no tigers show up, the connection between the farmer's actions and the lack of tigers is not causal because there are no wild tigers in Indiana. When economic times in a country are good, employment is high, and many people prosper, the country's leader will take credit for the strong economy but be hard pressed to offer a valid explanation, accompanied by convincing data, that his or her efforts were the sole cause of the robust economy.

Unfortunately, most examples of relationships in empirical political analysis that appear to be causal but are not are more difficult to recognize than those we just mentioned. In the following sections of this chapter, we will help you to determine systematically whether the relationships you hypothesize and observe are causal or only appear to be so, and how to elaborate on simple relationships in order to develop more detailed models of political behavior. We start with a discussion of relatively simple two variable hypotheses but move steadily to the consideration of more complex explanations of behavior that involve more than two variables.

Questions for Thought and Discussion

Do you believe it will ever be possible to find *causes* for human behavior in the same sense that medical researchers find causes for disease? What do you think are some obstacles to finding the causes of behavior? Which obstacles do you think will be most difficult to overcome?

■ Independent and Dependent Variables: The Direction and Strength of Relationships

Hypotheses, as pointed out in Chapter 3, are conjectural statements that contain at least two variables, but when the hypothesis is explanatory rather than simply descriptive, the variables have particular names and identities. The **independent variable** is the presumed cause of the behavior or attitude we are trying to explain. The **dependent variable** is the behavior or attitude we are trying to describe and explain—that is, the presumed effect. Note that we say *presumed* cause and *presumed* effect because the hypothesis is conjectural—an educated, logical guess about how people behave. We will not know whether the relationship posited in the hypothesis can be accepted until we have made our observations about the world around us—that is, collected and analyzed our data.

To repeat, the dependent variable is the behavior you are trying to explain; the independent variable is the factor you point to as the cause of that behavior. Consider this hypothesis: "Older U.S. citizens will be more concerned about the financial viability of Social Security than younger citizens." The independent variable is age of the citizen, and the dependent variable is level of concern about Social Security. The logic behind the hypothesis is that of self-interest. Older people are closer to receiving retirement benefits provided by the Social Security Administration, leading to more concern about whether promised benefits will be available when they retire, compared to younger citizens whose retirement is further in the future.

As touched on in Chapter 3, a hypothesis also indicates the **direction of a relationship** between the variables, positive or negative. In the example of Social Security, we are presuming a positive relationship: as age increases, concern increases. A negative relationship suggests that the two variables move in opposite directions: as the independent variable in the hypothesis goes up, for example, the dependent variable goes down. The following hypothesis illustrates a negative relationship: "Wealthier U.S. citizens will be less concerned about the financial viability of Social Security than less wealthy citizens"—as wealth goes up, concern goes down. As in the previous hypothesis, the dependent variable (the attitude we are trying to explain) is concern about financial viability of Social Security, but the independent variable is now the level of wealth of the individual and is hypothesized to be inversely related to the attitude. The logical basis of the relationship is still the same: self-interest. Those with more wealth will have more assets when they retire and less concern about Social Security benefits, which will be a smaller part of their retirement income than those with less wealth.

We must also consider the **strength of the relationship** expressed in the hypothesis. How strong a relationship between the variables should you expect? If, in our previous examples, we find one very old person with little concern about the financial viability of Social Security or one very rich person with a high level of concern, does that invalidate our two hypotheses? It does not—because in empirical political analysis you are not apt to find perfect correlations between variables. As discussed in both Chapters 1 and 2, empirical researchers assume a probabilistic world, one in which people generally tend to behave one way or another but where there will almost invariably be variations from what is hypothesized. You are unlikely to find a theory from which you can derive a hypothesis that will explain

To the Web

Exercise 6.1   Independent and Dependent Variables

The only way to recognize independent and dependent variables and understand the relationship between them is to read many hypotheses and try to identify which variable is which. In short, you must practice. The first exercise for this chapter requires you to review hypotheses and list the unit of analysis for each hypothesis, the independent and dependent variables, and the direction of the stated relationship. Go to the **DEPR Web Page,** click on **Web Exercises, Chapter 6,** then on **Independent and Dependent Variables.**

completely all of the behavior you observe. You might be able to explain 100 percent of relatively trivial behavior, but explaining simple behaviors is generally not worth the effort. We will examine the strength of observed relationships in more technical, quantitative terms in later chapters that cover data analysis.

Association Versus Causation

An important distinction must be made about the statement of relationships between variables in a hypothesis: that of **association** versus **causation,** briefly mentioned in Chapter 3. All hypotheses explicitly say the variables are associated, but only some hypotheses claim the variables are causally related, and understanding this distinction between association and causation is critically important. Association occurs when the independent and dependent variables move together—they covary—but the change in the independent variable is *not* bringing about the change in the dependent variable. On the other hand, causation occurs when the change in the dependent variable is as a direct result of changes in the independent variable. In the case of causation, the variables not only change together, but additionally, the dependent variable changes *due to* the changes in the independent variable.

A quick example might help. Over the years, we have written a large number of letters of recommendation for our students who apply to graduate school or other fields of professional study, such as law school. As we look over these letters, covering many years, we have noticed a stable pattern of students being admitted to excellent schools when we write excellent letters, mediocre schools when we write mediocre letters, and so on. This has led us to the following hypothesis: "The more positive letters of recommendation written by a professor, the better the professional schools to which his or her students will be admitted." Is this connection between level of quality of the letters and acceptances a matter of association or causation? While many college faculty would like to believe the relationship between the variables is causal, and while some students may indeed be accepted to graduate and professional schools on the strength of their letters of recommendation, it is more likely the hypothesis reflects an association between the variables. Students with higher undergraduate grade point averages (GPA) and better scores on standardized tests, such as the Graduate Record Exam or the Law School Admissions Test, will see two positive results: better letters of recommendation from their professors and admission to better schools. Those with lower GPAs and lower scores on standardized tests will find their letters not as strong and their acceptances coming from less outstanding schools. So while the quality of letters of recommendation and quality of the schools to which students are admitted vary together, they are probably not causally related, only associated. They vary together because they are both changing together as a result of other variables, such as GPA and standardized test scores.

■ Criteria for Causality

There are four criteria that need to be met if a researcher is to establish a causal relationship between variables, but we need to say right up front that meeting these criteria in empirical political research is, for all practical purposes, impossible. To demonstrate empirically a cause-and-effect relationship between variables is practically impossible because so many independent variables may affect the behavior you are trying to explain that accounting for all of them is an unrealistic expectation. In addition, how each independent variable individually affects the dependent variable, and how the independent variables themselves interact with one another, is extremely difficult to disentangle. The most effective way to attempt to demonstrate a cause-and-effect relationship empirically is the use of experimentation, which is not often employed by political scientists and has its own restrictions, and which we will cover in Chapter 12.

The first criterion for demonstrating a causal relation between variables is that the variables must be associated: They must change together. Second, the change in the independent variable must precede the change in the dependent variable in time; logically, the cause must come before the effect. While that seems simple enough, there are situations where the order of the variables is not clear, and it is difficult to determine which is the independent or dependent variable. For example, it may seem logical that one's friends will influence a person's political views, but it also seems logical that a person will choose friends with similar political views. Which is the independent variable—friends' political views or one's own political views? So one part of the job of a researcher in substantiating causality is to establish the **temporal order** of the variables. Third, the linkage between the variables must be plausible, have some logical connection with one another. This logical connection between the variables is based on the theory from which the hypothesis is derived or, in the case of induction, on the reasoning that originally identified patterns in observations. Without a theory to account for a logical explanation of the relationship between variables, establishing causation is not possible.

The fourth and final criterion for establishing causality is that the observed, empirical relationship between the variables cannot be explained away through the influence of other, competing independent variables. That is, you must be sure the observed relationship is not an association with the two variables covarying due to the presence of some missing third variable, such as our example of letters of recommendation. This is a problem that ultimately will be resolved through the use of theory and careful planning of your research, but to clarify the problem, we will first examine the ideal but unattainable objective we would like to achieve. In ideal terms, a causal hypothesis should satisfy the conditions of **necessity** and **sufficiency:** The observed changes in the independent variable would be both *necessary and sufficient* to bring about the observed changes in the dependent variable. Neither condition alone assures causality between the variables; both conditions must be satisfied.

Assume a researcher is trying to establish a causal relationship between the independent variable X and the dependent variable Y. Once he or she establishes the condition of necessity— that is, X must change for Y to change—he or she can say that changes in Y will not occur without changes in X. But other independent variables (such as W and Z) may also need to change along with X in order for Y to change. On the other hand, if only the condition of sufficiency is met, a change in X will indeed bring about a change in Y, but changes in other independent variables, such as W and Z, may also separately and independently cause changes in Y. Only when both conditions are present, when X is both necessary *and* sufficient to produce the observed change in Y, can the researcher claim a causal relationship between X and Y. When the two conditions are met, Y will change if, *and only if,* X changes.

Key Points

These are the four conditions required for establishing a causal relationship between two variables:

1. The variables must be associated; they must change together.
2. Change in the independent variable must precede the change in the dependent variable in time.
3. The linkage between the variables must be plausible, having some logical, theoretical connection with one another.
4. The observed relationship between the variables cannot be explained away through the influence of other independent variables.

Research Design

As mentioned, satisfying the conditions of necessity and sufficiency is the ideal—difficult to achieve in actual empirical research. In practice, researchers try to eliminate possible alternative independent variables that may be affecting the dependent variable under study, a formidable task given the large number of independent variables possibly having an impact on the dependent variable. This attempt to eliminate alternative explanations for changes in the dependent variable is part of a **research design,** which is a plan to show how the research questions under study will be answered. In the case of explanatory research, in which hypotheses are tested, a major component of your plan, or design, will be to show how you are controlling for the effects of extraneous independent variables.

There are two primary research design strategies to control for extraneous independent variables in attempts to eliminate alternative explanations for observed changes in the dependent variable. The first strategy is to factor these independent variables out of the design completely by isolating the individuals under study. This type of design is called an experiment and generally employs relatively few people in the study. How to set up experiments for testing hypotheses in political science, including controlling for extraneous variance, will be discussed in Chapter 12, which covers research using a small number of subjects. The second strategy is to build these independent variables right into the study to see if they have any demonstrated effect on the dependent variable. If they have no effect, they can be eliminated from consideration. This process of sifting through alternate independent variables that may account for changes in the dependent variable is called controlling for extraneous variance, and the alternative independent variables introduced into the research are called **control variables.** Using control variables as a strategy to eliminate alternative explanations for changes in the dependent variable is part of a research design referred to as a field study and is discussed at length in this chapter.

As discussed in Chapter 3, you will never be able to "prove" a hypothesis—you can only subject it to continuous attempts at falsification or disproof. As long as it withstands these efforts at falsification—that is, the original relationship is unaffected by the control variables—you will continue to accept it as the best explanation available of the behavior being studied. Introducing control variables into an empirical research project is the researcher's attempt to strengthen a hypothesis by subjecting it to further attempts at falsification.

To the Web

Exercise 6.2   Association and Temporal Order

The second exercise for this chapter asks you to think of (1) an example of a hypothesis that has variables that are associated but not causally related and (2) a hypothesis in which the temporal order of the variables is not clear. Some hints are provided. Go to the **DEPR Web Page,** click on **Web Exercises, Chapter 6,** then on **Association and Temporal Order.**

■ Null Hypothesis

A simple procedure to check for the first criterion of causality—that the variables must be associated—is to hypothesize that there is no relationship at all between the variables. A hypothesis stating no relation between the independent and dependent variables is called the **null hypothesis,** and rejection of the null hypothesis means there *is* an association between the variables and that the first criterion of causality has been met. (The null hypothesis is often designated by the term H_0.) Researchers evaluating publicly funded programs sometimes use the null hypothesis in attempting to determine if it is at least possible that some public policy is having its intended effect. A public health agency might hypothesize that there is no difference in the percentage of smokers who have quit smoking cigarettes among those who have completed a smoking cessation program and those not involved in the program. The null hypothesis would be "Smokers who complete a smoking cessation program are no more or less likely to quit smoking than smokers who have not enrolled in such a program."

Rejection of this null hypothesis based on data that smokers enrolled in the program were more likely to quit smoking would establish the first criterion of causality between the variables of program participation and smoking behavior: The variables are at the minimum associated. But other criteria for causality would also have to be considered, including the elimination of other possible explanations for the change in smoking behavior. (Smokers who enrolled in the program might be more motivated to quit, and the level of motivation accounts for their quitting rather than participation in the program.) On the other hand, if the null hypothesis were accepted, or rejected because smokers in the program were *less* likely to quit, the public health agency might consider spending its antismoking funds on another program. But testing the null hypothesis provides the minimal information of whether there is any association at all between the variables—in this instance, between program participation and intended change in smoking behavior.

To the Web

Discussions of Causation

For further discussion about causality, go to the **DEPR Web Page**, click on **Web Links, Chapter 6**, then on **Determinism** and **Causation**. For a consideration of the nature of causation assuming a probabilistic world, click on **Probabilistic Causation**.

To the Web

Exercise 6.3   Writing a Null Hypothesis and Considering Alternate Explanations

To more completely understand the idea of the null hypothesis, for this exercise you will write a null hypothesis about a public policy and then consider alternative hypotheses to the original. Go to the **DEPR Web Page**, click on **Web Exercises, Chapter 6**, then on **Writing a Null Hypothesis and Considering Alternate Explanations**.

Control Variables and Causality

One of the criteria mentioned previously for assuring a causal relationship is to be sure the changes in your dependent variable cannot be accounted for by independent variables other than one you have chosen. That is, you must ascertain the effect, if any, of other independent variables (control variables) on your dependent variable. The first problem in this area is deciding what other independent variables might be involved, what variables to control for. For example, if we hypothesize that U.S. presidents with a conservative political philosophy are more likely to use military force in foreign affairs than those with a liberal philosophy, we need to consider the possible effect of factors other than political ideology on presidential behavior. Clearly we have neither the time nor resources to control for every possible alternative independent variable (age? place of birth? height? parents' political ideology?) in explaining presidential behavior. One tongue-in-cheek suggestion for an alternative independent variable is shoe color: Those presidents who wear black shoes are more likely to use military force than those who wear brown shoes.

You have probably already decided that shoe color is a foolish suggestion because you see no logical connection between a president's shoe color choice and foreign policy. Your willingness to ignore shoe color as an independent variable means you have some sort of theory (probably implicit and not very well thought out) to explain how presidents behave, and shoe color is not part of that theory. And in part, that is how researchers decide on which variables to control for: theory. Without a theory to guide them, all factors about a situation will be equally relevant to a researcher. When empirical researchers bring a theory to bear on a situation, they can decide what is relevant and what is not and thus have a rational basis for choosing to control for some independent variables and not for others. In addition, researchers also use the existing literature in the field as a guide for choosing control variables. In your work, if others have demonstrated empirically a relationship between one or more independent variables and a dependent variable that you are now studying, those independent variables employed by others should probably be added to your research as controls. If you are exploring the relationship between religious preference and attitude toward abortion, for example, and research prior to yours in academic journals or books has shown that the level of education influences attitude toward abortion, you probably want to include education as a control variable for your hypothesis.

When working through control variables, researchers often find two types that may affect the original relationship: antecedent and intervening. An **antecedent variable** is one that logically precedes the original independent and dependent variables, having an influence on both of them. For example, in doing research about money and politics, one might hypothesize that candidates for U.S. Congress who spend more money than their opponents are more likely to win their elections. The researcher could obtain from the Federal Elections Commission the amount of money each candidate for U.S. Congress had spent in the last election in each of the 435 races for the House of Representatives and the 100 races for the Senate and from newspapers who won each of those races. Then by comparing the campaign expenditures to the electoral outcomes, the researcher could determine if in a majority of cases the candidate who had spent more money won the election.

Assuming a positive relationship is found, the researcher would have established an association between the variables, but not causation. In order to address the issue of causation, you need to eliminate other possible explanations by controlling for other independent variables. In this case, previous research has established that incumbents for congressional seats win more often than nonincumbent candidates *and* that incumbents generally receive more campaign contributions than their nonincumbent challengers. [1] In this research situation, incumbency is an antecedent variable that affects both the independent variable of campaign expenditures and the dependent variable of votes received. In diagram form, the relationships appear as follows.

Original Hypothesis

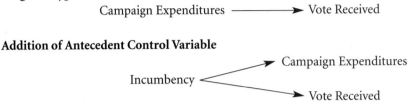

Campaign Expenditures ⟶ Vote Received

Addition of Antecedent Control Variable

Incumbency ⟶ Campaign Expenditures
⟶ Vote Received

The original hypothesis showed the two variables of campaign expenditures and percentage of vote received to be associated, but the addition of the control variable, incumbency, demonstrated that the association was coincidental. Therefore, at least one criterion of causality *cannot* be met; the relationship can be explained away by another independent variable. A connection between associated variables that appears to be causal but that further empirical research shows to be the result of an antecedent variable is called a **spurious relationship.** In the preceding example, empirical political scientists would say that the addition of the incumbency variable had shown the original two variables to be spuriously related.

The other type of control variable often found, an **intervening variable,** is one that is logically placed in between the independent and dependent variables of the original hypothesis. A simple example is the hypothesis expressing a positive relationship between the age of a child and reading ability. Older children generally read better than younger children, which expressed in diagram form would appear as follows: Age → Reading Ability. But we know that children normally attend school for nine or ten months out of each year and that reading ability improves with additional education. Children who did not attend school or were not home-schooled would likely not improve their reading skills over time. The addition of education as an intervening control variable would appear as follows: Age → Education → Reading Ability. In this illustration, age and reading ability among children are related through the intervening variable of education.

An example of an intervening variable in the professional literature of political science is provided by Ted Robert Gurr in *Why Men Rebel,* a work that tries to explain when revolution will occur in a political system. [2] He suggests that the outbreak of revolution is not, as some propose, directly related to economic or political hardship. He argues the hypothesis "the worse the economic and political conditions, the more likely a revolution will occur" is incomplete because revolution is not the *direct* result of political and economic conditions. Rather, the relationship between conditions and revolution is ameliorated by another, intervening variable: the political and economic expectations of the populace. Gurr reasoned that higher expectations among the population will produce revolutions in countries where the economic and political conditions are, in absolute terms, less onerous than in countries where no revolution occurs. This reasoning involves the presence of an intervening variable, individual expectations about conditions in the country. People who expect hard economic and political times and actually suffer those harsh conditions—that is, their expectations about reality and the reality they experience are in correspondence—are less politically dissatisfied, and therefore less likely to revolt, than those who anticipate better political and economic times but find somewhat less harsh conditions—that is, where their expectations of conditions are higher than what they find in reality. The expectations of the citizens are an intervening variable, as shown in this diagram: Economic/Political Conditions → Expectations of Population → Political Revolution.

In contrast to the illustration where an antecedent variable showed a relationship to be spurious, this example of trying to explain political revolution shows the two original variables are connected with the intervening variable of individuals' expectations. The original relationship is not wiped out but changed. Such altered findings when a control variable is added to the hypothesis are not unusual. In the next section we will explore how to handle such situations.

To the Web

> **Exercise 6.4   Assessing Causality**
>
> The fourth exercise for this chapter asks you to think in general terms about cause-and-effect relationships. An example from local politics in California is the basis for one question, while another asks you about voting turnout in congressional elections. Go to the **DEPR Web Page,** click on **Web Exercises, Chapter 6,** then on **Assessing Causality.**

Elaborating a Causal Hypothesis

As just pointed out, when causal hypotheses are subjected to a variety of control variables, one outcome is that the original relationship will turn out to be spurious, and the original hypothesis will be rejected. On the other hand, some control variables may have a substantive effect on the original relationship—not wiping it out but somehow altering it—thus revealing that the original hypothesized relationship is more complex than expected. An illustration of this situation was Gurr's research about political rebellion that involved an intervening variable.

In general, as a researcher rethinks his or her original hypothesis, other independent variables may loom that are believed to affect the behavior or attitude under study. When you reach that point in empirical research, you will need to theorize about how these other independent variables might fit into your research. This process of adding control variables (other independent variables) and theorizing about how they fit with the original hypothesis is called **elaboration.**

This process of subjecting hypotheses to a variety of control variables, of elaborating, requires imaginative thinking. Instead of simply accepting the confirmation of your hypothesis as evidence that your theory or logical explanation is correct or accepting the rejection of your hypothesis as an indication that the logic underlying your hypothesis is faulty, you must think through possible alternative explanations for why the dependent variable changes, and that takes imagination. That is, you should employ imaginative thinking to try to develop some alternate hypothesis to explain changes in the dependent variable. By suggesting and testing alternate hypotheses as possible explanations, you are going through a process that helps strengthen the causality of the original relationship and also provides an opportunity to elaborate on your original hypothesis. In addition, elaboration also allows for testing competing theories. If there are competing theories, each will point to a differing set of independent variables, and researchers can choose from both sets in an attempt to see which theory is more correct.

Simply assembling a list of causal factors—independent variables that individually have an influence on your dependent variable—is not enough. You must think through how all the variables in the study may fit together as a whole, including how the independent variables might be related to one another as well as to the dependent variable. Ideally, the result is a set of interlocking hypotheses that together expand upon, and spell out in more detail, the **causal chain** underlying the behavior you are seeking to explain. This process of elaboration is part of the wheel of science, moving from theory to observation by both deductive and inductive processes, described in Chapter 2.

An example of elaboration is found in the research of Warren Miller and Donald Stokes. [3] Their research was embedded in the normative questions surrounding the theory of representation. How should elected representatives vote in a legislative body— by following the mandate of their constituency, assuming they can determine what it is? Or should they follow the dictates of their own conscience, behaving consistently with what they personally believe to be in the best interests of the people they represent? Another choice would be somehow to combine these two styles of representation or develop yet other alternative methods of determining how to cast legislative votes. Miller and Stokes, moving away from the normative debate, instead studied these questions empirically. They were interested in determining how members of the U.S. House of Representatives actually made up their minds when casting roll call votes on bills when they came to the floor, and they used survey research data from the Survey Research Center at the University of Michigan to do so.

Their initial concern was with the connection between the attitudes of constituents in an individual Congress member's district toward an issue and the representative's roll call vote on that issue, diagrammed as: Constituency's Attitude → Representative's Roll Call Behavior. But Miller and Stokes, thinking imaginatively, proposed two new variables that had to be included to create a logical causal chain between the two original variables. First, as just suggested, even with a good-faith effort, members of Congress may not always know precisely the views of their constituents on each issue; instead they have only their *perceptions* of what their constituents think. So representatives can-

Figure 6.1
Miller and Stokes's Causal Chain Explaining Roll Call Vote

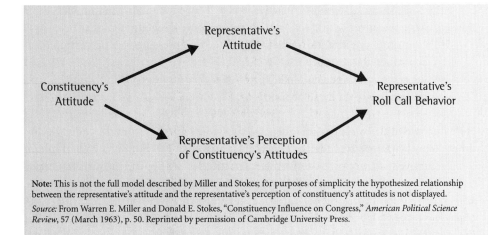

Note: This is not the full model described by Miller and Stokes; for purposes of simplicity the hypothesized relationship between the representative's attitude and the representative's perception of constituency's attitudes is not displayed.

Source: From Warren E. Miller and Donald E. Stokes, "Constituency Influence on Congress," *American Political Science Review*, 57 (March 1963), p. 50. Reprinted by permission of Cambridge University Press.

not vote on legislative matters directly based on what their constituents believe about the issue but only on what the congressmen think their constituents believe. That is the basis for one of the new variables: the representative's perceptions of the constituency's attitude. Second, as pointed out in the normative debate over representation, members of Congress may vote on the basis of their *own* views on an issue—that is, vote consistent with their own attitudes. The representative's attitude is the other new variable.

Now Miller and Stokes had three independent variables—constituency's attitude, representative's perception of constituency's attitudes, and representative's attitude— to explain the roll call vote of the representative. But how do the three independent variables logically fit together? Clearly, the representative's perception of his constituency's attitudes is very likely affected by the actual constituency's attitude, and the constituency's attitude may have an influence on the representative's own attitude. There are a variety of possible arrangements of the independent variables relative to one another and the dependent variable. Miller and Stokes produced the causal chain shown in Figure 6.1 to show how a representative came to cast a vote on the floor of the U.S. House.

The lines indicate which variables are hypothesized to be positively related. If any of the relationships were hypothesized to be inversely related, a minus sign would be placed next to the line. Notice in the model that constituency attitude is hypothesized to have no direct effect on roll call behavior. The effect of the constituency's attitude passes through the intervening variables of representative's attitude and representative's perception of constituency's attitudes. The causal chain involves four separate, but inter-locking, hypotheses (labeled as H1, H2, and so on).

H1 Constituency's attitude is positively related to representative's attitude.

H2 Representative's attitude is positively related to representative's roll call behavior.

H3 Constituency's attitude is positively related to representative's perception of constituency's attitude.

H4 Representative's perception of constituency's attitude is positively related to representative's roll call behavior.

Note that two of the variables are independent in one hypothesis but dependent in the other. Representative's attitude is a dependent variable in H1, but independent in H2. Representative's perception of constituency's attitudes is a dependent variable in H3, but independent in H4. Thus, Miller and Stokes have elaborated the original hypothe-sized relationship of constituency's attitude and representative's roll call behavior to in-clude two other independent, intervening variables that flesh out the causal chain. By the way, the survey data collected from congressmen and their constituents in 116 con-gressional districts confirmed each of the hypotheses and therefore the more complex causal chain proposed by Miller and Stokes.

Remember that these examples are of completed research and that after the fact the elaboration process seems logical and relatively easily accomplished. But consider-able effort (and sometimes anguish) is involved in research work such as this. When you begin your empirical research and finalize a hypothesis for testing, the effort to choose control variables for asserting your contention of causality and elaborating on the orig-inal relationship can be a lengthy and frustrating job. Be on guard against the "investment problem": becoming too committed to your particular hypothesis and transforming your-self into an advocate for it rather than a scientist testing it. We have seen many of our students (understandably) blinded to alternative expla-nations for political behavior because they became com-mitted to "proving" that their hypothesis was "right."

You will have to use your imagination to envision relationships among variables that are not immediately obvious, but such musings can be stimulated by reading about previous research in your area and talking with others engaged in empirical political research. The pro-fessional literature in the area will help you discover what other variables researchers in your area have worked with, as well as the theory and reasoning they utilized for the

To the Web

Exercise 6.5 Association and Empirical Evidence

The way to determine if two variables are associ-ated is to examine empirical evidence. This exercise gives you the first opportunity to see some empiri-cal evidence collected and analyzed to test hypothe-ses about political behavior. Go to the **DEPR Web Page,** click on **Web Exercises, Chapter 6,** then on **Association and Empirical Evidence.**

logic underlying their hypotheses. Discussing the logic underlying your hypothesis with fellow students and faculty, and seeking suggestions from them for new independent variables for alternate hypotheses, is one of the most effective methods for thinking about strengthening and elaborating on a hypothesis.

Conclusion

In this chapter, we moved from a consideration of simple two variable hypotheses to more complex assessments for understanding political behavior. The modest attempt to describe behavior has evolved into the task of explaining behavior, and understanding causal relationships underlies the effort to explain. Demonstrating causality between variables with empirical data is the ideal, pretty much impossible to achieve. But research efforts directed at showing causal relationships, even if not ultimately successful, will strengthen the explanatory power of hypotheses by eliminating some, if not all, alternative explanations for the behavior under study. In addition, introducing control variables to test for causality provides the opportunity to elaborate on the original hypothesis, providing a fuller, more richly textured picture of how political actors behave. Elaborating a hypothesis will require you to maintain your scientific objectivity, being careful not to cling tenaciously to your hypothesis. This can be achieved through review of previous research in the area and brainstorming on your part. The reward is to take pleasure in explaining some aspect of political behavior that except for your efforts would have remained unknown.

Elaboration is revisited in Chapters 16 and 17, where you will learn, in quantitative terms, how to determine the precise effect of adding more independent variables to your hypothesis. Fairly simple data analysis techniques will reveal to what extent your additional independent variables, individually and collectively, affect your dependent variable. But more immediately, in Chapter 7, you will learn how to transform abstract concepts into concrete measures of political reality.

Summary of the Main Points

- The independent variable in a hypothesis is the presumed cause of the dependent variable, which is the presumed effect.
- Independent and dependent variables may be either positively related or negatively (inversely) related.
- Variables are associated when they change together, but the change in one is not dependent on the change in the other. When variables are associated and the change in the dependent variable comes about because of change in the independent variable, they are causally related.
- The four conditions demonstrating a causal hypothesis are association, temporal order, plausibility, and elimination of competing independent variables

- A null hypothesis states that there is no relationship between variables.
- Control variables are additional independent variables added to a two-variable hypothesis in order to test for causality and/or elaborate on the original hypothesized relationship.
- An antecedent variable logically precedes both variables in a hypothesis; an intervening variable logically falls in between the two variables in a hypothesis.
- A spurious relationship between variables is one that appears to be causal, but the introduction of an antecedent variable demonstrates them to be only associated.
- Elaborating a hypothesis means adding additional independent variables to further explain the behavior or attitude under study.
- A causal chain is a sequence of variables logically interconnected that purports to explain a behavior or attitude.

Terms Introduced

antecedent variable	intervening variable
association	necessity
causal chain	null hypothesis
causation	research design
control variable	spurious relationship
dependent variable	strength of a relationship
direction of a relationship	sufficiency
elaboration	temporal order
independent variable	

Selected Readings

Blalock, Hubert M., Jr. *Causal Inferences in Nonexperimental Research.* New York: Norton Publishing Co., 1961.

Etheredge, Lloyd. "The Case of the Unreturned Cafeteria Trays" (Pamphlet), Washington, DC: American Political Science Association, 1976.

Kuhn, Thomas. *The Structure of Scientific Revolutions.* Chicago: University of Chicago Press, 1962.

Lave, Charles, and James March. *An Introduction to Models in the Social Sciences.* New York: Harper and Row, 1975.

Activities

Activity 6.1
Hypotheses, Variables, and Causality

1. Answer all of the questions for each of the three hypotheses that follow. What are the variables in the hypothesis? What is the unit of analysis? What is the direction of the

relationship? Do you think the variables are causally related? If so, explain the logical causal connection between the variables. If not, explain why you think there is no causal connection. Finally, write an alternative to each of the hypotheses, using a different independent variable.

- Women who run for elective office have higher levels of self-esteem than women who do not run for elective office.
- The greater the percentage of college graduates in a state, the greater the percentage of women in the state legislature.
- The more trees there are in a municipality, the lower the crime rate will be.

2. Write a hypothesis using residents of your home state as the units of analysis. What are the independent and dependent variables? What is the direction of the relationship? Explain why you think the variables are, or are not, causally related.

3. Write a hypothesis using nations as the units of analysis. What are the independent and dependent variables? What is the direction of the relationship? Explain why you think the variables are, or are not, causally related.

4. Choose a topic about politics that interests you, and write a hypothesis about some behavior or attitude in that area. What are the variables in the hypothesis? What is the unit of analysis? What is the direction of the relationship? Explain why you think the variables are, or are not, causally related.

Activity 6.2
Causal Chains

1. Look back at the two hypotheses concerning Social Security used as examples at the start of this chapter. The dependent variable in each hypothesis was attitude toward the financial viability of Social Security, with age the independent variable in one and personal wealth the other. Diagram what you think would be the relationship among these three variables, remembering that one of the independent variables was hypothesized to be inversely related to the dependent variable. Think of one more independent variable that you believe would affect the dependent variable, explain the logic behind your choosing that particular independent variable as opposed to some other, and add that variable to your diagram.

2. How do Political Action Committees decide which candidates for Congress they will support with campaign contributions? With PAC financial contributions to congressional candidates as your dependent variable, choose three independent variables that you think affect that choice, and diagram the relationship among all four variables. Write a hypothesis for each relationship imbedded in your diagram. Provide a rationale for your selection of each independent variable and explain the logic for the relationships among the four variables.

3. How do presidential candidates choose a vice-presidential running mate? With vice-presidential choice as your dependent variable, choose three independent variables that you think affect that choice, and diagram the relationship among all four variables. Write a hypothesis for each relationship imbedded in your diagram. Provide a rationale for your selection of each independent variable and explain the logic for the relationships among the four variables.

4. How do nations choose other nations for alliances, such as the North Atlantic Treaty Organization (NATO)? With choice of alliance partner as your dependent variable, choose three independent variables that you think affect that choice, and diagram the relationship among all four variables. Write a hypothesis for each relationship imbedded in your diagram. Provide a rationale for your selection of each independent variable and explain the logic for the relationships among the four variables.

Chapter 7

Conceptualizing, Operationalizing, and Measuring Variables

Learning Objectives

After completion of this chapter, students should be able to do the following:

Develop useful conceptual and operational definitions of political science concepts.

Describe and distinguish the levels of measurement of variables.

Explain validity of measurements and how it is established.

Explain reliability of measurements and how it is established.

Distinguish between indexes and scales designed to measure concepts.

Illustrate how moving from conceptualization to measurement of variables results in an operational hypothesis that has been deduced from an original conceptual hypothesis.

From Abstract Concept to Concrete Measurement

Research in political science usually starts with a vague theory or tentative generalization about the nature of political reality. To be useful, theories must be tested empirically through observation. But how can the abstract terms in a vague theory or conceptual hypothesis be transformed to measurements that produce concrete, accurate, and precise indicators of aspects of the real world? That is a crucial question for social science, and you will see that the transformation is accomplished through a number of steps. First it will be useful to provide an overview of the process with a substantive example.

143

Political alienation is one of the most important concepts in political science. Scholars since Aristotle have argued that the stability and life of a political system depend at least in part upon the support of citizens. When citizens are alienated from the political system, the results may include a refusal to participate in politics, noncompliance with laws, civil strife leading to the loss of life, and ultimately revolution. But what is political alienation, and how can it be measured? A first step in answering the question is surveying the literature (perhaps starting with specialized dictionaries and encyclopedias) to determine how others have used the term. An extensive search is not required to reveal that alienation is a very old term, originating in early Christian thought, the meaning of which has been the subject of literally hundreds of books and academic articles. [1] How can you sort out all of the different meanings and choose those that are most relevant to your theory? After carefully considering the variety of meanings, a first step is to focus on the *political* aspects of alienation.

While alienation is a concept that has been used to explain an assortment of dispositions and behaviors, political scientists have chosen to focus on a limited number of meanings. Ada Finifter identified a manageable number of dimensions about alienation that are relevant to explaining political behavior, including the degree of distrust in government, the sense of political powerlessness felt by citizens, and the feeling on the part of citizens that the political choices they are offered are meaningless. [2] Finifter's work helps to clarify the various aspects of the concepts of political alienation. You will decide which definitions of concepts to use, but your decision should focus on those meanings that are most closely related to the theory that is of interest to you and that are acceptable to scholars in that field. This process of deciding on what we mean by specific terms after a thorough investigation of the literature is called **conceptualization.** A second step in the process of moving from the abstract to the concrete is deciding which of your chosen definitions to use to test your theory. Your choice of a definition, or several definitions, involves a narrowing process from concept to several variables, sometimes called the process of developing a nominal definition. A **nominal definition** is one that is assigned to a concept by the researcher and is very much like a dictionary definition that uses words to define other words. There may be widespread disagreement about the many definitions of a concept, as is the case with political alienation, but at some point you must establish a working definition before you can proceed with your research. For example, you may acknowledge that political powerlessness and political meaninglessness are important components of political alienation, but for purposes of your research you decide to focus instead on political distrust. A nominal definition of political alienation that focuses particularly on distrust might be "the general feeling that government is no longer of the people, by the people, and for the people." [3] So the concept of political alienation has been narrowed to a single aspect. Later in the chapter we examine the advantages of considering more than one meaning in the process of developing variables and nominal definitions.

Once a nominal, or working, definition of a concept has been established, it is time to develop an operational definition. The process of **operationalization** is specifying the procedure that will be employed to measure that concept and is the point at which the concept is defined most precisely and its meaning becomes most clear. Operationalization always encompasses **measurement,** in which numbers are assigned to units of analysis or cases based on specified rules and procedures. The outcome of operationally defining a concept will be **indicators** that represent that concept in the real world. Operationalizing political distrust, which is our nominal definition of political alienation, makes us ask, "What empirical observations or indicators would lead us to believe that a person does not trust the government?"

In national surveys political distrust has been operationalized with these three questions.

Do you think that quite a few of the people running the government are a little
crooked, not very many are, or do you think hardly any of them are crooked at all?
  1. Hardly any
  2. Not many
  3. Quite a lot
  4. Don't know
  5. No Answer

How much of the time do you think you can trust the government in Washington to
do what is right—just about always, most of the time, or only some of the time?
  1. Always
  2. Most of the time
  3. Some of the time
  4. None of the time
  5. Don't know
  6. No Answer

Would you say that the government is pretty much run by a few big interests look-
ing out for themselves or that it is run for the benefit of all people?
  1. For benefit of all
  2. For a few big interests
  3. Other; depends
  4. Don't know
  5. No answer

The answers to these questions are the indicators of political distrust. Responses that "quite a lot" of officials are crooked, that government can be trusted "none of the time," and that government is run "for a few big interests" would *indicate* a high degree of political distrust. Other responses would indicate a lesser degree of political distrust. Using

Figure 7.1
From Concept to Measurement

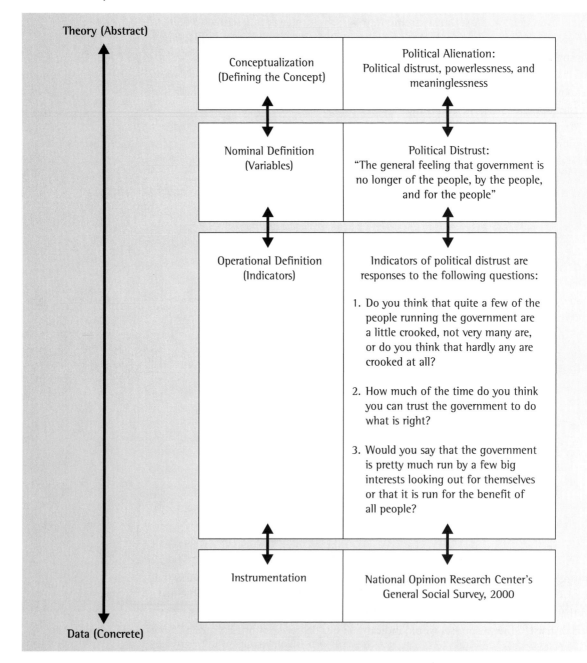

the answers to these three questions, respondents can be classified in terms of their comparative level of distrust.

The final step in the process of measurement is stipulating the instrument(s) or measuring device(s) that will be used to operationalize the concept. Political distrust was operationally defined with three survey questions designed to evoke indicators of the concept in the form of answers. But how and of whom will the questions be asked? Applying an operationalization is called **instrumentation,** encompassing the creation of the measurement device (in this case, the questions) and the means by which those devices will be employed (in this case, a scientific survey). The process of instrumentation would include designing the questionnaire, settling on a sample of possible respondents, and deciding whether to administer the survey face to face, over the telephone, or by mail. Using instruments and data sets developed by other scholars, as in our example of political distrust, is very efficient because it saves the time and effort necessary to develop one's own instrumentation. The three questions we used have been asked of a national sample of respondents in the General Social Survey by the National Opinion Research Corporation for many years. In later chapters we discuss in more detail the process of instrumentation and data collection.

A summary of operationalizing concepts is displayed in Figure 7.1. As the process moves from conceptualization to instrumentation, the concepts become less abstract and more concrete. Vague concepts defined only by other words become reflected by indicators that are susceptible to sensory observation. At this point we need to give more detailed attention to concepts and conceptualization and the process of operationalization and measurement, leaving alternative choices for instrumentation for later chapters.

Concepts and Variables

We noted in Chapter 3 that concepts are words and terms used to make sense of our experience. Since concepts are the building blocks of generalizations, we must consider their characteristics in more depth. Concepts are only mental images and do not exist in reality; they are not susceptible to sensory observation. Concepts such as freedom, racism, and revolution do not exist anywhere but in our minds—we cannot bring them into our classroom and present them during "Show and Tell." Concepts are important because they facilitate communication between people; in fact, language works only because we share mental images. When you tell someone to "look at that car," he or she constructs from personal experience a mental image of an object that resembles a car. Individuals are able to communicate with one another because their mental images of objects are similar, and they have agreed, along with everyone else who shares their language and experience, on the definition of most concepts. The terms used to describe objects and ideas have no real meaning, so consequently their usefulness is always determined by the extent to which there is agreement about their definition: how widely the mental images are shared. Since language changes with experience, the shared meanings of concepts are always tentative.

Obviously, people share a large number of mental images because they are able to use language to communicate. Communication is easier when we discuss concrete objects such as chairs, classrooms, and books, but unfortunately it is more difficult for social scientists who are interested in communicating about concepts that are not directly observable. Coming to an agreement about the meaning of "freedom" is much more difficult than agreeing about "tree." A *true* or absolute meaning of a concept like "freedom" does not exist, but the process of conceptualization is intended to produce at least some agreement among social scientists. Some concepts, however, are so contested that they may not be useful for communication and building generalizations.

Most concepts such as "freedom" and "equality" that are of interest to political scientists are complex because they are multidimensional and can take on many meanings. Political scientist Phillips Shively argues for the use of unidimensional concepts because the results of research should mean approximately the same thing to all people. Specifically, he contends that multidimensional concepts hamper communication, make measurement difficult, and ultimately result in ambiguous generalizations. [4] With regard to the latter problem, Shively suggests that because meanings of multidimensional concepts change over time, it is difficult to develop enduring generalizations. He points to the example of the concept "liberalism," showing how the meaning currently varies widely from person to person and has changed dramatically over time. Shively is certainly correct about the difficulty communicating with multidimensional concepts, but on the other hand, we believe their complexity reflects the complex reality of social behavior.

Avoiding multidimensional concepts means our generalizations will lack the richness and relevance that characterize politics. Concepts with a multidimensional meaning are certainly difficult to measure, but if defined with care, measurement of their dimensions is possible. In addition, as the meanings of concepts change, the usefulness of the generalizations (theories) of which they are a part may be diminished. As we noted in Chapter 1, however, all knowledge is tentative and likely to change. Generalizations must continuously be retested and modified.

We noted earlier that the process of conceptualization requires discovering and detailing as many possible meanings or dimensions of a concept as possible. The best approach to defining multidimensional concepts is to be extremely thorough about articulating possible meanings or variables. Once an exhaustive list of meanings is formed, you have to decide which one will be your nominal, or working, definition and then operationalized. The choice of working definitions may be based on the goal of developing a generalization or on an assessment of acceptability by scholars in the field. Taking into account the resources at your disposal to conduct your research (which are always limited), the greater the number of working definitions or variables that are developed and operationalized, the greater the likelihood that scholars will accept at least one of your "meanings."

A good example is the concept of religiosity. How do we know if a person is very religious? A common definition focuses on the frequency of attendance at religious services. A variable resulting from this conceptual definition might be that "religious people attend services more often than others." You might object that religiosity is a matter of belief and that a person can be very religious and not attend regular services. Or you might offer an alternative definition that focuses on prayer: "People who pray often are more religious than those who do not." One of your classmates might point out that your definition is inadequate because some religions mandate prayer several times per day, whereas others do not emphasize prayer. Does that mean that members of a religion that do not emphasize daily prayer are less religious? There are numerous other possible definitions of religiosity, but the point is that the more definitions or variables generated and operationalized, the greater the likelihood that you will capture more accepted meanings of the concept. Often there is no one meaning for complex concepts that is completely satisfying, so multiple definitions and composite measurements are necessary. Definitions should be constantly examined and improved—concept definition is a continuous process.

To the Web

Exercise 7.1   Defining Multidimensional Concepts

An important step in social and political research is developing definitions of multidimensional concepts. Exercise 7.1 requires that you consider some important concepts and develop more than one definition for each. You might want to use one of the specialized dictionaries mentioned in Chapter 4 or an online dictionary or encyclopedia. Go to the **DEPR Web Page**, click on **Web Exercises, Chapter 7**, then on **Defining Multidimensional Concepts.**

Questions for Thought and Discussion

Democracy is a concept and therefore exists only in our minds. What image do you form when you hear or read the word "democracy"? Describe some images that might come to mind among other people, perhaps in other countries. What types of images are most likely to be shared by individuals? What images might be the subject of debate?

Operationalization and Measurement

Earlier we noted that operationalization entails selecting observable phenomena (indicators) to represent the various dimensions of abstract concepts. When operationalizing concepts, which phenomena can actually be observed and which must be inferred is a factor. Abraham Kaplan discusses three classes of things that can be measured. [5] First, we perceive *direct observables* using the senses directly and simply, such as whether a candidate for office wears glasses. Second, *indirect observables* involve some logical inference on the part of the observer who must rely on indicators because he or she cannot see the phenomenon itself. For example, while it is possible to directly observe whether

To the Web

Exercise 7.2   Direct Observables, Indirect Observables, and Constructs

The ability to distinguish between the types of variables you need to operationalize is an important skill for you to develop. This exercise asks you to come up with some examples of each of the three types of variables described by Kaplan. To access the exercise, go to the **DEPR Web Page**, click on **Web Exercises, Chapter 7,** then on **Direct Observables, Indirect Observables, and Constructs.**

or not an individual votes, we normally rely instead on a check mark on a questionnaire where a person *indicates* the behavior in response to a question such as "Did you vote in the last election?" The operationalization of the concept of voting in the latter case requires an inference. Third, *constructs,* according to Kaplan, are theoretical concepts created through observation, but they cannot be observed directly or indirectly. An example of a construct is an orientation toward politics such as *alienation* that is constructed through the use of a number of indicators. Another construct is *democracy,* created by the conceptions of many individuals. Democracy cannot be directly or indirectly observed, but it can be operationalized by a composite of indicators. In the case of constructs, each separate indicator must be operationally defined and then detailed as to how they are combined to operationalize the overall concept.

Operational definitions are measurements of concepts. Earlier we defined measurement as the process of assigning numbers for values or properties of variables based on specific rules and procedures. A more comprehensive definition is offered by Edward Carmines and Richard Zeller: "Measurement is most usefully viewed as the process of linking abstract concepts to empirical indicants, as a process involving an explicit organized plan for classifying (and often quantifying) the particular sense of data at hand—the indicants—in terms of the general concept in the researcher's mind." [6] Most often, the strategy for operationalization and measurement is clear because concepts and variables naturally take on certain values, such as male and female for sex. The measurement of many other variables of interest to political scientists (indirect observables and constructs), however, involves choices. That is why Carmines and Zeller write about measurement as involving "an explicit organized plan."

Measurement of all but the simplest concepts requires you to make choices because the concept being measured is "in the researcher's mind." There are many choices to be made, but two examples should be sufficient. One decision that must be made concerns the range of variation of a variable or the number of values that will be assigned. Suppose you want to measure opinions about capital punishment. You could simply ask people to indicate agreement or disagreement with the following statement: "Capital punishment should be made illegal." The possible values of the variable might be "agree" or "disagree." You might decide instead that you want your measurement of capital punishment opinion to reflect the strength, as well as the direction, of the opinion. That can be accomplished by offering respondents the following responses: strongly agree, agree, disagree, and strongly disagree. The latter option offers a wider range of responses and measures both the intensity *and* direction of feeling about capital punishment.

You must also decide how many possible values that a variable can take on and how fine the distinctions between units of analysis need to be. If the goal is to measure party identification, respondents could be asked if they consider themselves to be Democrats, Republicans, or Independents. The results would be three gross categories indicating partisan affiliation. To make finer distinctions, Democrats and Republicans could be asked if they consider themselves to have strong or weak partisan attachments. Independents could be asked if they felt "closer" to the Republican or the Democratic party. Their answers would make finer distinctions between respondents in the measurement of their partisan identifications.

The precision and accuracy of measurements require still other types of choices that must be made. We subscribe to the cardinal rule stated by Phillips Shively that it is a "sin to waste information." [7] Measurements should always be as precise as the concept in the mind of the researcher allows. You can always produce simplified measures from more sophisticated measures but not vice versa. In measuring any opinion, you could combine those who said they "strongly agree" with those who said they "agree" to obtain a single category of agreement. But if you initially operationalized the attitude using only two categories, you could not expand them to more. In general, always try to develop measures that will provide the finest distinctions between units of analysis.

■ Precision: Levels of Measurement

The process of measuring actually involves cataloging and ordering phenomena, and the precision with which phenomena are classified is described by differing levels of measurement. **Levels of measurement** refer to the "organized plan" that is used to assign numbers to values of variables. These different levels ultimately determine how the data will be analyzed and the nature of the conclusions we can draw from that analysis. Each level of measurement has associated with it unique mathematical assumptions that affect choices for data analysis (covered in later chapters), so it is critical that you understand each of them.

Variables can be operationalized at one of four levels of measurement: nominal, ordinal, interval, or ratio. Nominal is the lowest level of measurement with the fewest mathematical properties and the smallest degree of precision, while ratio is the highest level with the greatest number of mathematical assumptions and the highest level of precision. So there is a hierarchy associated with levels of measurement. At the lower levels of measurement there are fewer assumptions and the statistical procedures used for data analysis with these lower levels of measurement are less sensitive.

The **nominal level of measurement** is the most primitive way to measure variables, producing a set of discrete categories to distinguish units of analysis. Nominal level measurements are mutually exclusive and collectively exhaustive, meaning that each case or unit of analysis fits into only one category and that the categories cover all cases. Many variables in political science research are measured at the nominal level, such as religious affiliation being measured with the categories Protestant, Catholic, Jewish, and Other. This measurement satisfies the characteristic of mutual exclusivity because no person can be placed in more than one category. The addition of the "Other" category ensures that the measurement is exhaustive and that every person will fit into some category. Note that the categories of religious affiliation have no direction: It cannot be said that Protestants have more or less religious affiliation than Catholics. The order of the values is arbitrary, and we could have just as well listed the religious affiliation categories as Protestant, Other, Jewish, and Catholic. For purposes of data analysis we would usually want to assign a number to each category, but for nominal levels of measurement the number assignments are arbitrary. Assigning a "1" to Protestants and a "2" to Catholics does not mean that Catholics have "more" religious affiliation. Other examples of variables measured at the nominal level are state of residence (Texas, Illinois, Washington), nationality (English, Japanese, Italian), sex (male, female), and party membership (Democrat, Republican, Other).

The **ordinal level of measurement** involves classification of units of analysis or cases into categories that have an inherent, hierarchical order. Measurements at the ordinal level are mutually exclusive and collectively exhaustive like those at the nominal level, but they also have the characteristic of ordinality: More or less of a variable can be measured, and the categories have direction. The measure of political distrust that we considered earlier is a good example of a variable measured at the ordinal level: "Do you think that quite a few of the people running the government are a little crooked, not very many are, or do you think hardly any of them are crooked at all?" Some possible responses are 1. Hardly any, 2. Not many, and 3. Quite a lot. Respondents are classified based on their beliefs concerning the number of people running the government who are crooked. Those who answered "Quite a lot" thought more officials were crooked than those who said "Not many," and those who responded "Not many" thought more were crooked than those who replied "Hardly any." It follows that those who said "Quite a lot" thought more were crooked than those who said "Hardly any." The measurement ranks respondents in terms of how many people running the government they believe are crooked. But the differences between categories are not exact, and we cannot say that the difference between "Hardly any" and "Not many" is the same as the difference between "Not many" and "Quite a lot." Another example of a variable commonly measured at the ordinal level is subjective social class.

Individuals may categorize themselves as being members of the working, middle, or upper class, mutually exclusive and collectively exhaustive categories that also serve to rank individuals by their self-perceived class. Upper class is higher than middle class, and middle class is higher than working class, but it is not known, however, whether the difference between working class and middle class is equivalent to the difference between middle class and upper class. Another example of a variable measured at the ordinal level is frequency of church attendance (daily, weekly, monthly, a few times a year, less than once per year, never), which ranks individuals from greater to lesser attendance. But the differences between rankings are not equivalent (daily versus weekly and monthly versus a few times per year), meaning precise differences among individuals on this variable cannot be determined. With ordinal measurement, whether we assign numbers to values for analytical purposes from low to high or high to low does not matter, but the numbers must correspond with the ranking of the categories.

The **interval level of measurement** not only categorizes and ranks (having all the properties of nominal and ordinal measurements), but it also determines *how much* more or less of a property one case has than another. Because interval levels of measurement have an arbitrary zero point, they have *additive* properties. A common example of measurement at the interval level is temperature on a Centigrade scale. The zero point on the scale is arbitrarily determined as the freezing point of water. It does not mean the absence of heat or cold, but a zero point allows us to determine that the difference between 10° and 20° is equivalent to the difference between 30° and 40°. Unlike measurements at the nominal and ordinal levels, we can determine the difference between objects. Political science does not use interval measurements very much. In fact, most measurements in the social sciences are at the lower levels (nominal and ordinal) or the ratio level, which we discuss next. Some social scientists treat ordinal measures of attitudes as if they have additive properties, but a great deal of controversy surrounds that issue.

The **ratio level of measurement** has multiplicative properties because it has a real zero point—zero means the absolute absence of the variable. Political scientists measure a large number of variables at the ratio level, such as variables involving money. The variable "gross annual income" has a real zero point: the absence of income. The measure also has multiplicative properties because a person with a gross annual income of $80,000 has twice the income of a person who earned $40,000. Other examples of variables measured at the ratio level are the population of cities, the number of votes received by a candidate, and the number of bills passed by Congress in a particular year. As a practical matter, empirical political analysts usually do not distinguish between interval and ratio levels of measurement. In fact, some methodologists simply ignore the ratio level or refer to both simultaneously as the *interval/ratio level*.

The most important point to remember about the levels of measurement is that using higher levels produces more precision. Always measure variables at the highest possible level because otherwise information will be lost. Let's consider an example of annual income. The left side shows the annual income of six individuals measured at the interval/ratio level, and the right side shows the ordinal level.

Individual	Income	Individual	Income
Jones	$100,000	Jones	High
Smith	$80,000	Smith	High
Johnson	$50,000	Johnson	Medium
Jackson	$40,000	Jackson	Medium
Green	$20,000	Green	Low
O'Brien	$15,000	O'Brien	Low

The measurement of the data on the left allows us to make precise comparisons of the six individuals. Given the actual income figures, we could easily categorize the six individuals into high-, medium-, and low-income groups as they appear on the left. If, however, we initially measured income at the ordinal level and categorized our six respondents into high, medium, and low groups when we collected the data, we would not be able to "recapture" the actual dollar amounts (measured at the interval/ratio level) for later analysis. In other words, variables measured at a higher level of measurement can be regrouped at a lower level for analysis but not the other way around.

The following examples related to television news illustrate different levels of measurement.

Nominal

Which network news program do you watch most frequently?

1. NBC
2. CBS
3. ABC
4. CNN
5. Fox
6. Other

Ordinal

How accurate do you think most news stories are?

1. Not accurate at all
2. Somewhat accurate
3. Mostly accurate
4. Always accurate

Interval/Ratio

How many hours of news programming do you watch on television each week?
_____ hours

You can see from these examples that the level at which a variable is measured is influenced by the nature of the phenomenon being studied. Some variables, such as which television news program a respondent views most frequently, can be measured only at the nominal level. The frequency of television viewing, however, can be measured at the ratio (hours per week) or ordinal (often, sometimes, never) level. Unless you have a good reason to do otherwise, you should always measure a variable at the highest level available to you because you will be preserving more options for later analysis.

Key Points

Variables are measured at four levels that range from low to high precision and sophistication:

- Nominal Level of Measurement—Defines mutually exclusive and exhaustive categories or values of a variable.
- Ordinal Level of Measurement—Defines mutually exclusive and exhaustive categories that can be ranked or ordered.
- Interval Level of Measurement—All of the characteristics of nominal and ordinal level measures but also additive because precise differences between rankings can be determined.
- Ratio Level of Measurement—All of the characteristics of the lower levels of measurement but also has a true zero point and multiplicative properties. Social scientists often ignore the differences between interval and ratio levels and refer to them in combination as interval/ratio.

To the Web

Exercise 7.3   Distinguishing Levels of Measurement

The ability to identify and distinguish levels of measurement is fundamental not only for operationalizing variables but also for data collection and data analysis. Exercise 7.3 asks you to identify some examples of variables that can be measured at different levels using the CIA World Factbook Web site. To access the exercise, go to the **DEPR Web Page**, click on **Web Exercises, Chapter 7**, then on **Distinguishing Levels of Measurement.**

Accuracy of Measurement

We now know that measurement means assigning values to units of analysis (cases) on the basis of indicators and that the goal of measurement is to generate indicators that accurately reflect a concept. Continuing with our example of television news, when we ask somebody, "How accurate do you think news stories are?" we are looking for a response (an indicator) that precisely reflects the opinion held by that individual. The opinion itself is not observable, and our measurement of it is unlikely to be perfectly precise. There will likely be a difference—hopefully a small one—between the answer given to the question and the opinion held by the person. This difference between the concept and its operational definition is called **measurement error** and is a general problem because *all* measurement leads to error. Physical measurements also produce error: Odometers in two cars will produce slightly different measurement values for the distance from Boston to San Francisco. The answer that a respondent provides concerning the accuracy of a news story can be attributed to two sources. The first is the actual perception of news accuracy by the individual, and the other is the error in the measurement of that opinion. Methodologists assert that an observed response (or score) to a question similar to the one about news accuracy is equal to the *true* or *real* opinion plus error. The goal of measurement is, of course, to reduce error, but it cannot be completely eliminated. Remember that a measurement is successful to the extent that it reflects a concept; achieving a goodness of fit between concept and measurement is the objective.

Measurement error is of two types. **Random error** occurs when chance factors affect the measurement of a concept. If we ask people to provide an estimate of their annual family income, they might not remember exactly how much money they made in the previous year and offer a rough estimate. If they were asked the same question again on another occasion, the estimate might be slightly different. They may not have been intentionally deceptive, but they gave different answers because of situational differences, such as when the question was asked, their level of distraction at the time, or the form of the question. The specific sources of random error are numerous, but in the long run, if the measures of concepts seem to reflect reality, we can assume the error associated with them is random. **Nonrandom error** is the result of the measurement process itself or perhaps confusion concerning what is being measured. An illustration of nonrandom error in the measurement process is the young woman interviewer who asks in a face-to-face interview, "Do you agree or disagree that sexism plays a role in inhibiting the career advancement of women?" The gender of the interviewer might systematically encourage a socially acceptable response, leading some respondents to indicate agreement when they actually disagreed. The response might differ if a male interviewer asked the same question.

Assuming that measurement error is always present and that no measurement perfectly reflects reality, the major concern of social scientists is the *extent* to which a measurement accurately reflects a concept. The problems we encounter in trying to achieve goodness of fit between our concepts and our measurements center on validity and reliability. **Validity** quite simply means the extent to which a researcher is measuring what, and only what, he or she intends to measure. The better that is done, the more valid the measure. **Reliability** refers to the stability and consistency of a measure. A measure is reliable to the extent that it produces the same results over repeated applications. Given these definitions, a measure can be invalid but reliable. If a bathroom scale always indicates ten pounds over the true weight, it reliably measures weight because it produces consistent results with repeated applications. The results are not valid, however, because

Figure 7.2
Throwing Darts: Measurement Error, Validity, and Reliability

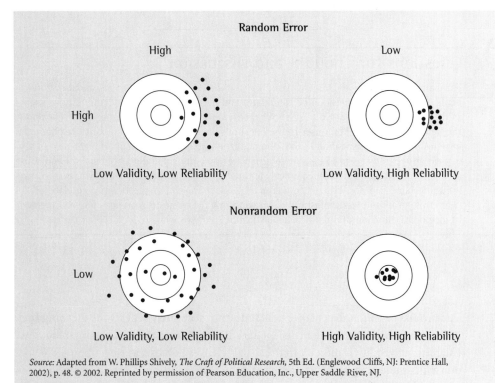

Source: Adapted from W. Phillips Shively, *The Craft of Political Research,* 5th Ed. (Englewood Cliffs, NJ: Prentice Hall, 2002), p. 48. © 2002. Reprinted by permission of Pearson Education, Inc., Upper Saddle River, NJ.

the scale is not measuring what it is supposed to measure: the actual weight. On the other hand, an unreliable measure can never be valid because if different results are obtained from repeated applications, the measure does not reflect the concept. In other words, reliability is a necessary, but not sufficient, condition for validity. The next task is to establish the validity and reliability of measurements. [8] The distinction and relationship between validity and reliability is illustrated in Figure 7.2. You can think about achieving an accurate measurement as analogous to the accuracy with which darts are thrown at a target. Obviously, the goal is to hit the bull's-eye every time. That would indicate the least amount of error and, in the case of measurement, high validity and high reliability. If all of your darts miss the bull's-eye but are grouped on one area of the target, then your throws produced approximately the same result, even if it's not the desired one. You reliably hit the same spot but not the bull's-eye (that is, you had high reliability but low validity). If your darts are scattered all over the target or scattered on one side or another, your shots were not accurate with respect to validity (closeness to the bull's-eye) or reliability (darts closely grouped).

Q Questions for Thought and Discussion

For many years the Survey Research Center at the University of Michigan has asked respondents their opinions of presidential candidates and parties using open-ended questions such as the following: "What do you like about the Democratic party?" "What do you dislike about the Democratic party?" Responses to the questions have been used to categorize respondents in terms of their sophistication in thinking about politics. Those who have a great deal to say in their answers and seem to be able to articulate some understanding of liberalism and conservatism are categorized as "ideological" and politically sophisticated. Those whose answers are abbreviated and do not seem to incorporate liberalism-conservatism are categorized as "nonideological" and less sophisticated. Do you think the question is an accurate measurement of ideological thinking and political sophistication? Why or why not?

▩ Validity

The process of *validation* ensures that a measure accurately reflects the meaning (held in the researcher's mind) of a concept and that no dimensions or aspects are ignored. Establishing validity is difficult in the social sciences because, as we have noted before, our most interesting concepts are very abstract and multidimensional. A key problem of measurement validity is that only measurements of a concept can be observed, not the concepts themselves, so it is impossible to directly compare the measurement with the actual concept. Still, to have confidence in the generalizations that are built from our concepts, we need to be as sure as we can that the differences we observe between units of analysis on variables reflect only differences in the actual concept and not error or differences on some other unmeasured variable. Validity can be established in a number of ways, some more useful than others, but because of the nature of concepts as mental images, we can never be sure that measurements are valid.

Face validity is asserted and not demonstrated empirically. Face validity means the measurement is consistent with an agreed definition (common mental image) of a concept. For example, there may be disagreement about the adequacy of measuring the wealth of a nation by determining the average income of families, but there is agreement that family incomes have something to do with a nation's overall wealth. If it were suggested that national wealth be measured by determining the number of soccer players per capita, most researchers would object, saying the idea made little sense. The measurement would lack face validity. Face validity is nothing more than agreement among observers that a measurement is germane to the concept.

Criterion-related validity, sometimes called predictive validity, is based on the ability of the measure to predict a related behavior. The Scholastic Aptitude Test is a measurement designed to assess "scholastic aptitude" and predict student academic success in college. When students actually enroll in college, their academic success is measured by grade point average. The better the SAT can predict individual educational outcomes such as GPA, the more valid it is. Criterion-related validity involves the measurement of two concepts: the one that is being validated and the criterion against which it is compared. Another example of criterion validity is found in the development of a measure of motivation to become involved in partisan activities. The measure would be correlated with actual activity in party organizations to determine the criterion-related validity level.

Another approach to establishing criterion-related validity is to use a "known group method." To measure attitudes concerning civil liberties, for example, administering a test to members of the American Civil Liberties Union would help establish criterion validity. If members of the ACLU did not score highly on the measure, its validity would be in question. Some empiricists distinguish between two types of criterion-related validity. **Predictive validity** is established when a measure is used to predict a behavior that occurs later in time, while **concurrent validity** is demonstrated if the predictor and criterion are measured at the same time. The use of SAT scores to predict grade point averages is an example of establishing predictive validity. The known groups approach to validating a civil liberties measure is an example of concurrent validity. Criterion-related validity is more useful in developing measures related to psychology and education because in the social sciences it is difficult to think of criterion variables for our abstract concepts. For example, what would be a criterion variable for political ideology?

Content validity has to do with whether a measure covers the full domain of the meaning of a concept. Carmines and Zeller provide an interesting example using arithmetic. A general measure of arithmetic skills using problems that only test addition but ignore subtraction, multiplication, and division will not have content validity. [9] Paying attention to content validity emphasizes the importance of fully defining a concept and its dimensions before measurements are developed. Political science departments often struggle with an issue of content validity when developing the means to assess the success of their programs. Tests of knowledge of political science are often developed to evaluate student learning, and this raises important questions (and often creates arguments) about what content should be included. At the heart of the matter is the definition of political science and which subfields are most important. Should the majority of the questions deal with American politics? International relations? Political philosophy? Comparative politics? Would a test of political science knowledge be invalid if there were no questions about empirical analysis?

The determination of content validity depends on the definition of the concept. In the past, scholars have defined the communications development of a nation by the quantity of print media (such as magazines and newspapers) and electronic media (such as radios, televisions, and telephones) per capita. Today this traditional definition would lack content validity because it does not take into account Internet users and cell phones per capita. In operationalizing concepts it is preferable to choose too many measures to represent the dimensions than too few. When only one or just a few dimensions of a concept are measured, a researcher should clearly define which dimensions are left unmeasured.

Construct validity focuses on how a measured variable relates theoretically to other variables. In political science, construct validity, as opposed to criterion-related ability, is more popular because of the lack of easily measured criterion variables. Construct validity is essentially the development of a hypothesis that is consistent with a theoretical expectation. The hypothesis is tested, and the measurement is said to be useful and valid if it is related to the other variable as the theory predicts. Such tests of construct validity offer evidence of the extent to which the measurement reflects the concept. A series of questions designed to measure religious fundamentalism might be evaluated for construct validity by testing the hypothesis that they are related to support for school prayers. Theory would lead you to expect more fundamentalist respondents to be stronger supporters of prayer in public places. No relationship between the variables would mean either that the measure of religious fundamentalism lacked validity or that the theory was incorrect.

Carmines and Zeller describe the necessary steps to ensure construct validity: (1) a theoretical relationship between the measure and another variable must be specified, (2) the empirical relationship must be examined, and (3) the empirical evidence must be interpreted in terms of how it clarifies the validity of the measure. [10] A single theoretically expected relationship between a measure and another variable should be interpreted as evidence of construct validity. Multiple relationships should be discerned to establish confidence in validity. A relationship inconsistent with theoretical expectations does not necessarily mean that a measure lacks construct validity because possible alternative explanations are that the theory is incorrect or that the measure of the "other" variable lacks validity. Despite the dependence on theoretical expectations and the validity of the other variable, construct validity is probably the most useful approach for the social sciences.

■ Reliability

Reliability is present when the same value is obtained each time a measurement is applied to the same phenomenon. Measuring the height of a table several times with a metal yardstick and finding the same height each time means the measurement is reliable. If the yardstick were constructed from soft rubber rather than wood or metal, each measure taken of the table would produce a slightly different height, and the measurement would not be reliable. From this simple example, reliability of measures may seem easy to establish, but unfortunately that is not so. Because reliability problems occur in such a wide variety of situations, tracking down the sources of error is difficult. There are, however, various methods for determining the reliability of measurements: Some are more practical than others.

The **test-retest method** applies a measurement to the same units of analysis (cases) at two different points in time to determine if the same results are produced. The difficulty with this approach is that real changes may take place between the time of a first measurement and the time of a second, perhaps resulting in a perfectly reliable measure being judged unreliable. For example, the person who is asked whether she approves of the president's goal to expand trade with Asian nations first indicates approval, but when she is asked the same question after a period of time, she indicates disapproval. Do the inconsistent responses mean that the question is an unreliable measure or that the person's opinion changed? Another factor that may influence test-retest reliability is that a respondent's response to the second application of the measurement may be influenced by the first. Using our preceding example, the person may have indicated approval both times the question was asked to appear consistent. If too much time passes between applications of the measure, real change is more likely, but if the time period is short, the initial application may influence the second.

The **alternative forms method** for establishing reliability is similar to test-retest, but it avoids the problem of the influence of experience when the measure is used the first time. The procedure calls for measuring the same variable more than once but using two different forms applied to the same units of analysis (cases) at different times. An example would be a test designed to measure knowledge of American politics. A pool of questions representing the breadth of knowledge would be written, and from that pool two sets would be randomly selected for the two forms. Similar scores for members of the group on the two forms would be evidence of reliability.

The **split-halves method** for establishing reliability calls for designing two measures of a concept and using them once on the same group of people. The test of knowledge of American politics can be used as an example. Forty multiple-choice questions measuring knowledge of American politics would be split into two subsets of twenty questions each. All forty questions would be given to a group of students at the same time, with the scores for each subset compared for equivalence. If the test is reliable, comparing the results of any combination of twenty questions with the other twenty should produce the same results.

The **subsample method** of assessing reliability focuses on comparing subsamples of a larger sample. A large sample is drawn, then randomly divided into two subsamples.

Because they are randomly drawn, the two subsamples can be assumed to be equivalent on all relevant characteristics. The complete test is then given simultaneously to both subsamples, and the similarity and differences between them is determined. Using our example of the forty-question test of knowledge of American politics, all forty questions would be given to the two subsamples. Because the subsamples are equivalent, reliability would be indicated by similarity in scores.

Q Questions for Thought and Discussion

You are on a committee that determines the menu for your college dining hall, and your assignment is to determine the food preferences of students. You decide to enlist twenty of your friends to interview students about what they like to eat. Interviews will take place in the dining hall and in dormitories. Since you need to determine just one piece of information, you and your friends ask just one question: "What do you like to eat?" Respondents' answers are recorded on notebook paper and the results tabulated to determine next month's menus. What are some possible threats to the *reliability* of your results?

Maximizing Validity and Reliability

Ideally, measures should be pretested for validity and reliability, but political scientists, compared with scholars in the fields of psychology and education, are not careful about pretesting the questions they use for surveys or experiments. The results are measures that may have little more than face validity and suspect reliability. As we have noted, if measures are unreliable, they will be invalid even if they have every appearance of reasonable reflections of a concept. Pretesting usually involves collecting data as part of the process of developing measures. It can be a slow, cumbersome, and costly effort that is frustrating because researchers are anxious to proceed with their project. But pretesting should always be a part of the process of operationalization if the validity and reliability of the measures chosen have not been established by others. Remember that the sources of error that threaten reliability and validity are numerous, but there are ways to reduce error and increase validity and reliability.

Using measurements of variables that have been constructed by others makes a lot of sense. Many concepts of interest to political scientists have been successfully measured and effectively used on a continuing basis for many years and have become the standard in the field. The set of survey questions to measure political efficacy (sense of political effectiveness) is one instance. The questions have been subjected to tests of validity and reliability and their strengths and weaknesses are well known. [11] The use of such standard measures contributes to the comparison of research findings and encourages replication. A number of sourcebooks contain measures of important variables, and in some cases information about validity and reliability is provided. Sourcebooks that focus on psychological rather than political variables are more numerous, so political scientists usually comb through previous research to find concepts measured by other scholars and to determine the extent to which validity and reliability have been assessed.

One threat to reliability and hence validity is the person who administers the measurement. Responses to questions, as in an earlier example of women's career advancement, are often influenced as much by the questioner as the question. Of course, we would not argue that intrusive methods of data collection such as survey research be abandoned, but one approach to reducing measurement error is to develop **unobtrusive measures** that reduce the impact of the observer. While recognizing the impossibility of completely removing the effect of the observer, we believe in trying to minimize that source of error. For example, measuring the attitudes of state legislators toward tax reform by gathering records of their roll call votes on the issue is less intrusive than asking them in an interview. Roll call votes are a behavioral rather than attitudinal measure and generally more valid and reliable than responses to a direct question. [12]

Yet another way to maximize reliability and validity is to develop multiple indicators of the same concept. We have pointed out that many concepts in political science are complex and multidimensional; multiple measures reduce error and contribute to more complete operationalization of a concept. Because different types of measures will contain different types of errors, the more measures employed and the more distinct they are from one another, the more likely they will not share the same sources of error. Multiple indicators also increase content validity by ensuring that more dimensions of the concept are measured. The forty-item test of knowledge of American politics is a good example of using multiple indicators. A poorly worded, three-item test would be unreliable and invalid, producing unwanted distortion and error in the final measurement of knowledge. Content validity would also suffer because the many dimensions of American politics could not be captured in three items. On the other hand, in a 100-item test, the error associated with three or four poorly crafted questions would be diluted by the other 96 or 97 items. Furthermore, 100 items would account for greater content validity because they would capture a larger proportion of the complexity of American politics.

Combining individual measures of a concept to produce a single value or score, such as the overall grade on an examination, is helpful. Composite scores reflect a diminishment in overall measurement error because the errors associated with each item cancel each other out, increasing validity. Composite measures are called **indexes** or **scales.** The terms are often used interchangeably, but there are some important differences. Indexes are constructed by a simple accumulation of values assigned to individual indicators. The composite measure of knowledge of American politics discussed previously is an index. A summation of correct answers on that test would range from zero correct to forty correct, and those who take the test can be compared in terms of their index scores. Indexes are most often used in political science to measure attitudes. A scale is similar to an index in that it is a multi-item measure, but it is constructed so *patterns* of responses can be discerned. They are specifically designed to distinguish the *intensity* among attributes. A common scale used to measure attitudes toward legalized abortion emphasizes the conditions under which abortions would be allowed. The series of items may include the following possible responses to the question "Do you agree or disagree that abortions should be allowed in the following circumstances?"

1. The woman's health is seriously endangered.
2. The pregnancy is the result of a rape.
3. The woman is not married.

A person who disagrees that abortion should be allowed when a woman's health is endangered would also likely disagree with permitting abortions in the other two circumstances. The three items would constitute a scale because they vary in intensity, and a pattern of responses should be discernible.

To the Web

Understanding Measurement: Precision and Accuracy

Social scientists are often preoccupied with the measurement of key concepts. Entire professional journals and many books are devoted to this complex process. We know that issues surrounding the precision and accuracy of measurement are often difficult for students to understand. There are some helpful Web sites that elaborate on the importance of and the problems with measurement. We have linked some of these useful and interesting sites to the Web Page. Go to the **DEPR Web Page**, click on **Web Links, Chapter 7,** then on **Understanding Measurement: Precision and Accuracy.**

From Conceptual to Operational Hypotheses

For most of this chapter we have focused on definitions and measurements for single concepts, but now we will return to hypotheses. Moving from a concept definition to operational definitions is a deductive process—a transition from the general to the more specific. Concepts are not meant to stand in isolation: They are useful only when linked together to form generalizations. So researchers usually find themselves defining and operationalizing at least two concepts contained in a conceptual hypothesis, and in that sense, they are simultaneously deducing operational hypotheses from the initial conceptual hypothesis.

The conceptual hypothesis "People with higher social status are more likely to participate in politics than those with lower status" contains two concepts: social status and political participation. This is the operationalization of the concepts.

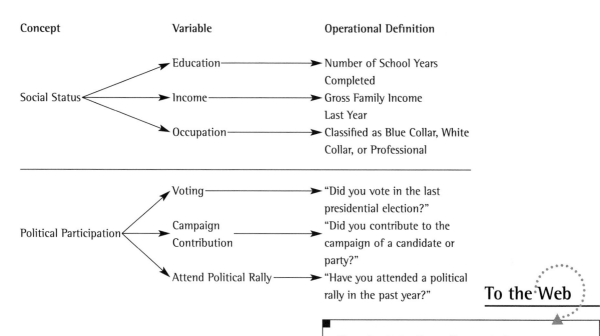

Concept	Variable	Operational Definition

Social Status → Education → Number of School Years Completed

Social Status → Income → Gross Family Income Last Year

Social Status → Occupation → Classified as Blue Collar, White Collar, or Professional

Political Participation → Voting → "Did you vote in the last presidential election?"

Political Participation → Campaign Contribution → "Did you contribute to the campaign of a candidate or party?"

Political Participation → Attend Political Rally → "Have you attended a political rally in the past year?"

We began with an abstract conceptual hypothesis, but after operationalizing the concepts and taking into account several of their dimensions, we can deduce nine possible operational hypotheses. Two of them are (1) the greater the number of school years completed, the more likely that person voted in the most recent presidential election, and (2) the greater a person's gross family income in the last year, the more likely that person made a contribution to a candidate or party. By collecting data to test the nine operational hypotheses and finding most of them to be confirmed, we could then conclude, through a process of inductive inference, that the original generalization of social status being related to political participation is supported.

To the Web

Exercise 7.4 From Conceptual to Operational Hypotheses

Concepts are important because they are related in conceptual hypotheses. As concepts are operationalized, operational hypotheses, which in turn are logical deductions of the original conceptual hypothesis, can be formulated. In this exercise you will state the seven additional operational hypotheses that follow from our operationalizations of social status and political participation. We have provided some additional conceptual hypotheses as well. You will develop operational definitions for the variables in these hypotheses and state operational hypotheses that result from your operational definitions. To access the exercise, go to the **DEPR Web Page**, click on **Web Exercises, Chapter 7**, then on **From Conceptual to Operational Hypotheses.**

Conclusion

In this chapter you learned about the process of defining and operationalizing concepts. Concepts are the building blocks of the generalizations and theories about the political world, so their precise definition is critical to the social scientific process. The definition of a concept proceeds deductively from the designation of a general meaning to the more specific terms in a hypothesis and finally to the exact description of how the concept will be measured. The measurement of concepts must be precise and accurate. Precision refers to the organized plan that is used to assign numbers to values of variables and the level of measurement achieved by that process. Accuracy is the extent to which measurements reflect the concepts they are intended to measure. Finally, you learned that as the dimensions of a concept are more narrowly defined, the result is a set of operational hypotheses that are deduced from the original generalization or conceptual hypothesis.

In Chapter 8 we turn to the end product of operationalizing and measuring variables: data. Data sets contain operationalized variables and are generally stored in computer files. We will help you learn how to access data sets and create your own so you will have the necessary empirical data available to test your hypotheses.

Summary of the Main Points

- Conceptualization entails discovering and detailing as many meanings and dimensions of a concept as possible.
- All dimensions of a concept should be operationalized.
- Decisions about measuring variables means making choices about the number and range of values to be assigned.
- Level of measurement reflects the precision with which you have classified phenomena.
- Variables should always be measured at the highest appropriate level.
- All measurement results in some error; the goal is to minimize nonrandom error.
- The problems you encounter in trying to achieve goodness of fit between concept and measurement center on validity and reliability.
- Maximize validity and reliability by using measures successfully employed in the past, those that are unobtrusive, and those with multiple indicators.
- The development of alternative operational definitions of concepts takes place concurrently with the development of operational hypotheses.

Terms Introduced

alternative forms method
conceptualization
concurrent validity
construct validity
content validity
criterion-related validity
face validity
index
indicator
instrumentation
interval level of measurement

levels of measurement
measurement
measurement error
nominal definition
nominal level of measurement
nonrandom measurement error
operationalization
ordinal level of measurement
predictive validity
random measurement error
ratio level of measurement

reliability
scale
split-halves method
subsample method

test-retest method
unobtrusive measures
validity

Selected Readings

Blalock, Hubert M., Jr. *Conceptualization and Measurement in the Social Sciences.* Beverly Hills, CA: Sage Publications, 1982.

Carmines, Edward G., and Richard A. Zeller. *Reliability and Validity Assessment.* Beverly Hills, CA: Sage Publications, 1979.

Hempel, Carl G. *Fundamentals of Concept Formation in Empirical Science.* Chicago: University of Chicago Press, 1952.

Shively, W. Phillips. *The Craft of Political Research,* 5th Ed. New York: Prentice-Hall, 2002.

Sullivan, John L., and Stanley Feldman. *Multiple Indicators: An Introduction.* Beverly Hills, CA: Sage Publications, 1979.

Webb, Eugene F., Donald T. Cambell, Richard D. Schwartz, and Lee Sechrest. *Unobtrusive Measures.* Chicago: Rand McNally, 1966.

Activity 7.1
Inferring Concepts from Measurements

Activities

In this chapter we focused on the transition from abstract concepts to concrete measurements—a deductive process. Sometimes research questions are guided by data that have been collected by others. As we shall see in later chapters, political scientists commonly test their hypotheses with data from surveys conducted by research organizations and from information compiled in volumes by organizations such as the United Nations and the U.S. Census. Implicit in each of these indicators is a concept. By learning to infer inductively what concept is being measured by a given indicator, you will be able to see the potential use of these data to test hypotheses. Here is a set of operationalizations of concepts. For each of the operationalizations, write down the concept it measures.

1. Survey question: "How many times a week do you drink an alcoholic beverage?"
2. Percentage of a nation's population that is literate
3. U.S. Senate roll call vote on eliminating estate taxes (Yea, No, Abstain, Absent)
4. Survey question: "I often feel lonely." Agree or Disagree.
5. Number of negative stories about political candidates in a local newspaper
6. Percentage of budgets of South American nations devoted to military expenditures
7. Survey question: "Most people can't be trusted." Agree or Disagree.
8. Attendance at concerts performed by heavy metal groups
9. Number of hours of sleep each night
10. Number of trips taken abroad each year by presidents

Activity 7.2
Identifying Levels of Measurement

What level of measurement—nominal, ordinal, or interval/ratio—describes each of the following variables?

1. Political ideology: very conservative, conservative, moderate, liberal, very liberal
2. Annual salaries of state governors
3. The number of years of service in the House of Representatives
4. Occupations of members of the state legislature
5. Job approval rating of the president: Strongly approve, approve, disapprove, strongly disapprove
6. Number of formal trade agreements negotiated each year (1980–1990) between the United States and Asian nations
7. Percentage of the vote received by winning candidates for the U.S. Senate
8. The order of finish of candidates in a presidential primary election: first, second, third, fourth, and so on
9. Whether a candidate for office is an incumbent or a challenger
10. The number of poor people per 1,000 population for selected counties
11. Populations of countries categorized as less than 20 million, 20 million to 50 million, more than 50 million
12. Presidential character classified as active-positive, active-negative, passive-positive, or passive-negative
13. Birth order of political leaders: first child, second child, third child, etc.
14. Expenditures per capita for education in the New England states
15. Languages spoken in Canada

Activity 7.3
Operationalizing Concepts and Hypotheses

At the end of the chapter we emphasized that as you operationalize concepts, you are also creating operational hypotheses that are logical deductions from the conceptual hypothesis with which you started. This activity is designed to show that once concepts are operationalized they can be used to construct operational hypotheses logically following from the original, conceptual hypothesis.

1. Conceptual hypothesis: Conservatives are more likely to oppose the creation of new government programs than are liberals.
   a. Write at least two operational definitions for each of the two concepts in the hypothesis: Political Ideology and Opinion on New Government Programs.

b. Using your operational definitions of the concepts, write at least two operational hypotheses.

c. Explain how your operational hypotheses logically follow from the original hypothesis.

2. Conceptual hypothesis: More democratic nations provide more social services to their citizens than less democratic nations.

a. Write at least two operational definitions of the two variables in the hypothesis: Extent of Democracy and Social Services Provided.

b. Using your operational definitions of the concepts, write at least two operational hypotheses.

c. Explain how your operational hypotheses logically follow from the original hypothesis.

3. Conceptual hypothesis: Nations that are experiencing economic growth are more likely to act aggressively toward their neighbors than those with economies in decline.

a. Write at least two operational definitions for each of the two concepts in the hypothesis: Economic Change and Aggression Toward Neighbors.

b. Using your operational definitions of the concepts, write at least two operational hypotheses.

c. Explain how your operational hypotheses logically follow from the original hypothesis.

4. Conceptual hypothesis: "Countries that experience inclement weather are more likely to be democracies than those that enjoy moderate weather."

a. Write at least two operational definitions of the two variables in the hypothesis: Type of Weather and Form of Government.

b. Using your operational definitions of the concepts, write at least two operational hypotheses.

c. Explain how your operational hypotheses logically follow from the original hypothesis.

Part 3

Data Collection

Chapter 8

Organizing and Managing Data

Learning Objectives

After completion of this chapter, students should be able to do the following:

Understand why data must be stored in computer files and analyzed with software designed for that purpose.

Define and explain the component parts of a data matrix.

Interpret a codebook to make sense of an existing data file and create an original codebook for their own data.

Create and enter the values of variables into an SPSS data file.

Know what a frequency distribution is and why that procedure is initially run on a data file.

Run and interpret a frequency distribution for a data set using SPSS.

Mounds of Data

In the previous chapter, you learned about moving from the conceptual to the operational level when doing empirical research and how to measure and quantify the variables in your research. The result of that effort is a set of quantitative data that you can use to test your hypotheses. Each variable and its measurement is a characteristic of whatever unit of analysis you are studying—individual, group, city, state, nation, or whatever. You may, for example, have survey data about individuals in the United States that include variables such as the respondents' ages, incomes, political party identifications, positions on public policy issues, attitudes toward political institutions, and so on. Or your data set may have nations as the unit of analysis with variables such as population, per capita income, literacy rate, level of democracy, percentage of national budget spent on defense, and more. But whatever your unit of analysis or variables, you will have far too much numerical information to keep track of by simply looking over written lists of respondents, states, or countries and the information you have available about them. You need to learn some basic technological skills about arranging and handling large amounts of quantitative data in order to test your hypotheses.

For example, surveys generally have, at the minimum, hundreds of respondents, with forty or fifty variables for each of those respondents. The norm is to have approximately 1,500 respondents. A survey with that many respondents and fifty questions would have 75,000 answers to record and keep track of. Clearly, managing and analyzing that much information without the help of a computer would be an endless task. In addition, there are even bigger sets of various types of quantitative data collected by governments, universities, private institutions, survey research centers, businesses, and individuals available to the public that cannot be accessed or reviewed without the use of appropriate technology.

Questions for Thought and Discussion

Some people criticize efforts to study behavior with numerical data, such as survey answers that are quantified and recorded in a computer file. They claim that using quantitative data "reduces people to a set of numbers" and is overly simplistic for describing and explaining human behavior. Do you agree with these criticisms? Why or why not?

You will use the five data sets that accompany this book for exercises and activities in this and later chapters. Two data sets are the results of surveys of national samples of American residents. Another is about the members of the U.S. House of Representatives in the 106th Congress. The final two data sets contain characteristics about the American states and countries, respectively. The data set titled "GSS2000depr" has results from the 2000 General Social Survey (GSS) conducted by the National Opinion Research Center. Included in the data set for this book are 342 variables from a random sample of 2,817 respondents. The other survey data set, titled "NES2000depr," contains results from the 2000 National Election Study (NES), a national survey of the American electorate conducted in presidential and midterm election years. We have selected 154 variables from the 2000 NES survey for the data set for this book; the sample size is 1,807. The "HOUSE106depr" data set has information on 39 variables for all 435 members of the U.S. House members elected in 1998. The data set with the fifty American states as the units of analysis, called "STATESdepr," has information on 153 variables. Finally, the "COUNTRIESdepr" data set has information on 79 variables for 208 countries.

Data Analysis Software

To the Web

Statistical Software Packages

SPSS and other software suppliers, such as SAS, S-PLUS, STATA, and MINITAB, provide considerable information about their products on their respective home pages. On occasion, you may have the opportunity to download demonstration programs so that you can try the product. Go to the **DEPR Web Page,** click on **Web Links, Chapter 8,** then on **Statistical Software Packages.**

Empirical political researchers organize, manage, and analyze large amounts of quantitative data, using readily available software, the most common of which is the Statistical Package for the Social Sciences, generally referred to by its acronym, **SPSS.** And while this software was initially written by and for social scientists over thirty years ago, it is now widely used in many business-related fields. SPSS is employed in health care, financial services, insurance, manufacturing, market research, the public sector, retail, and higher education. The use of SPSS in such a wide diversity of commercial and nonprofit activities points to both its flexibility and utility. Learning how to use SPSS will have practical implications beyond your work in empirical political analysis. Not only does it have applications outside the social sciences, it can also be used with data collected by you or others in formats different from SPSS. Data can be easily imported to SPSS from spreadsheets such as Excel or Lotus, databases such as Paradox or dBase, or even other statistical programs.

We will not explore the full potential of SPSS in this book. While it is a powerful program that can handle enormous data sets and perform complex statistical procedures, this book presents only the information required for basic analysis. Once you are comfortable with SPSS, you should be able to learn more complicated procedures easily. For empirical political analysts, software is one of the means to achieving the end of explaining human behavior. As empiricists studying political behavior, we want to use data to answer our questions about politics. Understanding how to employ software that manages and analyzes our data is necessary for answering those questions, but we do not want to get bogged down in the software as an end in itself. For political scientists, statistical software is only a tool, a means to the end of testing hypotheses and explaining political phenomena.

The Data Matrix

Once you have accessed and opened the SPSS program on your own or the school's computer system, you will see the screen pictured in Figure 8.1: the SPSS Data Editor Window. It is similar to "spreadsheet" programs used for budgeting and accounting, such as Excel or Lotus, with which you may be familiar. This screen represents what empirical political scientists call a **data matrix,** which is a template to organize quantitative data

Figure 8.1
Empty Data Matrix in SPSS Data Editor Window

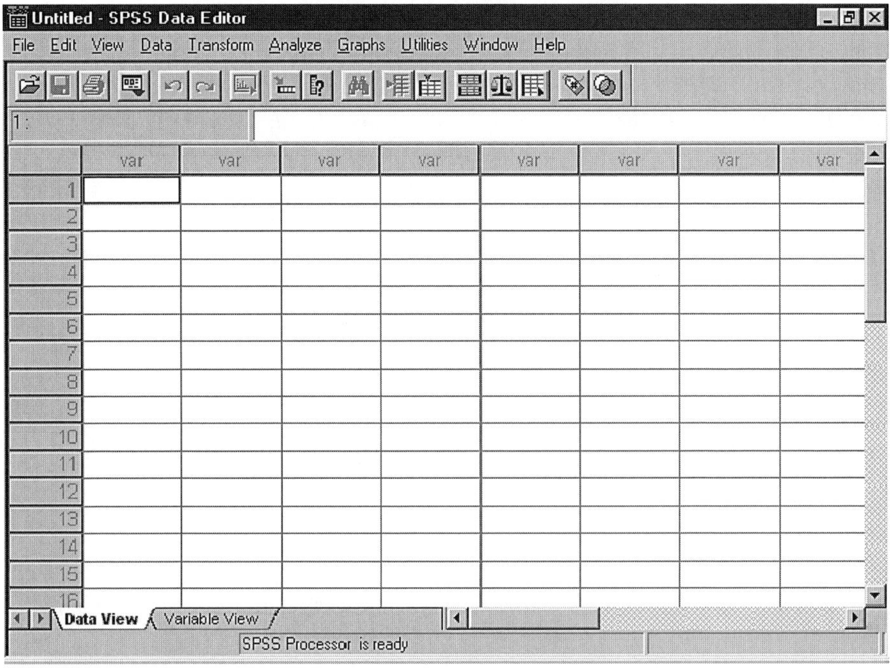

Courtesy of SPSS, Inc.

collected to test hypotheses. Whether using SPSS or any other software program, the data matrix is the basic format in which empirical data are organized. When you call up an SPSS **data file** that you want to use, the template of this data matrix will be filled with the information from that data file.

A data matrix, such as that in Figure 8.1, has three components. First, down the left side of the data matrix are the units of analysis—what it is you are studying. As you can see in Figure 8.1, the SPSS template has numbers listed there in anticipation of the researcher entering his or her data. If your data file consists of the results of a survey, the individuals who responded to the survey will be the units of analysis and will be listed by a number assigned to each respondent. The total number of rows, or lines, in the data set will be equivalent to the number of respondents in the survey. If you are testing a hypothesis about the American states, the states are your unit of analysis, and the column on the far left would have the (perhaps abbreviated) names of the states or in some cases the numbers one through fifty, each state having been assigned a number in alphabetical order. Second, across the top of the data matrix are the variables in the study, each column labeled "var" in Figure 8.1. When the data file is called up and fills the matrix, these compartments will contain the assigned names of the variables. **Variable names** in SPSS must be no more than eight characters long, so some names will not be complete words but abbreviations. The third section of the data matrix is composed of the cells created by the intersection of the variable columns and the unit of analysis rows that will be filled by the value of each variable for each unit of analysis. Finally, notice near the bottom left of the screen in Figure 8.1 the two terms "Data View" and "Variable View." These are two options, which we will explain a bit later, for how you want to view the information in the data file.

For now, direct your attention to Figure 8.2, a picture of an SPSS screen with the data matrix filled with data about the American states. SPSS always opens the file in the "data view" mode within the Data Editor. These data are from the "STATESdepr" data set provided along with this book. When you open the STATESdepr data file in SPSS, this is exactly what you will see on the screen. By looking at a particular column of the matrix— that is, down the cells under a specific variable name—you will see the value of that variable for every unit of analysis. Under the column "state," for example, you see a vertical sequence, arranged alphabetically, of the postal code letters for each state. Each of the fifty states has a unique two-letter code. The second column is titled "popsqmi," which is an abbreviation and the SPSS variable name for "population per square mile," a measure of the population density for each state. Alabama, the first state listed, has a population density of 79.6 residents. From the states appearing on the screen in Figure 8.2, you can see that Alaska (1.0 residents per square mile) and Idaho (12.2 residents per square mile) are less densely populated, while Connecticut (674.7 residents per square mile) and Delaware (344.7 residents per square mile) are more densely populated. You could calculate the average population density for the American states by adding up all these individual state values and dividing by fifty. Eventually, we will explain how you can use SPSS do this and many other kinds of arithmetic calculations more quickly and accurately than you could with a handheld calculator.

By looking down any column under a specific variable name in a data set, you can see the values of that variable for a particular state. Under "womleg96," the variable name for the percentage of women in a state's legislature, the percentage of women in each state's legislature in 1996 is indicated. As you can see for yourself, Alabama had 5 percent women in its legislature for that year, Alaska 14 percent, Arizona 27 percent, and so on. Other variable names running across the top of the screen include "repc88," the percentage of the vote received by the Republican party candidate for U.S. president in 1988; "dempc88," the percentage of the vote received by the Democratic party candidate for U.S. president in 1988; and "othrpc88," the percentage of the vote received by the candidates other than the Democratic and Republican parties for U.S. president in 1988. If you scrolled across the width of the entire data set, you would see variables names for all 153 variables in this data set—that is, all the information we have collected about the

Figure 8.2
SPSS Data Editor—Data View Option of States Data Set

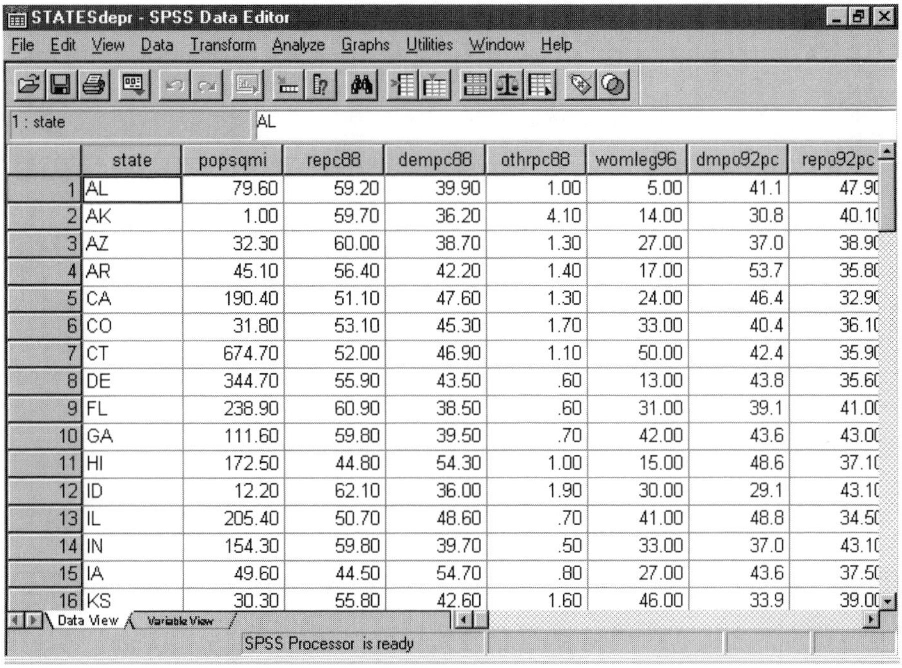

STATESdepr - SPSS Data Editor

File Edit View Data Transform Analyze Graphs Utilities Window Help

1 : state   AL

	state	popsqmi	repc88	dempc88	othrpc88	womleg96	dmpo92pc	repo92pc
1	AL	79.60	59.20	39.90	1.00	5.00	41.1	47.90
2	AK	1.00	59.70	36.20	4.10	14.00	30.8	40.10
3	AZ	32.30	60.00	38.70	1.30	27.00	37.0	38.90
4	AR	45.10	56.40	42.20	1.40	17.00	53.7	35.80
5	CA	190.40	51.10	47.60	1.30	24.00	46.4	32.90
6	CO	31.80	53.10	45.30	1.70	33.00	40.4	36.10
7	CT	674.70	52.00	46.90	1.10	50.00	42.4	35.90
8	DE	344.70	55.90	43.50	.60	13.00	43.8	35.60
9	FL	238.90	60.90	38.50	.60	31.00	39.1	41.00
10	GA	111.60	59.80	39.50	.70	42.00	43.6	43.00
11	HI	172.50	44.80	54.30	1.00	15.00	48.6	37.10
12	ID	12.20	62.10	36.00	1.90	30.00	29.1	43.10
13	IL	205.40	50.70	48.60	.70	41.00	48.8	34.50
14	IN	154.30	59.80	39.70	.50	33.00	37.0	43.10
15	IA	49.60	44.50	54.70	.80	27.00	43.6	37.50
16	KS	30.30	55.80	42.60	1.60	46.00	33.9	39.00

Data View Variable View

SPSS Processor is ready

Courtesy of SPSS, Inc.

states. If you scrolled down the entire data set, you would see the names and the rows of data for all fifty American states.

Figure 8.3 shows a different view of the STATESdepr file data in the SPSS Data Editor. We have clicked on the "variable view" toggle switch at the bottom left of the Data Editor screen, which has changed the screen from a view of the data to a description of the variables in the data set. Down the left-hand side of the Data Editor in the "variable view" mode are the variable names that were previously at the top of the screen in the "data view" mode. At the top are various descriptors of the variables. In the cells are the descriptive characteristics for each of the variables. The first column shows the variables names, and under the "Label" column, there is a fuller description of each variable. The SPSS variable name "repc88," for example, is now clearly labeled "Republican Percent of the Presidential Popular Vote, 1988." "womleg96" is more fully described as "Percent of Women in State Legislature, 1996." Other columns show more information about the variables. The "type" column reveals whether the variable is in letter (string) or number (numeric) form. Under "Width," you can see how many columns in

Figure 8.3
SPSS Data Editor—Variable View Option of States Data Set

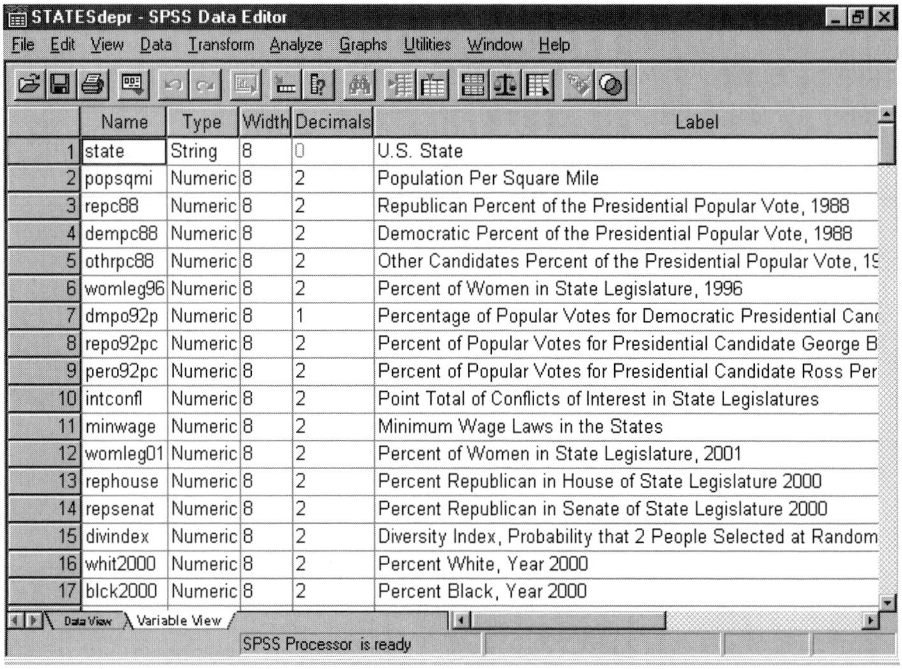

	Name	Type	Width	Decimals	Label
1	state	String	8	0	U.S. State
2	popsqmi	Numeric	8	2	Population Per Square Mile
3	repc88	Numeric	8	2	Republican Percent of the Presidential Popular Vote, 1988
4	dempc88	Numeric	8	2	Democratic Percent of the Presidential Popular Vote, 1988
5	othrpc88	Numeric	8	2	Other Candidates Percent of the Presidential Popular Vote, 1\$
6	womleg96	Numeric	8	2	Percent of Women in State Legislature, 1996
7	dmpo92p	Numeric	8	1	Percentage of Popular Votes for Democratic Presidential Canc
8	repo92pc	Numeric	8	2	Percent of Popular Votes for Presidential Candidate George B
9	pero92pc	Numeric	8	2	Percent of Popular Votes for Presidential Candidate Ross Per
10	intconfl	Numeric	8	2	Point Total of Conflicts of Interest in State Legislatures
11	minwage	Numeric	8	2	Minimum Wage Laws in the States
12	womleg01	Numeric	8	2	Percent of Women in State Legislature, 2001
13	rephouse	Numeric	8	2	Percent Republican in House of State Legislature 2000
14	repsenat	Numeric	8	2	Percent Republican in Senate of State Legislature 2000
15	divindex	Numeric	8	2	Diversity Index, Probability that 2 People Selected at Random
16	whit2000	Numeric	8	2	Percent White, Year 2000
17	blck2000	Numeric	8	2	Percent Black, Year 2000

Courtesy of SPSS, Inc.

the data matrix have been assigned to that variable; in this data set, every variable was assigned a standard eight columns, although not all variables filled up the columns that we assigned to it. The "Decimal" column tells you to how many decimal places the values of the variable have been calculated. The "State" variable, which is string and not numeric, has, of course, no decimal places. If you were to scroll across the width of the Data Editor screen in the "variable view" mode, other information—such as which numbers are used to indicate missing data—would be revealed about each variable.

Now look at Figure 8.4, a picture of an SPSS screen with the Data Editor filled with data about the members of the 106th U.S. House of Representatives from the "HOUSE106depr" file that accompanies this text. You are looking at the "data view" mode in Figure 8.4. The unit of analysis is no longer states but individual members of the U.S. Congress. Their names run down the left-hand column, starting with the honorable Mr. Callahan. Across the top, as when the States data filled the editor, are the variable names. The variables showing in Figure 8.4 are the representatives' party iden-

Figure 8.4
SPSS Data Editor Filled with "HouseData106" File Showing Information About the 106th U.S. House of Representatives in Data View Mode

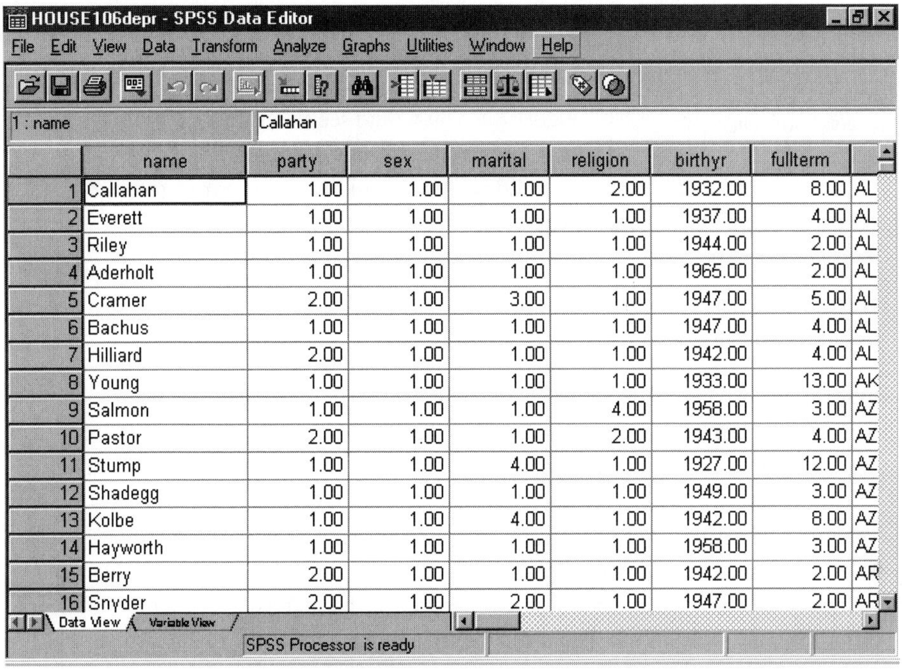

	name	party	sex	marital	religion	birthyr	fullterm	
1	Callahan	1.00	1.00	1.00	2.00	1932.00	8.00	AL
2	Everett	1.00	1.00	1.00	1.00	1937.00	4.00	AL
3	Riley	1.00	1.00	1.00	1.00	1944.00	2.00	AL
4	Aderholt	1.00	1.00	1.00	1.00	1965.00	2.00	AL
5	Cramer	2.00	1.00	3.00	1.00	1947.00	5.00	AL
6	Bachus	1.00	1.00	1.00	1.00	1947.00	4.00	AL
7	Hilliard	2.00	1.00	1.00	1.00	1942.00	4.00	AL
8	Young	1.00	1.00	1.00	1.00	1933.00	13.00	AK
9	Salmon	1.00	1.00	1.00	4.00	1958.00	3.00	AZ
10	Pastor	2.00	1.00	1.00	2.00	1943.00	4.00	AZ
11	Stump	1.00	1.00	4.00	1.00	1927.00	12.00	AZ
12	Shadegg	1.00	1.00	1.00	1.00	1949.00	3.00	AZ
13	Kolbe	1.00	1.00	4.00	1.00	1942.00	8.00	AZ
14	Hayworth	1.00	1.00	1.00	1.00	1958.00	3.00	AZ
15	Berry	2.00	1.00	1.00	1.00	1942.00	2.00	AR
16	Snyder	2.00	1.00	2.00	1.00	1947.00	2.00	AR

Courtesy of SPSS, Inc.

tification, sex, marital status, religion, birth year, and number of full terms served. As you can see, each House member's party identification has been labeled either 1, for Republican, or 2, for Democrat. The initial four members listed are Republicans and all are assigned 1's, while member Cramer, listed in the fifth position, is a Democrat and assigned a 2. We assigned Independents in the 106th Congress a value of 3. You could add up all the 1's in the "Party" column to determine how many members of the 106th Congress were Republicans, and do the same with the 2's and 3's to figure out how many Democrats and Independents were in that Congress.

Looking across the columns of Figure 8.4, you can see the other variables listed are "sex"—1. male, 2. female; "marital" for marital status—1. married, 2. single, 3. widowed, 4. divorced, and 5. separated; "religion"—1. Protestant, 2. Catholic, 3. Jewish, 4. Other, 5. Unspecified; "birthyr" for birth year—the year the member was born; and

To the Web

Exercise 8.1—Reading Data from an SPSS Data File

To make sure you understand how data in an SPSS data file are organized and displayed, you will be asked to search an on-screen representation of a data file to answer some questions about the units of analysis. Go to the **DEPR Web Page,** click on **Web Exercises, Chapter 8,** then on **Reading Data from an SPSS Data File.**

number of full terms served (SPSS variable name "fullterm")—the actual number of full terms served. By reading across the row next to a particular member's name, you can see all the data collected about that member for this data set. For example, in the eighth row is the member named Young—born in 1933, married, male, Protestant, Republican, and served thirteen terms. Snyder, the sixteenth member listed, was born in 1947 and is a single, male, Democrat, Protestant who has served two terms. If you were to scroll down the screen pictured in Figure 8.4, you would see a single line of data for all 435 members of the 106th Congress. By scrolling across the Data Editor, you would find there are a total of 39 variables for each of the members.

Codebooks

Where do all these numbers representing the sex, party identification, religion, and so forth of each member come from? In order to keep track of what information is in a data set and how those data are organized, a **codebook** is created by those who collect the information, revealing the format used to record the data electronically. A codebook tells a researcher how many cases are under study, what variables are included in the data set, the name (eight characters or fewer for SPSS) of each variable, the order in which the variables can be found across the top of the matrix, and the possible values each variable can take on. Without a codebook, a data set would be a large matrix of numbers without anyone being able to tell what they represented. Some codebooks are small, consisting of a single page, while others may fill an entire volume. Their size and complexity depend on how many cases and variables are included in the data set, as well as the sophistication of the operational definitions of the variables.

To the Web

General Social Survey Codebook

The General Social Survey (GSS), a survey of the American adult population done by the National Opinion Research Center (NORC) at the University of Chicago, was first administered in 1972. The complete codebook for all the survey items from 1972 to the present is very large. To explore this cumulative codebook for the GSS, go to the **DEPR Web Page,** click on **Web Links, Chapter 8,** then on **General Social Survey Codebook.**

A portion of the codebook for the data set on the U.S. House of Representatives that accompanies this book, fairly typical in its setup, is shown in Figure 8.5. It reveals the coding scheme we employed to organize and input to an SPSS data file the data we collected about the 106th Congress. The variables are listed in the order in which they appear across the top of the data matrix, or data file as it is called in SPSS. The SPSS variable names are listed in capital letters in quotation marks in the codebook and appear at the head of the column in which the variable information is stored. We tried to be obvious in our choice of variable names,

Figure 8.5
Codebook for Data File "HOUSE106depr"—Members of the 106th U.S. Congress

1. "NAME" (Last Name of Representative)
    Sources: Congressional Quarterly [CQ], *Almanac of American Politics,* and http://clerkweb.house.gov/106/
    mbrcmtee/members/mbrsalph/oalmbr.htm
2. "PARTY" (Political Party)
    Sources: CQ and http://clerkweb.house.gov/106/mbrcmtee/members/mbrsalph/oalmbr.htm
    1-Republican
    2-Democrat
    3-Independent
    Notes: Three Representatives changed party affiliation during the 106th Congress. Their final party affiliations at
    the close of the 106th session are included in this data set.
    -Rep. Martinez (CA 31st) changed his party affiliation from Democrat to Republican in 2000. His affiliation
    appears as Republican in this data set.
    Sources: <http://bioguide.congress.gov/scripts/biodisplay.pl?index=M000206> and <http://clerkweb.house.gov/
    106/mbrcmtee/members/mbrsalph/oalmbr.htm#G>
    -Rep. Forbes (NY 1st) changed his party affiliation from Republican to Democrat in 1999. His affiliation appears as
    Democrat in this data set.
    Sources: <http://bioguide.congress.gov/scripts/biodisplay.pl?index=F000257> and <http://clerkweb.house.gov/
    106/mbrcmtee/members/mbrsalph/oalmbr.htm#G>
    -Rep. Goode (VA 5th) changed his party affiliation from Democrat to Independent in 2000. His affiliation appears
    as Independent in this data set.
    Sources: <http://bioguide.congress.gov/scripts/biodisplay.pl?index=M000206> and <http://clerkweb.house.gov/
    106/mbrcmtee/members/mbrsalph/oalmbr.htm#G>
3. "SEX" (Sex)
    Source: CQ
    1-Male
    2-Female
4. "MARITAL" (Marital Status)
    Source: CQ, with <http://capwiz.com/c-span/bio/?id=40719> for Rep. Baca (CA 42nd)
    1-Married
    2-Single
    3-Widowed
    4-Divorced
    5-Separated
5. "RELIGION" (Religion)
    Source: CQ, with <http://capwiz.com/c-span/bio/?id=40719> for Rep. Baca (CA 42nd)
    1-Protestant
    2-Catholic
    3-Jewish
    4-Other
    5-Unspecified
6. "BIRTHYR" (Birth Year)
    Source: CQ, with <http://capwiz.com/c-span/bio/?id=40719> for Rep. Baca (CA 42nd)
    Four-digit year of birth
7. "FULLTERM" (Full Terms)
    Source: CQ
    # of full terms served and/or elected to
8. "STATE" (State)
    Source: CQ
    Two-letter postal abbreviation

using, for example, "name" for the member's name and "party" for the representative's party identification. Sometimes, however, the variable names are not quite so apparent. For example, the variable "natincrk" (not shown in Figure 8.5) is the median household income rank of the representative's district. In parentheses next to the variable name is a fuller description of that variable.

The values each variable can take on and the source of the information about the variable are also listed. For example, the variable "birthyr," as shown in Figure 8.5, is the birth year of the representative and was recorded as a four-digit number obtained from *Congressional Quarterly.* Religion has five possible values, and the description of each of those values is provided in the codebook: 1 means Protestant, 2 means Catholic, and so on. For the variable of sex, 1 means male and 2 means female. The codebook allows the person using the data set for testing hypotheses to know what each number value of a variable represents.

In some instances, an explanation of how a variable was recorded in the data set needs to be explained in the codebook. During the 106th Congress, three members changed their party identification. As you can see in Figure 8.5 under the variable name "PARTY," we have included a note that lists these Representatives, what switch in party each made, and how the data were recorded for each of them. Most data sets, by the way, have some information missing for some units of analysis, especially general surveys of the public. A respondent in a survey, for example, may answer all questions except the one about income. In situations of missing data on a variable, among other alternatives, a specific number can be assigned to indicate that the particular variable should be ignored for that case. In SPSS, you can designate any digit to represent missing data, but most often researchers choose either the digit nine or zero. A full version of the codebook for our data set on the 106th Congress, as well as the other data sets accompanying this book, are available on the Web page. The full codebooks will note any problems with missing data and the method employed to resolve them.

To the Web

Codebooks for the Data Sets Accompanying This Text

To see the codebooks for the five data sets accompanying this text, go to the DEPR Web Page and click on Data Sets and Codebooks.

Look back at Figure 8.4, which shows the SPSS data matrix filled with the information about members of the U.S. House. The data you see is consistent with the scheme laid out in the section of the codebook shown in Figure 8.5. The member's last name, the first variable, is entered in the first column, and the rest of the information about each member is recorded across the row in the appropriate columns next to his or her name: political party, marital status, religion, birth year, with the variable names of "sex," "marital," "religion," and "birthyr." Again, reading across each row will provide the description of one member of the House, and there are a total of 435 rows, one for each member. In general, codebooks guide the process of converting data from written to electronic form for storage and then allow others who access the data to figure out exactly what is in the data set and where it came from.

Key Points

A codebook tells a researcher the following:

- How many cases are under study
- What variables are included in the data set
- A description of each variable
- The source of the data for each variable
- The name (eight characters or fewer for SPSS) of each variable
- The possible values each variable can take on

Written codebooks are needed to enter the information about each variable into a data file, but once that data file is created, SPSS includes in electronic form most of the information from the codebook directly in that data file. By choosing the "variable view" mode in the Data Editor, much of the information about each variable from the codebook can be viewed on screen. Figure 8.6 shows the "variable view" of the HOUSE106depr file in the SPSS Data Editor. Just as with the STATESdepr data file, you can see the description of the first seventeen variables in the House data set, including the full variable label. The complete text of the codebook for the data, however, is not electronically embedded in the SPSS program. For example, you cannot find the original source of the data in the "variable view" mode of the Data Editor; that information can be gleaned only from the full text codebook.

As an alternative, you can quickly check the full label of an SPSS variable name from the "data view" mode of the Data Editor. As previously mentioned, the SPSS name applied to a variable is not always easily interpreted. Rather than having to switch to the "variable view" mode each time you want to check the full name of a variable, you can, while still in the "data view" mode, rest the cursor on a variable name at the head of a column in an SPSS data file and the full description of that variable name will become visible. In Figure 8.7, you can see a portion of the STATESdepr data file we looked at earlier. In this view, and while in the "data view" mode, we placed the cursor on the variable name "viocrime." After a second or two delay, the box you see under the variable name appeared with the full label for that variable: "Violent crime rate per 100,000 inhabitants, 1999." This is a handy option for when you are looking through large data sets and do not want to switch back and forth continually between the "variable" and "data" view modes in the Data Editor.

To the Web

Exercise 8.2   Examining Data About the U.S. House of Representatives

So far we have explained how data are organized and managed by pictures of computer screens and descriptions of what you can do with SPSS. Now you will see how SPSS actually works by completing an exercise using SPSS with some of the data accompanying this book. Go to the **DEPR Web Page**, click on **Web Exercises, Chapter 8**, then on **Examining Data About the U.S. House of Representatives**.

Figure 8.6
SPSS Data Editor Displaying "HouseData106" File About the 106th U.S. House of Representatives in Variable View Mode

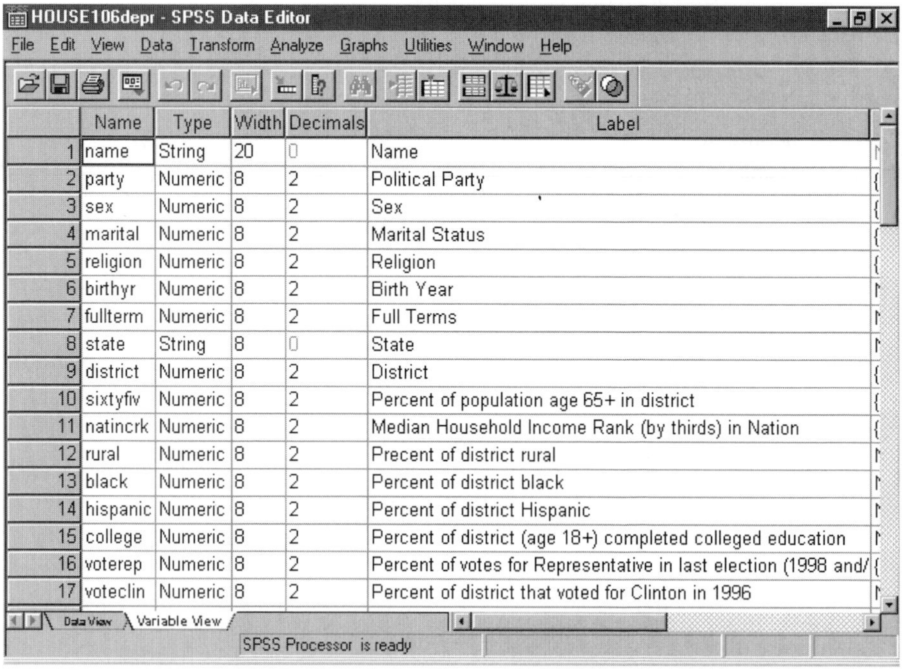

	Name	Type	Width	Decimals	Label	
1	name	String	20	0	Name	
2	party	Numeric	8	2	Political Party	
3	sex	Numeric	8	2	Sex	
4	marital	Numeric	8	2	Marital Status	
5	religion	Numeric	8	2	Religion	
6	birthyr	Numeric	8	2	Birth Year	
7	fullterm	Numeric	8	2	Full Terms	
8	state	String	8	0	State	
9	district	Numeric	8	2	District	
10	sixtyfiv	Numeric	8	2	Percent of population age 65+ in district	
11	natincrk	Numeric	8	2	Median Household Income Rank (by thirds) in Nation	
12	rural	Numeric	8	2	Precent of district rural	
13	black	Numeric	8	2	Percent of district black	
14	hispanic	Numeric	8	2	Percent of district Hispanic	
15	college	Numeric	8	2	Percent of district (age 18+) completed colleged education	
16	voterep	Numeric	8	2	Percent of votes for Representative in last election (1998 and/	
17	voteclin	Numeric	8	2	Percent of district that voted for Clinton in 1996	

Courtesy of SPSS, Inc.

▪ Creating Your Own Codebook and SPSS Data File

While there are lots of data sets available to test hypotheses that might interest you, including several accompanying this book, there may be occasions when you will want to collect your own data and create your own SPSS data file for your research. We will briefly outline here how to accomplish this task, but the necessary information and step-by-step instructions are available in the on-screen help section of SPSS, and you should look over those instructions carefully before you begin. Another option is to consult a printed user's guide to SPSS. [1] The help section in SPSS can be found, not surprisingly, by clicking on "Help" on the drop-down menu bar and selecting "Tutorial" from the drop-down menu. The tutorial window will appear with the word "Tutorial" highlighted. Then select "Data Editor" and "Entering numeric data." This set of instructions will give you an excellent overview of how to set up your own data file.

Figure 8.7
SPSS Data Editor in Data View Mode—Full Variable Label for Variable Named "Viocrime" Revealed When Cursor Put on Variable Name at Top of Column

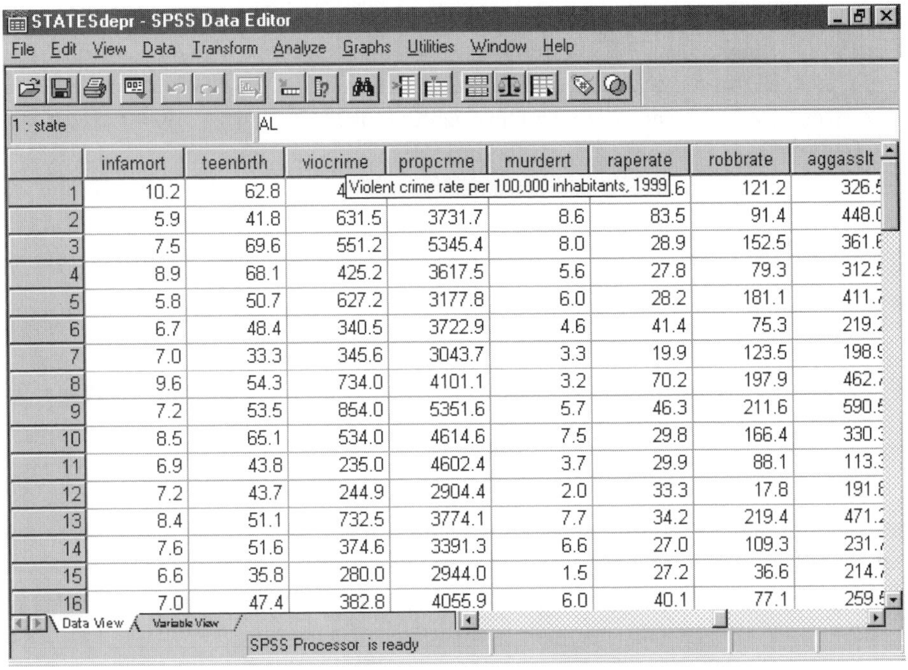

	infamort	teenbrth	viocrime	propcrme	murderrt	raperate	robbrate	aggasslt
1	10.2	62.8	4	Violent crime rate per 100,000 inhabitants, 1999	6		121.2	326.5
2	5.9	41.8	631.5	3731.7	8.6	83.5	91.4	448.0
3	7.5	69.6	551.2	5345.4	8.0	28.9	152.5	361.8
4	8.9	68.1	425.2	3617.5	5.6	27.8	79.3	312.5
5	5.8	50.7	627.2	3177.8	6.0	28.2	181.1	411.7
6	6.7	48.4	340.5	3722.9	4.6	41.4	75.3	219.2
7	7.0	33.3	345.6	3043.7	3.3	19.9	123.5	198.9
8	9.6	54.3	734.0	4101.1	3.2	70.2	197.9	462.7
9	7.2	53.5	854.0	5351.6	5.7	46.3	211.6	590.5
10	8.5	65.1	534.0	4614.6	7.5	29.8	166.4	330.3
11	6.9	43.8	235.0	4602.4	3.7	29.9	88.1	113.3
12	7.2	43.7	244.9	2904.4	2.0	33.3	17.8	191.8
13	8.4	51.1	732.5	3774.1	7.7	34.2	219.4	471.2
14	7.6	51.6	374.6	3391.3	6.6	27.0	109.3	231.7
15	6.6	35.8	280.0	2944.0	1.5	27.2	36.6	214.7
16	7.0	47.4	382.8	4055.9	6.0	40.1	77.1	259.5

Courtesy of SPSS, Inc.

Collecting a large amount of data, such as a survey of several hundred people, and organizing it into a data file take a long time and must be done with considerable attention to detail to avoid mistakes that will contaminate the data and foil your effort to test hypotheses. Such a project is impractical for a single college course. Professional telephone survey researchers have a most efficient process for organizing their data sets: collecting, coding, and inputting the data simultaneously. It is generally referred to as computer-assisted telephone interviewing, or CATI. Interviewers wearing telephone headsets sit at computer terminals. The computer has files that contain the phone numbers to be called, the survey questions to be asked, the codebook to organize the survey answers, and the data analysis software to store the coded information. The computer automatically dials the telephone numbers, and the interviewers read questions from the survey instrument that appear on the computer screen. As the interviewer types in the respondents' answers to those questions, they are organized and placed into a data file consistent with the scheme laid out by the codebook. This seamless process cuts down on mistakes made in transcribing information, and it saves time as well.

You probably did not budget for hiring a professional pollster for doing term papers, so if you are going to collect and input your own data, you need a different approach. A smaller data set, such as collecting data for ten to fifteen variables about the American states or countries, takes considerably less time and can probably be handled as part of a one-semester undergraduate project. Inputting your own data requires that you first create your own codebook that lays out the structure of the data file. Once you have decided and written down which variables to include, their order in the data set, the SPSS variable names (limited to no more than eight letters), and the **value labels** (up to 255 characters for each label) for each variable, you are ready to begin inputting the data.

When SPSS is first opened, as you saw in Figure 8.1, an empty data matrix appears, titled "SPSS for Windows Data Editor," at the very top of the screen. Data inputting takes place in this data editor window in the "Data View" mode. Click on the column in which you want to enter data and then click on the specific cell in which you want to enter a value. For example, if your variable in the first column is the name of the American states, you would type "Alabama" in the uppermost left cell, "Alaska" in the cell underneath, and so on through "Wyoming." SPSS will provide a unique variable number, starting with "VAR001," for each variable you enter, and it will appear automatically at the head of the column. When you want to assign your own variable name, switch to the "Variable View" mode of the Data Editor. In the instance of this example using the American states, you will see across the top row a description of the variable for which you had entered the data. Under the "name" column would be "VAR001." You can change the name of the variable by clicking on the cell containing its name, deleting the name assigned by SPSS, and typing in your own choice. For this example, you would likely delete the name "VAR001" and type in the word "State" as your SPSS variable name. Across the row now labeled "State," you would see some of the characteristics of the variable. Under the "Type" column, for example, would be the word "String" because SPSS would have recognized the values of the state variable (the names of the states you typed in) as containing letters, thus making it a string rather than a numeric variable.

The second variable in your personal data set about the American states, to be located in the second column, might be the number of prisoners in the state who are under a death sentence. You would type the numbers representing the number of prisoners on death row into the cell next to the name of the state you have already entered and then move to the "Variable View" in

To the Web

Exercise 8.3   Setting Up a Data Matrix and Codebook

This exercise is based on the idea that, especially when learning new ideas, it is best to start small. You are asked to write a very short survey, administer it to a very few people, develop a codebook to organize the survey results and store the data in an SPSS data file. Go to the **DEPR Web Page**, click on Web Exercises, **Chapter 8**, then on **Setting Up a Data Matrix and Codebook**.

the Data Editor to name and further define the variable. We have used the name "death-sen" for this variable in the States data set that accompanies this text. For states that do not have the death penalty, you would need to indicate that the data on the number of prisoners on death row was missing. We entered the numeral 9 to designate missing data for this variable. You would continue to enter values of variables for each state until all of your variables had been entered, at which point you would "save" the file. This is only a *very brief* description of the process, and we need to reemphasize that you should review the procedure for entering your own data in the on-screen "help" section of the program or a printed SPSS user's guide, or both. You will also find directions for importing data from other software applications in these sources.

Running a Frequency Distribution to Describe Your Data

When an empirical researcher opens a data file for the first time, he or she will initially run a procedure in SPSS called a **frequency distribution** to get an overview of the data. A frequency tells a researcher how many cases fall into each value of a variable, and a frequency distribution displays the frequencies for a group of variables in the data set. Figure 8.8 shows the frequency for the variable "religion" in the data set for the U.S. House, indicating how many House members fall into the five values of the variable "religion." A frequency distribution for variables measured at the interval or ratio level—continuous variables—will of course have many more categories. For the House members in the 106th Congress, for example, the youngest member was born in 1970 and the oldest in 1922, with a total of forty-five different categories for the variable "birthyr."

You will want to run an initial frequency distribution for your data file for a couple of reasons. If the file is one you have created yourself, your first task will be to **clean the data**—that is, check for errors that might have been made when the information about your variables was put into the data file. The most common mistake is entering the wrong value for a variable for one or more cases. If your frequency distribution for the data set on the U.S. House showed a member with the value label of 3 for the variable "sex," when 1 is a male, 2 is a female, and 9 is missing data, you would know someone had mistakenly entered a 3 for that variable. In general, if a value appears outside of the range of values assigned to that variable, you know an error has been made in entering the data. In addition, you can spot mistakes made in entering variable values for interval or ratio levels as well. If a respondent's age in a survey of adult Americans is recorded as 5, someone entered the data incorrectly or interviewed a precocious child by mistake. Of course, not all mistakes made in entering the data will be caught by running a frequency. If someone mistakenly enters a 1 for the variable "sex" when it should have been a 2, that error will not be revealed in the frequency distribution, and your data will incorrectly show one more male and one fewer female than it should. That is why great care must be taken in entering the data correctly in the first place.

Figure 8.8
SPSS Output Viewer for Frequency Distribution for the Variable "Religion" for the 106th U.S. House of Representatives

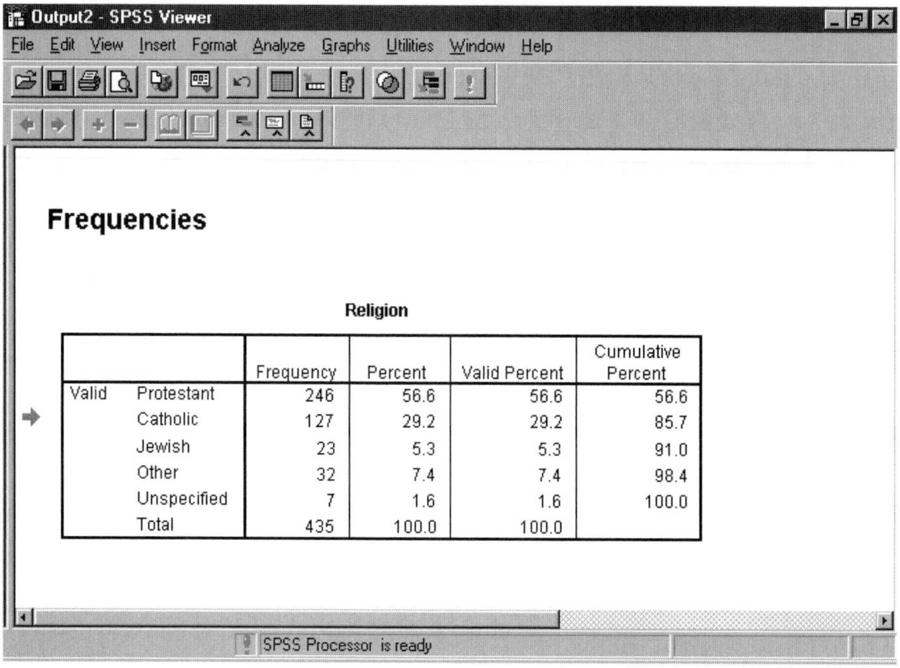

Frequencies

Religion

		Frequency	Percent	Valid Percent	Cumulative Percent
Valid	Protestant	246	56.6	56.6	56.6
	Catholic	127	29.2	29.2	85.7
	Jewish	23	5.3	5.3	91.0
	Other	32	7.4	7.4	98.4
	Unspecified	7	1.6	1.6	100.0
	Total	435	100.0	100.0	

Courtesy of SPSS, Inc.

The second reason for doing a frequency distribution is to get a sense of the range and distribution of answers for each variable in the study, whether or not you have collected the data yourself. The data file will be used to test hypotheses of interest to you, so you need to have a general idea of the variation in the data. If, for example, you are interested in using as a dependent variable an item from a survey that measures an attitude, you will want to determine how much variation there is in that attitude before you begin forming hypotheses. When a variable shows little variation, such as 98 percent of the respondents agreeing with a particular position and only 2 percent disagreeing, there is not much variation to explain. On the other hand, if respondents split evenly in their opinions on an item, there is a lot of difference in the sample for a researcher to try to account for. The same problem may occur when attempting to use a variable for explanation—that is, as an independent variable. In trying to account for differences in behavior based on race, for example, a frequency distribution of that variable showing fewer than 5 percent of respondents are African American or Asian American will tell you that not enough variation is present in that variable to show any relation to the behavior under examination.

Also, a frequency distribution may reveal a situation in which you will want SPSS to transform the values of a variable for your particular analysis of the data. An attitudinal variable operationalized with five responses—strongly agree, agree, neutral, disagree, and strongly disagree—with very few respondents answering at one or both the extremes—either strongly agree or strongly disagree—means combining some responses by "**collapsing**" the five categories into three may be advantageous. Respondents who answered "strongly agree" would be moved into the "agree" category, and those who answered "strongly disagree" would go into the "disagree" category. While on the one hand there would be less precision in your measurement of the attitude, on the other there would be enough respondents assigned to each category to make some meaningful comparisons. Also, at some point in your research, you may want to transform a variable from interval or ratio level measurement to ordinal, as discussed concerning annual family income in Chapter 7. This is a likely scenario when employing a data set collected by others, who may have had a different use in mind for their data than what you intend. Variables operationalized at the interval or ratio level can always be changed to categorical variables—for example, individuals' annual income from actual dollars into categories of "high," "moderate," and "low," as displayed in the example in Chapter 7. Remember, however, that transforming variables in the opposite direction, from categorical to continuous, is not possible. (Combining categories of values of variables is accomplished in SPSS by clicking on "Transform" on the drop-down menu bar and selecting **Recode.**) Running an initial frequency distribution on the data will alert you to these types of potential problems: variables with little or skewed variation and those operationalized differently from what you expected.

Conclusion

Operationalizing variables and collecting data require a researcher to be persistent and careful. But once these tasks are successfully completed, the researcher has at his or her disposal the information necessary to test hypotheses. Good data, well organized and stored in a useful format, are essential for determining whether descriptions and explanations of political behavior posited at the abstract, theoretical level have any basis in reality. Understanding how to get access to and handle electronically stored information is an indispensable skill for an empirical political analyst. You now have the fundamental knowledge necessary to get into and look over electronic data, and your skill in performing these tasks will increase over time with practice. In the next chapter we consider how units of analysis included in data sets are actually chosen in an attempt to make them as representative as possible.

Summary of the Main Points

- Large quantitative data sets are stored in electronic format and accessed with data analysis software, such as SPSS.
- A data matrix is the basic design in which data sets are stored.
- A codebook lays out the format for how data in a file are arranged.
- When an SPSS data file appears in the SPSS Data Editor, most of the codebook information is electronically embedded and available on-screen.
- In creating a new data file in SPSS, the values of the variables can be entered from the Data Editor Window.
- An initial frequency distribution is run on a data file to clean the data and examine the variation in individual variables.
- Without a well-organized and easily accessible data set, hypothesis testing is impeded.

Terms Introduced

cleaning data

codebook

collapse a variable

data file

data matrix

frequency distribution

recode a variable

SPSS

value label

variable name

Selected Readings

Einspruch, Eric L. *An Introductory Guide to SPSS for Windows.* Thousand Oaks, CA: Sage Publications, 1998.

Foster, Jeremy L. *Data Analysis Using SPSS for Windows Version 8.0–10.0: A Beginner's Guide.* Thousand Oaks, CA: Sage Publications, 2001.

Activities

Activity 8.1
Running a Frequency Distribution in SPSS

At this point, you need to learn how to do a frequency distribution using SPSS, and this activity will show you how to run a frequency distribution and interpret the results. Remember that SPSS has on-screen help if you need it during this exercise.

Open SPSS and open the "HOUSE106depr" file. Near the top of the screen, in the status bar area, click on "Analyze." When the gray drop-down menu appears under "Analyze," click on "Descriptive Statistics." When the menu appears to the side, click on "Frequencies." You are now looking at a new window titled in the status bar as "Frequencies." The small window to the left is the variable list from the data, organized alphabetically. Scroll through the variables until you find the variable "Party." Click on "Party." Click on the arrow button between boxes to move "Party" into the right-hand box. Click on the "OK" button and wait while SPSS calculates a frequency for this variable.

A new window titled "Output 1—SPSS Viewer" appears; the results of your data analysis are in this window. The first table lets you know if there are any missing values for your variable. In this instance there are not. The second table shows in the left-hand column the possible values of the variable and then, working across from left to right, the frequency (how many cases fall into each value of the variable), the frequency calculated as a percentage, the valid percentage (which will be different from the percentage column if there are any missing values), and the cumulative percentage. Look over the results and write down what number and percentage of House members in the 106th Congress were Republicans, Democrats, or Independents.

At the top of the screen, click on "Analyze" and repeat the above process for the variable "Marital," but before you click on the "OK" button this time, be sure to move the "Party" variable back into the left-hand box, or SPSS will do a frequency distribution for that variable again. You can do a frequency for as many variables in a data set as you want at one time by moving them all into the right-hand box at the same time. SPSS will do a frequency simultaneously for all the variables listed in the right-hand box.

To print your results, click on "file" near the top of the window and when the dropdown menu appears, click on "Print Preview" to see how many pages of output you have. Or simply click on "Print." A window titled "Print" appears. Click on the "OK" button to print. Exit SPSS.

Activity 8.2
More Frequency Distributions Using SPSS

1. Open SPSS and open the "GSS2000depr" data file. Run a frequency distribution for these four variables: "consci," "attend," "corrupt," and "expunpop." Print the results of your frequency distribution and write a short description of each variable, the values it can take on, and the number and percentage of respondents who fall into each category of the variable.
2. Go to SPSS and open the "COUNTRIESdepr" data file. Find five variables that are operationalized at the nominal or ordinal level of measurement. Once you have identified these five variables, run a frequency distribution for each of them. Print the results of your frequency distribution and write a short description of each variable, the values it can take on, and the number and percentage of countries that fall into each category of the variable.

Chapter 9

How to Achieve Maximum Representativeness: Sampling

Learning Objectives

After completion of this chapter, students should be able to do the following:

Explain the advantages of drawing representative samples.

Distinguish between probability and nonprobability samples.

Explain how simple random, systematic, and cluster samples are drawn.

Describe alternative nonprobability sample designs.

Compare and evaluate the strengths and weaknesses of different sample designs.

Calculate sampling error and determine sample sizes.

Choosing Representative Units of Analysis

As noted in Chapter 2, we are all scientists because we use our senses to make observations of phenomena (collect data) with the goal of developing useful generalizations. The conclusions that we draw from these observations are usually based on incomplete information because we rely almost exclusively on readily available observations. There are numerous examples of the use of convenient, available information to draw conclusions that might be incorrect, such as the practice of journalists, especially television news reporters, of stopping people on street corners to ask opinions about political figures or issues that are in the news. The implication is that the opinions of the "people on the street" represent the views of the larger community. Common sense tells us that the people who are conveniently walking down the street and who agree to talk to a reporter are likely not *representative* of other members of the community who may be at home or at work when the interviews were conducted. A reporter's conclusions based on people-on-the street interviews would be accurate only to the extent that there is a strong correspondence between the views of those interviewed and the members of the larger community. In choosing people on the street to interview, a reporter is *sampling* public opinion. In this chapter we focus on the problems associated with this practice of selecting a small number of units of analysis in an attempt to accurately represent the larger group about which we wish to generalize.

Sampling is necessary because it is usually impractical in terms of both time and money to collect information from a large population. A journalist could not realistically interview every person in town about the issue of the day. But while from the standpoint of accuracy it would always be preferable to collect information from an entire population, a scientifically selected sample can be surprisingly representative. As we shall see, how representative a sample is of some larger group is determined for the most part by its size and the method of selection. Many of you may be skeptical about the accuracy of a sampling, wondering how 1,500 people can produce valid conclusions about the opinions and characteristics of millions of people. We hope that by the time you have completed this chapter, you understand that no magic is involved, because sampling done correctly is a rigorous and precise scientific procedure. The issues we must resolve in designing a sample include how it will be selected, the number of cases required, and the estimation of error with respect to representativeness.

The Concept and Terminology of Sampling

Let's begin with a simple example. Suppose you want to determine the percentage of students at your university who took an American Government class in high school. One approach would be to obtain a list of all of the students at your university, contact them, find out if they had taken American Government, and then calculate the desired percentage (the number of students who took American Government divided by the total number of students and then multiplied by 100). A more economical approach might be to carefully select a few hundred students, contact them, ask them if they had taken American Government, and then calculate a percentage that would be an *estimate* of the percentage for the entire student body.

The first approach involves taking a **census,** whereas the second approach is an example of taking a sample. A **sample** is a subgroup of a population that is chosen for analysis. A **population** (sometimes called a *universe*) is a group of cases about which you wish to generalize. In the preceding example the population is all students at your university. You are probably most familiar with the idea of sampling populations of people for purposes of public opinion polling, but social scientists are interested in developing generalizations about a wide variety of objects, such as political parties, countries, cities, newspaper stories, campaign commercials, Web sites developed by interest groups, legislators, and government agencies. The entity about which the researcher collects information is called an **element** (or sometimes a *unit*). A population is simply an aggregate of elements. In the case of our example about your university, each student at the school is an element of the population of students. To offer another example, if you were interested in developing a generalization about the previous political experiences of members of the British House of Commons compared to the U.S. House of Representatives, the population would be defined as all the current members of those legislative bodies, and each member would be an element of that population.

The decision to collect information from a sample instead of from the entire population almost always involves a number of practical considerations. The greatest accuracy is ordinarily achieved by collecting data from an entire population, and when the size of that population is relatively small and an accurate and comprehensive list of elements exists, the selection of a sample is unnecessary. For example, to test a hypothesis relating economic development and voting behavior concerning human rights of the member states in the United Nations, a sample of nations is not necessary. A list of members of the United Nations is readily available, and the number is not so large that data collection would be costly. On the other hand, public opinion surveys are often taken to develop generalizations about populations containing a large number of people, and the cost in time and money of surveying a large population is usually prohibitive.

Sometimes it is impossible to collect data from an entire population. Suppose you wanted to analyze all of the newspaper reports in a given year of election campaigns in which a female candidate faced a male candidate. There would certainly be a finite number of such reports that could be described as a population of newspaper stories, but no comprehensive list would be available. In such a case a representative sample of stories would be need to be selected. Samples are used for the sake of reducing cost and convenience, but there are always trade-offs. Using a sample instead of the population saves time and resources, but accuracy is always compromised.

An important step in any social research project designed to develop generalizations is to define the theoretical population. How the population is defined will ultimately determine the breadth and utility of generalizations that are derived from a study. For example, a finding that women included in a survey sample of voting age adults of Washington State are more supportive of gun control legislation than men cannot be generalized to the entire United States; the specification of the population from which the sample was drawn limited the ability to generalize. Careful specification of a population should include the definition of elements and time. Let's return to the example of students at your university who took an American Government course in high school. The definition of the **theoretical population** would seem to be obvious. But is it? Who would be included in the population of university students? Would you include graduate students? Part-time students who take only one course per semester? Students who are not pursuing degrees? Would you be satisfied with including students who are currently enrolled, or should students who attended the university in previous years be included? You would obviously prefer to generalize about the largest population possible, but practical considerations are limiting. Few researchers take into account time when specifying a population, but an exception is the use of preelection polls used to determine which candidates are ahead and behind. In the weeks prior to an election, pollsters are careful to point out that their results are simply a "snapshot" of how candidates are doing at a particular point in time. The preceding examples are subject to the same limitations. Generalizations about the relationship between gender and gun control legislation, as well as the proportion of students who have taken a high school American Government course, would technically be applicable only to the particular time when data were collected.

Often you cannot be certain that every element in a population has a chance to be selected in a sample. For that reason we often make a distinction between a theoretical population and a study population. The **study population** is the group of elements (**sampling elements**) from which a sample is actually drawn. A sampling population may be hypothetical or enumerated. A complete list of elements of large populations, such as all voting age individuals in the United States, could not be enumerated. Still, a sample population could include all who are voting age. Some populations, such as all members of state legislatures in a particular year, are enumerated and constitute a well-defined sampling population.

The enumerated list of elements in a study population is called a **sampling frame.** Too often little attention is given to the fact that the representativeness of a sample is determined by the quality and comprehensiveness of the sampling frame. Potential sampling frames should be carefully examined to determine their correspondence with the theoretical population. A famous example of a lack of correspondence between a sampling frame and theoretical population was a preelection poll taken by the *Literary Digest* in 1936. The *Literary Digest* was a popular news magazine that used a survey method of sending sample ballots printed on postcards to people who appeared on lists obtained from telephone directories and automobile registration lists. Their method of polling had successfully predicted the outcomes of the presidential elections in 1920, 1924, 1928, and 1932. In 1936, the sampling frame was expanded in size to more than 10 million people, and over 2 million postcard/ballots were returned indicating that Alf Landon would defeat Franklin Roosevelt by a 14 percent margin. The actual election result gave Roosevelt a 22 percent margin of victory. Obviously, the sampling frame based on telephone directories and automobile registrations did not adequately reflect the population of potential voters. In the depths of the Great Depression in 1936, wealthy voters were most likely to have telephones and own automobiles and also more likely to vote Republican.

We have been describing an ideal situation where theoretical populations can be accurately enumerated by sampling frames and where samples accurately reflect the theoretical population. The reality is that accurate representation of broad populations by samples is difficult to achieve. Political researchers must be ready to accept limitations imposed by the availability and completeness of sampling frames, as well as the costs of data collection. For example, for a study of political tolerance in the former U.S.S.R., James L. Gibson and Raymond M. Duch set the original goal of selecting a sample of residents from all of the territory within the European U.S.S.R. Due to political unrest and the costs of obtaining data, however, they were unable to sample Azerbaijan and Kazakhstan. Appropriately, in a footnote to their study the authors pointed out that generalizations based on their work could not include those regions. [1] Another study, conducted by Charles L. Davis and James G. Speer and aimed at determining support for political regimes, sampled 1,019 workers in five cities in Mexico and four cities in Venezuela. Interviews were conducted in five work settings. [2] While both studies produced interesting results, it is unclear how the parameters of the populations were defined and therefore what generalizations from the data collected were appropriate. Studies such as these are commonplace in the literature of political science, so you must give careful attention to descriptions of populations and samples completed by others to determine what generalizations are acceptable. Social scientists commonly use available lists of elements as sampling frames that effectively define their populations. For example, a researcher might describe the process of selecting a sample from a list provided by a national interest group of its local officers. If there is little or no discussion of the intended theoretical population for the study, you must critically examine any generalizations and conclusions that are drawn.

At this point we need to reemphasize that the goal of taking a sample is to represent accurately the characteristics of a defined theoretical population. Actual characteristics of populations are referred to as **parameters.** Characteristics of samples are called **statistics.** In essence, statistics derived from samples are *estimates* of population parameters. The estimates are seldom perfectly precise, and **sampling error** is the difference between the sample statistic and the population parameter. If, for example, 72 percent (population parameter) of all campaign commercials in an election year are negative in tone, but a sample carefully drawn from a list of all commercials reveals that 60 percent (sample statistic) were negative, the sampling error is 12 percent. We will give more attention to sampling error later in this chapter. At this point, we only want to remind you that the representativeness of samples is strongly related to both sample size and the means of selection. Figure 9.1 provides a summary of sampling terminology.

Types of Samples

Probability and nonprobability samples are very different. In a **probability sample** all members of a population have an equal and independent chance of being selected for the

Figure 9.1
The Concept of Sampling

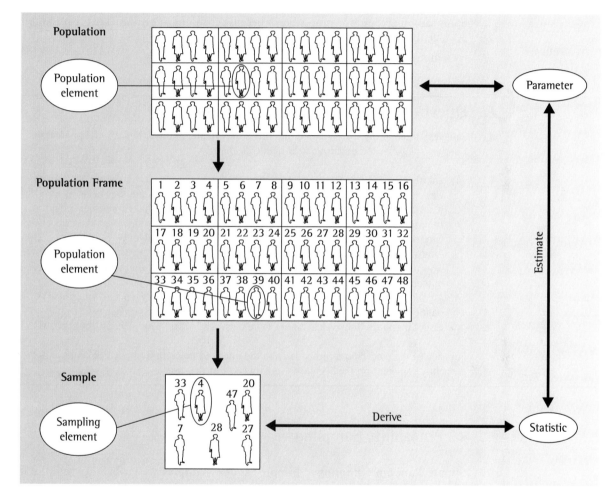

sample. Perhaps more important, a researcher can calculate and know the probability of any member of the population being included in the sample. **Nonprobability samples** are those where elements are selected at the discretion of the researcher and offer no guarantees against selection bias. Probability samples are always preferable to nonprobability samples for several reasons. First, they are more representative because they avoid the selection biases that may result from the discretion and control of the researcher over inclusion of elements. Second, a properly selected probability sample will allow a researcher to estimate sampling error—the extent to which sample statistics differ from population parameters. Estimating sampling error for nonprobability samples is impossible.

Despite the overwhelming advantages of probability samples due to representativeness, political scientists sometimes employ nonprobability samples because developing sampling frames is impossible or because economy or convenience is paramount. We will discuss some of types of nonprobability sample designs after covering probability sampling.

Questions for Thought and Discussion

Samples should always be evaluated in terms of how representative they are of a population. Consider the following descriptions of data collection.

1. Shortly after the completion of a debate between presidential candidates, CNN asks its viewers to log on to its Web site and cast a vote for the candidate they believed won.
2. A social scientist is interested in study habits of college and university students. She carefully chooses a sample of colleges and then instructs her interviewers to stand at the entrances of college libraries and interview thirty "typical" students.
3. An expert on American elections knows that no Republican in the past 100 years has won the presidency without winning the vote in Ohio. He says that he can predict the outcome of a presidential election by conducting a preelection poll in Ohio.
4. A political psychologist asks his students to volunteer for an experiment concerning political persuasion. Based on his experiment using his students for subjects, he concludes messages that evoke fear are more persuasive than those without fear appeals.

For each of the preceding projects describe the intended theoretical population and sample elements. Comment on the likely representativeness of the sample.

■ Probability Sampling

Simple Random Sampling. **Simple random samples** are probability samples in which each element and every possible combination of elements in a sampling frame have an equal likelihood of being selected. Simple random sampling requires a list of all elements in the sample population. Once that list is obtained, actually drawing the sample is simple and straightforward. Each element is given a unique number, and those assigned numbers are chosen based on a random process. How many elements are chosen—the sample size—will be discussed later.

Random choice of sample can be accomplished in two ways. The first, which is more appropriate if the total population is small, is a simple lottery. Numbers can be written on slips of paper corresponding to those assigned to **population elements,** the papers put in a fishbowl or box, and then chosen without looking until the desired sam-

Table 9.1
Table of Random Numbers

94	91	72	74	41	11	15	18	22	41	58	14
23	17	61	99	58	12	02	15	10	21	41	87
85	91	33	20	31	06	52	64	10	71	94	71
20	13	14	91	85	28	12	01	65	15	71	75
44	51	11	24	41	25	15	32	03	18	33	61

Source: This table was generated using *Research Randomizer* available at http://www.randomizer.org/, sponsored by the Social Psychology Network.

ple size is reached. A more common way to chose a random sample is to have a computer generate a table of random numbers. An extract from a table of random numbers is reproduced in Table 9.1. The point of entry of the table should be determined randomly, but in practice most people simply place their finger at some point in the table and then read the number moving down a column or across rows. The numbers are recorded until the desired sample size is reached. For the purpose of illustration, let's assume that you wish to draw a sample of ninety elements and your finger has fallen on the number 23 in the first column and second row. You would select your sample reading across to include elements numbered 23, 17, 61, 99, 58, 12, 02, 15,10, 21, 41, and 87. If your desired sample size is three digits, you could use, for example, the first three digits in the first row of the table and read down the column: 949, 231, 859, 201, and so on.

To the Web

Generating Random Numbers

There are a number of Web sites that can be used to generate a table of random numbers and, ultimately, random samples. Some of the best sites provide tutorials. Try generating a small table of random numbers at one of these useful sites. Go to the **DEPR Web Page**, click on **Web Links**, Chapter 9, then on **Generating Random Numbers**.

While the process of selecting a simple random sample seems easy, the practical difficulty of identifying and numbering each element in a population limits its use. Many populations of interest to political scientists are too large to enumerate. Assigning a unique number to every registered voter in California, for example, would be impractical even if it were possible. Another obstacle to simple random sampling is difficulty in obtaining complete and accurate lists of populations of interest. Our earlier example of the population of newspaper stories about female candidates for public office is an instance of this difficulty. Still, when sample populations are small, or especially when numbered lists are available, selecting a simple random sample is advisable.

Systematic Samples.   As we noted, if the desired sample is large, simple random sampling can absorb appreciable time and effort because each element in the population must be assigned a unique number and a table of random numbers created or consulted. A labor-saving variant of simple random sampling is **systematic sampling,** which involves selecting every *n*th element on a list for inclusion in the sample. For example, if you wish to draw a sample of 100 from a list of 1,000 officials in the Swedish Social Democratic party, you would select every tenth name. The sampling begins with some random process to choose a starting number from the list. The number chosen would represent the first official included in the sample, followed by every tenth official on the list. Because the list of numbers was entered randomly, each party official had an equal likelihood of being selected.

Systematic sampling usually begins with a decision about the desired sample size followed by counting the number of elements in the population. The **sampling interval** is determined by dividing the total number of the population by the desired sample size. The population of 1,000 Swedish Social Democrats would be divided by the desired sample size of 100, producing a sampling interval of 10. The **sampling ratio** is the proportion of the population that is sampled—for our Swedish officials, 100/1,000, or 10 percent. Systematic samples are empirically equivalent to simple random samples, and for that reason, most researchers prefer the simpler method.

Possible sources of bias in systematic sampling include periodicity, which may occur when a list of elements is organized in a cyclical pattern or using a particular characteristic. If the names on the list of Swedish party officials were organized into groups of five, with the head of the party for a local district listed first, then sample selection beginning with the first name on the list would produce a biased sample consisting only of local party heads. Likewise, if selection started with a number other than one, local party heads would be excluded from the sample. Before selecting a systematic sample, the list of population elements should be carefully examined to search for organizational patterns that might produce bias.

To the Web

Exercise 9.1   Selecting a Random and a Systematic Sample

This exercise asks you to select a random sample and then a systematic sample from a sampling frame consisting of the fifty states. To access the exercise, go to the **DEPR Web Page,** click on **Web Exercises, Chapter 9,** then on **Selecting a Random and a Systematic Sample.**

Stratified Sampling.   Stratified sampling requires dividing a population into groups, called strata, and then selecting a probability sample from elements within each stratified group. Stratified sampling can be carried out to ensure that samples of subgroups are proportional to their representation in the population. This procedure is called **proportionate stratified sampling.** If you were interested in comparing Democrat and Republican precinct captains, you would divide the population into two groups based on party affiliation and then select a simple random sample or systematic sample from each of the respective party groups. The resulting sample size drawn from each group would be proportionate to its presence in the population (see Figure 9.2). The advantage of proportionate stratified sampling is that homogeneous populations produce samples

Figure 9.2
Stratified Sampling

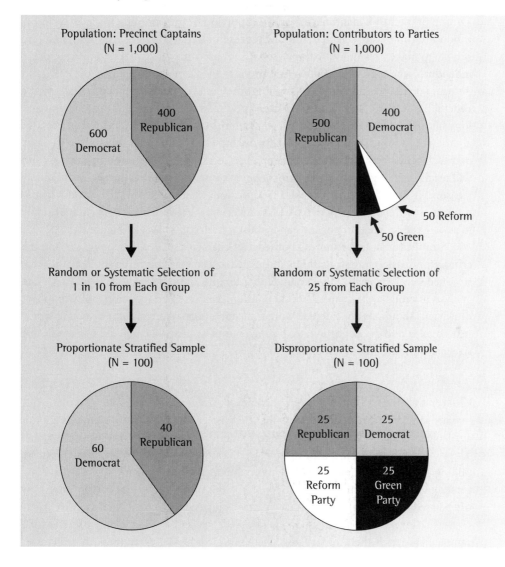

with smaller sample errors than do heterogeneous populations. Each of the two sub-samples selected would be homogeneous with respect to the variable of interest: party affiliation. When the two subsamples are combined into a single sample and comparisons are analyzed regarding party affiliation, sampling error will be smaller than if the entire population had been sampled. In a sample stratified by party affiliation, the sampling error would be reduced to zero for that variable.

Stratified sampling can also be used to ensure that groups in a population are adequately represented in the sample. **Disproportionate stratified sampling** is used when a group of interest constitutes a very small portion of the sampling frame. If a simple random sample were selected, too few representatives of the group would be in the sample to make meaningful comparisons. Suppose you were interested in comparing individuals who made financial contributions to the Democrat, Republican, Green, and Reform parties. Simple random sampling from a list of contributors provided by the Federal Election Commission would likely produce a sample with lots of Democrat and Republican contributors but very few contributors to the Green and Reform parties. An alternative approach would be to select subsamples of equal size from each of the four parties. Essentially this involves oversampling Green and Reform party contributors and will produce enough Green and Reform party contributors to make meaningful comparisons. It should be obvious that disproportionate stratified sampling produces disproportionate representation in the final sample, making it necessary to weight the sample to restore the original proportions and adjust for selection bias (see Figure 9.2). [3]

Stratified sampling requires knowledge of characteristics of the population and the criteria for division into strata should be related to a key variable being studied. As noted, stratified samples may be more accurate than simple random samples and may facilitate analysis of groups whose members are not numerous in the population, but a couple of drawbacks should be considered. More time and effort are involved in selecting stratified samples, and disproportionate stratified sampling generally requires a larger sample size than simple random sampling.

Cluster Samples.   Often it is not possible or feasible to select simple random or systematic samples from a population either because lists of population elements are not available or the population is too large to generate a numbered list for a sample frame. The latter problem occurs, for example, when samples are needed for public opinion polling. An alternative approach that approximates probability sampling is called cluster sampling. **Cluster sampling** divides populations into a large number of groupings—often based on geographic boundaries—called clusters. From the comprehensive list of clusters a simple random or systematic sample is selected. A list of elements within the sampled clusters is then constructed, and a sample is chosen from them. When cluster sampling proceeds through a series of stages, as it often does, it is called **multistage cluster sampling.**

An example of multistage cluster sampling is shown in Figure 9.3. Suppose you want to draw a sample of middle school students in California who are currently taking an American Government course. No comprehensive list of American Government stu-

Figure 9.3
Multistage Cluster Sampling

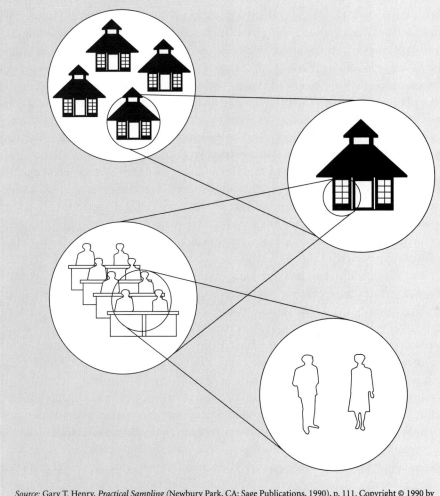

Source: Gary T. Henry, *Practical Sampling* (Newbury Park, CA: Sage Publications, 1990), p. 111. Copyright © 1990 by Gary T. Henry. Reprinted by permission of Sage Publications.

dents is likely to be available, and it would be enormously expensive to construct one. However, the California State Department of Education probably can provide a list of middle schools, which could serve as an initial sampling frame. A simple random sample would be taken of middle schools and, from among the schools selected, lists of classes assembled. A simple random sample of classes would be selected from that list, and in turn, a complete list of students would be generated from the selected classes. Finally, a simple random sample of students would be selected from the list.

Survey research organizations ordinarily use multistage cluster sampling to draw, at the final stage, a sample of households or dwellings. The first stage may begin with a map of the United States that divides the nation into equally populated areas, the most convenient of which are congressional districts. The multistage process of listing elements in clusters and sampling each proceeds from congressional district to voting precincts to city blocks and, finally, to households. Of course, public opinion researchers are looking to interview people within the sampled households, but since it would be impossible, or at least very inefficient, to list all occupants of the sampled households, interviewers are given instructions concerning whom will be interviewed. The instructions, containing specific decision rules implementing quotas based on gender, age, and family standing, are generally on a card carried by the interviewer. [4]

Multistage cluster sampling has obvious advantages. Researchers are relieved of the task of compiling and counting large lists of elements. Multistage sampling is cost efficient when the research project involves face-to-face interviews of respondents. And because, in the last stage of sampling, respondents (or households) will be clustered geographically, transportation costs are greatly reduced. The efficiency of multistage cluster sampling, however, is balanced with a loss of accuracy. Each stage of the sampling process involves an addition to total sampling error—the larger the number of stages, the greater the error. This means that larger samples are needed, compared to simple random sampling, to achieve an acceptable level of error. Sampling error can be reduced in multistage cluster sampling by creating a large number of clusters with fewer elements, as opposed to a small number of clusters with many elements. Of course, increasing the number of clusters reduces efficiency, so there is a trade-off. You must be careful to ensure that clusters contain approximately the same number of elements, or they must be sampled so that the probability of being included in a sample is proportional to the population. If clusters do not contain an equal number of elements and are sampled randomly, then a complicated weighting procedure must be applied to ensure representativeness. [5]

A recent study emphasized the need for caution in using multistage cluster sampling to sample households or dwellings. For years the General Social Survey conducted by the University of Chicago found that men claimed to have more sexual partners than women. Researchers pointed out that, for the population considered as a whole, men and women must have an equal number of partners. How could they account for this discrepancy? It turns out that the surveys did not measure the sexual activities of prostitutes; the professionals who perform sex for profit were ignored because the sample was taken from people who lived only in households, excluding those who lived in motels, shelters, and rooming houses. [6]

Telephone Samples. The most common means of conducting public opinion surveys is through telephone interviews. Obtaining samples of respondents by first sampling telephone numbers presents some unique challenges, but it has some important advantages that include speed and cost. Researchers are often interested in quickly learning the public's opinion about a current event. For example, the major television networks can interview a large sample of respondents by telephone about their views on a presidential candidate debate and present the results to their audience within an hour. A second advantage is cost. Telephone interviews are substantially less expensive to conduct than face-to-face interviews because no transportation costs are involved.

Those who sample telephone numbers face a variety of challenges. One potential difficulty is class bias: Poor families are less likely to have telephones, although 95 percent of households now have a telephone. [7] Sometimes telephone directories are used as a sampling frame, and systematic samples are selected. Potential problems here are out-of-date directories (many people change residences and phone numbers within a year) and unlisted phone numbers. One estimate is that about 30 percent of households in the United States have unlisted telephone numbers. [8] Using telephone directories for national or even statewide samples would be extremely cumbersome, but in some cases they might be used efficiently for a sample of a small community. One way of dealing with unlisted numbers is to use the "add a digit" approach. For every number sampled from a directory, the last digit is randomly replaced with a number ranging from zero to nine. This method will result in the inclusion of unlisted numbers.

Most telephone pollsters use a procedure called **random digit dialing;** random numbers are generated, usually by computer, to obtain telephone numbers. If ten-digit numbers (a seven-digit telephone number plus area code) are selected completely at random, many (about four out of five) calls will be placed to nonworking numbers. In the interest of efficiency most pollsters use stratification combined with a form of multistage sampling to obtain a representative sample of numbers. Nationwide samples usually begin with sampling from a list of area codes. Three-digit central office exchanges are randomly sampled within those selected area codes, and random four-digit suffixes are added, producing a complete, randomly selected phone number. Often it is possible to obtain information on how many central office exchanges are in use for each area code so samples can be chosen in proportion to actual numbers. Respondents are not sampled randomly through this method of random digit dialing. Once a telephone is answered, interviewers use screening questions based on predetermined decision rules to decide which member of a household will be interviewed. To avoid arbitrary choices, interviewers are often instructed to interview the member of the household who most recently celebrated a birthday.

Technology and affluence have contributed to the difficulty in extracting a representative sample of respondents by sampling telephone numbers. These days phone calls often lead to an answering machine or voice mail. Many people use answering machines to screen incoming calls before deciding to pick up. To achieve a representative sample, interviewers must call back these numbers until a respondent is reached and an interview is completed. There is a great deal of variability among pollsters regarding the number of attempts made to reach respondents; time constraints placed on completion of projects reduces the likelihood of callbacks. And we have to wonder about the extent to which a sample is biased if it includes only those who answer their phones. Other problems include the increasing use of cell phones, numbers dedicated to computer modems or fax machines, and number portability. Of course, it is important to acknowledge that a phone number may no longer represent a household located in a specific place. Telephone pollsters use screening questions to deal with these new problems, but a great deal of uncertainty about sample representativeness persists.

Key Points

Probability samples are those that permit the estimation of sample error. These are the major types:

- Simple random samples, in which units of analysis are selected based on a random procedure.
- Systematic samples, in which every *n*th unit of analysis is selected to obtain the desired sample size.
- Stratified samples, in which populations are separated into groups based on known characteristics and random samples are chosen from each group.
- Cluster samples, in which random samples are taken in stages from aggregations of units of analysis of decreasing size.
- Random digit dialing, in which telephone numbers are units of analysis sampled though a random process.

◼ Nonprobability Sampling

There may be situations where is it not necessary, feasible, or appropriate to select a probability sample. If the goal of research is to generalize about characteristics of populations, a probability sample is always preferable. Nonprobability samples may be appropriate, however, if the goal of research is exploratory with the aim of developing hypotheses that might later be tested with analysis of probability samples. They are also appropriate for rare occasions when a population of interest is so poorly defined that it would be impossible to draw a probability sample. Increasingly, scholars are using **qualitative research methods,** where the goal is not to develop generalizations about large populations but instead to gather insights that can be provided by specific individuals or groups about how they relate to their environment or see the political world. In qualitative research the concern is more with "choosing cases" (sometimes with the goal of explicitly including those who are *not* representative of a population) than sampling to develop general conclusions. Social scientists use a variety of nonprobability sample designs. All of them must be judged in terms of the goals of the specific research. They have severe limitations if the goal is representativeness and generalizability but may be perfectly appropriate in other circumstances.

Convenience Sampling.   The selection of the most available elements in a population is **convenience sampling,** sometimes called accidental or haphazard sampling. Journalists asking people on the street their opinions on an important issue or university professors distributing questionnaires to students in their classes are good examples of this approach. Additionally, convenience sampling is often used for methods of data collection other than surveys. A political scientist, for example, might be interested in how much newspaper coverage is given international versus domestic politics and select stories from the local paper because of their availability. Political psychologists, as a common practice, conduct experiments using student volunteers as subjects. The drawback with all convenience samples is the inability to evaluate how biased or representative they are. Making inferences from them to populations is perilous. Convenience samples may be appropriate for pretesting survey questions or engaging in exploratory research, but in general they should be avoided, and when encountered in reports of published research, treated with skepticism.

Judgmental Sampling.   In **judgmental samples,** sometimes called purposive samples, the researcher selects sample elements he or she believes to be representative of a population. In some instances an expert on a subject will choose the sample. For example, a superintendent of schools for a large city might choose for a sample schools that in his or her judgment are representative of all others. The difficulty with this approach is that experts will almost always disagree. Another example is when survey interviewers are sent to locations selected by experts and instructed to question a certain number of "typical" people, an instruction so vague as to be meaningless. Judgmental samples, like convenience samples, are selected in such a way that it is impossible to estimate sampling error. The risks involved in making inferences to populations are unknown. Obviously, judgmental samples selected with the goal of achieving representativeness of some population should be considered with suspicion.

Judgmental samples can be appropriate and useful when the primary goal of selecting cases is not necessarily to achieve representativeness. When populations are difficult to define and elements are difficult to locate, for example, it may be necessary to use an extraordinary approach. If you were interested in examining the political attitudes of fans of professional wrestling (this is not a trivial question given the success of Jesse Ventura of Minnesota), you might have to attend some wrestling matches and attempt to choose typical fans to interview. Finding "average" wrestling fans is unlikely, but no other approach would be available. Judgmental sampling may also be used for qualitative and intensive approaches to studying politics where there is no real intention to generalize to a larger population of people. A good example of this use of judgmental sampling can be found in *Political Ideology* by political scientist Robert Lane, who used his judgment to choose a very small sample of working-class men to interview intensively about politics. [9] Judgmental samples may also be appropriate for studies involving intensive interviews of political elites. A political scientist would likely be in the best position to judge who should be included in a small sample of state legislators who specialize in environmental policymaking. In Chapter 12 we will discuss some examples of intensive and qualitative approaches. We will see that for researchers to use their judgments in selecting participants for studies, using Q-methodology or focus groups is appropriate.

Quota Sampling.　　In **quota sampling** elements are chosen in proportion to their representation in a population. The process of quota sampling begins with a listing of known distributions of characteristics of elements of a population, such as gender, race, or age. Census data may reveal, for example, that 60 percent of a population is female, 40 percent male, 65 percent older than thirty-five, and 35 percent thirty-five years of age or younger. Based on those figures interviewers might be given quotas so that a proportional number of those interviewed are females older than thirty-five, males thirty-five or younger, and so on. Within the constraints of the established quotas (usually presented to interviewers on written quota forms) interviewers select a convenience sample. The goal is for the sample to match the population with respect to quota characteristics.

A problem with quota sampling is that it *seems* scientific. But in fact quota samples are not probability samples, and sampling error cannot be estimated because the individual respondents within the quota category are not randomly chosen. Even complex quota schemes involving a relatively large number of characteristics cannot eliminate potential bias (see Figure 9.4 for an example). In the end it is interviewers who choose respondents, and they are likely to introduce bias by their choices. If you were an interviewer and were given a choice to select a respondent on the first or fifth floor of an apartment building with no elevator, what would you do? We would choose not to walk up five flights of stairs, and those potential respondents who live in inconvenient places would be left out of the sample. Ultimately, interviewers will select the people they want

Figure 9.4
Quota Sampling

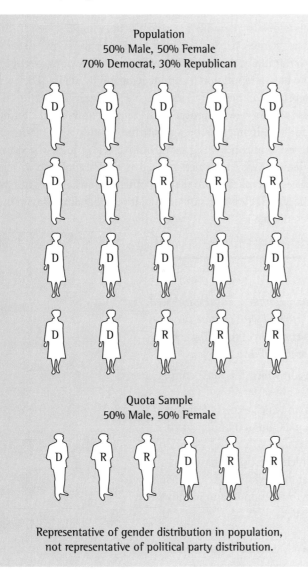

Population
50% Male, 50% Female
70% Democrat, 30% Republican

Quota Sample
50% Male, 50% Female

Representative of gender distribution in population,
not representative of political party distribution.

to interview, usually those who are most like themselves. A quota sample may appear to be representative of a population, but we know for sure that is the case only with respect to the characteristics that influenced choice of respondent. Just because a sample mirrors a population on selected demographic characteristics, such as age, you cannot assume that it accurately represents other characteristics, such as opinions on issues.

Snowball Sampling.   One other type of nonprobability sample deserves mention. **Snowball sampling** begins with a small number of respondents who then identify others with similar characteristics or interests. Some researchers have used snowball samples to study community power. Initially, the researcher will identify key nongovernmental elites in a community who have a reputation for influencing public affairs. They will be interviewed and asked to provide names of others who, like themselves, are elites in the community. As the process of interviewing proceeds, the sample grows in size. Snowball sampling is most useful for identifying members of difficult-to-locate populations. For example, if you were interested in conducting a study of American men who deserted the military during the Vietnam War and settled in Sweden, you might begin with just a few identifiable interviewees and ask them to identify others. Snowball samples, while useful in some extraordinary situations, are similar to all nonprobability samples in that sampling error cannot be estimated.

Key Points

Nonprobability samples are common, but results based on their use must be interpreted with caution because they do not permit the estimation of sampling error. These are the types of nonprobability samples:

- Convenience samples, in which the most convenient units of analysis are selected.
- Judgmental samples, in which experts or perhaps interviewers select sample units that appear to be representative.
- Quota samples, in which selection is based on membership in predetermined groups. The goal is to match the sample to the population in terms of specific characteristics.
- Snowball samples, in which respondents initially included in a judgmental sample suggest additional respondents who would be appropriate for inclusion. Used to study members of hard-to-find populations.

Sample Error and Sample Size

■ Sampling Error

We mentioned earlier that the difference between an estimate represented by a sample statistic and a population parameter is total sampling error, consisting of two parts: sampling bias and random sampling error. Sampling bias represents those differences between a statistic and a parameter that can be attributed to systematic errors in the way the sample is drawn. The nonprobability samples that we described are threatened by systematic sampling bias because experts or interviewers make the ultimate decision about what population elements are included. Because sampling units are chosen subjectively, sampling bias cannot be controlled. If a sampling design is flawed, no increase in sample size can reduce the possibility of bias. Furthermore, it is impossible to estimate the extent of systematic sampling bias so that adjustments can be made in inferences about a population. The only way to eliminate sampling bias and avoid the obtrusiveness of individual choice is to use probability samples that are based on random selection.

In contrast to sampling bias, random sampling error can be estimated and controlled if probability sample designs are used. Sample statistics inevitably are different from the parameters of a population, and different samples will produce different sample statistics. This important fact is easy to overlook because the figures based on the results of a single sample survey are often reported as if they are certain. For example, a newspaper story may report that a survey reveals that 67 percent of the adult population of a state supports stricter gambling laws. The report would be misleading because no sample can produce such precise estimates, and additional or alternative samples would produce different figures. If the survey were taken from a probability sample, however, it would be possible to estimate the accuracy of the figure of 67 percent and therefore determine how confident one is that it reflects the actual population parameter.

Inevitable questions about sampling include "How is it possible that the entire population of American adults can be accurately represented by a sample of fewer than 2,000?" and "How large should a sample be?" To answer these questions, the factors that determine random sampling error need to be understood. As we have noted, parameters of study populations are generally not known, so random sampling error must be estimated to surmise the accuracy of results. Suppose we are interested in determining what percentage of the state legislators in the United States are lawyers. The actual percentage (population parameter) is unknown, and unlikely to become known, because the size of the population of state legislators is very large. However, random samples of state legislators could be selected and estimates determined for each separate sample. Figure 9.5 shows how proportions from five samples of state legislators might differ from the actual

Figure 9.5
Random Sampling Error

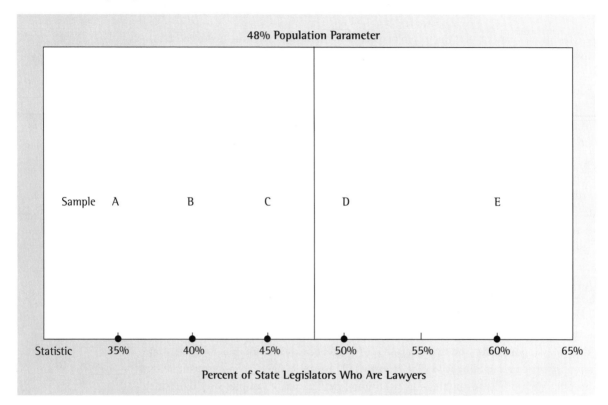

percentage of lawyers. The differences between the sample estimates and the actual percentages represent sampling error.

How much sampling error is present in any sample is a function of three factors: (1) the confidence level, (2) the homogeneity of the population, and (3) the sample size. Formulas to calculate random sampling error or, alternatively, the size of the sample needed to produce a specific value for random sampling error include these three factors. Random sampling error is estimated by using one of two formulas: one for averages (or means) and the other for proportions. [10] The following formula is used to estimate sampling error (SE) for proportions.

$$SE = (1.96)\sqrt{\frac{p(1-p)}{n}}$$

SE represents the degree of expected proportionate sampling error. The value 1.96 is the standard z-score, used in conjunction with the normal curve, to produce a confidence interval of 95 percent. The full meaning and calculation of this figure will be considered in Chapter 13. The sample size is represented by *n*, and the sample proportion (the proportion of the population in one category if the variable of interest has only two values) by *p*.

Let's consider each element in the formula. Proportionate sampling error (SE) that is derived from the equation is expressed as a percentage. If in the example shown in Figure 9.5 a sample of 600 state legislators was selected, and the statistical estimate of 45 percent lawyers was derived, sampling error would be approximately ±4 percent. That means that it is highly likely that the actual proportion of lawyers in the population of state legislators lies between 41 percent and 49 percent. As we noted, the z-score of 1.96 represents a confidence interval of 95 percent. Most scholars are willing to accept the 95-to-5 odds that their sampling error is accurately estimated. Our interpretation of the statistical estimate of 45 percent lawyers in state legislatures would be interpreted as follows: "In 95 out of 100 samples that could be drawn, the actual proportion of lawyers would fall between 41 percent and 49 percent." We could increase the confidence level to 99 percent by using a z-score of 2.58. Examining the formula, you will see that the sampling error is increased by increasing the confidence level. If you want to be more confident that your sample statistic is an accurate approximation of the population parameter, you must accept the trade-off of increasing the sampling error.

The $p(1 - p)$ term in the formula represents the degree of variability in the population that is sampled. The more homogeneous a sample, the more accurate estimates of the population will be. To take an extreme example, suppose that every state legislator in the United States is a lawyer. In this instance, $p(1 - p)$ would be 1.0 (0), which equals 0, which is no variability at all. If that were the case, a sample of one legislator would be sufficient to accurately represent the proportion of state legislators who are lawyers; sampling error would be zero. If, on the other hand, the proportion of lawyers to nonlawyers is perfectly split into two equal groups, the likelihood of making an accurate estimate (the odds) would be the least favorable of all proportional splits. In fact, every element in the population would have to be included to result in a sample error of zero. In most cases the degree of homogeneity of a population with respect to characteristics of interest is unknown, so *p* is conservatively set at .50 (perfect heterogeneity) for the purpose of estimating sampling error.

The *n* term in the formula represents the sample size. Since it is the denominator in the formula, increasing sample size reduces the estimate of sample error. In fact, the key ingredient in determining sample error is the size of the sample. A counterintuitive aspect of sampling is that the relationship between sample size and sampling error is in most circumstances unrelated to the size of the population. A sample of 1,500 registered voters drawn from the entire population of the United States is just as accurate as the same number drawn from a small state like Rhode Island. The proportion of the population that is represented in the sample, the sampling ratio, would have to exceed more than 10 percent before error would be reduced substantially.

An illustration of the application of the formula should clarify how each of the elements is related to sampling error. Assume that we have taken a simple random sample of 600 state legislators. We wish to determine sampling error at the 95 percent confidence level and we assume maximum heterogeneity (a 50 percent to 50 percent split) in the population with regard to the proportion of the population who are lawyers. The sampling error would be calculated as follows:

$$SE = (\pm 1.96)\sqrt{\frac{.50(1 - .50)}{600}}$$
$$= \pm .0398 \text{ or } 3.98\% \text{ rounded to } 4\%$$

◼ Sample Size

A number of factors need to be considered in determining the sample size that is appropriate for any particular research project. The first questions any researcher must ask is "How much error am I willing to tolerate?" and "How confident in my results must I be?" The answers to those questions vary and are mitigated by the costs of drawing larger samples. (In survey research involving face-to-face interviews, additional costs can amount to as much as $100 per additional respondent sampled.) If you are interested in predicting the outcome of an election and your reputation depends on your accuracy, you may want to invest in a large sample. If you are conducting an initial test of a tentative hypothesis, you might be willing to tolerate more error in order to reduce costs. The formula for determining what sample sizes are needed for alternative levels of tolerated error and confidence levels is a rearrangement of the formula for determining sample error.

Let's assume that we wish to draw a sample of state workers in Oregon to compare attitudes of males and females. We want to achieve a proportionate sampling error of ± 3 percent at the 95 percent level of confidence, and personnel records indicate that about 60 percent of state workers are men. We would use the following formula for our calculation.

$$n = \frac{1.96^2 [p(1-p)]}{SE^2}$$
$$n = \frac{1.96^2 [.60(1-.60)]}{.03^2} = \frac{3.84 (.24)}{.0009}$$
$$= 1,024 \text{ state workers}$$

Table 9.2
Simple Random Sample Size for Several Degrees of Precision

	CONFIDENCE LEVELS	
Tolerated Error	95 Samples in 100	99 Samples in 100
1%	9,604	16,587
2%	2,401	4,147
3%	1,067	1,843
4%	600	1,037
5%	384	663
6%	267	461
7%	196	339

Source: Charles H. Backstom and Gerald Hursh-Cesar, *Survey Research,* 2nd Ed. (New York: John Wiley and Sons, 1981), p. 75. © 1981. Reprinted by permission of Pearson Education Inc., Upper Saddle River, NJ.

Instead of applying the formula for estimating random sampling error and determining sample sizes, most researchers consult a sampling table such as Table 9.2. Sampling tables show the relationship between various sample sizes, estimated sampling error, and confidence levels. Examining Table 9.2 reveals, for example, that a sample of 1,067 has an estimated sampling error of ±3 percent at the 95 percent confidence level. This *n* is slightly larger than the example of the Oregon state workers because it assumes maximum variability, a 50 percent to 50 percent split, rather than the 60 percent to 40 percent split assumed for males versus females among the Oregon population of state workers. Looking at the table from the perspective of determining sample size, you can see, for example, that if you desire accuracy associated with a ±2 percent sampling error at the 95 percent confidence level, you must draw a sample that equals or exceeds 2,401.

To the Web

Exercise 9.2   Calculating Sample Error and Sample Size

This exercise asks you to demonstrate that you can calculate sample error for various sample sizes and levels of confidence. It also asks you to calculate sample sizes necessary to achieve different levels of confidence. Knowledge of how to do these calculations will help you understand the relationship between the determinants of sample error. To access the exercise, go to the **DEPR Web Page,** click on **Web Exercises, Chapter 9,** then on **Calculating Sample Error and Sample Size.**

There are just a few additional considerations that should be taken into account when determining sample size. The first has to do with the sampling ratio. If the sampling ratio is relatively large, then error is overestimated by the formula we have used and the figures shown in Table 9.2. In other words, accurate inferences concerning small populations may be made with relatively smaller samples. A second consideration concerns the homogeneity of the population. Sometimes information is available on population diversity. If it is known that a population is homogeneous, then a smaller sample may be appropriate. This is often the case with stratified samples. A third consideration is the use of multistage samples, when random sampling error accumulates with each additional stage. As a result, a larger sample is often necessary to counteract the increasing error added with each stage. A final consideration has to do with the goals of the researcher. Subsets of the whole sample will sometimes be analyzed separately, and the sampling error based on these subsets is always higher than for the entire sample. For example, a random sample of about 1,100 state legislators would have a sampling error of about ±3 percent. If you were interested in separately analyzing female state legislators in your sample, however, and only 200 legislators in your sample were female, tolerated error for the subset would rise to about ±7 percent. When determining sample size, how many categories or subsets will ultimately be analyzed should be considered. The more variables you wish to study and the more values that each variable contains, the greater the sample size must be to ensure representativeness and the accuracy of comparisons.

We believe that oversampling by 10 to 15 percent will alleviate most potential problems. If your goal is a sampling error of 6 percent and a confidence interval of 95 percent, sample more than the required 267 cases in anticipation of unforeseen difficulties. Predicting how much information will be missing (for example, an individual respondent's refusal to answer one or more questions on the survey) or how many variables or subsets may ultimately be analyzed is a difficult challenge, so erring on the high side of what sample size is needed is the better choice.

To the Web

Polling Fiascos and Sampling Error

Earlier we mentioned the famous (or infamous) *Literary Digest* poll of 1936. There are other examples of polling fiascos. Some polling errors have been attributed to poor sampling techniques, while others can be attributed to problems such as the wording of survey questions (we will discuss survey research in Chapter 10). The *Why Files* Web site at the University of Wisconsin provides an interesting discussion of famous polling fiascos and an extended discussion of sampling error. To access the site, go to the **DEPR Web Page**, click on **Web Links, Chapter 9**, then on **Polling Fiascos and Sampling Error**.

Conclusion

In this chapter we focused on the purposes and processes of sampling. Samples are selected because it is often not possible to collect information about an entire population that is of theoretical interest. Since samples are subsets of a population and there is a desire to generalize about the larger group, the goal of sampling is to achieve representativeness. Representativeness is determined by the method used for selection and sample size. It is always preferable to obtain a probability sample because error can be estimated and representativeness assessed. We reviewed and evaluated a number of methods that can be used to obtain probability samples. We learned that even with probability samples there can be sampling error. We also learned, however, that sampling error in probability samples can be estimated with some accuracy with some simple calculations. We also noted that nonprobability samples are often used by social scientists. We urged you to be critical of the findings of studies that use nonprobability samples because with them error cannot be estimated and therefore representativeness cannot be evaluated. Findings produced with nonprobability samples, while they may be interesting and useful, cannot be safely generalized beyond the sample itself.

In Chapter 10, you will learn about how surveys are done once the sample has been chosen, including how to administer surveys, write questions, and assure maximum participation. In addition, we will help you with finding survey data collected by others that are available for public use.

■ Sampling is necessary because it is often not possible to collect information from all elements of a study population.

■ Samples should always be evaluated in terms of their representativeness.

■ Sample representativeness is a function of the size of samples and how they are selected.

■ Probability samples are always preferable to nonprobability samples because sampling error can be estimated.

■ Total sampling error consists of sampling bias and random sampling error.

■ Estimates of sample error for probability samples are based on the size of the sample, the heterogeneity of the population, and desired level of confidence in the estimate.

■ The size of the sample is based on acceptable levels of sample error, the level of confidence desired in the sample error estimate, the heterogeneity of the population, the size of subgroups to be analyzed, the number of variables to be employed, and research costs.

Summary of the Main Points

census
cluster sampling
convenience sampling
disproportionate stratified sample
element
judgmental sample
multistage cluster sampling
nonprobability sample
parameter
population
population element
probability sample
proportionate stratified sampling
qualitative research methods
quota sampling

random digit dialing
sample
sampling element
sampling error
sampling frame
sampling interval
sampling ratio
simple random sample
snowball sampling
statistics
stratified sampling
study population
systematic sampling
theoretical population

Terms Introduced

Selected Readings

Henry, Gary T. *Practical Sampling*. Newbury Park, CA: Sage Publications, 1990.

Kalton, Graham. *Introduction to Survey Sampling*. Beverly Hills, CA: Sage Publications, 1983.

Kish, Leslie. *Survey Sampling*. New York: John Wiley and Sons, 1965.

Lavrakas, Paul J. *Telephone Survey Methods: Sampling, Selection, and Supervision*. Newbury Park, CA: Sage Publications, 1987.

Yamane, Taro. *Elementary Sampling Theory*. Englewood Cliffs, NJ: Prentice-Hall, 1967.

Activities

Activity 9.1
Evaluating Samples Reported in Articles in Professional Journals

The following are descriptions of samples taken from studies reported in social science professional journals. After reading each one, (1) describe the theoretical population that is sampled, (2) describe the sample elements, and (3) critically comment on the representativeness of each sample.

1. "The first study, providing a representative sample of German youth and young adults from age fifteen to thirty was conducted by SINUS/Infratest under contract from the Federal Ministry of Youth Family and Health. It was conducted in July and August 1982 and includes over 2,012 individuals, of whom about 1,474 were between fifteen and twenty-four. The second sample survey makes use of a quota sample of 1,472 young people (aged fifteen to twenty-four) and was conducted in April and May 1984." (Watts, Meredith W. "Orientations Toward Conventional and Unconventional Participation Among West German Youth," *Comparative Political Studies,* 23 [October 1990], 287–288.)

2. "Face to Face interviews were conducted with 1,393 respondents in twenty-one regions of Russia during November through December 1992 by ROMIR (Russian Public Opinion and Market Research). The referent population was permanent residents of the Russian Federation, aged eighteen and older. The multistage sample was stratified first by regions and then by cities and villages, with a probability proportionate to unit size. Respondents were drawn randomly with each sampling point. The response rate was 79.5 percent; 10.5 percent of the sample could not be located or were unable to participate in the survey; 11 percent refused. Interviewers made three attempts to contact each respondent. (Bahry, Donna, Cynthia Boaz, and Stacy Burnett Gordon. "Tolerance, Transition, and Support for Civil Liberties in Russia," *Comparative Political Studies,* 30 [August 1997], 492.)

3. "This study focuses on the individual votes of the Supreme Court justices in eight states (Arizona, California, Kentucky, Louisiana, New Jersey, North Carolina, Ohio, and Texas) from 1983 to 1988 in the death penalty decisions issued by these courts. We selected these particular state supreme courts for evaluation because they exhibit

substantial variability in their propensity to uphold death sentences. These courts also exhibit wide and sufficient variation in all variables to be examined in this analysis." (Hall, Melinda Gann, and Paul Brace. "Justices' Responses to Case Facts: An Interactive Model," *American Politics Quarterly,* 24 [April 1996], 244.)

4. "Data for this study came from a survey administered to a convenience sample of 520 undergraduate students at a large public university in the midwestern United States. The survey, which was conducted during March and April 1997, consisted of a self-administered questionnaire on topics that included beliefs about the characteristics of various media, general attitudes toward computer technology, frequency and patterns of using the World Wide Web, and estimates of time spent using various media." (Althaus, Scott L., and David Tewksbury. "Patterns of Internet and Traditional News Media Use in a Networked Community," *Political Communication,* 17 [January–March 2000], 29.)

5. "It was decided therefore to conduct a content analysis of news about Land Day. The analysis covered the years 1977 (the year following the first confrontation) to 1997 in two newspapers, *Yediot Ahronot* and *Ha'aretz. Yediot Ahronot* has a more 'popular' format and is by far the best selling newspaper in Israel. *Ha'aretz* is considered a 'quality' newspaper and is read mostly by social and political elites of the country, and has a more subdued, intellectual format. All relevant articles that appeared in *Yediot Ahronot* and *Ha'aretz* during the two weeks before and after Land Day were included in the analysis. A total of 167 articles appeared in *Ha'aretz* and 199 in *Yediot.* (Wolfsfeld, Gadi, Eli Avraham, and Issam Aburaiya. "When Prophesy Always Fails: Israel Press Coverage of the Arab Minority's Land Day Protests," *Political Communication,* 17 [April–June 2000], 120.)

6. "A sample of MTV commercials was recorded on videotape during five weekdays in mid-November 1991. Six hours of MTV programming were recorded each day, half between the hours of 3:00 and 6:00 P.M. and half between the hours of 9:00 and midnight, the hours (after school and late evening) when adolescents are most likely to watch MTV. In total, 550 commercials were recorded. Eliminating repeat commercials, the final sample consisted of 119 individual commercials." (Signorielli, Nancy, Douglas McLeod, and Elaine Healy. "Gender Stereotypes in MTV Commercials: The Beat Goes On," *Journal of Broadcasting and Electronic Media* [Winter 1994], 93.)

7. "For purposes of analysis, we used data from a probability survey conducted by the University of Kentucky Survey Research Center, which interviewed 501 adults in the greater Lexington, Kentucky, area. Respondents were selected through a variant of random digit dialing procedures between June 22 and July 5, 1994. Because the survey was initially designed to examine whites' attitudes toward race and crime, only white adults participated." (Hurwitz, Jon, and Shannon Smithey. "Gender Differences on Crime and Punishment," *Political Research Quarterly,* 51 [March 1998], 96.)

Activity 9.2
Evaluating Samples Reported Along with Poll Results by the Popular Press

The results of public opinion polls are reported by the news media nearly every day. Accurate and complete reporting of polls requires a description of the sample used. Locate and record reports of public opinion polls provided by a national newspaper like the *New York Times* or *Washington Post,* a local newspaper, a network television news organization, and a local television news station. Evaluate the information provided by each in terms of samples. What additional information could have been provided so you could evaluate the representativeness of the samples?

Activity 9.3
Using SPSS to Select a Random Sample

SPSS allows you to select random subsamples from existing sets of data. This facility can be used to help you understand the nature of sampling error.

1. Open SPSS and then open the "COUNTRIESdepr" data file.
2. Run a frequency distribution for the variable freestat (Freedom Status) and record the percentage of countries that are categorized as "free." (See Exercise 8.4 if you need to review how to run a frequency distribution.)
3. Click on "Data," then on "Select Cases."
4. In the "Select Cases" box select "Random sample of cases," then click on "Sample."
5. In the "Select Cases: Random Sample" box under sample size select "Approximately," type in 20%, and then click "Continue." In the "Select Cases" box click "OK."
6. Run a frequency distribution for your selected sample for "freestat" and record the percentage of countries that are categorized as "free."
7. Calculate the total sample error for your sample by calculating the difference between the percentage categorized as "free" for the entire data set and the percentage categorized as "free" for your random sample.
8. Repeat the process of sampling four more times and calculate total sample error for each sample.
9. Draw a chart similar to Figure 9.5 to demonstrate total sampling error. Plot the percentage of countries for the entire sample categorized as "Free" as the population parameter. Indicate the statistical estimate of the percentage of nations that are "Free" for each of your five samples.

Activity 9.4
Selecting Student Samples

Recall that one of the examples we used early in the chapter involved sampling college or university students who had taken an American Government course in high school.

1. Describe how you would select a simple random sample of 400 students at your college or university. Be sure to describe your population and sampling frame.
2. Describe how you would select a similar sample of 400 students using systematic sampling.
3. Assume for a moment that no comprehensive list of students is available, but you are primarily interested in generalizing about students who reside on campus. Describe how you would design a multistage cluster sample to obtain a sample of 400 students.

Chapter 10

Collecting Data Using Surveys

Learning Objectives

After completion of this chapter, students should be able to do the following:

Write open- and closed-ended questions to gather information from respondents.

Evaluate the quality of survey questions and describe the types of problems that arise from inappropriate question wording.

Construct a questionnaire or interview form, taking into account question order, formatting, and planned coding procedures.

Compare the advantages and disadvantages of various methods of administering (mail, face-to-face, and telephone) surveys.

Describe the techniques that can be used to maximize return rates for questionnaires distributed by mail.

Identify some sources of survey data collected by others and available for secondary analysis.

Acquiring Survey Data

We begin our consideration of data collection, appropriately, with survey research because public opinion polls have become familiar parts of our lives. Newspapers, magazines, and television newscasts regularly present the results of one poll or another, telling us who is going to win the coming election, or who is the most popular actress on television, or what Americans think about a current international crisis. We have all filled out questionnaires, and most of us have been interviewed in person or over the telephone. Surveys are conducted for a wide variety of purposes. The news media use them for news gathering (and news making), businesses use them to develop marketing strategies, candidates use them to develop campaign strategies, and government agencies use them to obtain information about desired services and the effectiveness of programs. As social scientists we are most concerned with using survey research to test hypotheses and to develop generalizations, but as citizens and consumers, it is important that we acquire enough knowledge of the process to be able to critically evaluate information from polls that confront us every day.

Our primary goal in this chapter is to review the process of conducting surveys for purposes of testing hypotheses. We describe how to write questions, design a questionnaire, and the variety of ways surveys are administered to respondents. Many social scientists have noted that the construction and administration of surveys is both an art and a science. The development of a survey instrument can be a complex process that must be undertaken with care to reduce error. Detailing every aspect of survey design is beyond the scope of this text. Before developing a survey you should consult some of the many useful reference books on the subject, a number of which are listed at the end of this chapter. A secondary goal of this chapter is to make you aware of some of the numerous sources of survey data that have been culled by others and are available at little or no cost. If you examine articles in political science journals that analyze survey data, you will find that most focus on data that has been collected by large survey organizations rather than by the authors themselves. Many of the questions required to test hypotheses of interest to us have been asked by others who have the resources to survey large national samples. Several of the large survey data sets that are currently available accompany this book. We will show you how to locate others.

Survey research is a method of collecting information by directly asking people questions concerning their personal background characteristics, opinions, knowledge, and behavior so that generalizations can be developed about a population. [1] *Background characteristics* include information such as age, marital status, income, religious affiliation, and membership in groups. *Opinions* and *attitudes* are orientations people have concerning ideas or objects such as a contemporary issue like capital punishment or a political figure like Hillary Clinton. While opinions are usually held about specific ideas or objects, more general attitudes may be associated with a set of related ideas or objects, such as Democratic party candidates. *Knowledge* might include awareness of current events or the operation of governmental institutions such as the Electoral College. *Behavior* includes self-reports of things people have done—for example, how often they attended religious services in the past year or how much they contributed to a particular charity.

The development of questions for a survey is essentially a process of operationalization and measurement. The goal, as we discussed in Chapter 7, is to create questions that accurately reflect a concept. Issues of reliability and validity are paramount in evaluating possible survey questions. The process by which the questions are presented to respondents on a self-administered questionnaire, or through interviewing, is also crucial to the validity and reliability of results. We begin by discussing the process of developing useful questions and then options for presenting them to respondents.

Developing Questions

Question Form

Survey questions are either open-ended or closed-ended. **Open-ended questions** allow respondents to structure their own answers using their own words. **Closed-ended questions** provide respondents with a limited number of alternative answers from which they must choose. Each of the question forms can be used to obtain all of the types of substantive information previously mentioned: background characteristics, opinions/attitudes, knowledge, and self-reports of behavior. While each form has its advantages and disadvantages, most questionnaires contain more closed-ended than open-ended questions for reasons of efficiency in handling data. **Filter questions** (sometimes called screening questions) are designed to separate respondents into groups based on a characteristic or opinion, such as likely voters in an upcoming election. **Contingency questions** are asked of respondents who replied in a specified way to a filter question. These two types of questions can be either open-ended or closed-ended.

Open-Ended Questions.   Open-ended questions are a flexible means for obtaining any type of information from a respondent. Here are some common examples.

> *Other than American, what nationality do you consider yourself?* (Social Background)
> *What do you consider the most important problem facing the nation today?* (Opinion)
> *What are the names of the U.S. senators who represent your state?* (Knowledge)
> *How many times in the past year have you checked out books from your public library?*
>   (Behavior)

Each of the questions provides respondents with the opportunity to use their own words for their answers. Note that each question seeks answers that may be numerous, unanticipated by the researcher, or require the respondent to provide knowledge based on recall and not simply recognition.

Open-ended questions have some important advantages. They allow respondents to have their say without being forced to choose from among a number of categories developed by the researcher. They are also very useful when responses to a question are likely to be numerous and difficult to specify: Researchers are often surprised by some of the answers respondents volunteer in response to open-ended questions. Because they allow for elaboration and often require justification for answers, open-ended questions can sometimes shed light on *how* respondents think about important political issues in addition to *what* they think.

There are also a considerable number of disadvantages associated with open-ended questions, leading to their declining use by researchers. They are costly, taking up valuable space on a questionnaire, requiring more interview time, and demanding considerable more effort for data organization and management than closed-ended alternatives. Open-ended questions require more space to record answers than closed-ended questions, often limiting the number of questions that can be asked. By asking a large number of questions that require lengthy answers, respondents are more likely to grow weary of the process and break off the interview or fail to complete a self-administered questionnaire. The result is loss of information. Error and bias can result from interviewers incorrectly or incompletely recording information. Because open-ended questions are difficult to code, organizing the data collected using open-ended questions is cumbersome. The researcher usually sorts answers into a small number of categories. In that process, the original meanings of responses are often lost, and problems with reliability arise because different coders may place the same type of answer in different categories. Open-ended questions on self-administered questionnaires are frequently biased in favor of those with strong writing skills and those who are comfortable expressing their views in writing. While survey researchers disagree about the relative merits of open-ended questions, their use in comparison to questions with structured answers is increasingly limited.

Closed–Ended Questions.   As with open-ended questions, closed-ended questions with fixed responses can be used to collect any type of information from a respondent. The following are some examples that are commonly used in political science research.

Do you consider yourself PROTESTANT, ROMAN CATHOLIC, JEWISH, or what?
  (Social Background)
How much of the time do you think you can trust the government in Washington to
  do what is right—JUST ABOUT ALWAYS, MOST OF THE TIME, or ONLY
  SOME OF THE TIME? (Opinion/Attitude)
How much attention did you pay to news about the campaign for President—A
  GREAT DEAL, QUITE A BIT, SOME, VERY LITTLE, or NONE? (Behavior)
For each statement below, just check the box that comes closest to your opinion of how
  true it is.
In your opinion, is the following statement DEFINITELY TRUE, PROBABLY TRUE,
  PROBABLY NOT TRUE, or DEFINITELY NOT TRUE? Using coal or gas con-
  tributes to the Greenhouse Effect. (Knowledge)

Closed-ended questions have been developed in a wide variety of formats. You will recall from the discussion of measurement in Chapter 7 that even the lowest level of measurement, the nominal level, must include categories that are *collectively exhaustive* and *mutually exclusive*. The construction of closed-ended questions must reflect this pattern: All possibilities for answers must be included. A category such as "other" should be included to cover potential answers not anticipated (see the preceding questions concerning religious affiliation). Be careful to avoid questions for which a respondent might reasonably choose more than one response: "Please indicate which media you use to obtain information about politics—newspapers, magazines, television, radio, other." Clearly, a respondent might choose two or more of these information sources. Multiple responses to single questions complicate data organization, management, and analysis, so construct separate questions with mutually exclusive answers.

We must give some special attention to the construction of closed-ended questions that measure opinions and attitudes. Since opinions exist only in the minds of respondents, they cannot be directly observed. [2] Hence, social scientists must infer opinions from observed behavior. One way that behavior is stimulated and then observed is through a survey question. To understand how opinions might be measured, you need to have some understanding of how opinions are defined and described. Think of an opinion as an orientation toward an object, which may be something tangible like an automobile or a political leader like President Bush. We also have opinions about intangible objects, like a political idea such as the legalization of marijuana. Our opinion of an object may include a number of dimensions, but for purposes of measurement we will focus on two: direction and intensity.

Direction has to do with positive or negative evaluation of the object. We may agree or disagree with the legalization of marijuana, and we may like or dislike President Bush. Intensity reflects the degree of that positive or negative evaluation. A person who strongly agrees that marijuana should be legalized may have an orientation toward the subject that is equal in intensity to that of a person who strongly disagrees with legalization. Likewise, a person who very strongly likes President Bush has a view that is equally intense as one who very strongly dislikes him. The most useful survey questions that measure inions indicate both the direction of the evaluation of the object as well as the intensity of feeling. Survey researchers may depend on single questions to measure an opinion or combine many questions to form indexes or scales in order to increase measurement reliability and validity. For our purposes, it is sufficient to provide some examples of closed-ended question formats that can stand alone or be used for the construction of indexes and scales.

A very common format for survey items is the Likert response format (named after its creator Rensis Likert). [3] Instead of asking a question, Likert items provide an affirmative statement about an opinion object followed by specified response categories. of 1. strongly disagree (or disapprove, oppose, etc); 2. disagree; 3. uncertain (or neutral, unsure); 4. agree; 5. strongly agree (or approve, support, etc.) Responses to the statement indicate evaluation of the object (agreement or disagreement) and intensity of feeling or strength of opinion (strong agreement or weak agreement). Here is an example of a Likert item that measures a specific opinion about American courts.

The courts in America generally guarantee everyone a fair trial.
1. *Strongly disagree*
2. *Disagree*
3. *Undecided*
4. *Agree*
5. *Strongly agree*

This item narrowly focuses on the ability of courts to guarantee a fair trial. Other items might be constructed to measure opinions on court efficiency, power, or honesty. If the additional items were combined with this one, a resulting scale might measure a more general attitude toward courts.

The semantic differential format is used less frequently than Likert's, but it has some useful characteristics. It employs bipolar adjectives arranged at opposite ends of a continuum to measure the direction and intensity of opinions toward objects. While the number of response categories used can vary, a seven-point scale is most common. The following are examples of how semantic differential items might be used to measure opinions regarding American courts.

American courts are:

Fair	___	___	___	___	___	___	___	*Unfair*
Powerful	___	___	___	___	___	___	___	*Weak*
Effective	___	___	___	___	___	___	___	*Ineffective*
Active	___	___	___	___	___	___	___	*Passive*

Research on semantic differential items has shown that there are three dimensions that most respondents use to appraise opinion objects: evaluation, potency, and activity. In the preceding examples, American courts can be assessed along those dimensions: evaluation (fair-unfair and effective-ineffective), potency (powerful-weak), and activity (active-passive). As with the Likert format, semantic differential items can be combined into indexes and scales to improve reliability and validity. [4]

A number of visual devices have been employed to measure the direction and intensity of opinions. These devices are most useful for questions asked face to face by interviewers and/or when more than five possible response categories are offered. Two such devices are the *numerical rating scale* and the *feeling thermometer*. The former permits respondents to indicate the closeness of their opinion to two, opposite sides of an issue. The continuum looks very much like the one used with the semantic differential. The following is a numerical rating scale, again designed to measure opinion concerning American courts:

> *Some people believe that the courts are too lenient when it comes to sentencing people who have been convicted of crimes. Others believe that the courts are too harsh. The following is a scale from 1 to 7. Think of a score of 1 as meaning the courts are too harsh on convicted criminals and a score of 7 meaning that courts are too lenient. What score between 1 and 7 comes closest to the way you feel? (Circle one.)*
> *Courts are too harsh.*   *Courts are too lenient.*

| 1 | 2 | 3 | 4 | 5 | 6 | 7 |

The numerical scale can be placed directly on a questionnaire that is to be self-administered or printed on a card that is shown to the respondent for a face-to-face interview.

Feeling thermometers are especially useful for measuring the general images of groups and individuals. The visual device is analogous to a thermometer and asks respondents to indicate how "warm" or "cold" they feel about opinion objects on a 100-point scale. This approach efficiently collects a large amount of information while using little space on a questionnaire. The image of a thermometer is presented to respondents, and they are asked to use the scale to indicate their views of a large number of groups, institutions, or political figures. Figure 10.1 shows an example of how a feeling thermometer might be used to measure images of the American criminal justice system.

These are just a few of the most common formats that can be used for constructing closed-ended questions. Regardless of their form, they share some advantages and disadvantages. Their advantages have to do with efficiency. They can be administered quickly and easily, and comparison of response categories is simple and straightforward. They facilitate data organization and management, so that results can be analyzed quickly. Furthermore, respondents are often more willing to answer some personal questions, such as family income, if they are given options in the form of categories rather than having to directly state their annual income or other personal information. The disadvantages of closed-ended questions have to do with the constraints put on respondents and the dangers of encouraging artificial or unrealistic answers. Closed-ended questions tend to sacrifice depth and richness of information by forcing people to make choices they might otherwise not make if given more freedom. Fixed responses to opinion questions force people to decide where they stand, and a possible result of that process is the expression of an opinion that a respondent does not actually hold. In such a situation, the researcher is, in effect, encouraging respondents to "manufacture" an opinion. [5] Thus, the choice of closed-ended versus open-ended questions involves

Figure 10.1
A Feeling Thermometer

We would like to get your feelings about the American criminal justice system. When I read the name of an institution or group, we would like you to rate it on what we call a feeling thermometer. Ratings between 50° and 100° mean that you feel favorably or warm toward the institution or group; ratings between 0° and 50° mean that you do *not* feel favorably or warm toward the institution or group. If you do not feel particularly warm *or* cool, an appropriate rating would be 50°. First, let's consider the United States Supreme Court: How warm would you say you feel about it?

Warm

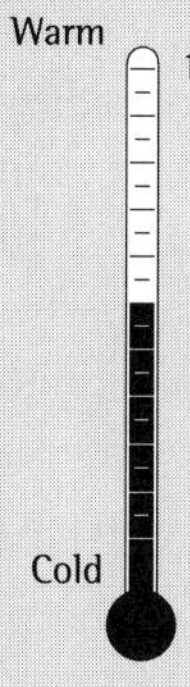

100° Very warm feeling (very favorable)
85° Quite warm feeling (quite favorable)
70° Fairly warm feeling (fairly favorable)
60° Slightly warm feeling (slightly favorable)
50° No feeling (neither favorable nor unfavorable)
40° Slightly cold feeling (slightly unfavorable)
30° Fairly cold feeling (fairly unfavorable)
15° Quite cold feeling (quite unfavorable)
0° Very cold feeling (very unfavorable)

Cold

1. Supreme Court   _____°
2. Prosecutors   _____°
3. Defense Attorneys   _____°
4. State Trial Courts   _____°
5. Police Officers   _____°

Source: Adapted from Seymour Sudman and Norman M. Bradburn, *Asking Questions: A Practical Guide to Questionnaire Design* (San Francisco: Jossey-Bass, 1985), p. 159. Copyright © 1982 by Jossey-Bass, Inc., Publishers. This material is used by permission of Jossey-Bass, Inc., a subsidiary of John Wiley & Sons, Inc.

some important trade-offs. What is gained in efficiency from using closed-ended questions may be countered by the loss of depth and accuracy.

Filter and Contingency Questions.   There will be occasions when you want to direct questions to respondents who have particular characteristics or opinions. You may, for example, want to question only parents to determine if their children had taken a sex education course in school. You will recall that *filter questions* are used to determine which *contingency questions* will be asked of respondents. Filter and contingency questions facilitate completion of a questionnaire because you can spare respondents being asked questions irrelevant to them. They are also useful for identifying respondents likely to have the most informed opinions on important issues. The following filter and contingency questions are meant to identify respondents who might be especially informed about a key issue.

> *Have you been following the news about proposals made by the president to change the Social Security system?*
> [ ] *Yes*
> [ ] *No*

If yes: Do you think the system should be changed so that taxpayers would be able
to invest a portion of their Social Security contributions in individual retirement
programs, or should the Social Security system remain unchanged?
[   ] Permit investment in individual accounts
[   ] Remain unchanged
If no, skip to the next question.

To the Web

Exercise 10.1   Writing Survey Questions

This exercise asks you to write open- and closed-ended survey questions to measure several attitudes and behaviors. At this point it is important that you practice writing questions in a variety of formats. Later we will focus on writing questions in ways that maximize validity and reliability. To access the exercise, go to the **DEPR Web Page,** click on **Web Exercises, Chapter 10,** then on **Writing Survey Questions.**

Combinations of filter questions and contingency questions are almost always developed in a closed-ended format. The preceding example involves a simple division of respondents, but more complex sets of contingency questions are common. Some filter questions have as many as four or five possible responses, each followed by a different contingency question. Filter and contingency questions can be used to create very complex, multistep branching formats for questionnaires.

■ Focus on Content: Appropriate Question Wording

Once you have decided on the appropriate format for asking questions, you must develop wording that will produce valid and reliable results. Crafting questions is critical because the wording affects the responses you will obtain. A good example of different questions on the same topic concerns presidential performance approval and is provided by Weisberg, Krosnick, and Bowen. The Gallup Poll asks respondents, "Do you approve or disapprove of the way the president is handling his job as president?" The Harris Poll question asks, "How would you rate the job the president is doing?" These two questions produce different results about presidential performance that would lead to quite different interpretations of the public's opinion about the president. [6] Extensive research has been done on the subtle influences of question wording on responses, but our goal in this book is only to provide you with general guidelines to help you avoid obvious mistakes. [7] We will describe, accompanied by examples, some common problems with question wording. [8]

Biased Questions.   Biased or loaded questions should be avoided because they suggest to respondents that one answer is more appropriate or desirable than another. Biased questions may contain emotionally loaded terms, provide opinionated response categories, or lead a respondent toward a particular answer. Here are examples of each type with suggested improvements.

Poor:	*Do you favor or oppose the elimination of our unfair system of taxation?*
Improved:	*Would you favor or oppose a bill that revised the present system of taxation?*
Poor:	*Do you agree that the courts should treat convicted criminals more harshly?*
Improved:	*Some people believe that the courts are too lenient when it comes to sentencing those convicted of crimes. Others believe that the courts give appropriate sentence or are too harsh. What is your view? Are the sentences usually too lenient, about right, or too harsh?*
Poor:	*Most people believe that the government should establish a national health-care plan. What is your view?*
Improved:	*Some people believe that the government should establish a national health-care plan, while others believe that the government should not be involved in health care. What is your view?*

Questions for Thought and Discussion

Consider the distributions of responses to three items concerning opinion on abortion. These questions were included on a survey conducted in 1985.

What do you think about abortion? Should it be legal as it is now; legal only in such cases as saving the life of the mother, rape, or incest; or should it not be permitted at all?

Legal as is now	40%
Legal only to save mother, rape, or incest	40%
Not permitted	16%
Don't know; not ascertained	4%

Which of these statements comes closest to your opinion? Abortion is the same as murdering a child, or abortion is not murder because a fetus isn't really a person.

Murder	55%
Not murder	35%
Don't know; not ascertained	10%

Do you agree or disagree with the following statement? Abortion sometimes is the best course in a bad situation.

Agree	66%
Disagree	26%
Don't know; not ascertained	8%

What conclusions could be drawn about public opinion on the issue of abortion in 1985? In what ways might your conclusions be influenced by the wording of the questions?

Source: Herbert Asher, *Polling and the Public,* 4th Ed. (Washington, DC: CQ Press, 1998), p. 98. Copyright © 1998. Reprinted by permission of CQ Press.

Ambiguous Questions.   Survey questions should be clear, simple, and free of jargon or technical terms. The goal is to use words that have the same meaning for the researcher and all respondents. Ambiguous questions are those that contain words that have double meanings or are unfamiliar to respondents. Ambiguity also results when questions are too general with respect to location or time.

Poor: *Do you support or oppose a progressive income tax?*
Improved: *Some states have a form of income tax where people with higher incomes pay a higher tax rate than those with lower incomes. Would you support or oppose such a plan for your state?*

Poor: *What is your income?*
Improved: *What was your total family income last year?*

Poor: *How often do you watch the news on television?*
Improved: *How many times in the past week did you watch the news on television?*

Double-Barreled Questions.   Double-barreled questions are those with compound meanings. They are actually two questions in one that make it impossible for the respondent to answer with a simple "yes" or " no." If a respondent does provide an answer, you cannot determine which part of the question stimulated the response.

Poor: *Should Congress cut taxes and increase defense spending?*
Improved: *Should Congress cut taxes?*
            Should Congress increase defense spending?

Negative Questions.   Questions that are stated negatively are confusing and may result in misinterpretation. Respondents will often miss the negating term and answer the question as if it were an affirmative question. It is better to word questions positively and then create alternative answers so the respondent can answer positively or negatively.

Poor: *Do you agree or disagree that speed limits on interstate highways should not be lowered?*
Improved: *Do you agree or disagree that speed limits on interstate highways should be lowered?*

Questions That Encourage Socially Desirable Responses.   Questions that seek to obtain sensitive information such as income, family life, or even unorthodox political views must be crafted with care. Survey respondents usually want to portray themselves in a positive light and may be reluctant to reveal accurate information about some subjects. Questions that request an answer that would reveal a socially undesirable trait or opinion also must be carefully worded to avoid receiving false information.

Poor:	*Did you vote in the last election?*
Improved:	*Some people voted in the last election, but others did not. How about you? Did you vote in the most recent election?*
Poor:	*Blacks have not achieved income levels equivalent to those of whites in America because they lack a work ethic. Do you agree or disagree?*
Improved:	*Blacks have not achieved income levels equivalent to those of whites in America. Which of the following do you believe is the best explanation for the disparity in incomes.*
	1. Blacks in America lack a work ethic.
	2. Blacks have been victims of prejudice and discrimination throughout our history.

Questions That Assume Respondent Knowledge.   Respondents should be competent to answer questions. It may not be reasonable to expect respondents to produce accurate information about all areas of their lives or to provide informed opinions on all topics. Researchers have found that respondents, given the opportunity, will indicate that they have an opinion about a subject that they know nothing about. In fact, they will "construct" an opinion in response to a question so that they will not appear uninformed. In situations where a respondent's recall of past behaviors or of precise information is unlikely, the question can only ask for rough estimates or more general information. Precise knowledge of gross family income or what was learned in a fourth-grade social studies class is knowledge not normally kept in a respondent's current memory. But respondents should be able to make an estimate of annual income and remember whether or not they ever studied civics. Providing definitions of unfamiliar terms in questions can sometimes improve respondent competence. Filter questions can also be used to distinguish respondents who are competent to answer questions that assume some knowledge.

Poor:	*How many hours per week do you spend watching television?*
Improved:	*About how many hours do you spend watching television each day?*
	1. 0 to 1 hour
	2. 2 to 4 hours
	3. 5 hours or more
Poor:	*Do you agree or disagree that a proportional representation system should be established for the city council?*

Improved: *Do you agree or disagree that the system of representation on the city council should be changed so that seats are assigned to political parties proportional to the percentage of votes they receive in an election?*

Poor: *Do you agree or disagree that the town should set aside funds for a land trust to preserve open space?*

Improved: *Have you read or heard anything about the proposal in town to create a land trust to preserve open space?*
             If the answer is yes: Do you agree or disagree with the proposal to set aside funds for a land trust to preserve open space, or do you not have an opinion on this issue?

Questions of Excessive Length.   We have emphasized avoiding ambiguity and lack of specificity in writing questions. Many of the preceding improved questions are more lengthy than the originals, but we do not want to create the impression that lengthy questions are more desirable. In fact, the opposite is true: Excessively long questions should be avoided. The longer the question, the more likely respondents will become confused or simply lose patience and not give it their full attention. Long questions are more likely to contain many of the errors we just listed. Short questions are best.

Poor: *If at some time in the future a member of the state legislature were to draft legislation creating a new agency to regulate the disposal of hazardous waste, and the State Senate and State House of Representatives approved it, would you urge the governor to sign it into law?*

Improved: *Should a new state agency be created to regulate the disposal of hazardous waste?*

To the Web

Exercise 10.2   Improving the Wording of Survey Questions

Poor wording of survey questions can result in measurements that lack validity and reliability. This exercise presents you with a series of poorly written questions. It asks you to explain why they are poorly written and to offer improvements by rewriting. To access the exercise, go to the **DEPR Web Page**, click on **Web Exercises, Chapter 10**, then on **Improving the Wording of Survey Questions**.

Key Points

Avoid the following when developing survey questions:

- Biased questions that suggest a desirable answer
- Ambiguous questions in which words may not have the same meaning for all respondents
- Double-barreled questions that are really two or more questions in one

- Negative questions for which respondents might miss the negating term
- Questions encouraging socially desirable responses
- Questions assuming that respondents are knowledgeable about a subject
- Questions of excessive length

Using Questions Developed by Others

"Why reinvent the wheel?" is a question you have probably heard. The question implies that looking for available solutions to problems is better than first trying to invent a new one. This is definitely the case with writing survey questions. Whenever possible, it makes sense to use existing, standard survey questions developed by other researchers. Major survey research organizations have been writing and asking questions for many years, and they have refined their work over time. You might as well take advantage of their experience and expertise. In addition to saving time and effort, the use of standard questions has other important benefits. First, direct comparisons with earlier research are made possible. In Chapter 2 we saw how scientific generalizations are developed through replication of earlier studies, and the use of equivalent questions in survey research facilitates replication. The repeated use of the same questions provides the information necessary to establish reliability. Finally, using standard questions not only allows for comparability with earlier studies but also facilitates comparisons across time, making it possible to discern trends. Here are some useful sources of standard survey questions.

General Social Surveys, 1972–2000: Cumulative Codebook. Chicago: National Opinion Research Center, 2000.

Miller, Delbert. *Handbook of Research Design and Social Measurement,* 6th Ed. Newbury Park, CA: Sage Publications, 2002.

Robinson, John P., Phillip R. Shaver, and Lawrence S. Wrightsman, *Measures of Personality and Social Psychological Attitudes.* San Diego: Academic Press, 1991.

Robinson, John P., Phillip R. Shaver, and Lawrence S. Wrightsman, *Measures of Political Attitudes.* San Diego: Academic Press, 1999.

To the Web

Online Sources for Survey Questions

Standard survey questions can be found on Web sites as well as source books. Some organizations have developed "question banks" with elaborate search engines. Codebooks for data sets such as the General Social Survey and the National Election Studies are also a useful online source of survey questions. To access some of these sources, go to the **DEPR Web Page,** click on **Web Links, Chapter 10,** then on **Online Sources for Survey Questions.**

Assembling the Survey Instrument

After deciding on the format and wording of individual questions, the survey questionnaire, or instrument, must be constructed. This involves writing the introduction, determining the order of questions, designing the physical layout or format, and pretesting to detect any problems or possible sources of error. Survey instruments vary somewhat in structure, depending on whether they will be self-administered or read to respondents by an interviewer. Regardless of how questionnaires are administered, the order in which questions are asked and the ease with which answers can be recorded by respondents or interviewers affect reliability and validity. An overview of questionnaire construction follows, but we urge you to consult the reference works at the end of the chapter for detailed accounts of how to assemble effective survey instruments.

Introduction and Instructions

Both interview forms and self-administered questionnaires begin with an introduction for the respondent. The introduction should contain the purpose of the survey, the name of the sponsor, a promise that all answers will be held in confidence (see the discussion of research ethics in Chapter 3 for a distinction between anonymity and confidentiality), and clear directions on how to answer the questions. A major goal of the introduction is to convince respondents that it is worth their time and effort to answer all of the questions. Respondents are often encouraged to participate by stressing the contribution their participation would make to scientific knowledge or by appealing to their altruism by focusing on the needs of the researcher. Naming a prestigious and well-known sponsor, such as a university, often encourages participation as well. Also included in introductions are emphases on the voluntary nature of participation in the survey and deadlines for completion and return of self-administered questionnaires. Introductions should be brief, simply worded, serious, neutral, nonthreatening, and matter-of-fact. [9] Overly elaborate introductions can in some instances create confusion among respondents and encourage socially desirable responses.

Most survey instruments contain a variety of forms of questions, each of which should be introduced by a set of instructions. For example, when a transition is made from a set of open-ended questions to Likert format closed-ended questions, respondents must be instructed on how to answer the questions by circling or checking an answer on a self-administered questionnaire or orally answering a question that is read to them. Transitions between question types can be accomplished in a conversational tone, such as "Now we are interested in your opinion about the qualities you believe would be ideal for a mayor of your city. Please read each of the following qualities and indicate whether you think they would be very important, important, or not very important in a mayor."

Special care must be given to writing instructions for filter and contingency questions. These types of questions can be especially confusing on a self-administered questionnaire, so respondents must be given explicit instructions on which questions to skip and which ones they should answer next. On both interview forms and questionnaires, arrows can sometimes be used to lead interviewers and respondents from question to question.

Question Order

The sequence of questions can influence answers, but more importantly, it may determine whether a respondent completes a self-administered questionnaire or an interview. Most experts recommend beginning with easy, nonthreatening questions that are of relevance to the respondent. The most difficult questions and those requesting sensitive information are left for the end of the survey. As respondents answer questions and progress through a survey, they accumulate information—learning takes place. Each question pondered and each answer provided may influence answers to questions that follow.

Two common problems that can be avoided by careful sequencing of questions are saliency bias and consistency bias. **Saliency bias** occurs when a question brings a particular issue or behavior to a respondent's attention. Once the respondent is alerted, the answers to later questions may be biased. For example, if early in an interview respondents are asked specific opinions about the problem of air pollution in their community, they are more likely to mention environmental issues in response to a later, more general open-ended question about community problems. **Consistency bias** occurs when respondents are inclined to answer questions in a way that makes them appear logical and consistent. Suppose a respondent was asked to agree or disagree with the statement "Every citizen has an obligation to vote" and responds in agreement. If the next question is "Did you vote in the election last November?" the respondent, in fear of being revealed as inconsistent, would be reluctant to admit that she did not vote, even if she didn't. Saliency bias can be reduced by placing general questions about topics earlier in a survey instrument than more specific opinion items. Consistency bias can be reduced by placing questions that respondents might see as related in different parts of the survey instrument.

Response set bias occurs when respondents are confronted with a series of questions that have identical response categories. If such questions are numerous, respondents may, through acquiescence, provide the same answers without paying careful attention to each question. If, for example, a long series of questions designed to measure political ideology were all worded so agreement indicated a conservative viewpoint, after a while a conservative respondent might simply indicate agreement without carefully considering each question. In this example, response set bias could be reduced by wording items so that in some instances agreement indicates a conservative response, while in others it indicates a liberal response.

The goal of question sequencing is to make the process of answering questions as easy as possible for the respondent and to encourage accurate and complete responses. There should be a natural progression from one question to the next. The idea is to keep the respondent engaged, interested, and cooperative. In addition to the introduction, there are three parts to most survey instruments: warm-up questions, main questions, and demographic questions.

Nonthreatening warm-up questions that are easy for respondents to answer should be placed first in order to involve respondents and put them at ease. Leave questions requiring more thought or sensitive information for later. Of course, the opening questions should be relevant to the purposes of the study; questions eliciting responses that will not be used should be avoided. If respondents are interviewed, open-ended questions that all respondents can answer are good starters, such as, "What do you think are the most important problems facing your community?" Open-ended questions that require more than a few written words should be avoided at the beginning of a self-administered questionnaire. Sometimes a background question that does not require highly personal information can be used to break the ice—for example, "How long have you lived in this community?"

The main questions on a survey instrument usually focus on measuring opinions, knowledge, and behavior. They usually require the respondent to recall information or to engage in some reflection before providing answers, so they should appear after a series of "easy," nonchallenging questions. Questions are best organized by topic, following a logical sequence. Once you get a respondent thinking about a particular topic, it makes sense to complete all of the questions about that topic. Switching from topic to topic confuses people and interrupts the flow of the survey. Questions should proceed from the general to the more specific in order to avoid saliency and consistency bias.

Generally, demographic questions should be asked at the end of a survey instrument. While some personal information such as marital status, religion, and education may be readily answered by most respondents, many people are reluctant to answer questions about their personal and financial affairs. A question perceived as sensitive, such as one that requests an estimate of family income, would more likely be answered at the end of an interview after a respondent has become familiar and comfortable with the process. If asked at the end of an interview, a refusal to answer a sensitive question will not set a pattern for refusing to answer other questions. Sometimes demographic questions are needed to filter respondents into groups of respondents who will be asked contingency questions. For example, a researcher wants to pose a different set of questions about religion to Protestants and Catholics. If that were the case, a question asking about religious identification should appear early in a questionnaire. Even if demographic items have to appear early in the questionnaire, they should be preceded by some warm-up questions.

Format

Once the sequence of questions is determined, the physical format of the survey instrument needs to be considered. Formatting arranges the questions into topic groups, determines spacing between questions, and uses arrows, boxes, and capital letters to clearly direct the interviewer and respondent through the intended question sequence. Additionally, consideration must be given to those who will code the results; questionnaires can be precoded to facilitate data organization and analysis. The format is most important for self-administered questionnaires because, in the absence of an interviewer, the respondent needs to fully comprehend, without outside help, what is being requested.

A great deal has been written about the design of questionnaires and interview schedules, including such factors as the formatting and spacing of questions, means of routing respondents and interviewers through the survey instrument, the clarity and size of type, the use of color, and organization into booklet form. [10] The design of questionnaires differs in a number of respects from that of interview schedules. Here are a few general guidelines and suggestions.

- Do not crowd questions. Leave enough space so that there is room for interviewers to record the answers to open-ended questions and to prevent respondents from checking the wrong box or circling the wrong answer.
- On interview forms, differentiate between instructions and words that are to be read to respondents by the interviewer. Instructions can be printed in capital letters and questions in lowercase, for example.
- Each question should be numbered and subparts lettered. This will prevent questions from being skipped over.
- On interview forms use visual cues like boxes and arrows for directions for filter and contingency questions. This helps interviewers understand what they should read next.
- Organize the survey instrument in a booklet format for ease of turning pages.
- Avoid splitting questions onto two pages.
- Organize questions with similar response patterns into a matrix format to save space on questionnaires.
- In face-to-face interviews, save space by using cards to show scales.
- Keep filter questions and contingency questions to a minimum on self-administered questionnaires.

Some experts argue that the number of sheets of paper used for a survey instrument is less important than making sure it is uncluttered, with plenty of room to record answers. While that is probably true for interview schedules, the number of pages of a self-administered questionnaire more likely influences completion rates. The number of questions included on the instrument is a separate matter; generally, the greater the number of questions asked, the lower the completion rate. This is especially the case with self-administered questionnaires and telephone-administered interviews.

Pretesting

Every survey instrument should be **pretested**—that is, tried out on the very least a dozen or so respondents to detect any problems. After pretesting, interviewers are usually debriefed to determine any difficulties in reading questions and recording responses. Completed pretest survey instruments can be examined to determine problems with instructions, question wording, format, and especially filter and contingency questions. Finally, pretesting is necessary to determine the amount of time it takes to complete the survey. Pretesting almost always results in some adjustments and often leads to the exclusion of some questions in order to advance completion time.

Administering the Survey

The three primary ways to collect survey data are face-to-face interviews, telephone interviews, and self-administered questionnaires. The preferred mode of data collection is directly related to the research question, sampling frame, characteristics of the sample, and the availability of staff and facilities. [11] Obviously, financial costs and time constraints are also important considerations. The choice influences the types of questions that can be asked and response rates. In addition, which approach to the collection of survey data is appropriate depends on your research goals.

Face-to-Face Interviews

The distinctive feature of the **face-to-face interview** is the social interaction between the interviewer and the respondent; one person asks the questions, and the other provides answers. Emphasis is on the ability of the interviewer to get respondents to agree to participate in the survey and then develop a personal rapport so that answers are candidly and accurately provided. The ultimate success of the survey depends on interviewer demeanor and skill. Effective interviewers are those who put the respondent at ease, are completely familiar with the questions, and accurately record responses.

If face-to-face interviews are your chosen mode of data collection, recruiting, training, and supervising of interviewers are major tasks. Finding interviewers can be a chore. You can recruit volunteers, use staff members from an organization interested in the results of the survey, hire your own, or rely on professional interviewers from a commercial organization. Training usually involves the development of general interviewer skills, including problem solving, ensuring familiarity with the survey instrument, and instructions on how to select respondents. [12] Once interviewers are in the field, they must be monitored and supervised. All of these processes involve a substantial and often prohibitive investment of time and money. At one time face-to-face interviews were the dominant approach to data collection by professionals, but they are becoming less common. Face-to-face interviews have the following advantages.

- They are the most effective way to gain cooperation with respondents.
- Longer survey instruments with more questions are possible compared to telephone interviews and self-administered questionnaires distributed by mail. Respondents are more reluctant to break off interviews in a face-to-face situation.
- Because of the rapport that is established, open-ended questions are easier to use. Probing for elaboration of responses is also facilitated.
- Visual cues, such as feeling thermometers, are more smoothly employed.
- A greater variety of question formats is possible.
- Response rates are usually higher than with other methods.
- Interviewers control and monitor the conditions under which answers are given.

Face-to-face interviews have the following disadvantages.

- They are the most costly mode of data collection.
- Interviewer effects—answers may be biased by characteristics of the interviewer or interviewer demeanor.
- It takes more time to collect data than it does with telephone interviews.
- Respondents may be reluctant to answer questions requesting personal information in the presence of an interviewer.

■ Telephone Interviews

Telephone surveys have gained in popularity among professional researchers because of their economy and the speed with which they can be completed. Telephone interviews are very similar to face-to-face interviews, but some procedural differences should be emphasized. They are generally conducted from a single site, usually a single room, where many interviewers may be simultaneously interviewing respondents from a nationwide sample. [13] Professional organizations use computer-assisted telephone interviewing

(CATI), during which interviewers wearing telephone headsets sit in front of computer screens. A computer program, using a process called random digit dialing, dials the number of a household. The interviewer makes contact, reading instructions and questions from the screen. Responses are typed on the keyboard. The CATI program will alert the interviewer about any recording errors. As interviews are conducted and answers recorded, the responses are automatically organized into a data file for analysis. [14]

Telephone surveys require less extensive interview training than face-to-face interviews, and personal characteristics of the interviewer are not an issue. Each interviewer completes more interviews because the operation is centralized and no transportation time is involved. Supervisors have more control over the process and are in a position to make corrections if problems arise.

Telephone interviews have the following advantages.

- Costs are about half those of face-to-face interviews.
- Projects can be completed quickly.
- It is easier to monitor and supervise interviewers because they are centrally located and fewer in number.
- Interviewer bias effects are minimized compared to face-to-face interviews.
- Response rates are higher than with self-administered mail questionnaires and may approach those of face-to-face interviews.
- Respondents are more forthcoming when asked sensitive questions.

Telephone interviews have the following disadvantages.

- Sample limitations—those without telephones are omitted. Each completed interview involves many tries (perhaps one in twelve is successful). Those who consent may differ substantially from those who do not answer because of caller identification or avoidance of telemarketers.
- There are fewer comments in response to open-ended questions.
- There are limits on possible response alternatives and use of visual aids.
- Respondents are less motivated than those who are interviewed in person or who complete self-administered questionnaires.

▨ Self-Administered Questionnaires

An alternative to the use of interviewers is to ask respondents to complete **self-administered questionnaires.** There are several ways in which questionnaires can be distributed to respondents for self-administration, but the most common is through the mail. The major challenge facing the researcher who plans to use mailed questionnaires is the return rate. Depending on the sampling frame and other circumstances, return rates for mailed questionnaires range from 10 to 50 percent. It is unusual for more than half of those mailed to be returned to the researcher. A great deal of research dealing with ways in which respondents can be encouraged to return mailed questionnaires has been done. Attention has been given to factors such as the number of reminders, the type of appeal in the cover letter, the offering of gifts, and the use of stamps. If you plan to distribute a questionnaire by mail, you should consult references that give a detailed description of how to increase return rates. [15]

Distributing and collecting questionnaires by mail is fairly straightforward. Questionnaires, a cover letter of explanation, and a stamped return envelope are mailed to respondents. Returned questionnaires are carefully monitored. Usually after two or three weeks those who have not returned their questionnaires are sent a reminder letter or postcard. After a month to six weeks a third mailing including a new questionnaire is sent to the remaining respondents who have not replied. Coding and organization of data can proceed as the questionnaires are returned.

Depending on the purpose of a study, questionnaires can sometimes be administered to groups of respondents gathered in one place rather than mailed. For example, if you were conducting a survey of delegates to a county political party convention, you might gain permission to distribute questionnaires during meetings and ask respondents to complete and place them in a box as they exit. Another alternative is to have a researcher hand-deliver questionnaires to the homes of respondents and then pick them up later. This latter alternative is, of course, more costly than delivery through the mail. Both distributing questionnaires to groups of respondents and hand delivery increase response rates, but among professional researchers who are attempting to reach members of a diverse sample, mail delivery is more common.

Self-administered questionnaires delivered by mail have the following advantages.

- Process is relatively inexpensive, so larger samples can be surveyed.
- Since there are no interviewers, interviewer effects and bias are not issues.
- Candid responses are more likely to questions requesting sensitive information.
- Respondents have the time to develop thoughtful answers.
- Questions with answers that fall in many complex categories can be included.
- Questions using visual aids are possible.

To the Web

Conducting Surveys Using the Internet or Fax Machines

New technologies have added to the ways in which surveys can be delivered. It is not unusual to find questionnaires posted on Web sites for completion or distributed by e-mail for return. Fax machines have also been used as a means for distributing self-administered questionnaires. Obviously, the use of new technologies has implications for study populations, samples, and the accuracy of generalizations. Scholars and market researchers are engaged in a vigorous debate about the utility of online and fax surveys. To access a summary of the issues of concern, go to the **DEPR Web Page,** click on **Web Links, Chapter 10,** then on **Conducting Surveys Using the Internet or Fax Machines.**

Self-administered questionnaires delivered by mail have the following disadvantages.

- Low response rates—the researcher cannot be sure that those who return questionnaires do not differ on a wide variety of characteristics from those who do not.
- Data are collected over a relatively long period of time.
- Questionnaires usually have to be short to encourage completion and return.
- It is necessary to limit the number of open-ended questions.
- The researcher cannot be sure that it was the addressee who completed the questionnaire.
- Questions assessing knowledge cannot be asked (respondents can look up answers).
- A mailing list is required for a sampling frame.
- They assume that respondents have adequate reading and writing skills.

Secondary Analysis of Survey Data

By now you should have noticed that survey research projects are major undertakings. In fact, it is extremely unlikely that you will ever personally conduct a large-scale survey, especially if you are not affiliated with a professional research organization. Full-scale survey research projects entail levels of funding that are beyond the reach of most of us and consume so much time and effort that they are impractical modes of data collection. Answering research questions by analyzing survey data is still possible, however, because survey data collected by others are widely available. The analysis of data collected by other researchers is called **secondary analysis.** Even a cursory examination of articles in the professional political science literature will reveal that secondary analysis of survey data is considerably more common than the analysis of data authors have collected themselves.

Finding survey data appropriate for testing hypotheses of interest to us is facilitated by the existence of **data archives** that are maintained by large universities and other organizations. They are much like libraries, storing data sets that are provided to scholars for a fee or in some cases for free if a project was publicly funded. Virtually all of the important social science data archives now maintain their inventories online. Some online inventories contain search engines that can assist in the location of useful data sets by using keywords found in survey questions. Most archives include abbreviated and complete copies of codebooks that can be searched. In some instances, simple data analysis can be done right at an archive's Web site. Ordinarily, a full data set in SPSS or other software formats can be directly downloaded

To the Web

Obtaining Survey Data for Secondary Analysis

A surprising number of sets of survey data are easily obtainable from online data archives. The archives vary with regard to the extent to which data sets are indexed and the ease of downloading. The linkages we provide on our Web page emphasize sites where data are provided without cost and are easy to download. To access survey data, go to the **DEPR Web Page,** click on **Web Links, Chapter 10,** then on **Obtaining Survey Data for Secondary Analysis.**

to your computer. We provide linkages on our Web page to some of the most important and useful sites that contain survey data.

You should be critical in the use of available survey data for secondary analysis. Before choosing a data set to examine, consider carefully the sample and how it was selected, making sure that the sample is adequate for the hypotheses you want to test. Look over questions closely because validity is always an issue when using data collected by others. Often you will find a question that closely, but not precisely, measures the concept of interest to you. Make sure the survey items you examine actually measure the concepts you want to relate in your hypotheses.

Conclusion

Survey research has played a key role in the development of scientific approaches to the study of politics. As a method of data collection it has some important strengths, but it also has weaknesses that are often overlooked. It is especially useful for describing large populations. That the essence of the method involves asking respondents questions is an important factor in its contribution to knowledge because, in general, much more can be learned from people by asking them questions as opposed to simply observing their behavior. Another strength is that many questions covering a wide variety of topics can be included on a single instrument.

One of the strengths of survey research is also a weakness. Because questions are asked of respondents, we are dependent on self-reports for information, raising important issues of validity and reliability. Respondents may not be truthful, or questions may be misinterpreted. Survey research involves contact with a large number of respondents for a short period of time. Usually respondents are asked to answer standardized questions. All of this produces a grossly simplified portrait of a person's attitudes and behaviors. In fact, questions may provide a false portrait of individual views by creating attitudes. Finally, we often forget that surveys are mere snapshots of opinions at a specific point in time. Opinions and behavior change, but few surveys measure individual dispositions and characteristics at several points in time.

In the next chapter, we consider using data from published sources for testing hypotheses. These data often describe units of analysis other than individuals, such as cities, states, or countries, and generally can be obtained for little or no cost.

Summary of the Main Points

- Survey research is a method of data collection in which questionnaires are administered to a sample of respondents to assess their background characteristics, opinions, knowledge, and behaviors.
- Survey questions are either open-ended, with respondents structuring their own answers, or closed-ended, with respondents choosing from among answers structured by the researcher.

- Writing survey questions is an exercise in operationalization. A great deal of care must be taken to avoid problems of validity and reliability.
- Employing survey questions that have been developed by other researchers is productive.
- Surveys can be presented to respondents in face-to-face interviews, over the telephone, or distributed by mail for self-administration.
- A great deal of survey data is available for secondary analysis.

Terms Introduced

closed-ended questions

consistency bias

contingency questions

data archives

face-to-face interviews

filter questions

open-ended questions

pretesting

response set bias

saliency bias

secondary analysis

self-administered questionnaires

survey research

telephone surveys

Selected Readings

Babbie, Earl R. *Survey Research Methods,* 2nd Ed. Belmont, CA: Wadsworth, 1990.

Backstrom, Charles H., and Gerald Hursh-Cesar. *Survey Research,* 2nd Ed. New York: John Wiley and Sons, 1981.

Converse, Jean M., and Stanley Presser. *Survey Questions: Handcrafting the Standardized Questionnaire.* Newbury Park, CA: Sage Publications, 1986.

Fowler, Floyd J. *Survey Research Methods,* Rev. Ed. Newbury Park, CA: Sage Publications, 1988.

Labaw, Patricia. *Advanced Questionnaire Design.* Cambridge, MA: Abt Books, 1980.

Mangione, Thomas W. *Mail Surveys: Improving the Quality.* Newbury Park, CA: Sage Publications, 1995.

Peterson, Robert A. *Constructing Effective Questionnaires.* Newbury Park, CA: Sage Publications, 1999.

Sudman, Seymour, and Norman M. Bradburn. *Asking Questions: A Practical Guide to Questionnaire Design.* San Francisco: Jossey-Bass, 1985.

Weisberg, Herbert F., Jon A. Krosnick, and Bruce D. Bowen. *An Introduction to Survey Research and Data Analysis,* 2nd Ed. Glenview, IL: Scott, Foresman and Company, 1989.

Activity 10.1
Constructing a Questionnaire

The objective of this activity is to develop a survey research instrument and to plan for the organization, management, and analysis of the data to be collected.

1. Develop a questionnaire to test a number of hypotheses of interest to you. Your survey must include an introduction and at least sixteen (16) questions, including the following.
   a. At least two must be open ended.
   b. At least five must measure social background characteristics.
   c. At least six must measure attitudes and opinions.
   d. At least two methods must be used to measure opinions.
   e. At least one question must involve more than ten response categories.
   f. At least two questions must be a combination of a filter question and a contingency question.
2. Develop a codebook to accompany your survey instrument. The codebook should include coding categories for your open-ended questions.
3. State five hypotheses that relate variables measured by your questions.

Activity 10.2
Accessing Data for Secondary Analysis

1. Using your browser to go to the World Wide Web, locate SDA: Survey Documentation and Analysis: http://csa.berkeley.edu:7502.
2. Examine the codebooks for the data sets located in the archive.
3. Choose one of the data sets to use for this activity (we recommend GSS or National Election Study for a single year).
4. Select "Browse codebook" in this window and click "Start."
5. Locate three questions that measure social background characteristics. Record the variable names for those questions.
6. Locate three questions that measure opinions, each of which uses a different question format. Record the variable names for those questions.
7. Locate three questions that measure behavior. Record the variable names for those questions.
8. Click back and select "Download a customized subset of variables/cases." Click "Start."
9. Select Data definitions for SPSS.
10. Enter the names of the nine variables you have chosen in the "Select VARIABLES to include" box. Click "Continue" at the top of the page.

11. Check the variables to make sure they are the ones you selected. If they are correct, click on the "create the files" button.

12. Download the three files ("data," "codebook," and "SPSS file") into your computer by following the instructions on the page. RENAME your "SPSS file" to "activity10.sps." The "sps" extension will allow the SPSS software to read that file directly.

13. Open SPSS and click on "file," then "open," then "synatx." When the dialog box opens, find the "activity10.sps" file where it has been stored on your computer.

14. Within the "activity10" synatx file, go to the DATA LIST portion, find the command line "FILE=x" and replace the "x" with the name of the data file you downloaded from the Berkeley site. Be sure to include the file structure. For example, if the name of your file is "PoliSci" and it was stored in the "My Documents" folder of your hard drive, you would type in "c:\mydocuments\PoliSci".

15. At the bottom of the "activity10" syntax file, go to the "SAVE OUTFILE=y" command and replace "y" with the name of the file you wish to assign your new SPSS data file (e.g, "mydata.sav").

16. Using SPSS, run a frequency distribution for each of your nine variables. If necessary, see Chapter 8 for a review of running a frequency distribution in SPSS.

Chapter 11

Collecting and Organizing Data from Published Sources

Learning Objectives

After completion of this chapter, students should be able to do the following:

Identify and locate data from published sources that describe a variety of units of analysis.

Describe the advantages and disadvantages of using data from published sources.

Evaluate the utility of data from published sources for testing hypotheses.

Code and organize data from published sources so that it is ready for analysis using statistical software such as SPSS.

Describe the process of collecting and analyzing the content of mass-media messages.

Describe the strengths and weaknesses of content analysis.

Previously Collected Data

In the last chapter we noted that collecting data through surveys requires extensive financial resources and large amounts of time that usually are not available to professional political science researchers, not to mention undergraduate students. We suggested that survey data collected by others can easily be obtained and subjected to secondary analysis at a fraction of the cost of an original survey. In this chapter we discuss the collection of data from published sources—data collected by others and made available to the public—and messages that can be collected from print and electronic media. These data can usually be obtained without financial cost, but sometimes they require a great deal of effort to locate and prepare for analysis.

Discussing the types of published data in terms of units of analysis is the most useful way to approach this topic. Social scientists often distinguish between *levels of analysis*. The **macro level of analysis** usually refers to units that are defined geographically, such as countries, states, provinces, counties, congressional districts, cities or towns, and census tracts. These geographical boundaries are usually determined by political processes such as diplomacy, war, or legislation. Some, like the borders of countries, define important political units, whereas others, like the census tracts created by the U.S. Census Bureau, are designed for purposes of convenience in data collection. The **micro level** refers to a focus on people as units of analysis. Data collected by surveys, intensive interviews (to be discussed in the following chapter), or from biographies and public records are examples of a micro approach. In between macro and micro levels of analysis are organizations such as interest groups, political parties, government agencies, and nongovernment organizations (NGOs). Published data are available to describe units of analysis at all three levels.

Another form of published data are media messages. The units of analysis of media messages may include stories, paragraphs, words, and images. Media messages may be found in hard copy form, such as books, magazines, court reports, and newspapers, or in electronic form, such as television, film, videos, radio, and the World Wide Web. The collection and analysis of media messages is called **content analysis.** We begin with a discussion of published data concerning geographical units, organizations, and individuals and go on to an introduction to content analysis.

Published Data

Locating Published Data

Finding sources of published data involves strategies similar to those that were outlined in Chapter 4, where we discussed building a bibliography about a research topic. You should begin with a search of library resources, but the approach differs somewhat from that taken in building a bibliography. Building a bibliography means searching subject indexes using keywords related to your topic or chosen variables, and this approach will produce some sources of published data. But you should also think in terms of your units of analysis because data are often published by governments and other organizations in volumes that include a broad array of substantive variables. The very useful *Statistical Abstract of the United States* published by the U.S. Census Bureau, for example, contains data on subjects ranging from crime rates in the states to election results to state spending on education. A subject search for "crime rates" or "education spending" would not turn up the *Statistical Abstract.* A subject search for "state governments," however, would eventually reveal *The Book of the States,* published by the Council of State Governments, another very rich data source. Initially, the best approach to finding published data is to undertake a thorough literature review, paying special attention to the data sources used by other scholars. Additionally, you should familiarize yourself with important sources of published data such as the United States Census, the United Nations, and Congressional Quarterly, Inc. Hard copy volumes of published data are generally found in close proximity in the reference (noncirculating) section of the library.

The use of search engines to probe the World Wide Web for data sources should focus on organizations that publish data and specific variables. For example, the United Nations Web site reveals abundant sources of data published online and in hard-copy volumes. The UN's *Demographic Yearbook* contains valuable data on social and economic characteristics of nations. Alternatively, a search focused on a substantive topic such as "human development" will eventually lead you to the *Human Development Report,* which contains additional data published by the United Nations. As with library searches, there are many paths to data published on Web sites. Pay close attention to procedures for limiting searches and be creative and flexible in using keywords. Always keep a careful record of the sources of data you locate. Sometimes you will come across a reference to a potentially useful Web site, but when you access it, you will not find the expected data. If this happens, a good strategy is go back to the first page of the site to determine if the link to the data has changed. Some sites have their own search engines to help you locate data. Organizations tend to move data around within their sites from time to time, so be persistent about finding what you need.

Evaluating the Usefulness of Published Data

Organizations publish in different formats. You must take care to select data that are easily accessible and appropriate for testing the hypotheses of interest to you. One consideration is the medium of publication because it is closely related to accessibility and the effort necessary to organize the data and make it ready for analysis. Data are published in hard copy, such as statistical yearbooks or periodicals, and electronic formats. The hard-copy data are produced in raw form, requiring them to be coded and written to a data matrix such as the SPSS data files we discussed in Chapter 8. On occasion, data in hard-copy volumes are organized in a data matrix with units of analysis on the rows and variables on the columns, making the transfer of data to an electronic format relatively easy either by hand or by optical scanner. Unfortunately, most published data—especially biographical information—must be laboriously collected, coded, and put in electronic format. Happily, there is a trend toward publishing data in more accessible formats. Most U.S. Census data are available either in hard-copy volumes or on CDs and, most conveniently, at the Bureau of the Census Web site as well, where they can be easily downloaded or cut and pasted into SPSS data matrices. Huge amounts of data are available and ready for secondary analysis from repositories such as the Inter-university Consortium for Social and Political Research at the University of Michigan. Using data that are ready for analysis is obviously more efficient and should be done whenever possible.

Evaluating the reliability of data collected from published sources is important. Reliability, you will recall, has to do with the extent to which the same results are produced if measures are taken at different points in time or by different researchers. When using data collected by others, you have to consider factors such as the motives and credibility of sources. In most instances, the published data that we use were collected by people or organizations who were not interested in social science research. Most are interested in publishing accurate information that can be used by policymakers or the mass media. The International City Management Association, for example, publishes the *Municipal Year Book* to provide information to its members and other city administrators. The data contained in the *Year Book* are considered reliable and accurate, and city managers depend on it for their decision making. Political scientist Ted Robert Gurr points to a common problem called "self-serving error": when a government agency or organization provides a "firm estimate," reflecting the opinion of officials about what the figure should be. While often benign, these errors sometimes involve government officials inflating such data as economic figures or literacy rates in order to protect individual and national reputations. [1] Threats to the reliability of published data can also be attributed to human error, bias in the process of recording and reporting, or simple censorship.

Recall that the issue of validity concerns the extent to which a measure accurately reflects the concept it is supposed to represent. The use of published data often presents a challenge to validity because you do not create the measures yourself, but search through existing data for those that most accurately reflect some concept that interests you. As we pointed out in Chapter 7, many of these concepts are multidimensional and less than concrete. By carefully and thoroughly defining a concept, you can evaluate the validity of alternative indicators. As a practical matter, however, the availability of indicators may influence the definition of concepts. Justifying the use of an indicator and making the case that there is a good match between indicator and concept is important for content validity. For example, choosing an indicator like "personal computers per capita" to compare the levels of modernization of countries might ignore aspects of modernization such as transportation and distribution of wealth, threatening content validity.

Questions for Thought and Discussion

Suppose that you were interested in comparing the quality of life in countries in Europe. How would you define "quality of life"? Describe some of the indicators that might be available to differentiate countries in terms of your definition. Which indicators would be the most valid?

When discussing the representativeness of samples in Chapter 9, we mentioned that little attention is given to how representative sets of data are with respect to time. A public opinion survey of a sample of registered voters, for instance, is simply a "snapshot" of opinion at a particular point in time. Care must be taken when generalizing about opinion at times earlier or later than the survey. You must be even more cautious when using data from published sources that describe a full population such as all the states in the United States or all the members of the U.S. House of Representatives. While we need not be concerned with sample error when dealing with populations, published data usually describe characteristics and behavior from the past. In fact, most collections of data are not published annually. In some cases, the exact date on which the data were collected is not relevant to your hypotheses, but in many instances it can make a substantial difference in your generalizations. Data collected in 1988 about the political characteristics of the countries in Eastern Europe, for example, would not have reflected the conditions in 1992—only four years later. Be sure to take into account when data were collected and cite the dates when describing how your concepts are operationalized.

Key Points

In evaluating the usefulness of data from published sources, take the following into account.

- Format for ease of collection and coding (are units of analysis on rows and variables on columns?)
- Medium (hard copy, CD, Web site, or downloadable and ready for analysis?)
- Credibility of sources (what was the original purpose for collecting of the data?)
- Validity (to what extent do the indicators reflect the concept that interests you?)
- Timeliness (is the time frame when data were collected relevant to your hypotheses?)

Collecting and Organizing Published Data

In Chapter 8 we saw how to place data in a data matrix and develop a corresponding codebook. The examples were in SPSS format. When using published sources, you will likely have to select, organize and prepare data for analysis yourself. We noted previously that data collected by others is increasingly made available in electronic formats, such as on

Figure 11.1
Codebook and Coding Form

Codebook

1 "COUNTRY" (Country Name)
   Country name
   Source: <http://www.un.org/Depts/unsd/social/hum-set.htm>

2 "POLRIGHT" (Political Rights Score, 1999–2000)
   Seven-point scale measuring political rights, 1999–2000.
   Source: <http://www.freedomhouse.org/research/freeworld/2000/table1.htm;
   http://www.freedomhouse.org/research/freeworld/2000/table2.htm>

   1-Most Free to 7-Least Free

3 "CIVILLIB" (Civil Liberties Score, 1999–2000)
   Seven-point scale measuring civil liberties, 1999–2000.
   Source: <http://www.freedomhouse.org/research/freeworld/2000/table1.htm;
   http://www.freedomhouse.org/research/freeworld/2000/table2.htm>

   1-Most Free to 7-Least Free

4 "FREESTAT" (Freedom Status, 1999–2000)
   Three-point scale based on combination of political rights score and civil liberties score.
   Source: <http://www.freedomhouse.org/research/freeworld/2000/table1.htm;
   http://www.freedomhouse.org/research/freeworld/2000/table2.htm>

   1-Free
   2-Partly Free
   3-Not Free

5 "BIRTH" (Birth Rate)
   "Births per 1,000 population, 2000.
   Source: Table 008: Vital Rates and Events. <http://www.census.gov/cgi-bin/ipc/idbagg.
   original search screen address: http://www.census.gov/ipc/www/idbagg.html>

5 "DEATH" (Death Rate)
   "Deaths per 1,000 population, 2000.
   Source: Table 008: Vital Rates and Events. <http://www.census.gov/cgi-bin/ipc/idbagg.
   original search screen address: http://www.census.gov/ipc/www/idbagg.html>

Country	polright	civillib	freestat	birth	death
Afghanistan	7	7	3	41.8	18.0
Albania	4	5	2	19.5	6.5
Algeria	6	5	3	23.1	5.3
American Samoa	1	1	1	25.8	4.3
Andorra	1	1	1	10.6	5.3
Angola	6	6	2	46.9	25.0

CDs, that facilitate collection, organization, and analysis, but much data are still obtained from hard-copy volumes. Therefore, we must discuss the development of codebooks and data matrices that facilitate the transfer of data from hard copy to electronic formats.

Codebooks should be developed before the process of collecting data from published volumes begins. Remember that codebooks contain lists of variables in the order they appear in the data matrix. Your codebook should provide a title or name for each variable and a brief description that indicates the source of the data and the date collected. The range of values might also be indicated in the case of interval/ratio–level variables and value names in the cases of nominal- or ordinal-level variables. Record keeping is especially important if you construct your data set from several different published sources. Your codebook should provide enough information so that another person would know, without talking to you, exactly where to find values for each variable and where to place those values in the data matrix.

Your data matrix can be constructed on any type of paper with grids, such as graph paper. To ease the process of collecting and recording values of variables, the names of units of analysis should be listed on the rows and variable names on the columns. An example of a portion of a codebook and related data matrix for characteristics of countries is shown in Figure 11.1. (Note that we used the name of each country to identify units of analysis. Each unit of analysis was assigned a unique identification number and placed in the first column of the data matrix.) Once all of the data are recorded from hard-copy volumes, they can be transferred to an electronic format using SPSS or a spreadsheet that can be read by statistical software. The process we have described can be laborious. If the data you need for analysis can be found in electronic format or scanned from hard copy to a format that can be read by SPSS or other statistical software, we recommend that you avoid collection and inputting by hand. Each step in the process that can be avoided will reduce the likelihood of recording error.

Published Data on Geographic Regions or Organizations

When variables describe a population or a group, they are often referred to as **aggregate data,** but the term *aggregated* is not always correctly applied to variables that describe geographical subdivisions such as cities and countries or groups such as schools or political parties. Political scientist Richard Merritt points out that the term has been applied not only to characteristics of an entire population or organization but also to aggregate characteristics of individuals. More specifically, **summation variables** are those that were created by combining characteristics of members of a region or group. Examples include the number of homicides that take place in a city in a given year or the number of bills passed by the lower house of a state legislature during a session. **Syntality variables** are those that describe the qualities of a region or group as a whole, such as American cities being described as having city manager, mayor-council, or commission forms of government. Another example is interest groups that may be described, as a whole, as democratic or oligarchic organizations. [2] Merritt describes six different types of aggregated data, noting they vary considerably with regard to accessibility, reliability and validity. [3]

Census data are collected by governments through questionnaires distributed to the entire population. In addition to population counts, a great deal of information about demographic characteristics, such as educational level, income, residence, occupation, race, and living conditions, is also acquired. The results of a census are routinely conveyed in summary form in statistical yearbooks and reports. The United States Census reports the average number of school years completed by adults for the nation, states, congressional districts, counties, metropolitan areas, and cities. Compared to other types of published data, census data are easily accessible and highly reliable.

Governmental and quasi-governmental statistics are produced by government agencies other than the census and by professional organizations that provide services to government officials or report government actions. The Federal Bureau of Investigation (FBI) produces an annual *Uniform Crime Report* in which statistics on crimes committed in the United States during the previous year are summarized. The FBI gathers these statistics from state and local officials and compiles them in the report. The quasi-governmental Council of State Governments publishes *The Book of the States* as a reference volume. Many nonprofit associations publish data on political, social, and economic trends of interest to social scientists. Private organizations also publish data about the government; the *Almanac of American Politics,* in which you can find information about states, congressional districts, and the people who represent them is a good example.

Survey data can be summarized for geographical areas and organizations, insofar as equivalent questions are used, samples are similar, and surveys are taken at about the same time. The *Eurobarometer,* established in 1973, is a public opinion survey carried out two to five times per year in European countries. Summary figures from the country surveys are directly comparable. [4] Political scientists in the United States have also been able to use survey data to describe public opinion in the states and relate it to public policy outcomes. [5] An innovative study surveyed party officials in the states and used the results to develop scores describing state level party organizations. [6] With some effort, you could piece together the results of public opinion surveys in quite a large number of countries and develop aggregate indicators.

We discuss content analysis more fully later in this chapter, but at this point we must note that the results of analyses of media content can be used to characterize such units of analysis as countries, states, cities, or political organizations. A famous example is David McClelland's content analysis of children's readers in forty-one countries to determine each nation's emphasis on personal achievement. [7] More recently, a content analysis conducted by Pippa Norris of the Web sites of parliaments in 149 countries was able to assess the level of democratization in these nations. [8] As the technology and software that are used to conduct content analyses become more sophisticated, we are likely to see an increase in the use of media messages to characterize political units like countries and interest groups.

Event statistics are another type of data that have been used to describe political units such as cities, states, or countries. As the name implies, events are recorded and characterized for collectivities. The most common use of event data has been to record incidents reflective of political instability, like demonstrations, riots, resignations of government officials, and wars between nations. These types of events are not usually recorded in census reports or government-sponsored publications. Collecting event data is very much like content analysis in that scholars must use as sources news indexes such as the *New York Times Index* or annual volumes that publish a review of international events. Ted Robert Gurr, a leading authority on civil strife, provides a thorough discussion of how to collect data about civil strife and create indicators from that data. [9]

Judgmental data are based on the opinions of experts in categorizing collectivities on the values of a particular variable. Judgmental data requires careful definition of a variable accompanied by rules for use by the experts. The most common use of judgmental data is classifying political systems into types, such as Seymour Martin Lipset's work of distinguishing European and Western Hemisphere political systems as democracies, stable dictatorships, or unstable dictatorships and then exploring the social-economic characteristics of each. [10] Recently, much more sophisticated typologies of government forms have been developed using judgmental data. [11]

To the Web

Exercise 11.1—Identifying Different Types of Variables that Describe Collectivities

It is important to distinguish different types of data that describe collectivities like countries and cities. This exercise involves the examination of two data sets that accompany this book—COUNTRIESdepr and STATESdepr—using SPSS to identify different types of variables. To access the exercise, go to the DEPR Web Page, click on Web Exercises, Chapter 11, then on Exercise 11.1—Identifying Different Types of Variables That Describe Collectivities

Key Points

There are six types of data that describe geographical regions or organizations:

- *Census data* are collected from the entire population within a geographic area and are reported in summary form.
- *Governmental and quasi-governmental statistics* are reported by government agencies other than the census and by professional organizations.
- *Survey data* are summarized for geographical regions or organizations.

- *Summaries of media content* are transmitted within a geographical area or within an organization.
- *Event statistics* summarize events, such as crimes, that occurred during a specified time period within a geographical area.
- *Judgmental data* are constructed from the opinions of experts about the characteristics of geographical areas or groups.

Sources of Published Data that Describe Collectivities

The sources of data that describe collectivities are so numerous that we cannot even begin to name them all. Much is still available only in hard-copy form, but increasingly you can find the data you need online. Some of the political science Web pages covered in Chapter 4 are especially useful portals for locating data-rich Web sites. While we are sure there are a number of good starting places for your search for online data, we find Robert Duval's Web page to be especially valuable. Also helpful is the data source search engine found at the Social Science Data Collection at the University of California at San Diego. Links to all of the sites mentioned (and more) in the discussion that follows can be found on the DEPR Web site.

Characteristics of Governments and Event Data for Nations.   The primary source of data for demographic characteristics of nations is the United Nations. A lot of data is available online from the UN Web page. Hard-copy volumes include the *Demographic Yearbook, Statistical Yearbook,* and *UNESCO Statistical Yearbook.* UN data concerning human development and human rights are available in the *Human Development Report.* A somewhat dated, but still useful, volume that contains social, economic, and political indicators is the *World Handbook of Political and Social Indicators,* by Charles Lewis Taylor and David A. Jodice (New Haven: Yale University Press, 1983). Each year the Center for Comparative Political Research of the State University of New York at Binghamton and the Council on Foreign Relations publishes the *Political Handbook of the World.* This volume has a great deal of political information about nations. Up-to-date country profiles and data can be found in the Central Intelligence Agency's *World Fact Book.*

Worthwhile sources of judgmental data about nations are Freedom House, a non-profit organization that annually rates the nations of the world in terms of a number of democratic characteristics, and the Heritage Foundation, which rates nations in terms of economic freedom. The World Bank provides economic, and some political, data in its hard-copy volumes *World Development Report* and *World Tables* and at its Web site. The best source for data on military expenditures is Ruth Leger Sivard's *World Military and Social Expenditures* (Leesburg, VA: WMSE Publications). Current data on election results, both participation and outcomes, are difficult to obtain. A good source of historical data is *The International Almanac of Electoral History* by Thomas T. Mackie and Richard Rose (Washington, DC: CQ Press, 1991). Data on electoral participation can be found in *Voter Turnout from 1945–Date: A Global Report on Political Participation,* published by the International Institute for Democracy and Electoral Assistance. The *International Relations Data Site,* created and maintained by Paul Hensel of Florida State University, is a worthwhile index of data with numerous links to data concerning wars, treaties, alliances, and international trade.

Data on the United States and Its Geographical Subdivisions.   The most comprehensive source of data that describe American states, counties, cities, and congressional districts is the U.S. Census. The best place to begin a search for key variables is the *Statistical Abstract of the United States* that is issued each year by the Department of Commerce. Also important are the *State and Metropolitan Area Data Book* and the *County and City Data Book.* The *Book of the States* published by the Council on State Governments is full of useful tables describing state political characteristics and policy outcomes. *State Rankings: A Statistical View of the 50 United States* (Lawrence, KS: Morgan Quitno Corp., 1990–Date) and Congressional Quarterly's *State Fact Finder* (Washington, DC: CQ Press, 1993–Date) are also good sources for state data. In addition to the U.S. Census, the *Municipal Year Book,* published by the International City Managers Association, has lots of data about urban areas. The Department of Housing and Urban Development provides access to a large amount of social, economic, and crime data about cities at its *State of the Cities* Web site. The results of federal elections for the U.S. House and Senate since 1849 are reported in the *Guide to U.S. Elections. America Votes* has published both federal and some state-level election results since 1952. Both are published by Congressional Quarterly, Inc. Data on crime in cities, counties, and states are reported each year in the FBI's *Uniform Crime Reports.* In addition to governmental and quasi-governmental sources of data, some private groups rate the states by key characteristics and policies. The online newspaper *Education Week* grades the states on support for education and levels of educational achievement. *Governing.com,* another online newspaper, grades cities on government performance.

Data on Political Organizations.   Data for describing political organizations is a bit more difficult to locate and prepare for analysis. The Census Bureau publishes a

To the Web

Census of Governments with data about federal agencies as well as state and local governments. Kenneth Janda's *Political Parties: A Cross-National Survey* (New York: Free Press, 1980) is dated but still a very worthwhile source of data on political parties. Information about interest groups that is accessible and ready for analysis is very scarce. Two sources on political action committees (PACs) that provide some information are Congressional Quarterly's *Federal PACs Directory* (Washington, DC: CQ Press, 1998–Date) and *The PAC Directory* (Cambridge, MA: Ballinger Pub. Co., 1982–Date). In recent years political scientists have given a great deal of attention to nongovernmental organizations (NGOs). The United Nations keeps a database of information about the organizations that have consultative status with its Economic and Social Council.

Online Sources of Data That Describe Collectivities

There are numerous online sources of published data. All of the Web sites we have discussed in this section are linked to the DEPR Web page, along with many other sources. To access these linkages, go to the **DEPR Web Page,** click on **Web Links, Chapter 11,** then on **Online Sources of Data That Describe Collectivities.**

■ Cautions About Using Published Data Describing Collectivities

Missing Data.   You should always be concerned about missing data. When respondents in a survey refuse to answer certain questions, for example, you have to wonder whether your findings based on the data are affected. You can only hope that the missing responses are distributed randomly and not related to the variables included in your analysis. Missing data can be an important problem when collecting from published sources because you rely on others to complete your data set. Data can be missing simply because of unavailability or reasons that may be political. For example, some countries might not collect data on ownership of televisions, so it would be impossible to obtain a figure on televisions per capita. Likewise, some countries might not want to reveal their military expenditures for a particular year. As you collect data that describe geographical units of analysis, you should note the gaps in your data matrix to see if the missing data fall in a pattern or seem to be distributed randomly. If there is a great deal of missing data for a particular indicator, you should probably try to find an alternative measure for that variable. If there is a pattern to the missing data (for example, authoritarian regimes not reporting defense expenditures), you have to consider whether analysis of an incomplete data set will distort your findings.

There are several ways to treat missing data during analysis. You can exclude cases with missing data casewise—that is, individual cases are excluded (ignored) only for analyses of variables where values are missing. You can also exclude listwise—cases with missing values are excluded from all analyses. The advantage of casewise exclusion of missing data is that you retain a larger number of cases, but since different analyses will be done on different cases (and total numbers), there will be a loss of comparability between analyses. Listwise deletion of cases ensures that all analyses will be conducted on the same cases. It may result in a much smaller data set, however, since a case is excluded if it is missing a value on *any* variable included in the analysis. You can also replace missing values with some type of estimate, such as the average value calculated from all the cases that contain data on the variable. There are other more sophisticated ways to develop estimates for missing data that are beyond the scope of this book.

Ecological Fallacy.   The analysis of data that describe collectivities can lead to errors in inference. An **ecological fallacy** occurs when relationships found between characteristics of groups are used for drawing conclusions about individuals. It is tempting to make inferences that result in an ecological fallacy because many variables in data sets where units of analysis are states, cities, or countries describe aggregated characteristics of individuals. For example, a well-established generalization about individuals is that people with higher levels of education are more likely to participate in elections by voting. This generalization has been confirmed many times using survey data. If we collected data for the fifty states on the proportion of the adult population who had completed college and the proportion of the eligible population who voted in the last gubernatorial election, we would likely find a positive relationship between the two variables. The proper conclusion we could draw from such a finding would be that *state*s with a highly educated population tend to be those with a large proportion of citizens who turn out to vote. We could not conclude from data with states as the units of analysis that "people with college degrees are more likely to vote."

A good example of the commission of an ecological fallacy is a classic study by James Q. Wilson and Edward C. Banfield on the concepts of "public-regardingness" and "private-regardingness" as motivations for voting behavior. Public-regardingness was defined as voting behavior that reflected a concern for the community, while private-regardingness reflected a concern with self and family. Banfield and Wilson chose wards (electoral districts) in cities such as Cleveland and Chicago for their units of analysis. They examined relationships between aggregated background characteristics from the census such as the "proportion of citizens of foreign stock" and ward voting patterns for expenditures on city services such as parks and veteran's bonuses. They concluded that voters with certain characteristics (upper-income Anglo Saxons) were more public-regarding in their voting decisions than other groups (Poles and Czechs). [12] Banfield and Wilson were interested in relating personal social

To the Web

Exercise 11.2—Collecting, Organizing, and Coding Data from the 2000 U.S. Census

This exercise involves collecting, organizing, and analyzing data describing the states. The source of the data is the 2000 U.S. Census. You will navigate the U.S. Census Web site and choose some variables that describe the states. You will then create a codebook, enter the data onto a coding form, transfer the data to an SPSS file, and complete a simple statistical analysis that summarizes your data set. To access the exercise, go to the **DEPR Web Page**, click on **Web Exercises, Chapter 11**, then on **Exercise 11.2—Collecting, Organizing, and Coding Data from the 2000 U.S. Census.**

characteristics of voters to personal orientations toward their community (public-regardingness), but they inappropriately inferred from aggregate data a relationship between individual social background characteristics and an important attitude.

Published Data on People

Studies of the mass public almost always involve the use of surveys. While we can point to studies of party leaders, lobbyists, and state legislators that employ surveys, political elites are often reluctant to complete surveys that ask them to indicate their background characteristics, attitudes, and behavior. Since elites are prominent people, however, their backgrounds and behaviors are often a matter of public record. Unfortunately, the process of collecting, organizing, and managing the data from published sources that can be used to connect social background to behavior is very cumbersome. The collection of background data generally means perusing biographical directories and coding information on forms before putting it all into electronic format. With some exceptions, the collection of behavioral data requires a similar amount of work. Still, quantitative research on the behavior of political elites is worth the effort. Most political scientists would agree that elites should receive more research attention because of their impact on public policy and, ultimately, the lives of citizens.

Sources of Published Data That Describe Political Elites

Political Candidates.　With the continuing development of the Web, it is easier to locate biographical data about candidates for office in the United States. Virtually every candidate for higher office, such as Congress and governor, maintains his or her own Web site that can be located through portals, such as the one provided by *Project Vote-Smart,* or by using a search engine. Information on candidate fundraising and expenditures is provided by the Federal Elections Commission.

Members of Congress.　Biographical information on members of Congress can be found in the biennial volumes *Politics in America* and the *Almanac of American Politics.* In addition to the biographical information, these volumes include data on the characteristics of Congressional districts and states, member votes on key roll calls, and ratings by interest groups. Most of the information found in these two volumes, plus the results of all roll call votes in Congress, can also be found online at the Web site maintained by the clerk of the U.S. House of Representatives and the U.S. Senate Web site.

Roll call votes are reported in the *Congressional Quarterly Weekly Reports* and compiled at the end of each year in the *Congressional Quarterly Almanac.*

Members of the Judiciary.   The texts of opinions and voting on decisions of the U.S. Supreme Court are found in the *United States Reports* (U.S. Government Printing Office) and summaries of decisions rendered by lower federal courts and state courts in the *Decennial Digest.* Online sources of court decisions, however, are often more accessible. We recommend the U.S. Supreme Court Multimedia Database, maintained by Jerry Goldman of Northwestern University, and the Cornell University Law School Legal Information Database. Biographical information about current and past Supreme Court justices and caseloads can be found at the Court's Web site.

Presidents and Members of the Executive Branch.   There is not a great deal of quantitative information about the presidency and the executive branch. Some hard-copy sources of data include Congressional Quarterly's *Guide to the Presidency,* Joseph Nathan Kane's *Facts About the Presidents,* and Lynn Ragsdale's *Vital Statistics on the Presidency.* Robert Sobel has edited some very functional biographical volumes, including the *Biographical Directory of the United States Executive Branch, 1774–1989* and *Biographical Directory of the Council of Economic Advisers.* Background information about some U.S. ambassadors can be found in *Notable U.S. Ambassadors Since 1775: A Biographical Dictionary,* edited by Cathal J. Nolan.

Elites Outside of the United States.   There are various biographical directories that provide information about elites in many areas of social and political life. A useful source of lists of world rulers and information about their terms in office is Rulers.org. Biographies of world leaders can be found at a Web site called World Statesmen, while those for international women leaders can be found at the Web site Women World Leaders. One group of hard-copy directories that is widely used is the *Who's Who* series (for example, *Who's Who in Africa South of the Sahara*). Online encyclopedias can also provide worthwhile biographical information. Try the online *Encyclopedia Britannica* or *Encyclopedia.com.* The parliaments in most countries now maintain Web pages with links to the votes and biographies of members. The British House of Commons site has plentiful information about member characteristics and voting patterns.

To the Web

Online Sources of Data About Individuals

There are many additional Web sites that contain data about political elites. All of the Web sites mentioned in this section are linked to the DEPR Web page, along with many other sources. To access these linkages, go to the **DEPR Web Page,** click on **Web Links, Chapter 11,** then on **Online Sources of Data About Individuals.**

Media Messages: Content Analysis

The classic question for communications scholars, which is equally relevant for those of us who are interested in politics, is "Who says what to whom with what effect?" [13] The data collection technique appropriate for answering the "what" part of the question is called content analysis and has been defined as "a multipurpose research method developed specifically for investigating any problem in which the content of communication serves as the basis of inference." [14] Content analysis is truly a multipurpose method because it can be applied to any form of recorded communication: books, newspapers, magazines, television programs, poems, paintings, presidential speeches, legal documents such as Supreme Court opinions, Web sites, radio talk shows, campaign advertisements, political party platforms, letters, government documents, and political posters. Any recorded message can be objectively, systematically, and quantitatively analyzed.

The content analysis of recorded messages can be used in its own right or in conjunction with other means of data collection to test a diversity of hypotheses. For example, Jisuk Woo was interested in how Korean television news "framed" the Korean presidential elections of 1987 and 1992. Through a systematic examination of the themes of election news stories, he found that the television networks framed events to emphasize the ruling party's vision of eliminating dissenting perspectives and narrowing the range of discussion. [15] Content analysis is also used to test hypotheses relating characteristics of the source or communicator with the message. Darrell West and others, as an example, have related the content of political campaign television advertisements (positive versus negative or policy versus personal) to the characteristics of the candidates that sponsored them. [16] Finally, a major concern of studies of political communication has been the effects of communication content on political attitudes and behavior. In this genre, Thomas Patterson has found that unfavorable news stories about political candidates tend to produce negative opinions of candidates among voters. [17]

We begin with a brief overview of the process of content analysis and some examples of how it is applied to different topics. Content analysis usually begins with the formulation of a research question and the definition of variables. If you are interested in comparing the ideological content of editorial positions taken by the *New York Times* with those of another newspaper, you must come up with an operational definition of editorial liberalism-conservatism. Once your variables are defined, you will develop a coding form to collect data about the editorials, such as the date published, the substantive issue, and the ideological position taken. Next, since you cannot read every editorial ever published, you will have to decide on how you will sample issues of the newspapers and the editorials within. You must decide to limit your reading to specific dates and perhaps take a random sample of editorials. Your data will be collected by reading the sampled editorials and recording the values for your variables. Finally, you will put your data into machine-readable format and test your hypothesis, using appropriate statistical software. As you will see from the following examples of research, regardless of the medium studied, content analysis follows these basic steps.

Three Examples of Content Analysis

Elite Discourse During the Cold War.   During the Cold War, did presidential rhetoric about nuclear weapons and the former Soviet Union influence the growth of protest movements? Or did protest movements concerning national security issues influence presidential rhetoric? To answer these questions David S. Meyer conducted content analyses for the years 1945 to 1960 of presidential State of the Union Addresses and articles published in the professional journals *Foreign Affairs* and *Scientific American* to determine how discussions among elites of national security issues were "framed" by social movements and protest. He analyzed *New York Times* articles for the same years to determine the degree of coverage of nuclear weapons opposition. As he read the presidential addresses and articles in the journals, he added a point for the presence of statements that confronted the Soviet Union or emphasized nuclear weapons, while subtracting a point for conciliatory statements or mentions of nuclear arms control. With this scale, he was able to characterize the rhetoric in each year as "Cold War" (confrontational), "Common Security" (conciliatory), or "Managed Rivalry" (confrontational, tempered by offers to negotiate). In analyzing relationships between political climate and rhetoric over the years of the Cold War, Meyer found that presidential rhetoric both influenced protest and dissent and was, in turn, influenced by them. When the president's rhetoric emphasized the Cold War in a State of the Union Address, it was usually followed by protests (indicated by the number of *New York Times* stories and dissenting articles in *Foreign Affairs*). On the other hand, presidential rhetoric in State of the Union Messages seemed to move in the direction of an emphasis on "Common Security" in response to a political climate of protest and articles published in *Foreign Affairs* and *Scientific American*. While the relationships were not crystal clear, Meyer was able to show through the use of content analysis that political climates and expert opinion influenced presidential statements and vice versa. [18]

Cops, Suspects, and Race on "Reality" Television Programs.   Do those popular "reality-based" police shows on television actually reflect the real world of law enforcement? Mary Beth Oliver was interested in how shows such as *Cops, America's Most Wanted,* and *Top Cops* represented criminal suspects, police, and their behaviors. More specifically, she was interested in portrayals of race and aggressive behavior of characters. She chose to content-analyze five programs recorded during the fall of 1991: *America's Most Wanted, Cops, Top Cops, FBI, the Untold Story,* and *American Detective.* Her units of analysis were characters who appeared on the programs. Five undergraduate coders viewed the programs and recorded the following information about each character that appeared: gender, race (white, black, Hispanic, Asian, or other), character portrayal (police or suspect), and whether one of four types of aggressive behavior (verbal aggression, threat of physical aggression, unarmed physical aggression, or armed physical aggression) was inflicted or received. Oliver found that whites were more likely to be portrayed as police, and blacks and Hispanics were more likely to be portrayed as suspects. Police were more likely to engage in aggressive behavior than suspects. Furthermore, blacks and Hispanics were more likely to be the victims of aggressive behavior on the part of police than white suspects. Coding the types of crimes portrayed on the programs indicated an emphasis on violent crimes and police success in their resolution. These findings, based on the content analysis, led Oliver to suggest that viewing reality-based police shows might be associated with unrealistic attitudes about the nature of crime in society, police effectiveness, and exaggerated estimates of the proportion of minorities who are engaged in criminal activity. [19]

Characteristics of Countries with Elaborate Parliamentary Web Sites. Earlier, when we discussed the types of data that can describe geographical areas, we mentioned a content analysis of parliamentary Web sites conducted by Pippa Norris. Her study deserves a closer examination. Norris is interested in the possibility that the Internet might revive democracy by providing increased opportunities for citizens to gather information about politics and communicate with government officials. With the use of search engines she found that 98 out of 178 nations worldwide had parliamentary Web sites. As you would probably expect, democratic countries and those with a high degree of human development were most likely to have such sites. She then carefully read the material on each of the sites and classified the content on a yes/no basis according to the presence of forty-eight types of content (including complete constitutional text, parliament's e-mail address, opportunity for sending feedback, and a full record of parliamentary proceedings). After coding each country for the forty-eight types of content on its parliamentary Web site, she created two indexes, one measuring the extent to which Web sites provided information and the other how strongly communication was emphasized. She then examined relationships between the levels of democratization of countries, human development, and the extent to which parliamentary Web sites provided information and opportunities for communication. She concluded that democratic countries were more likely to provide both

To the Web

Examples of Research Using Content Analysis

There are some very useful online annotated bibliographies of research using content analysis, as well as a listserv where contemporary research using content analysis is discussed and reports of recent studies are reviewed. To access some of these resources, go to the **DEPR Web Page**, click on **Web Links, Chapter 11**, then on **Examples of Research Using Content Analysis.**

information and opportunities for communication. Human development and the size of the population seemed to have no influence on the content of Web sites. Not surprisingly, in countries where a relatively large proportion of the population is online parliamentary Web sites provide more information. This is a good example of a cutting edge study using content analysis to suggest that use of the Internet may change the way political communication will take place in representative democracies. [20]

The Process of Content Analysis

Specification of the Research Question and the Population.   As with all methods of data collection, you must begin content analysis with a specification of a research question and the population or universe about which you want to generalize. If the question is "Are Democratic or Republican candidates more likely to sponsor negative campaign advertisements?," you would consider how to limit your question and the resulting population to which you want to generalize. Do you want to focus on candidates for national office? Should you limit your analysis to particular years? While you will want to generalize to candidates running for differing offices at various times, you will need to narrow your focus to go about collecting data. Recorded campaign commercials would be most accessible for candidates for the most visible offices, such as president, Congress, and governor, and the most complete compilations of campaign commercials would focus on recent years.

Taking a Sample of Units of Observation and Recording Units.   In Chapter 9, we discussed the ways in which units of analysis can be sampled from a larger population or universe. In content analysis the idea of units of analysis can be confusing, and sampling can occur at more than one stage of the research. A distinction is often made between **units of observation** and **recording units,** which in some instances are one and the same. For example, Norris sampled parliamentary Web sites as units of observation and also treated them as recording units when she collected data about the types of information they included. On the other hand, in her study of reality police shows, Oliver sampled television programs as units of observation, but she collected information about the characters that appeared on the programs. In Oliver's analysis the characters were the recording units. Sampling of units of observation is often necessary in content analyses because, in most instances, we cannot view every television program or campaign commercial, read every newspaper article, or listen to every radio program in the population we have defined.

All of the methods discussed in Chapter 9 can be used to sample units of observation. We could list and take a simple random sample or a systematic sample of editorials published in the past year in the United States in newspapers with circulations of more than 50,000. Additionally, we could stratify the sample so that every state in the United States is represented. Most often a judgmental or convenience samples of units of observation is taken. That was the approach taken by Oliver when she chose to have her coders view all of the "reality-based" police programs aired during the fall of 1991. Meyer was also engaged in judgmental sampling when he chose to read and analyze the State of the Union Addresses delivered by presidents during the Cold War. His judgment was that State of the Union Addresses were representative of presidential discourse. A study of campaign commercials would also require sampling, probably with an emphasis on availability of recordings.

After you decide how you will sample units of observation, you must choose and sample recording units. As we already noted, units of observation may serve as recording units. If you were to pursue your study of party affiliation and negative campaign commercials, the commercials themselves would serve as both units of observation and recording units. However, it is very common in content analysis to sample units of observation but choose different recording units. Recording units can include words, sentences, paragraphs, pages, or themes in written communications like magazine articles, books, or political party platforms. They can be segments, stories, or people portrayed on television news broadcasts, characters on television entertainment shows, or images in paintings or political cartoons. Once units of observation are sampled, recording units can be sampled using the familiar methods. Thus, sampling can occur at different stages, beginning, for example, with news magazines, then articles in the sampled magazines, and then themes found in the articles. Content analyses commonly include all of the recording units found in units of observation. Oliver chose to gather information about all of the characters portrayed in her sample of "reality-based" television programs. Likewise, Meyer decided to examine all of the articles published in *Foreign Affairs* during the Cold War.

Defining Variables and Categories of Content.   Establishing categories of media content is essentially a process of conceptualization and operationalization. Variables have to be clearly defined and the rules regarding measurement plainly specified. For the purposes of constructing categories, Holsti distinguishes between manifest and latent content. **Manifest content** is visible surface content that easily lends itself to the development of categories and counting, such as a content analysis of campaign advertisements that counts the number of times the opponent's name is mentioned. Meyer analyzed manifest content when he counted the number of stories dealing with protests of nuclear weapons each year. The advantage of restricting content analyses to manifest content is increased reliability. Since messages are easily observed and counted, there would likely be little disagreement among coders. **Latent content** refers to the deeper meanings of media messages. You might want to conduct a content analysis of newscasts to determine whether network anchormen Dan Rather, Tom Brokow, or Peter Jennings is the most liberal. To undertake such an analysis you would have to carefully define liberal-conservatism in such a way as to produce agreement among coders and those who might read your results. Clearly, focusing on the latent content of communications is more interesting, but since the focus is on the meaning of messages, there are likely to be disagreements among coders about how those message should be categorized. The result is a threat to reliability.

Questions for Thought and Discussion

Suppose you are interested in testing the hypothesis that Republican candidates for the U.S. House of Representatives are more likely than Democrats to produce and air negative campaign advertisements. Develop conceptual and operational definitions of "negative" and "positive" campaign ads so your coders will be accurate in their classifications.

Like all processes of measurement, classifications must be exhaustive and mutually exclusive—there must be a category or value for every message, and no message should fit into more than one category. Different levels of measurement can be used in operationalizing variables representing aspects of content. In a content analysis of campaign advertisements, you might record whether the sponsor is a Democrat or Republican. This would be an example of measurement at the nominal level. A five-point scale ranging from very positive to very negative for coders to use to characterize the content of advertisements would be measurement at the ordinal level. Finally, a count of the number of times the opponent's name is mentioned is the interval/ratio measurement.

Developing an Instrument for Recording Data.   The collection and categorization of media messages is essentially a coding operation. The goal is to develop a coding form that is easy for coders to use in order to reduce the number of errors. The coding forms should facilitate the ease of transferring data to a machine-readable format. If your content analysis focuses on the manifest content of print media and involves simple classification and counting, your coding form should resemble a data matrix with recording units listed by row and variables by column. Figure 11.2 shows a coding form that might be used to study changes in the amount of attention given to international versus domestic news by *Time Magazine* over the past fifty years. Note that the data can easily be transferred to an SPSS data matrix or a spreadsheet.

If the measurement of one or more of your variables involves categorizing latent content from a electronic medium such as television, it makes sense to develop a coding form for each recording unit. A form for each recording unit can be precoded to ease

Figure 11.2
Coding Form for a Study of Magazine Articles

Magazine ID	Magazine 1. *Time* 2. *Newsweek*	Publication Year	# Articles/ Domestic News	# Articles/ International News	Column Inches Domestic News	Column Inches International News

To the Web

Exercise 11.3—Analyzing the Content of Newspaper Web Sites

In this exercise you will conduct a content analysis of newspaper Web sites. Your focus will be on testing the hypothesis that "national newspapers" report more international news than "nonnational newspapers." You operationally define "international" and "domestic" news, examine a sample of Web sites, and record the data necessary to test the hypothesis. To access Exercise 11.3, go to the **DEPR Web Page,** click on **Web Exercises, Chapter 11,** then on **Exercise 11.3—Analyzing the Content of Newspaper Web Sites.**

transfer to an electronic medium. Figure 11.3 shows a coding form that might be used for each of the television campaign commercials included in a sample. Generally, the more coders that are used, the better. A proportion of messages should be coded by more than one coder to establish reliability, especially if latent content is being coded. No content analysis should proceed without a thorough pretest which will reveal any problems with the understanding of definitions of variables and coding procedures. The pretest will also provide guidance in developing coding forms that are easiest to use.

Any discussion of content analyses must include the contributions of technological advances to the method. Optical scanners, new software, and search engines have created opportunities to use computers to conduct content analysis. Scanners can convert hardcopy texts to electronic formats so the text can be analyzed using software such as *Diction 5.0,* a text analysis program that can search out and determine the tone of

Figure 11.3
Coding Form for a Study of Televised Campaign Commercials

Advertisement Number _____

Sponsor: _____ 1. Democratic Candidate _____ 2. Republican Candidate _____ 3. Other Group

Office: _____ 1. U.S. Senate _____ 2. U.S. House _____ 3. Governor _____ 4. Other

Major Substantive Emphasis:
_____ 1. Personal Qualities of Candidate
_____ 2. Personal Qualities of Opponent
_____ 3. General Policy Position of Candidate
_____ 4. General Policy Position of Opponent
_____ 5. Specific Policy Position of Candidate
_____ 6. Specific Policy Position of Opponent
_____ 7. Other

Overall Tone:

Negative _____ _____ _____ _____ _____ _____ _____ Positive
       1   2   3   4   5   6   7

a verbal passage. A very useful Web site called *Content Analysis Resources* lists more than twenty-five software programs designed to conduct content analyses. It is also possible to use your Web browser and search engines to generate word counts for documents and to determine the proximity of words and phrases within documents. Clearly, content analysis will increasingly become a more sophisticated method of data collection and analysis.

Cautions Concerning Reliability and Validity

A major concern for those who use content analysis is the reliability of the subjective responses of coders to media messages. Reliability is a special problem when latent content is categorized and coders have to focus on "meanings." When the focus is on manifest content and coders are concerned with measuring time or space, counting words, paragraphs, or stories reliability is a lesser concern. As noted previously, the most effective way to increase confidence in the reliability of the results of content analyses is to establish **intercoder reliability,** which exists when at least two coders reach a consensus about the categories in which media messages should be placed. If more than one coder classifies the same messages, then it is possible to use statistical processes to measure the extent to which they agree on "meanings." The creation of clear definitions of categories and the proper training of coders, using a large number of examples, usually increases intercoder reliability.

You will recall that issues of validity concern the extent to which your indicators actually reflect the concepts you intend to measure. Implicit in content analysis is the idea that media messages reflect the real and intended views of the communicator. The problem is that communications are not always reflective of communicator views or intentions. We all know that candidates for office will communicate messages that do not reflect their views but may enhance their goal of winning office. We also know that media may distort some messages so the resulting communication is not consistent with the intentions of the communicator. A common tactic used in campaign advertisements is to distort statements made by opponents. Always ask yourself if the content being studied really reflects the views and intentions of communicators.

Conclusion

In this chapter we have focused on the collection of data from published sources. Many public and private organizations collect and report data that can be used to test hypotheses about politics. Published data are available that describe geographical entities such as countries and cities, organizations such as political parties and interest groups, and individuals such as legislators. These data are often available at little or no financial cost but may involve considerable time and effort to gather and prepare for analysis. While published data are available, you should be aware that there may be problems with validity and reliability. Still, we urge you not to overlook published data for your research because collecting your own data through surveys or other methods is usually not feasible for beginning researchers.

We also focused on the analysis of communication content in this chapter. Although content analysis is not as widely used by political scientists as other methods of data collection, it is very revealing for answering questions concerning the nature of political communication. It can also be used in conjunction with other procedures such as survey research to examine the effects of media messages. Content analysis is an economical and time-efficient procedure that can be employed by beginning researchers.

Summary of the Main Points

- A great deal of diverse published data useful for testing hypotheses about politics are available for little or no cost.
- Published data are available that describe geographical units of analysis such as countries and cities, organizations such as political parties, and individuals such as legislators.

- The types of data that describe geographical units of include census data, governmental and quasi-governmental statistics, survey data, summaries of communication content, event data, and judgmental data.
- Ecological fallacy refers to instances where analysts inappropriately infer characteristics of individuals from data that describe collectivities, such as counties or political parties.
- Content analysis is the collection, organization, and analysis of recorded media messages.
- Doing content analysis includes specifying a research question and theoretical population, sampling units of observation and recording units, defining variables and categories of content, and developing an instrument for recording communications content.
- Intercoder reliability is important to establish in content analysis because of a concern that coders might interpret and categorize the same content in different ways.

Terms Introduced

aggregate data
census data
content analysis
ecological fallacy
event statistics
intercoder reliability
judgmental data
latent content

macro level of analysis
manifest content
micro level of analysis
recording units
summation variables
syntality variables
units of observation

Selected Readings

Gurr, Ted Robert. *Politimetrics: An Introduction to Quantitative Macropolitics.* Englewood Cliffs, NJ: Prentice-Hall, 1972.

Holsti, Ole R. *Content Analysis for the Social Sciences and Humanities.* Reading, MA: Addison-Wesley, 1969.

Krippendorff, Klaus. *Content Analysis: An Introduction to Its Methodology.* Beverly Hills, CA: Sage Publications, 1980.

Lee, Raymond M. *Unobtrusive Methods in Social Research.* Buckingham: Open University Press, 2000.

Stewart, David W. *Secondary Research* Beverly Hills, CA: Sage Publications, 1984.

Webb, Eugene.J., Donald T. Campbell, and Richard D. Schwartz. *Nonreactive Measures in the Social Sciences.* Boston: Houghton Mifflin, 1981.

Weber, Robert P. *Basic Content Analysis.* Beverly Hills, CA: Sage Publications, 1985.

Activities

Activity 11.1
Location of Data from Published Sources

In this chapter we reported a large number of data sources. Data can be found in hard-copy publications in the references section in libraries and on Web sites created by numerous governmental, quasi-governmental, and private organizations. Here is a list of variables that describe units of analysis. Locate the data described and write down the precise location (bibliographic reference or Web address).

1. The percentage of the vote received in the most recent election by members of the House of Representatives
2. The most current data on life expectancy of citizens in African countries
3. The number of homicides that occurred in Californian cities in 1998
4. Roll call votes in the U.S. Senate in the past five years dealing with an environmental issue
5. The most recent data describing the number of telephones per capita for countries
6. Which states have set term limits for their governors
7. Judgmental data describing democratic characteristics of countries
8. The vote received by the two major parties in the most recent election in a country in Europe
9. The percentage of citizens who hold bachelors degrees in each of the counties in Montana
10. How many presidents previously served in the U.S. Senate

Activity 11.2
Preparing to Collect and Analyze Data

Suppose you were interested in determining the characteristics of states with divided governments (the governorship and at least one house of the state legislature are controlled by different parties). You need to collect data for the states including the following variables: party affiliation of the governor, party that controls the lower house of the legislature, party that controls the upper house of the legislature, regional location of the state, percentage of the state's adult population that has not completed high school, the percentage of the state's population who live in urban areas, and the percentage who are employed in manufacturing. Create a codebook and a recording form that can be used to collect and organize your data. Locate sources for these data and record them on your coding form. Create an SPSS data set (see Chapter 8).

Activity 11.3
A Content Analysis Project

Consider the following hypothesis.

> "Female characters in television drama programs are less likely to occupy positions that are subordinate to male characters than female characters in situation comedies."

Develop a research design using content analysis to test the hypothesis. Describe how you would sample observation units of analysis and recording units. Conceptualize your key variables and create coding categories. Develop a coding form to collect the data necessary to test the hypothesis. View at least three television dramas and three situation comedies. Code the information necessary to test the hypothesis. Write a brief essay indicating whether your data support the hypothesis.

Chapter 12

Studying Only a Few Cases: Intensive Approaches

Learning Objectives

After completion of this chapter, students should be able to do the following:

Explain the fundamental distinction between extensive and intensive analysis.

Understand the logic of experimentation in controlling extraneous independent variables.

Understand and explain the differences between internal and external validity.

Distinguish among different experimental designs and quasi-experiments.

Explain Q-technique as an approach to understanding political attitudes and dispositions and distinguish it from extensive approaches.

Understand what a focus group is and how it is employed in empirical research.

Extensive and Intensive Approaches

In Chapter 2 we pointed out that a goal of social science is to develop generalizations that are useful for explaining human behavior. The greater the applicability of the generalizations that we develop with respect to cases (people, cities, states, countries, newspapers, etc.) and with respect to time, the greater their utility for understanding the social and political world. Since we wish our generalizations to be extensive in applicability, it would seem to make sense that the research we conduct to develop them should be based on large numbers. Indeed, we showed in Chapter 9 that large samples permitted more accurate generalizations about populations. Social science opinion would certainly come down on the side of analyzing large numbers, but in this chapter we will point to some fundamental distinctions between extensive and intensive approaches to political analysis and show that the intensive study of small numbers of cases can contribute greatly to our knowledge of political behavior.

Intensive analysis in political science can be traced to Harold Lasswell, who was greatly influenced by psychoanalytic theory developed by Sigmund Freud. More than forty years ago Lasswell distinguished between extensive and intensive observational standpoints. [1] **Extensive approaches** are distinguished by their cursoriness—the contact between the researcher and respondent is brief, relatively little information is obtained, and responses are simple. A survey project involving a large representative sample is the best example of an extensive approach. A relatively small amount of information is obtained from a large number of people in a brief period of time in the form of responses to simple questions with prestructured answers. In contrast, the **intensive approach** involves researcher contact with a small number of respondents over an extended period of time where a wide variety of information is obtained. The intensive approach is usually epitomized by the in-depth psychological interview, but there are a variety of approaches that emphasize close examination of only a few subjects.

Studies of single cases or a small number of cases are often seen as useful only for purposes of exploring new hypotheses or when more extensive studies are not possible. Furthermore, some would argue that their findings can only be suggestive but not generalized. We believe, however, that extensive and intensive approaches can be complementary and not conflict with each other. Robert Yin, an advocate of the study of *single* cases, argues that a focus on a small number of cases is most appropriate when trying to answer the "how" or "why" questions that are at the heart of explanation.[2] Steven Brown argues forcefully that "extensive methods are eminently suited for counting things and computing proportions which exist in the universe at large, and there is no denying that science made a real advance when its practitioners learned to count. Intensive methods, however, are best equipped to determine which things are worth counting in the first place." [3] Depth in the understanding of political behavior is most likely to come from the intensive analysis of individuals and events. Brown concludes that "the number of cases one chooses to observe depends for its scientific credibility on the conceptualization of the problem, the structure of the observation, the significance of the cases chosen, the use to which the results are to be put." [4] Intensive approaches may be more appropriate for understanding complex human behavior, whereas extensive approaches may be more appropriate for generalizing, but those goals do not seem inconsistent to us.

Among the intensive approaches that have been used in political science over the years, we will focus, for purposes of illustration, on case studies, experimentation, Q-technique, and focus groups. Our view of what constitutes an intensive approach is broader than those that focus on just a few cases examined with respect to a very large number of characteristics over a long period of time. The analysis of data from in-depth interviews and life histories certainly is consistent with our definition, but we also include other approaches where a small number of respondents are observed closely. An example is an experiment, where just a few variables are measured for a small sample of subjects, but manipulations are possible and control of extraneous factors taken into account in ways that are not possible when extensive approaches, such as field studies using survey research, are used. When you conclude this chapter we hope you appreciate that a comprehensive science of politics requires both extensive and intensive approaches.

Case Studies

Case studies involve examining, usually in considerable detail, a single case on only one occasion. Examples of topics for case studies include individual political groups or movements [5], labor unions, [6] cities [7], and political processes. [8] At one time, case studies were considered to be a poor way to conduct empirical research because the approach emphasized description and largely ignored attempts at explanation. They were seen as unscientific because using an individual case for study precluded comparisons necessary for testing hypotheses. While they might provide rich, detailed descriptions of events, case studies were seen as contributing to a wider empirical approach only by generating tentative hypotheses for later testing with more complete, comparative data. In addition, they were seen as less rigorous than other types of research designs because the conditions under which the data were collected and the operationalization of the variables were often highly individualized and not always made explicit, making replication difficult. And as with all small sample research, there was concern to what extent any findings could be generalized beyond the case under study. [9]

The case study approach, if done with care and within a theoretical framework, can make an important contribution to the empirical study of political behavior: explanation. As defined by Robert Yin, a case study is an empirical inquiry "that investigates a contemporary phenomenon within its real-life context; when the boundaries between phenomenon and context are not clearly evident; and in which multiple sources of evidence are used." [10] In this sense, case studies allow an inquiry to reflect a more complete environment within which events under study are taking place. The events are not studied in isolation from the context in which they occur and the researcher can rely on varied evidence, including direct observation, in-depth interviews, and relevant documents. As such, while the generalization of findings may be constrained due to the single case, the explanation of why the events happened is enhanced. The ultimate goal of empiricism is the explanation of behavior, and in this sense, case studies make contributions of theoretical importance rather than substantive findings that can be extended to other areas. In addition, if the case is chosen carefully to examine relationships previously discovered in extensive research, such as that using surveys, important theoretical considerations can be analyzed in greater detail than possible in extensive research. Under the right circumstances, the case study can indeed allow the "how" and "why" questions to be explored in more depth.

An excellent example of case study research is Theda Skocpol's analysis of President Clinton's health-care reform efforts during his first term in office. [11] The case under study was Clinton's Health Security measure proposed in September 1993, which was ultimately defeated in Congress. Health-care reform had been a central theme of Clinton's 1992 campaign for president, and Skocpol explains both why it was defeated and what the whole episode reveals about larger forces at work in American politics.

Consistent with the preceding definition, Skocpol employed multiple sources of evidence: scholarly works on U.S. politics, memoirs of key actors, reports on public opinion data, White House documents, presidential speeches, memoranda, personal interviews, interest group publications, newspaper articles, and even political cartoons, which are spread liberally and with good effect throughout the book. She was less interested in describing what individuals were doing to support or oppose the Health Security proposal and more concerned with how this particular case illuminated some basic patterns in American politics—that is, how the relatively narrow events surrounding health-care reform in 1993–1994 supported broader generalizations about all of American national politics. The defeat of health care reform, according to Skocpol, was a reflection of two larger forces in American politics: political partisanship and ideology. Conservatives—in this case Republican members of Congress with fond memories of the Reagan era—wanted less government and partisan control of both houses of Congress. Defeat of Clinton's health-care reform program would contribute to both ends by blocking further government involvement in health care and embarrassing a Democratic president. Liberals, who were for the most part Democrats, wanted government administered health coverage and to retain their partisan control of both the House and Senate. For them, passage of reform would fulfill Clinton's campaign pledge and hopefully produce a popular government program for which Democrats could take credit. The reform plan was defeated, and in 1994, the Republicans seized control of the U.S. House. The fight over health-care reform was really a skirmish in the larger battle over the size of the national government and party control of the U.S. Congress. In this sense, Skocpol effectively employed a case study design to illuminate a more general understanding of American political processes.

Experimentation

Experimentation is the research method best suited for assessing causal relationships. As discussed in Chapter 6, when testing a hypothesis, causality is impossible to demonstrate empirically. The major problem for the research described in Chapter 6 is eliminating possible competing explanations for the behavior under study. Also as described in Chapter 6, the way to confront this difficulty in extensive approaches, employing survey or aggregate data in a field study design, is to introduce additional independent variables into the analysis. The result is to either eliminate some independent variables as possible causes or to elaborate the hypothesis with the additional independent variables that are shown to be related to the dependent variable. The logic involved in assessing causality with experimentation takes the opposite tack of that described in Chapter 6 for large sample studies. When using experimental research designs, the researcher tries to devise a study that will factor out extraneous independent variables and eliminate their effect on the dependent variable prior to the research being conducted. This requires the researcher to have control over the independent variable, which is the hallmark of an experiment. Experiments are not widely used in political science, compared to extensive approaches, but can be very effective for testing hypotheses in the right circumstances.

Logic of Experiments

Experiments have four essential elements: (1) researcher control over the independent variable; (2) a **pretest** and a **posttest** of the subjects on the dependent variable; (3) use of at least two groups of subjects, an **experimental group** and a **control group;** and (4) **random assignment** of subjects to experimental and control groups. These four characteristics constitute what is known as a "classic" experiment. Each element is part of an overall effort to isolate the effect of the independent variable on the dependent variable, excluding the effects of all other possible factors except the experimental treatment on the dependent variable. Experiments often take place in a controlled setting such as a laboratory or classroom, but as you will see later in this chapter, some are conducted in real social settings.

Consider testing the hypothesis that individuals who see a television campaign commercial about candidate Jones have more favorable attitudes toward the candidate than those not seeing the commercial. A researcher, having control of the independent variable (one essential element of an experiment), could show the commercial to a small group of subjects and then measure their attitudes toward candidate Jones. This is called a **simple posttest design** experiment, and it has severe shortcomings. Positive attitudes toward the candidate might indicate the commercial had its intended effect, but certainly variables other than exposure to the commercial could affect the attitude. What can the researcher do about other independent variables, or **confounding factors** as they are sometimes called in experiments, that might be affecting the attitudes of the subjects toward the candidate? That is, how can the researcher control for other, extraneous independent variables? The other three essential elements of an experiment just listed can be added to eliminate some possible confounding factors.

In our example of the campaign commercial, perhaps the more positive attitudes of the experimental group were due not to the commercial but to already positive attitudes held by the people prior to seeing the commercial. The use of a pretest would control for this possibility. The same measurement of attitudes about the candidate would be given to the subjects prior to the viewing of the commercial—that is, they would be pretested. When the pretest score is subtracted from the measurement of attitudes after viewing the commercial (the posttest), the difference would be the effect of the commercial. Any effect of attitudes that subjects held prior to the viewing would be factored out of posttest measurement of the attitude.

Another potential problem is the experimental process itself affecting attitudes toward the candidate. Subjects might, for example, be impressed by the whole experimental procedure devoted to the commercial, and that might lead to a more positive evaluation of the candidate, independent of the effect of the commercial. To factor out this effect, a control group would be added to the experiment. Subjects in the control group would also be pre- and posttested but would not see the commercial. A comparison of the difference between the pre- and posttest scores of the experimental and control groups would reveal any effects the experimental process itself had on the dependent variable. The effect of the commercial, the independent variable, on attitudes toward the candidate, the dependent variable, would consequently be further isolated from another possible set of confounding effects.

Finally, differences in attitudes between the two groups may be due to individual differences of subjects in the two groups. Maybe the experimental group has some characteristic not in the control group that produces more positive attitudes toward the candidate. This potential difficulty is resolved by random assignment to the groups, which means that each subject in the experiment has an equal chance of ending up in either the experimental or control group. The reason for this random assignment is not to make either group representative of some larger population, as random selection is used in survey research, but to assure that the members of the experimental and control groups have nothing in common except membership in that group. That being the case, there is no characteristic common to one group or the other that could affect scores on the dependent variable, meaning one more confounding factor is eliminated from the analysis. In fact, Campbell and Stanley argue that if random assignment is used, a pretest of the attitude is not necessary because the groups are equivalent. [12] Comparison of experimental and control group pretest scores, however, can reassure a researcher that the two groups do not differ on the attitude or behavior under study prior to the experimental group receiving the treatment.

Making use of these four essential elements of an experiment is called a **classic experimental design** (see Figure 12.1). One additional procedure sometimes employed in classic experiments is to exclude possible effects of the person conducting the experiment by having subject assignment to the experimental or control group delegated to someone other than the major researcher and not revealed until the results of the experiment are analyzed. This final safeguard produces what is known as a "double blind" experiment in which neither subjects nor the experimenter know which subjects are in the control or experimental group.

Understanding the logic of experiments provides insight into the essential logic of the scientific method. For political scientists who want to test a cause-and-effect

Figure 12.1
Diagram of Classic Experiment

Experimental Group	Random assignment	Pretest of dependent variable	Receive experimental treatment	Posttest of dependent variable	Effect (posttest) – (pretest)
Control Group	Random assignment	Pretest of dependent variable		Posttest of dependent variable	Effect (posttest) – (pretest)

$$\text{Experimental Effect} = \left[\left(\begin{matrix} \text{Experimental group} \\ \text{posttest score} \end{matrix} \right) - \left(\begin{matrix} \text{Experimental Group} \\ \text{pretest score} \end{matrix} \right) \right] - \left[\left(\begin{matrix} \text{Control group} \\ \text{posttest score} \end{matrix} \right) - \left(\begin{matrix} \text{Control group} \\ \text{pretest score} \end{matrix} \right) \right]$$

relationship, an experiment is the best research design. Methods that employ survey or aggregate data handle the problem of extraneous variance by adding more independent variables that might affect the dependent variable, all along recognizing that the model will never fully assess cause and effect. If you were to test the hypothesis about the effect of candidate Jones's campaign commercial with survey data, you would definitely want to include other independent variables possibly affecting attitudes toward the candidate, such as each respondent's previous knowledge of the candidate and party identification of both the candidate and respondent as controls. The more fully you want to account for differences in attitudes toward candidate Jones among the respondents, the more independent variables you need to add. Experiments, as you have seen, take the opposite direction, trying to factor out extraneous variables with the design of the research rather than building them in. The goal of experiments is to eliminate the possibility of alternative explanations rather than trying to account for them with additional independent variables.

Key Points

These are the essential characteristics of an experiment:

- Researcher control over the independent variable
- Pretesting and posttesting of the subjects on the dependent variable
- Use of at least two groups of subjects: an experimental group and a control group
- Random assignment of subjects to experimental and control groups

Internal Versus External Validity

Not all hypotheses are amenable to experimental research. You must have control over the independent variable—often not possible in empirical research involving politics. Also, experimentation is better for explanation than description, while the reverse is true when using survey data of larger groups of people. This contention between explanation and description is generally set in the context of internal versus external validity. Empiricists use the word *validity* in two different ways. Part of operationalizing or measuring variables, covered in Chapter 7, is concern with the validity of measurement—that is, how accurately the operational definition of a variable reflects the concept being studied. In the current context of research design and experimentation, researchers are also concerned with the validity of the conclusions drawn from the study. First, how confident can you be that the variables shown empirically to be associated are indeed causally related? The answer to this question is the level of internal validity of the study. On the other hand, how confident is the researcher that the findings of the study can be generalized to other circumstances, situations, or times? The answer to this second question is the level of external validity. **Internal validity** asks how well cause-and-effect relationships have been established, while **external validity** asks how far the findings can be extended beyond the immediate study. In general, as internal validity increases, external validity decreases and vice versa. Experiments rank high in internal validity but low in external validity, while extensive approaches based on survey or aggregate data have more external validity but less internal validity. Some threats to internal validity can be controlled with more elaborate experimental designs, some of which are described in the next section, but other threats are more difficult to control. External validity is not a primary objective of experimental research, but field experiments, also discussed in the next section, provide a small measure of external validity.

To the Web

Experimental Research

For two general discussions of research using experimental designs, go to the **DEPR Web Page,** click on **Web Links, Chapter 13,** then **Research on Methods Knowledge Base** and **Continuous Learning Project.** To participate in an online experiment, click on **Chapter 13,** then **Online Experiment.** For useful software in randomly assigning subjects to groups when setting up an experiment, click on **Randomizer.**

Other Types of Experiments

We have discussed only two types of experiments thus far: simple posttest and the classic two-group design described when we explained the logic underlying experimentation. The simple posttest design has considerable difficulty controlling for internal validity, but the classic design greatly improves internal validity by having pretests, a control group, and random assignment. Other designs take account of other factors, such as the number of the values of the dependent variable and some of the lesser threats to internal validity. We will describe five other experimental designs and how each is employed: Solomon

Figure 12.2
Diagram of Solomon Four Group Design Experiment

Experimental Group 1	Random assignment	Pretest of dependent variable	Receive experimental treatment	Posttest of dependent variable
Control Group 1	Random assignment	Pretest of dependent variable		Posttest of dependent variable
Experimental Group 2	Random assignment		Receive experimental treatment	Posttest of dependent variable
Control Group 2	Random assignment			Posttest of dependent variable

four group, multigroup, multigroup time series, factorial, and field experiments. These are the most common designs employed in political science and related fields.

The **Solomon four group design** adds two extra groups to the classic design—one experimental and one control—for a total of four groups in order to increase internal validity. This design controls for another potential source of error: the effect of interaction between pretests and experimental treatment or between pretest and posttest for the control group. In the classic design, both the experimental and control groups are pretested. This may lead to the subjects in the experimental group being sensitized to the experimental treatment they receive. In our example of determining the effect of a campaign commercial on the attitude toward candidate Jones, the pretest might signal to the subjects the intended message of the commercial, and they would pay closer attention to the message in the commercial in a way they otherwise might not have if they hadn't been pretested. If the pretest asks about truthfulness, and the commercial is designed to enhance that quality of candidate Jones, the subjects might be more likely to respond to the intended message of the commercial. To control for this possible interaction, the Solomon four group design adds a second experimental group that is not pretested. In this added experimental group, there can be no interaction between the pretest and the treatment. A second control group is also added that is not pretested, only posttested, to account for possible interactive effects between the control group pretest and the control group posttest.

Results of the Solomon four group design are evaluated by making four comparisons, as seen in Figure 12.2. Using our example of the effect of a campaign commercial, and assuming the commercial produced the intended effect, the posttest attitude in experimental group #1 should be more positive toward the candidate than the pretest

Figure 12.3
Diagram of Multigroup Experiment

Experimental Group 1	Random assignment	Pretest of dependent variable	Receive experimental treatment/level 1	Posttest of dependent variable	Effect (posttest) – (pretest)
Experimental Group 2	Random assignment	Pretest of dependent variable	Receive experimental treatment/level 2	Posttest of dependent variable	Effect (posttest) – (pretest)
Control Group	Random assignment	Pretest of dependent variable		Posttest of dependent variable	Effect (posttest) – (pretest)

attitude. Second, the difference between the pretest attitude score and posttest attitude score of experimental group #1 should be greater than the difference between the pretest attitude score and posttest attitude score of control group #1. So far, this is the classic experiment design. But now two more comparisons can be made to rule out interactive effects. Third, the experimental group #2 posttest score should be greater than the posttest score of control group #1. Fourth, and finally, the experimental group #2 posttest score should be greater than the posttest score of control group #4.

The **multigroup design** is used when the independent variable has more than two values; an additional experimental group is added for each value of the independent variable beyond two. By adding groups, this design takes account of possible differences in the independent variable arising from subjects receiving different levels of the independent variable. In the preceding example of the effect of campaign commercials, there may be cumulative effects of repeated exposure to the commercial. A multigroup design would add experimental groups, each of which had seen the commercial more than once—for example, a second experimental group who would see the commercial twice, a third group who viewed it three times, and so on. All of the essential elements of a classic design remain, except there are additional experimental groups. A diagram of a multigroup design is shown in Figure 12.3.

One of the difficulties of experimental research is uncertainty about how long the effect of a treatment might take to show up and how long the effect of the treatment might last. As experiments are often completed in a single session with only one pre- and posttest of the experimental group, researchers may either miss the effect of an independent variable because it shows up after the posttest or overestimate the effect of the independent variable because that effect is extinguished in a short period of time. **Multigroup time series designs** (see Figure 12.4) are fashioned to help alleviate this problem by having multiple pretests and posttests for the subjects. Any trends in the

Figure 12.4
Diagram of Multigroup Time Series Experiment

Experimental Group	Random assignment	Pretest #1	Pretest #2	Pretest #3	Receive experimental treatment	Posttest #1	Posttest #2	Posttest #3
Control Group	Random assignment	Pretest #1	Pretest #2	Pretest #3		Posttest #1	Posttest #2	Posttest #3

behavior or attitude under study can be observed and differential effects of the independent variable over time can be examined.

Factorial designs are used to assess the effect of more than one independent variable and the possible interactive effects of those variables. Factorial design experiments are among the most widely used in political science. The simplest factorial design is 2 × 2— that is, two independent variables, each of which takes on two values—but factorial designs with more than two independent variables or variables with more than two values can be employed. An example of a 2 × 2 factorial design might be a state health department trying to determine which is the more effective policy for helping people to stop smoking: one-on-one counseling with a health professional or group meetings with other smokers trying to quit. A factorial design experiment could be employed to determine the effect of each method individually and the effect of both simultaneously. Twenty people would be randomly assigned to individual counseling, twenty to group meetings, twenty to both, and twenty to no treatment at all. One set of possible results is shown in Figure 12.5.

The effect of each independent variable (called a **main effect**) can be observed in the row and column totals. Those attending individual counseling had a higher success rate for quitting smoking—55 percent—than those who did not—30 percent. Attending group meetings also yielded more success—57.5 percent—versus those not attending group meetings—27.5 percent. Each separate treatment, therefore, is positively related to the dependent variable. The four cells within the table reveal the **interactive effect** of the variables. When subjects received neither treatment, 25 percent stopped smoking. When subjects received individual counseling but attended no group meetings, the percentage of subjects who stopped smoking increased to 30 percent. Attending group meetings without individual counseling produced a 35 percent success rate. For those who received both treatments, the success rate is 80 percent, indicating the positive interactive effect of the two variables on the dependent variable. Results such as these would be beneficial for decision makers in the health department concerning decisions about which smoking cessation programs to fund.

Figure 12.5
Results of a Factorial Design: Percentage Success Rates of Differing Treatments on Smoking Cessation

| | INDIVIDUAL COUNSELING | | |
Group Meetings	Yes	No	Total
Yes	80% (16/20)	35% (7/20)	57.5% (23/40)
No	30% (6/20)	25% (5/20)	27.5% (11/40)
Total	55% (22/40)	30% (12/40)	

Source: Simulated.

A factorial design was employed by Geva and Hanson in their study concerning perceptions of, and public approval of force against, another nation. According to them, "Experimentation . . . is penetrating slowly to the arsenal of acceptable research methodologies in political science and the study of international relations. Indeed, experiments are sometimes the only way to investigate hypothetical political events. . . ." [13] Undergraduate students from an American university (N = 60) and individuals drawn from the wider community where the university was located (N = 76) were employed as subjects. They were exposed to a written description of a hypothetical inter-nation regional conflict that provided an opportunity for American military involvement. The three independent variables, or experimental manipulations, were similarity of the target nation to the United States (similar versus dissimilar), extent of aggression used by target nation (economic sanctions versus military invasion), and participant (student versus community resident). This is a 2 × 2 × 2 factorial design—that is, three independent variables, each with two values. There were two dependent variables, rating of the regime type (10-point scale, nondemocratic to democratic) of the target nation and approval of the use of force against that country, measured on an 11-point scale. The effects of each independent variable on the two dependent variables can be determined, and because it is a factorial design, the simultaneous, interactive effects of the independent variables can be assessed as well.

Field experiments take place outside the laboratory in a real social setting, and as a result have somewhat higher external validity than laboratory experiments. Alan S. Gerber used a field experiment with a factorial design to examine the effects of three experimental treatments—personal canvassing, telephone calls, and direct mail appeals—on voter turnout in New Haven, Connecticut. [14] He created a data set of all households in the city with one or two registered voters (29,380 people) whose participation in the 1998 election could be determined from public records. People in the sample were randomly assigned to a control group receiving no treatment or experimental groups receiving, shortly before the November 1998 election, one of the treatments or a combination of them. Voting rates for the group who received no treatment were then compared at the time of the election, with the various groups receiving one or more treatments.

Program evaluation, a component of the study of public administration, attempts to measure the effect of social and political programs on the intended clients, often using field experimental designs. Program evaluation is used by public officials to determine how efficiently programs mandated by legislation are operated and to what extent they are achieving their stated objectives. Foundations and other private funding agencies generally require that organizations receiving monies undertake evaluations to determine the effectiveness and cost efficiency of their programs. The ideal in assessing effectiveness is to develop an experimental research design in which those targeted to benefit from the program—the experimental group—are compared to those who are not covered—the control group.

An example of a field experiment in program evaluation was done by Grossman and Tierney to measure the effect of mentoring in the context of the Big Brothers and Big Sisters Program. (15) Eight local agencies in various parts of the United States were selected for study. Using random assignment, 571 youths were placed in an experimental group and each of them matched with a Big Brother or Sister. At the same time, 567 youths were put into a control group and placed on an eighteen-month waiting list for a mentor. The groups were given a baseline questionnaire at the start of the program that was compared with a follow-up questionnaire at the end of eighteen months. Characteristics such as academic performance, antisocial behavior, family/peer relationships, and self-concept served as the dependent variables. All of the essential elements of an experiment are present in the Grossman and Tierney design: researcher control of the independent variable, both experimental and control groups, random assignment of subjects, and pre- and posttesting. It differs from a classic design only in that it was set in the field rather than the laboratory. However, because of the field setting and the extended time between the pre- and posttesting, the threat to internal validity for field experiments, such as those often employed in program evaluation, is greater than those in a laboratory or other controlled setting. [16] We will discuss only three of the most obvious threats to internal validity.

The primary goal of experimental methodology is to make sure the only difference between the experimental and control groups is exposure to the independent variable, but research in the field that extends over a long time exposes subjects to many other influences. This is the problem of **history:** Other events occurring in the lives of the subjects during the time of the experiment might affect individual scores on the dependent variable. Over the eighteen months of the experiment, the youths in the mentoring experimental group very likely had experiences that impacted their academic performance, social behavior, family/peer relationships, and self-concept other than their relationship with their mentor. **Maturation** is also a problem: People change over time, and those who were alike at the start of an experiment may not be as similar months later, quite apart from whether they received the experimental treatment or not. In addition, over time subjects may drop out of the experiment, and this **experimental mortality** may produce differences between the experimental and control groups that are erroneously attributed to the experimental treatment. These concerns do not necessarily invalidate field experiments or any other experimental design to which they apply, but, as a researcher, you must keep in mind that even with all your efforts to control confounding factors, threats to internal validity such as these must be recognized and acknowledged in discussions of your findings.

Key Points

Different types of experimental research include the following:

- Simple posttest design
- Classic two-group design
- Solomon four group design
- Multigroup design
- Multigroup time series design
- Factorial design

■ Quasi-Experiments

"True" experiments, those that contain the four essential elements, may not always be possible, especially for experimental research done in the field. Some aspects of experimentation, such as random assignment of the subjects to experimental and control groups, could be impossible to achieve. In such cases, the experimental approach need not be completely abandoned; you can use as many elements of experimentation as are feasible to produce what is called a "**quasi-experiment.**" While failure to implement each component of a "true" experiment will decrease internal validity, by maintaining as many elements as possible, you may learn more about the behavior or attitude under study than from other methodological choices available to you.

Burgess et al. wanted to examine the differing effects of two types of voting pledge cards sent out as part of MTV's "Rock the Vote" efforts to increase voting turnout among young people in the 1996 presidential election. [17] This strategy was undertaken by "Rock the Vote" prior to the start of the academic research, so the two groups receiving the different cards were not chosen by random assignment, an essential ingredient of experimentation. But having two distinct, identifiable groups with different types of cards allowed Burgess and her colleagues to conduct a "quasi-experiment" that compared the voting behavior of one group with the other, even though random assignment was not employed. The data about voting behavior, the dependent variable, were collected using a survey of those who had received both types of cards and allowed for the introduction of control variables to test alternative explanations to the effect of the pledge cards for differences in behavior between the groups. And while the internal validity of the work certainly suffers because the groups were not created with random assignment, the resulting study has considerable value. When researchers find identifiable groupings of people, such as those who received pledge cards from "Rock the Vote" arranged nonrandomly by someone other than those conducting the research, the situation is often referred to as a **natural experiment.** When subjects are not randomly assigned to groups, those not receiving the experimental treatment are generally referred to as being in the **comparison group** rather than the control group.

One alternative when random assignment is impossible to carry out is to "match" a comparison group to the experimental group on as many relevant characteristics as possible. This matching process can be accomplished on a one-to-one basis: Each person in the experimental group is matched to an individual in the control group or on an aggregate basis, where the average characteristics of the two groups are matched, for example, by mean age. Simon and Merrill used matching in trying to assess the effects of the Kids Voting USA civics curriculum used by students in grades from kindergarten through high school on their parents' likelihood of voting. [18] Voting turnout in areas where the program was implemented were matched on racial, socioeconomic, and partisan variables (factors likely affecting voting turnout) with areas that did not use the curriculum. By limiting the comparison of voting turnout to those areas similar to where the Kids Voting USA civic curriculum was employed, the researchers were trying to use principles of experimentation to control for extraneous independent variables.

To the Web

Exercise 12.1   Evaluating Experimental Research Designs

Sometimes it is difficult for inexperienced researchers to recognize if studies have problems with their research design, or alternatively, how the weakness of a particular design limits conclusions that can be drawn from the findings. This exercise describes two experimental research designs and asks you to analyze them on critical points. Go to the **DEPR Web Page,** click on **Web Exercises, Chapter 12,** then on **Evaluating Experimental Research Designs.**

■ Reminders About Ethics in Experiments

In Chapter 3, we discussed ethical considerations in political science research. In addition to keeping in mind general principles such as doing no harm, you need to be sensitive to some particular concerns when doing experiments. Here are some reminders. First, any research involving human subjects should be approved in advance by the Institutional Review Board (IRB) at your college or university. The board will likely provide guidelines specific to your institution about how you must treat any subjects you work with in an experiment. Second, because experiments often involve deception of some kind, you need to get the subjects' *informed consent* prior to the experiment and fully *debrief* them when their participation is completed. Informed consent means subjects, before agreeing to participate, clearly understand the purpose of the study, who is conducting the study, the type of information that will be requested, and the risks involved. A written consent form usually emphasizes the voluntary nature of participation, the maintenance of anonymity or confidentiality, and an offer to provide a summary of findings when the research is over. During *debriefing,* subjects are provided an explanation about the nature of the experiment immediately after the subjects' activities are completed. Finally, "right to service" is a concern, especially when doing experimental research to evaluate public programs. In the Grossman and Tierney evaluation of the Big Brothers and Big Sisters Program, 567 young people were deliberately not matched with a mentor until eighteen months later as part of the experimental procedure. The findings of the study demonstrated positive effects of having a mentor, so the young people in the control group were, because of the experiment, denied benefits provided to those in the experimental group.

Q-Technique

Q-technique is an intensive approach to data collection aimed at the study of human subjectivity. It is a very useful approach for determining the ways in which an audience is segmented with regard to complex issues and perspectives. When we use the term *subjectivity* with reference to Q-technique, we mean that respondents communicate their points of view as they relate to their own personal frames of reference. This approach contrasts with extensive methods such as survey research that emphasize the researcher's conceptualizations (of such concepts as political alienation or conservatism) as a frame of reference and where inferences are drawn about viewpoints of a population based on previously structured responses. Since Q-technique is concerned with *how* an audience is segmented and *how* people think about political and social issues, it does not rely on a large sample of respondents (most studies use thirty to forty). Unlike survey research, the concern is not with the proportion of persons in a population that hold a variety of points of view but with the number of viewpoints, their nature, the similarities and differences among them, and the ways in which respondents with each viewpoint think and feel. Scholars who use Q-technique argue that knowledge of how people think about political issues and how viewpoints are distinguished should precede the determination of the proportion who subscribe to each perspective. [19]

Q-technique allows a respondent to communicate his or her subjective point of view on a subject of importance through an instrument called a **Q-sort.** The Q-sorting process is accomplished by a respondent systematically rank ordering a set of stimuli (usually statements about an issue) according to specific instructions. Ordinarily a respondent is given a set cards (as few as 20 to as many as 100) on which are printed statements about an issue. He or she is instructed to sort them along a continuum ranging from "most characteristic of my point of view" to "least characteristic of my point of view." The resulting Q-sort is a respondent's representation of a subjective perspective on the subject of interest and is the result of a process of relating alternative statements to each other. Most studies using Q-technique are based on a small sample, perhaps thirty or forty people. Following completion of Q-sorts, the results are coded and a statistical procedure called factor analysis is used to distinguish groups of respondents who share points of view, those who sorted the statements in approximately the same way. The groups are then compared in terms of how they sorted the statements: Generally, a "typical Q-sort" is constructed for each group to distinguish differences in points of view.

You should recognize by now that Q-technique, compared to other approaches we have discussed in earlier chapters, is based on different assumptions and seeks to answer different questions. The goal of the approach is not to generalize about the proportion of a population that has a particular characteristic or holds a particular point of view. While approaches such as survey research emphasize collecting a relatively small amount of information from a large number of people, Q-technique emphasizes collecting a large amount of information about a single topic from a small number of people. After our emphasis on large numbers of respondents and the goal of generalizability, it may seem to you that Q-technique is not scientific. A more detailed description of the process of Q-technique and an illustration should help you see that this intensive approach is not inconsistent with extensive approaches—it simply answers different questions.

▧ Overview

Q-samples.   While survey research is based on obtaining representative samples of respondents, Q-technique is concerned with sampling communications about issues of interest. For example, if you are interested in distinguishing and understanding the variety of viewpoints on the issue of the possibility of peace in the Middle East, you would probably want to ensure that every possible viewpoint is represented. The process of developing a **Q-sample** on the subject would involve collecting as many statements as possible from such sources as newspaper reports of statements by leaders in the region and elsewhere, editorials on the subject in major newspapers, letters to the editor, articles in opinion magazines, and perhaps interviews with political leaders and scholars. The usual approach is to collect a large number of statements and then select a subset, the Q-sample or statement sample, for the Q-sort that represents every conceivable point of view. Often a balanced factorial design is developed so that a representative Q-sample of the debate can be achieved. For example, a Q-sort examining attitudes about peace in the Middle East should contain at least a balance of pro-Israel and pro-Palestinian statements. There are probably other relevant dimensions or criteria that should be considered as well. Once a Q-sample of statements is selected, they are printed on individual cards or slips of paper.

P-samples. The **P-sample** (or person sample) used in Q-technique is usually not selected with an eye toward representing a population but with the goal of including representatives of every possible point of view. P-samples are usually small, since on any given subject there are unlikely to be more than a half dozen distinct perspectives. Once three or four respondents who share a perspective are represented in the P-sample, it makes no sense to add others who share the point of view. The goal of Q-technique, as stated earlier, is not to count the number of people who hold a point of view but to distinguish different perspectives. Systematic criteria can be applied to select P-samples, and factorial designs are often used. For example, in selecting a P-sample for a Q-study of perspectives on peace in the Middle East, it would seem appropriate to include Jews, Arabs presenting a variety of nations, and those who represent neither group. Other criteria for selection of the P-sample might focus on occupation, age, and region of residence.

The Sorting Operation and Conditions of Instruction. Q-sorting itself is a process of respondents sorting statements that are printed on cards or slips of paper along a continuum according to specific conditions of instruction. The instructions are most often simply stated as follows: "Please sort the items according to those with which you *most strongly disagree* (−4) to those with which you *most strongly agree* (+4)." Respondents are commonly instructed to sort the statements in terms of a distribution in which fewer items are placed at the extreme points on the continuum and more in the center. The following is an example of a continuum with the number of statements to be placed under each score. The upper row of numbers represents direction and strength of the attitude about a statement; the lower row of numbers indicates how many of the forty-eight total statements the respondent should place under each level of agreement or disagreement.

Most Strongly Disagree							Most Strongly Agree	
−4	−3	−2	−1	0	+1	+2	+3	+4
3	4	6	7	8	7	6	4	3

This "forced distribution" of statements requires respondents to make distinctions between statements of opinion and to indicate clearly the statements they feel most strongly about.

Distinguishing Points of View.   After each respondent completes the Q-sorting process, the results are coded and subjected to statistical analysis. Usually a statistical process called factor analysis (a description of factor analysis is beyond the scope of this book) is used to group respondents based on how the statements are sorted. [20] Those who sorted the statements in approximately the same way share points of view on the issue. There are seldom more than six independent perspectives on even the most complex issues. The task of interpreting and distinguishing points of view focuses on where statements were placed on the continuum. An analysis of which statements distinguish each viewpoint reveals both the nature of each perspective and the differences between perspectives.

■ Using Q-Technique to Distinguish Conceptions of Representation

An example of a study of delegates to the national party conventions should help demonstrate how Q-technique can be used to explain *how* people think about key issues. One study sought to answer the question "In what ways do delegates to the national party conventions conceive of their roles as representatives?" [21] Research on legislators suggested some possible answers. It is possible that some delegates to the national conventions take the role of "trustee" and attempt to act in the best interest of their constituents, while others take the role of "delegate-servants" and attempt to act as their constituents would. A Q-sample of thirty-six statements was selected that took into account the two representative roles (trustee or delegate), perceived constituencies (district, state, party officials, candidates, demographic groups, and interest groups), and types of issues (foreign policy, economic issues, and social issues). Figure 12.6 shows the factorial design that was used to select a balanced Q-sample. Statements were collected from party officials, former delegates, and the political science literature on parties; they were rewritten to reflect each combination. The following are examples of some of the Q-sample statements.

> "As a delegate to a party convention I would feel bound to represent the views of the candidate on matters of foreign policy." (Delegate/Candidate/Foreign Policy)
>
> "I feel that with respect to economic issues I should speak my own mind and not follow the dictates of my party." (Trustee/Party Officials/Economic Issues)

Figure 12.6
Factorial Design of a Representation Q-Sample

Main Effects		Levels	
Role Orientation	(a) Trustee		(b) Delegate
Constituency	(c) District	(d) State	(e) Party Officials
	(f) Candidate	(g) Demographic Group	(h) Interest Group
Issues	(i) Foreign Policy	(j) Economic Issues	(k) Social Issues

(A) (B) (C) = (2) (6) (3) = 36 Statements

Source: James M. Carlson and Richard M. Martin. "Conceptions of Representation: A Study of Delegates to the 1984 Party Conventions," *American Politics Quarterly,* 15 (July 1987): 355. Copyright © 1987 by Sage Publications, Inc. Reprinted by permission of Sage Publications.

> "On social issues, the important thing is that the will of the citizens of my state is represented." (Delegate/State/Social Issues)

A diverse P-sample of thirty-six delegates to the 1984 Democratic and Republican National Conventions sorted thirty-six statements printed on small cards along a continuum ranging from "most disagree" (-4) to "most agree" ($+4$). When the Q-sorts were coded, placed in a data matrix and subjected to statistical analysis, each of the party delegates was found to be part of one of four distinct groups representing different perspectives on representation. The four perspectives could be distinguished by the placement of statements along the continuum. Let us examine the four points of view and make comparisons based on the distinctive emphases given to statements. (The placement of statements by the four groups are in parentheses.)

The first group of party delegates were *Trustees,* and compared to the other three groups, they agreed with the following statements.

> "It is my belief that those people from my district and community expect me to act as I see fit to help them be better off economically." ($+\mathbf{4} +1 +1\ 0$)
> "Even though the leaders of my party might take a particular stand, I feel I should exercise my own judgment with respect to issues of foreign policy." ($+\mathbf{4}\ 0 +1 +1$)

The second group seemed to be concerned about representing *group interests.*

> "In economic matters I am a delegate, a representative of my interest group." ($-3 +\mathbf{4} -1 +1$)
> "I am obliged to represent the views of people like myself (women, union members, etc.) on issues such as abortion and affirmative action." ($-3 +\mathbf{3} -1 -2$)

The third group saw representation as a *matter of conscience.*

"If my own views on social issues such as abortion conflict with the views held by
a candidate I pledged to support, I would vote own conscience on the issue."
$(+1 +1 +4 +1)$

"Even if I were selected as a delegate to represent the views of a candidate I support,
I would vote my conscience on foreign policy issues." $(+1 -1 +4 -2)$

The fourth group consisted of *delegate-servants.*

"With respect to social issues, I was elected to act as the people back home would
want." $(-1 -1 -2 +4)$

"I feel that my votes at conventions should reflect the social needs of the people
in my district or community." $(0 +1 +1 +3)$

The analysis of Q-sorts thus revealed four unique perspectives on how delegates view
their representative roles at national party conventions. There may be other perspectives that were not represented by those included in the P-sample, but Q-technique provided delegates with the opportunity to indicate how they viewed their roles. Some
perspectives were revealed that had not been anticipated by earlier studies.

▓ Disadvantages and Advantages

You may encounter objections to Q-technique procedures. Critics often do not understand the fundamental distinction between intensive and extensive analysis and object
that the results of Q-studies are not generalizable to wider populations. The goal of Q-
technique is not to permit generalizations, as you would expect from a survey-based study.
The goal instead is to determine how audiences are seg-
mented based on subjective interpretations of events or
issues. Extensive approaches may logically follow studies using Q-technique. After viewpoints regarding issues
are operationalized by respondents who participate in
Q-studies, it may be appropriate to use surveys to establish what proportion of a population holds a particular
point of view or what variables are associated with specific viewpoints. More often, Q-studies are followed by
intensive interviews designed to deepen understanding
of individuals who represent different points of view.

Q-technique may be a good starting point for studies of public or elite opinion or personality and politics.

To the Web

Exercise 12.2   Writing Q-Sort Statements

Writing statements for use in a Q-sort forces a researcher to consider the full domain of a concept.
The subjects must have a wide scope of statements
to sort. This exercise will give you practice in writing
statements for a Q-sort, helping you to understand
how Q-technique allows subjects to reveal their
subjective point of view within the context of their
personal frames of reference. Go to the **DEPR Web
Page,** click on **Web Exercises, Chapter 12,** then on
Writing Q-Sort Statements.

It is a technique that is relatively simple to use. Compared to other approaches, data collection is not very costly with respect to financial resources or time. Finally, Q-technique can be used to examine a wide variety of dispositions of interest to political scientists. [22]

Focus Groups

Focus groups, generally consisting of no more than fifteen members and sometimes considerably fewer, are brought together to discuss some topic in order for the researcher to learn how people think about that topic. They are used most often in market research for commercial products and by political campaign consultants during elections, but they are also a legitimate and helpful research tool for empirical political scientists. A trained moderator asks specific questions and guides the resulting discussions. A transcript of the discussion is kept, and often the entire session is videotaped. The members are usually homogeneous on some characteristic such as age, occupation grouping, or other criterion related to the research. The key to a successful focus group is the interactive discussion among group members to elaborate on some point, making a good moderator an integral component in the success of the focus group.

If experiments are designed to explain, then focus groups were originally employed to explore, both for possible directions in which to pursue more quantitative research as well as for interpretation of quantitative data already collected. Topics might include a discussion of the complexities of some concept that would ultimately be operationalized on a survey instrument or the differing interpretations of particular survey findings. In line with this thinking, Morgan argues such groups can be used to generate both theories and explanations. [23] But they are also seen as a way to observe interaction among people that is important in understanding political behavior that is not possible to observe using more traditional empirical methodology.

Rosenthal used focus groups as one part of her research strategy for studying women leaders in state legislatures. She employed what she called a "triangulated approach" that included the quantitative analysis of survey data collected from legislative committee chairs and fieldwork in state legislatures. To supplement the survey data, and providing the third side of the triangle, was the use of focus group data from twenty-six women and twelve men representing twenty-four different states. Three groups were employed: one all female, one all male, and one mixed. All focus group participants were chairs of state legislative committees. The focus groups "were designed to provide elaboration and insight into the survey results." [24] But the groups also discussed the meaning of such complex concepts as consensus and perceptions about gender differences, adding a depth and complexity to the data that would not be possible with more cursory interaction with subjects.

Another use of a focus group is to explore the dimensions of behavior revealed in a discussion among individuals that might not otherwise be evident when observing the same people individually. For example, Marion Just et al. used this methodology in studying the effect of the media in the 1992 presidential campaign. She and her colleagues conducted focus groups using individual citizens who did not have strong partisan or ideological loyalties. The group members were shown excerpts from television news and campaign commercials, and the resulting "discussions allowed [the researchers] to examine the potential for interpersonal communication in the construction of political meaning." [25] Because the meaning of political messages funneled through the mass media may be fashioned, in part, through interpersonal communications, focus groups provided the vehicle through which to examine that interaction in a controlled setting. Obviously, such interactive processes cannot be directly observed with traditional, individual, survey research interviews of respondents, but by using focus groups, the process of constructing meaning from political messages becomes visible.

Focus groups have the obvious limitations of other intensive approaches: limited generalizability, an artificially controlled setting, and concern about prolonged, close contact with members influencing the behavior under study. Added to those concerns is the inherently subjective interpretation of the transcript of the group meeting. Transcripts are not quantified for analysis but perused for patterns or themes, certainly a more subjective process of analyzing data than experiments, Q-sorts, or extensive approaches. [26]

To the Web

Using Focus Groups

To read a discussion on how university administrators use Q-methodology for research about administering student affairs, go to the **DEPR Web Page**, click on **Web Links, Chapter 12**, then on **Student Affairs Journal—Online**. A review of focus group research is provided by the University of Surrey, England. Click on **Focus Group Research Review**.

Conclusion

Intensive approaches are important methodological tools for the empirical political scientist. Q-sorts, experimentation, case studies, and focus groups allow the empirical study of attitudes and behavior from a perspective different from that of more extensive approaches. Each approach has its strengths, and depending on the objective of the research, can be effectively employed to answer empirical research questions. All these intensive approaches take some imagination to design and implement. As you become more familiar with empirical research by reading the professional literature and doing your own data-based work, you will more easily recognize opportunities to employ aspects of intensive analysis in testing hypotheses of interest to you.

The next chapter begins our discussion of data analysis, how to work through your data to look for evidence of the relationships you have hypothesized. Chapter 13 covers the initial stage of that process: how to describe and summarize a single variable. Chapters 14 through 16 describe techniques of data analysis for testing hypotheses. Chapter 17 discusses how likely it is that a relationship confirmed with sample data is also found in the population from which the sample was drawn.

- Extensive approaches obtain relatively little information from a large number of people in a brief period, whereas intensive analysis gathers a wider variety of information from a smaller number of respondents over more time.
- Case studies examine, usually in considerable detail, a single case on only one occasion.
- Experimentation is the research method best suited for assessing causal relationships; extraneous independent variables are factored out, and their effect on the dependent variable is eliminated.
- Experiments have four essential elements: researcher control over the independent variable, pretesting and posttesting of the subjects on the dependent variable, use of at least two groups of subjects: an experimental group and a control group, and random assignment of subjects to experimental and control groups.
- Internal validity is the extent to which a research design assesses cause and effect; external validity is the extent to which study findings can be generalized.
- The four essential elements of experimentation produce a classic experimental design; additional designs account for other possible sources of extraneous variance, different numbers of values for the independent variable, and the use of more than one independent variable.
- A quasi-experiment is research similar to experimentation but lacking at least one of the four essential elements.
- Q-technique is an intensive approach that is designed to measure subjectivity. It is useful for determining how audiences are segmented and allows respondents to model their points of view regarding issues based on their own perspectives.
- A focus group is a small number of people brought together to discuss a specific subject, led by a moderator, to learn what and/or how people think about that topic.

Terms Introduced

case studies
classic experimental design
comparison group
confounding factors
control group
experimental group
experimental mortality
extensive approach
external validity
factorial design
field experiment
focus group
history

intensive approach
interactive effect
internal validity
main effect
maturation
multigroup design
multigroup time series design
natural experiment
P-sample
posttest
pretest
program evaluation
Q-sample

Q-sort   random assignment
Q-technique   simple posttest design
quasi-experiment   Solomon four group design

Selected Readings

Boruch, Robert F. *Randomized Experiments for Planning and Evaluation: A Practical Guide.* Thousand Oaks, CA: Sage Publications, 1997.

Brown, Steven R. *Political Subjectivity: Applications of Q Methodology in Political Science.* New Haven, CT: Yale University Press, 1980.

Kinder, Donald R., and Thomas Palfrey, Eds. *Experimental Foundations of Political Science.* Ann Arbor: University of Michigan Press, 1993.

Kruger, Richard. *Focus Groups: A Practical Guide for Applied Research,* 2nd Ed. Thousand Oaks, CA: Sage Publications, 1994.

McKeown, Bruce, and Dan Thomas. *Q Methodology.* Newbury Park, CA: Sage Publications, 1988.

Stewart, David W., and Prem N. Shamdasani. *Focus Groups: Theory and Practice.* Newbury Park, CA: Sage Publications, 1990.

Activities

Activity 12.1
Designing a Classic Experiment

A public interest group has produced a fifteen-minute videotape designed to increase voting participation among young people aged eighteen to twenty-four but is not sure the tape will produce the desired effect. Sketch a classic experimental design to test whether the videotape is likely to increase voting turnout among eligible voters in the targeted age group.

Activity 12.2
Designing an Experiment for Evaluation

A state university is trying to improve efficiency by making sure that students who have signed up for a meeting with their academic adviser actually show up. Only 60 percent of the students arrive at their scheduled time. Two suggestions for increasing that percentage are to (1) e-mail each student a reminder of the meeting date and time the day before the meeting or (2) telephone the student with the reminder the evening before the scheduled meeting. Explain how to use a field experiment to assess the effect of each suggestion separately, as well as the effect of using both suggestions, compared to doing nothing at all.

Activity 12.3
Designing an Experiment for a Hypothetical Situation

After Hillary Clinton moved to New York to run for the U.S. Senate from that state, many people wondered what the effect of her being a "carpetbagger" would have on the likelihood of New York residents voting for her. The problem for doing an empirical research project on this topic is that there are very few actual "carpetbagger" cases to study. Using the idea of presenting hypothetical situations to subjects as described in the Geva and Hanson study about support for the use of force in foreign relations, design an experiment that would isolate the effect of "carpetbagging" on the likelihood of subjects voting for a candidate who moved to a state for the sole purpose of seeking elective office rather than a candidate who was an established resident of the state.

Activity 12.4
Points of View Emerging from a Q-Sort

The following is a set of Q-sort statements that subjects were asked to sort along a continuum from -5 (most strongly disagree) to $+5$ (most strongly agree). Two points of view emerged from the Q-sorting observation. Let's call the points of view perspective #1 and perspective # 2. The scores the two groups gave each statement are in parentheses. Write a brief essay distinguishing and explaining the two points of view.

1. Government should adopt stricter standards for clean air and water even if it forces businesses to raise the prices of their products. $(-1\ -5)$
2. Schools should be allowed to teach scientific creationism—that the world was created all at once by God and has not changed much since then. $(+4\ -3)$
3. Government should see to it that every person has a good standard of living. $(+1\ -5)$
4. Government should ban abortions except in cases where the life and health of the woman are in danger. $(+4\ -3)$
5. Government should have stricter penalties for people who use and sell drugs such as marijuana and cocaine. $(+5\ -2)$
6. Government should stop regulating business and protecting the consumer and let business regulate itself. $(-1\ +5)$
7. The government in Washington is trying to do too many things that should be left to individuals and private businesses. $(+1\ +5)$
8. Government should regulate the health and safety of working conditions. $(0\ -4)$

Part 4

Analyzing and Reporting Results

Chapter 13

How to Describe and Summarize a Single Variable

Learning Objectives

At the conclusion of this chapter, students should be able to do the following:

Identify the differences among univariate, bivariate, and multivariate statistics.

Understand what is meant by descriptive statistics.

Calculate and interpret a frequency distribution, a range or interquartile range, a mode or modal category, a median or a median grouping, an arithmetic mean, a standard deviation, and a z-score.

Understand why measures of central tendency and measures of dispersion are used in univariate analysis.

Define a normal distribution.

Explain the importance of the standard deviation in probability sampling and comparison of scores from distributions.

Why Statistics?

The next-to-the-last step in completing an empirical research project is analyzing the data you will use to test your hypotheses. Once that is done, only the task of writing up the results of your project remains. Some students worry about data analysis because it involves the dreaded word "statistics" and some mathematical equations. Statistics are simply useful summaries that communicate key information about your data and the hypothesized relationships between variables that you want to test. What is covered in the next few chapters is not that difficult, and if done correctly, statistical analysis of your data will allow the clearest presentation of your findings in the most efficient way. With the appropriate data analysis techniques, you can present a lot of information about what you have studied in a relatively small space.

Every day you use statistics to summarize information in your life without even realizing it. The quality of all your academic work is summarized by a number that ranges between 0 and 4: your grade point average, or GPA. Your performance on all of the class presentations, homework, quizzes, papers, examinations, and so on—in all the courses you have taken—is summarized in your GPA. That GPA will determine your rank in class—another statistic. It is those statistics—GPA and rank in class—that employers will use to evaluate your competence when you apply for a job and that graduate or professional schools will require to determine your qualification for admission. They are statistical summaries of how successful you have been in all the courses you have taken as an undergraduate student.

Statistics are used to summarize information in many areas of society familiar to us. Sports fans effectively utilize statistics. How well the hockey, soccer, or lacrosse goalie plays is summarized by his or her goals against average: the number of goals allowed divided by the number of games played. Goalies in all these sports can be evaluated one to the other by comparing their goals against average. Who is the best basketball player in a particular league? Perhaps you want to compare players' scoring and rebounding averages, turnover-to-assist ratio, and number of steals per game. All of these are statistical summaries of a player's performance that help to evaluate how well one player performs in comparison to others.

Statistics also play an important role in the daily life of business and finance. The Dow Jones Industrial Average and the Standard and Poor's 500 Index are popular indexes of performance of the New York Stock Exchange. Each provides a statistic that summarizes the performance of a particular group of stocks traded on the New York Stock Exchange. Retailers want to know information such as the average daily income of their various outlets to evaluate the performance of each relative to the others. Statistical studies are used in product development and distribution (how to get a product somewhere at the lowest price in the least time) to save time and money.

People who follow sports or who work in business and finance are interested in quantitative analysis and statistics not as an end in itself but with how this quantitative information and data analysis techniques can help them better understand their area of interest or solve problems confronted in their daily work. We also are interested in statistics only to help you clearly present the

To the Web

Web Sites About Statistics

To find a quick reference for the definition and explanation of statistics terminology, go to the **DEPR Web Site**, click on **Web Links, Chapter 13**, then on **Internet Glossary of Statistical Terms**. The Statistics Virtual Library provides links to every facet of statistics: university statistics departments throughout the world, news groups, government and private statistics institutes, online educational resources, and more. Click on **World Wide Web Virtual Library: Statistics**.

data you are working with in your attempt to describe and explain political behavior, not as an end in itself. When these techniques are employed to test an original hypothesis of interest to you, with the result that you can see explicitly in quantitative terms whether to reject or accept that hypothesis, there is a great deal of satisfaction in realizing that you have indeed created knowledge and, at that moment, know something that no one else does. It's a good feeling, and learning how to analyze data correctly will allow you to experience it. [1]

How Many Variables at What Level of Measurement?

When analyzing quantitative data, you need to keep in mind two questions: "With how many variables am I working?" and "What level of measurement have I achieved with each operational definition of these variables?" If your answer to the first question is "one," you will be doing **univariate** statistical analysis and calculating **descriptive statistics.** Because you are working with only one variable, you will be limited to describing rather than trying to explain behavior by testing hypotheses that, of course, have at least two variables. If, however, the answer to how many variables you are working with is "two," you will be doing **bivariate analysis,** trying to determine quantitatively if there is any relationship between the independent and the dependent variable in the hypothesis that you are testing. Using three or more variables in your data analysis—one dependent variable and at least two independent variables—is called **multivariate analysis.** We will cover only univariate analysis in this chapter. Bivariate and multivariate data analyses are covered in Chapters 14 to 17.

In this chapter, we discuss how to analyze data for single variables. Doing univariate analysis will provide a summary description (remember, univariate analysis involves only descriptive statistics) for the variables you would be employing to test your hypothesis. Descriptive statistics are valuable because they allow you to summarize a lot of information with just one or a few numbers. In most instances, you will be working with so many cases that a close examination of data for each individual case you are studying will be impossible. For example, if you are trying to summarize the information about the age of residents of an entire nation or of an American state, or even a survey research sample of a few hundred people, looking at the age of each individual in those groups and trying to describe what you have observed in words will confuse, not clarify, your understanding about the age of the people in your study. A better method of describing the age of any of these groups is to determine the "average" age of all group members and use that number as a description for the entire group. As you might expect, the use of different types of averages is a main component of univariate analysis and descriptive statistics.

Now that we have answered the first question for the purposes of this chapter—that is, we are working with one variable doing univariate analysis—we need to consider the second question about level of measurement. As discussed in Chapter 7, variables can be measured at four different levels: nominal, ordinal, interval, and ratio. In this chapter, you will learn about appropriate statistical techniques for summarizing information about single variables measured at each of these levels. We will start with nominal and ordinal level measurement.

Key Points

Describing and summarizing a single variable:

- Univariate analysis is examining data for only a single variable.
- Univariate analysis, because it involves only one variable, is called descriptive statistics.
- Descriptive statistics summarize information about a variable with just one or a few numbers.
- Which specific descriptive statistics to employ depends on the level of measurement achieved with the operational definition of the variable being described.

Variables Measured at the Nominal and Ordinal Levels

As you should recall, nominal measurement is placing units of analysis, such as individuals in a survey, into mutually exclusive categories. There is no determination of one unit having more or less of some characteristic (the variable under study) than others. Gender, place of residence, and religious grouping are all nominally measured variables for individuals. If the unit of analysis is American states, nominally measured variables include method of selecting state judges (election or appointment), region of the country (northeast, southwest, and so on), and political culture (individualistic, moralistic, traditionalistic). [2] Type of government for American cities (strong mayor/council, weak mayor/council, manager/council) or for nations (monarchy, presidentail system, and so on) is also a nominal level variable.

Variables measured at the ordinal level rank order the units of analysis along some continuum from more to less, reflecting that some units have more or less of a characteristic, but the exact distance between each of the ranks cannot be precisely determined.

Likert items designed to measure individual attitudes and place survey respondents into the categories of strongly agree, agree, neutral/no opinion, disagree, and strongly disagree provide ordinal level measurement. Cities ranked and placed into four categories of desirability for retirement living (very desirable, desirable, undesirable, very undesirable) or nations ranked and grouped according to their commitment to human rights (strong commitment, moderate commitment, weak commitment) are both examples of ordinal level measurement. Univariate statistics describing nominally and ordinally measured variables are the frequency distribution, the modal category, and the median.

■ Frequency Distribution

We originally encountered frequency distributions in Chapter 8 when we discussed managing large data sets and cleaning the data. In its simplest form, a frequency distribution lays out the values for a single variable and indicates the number of cases within each of those values. The categories for the variable into which cases will be placed must be mutually exclusive and collectively exhaustive; that is, each case must fit into only one category and the categories taken together must account for all the cases under study. In Chapter 8 we employed frequencies to make sure values had been entered correctly into the data matrix and to get a very general sense of the data with which you are working. In this chapter, we consider frequency distributions in much greater detail for the purpose of describing a single variable.

For sex of respondents in a survey sample, the frequency distribution would list the two categories of male and female and how many of the respondents fell into each category. For judicial selection in the American states, as suggested previously, the categories would be "appointed" and "elected," and the frequency distribution would result in the fifty states being placed into one of those two categories. In our example of the ordinally measured variable of the ranking of nations according to their commitment to human rights, all the nations under study would be placed into one of the three categories of strong, moderate, or weak, and the totals for each category shown.

Three examples of a frequency distribution from the 2000 General Social Survey, for gender, political party identification, and age are shown in Table 13.1. Sex is a nominal level variable with only two values and is called a **dichotomous variable.** The variable of party identification in this table has three values: Democrat, Republican, and Independent (collapsed from eight categories) and is also measured at the nominal level. The third variable, age, could be measured at the interval level, but in this instance it is operationalized at only the ordinal level. Often interval level data, such as age, are collapsed into categories at the ordinal level. If there are a large number of cases and many individual values for the variable, as is the case with age, presenting them all separately

Table 13.1
Frequency Distribution for Sex, Party Identification, and Age

	Frequency:
Variable: Sex	Frequency:
Values:	Number of Observations
Male	1,229
Female	1,588
Total	2,817
Variable: Party Identification	Frequency:
Values:	Number of Observations
Democrat	921
Republican	684
Independent	1,152
Total	2,757
Variable: Age	Frequency:
Values:	Number of Observations
18–29	526
30–39	610
40–49	634
50–59	408
60–69	273
70+	358
Total	2,809

Note: Party identification recoded to three values; "other party" category left out.

would take an enormous amount of space and, in the end, be confusing rather than clarifying. By collapsing, or ordinally grouping, the data into a smaller number of categories, a clearer representation of the data in the frequency distribution is provided. For all the variables in Table 13.1, the number of cases, or observations, falling into each category is displayed, as is the total number of cases. The frequency distributions for these variables provide summary descriptions of sex, party identification, and age of respondents in the General Social Survey sample for 2000.

A frequency distribution is virtually always accompanied by an additional column of numbers showing the proportion, or percentage, of cases that fall into each category. These proportions are calculated by dividing the number of observations in each category by the total number of observations. Percentages are determined by multiplying the proportions by 100. The percentages are usually easier to read and remember than raw figures, and they are more meaningful when comparing populations of different size. Saying that 500,000 people in Rhode Island oppose a particular government policy, for example, is quite different from the same number, or frequency, showing opposition in California. In Rhode Island, 500,000 people is about 50 percent of the entire population, whereas in California it is less than 2 percent of the state's population.

Also, frequency distributions often include a column showing the **cumulative percentage** of cases, the additive percentage of cases included with each additional category, or value, of the variable that is displayed. Finally, the description of a single variable employing a frequency distribution will often show that some cases have data missing. Frequency distributions calculated by most statistical software programs, including SPSS, list the frequency of "missing data" for a variable but provide a column titled "valid percentage" that shows the percentage of cases in each category of the variable after all missing data have been excluded.

Figure 13.1 is a replica of an SPSS frequency distribution output for a variable from the 2000 General Social Survey concerning the respondents' attitudes toward how harshly courts deal with criminals. It shows the values or categories of the variable (too harsh, not harsh enough, about right), the frequency for each value, the percent of cases within each value, the valid percent of cases within each value, and the cumulative percentages for each additional value or category of the variable. The first column is the frequency of responses and shows there are 209 respondents who feel the courts are too harsh, 1,913 respondents who believe the courts are not harsh enough, and 436 people who think the harshness of treatment in the courts is about right. There are 259 missing values on this variable: 240 respondents answered "don't know" (DK), and 19 provided no answer (NA) at all. The second column, labeled "percent," calculates the percentage of each of these responses as a function of the entire sample of 2,817 respondents. As you can see, 7.4 percent of the respondents felt that the courts were too harsh, 67.9 percent not harsh enough, 15.5 percent thought the treatment was about right, 8.5 percent answered "don't know," and .7 percent provided no answer to the question. As indicated in Figure 13.1, those individual percentages total 100 percent. The third column titled "valid percentage" drops the missing values (DK and NA responses) from the analysis and refigures the percentages based only on those who provided answers to this particular question. These adjusted percentages, the valid percentages, are 8.2 percent answering that the courts were too harsh, 74.8 percent saying the courts were not harsh enough, and 17.0 percent believing the courts were acting just about right. In most situations such as this, one should use the valid percent column figures to describe the variable. Reading down the final column on the far right shows the cumulative percentage of cases as the total number of cases in each value is added to the previous case total. The sum of both the frequencies for the responses "too harsh" and "not harsh enough" is 2,122, constituting 83.0 percent of the cases, and when the 436 cases in the "about right" category are added, all 100 percent of the valid cases are accounted for.

The results of frequency distributions may also be displayed in graph or chart form, as well as in tables. Most commonly, frequencies are displayed in pie charts (also referred

Figure 13.1
SPSS Output Viewer Showing Frequency Distribution
of Variable from 2000 General Social Survey

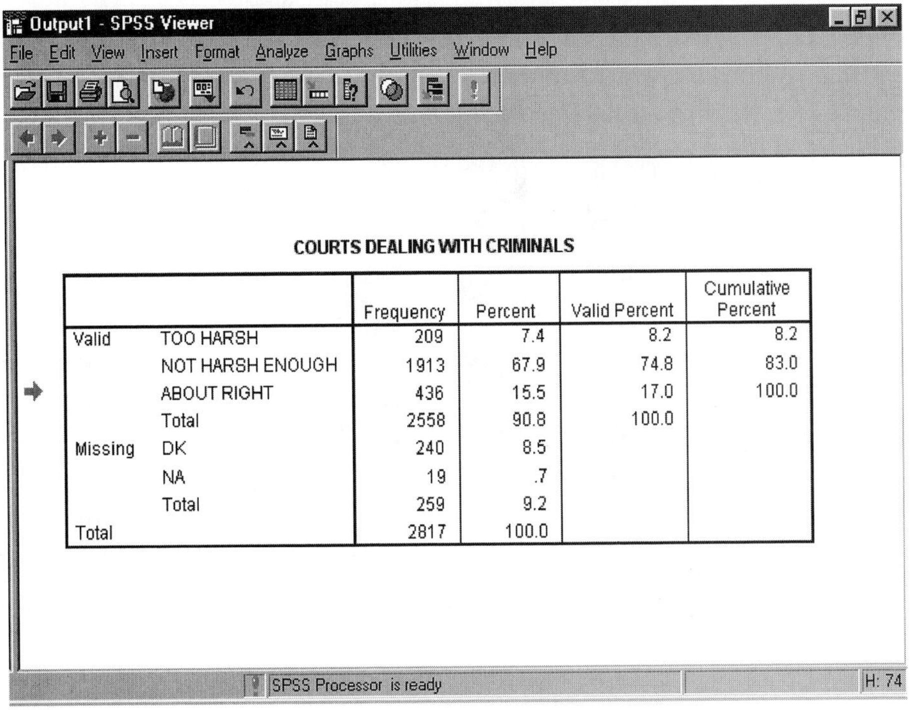

COURTS DEALING WITH CRIMINALS

		Frequency	Percent	Valid Percent	Cumulative Percent
Valid	TOO HARSH	209	7.4	8.2	8.2
	NOT HARSH ENOUGH	1913	67.9	74.8	83.0
	ABOUT RIGHT	436	15.5	17.0	100.0
	Total	2558	90.8	100.0	
Missing	DK	240	8.5		
	NA	19	.7		
	Total	259	9.2		
Total		2817	100.0		

Courtesy of SPSS, Inc.

to as a circle graph) or bar graphs. Figure 13.2 shows both a bar graph and pie chart for the frequency distribution of age displayed in Table 13.1. For the bar graph, each bar represents the number or percentage of cases falling into each category or value of the variable. In a pie chart, each "slice" of the pie represents the frequency of cases for each value of the variable. Such visual displays can help you describe the distribution of values on your variables in a way that is both pleasing to the eye and elucidating for your analysis. [3]

■ Measures of Central Tendency and Dispersion

You have now seen how to display a frequency distribution in table, graph, and chart forms as part of describing a variable measured at the nominal or ordinal level. On occasion

Figure 13.2
Bar Graph and Pie Chart for Distribution of Age

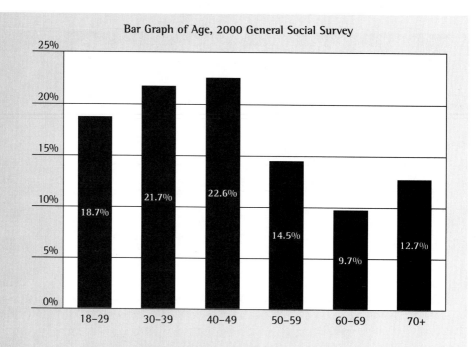

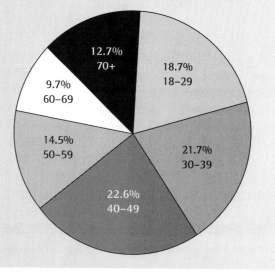

you will need to present that information in even more condensed form because you have a large number of cases or because you want to compare the contents of two or more frequency distributions. This is done regularly with variables measured at the interval or ratio level but less often with variables measured at the nominal or ordinal level. These descriptive statistics summarize the frequency distribution with one or two numbers.

If, for example, you asked one of your professors how the students in your class did on the midterm examination, you would not expect her to provide the score of each student in the class. A frequency distribution indicating what percentage of students fell into each category of grades (2 percent received A's, 4 percent received A–'s, and so on) would be more helpful. But if you wanted to know how your class performed on the midterm exam compared to another section of the course or compared to last semester's class, a descriptive statistic would be helpful. In this example, the instructor might tell you the "average" grade for each class or section, allowing you to compare the performance of one group with another. But note that the use of a descriptive statistic does not reveal any of the specific scores used to calculate the statistic. When the professor compares the average score on the midterm examination from your section with that of another section of the same course, you will not know how any student's individual score on the exam compares to any other student's individual score. In this example, the professor has likely made a deliberate choice, for reasons of confidentiality, to mask the individual scores.

The types of "averages" or **measures of central tendency** that you can employ depends, as discussed previously, on what level of measurement you have achieved with each variable. These measures of central tendency summarize the entire frequency distribution by showing what values tend to the middle of the distribution. On the other hand, **measures of dispersion** indicate how widely diffused the scores are as a whole. In simple terms, measures of central tendency help you determine where the middle of the data is, and measures of dispersion help you figure out how compact or spread out the cases are.

■ Mode, Median, Range, and Percentile

For variables operationalized at the nominal level, the measure of central tendency is the **mode** or **modal category,** the category that contains the greatest number of cases. In Table 13.1, "female" is the modal category for sex and "independent" is the modal category for party identification. A measure of dispersion for nominally measured variables is the proportion of the cases in the modal category; the smaller the proportion, the greater the dispersion. The least amount of dispersion would have all the cases in one category: The modal category would contain 100 percent of all the cases, and there would be no variation in scores on the variable. The greatest amount of dispersion would have an equal percentage of cases in each category of the variable.

Because ordinally measured variables, unlike those measured at the nominal level, involve the units of analysis having a greater or lesser amount of some characteristic, the scores are arranged in order from highest to lowest. The **median** is the middle score in such a distribution and used as another measure of central tendency for variables measured at the ordinal level. Half of the scores in the distribution lie above the median, and half lie below. Whichever category contains the middle score is called the **median group.** Distributions of an ordinally measured variable, like nominal variables, also have a modal category. For the variable of age displayed in Table 13.1, the median would be calculated as follows. Because there are 2,809 respondents, the middle observation of the scores ordered from highest to lowest would be 1,405. There are 1,404 scores below this value and 1,404 scores above this value. Respondent 1,405 falls into the 40–49 age category, so that is the median age group for the distribution. The person with the middle score in the distribution is in that category. The modal category, the one containing the most scores, is also 40–49. That category has 22.6 percent of the valid scores. In the example of the scores on the midterm examination, the professor might tell you the modal score and median scores were "C," indicating more students in the class received that grade than any other and that grade divided the scores on the exam into the upper and lower halves.

A measure of dispersion for ordinal-level variables is the **range,** which is the difference between the highest and lowest value in the distribution. Because the range is very sensitive to an extreme value at one end of the distribution or the other, midrange measures have been developed that eliminate considering part of the low and high ends of a distribution. One of these is the **interquartile range,** and it is often used to describe the distribution of scores for a variable measured at the ordinal level. The interquartile range delineates the range of values within which the middle 50 percent of the scores are found. This is accomplished by eliminating from consideration the first quartile—the bottom 25 percent of the scores—and the fourth quartile—the top 25 percent of the scores. What's left is the middle 50 percent of the observations, eliminating any extreme values at either end of the distribution. For the ordinally grouped variable of age in Table 13.1, the interquartile range is 30–39 to 50–59. One-fourth of the 2,809 respondents is equal to 702; omitting those respondents (the first quartile) from the lower end of the distribution puts the low score in the 30–39 age group. Eliminating the top quarter of respondents, the 702 respondents at the upper end of the distribution, puts the high score in the 50–59 age group. That makes the interquartile range "30–39" to "50–59"; the middle 50 percent of the cases in the distribution are within that range.

More generally, lots of data for individual variables with which you are probably familiar are reported in **percentiles,** a value below which a certain percent of the distribution is found. If you were ranked in the 65th percentile on the verbal score of the College Board SATs, it means that 65 percent of those individuals who took the exam scored lower than you did. You were in the top 35 percent of the distribution. Students

who take the Graduate Record Exams or the Law School Admission Test will also find
their scores reported in percentiles, indicating where they stand in percentage terms relative to all others in the distribution of raw scores. The
interquartile range is a particular case of reporting scores
in percentiles—that is, the range from the 25th to the
75th percentile.

   To summarize, the measure of central tendency for
nominal-level variables is the modal category, but for ordinal-level variables both the modal category and the
median grouping can be used. Measuring the dispersion
of a frequency distribution of a nominally measured
variable is limited to the percentage of cases in the modal
category, but for ordinal-level variables, dispersion can
be estimated from the range and the interquartile range.

To the Web

**Exercise 13.1   Frequency Distributions
for Nominal and Ordinal Variables**

This exercise requires you to look at two frequency
distributions from real data, determine what level
of measurement is reached with each variable, and
figure out appropriate statistics for assessing central
tendency and dispersion for each. Go to the **DEPR**
Web Site, click on **Web Exercises, Chapter 13,**
then on **Frequency Distributions for Nominal and
Ordinal Variables.**

Variables Measured at the Interval and Ratio Levels

Variables measured at the interval and ratio levels can be summarized more precisely than
those measured at lower levels because the operational definitions themselves are more
precise. Now the values of the variable are not only ranked, as with ordinal-level measurement, but the explicit distance between each rank is also known. The numbers representing measurement at the interval or ratio level have mathematical properties: They
can be added, subtracted, multiplied, and divided. This allows for measures of central
tendency and dispersion for these types of variables that are less equivocal and more
exact. Measures of central tendency for interval and ratio-level variables are the mode,
the median, and the **arithmetic mean.** The most common and most useful measure of
dispersion is the **standard deviation.**

■ The Mean

As you know, the mode and median can be used to describe distributions of nominal-
and ordinal-level data. But because interval- and ratio-level data are measured more precisely, the mode and median are reported as specific, individual numbers rather than as
a modal category for nominal variables or a median grouping for ordinal variables. With
interval- or ratio-level measurement, the mode (the score that occurs most frequently) and
the median (the middle score) are single numbers. Look at Figure 13.3, which shows the
distribution of the percentage of the vote received by Bill Clinton in the 1996 presidential
election in the 435 U.S. House of Representatives districts. This frequency distribution

Figure 13.3
Frequency Distribution of Percentage of 1996 Presidential
Vote Received by Bill Clinton in U.S. House Districts

	Frequency	Percent	Cumulative Percent		Frequency	Percent	Cumulative Percent
26.00	2	.5	.5	58.00	13	3.0	80.0
27.00	1	.2	.7	59.00	9	2.1	82.1
28.00	2	.5	1.1	60.00	6	1.4	83.4
29.00	4	.9	2.1	61.00	8	1.8	85.3
30.00	1	.2	2.3	62.00	4	.9	86.2
31.00	3	.7	3.0	63.00	5	1.1	87.4
32.00	2	.5	3.4	64.00	4	.9	88.3
33.00	4	.9	4.4	65.00	5	1.1	89.4
34.00	4	.9	5.3	66.00	3	.7	90.1
35.00	7	1.6	6.9	67.00	2	.5	90.6
36.00	6	1.4	8.3	69.00	1	.2	90.8
37.00	15	3.4	11.7	70.00	3	.7	91.5
38.00	12	2.8	14.5	71.00	3	.7	92.2
39.00	10	2.3	16.8	72.00	1	.2	92.4
40.00	7	1.6	18.4	73.00	2	.5	92.9
41.00	22	5.1	23.4	74.00	2	.5	93.3
42.00	14	3.2	26.7	75.00	2	.5	93.8
43.00	15	3.4	30.1	77.00	1	.2	94.0
44.00	15	3.4	33.6	79.00	2	.5	94.5
45.00	23	5.3	38.9	80.00	2	.5	94.9
46.00	22	5.1	43.9	81.00	5	1.1	96.1
47.00	22	5.1	49.0	82.00	2	.5	96.6
48.00	13	3.0	52.0	83.00	1	.2	96.8
49.00	17	3.9	55.9	84.00	1	.2	97.0
50.00	20	4.6	60.5	85.00	4	.9	97.9
51.00	14	3.2	63.7	86.00	4	.9	98.9
52.00	13	3.0	66.7	87.00	1	.2	99.1
53.00	14	3.2	69.9	91.00	1	.2	99.3
54.00	9	2.1	72.0	92.00	1	.2	99.5
55.00	9	2.1	74.0	93.00	1	.2	99.8
56.00	3	.7	74.7	95.00	1	.2	100.0
57.00	10	2.3	77.0	Total	435	100.0	

Source: Doing Empirical Political Research, "HOUSE106depr" data set.

was calculated from the "HOUSEdepr" data set that accompanies this text. This is ratio-level measurement, and with all 435 individual scores listed, making sense of the distribution of this variable without the use of descriptive statistics would be difficult.

The modal score is 45 percent: 23 representative districts had 45 percent of its voters choose Bill Clinton. The median score is 48 percent because that is the score that divides the 435 cases in half. Measures used for ordinal-level variables can also be employed with interval- and ratio-level data, so the range is 69.0, the difference between the highest (95) and the lowest (26) scores in the distribution. And by looking at the cumulative percentage column, you can determine which scores fall into any particular percentile and determine the interquartile range, which in this distribution is 42 to 57. But the most appropriate and most familiar measure of central tendency for this distribution is the arithmetic mean. You need to be cautious, however, when using the mean with interval/ratio data. If the data are skewed and do not approximate the **normal curve** (a symmetrical, bell-shaped frequency distribution), it is better to retreat back to ordinal-level measures or use the median as the measure of central tendency.

To calculate the mean, sum the values of a variable for each case and divide by the number of cases.

$$\text{Arithmetic mean} = \overline{X} = \frac{\Sigma X}{N} = \text{Sum of values/Number of cases}$$

where

$\overline{X}$ is the mean and is referred to as "X bar."
X is the value of the variable for each case.
N is the number of cases.
Σ (the Greek capital letter sigma) means to sum what follows.

The mean of the distribution in Figure 13.3 is 50.4 percent—that is, the mean vote received by Bill Clinton across all 435 House electoral districts.

■ The Standard Deviation

The mean, standing alone, may be a misleading descriptive statistic because markedly different distributions can produce the same mean. Here is an extreme, hypothetical example of improperly relying on only the mean to describe a distribution. Let's assume there is an outbreak of influenza in a state, and the health department is trying to get a handle on who is getting the flu so they can recommend which individuals in the state population are most threatened and should be immunized. The health director is informed by researchers only that 200 flu cases have been reported and that the mean age of the people getting the flu is forty-five years old. One age distribution that would produce a mean of 45 is if every person who had the flu was that exact age. In that case, the mean would be a perfect description of the distribution. But what if this influenza were attacking only the very young and the very old? If 100 of the people who had the flu were 2 years old and the other 100 people were 88 years old, the mean age would again be 45 years. (The sum of the ages of those 200 people is equal to 9,000. When divided by 200, the number of cases, the mean age is 45 years old.) In this latter case, the mean is a very poor description of the age of people who have the influenza. The health director, and anyone else employing the mean as a descriptive statistic for a frequency distribution they have not or cannot examine in its entirety, needs more information about the age of the people getting the flu than that provided only by the mean.

Whenever the mean is calculated for any distribution, just a few extreme values at either end of the distribution can render the mean a poor descriptor of that distribution. If the career placement office at a university is trying to describe the starting salaries of last year's liberal arts graduates, and one of them signed a multimillion-dollar professional sports contract, the mean would provide an artificially high description of starting salaries. In this situation, the median would be a better descriptive statistic to employ. In general, the additional information you need to go along with the mean are other measures of central tendency (the mode and the median) as well as a measure of dispersion you have already seen: the range. For the distribution reported in Figure 13.3, the median (48), the mean (50.4), and the mode (45) are fairly close, indicating pretty clearly what values tend toward the middle of the distribution. In addition, and most important, interval- and ratio-level data allow you to calculate the standard deviation as another measure of dispersion.

The standard deviation measures dispersion by indicating how far scores in the distribution differ from the mean. The further individual scores are from the mean, the larger will be the standard deviation. The closer individual scores are to the mean, the smaller will be the standard deviation. The smaller the standard deviation, the better the mean is as a descriptor of the center of a frequency distribution. This is the formula for the standard deviation.

$$\text{Standard deviation} = \sqrt{\frac{\Sigma(X - \bar{X})^2}{N}}$$

As you can see from the formula, the standard deviation is calculated by subtracting the mean from each score to obtain the **deviation score.** These deviation scores will always add up to zero, but because we are interested only in the amount of the deviation and not the direction, we can ignore the signs. This could be accomplished by using the absolute value of the scores, but the formula accomplishes the same end by squaring each deviation score and eliminating all minus signs. [4] The mean of these squared scores is then calculated in the usual way by summing them and dividing by the number of cases. Now we have the mean of the squared deviation scores, also called the **variance,** and when we take the square root of that mean, the result is the standard deviation. [5] The greater the dispersion of the scores around the mean, the higher will be the values of

Table 13.2
Calculation of the Standard Deviation

Score (X)	Mean Score on Exam ($\bar{X}$)	Deviation Score (X–$\bar{X}$)	Deviation Score Squared (X–$\bar{X}$)^2
94	75	19	361
86	75	11	121
83	75	8	64
80	75	5	25
76	75	1	1
76	75	1	1
73	75	−2	4
72	75	−3	9
64	75	−11	121
63	75	−12	144
58	75	−17	289
			Sum = 1,140

Sum of squared deviation scores $\Sigma(X–\bar{X})^2 = 1,140$

Mean of squared deviation scores $\Sigma(X–\bar{X})^2/N = 103.6 =$ Variance

Square root of mean squared deviation scores $= \sqrt{103.6} = 10.2 =$ Standard deviation

Source: Simulated.

the variance and the standard deviation. If all the values in the distribution are the same, as in the example of all 200 people getting the flu being forty-five years old, the standard deviation will be equal to zero. The standard deviation is important not only as a measure of dispersion for distributions of variables operationalized at the interval or ratio level, but it also is pivotal to the computation of other, more advanced statistics. The calculation of the standard deviation for the distribution in Table 13.2 is as follows.

1. Calculate the mean of the distribution: $\bar{X}$.
2. Subtract the mean from each score to obtain a deviation score: (X–$\bar{X}$). This shows how far each individual score in the distribution is from the mean.
3. Square each deviation score: (X–$\bar{X}$)^2.
4. Sum the squared deviation scores: Σ (X–$\bar{X}$)^2.
5. Divide the sum of the squared deviation scores by the number of cases: $\Sigma(X–\bar{X})^2/N$. This is the variance.
6. Take the square root of the number calculated in step 5. This is the standard deviation.

The variance of the distribution in Figure 13.3—percent of vote for Clinton in 1996 for each U.S. House district—is 162.7, and the standard deviation is 12.75.

To the Web

> **Exercise 13.2   Frequency Distribution for Interval and Ratio Level Data**
>
> This exercise requires you to look at data that reaches at least interval level of measurement. You will be asked to figure out and explain specific measures of central tendency and dispersion. Go to the DEPR Web Site, click on **Web Exercises, Chapter 13,** then on **Frequency Distribution for Interval and Ratio Level Data.**

The interpretation of a particular standard deviation, whether it is considered large or small, is dependent on recognizing something about the distribution of scores and the mean from which it was calculated. A standard deviation of 3.1 would be considered large for a distribution of scores on a seven-point Likert item with a mean of 3.8. In this instance, there is a great deal of variation in the scores around the mean. But the same standard deviation, 3.1, for the age of a random sample of the general population of the United States with a mean of 46.2 would be considered very small. Most cases for this age distribution would be clustered closely around the mean.

Q Questions for Thought and Discussion

During a political debate for governor, two candidates both claim to be talking about the "average" income for families in the state but cite different dollar amounts. Is one candidate necessarily misinformed or misleading the audience? Or is it possible that both candidates are correct?

■ The Standard Deviation and the Normal Curve

The standard deviation is used in inferential statistics; it provides the basis for probability sampling. It is also used for comparing individual scores from different normal distributions as well. The normal distribution, as mentioned previously, is a bell-shaped frequency distribution, sometimes called a bell curve. For such a distribution, shown in Figure 13.4, the mean, the median, and the mode all have the same value and are found at the center of the distribution. In addition, and key to understanding how probability sampling works, a fixed proportion of the cases are found between the mean and any distance from the mean measured in standard deviation units.

The mean of the distribution (which in the case of a normal distribution—remember—is the same as the median and the mode) divides it precisely in half: 50 percent of all the scores are above the mean and 50 percent are below the mean. As you move away from the mean in either direction, a certain proportion of the cases fall under that area of the curve. For example, the area between the mean and one standard deviation above the mean accounts for 34.13 percent of all the scores in the distribution. The same proportion of scores are between the mean and one standard deviation below it, which means that one standard deviation on either side of the mean accounts for 68.26 percent of the

Figure 13.4
Proportions of Cases Under Areas of the Normal Curve

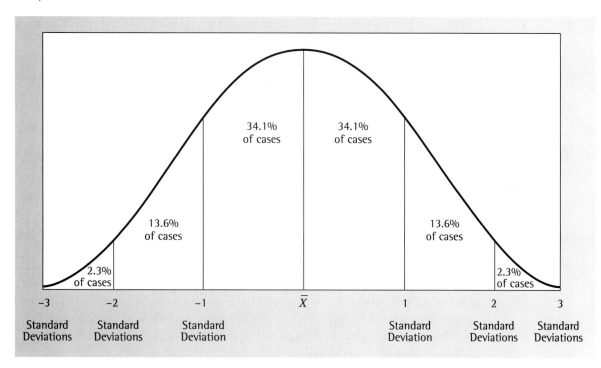

scores. Figure 13.4 shows what percentage of scores lie within any range of standard deviation units. What is important for probability sampling is that 95 percent of the scores lie between the mean and 1.96 standard deviation units on either side of the mean; 99 percent are between plus or minus 2.58 standard deviation units of the mean. That is how sampling error and confidence intervals are determined in drawing random samples.

■ The Standard Deviation and Probability Sampling

Remember in Chapter 9 that we provided the formula for determining the sampling error for any size random sample at a specific confidence level.

$$\text{Sampling error} = \pm 1.96 \sqrt{\frac{p(1 - p)}{N}}$$

The same formula, we pointed out, can be used for establishing the necessary sample size for some predetermined tolerated sampling error at a particular confidence level. We mentioned in Chapter 9 that most random samples had confidence intervals of 95 percent. Now you can see why the value ±1.96 is employed: It is the distance in standard deviation units on either side of the mean of a normal distribution that accounts for 95 percent of the cases.

When determining the sampling error for any size random sample, empirical political scientists think about the sample they have drawn as only one among many they *could* have drawn. Instead of drawing one sample and estimating a population mean (such as the age of the population) from that single sample, they could have drawn another sample or a few more samples or even an infinite number of samples. If they were to average the means of the two samples or the few samples or the infinite number of samples, they would become increasingly more confident that their estimate was closer to the actual population mean. Indeed, drawing an infinite number of samples, calculating the mean for each, and plotting all of those individual means will produce a normal distribution—and the mean of that distribution will be equal to the population mean. Thinking in these terms, the empirical political scientist now asks, "Where does my one, individual sample mean lie in that normal distribution of the possible infinite number of sample means? Is it close to the center of the distribution, near the mean, which would make the sample estimate very close to the population parameter? Or is it out at the end of the distribution, near one of the tails, making the sample mean a very poor estimate of the population mean?" The answer can only be provided in probabilistic terms, based on the standard deviation, about how far that empiricist's one sample mean is from the mean of the hypothetical distribution of sample means.

With these considerations in mind, the empirical political scientist can estimate where the sample with which he is working falls in the hypothetical distribution of sampling means. The standard deviation of the distribution of sampling means, also called the **standard error,** is equal to $\sigma/\sqrt{N}$, where σ is the standard deviation of the population and N is the size of the sample. The population standard deviation (σ), of course, is unknown. But because most of the sample mean values in the distribution will cluster around the true population mean, the empirical political scientist can substitute the standard deviation of the sample (s) with which he is working as an approximation of the standard deviation of the population. So, for example, if someone took a sample of 100 lobbyists registered in the state of Arizona and found that the mean age of the sample was 51 years with a standard deviation of 18, what would that tell you about the age of the population of registered lobbyists in that state? Using our formula,

$$\text{Standard error} = s/\sqrt{N} \quad \text{or} \quad 18/\sqrt{100} = 18/10 = 1.8.$$

Consequently, as shown in Figure 13.4, because 68 percent of the scores in a normal distribution fall between plus or minus one standard deviation around the mean, we can say that we are 68 percent confident that the true population mean lies somewhere between $51 + 1.8$ years and $51 - 1.8$ years—that is, between 52.8 and 49.2. If we wish to be 95 percent confident that we have identified the range of the true population mean (that is, we want to set the confidence interval at 95 percent) we need to move to 1.96 standard deviations around the mean—that is, $1.96 \times 1.8 = 3.53$. Adding that to the mean gives an upper limit of 54.53, while subtracting that number from the mean gives us a lower limit of 47.47, allowing us to say that we are 95 percent confident that the actual mean age of all lobbyists in Arizona lies somewhere between 54.53 and 47.47. Note that as the sample size increases, the denominator of the formula becomes larger, reducing the size of the standard error for samples with similar variance. With a conversion of the same formula (solving for $N = s^2 \, [p(1 - p)]/\sqrt{\text{Sampling error}}$), as pointed out in Chapter 9, we can calculate precisely the sample size required for any given sampling error.

▓ Standard or z-scores

The standard deviation can also be used to compare individual scores in any normal distribution with individual scores from any other normal distribution. The original scores in the distributions need only be converted into standard deviation units, called **standard scores** or **z-scores.** But remember this works only for scores that are normally distributed. A z-score is the number of standard deviation units that a score differs from the mean. A z-score of 1.4, for example, indicates that the score is 1.4 standard deviations above the mean, while a z-score of -2.0 is two standard deviations below the mean. This is the formula for calculating a z-score.

$$z = (X - \overline{X})/s$$

where

   X is a single score.
   $\overline{X}$ is the mean of all the scores.
   s is the standard deviation of the scores.

Expressing the scores in standard deviation units is what allows the comparison of scores from two distributions. This is why standardized test scores of students are comparable even if they took different exams at different times. For example, the College Board

To the Web

Interactive Exercises That Show Areas Under the Normal Curve

Both of these Web sites help you see clearly how much of an area under the normal curve is contained between differing standard deviation units above or below the mean by allowing you to change their values. Go to the **DEPR Web Site**, click on **Web Links, Chapter 13**, then on **Seeing Statistics** and **Normal Distribution Calculator**.

SATs are taken by thousands of students at one time, producing a normal distribution of scores each time the examination is administered. In rough terms, the scores reported by the college board that range from 200 to 800 are standard scores or z-scores, the distance from the mean in standard deviation units that any individual student's score lies. Consequently, students taking the SATs at different times have scores that are comparable because they are reported in terms of a student's placement in the distribution of scores relative to the mean. The same holds true for scores reported for most standardized testing done with large numbers of people; by converting original scores to z-scores, any individual's score can be expressed as a distance from the center point of a normal distribution.

Conclusion

Statistical analysis is one of the final steps in doing empirical political research, and you now have a good sense of how statistical techniques are employed to describe a single variable. When there is just too much data to visually scan, which is virtually always the case, measures of central tendency and dispersion can help describe a frequency distribution clearly and concisely. For doing your own data analysis, you need to understand which descriptive statistics are appropriate to use in a particular instance. For reading the results of others' empirical work, you must know how to interpret these statistics when you encounter them. Trying to memorize the formulas, in our opinion, is not a productive effort because you can always find them listed in this book or in other locations. Understanding when to use which statistic and how to interpret statistics are, on the other hand, important and useful skills. Bivariate data analysis and statistics, used to test hypotheses, are introduced and explained in the next two chapters.

Summary of the Main Points

■ Univariate statistics, also called descriptive statistics, are used to describe one variable.

■ Measures of central tendency are used to describe frequency distributions by indicating what scores tend toward the middle of the distribution; measures of dispersion describe frequency distributions by indicating how widely diffused the scores are.

■ Which univariate statistics to use depends on the level of measurement achieved with the variable.

■ For nominally measured variables, the measure of central tendency is the modal category, and the measure of dispersion is the proportion of cases in that modal category.

- For ordinally measured variables, the measure of central tendency is the median grouping, and the measures of dispersion are the range and the interquartile range.
- For roughly normal distributions with variables measured at the interval or ratio level, the measure of central tendency is the mean, and the measure of dispersion is the standard deviation.
- Understanding which statistics to employ and how to interpret them is more important than memorizing formulas.

Terms Introduced

arithmetic mean
bivariate analysis
cumulative percentage
descriptive statistics
deviation score
dichotomous variable
interquartile range
measures of central tendency
measures of dispersion
median
median group
modal category
mode
multivariate analysis
normal curve
percentile
range
standard deviation
standard error
standard score
univariate statistics
variance
z-score

Selected Readings

Blalock, Hubert M., Jr. *Social Statistics.* New York: McGraw-Hill, 1979.

Huff, Darrel. *How to Lie with Statistics.* New York: Norton, 1954.

Kranzler, Gerald, and Janet Moursund. *Statistics for the Terrified,* 2nd Ed. Upper Saddle River, NJ: Prentice Hall, 1999.

Meier, K. J., and J. L. Brudney. *Applied Statistics for Public Administration,* 4th Ed. New York: Harcourt Brace, 1997.

Phillips, John L., Jr. *How to Think About Statistics,* 5th Ed. New York: W. H. Freeman and Company, 1996.

Weisberg, H. F. *Central Tendency and Variability.* Newbury Park, CA: Sage Publications, 1992.

Activities

Activity 13.1
Calculating the Mean and Standard Deviation

The objective of this exercise is to more completely understand the logic of a standard deviation by calculating one by hand. You will need a calculator to complete this exercise. Following the example in Table 13.2, calculate the mean and standard deviation for the following distribution: 28, 30, 34, 38, 41, 41, 43, 48, 54, 58, 61.

Activity 13.2
Using SPSS for Describing Frequency Distributions

The objective of this activity is to learn how to create frequency distributions with appropriate measures of central tendency and dispersion, using SPSS. To that end, go to SPSS and open the "HOUSE106depr" data file. Near the top of the screen, in the status bar area, click on "Analyze." When the drop-down menu appears under "Analyze," click on "Descriptive Statistics." When a box appears to the side, click on "Frequencies."

You are now looking at a new window titled "Frequencies." The small window to the left is the variable list from the data, organized alphabetically. Scroll through the variables until you find the variable "Religion." Click on "Religion," and it will be highlighted. Click on the arrow button between the boxes to move "Religion" into the right-hand box. Then click on the "Statistics" button; notice the choice of measures of central tendency and measures of dispersion available for you to use. Because religion is a nominal level variable, check off only "Mode," and then click on "Continue." Next click on the "Charts" button, which will give you the choice of creating a bar chart or a pie chart. Check off "Pie chart." Another choice in this window is for chart values—frequencies or percentages. Check off "Percentages." Click on the "OK" button. Click "OK" again and wait while SPSS calculates a frequency distribution, mode value, and pie chart for the variable religion.

A new window titled "Output—SPSS Viewer" appears; results of your data analysis are in this window. The first table lets you know if there are any missing values for your variable and the value of the mode that you requested. The second table, similar to what is shown in Figure 13.1, shows in the left-hand column the possible values of the variable and, working across from left to right, the frequency, the frequency calculated as a percentage, the valid percentage, and the cumulative percentage. The percentage in the modal category, 56.6%, is the measure of dispersion.

At the top of the screen, click on "Analyze," and repeat the preceding process for the variable "ptyunity," which stands for party unity and is the percentage of time that the representative voted with a majority of his or her party. But *before* you click on the "OK" button this time, be sure to move the "Religion" variable back into the left-hand box, or

SPSS will do a frequency distribution for that variable again. You can do a frequency for as many variables in a data set as you want at one time by moving them all into the right-hand box at the same time. SPSS will do a frequency simultaneously for all the variables listed in the right-hand box, but remember that variables operationalized at different levels will require you to choose different measures of central tendency and dispersion. Because party unity is measured at the interval level, you will choose different options for central tendency and dispersion measures.

Click on the "Statistics" button and check off mean, median, mode for measures of central tendency and range, variance, and standard deviation for measures of dispersion. Click on "Continue." Click on the "Charts" button, and check off "Bar chart" and "Frequencies." Click on the "OK" button, and wait while SPSS calculates a frequency distribution, measures of central tendency and dispersion, and a bar chart for the variable of party unity.

To print only partial results of your SPSS output, such as only one table, right-click on that table and a box will appear around it. For example, when doing a frequency distribution of a variable with many values that produces a very large table that might take up several pages, you may want to print only the table reporting your measures of central tendency and dispersion. Click on "File" near the top of the window, and when the drop-down menu appears, click on "Print." A window titled "Print" appears. Click on "Print preview" to see if only the table you have designated appears. Click on the "OK" button to print.

Write a brief description of the frequency distributions of religion and party unity for U.S. House members, making use of all the measures of central tendency and dispersion for each variable.

Chapter 14

Constructing and Interpreting Bivariate Tables

Learning Objectives

After completion of this chapter, students should be able to do the following:

Recognize and name the component parts of percentage tables.

Read and interpret the data in percentage tables.

Construct different types of percentage tables to display data and show relationships in one's own data.

Calculate and interpret the lambda and gamma statistics that summarize relationships displayed in percentage tables.

Tables Tell Us a Lot

Most people have seen simple **percentage tables** in books or other scholarly works as students or in a variety of news sources. Many undergraduates use tables in preparing their term papers, although not always with the same intention as empirical researchers. Sometimes when students are assigned a term paper requiring a certain minimum length—twenty pages, for example—they come up one or two pages short. One solution to this problem is to search various sources for a table that is at least tangentially related to the paper topic, copy and reference it, and place it alone on a separate page in the term paper, and then do that as many times as necessary until you have the required number of pages. While this may be an effective strategy for achieving the short-range goal of filling pages, it does nothing to improve either the quality of the research in, or the grade assigned to, that term paper.

Actually, a better reason for using tables in research reports of any kind, including term papers, is to save space rather than fill it. Percentage tables are a very effective method for presenting nominal- and ordinal-level data in a condensed format that the reader can easily understand. If, as the saying goes, one picture is worth a thousand words, then one well-constructed percentage table is worth at least a few long paragraphs. Rather than simply comparing actual, raw numbers in different cells of the table, percentages are employed so meaningful comparisons can be made between or among groups of differing size.

Social scientists organize and summarize nominal and ordinal data in percentage tables to test hypotheses. Recall that a useful hypothesis is one that states a relationship between two variables, and examining a percentage table should easily reveal what hypothesis the table was constructed to test. Percentage tables are specifically designed to display relationships between variables measured at the nominal or ordinal level. You may also recall that relationships between variables expressed in hypotheses can be characterized in terms of their strength and direction.

Strength is the extent to which variables change together. A perfect relationship is one in which a change in the value of one variable is always accompanied by a change in the value of another variable. **Direction,** on the other hand, has to do with how variables change. If the values of two variables change in the same direction, there is a direct or **positive relationship.** The height and weight of people is a good example: Generally, taller people are heavier and shorter people are lighter. That is, the relationship between height and weight is generally positive. When the values of the variables move in opposite directions, there is an inverse or **negative relationship.** The weather in U.S. cities is one example: As the number of sunny days per year increases, the number of inches of rain each year decreases. Strength and direction of relationships, however, are not necessarily related. Any combination of strength and direction may be reflected in the relationship between variables. Percentage tables are helpful because they can always be used to find the strength and direction of relationships between variables.

Percentage tables are used in virtually every professional and business field a student might enter after college. All parts of modern society are data driven in one sense or another, and whatever career one chooses, understanding basic principles of data analysis will be an important aspect of your personal portfolio. Even if you are never required to conduct data analysis or create percentage tables, the probability is very high that you will find such tables strewn throughout reports, studies, and other documents on which complex decision making rests. The ability to read and make sense of percentage tables is a valuable skill in most modern professions.

Characteristics and Construction of Bivariate Tables

The key to understanding percentage tables is to know that the design of the percentage table follows a few basic principles, reflective of what most empirical researchers do in their work. If everyone follows these principles, and most do, it takes less effort and time

Table 14.1
Relationship Between Sex and Attitude on Health Spending, Raw Numbers

Health Spending Is	SEX		Total
	Male	Female	
Too little	421	589	1,010
About right	160	159	319
Too much	24	26	50
Total	605	774	1,379

Source: General Social Survey, 2000, National Opinion Research Center.

To the Web

Washington Statistical Society

For a more general introduction to the presentation of data, see *A Guide to Good Graphics,* by the Washington Statistical Society. Go to the **DEPR Web Page,** click on **Web Links, Chapter 14,** then on **Washington Statistical Society.**

to read and understand one another's tables. Following are the basic characteristics of a well-constructed percentage table designed to show the relationship between two variables. Such a table, with one independent and one dependent variable, is called a bivariate table.

- The table can stand on its own, containing enough information for the reader to understand it with little or no accompanying text. In fact, the reader should be able to discern the hypothesis tested in the table by examining the labels.
- The table has a title describing the content.
- The table is easier to read if the independent variable is placed along the top of the table and the dependent variable runs down the left side of the table.
- Percentages should run down the columns, totaling 100 percent.
- Comparisons for the purpose of identifying relationships between variables are made across the columns—that is, across the categories of the independent variable.

Crosstabulation of variables means classifying units of analysis in terms of their values on two variables. Table 14.1 shows how a sample of 1,379 adults can be classified in terms of their sex and attitudes on health spending. The table tells us that 421 males and 589 females believed that too little was being spent on health care, for a total of 1,010 adults who felt that way. The table also shows us that there were a total of 605 males and 774 females who responded to this question. Obviously, there are fewer males to indicate their opinion on health-care spending. Because of the imbalance of males and females, Table 14.1 is not useful for making the comparisons necessary for examining

Table 14.2
Relationship Between Sex and Attitude
on Health Spending, with Percentages

	SEX	
Health Care Spending Is	Male	Female
Too little	69.6%	76.1%
	(421)	(589)
About right	26.4%	20.5%
	(160)	(159)
Too much	4.0%	3.4%
	(24)	(26)
Total	100%	100%
	(605)	(774)

Source: General Social Survey, 2000, National Opinion Research Center.

the relationship between sex and opinions on health-care spending. To control for the unequal number of males and females, percentages must be computed, as shown in Table 14.2.

Table 14.2 is a bivariate percentage table that meets the criteria of a well-constructed table outlined previously, and much can be learned from such a table. It is easiest to read a bivariate table beginning from the outside and working inward. The title informs us that the table shows the relationship between sex and attitude on health spending, and as any useful title, indicates what variables are included in the table. You can even make an educated guess from the title what hypothesis is being tested in the table. Moving inward from the title, you see what are called identifiers. The two variables and their values are clearly labeled. The variable of sex, with its two values of "male" and "female," is placed at the top of the table, and attitude on health spending, with the values of "too little," "about right," and "too much," are on the left side of the table.

Focusing on the numbers in the table, you can see at the bottom that the totals for males (605) and females (774) are presented with an indication that each number represents 100 percent of each sex. The general rule for calculating percentages in a table is to use the total number of cases within categories of the independent variable as a basis for calculation. In other words, tables are percentaged within categories of the independent variable—in this case, "male" and "female." Table 14.2 shows that 421 males out of a total of 605, or 69.6 percent, believed that too little was being spent on health care. The percentages in the column for males, and females as well, total 100 percent. The independent variable and dependent variable in a table can be identified in this manner;

percentages always add up to 100 percent within values of the independent variables in a bivariate percentage table. Note that the independent variable is at the top of the table and values of that variable are represented by the column headings.

For each cell of the table the actual numbers (N's) and the percentages are both included. But including both is actually not necessary as long as the total numbers are given at the bottom of the table. For example, it would be possible to determine how many males said too little was being spent on health care by multiplying 605 by 69.6 percent and arriving at 421.

Once the independent and dependent variables are identified, it is possible to read and interpret the table. The general rule is that tables are percentaged *within* categories of the independent variable and read *across* categories of that variable. It appears that Table 14.2 is testing a hypothesis relating sex and attitude on health care spending and shows that 69.6 percent of males, compared to 76.1 percent of females, said that too little was being spent on health care. Likewise, 4.0 percent of males said too much was being spent on health care, compared to 3.4 percent of females. Being female increases the likelihood that a person will say too little was being spent on health care. A rough evaluation of the strength of the relationship can be made by calculating the percentage differences between males and females; in the case of saying too little was being spent on health care, the absolute difference is 76.1 percent − 69.6 percent = 6.5 percent. The larger the percentage difference, the stronger the relationship.

To the Web

Exercise 14.1   Constructing a Percentage Table from Raw Numbers

Understanding how to read and interpret percentage tables is easier after constructing several of them on your own. We have provided an exercise that will help you set up and read your own percentage table. Go to the **DEPR Web Page,** click on Web Exercises, Chapter 14, then on Constructing a Percentage Table from Raw Numbers.

▨ Evaluating the Direction and Strength of Relationships

Bivariate percentage tables are most useful for testing hypotheses that state a relationship between variables that are measured at the nominal level or the ordinal level, with relatively few values. (Of course, interval- and ratio-level variables can be collapsed into fewer categories and treated as ordinal.) Well-constructed hypotheses state how variables are related by indicating the direction in which they will covary, and it is important to emphasize how one distinguishes direction and strength in reading percentage tables.

A relationship is positive if two variables move in the same direction and negative if they vary in opposite directions. Table 14.3 displays a positive relationship between two variables. The independent variable is education, and the dependent variable is income because the percentages in the columns, within categories of education, add up to 100 percent. You can assume that Table 14.3 tests the hypothesis that people with higher levels of education tend to have higher levels of income. Let us compare the percentage

Table 14.3
Education and Annual Income

Annual Income	EDUCATION		
	Grade School	High School	College
Less than $20,000	64%	32%	22%
$20,000–60,000	24%	46%	31%
More than $60,000	12%	22%	47%
Total	100%	100%	100%
	(450)	(887)	(256)

Source: Simulated.

of those who earned more than $60,000 by levels of education: 12 percent of those with a grade school education earned more than $60,000 compared with 22 percent of those with a high school education and 47 percent of those with a college education. Table 14.3 displays a positive relationship between education and income because as respondents' education increases, their income also increases.

There are two ways to evaluate the strength of the relationship between two variables. The first, as just discussed, is to calculate the percentage differences across categories of the independent variable. It is easiest to compare the highest and lowest category for a row to get a rough idea of the strength of a relationship. For example, when comparing people who made less than $20,000 per year, the absolute difference between those with a grade school education and those with a college education is 42 percent (64 percent − 22 percent), quite a substantial difference that indicates a strong relationship between the variables. Another way to get a general idea of the strength of a relationship is to compare the percentages in opposite corners. If the percentages are relatively large in two of the corners (64 percent and 47 percent in Table 14.3) compared to the opposite corners (12 percent and 22 percent), the relationship is strong.

It is also important to understand the nature of negative relationships. Table 14.4 displays a negative relationship between two variables. Education is the independent variable, and degree of political cynicism the dependent variable. because the percentages add up to 100 percent within values of education. It appears that a hypothesis tested by the table would be that people with higher levels of education are more likely to display lower levels of political cynicism than those with less education. Compare the percentage of people with high levels of political cynicism across levels of education: 63 percent of people with a grade school education have high levels of cynicism compared to 24 percent of those with a high school education and 17 percent of those with a college

Table 14.4
Education and Political Cynicism

| | EDUCATION | | |
Political Cynicism	Grade School	High School	College
Low	14%	35%	62%
Medium	23%	41%	21%
High	63%	24%	17%
Total	100%	100%	100%
	(450)	(887)	(256)

Source: Simulated.

education. This is a negative relationship between education and political cynicism; as educational level increases, levels of political cynicism decrease. The relationship appears to be quite strong with an absolute percentage difference between those with a grade school education and those with a college education of 46 percent (63 percent − 17 percent).

Finally, it is important to be able to recognize a lack of relationship in bivariate percentage tables. Table 14.5 shows no relationship between two variables. The independent variable is pet ownership, and the dependent variable is partisan affiliation because the percentages are calculated within values of pet ownership. The table appears to test a hypothesis relating pet ownership with partisan affiliation—perhaps dog owners are more likely to be Republicans than cat owners. An examination of the percentage who are Democrats among dog owners (36 percent) versus cat owners (38 percent) versus those who own both a dog and a cat (35 percent), and those with no pets (37 percent) reveals that choice of pet has nothing to do with the choice of political party. None of the percentage differences, calculated across categories of the independent variable, exceed 4 percent. Table 14.5 displays an absence of a relationship and would fail to support a hypothesis linking pet ownership to party affiliation.

Measures of Association

The examples of positive, negative, and weak or nonexistent relationships displayed in Tables 14.3, 14.4, and 14.5 are *not* typical of what is usually found when constructing tables to analyze data. Results are usually not so clear cut. One way to summarize the strength and direction of the relationship between the independent and dependent vari-

Table 14.5
Pet Ownership and Partisan Affiliation

Partisan Affiliation	PETS OWNED			
	Dog	Cat	Dog and Cat	No Pets
Democratic	36%	38%	35%	37%
Independent	24%	22%	21%	22%
Republican	40%	40%	44%	41%
Total	100%	100%	100%	100%
	(235)	(341)	(67)	(400)

Source: Simulated.

ables displayed in a bivariate percentage table is to calculate a single, summary statistic called a **measure of association.** There are several measures of association employed to summarize the findings of a percentage table, but we will talk about only two: **lambda** for variables measured at the nominal level and **gamma** for variables at the ordinal level. [1] Lambda does not indicate direction (positive or negative) of the relationship because nominal variables are categorical and do not indicate whether the unit of analysis under study has more or less of some characteristic, only that they are different from one another. As a consequence, the value of lambda ranges from 0 to 1, with distance from zero indicating strength of the relationship. On the other hand, the gamma statistic, used for variables measured at the ordinal level, ranges from -1 to $+1$, with the sign indicating the direction of the relationship and the distance from zero the strength of the relationship between the variables. Statistical interpretations of the relationship between variables measured at the interval- or ratio-level variables are discussed in Chapter 15.

Both lambda and gamma are based on the idea of **proportionate reduction of error.** [2] With a simple frequency distribution of one variable from a survey, for example, the most accurate way to guess the value on that variable of any single person in the sample would be to choose the modal response, which would lead to the number of guessing errors being equal to the total number of responses minus the modal value. Reduction of error means how much more accurately you could guess the value of that variable for any person in the sample by crosstabulating the distribution of responses to that variable across the categories of some independent variable. Were the number of errors reduced by the crosstabulation, and if so, by how much? The greater the proportion of error reduction, the stronger the relationship between the variables displayed in the percentage table.

Table 14.6
Hypothetical Relationship Between Sex and Party Identification

| | SEX | | |
Party Identification	Male	Female	Total
Democrat	411	922	1,333
Republican	650	415	1,065
Total	1,061	1,337	2,398

Source: Simulated.

Questions for Thought and Discussion

In Chapter 6, an important distinction was made between *association* and *causation*. Lambda and gamma are measures of association, not causation. What else is required to demonstrate causation between two variables after they are shown to be strongly related in a percentage table?

Lambda.   Table 14.6 shows there are 1,333 Democrats and 1,065 Republicans under study. If you were trying to guess the party identification for any single respondent based on just that frequency distribution, the most accurate method would be to always guess Democrat, the modal response. Using that approach, you would make 1,065 errors, (2,398 − 1,333), equivalent to the number of Republicans you misidentified as Democrats. But if you knew about the data shown in Table 14.6 and knew the sex of each person whose party identification you had to guess, would your errors be reduced? Certainly— because for every male you would guess Republican, the modal response, and make 411 errors, the number of males who are Democrats. For each female you would guess Democrat, the modal response, and make 415 errors, one for each woman who is a Republican. That's a total of 826 errors, down from 1,065, when you knew only the frequency distribution of the party identification variable. The variable of sex, therefore, has allowed you to reduce your errors in predicting the party identification of any single respondent.

The calculation of lambda, used for nominal level variables, is reflective of this logic. The number of fewer errors—in this example, 239 (1,065 − 826)—is divided by the total errors from knowing only the frequency distribution of party identification: 1,065. And 239/1,065 = .224, the value of lambda and the proportionate reduction of error achieved with the independent variable. The general formula for calculating lambda is: (number of fewer errors using second variable)/(number of errors knowing only the distribution of original variable).

Table 14.7
Education and Annual Income, with Cell Counts

| Annual Income | EDUCATION | | |
	Grade School	High School	College
Less than $20,000	64%	32%	22%
	(288)	(284)	(56)
$20,000–$60,000	24%	46%	31%
	(108)	(408)	(79)
More than $60,000	12%	22%	47%
	(54)	(195)	(121)
Total	100%	100%	100%
	(450)	(887)	(256)

Source: Simulated.

Gamma.   Gamma, used for variables measured at the ordinal level and ranging from −1 to +1, is a bit more complicated because you are trying to guess about pairs of cases. If you are hypothesizing a positive relationship, your guess is that if one person is placed in a higher category of the *independent* variable than another person, the first person will be placed in a higher category of the *dependent* variable than the second person as well. For example, if one hypothesized that increased education is associated with increased income, as expressed in Table 14.3, you would expect someone with more education than another person would also have more income than that other person as well. Gamma is the proportion of the paired comparisons that fit the hypothesized configuration. It is calculated by comparing the number of pairs having the same ranking with number of pairs having the opposite rankings on the two variables; ties are not counted. The actual calculation of gamma is not difficult but it is cumbersome, as demonstrated by calculating its value for Table 14.3, reproduced in Table 14.7 with cell counts filled in.

If the lowest values of the two variables are in the upper left-hand corner of the table, as in Table 14.7, to determine the number of pairs having the same ranking on the two variables, the frequency of each cell is multiplied by the sum of all the cells below and to the right of it. Adding these products produces the sum of all the pairs having the same ranking. For Table 14.7 the number of pairs with the same ranking is 288(408 + 195 + 79 + 121) + 108(195 + 121) + 284(79 + 121) + 408(121) or 231,264 + 34,128 + 56,800 + 49,368 = 371,560.

To compute the pairs having the opposite ranking, the frequency of each cell is multiplied by the sum of the cells appearing below and to the left of it. Adding these products produces the sum of all the pairs having the opposite ranking. For Table 14.7, the computation is $56(108 + 54 + 408 + 195) + 79(54 + 195) + 284(108 + 54) + 408(54)$ or $42,840 + 19,671 + 46,008 + 22,032 = 130,551$. The formula for calculating gamma is as follows:

$$\text{Gamma} = \frac{\text{Same direction pairs} - \text{Opposite direction pairs}}{\text{Same direction pairs} + \text{Opposite direction pairs}}$$

Plugging in the numbers we have computed for Table 14.3

$$\frac{371,560 - 130,551}{371,560 + 130,551} = \frac{241,009}{502,111} = +.48$$

The positive sign is indicative of the positive association between the variables you saw by examining the table. The actual value of gamma, .48, means that 48 percent more of the pairs examined had the same ranking than the opposite ranking. Fortunately, for effective use of your time, both lambda and gamma (as well as other measures of association not covered here) can be calculated by SPSS or other statistical software packages each time you run a crosstabulation and produce a percentage table. There are two activities at the end of the chapter that will teach you how to do that.

◼ Statistical Significance

Although they are useful for summarizing the relationship between variables in a table, these measures of association do not provide a determination of whether you should accept or reject the hypothesis displayed in the table. In most instances, crosstabulation is used to analyze data from a sample, not a population. The percentage difference necessary to conclude that a hypothesis is confirmed and reflects a relationship between the variables in the population from which the sample was drawn is often dependent on the size and nature of that sample of observations. Whether relationships between variables found in samples also exist in the population is a question of statistical significance. We will discuss in Chapter 17 tests of statistical significance that aid in the process of drawing conclusions about whether relationships in a sample are strong enough to warrant rejection of the null hypothesis in the population—that is, concluding that the variables shown to be related in the sample reflect the same relationship in the population. At this point, you need only to understand the nature of relationships between variables as they are displayed in percentage tables and can be expressed by measures of association.

Key Points

A well-constructed bivariate percentage table has the following features:

- It contains enough information to require only a little or no accompanying text.
- It has a title that describes the content.
- It is easier to read if the independent variable is placed along the top of the table and the dependent variable runs down the left side of the table.
- It has percentages running down the columns, totaling 100 percent.
- It is read to identify relationships between variables by comparing across the columns.

Alternative Means for Organizing Percentage Tables

We mentioned that well-constructed percentage tables are those where the independent variable is placed at the top of the table and percentages add to 100 percent from top to bottom of columns. (See Key Points.) We prefer this construction because we believe it is easier and more familiar to read from left to right. The construction of tables is ultimately a matter of taste or convenience, however, and they are sometimes organized with the dependent variable on the top and percentages calculated across. At times the table may even be abbreviated because the independent variable will have many more values than the dependent variable, leading to space constraints on the printed page. You must learn to recognize tables that are not in the format we just discussed. Table 14.8 is an example of a table in which the independent variable is at the side and the dependent variable is represented in the columns. In Table 14.8, the independent and dependent variables must be identified by determining the direction in which the table is percentaged. The percentages add to 100 percent across the table, so in this instance the independent variable, found on the left side and represented in the rows, is religious affiliation. Since the table is percentaged across, it must be read from top to bottom. It is appropriate to compare the religious groups in terms of the percentage who are Democrats: 45 percent of Protestants are Democrats compared with 58 percent of Catholics, 86 percent of Jews, and 52 percent of Others. Note that the 45 percent in the table indicates that 45 percent of Protestants are Democrats and *does not* indicate that 45 percent of Democrats

Table 14.8
Religious Affiliation and Party Preference

| | PARTY PREFERENCE | | |
Religious Affiliation	Democrat	Republican	Total
Protestants	45%	55%	100% (650)
Catholics	58%	42%	100% (280)
Jews	86%	14%	100% (102)
Others	52%	48%	100% (89)

Source: Simulated.

Table 14.9
Religious Affiliation and Party Preference (Abbreviated)

Religious Affiliation	Percentage of Religious Group Affiliated with the Democratic Party	
Protestants	45%	(N = 650)
Catholics	58%	(N = 280)
Jews	86%	(N = 102)
Others	52%	(N = 89)

Source: Simulated.

are Protestants. The latter interpretation would be correct only if the percentages added to 100 percent in the columns. The important point in examining Table 14.8 is that while the independent variable is usually placed at the top of bivariate percentage tables, the only way to ensure a correct identification of variables is to determine the direction in which the table is percentaged. To make matters a bit more complicated, it is not unusual for publishers who are interested in saving a line of text to leave out the column or row indicating 100 percent. It is left to the reader to add the percentages in each direction to be certain which variable is independent and which is dependent.

Often in the interest of simplicity and conserving space, bivariate tables are abbreviated. This is usually accomplished by displaying the percentages for only one value of the dependent variable. Table 14.9 is an abbreviated version of Table 14.8.

It takes some effort to determine that the independent variable in this table is religious affiliation, but most readers understand that the remainder of each religious group affiliate with the Republicans or some other party. Once you have determined that the independent variable is religious affiliation, it is easy (perhaps easier than in the full table) to compare the religious groups in terms of their party affiliation. Note that no information is lost in Table 14.9 and that Table 14.8 can be fully reconstructed from its contents. For example, to determine what percentage of Protestants are Republican one need only subtract 45 percent from 100 percent (the total) to obtain 55 percent. Reduced or abbreviated tables may at first glance seem more difficult to understand because of what is omitted, but with some practice most people consider them easier to comprehend.

Conclusion

Bivariate table construction ordinarily follows some basic rules about placement of variables and direction in which to calculate percentages. Generally, percentages run down the columns, and you compare across the rows to see any effects of the independent variable. Remember, however, that you will find exceptions to these rules, so you need to examine tables carefully to be sure you have interpreted them correctly. You have now learned enough about data analysis to test a hypothesis on your own. By performing a crosstabulation and constructing a percentage table from the results, you can determine if a relationship you have hypothesized is present in the nominal or ordinal data you have analyzed. An appropriate measure of association, such as lambda for nominal data or gamma for ordinal data, will help you interpret and summarize the direction and the strength of your findings from the data analysis. These are measures of association, however, not causation, so without meeting the other criteria for causality you cannot claim to have found a causal relationship no matter how large the values of lambda or gamma. In addition, if you are working with sample data, finding a relationship in that sample data does not necessarily mean you will find the same relationship in the larger population. How likely a relationship in a sample also exists in the population from which the sample was drawn is a matter of statistical significance and will be covered in Chapter 17.

We will turn our attention in Chapter 15 to examining bivariate relationships when your variables are measured at the interval/ratio level. More precise measurement of the variables allows for more precise data analysis to test for hypothesized relationships in your data. In Chapter 16 we will introduce you to analyzing data when you have more than one independent variable.

Summary of the Main Points

- Percentage tables are useful for summarizing information about the distribution of variables and relationships between variables. They are found in nearly every type of publication from reports of social science research to business reports to popular news magazines.
- Tables are most easily understood if the title and identifiers clearly label the variables with the independent variable at the top and the dependent variable at the side.
- Tables should be read initially from the outside working in. The title should be read first, followed by the identifiers indicating variable names, then value labels, then the marginals (row and column totals), and finally the percentages.

■ Percentages in bivariate tables are calculated within values of the independent variable. In reading the table, comparisons are made across categories of the independent variable.

■ Bivariate percentage tables can show both the strength and direction of relationships between variables.

■ Lambda is a statistic used to show the strength of a relationship between nominal-level variables displayed in a percentage table; similarly, the statistic gamma is used for ordinal-level variables.

■ Frequently tables are constructed with the independent variable on the side and the dependent variable on the top, or they are abbreviated. Care must be taken in those instances to identify independent and dependent variables.

Terms Introduced

crosstabulation
direction of a relationship
gamma
lambda
measure of association

negative relationship
percentage tables
positive relationship
proportionate reduction of error
strength

Selected Readings

Champney, Leonard. *Introduction to Quantitative Political Science.* New York: HarperCollins, 1995.

Diamond, Ian, and Julie Jeffries. *Beginning Statistics: An Introduction for Social Scientists.* Thousand Oaks, CA: Sage Publications, 2000.

Activities

Activity 14.1
Understanding the Information in a Table

Consider Table 14.10.

1. Name the variables in the table.
2. Which is the independent variable?
3. Which is the dependent variable?
4. What are the values of the independent variable?
5. What are the values of the dependent variable?
6. Calculate the appropriate percentages in order to determine the effect of the independent variable on the dependent variable.
7. Write a paragraph describing the information in the table; conclude with a hypothesis that reflects the relationship between the variables.

Table 14.10
Relationship Between Political Ideology and Attitude on Business Regulation

Less Government Regulation of Business	POLITICAL IDEOLOGY		
	Liberal	Moderate	Conservative
Favor	126	222	278
Neutral	106	178	98
Against	72	74	72
Total	304	474	448

Source: General Social Survey, 1996, National Opinion Research Center.

Activity 14.2
Percentage Tables and Hypotheses

Consider Table 14.11.

1. Name the variables in the table.
2. What is the independent variable?
3. What is the dependent variable?
4. How many Liberals are Democrats?
5. State a hypothesis that is tested by the table.
6. Write a paragraph referring to actual percentages in the table and calculating percentage differences to determine the strength of the relationship indicating if the hypothesis is supported by the data.

Table 14.11
Political Ideology and Vote for Governor

Political Ideology	PARTY OF CANDIDATE		Total
	Democrat	Republican	
Liberal	62%	38%	1,850
Moderate	50%	50%	1,231
Conservative	31%	69%	1,113

Source: Simulated.

Activity 14.3
Creating a Bivariate Percentage Table
with Nominal Level Variables, Using SPSS

The objective in this activity is to create a percentage table using the software package SPSS, introduced in Chapter 8. We will employ a procedure in SPSS called crosstabulation, or "crosstabs," to create the table with two variables measured at the ordinal level and calculate a lambda to summarize the relationship displayed in the table.

Go to SPSS and open the data file containing the General Social Survey for 2000; the SPSS file name is "GSS2000depr." The dependent variable will be the respondent's feelings about walking in his or her neighborhood at night. The SPSS variable name is "fear" and has two values, "yes" and "no." The independent variable will be the respondent's sex: SPSS variable name "sex," with values of "male" and "female."

Click on "Analyze" near the top of the page; when the box appears under "Analyze," click on "Descriptive Statistics"; when a box appears to the side, click on "Crosstabs." Now you are looking at a new window titled in the status bar, "Crosstabs." Scroll through variables on the left and highlight "fear." Use the arrow button to move "fear" into the box titled "Row(s)"; this will be your dependent variable.

Scroll through the variables on the left again and highlight "sex." Use the arrow button to move "sex" into the box titled "Column(s)"; this will be your independent variable. Click on the "Cells" button at the bottom of the window. Now you are looking at a new window titled in the status bar, "Crosstabs: Cell Display." In the small box titled "Percentages" click on "Column" so that a check mark appears; this will ensure that percentages in the table are calculated down the columns. Click on the "Continue" button. Now you are back at the window titled "Crosstabs."

Click on the "Statistics" button at the bottom of the window. Now you are looking at a new window titled "Crosstabs: Statistics." In the outlined area titled "Nominal," click on "lambda"; this will ensure calculation of that statistic. Click on the "Continue" button. Now you are back at the window titled "Crosstabs." Click on "OK."

A window titled "Output—SPSS Viewer" appears; the results of your data analysis examining the relationship between sex and attitude toward walking in the neighborhood at night are in this window. Scroll through the results, noting what percentage of men and women are afraid or not afraid to walk in the neighborhood at night. Note under the percentage table the value of lambda calculated for the relationship displayed in the table.

Print the output generated by SPSS and write a brief summary of the information found in the table, describing the relationship between sex and attitude toward walking at night.

Activity 14.4
Creating a Bivariate Percentage Table
with Ordinal Level Variables, Using SPSS

Proceed as in Activity 14.3, but this time choose as your dependent variable "conlegis," which is the level of confidence the respondent has in Congress with values "great deal," "only some," and "hardly any." For your independent variable, use "agequart," respondents grouped by the following age categories: 18–32, 33–43, 44–57, and 58 and older. Because you have ordinal-level data, have SPSS calculate a gamma instead of a lambda statistic, as you did in the previous exercise.

Chapter 15

Graphing and Describing Linear Bivariate Relationships

Learning Objectives

After completion of this chapter, students should be able to do the following:

Verbally describe the logic underlying regression and correlation analysis.

Understand how to construct and read a scatterplot and determine if regression analysis is appropriate to use.

Understand each component of an equation that describes a straight line.

Grasp what the slope and Y-intercept of a regression equation reveals about the relationship between two variables.

Define a beta weight and explain why it is used in regression analysis.

Explain the logic behind the Pearson correlation coefficient and how it reveals the strength of a relationship in regression analysis.

Relationships Between Two Interval/Ratio Variables

To test hypotheses that link two variables measured at the interval or ratio level, **linear regression analysis,** rather than crosstabulation as described in Chapter 14, is employed. [1] The term *regression* comes from the phrase "regression to the mean," a statistical phenomenon first recognized over 100 years ago. It is a process in which cases that have an extreme value on a measure tend *naturally* to regress toward a more average value in later measures of the same variable. [2]

Linear regression sounds more complicated than it actually is. Such analyses begin by graphing the two variables on a scatterplot, fitting a straight line to the pattern of the plot (that's why it is called *linear* regression), using the slope of the line to describe the association between the two variables and calculating another statistic, called a **Pearson correlation coefficient,** to determine the strength of the association described by the line. As we said, it sounds more complicated than it is. We will go through the procedure slowly, making sure you understand each step in the process before moving on to the next.

When we considered descriptive statistics for interval and ratio level data in Chapter 13, we pointed out that they could be more precise than those used with nominal- and ordinal-level data because interval and ratio variables were operationally defined with more exactness. Quantifying variables at the interval or ratio level produces numbers that have mathematical properties—they can be added, subtracted, multiplied, and divided. This increased precision is important for bivariate as well as univariate analysis. As you learned in the previous chapter, bivariate analysis with nominal- and ordinal-level data means crosstabulation with results shown in percentage tables. The organization of the tables reflects the level of measurement of the variables. The independent variable is arranged in nominal or ordinal categories across the top of the table, while categories of the dependent variable run down the side of the table. Sometimes these categories are quite broad, grouping large numbers of observations into one category. Units of analysis are clustered in the resulting cells. The relative imprecision of the measurement is reflected in the number of cases that are found in each cell of the table.

But just as measures of central tendency used to describe interval and ratio level are individual numbers (mean, median, mode), bivariate analysis of these variables as well is undertaken with more precise measurement of the variables. If the unit of analysis is the individual instead of grouping people into age categories, resulting in ordinal measurement, each person is classified by precise age on his or her last birthday, such as thirty-two years old or forty-eight years old. (Even more precision is possible by determining a person's age in months rather than years, but unless one is studying relatively young children—preschoolers, for example—such fine distinctions are generally not necessary.)

■ The Scatterplot

Consequently, bivariate analysis that is more precise than crosstabulation is possible with interval- and ratio-level data—you can do linear regression analysis. First, instead of setting up percentage tables, the data are organized on a graph, with the independent

Figure 15.1
SPSS Scatterplot for State Lobbyists: Percent of Lobbyists
Known on a First-Name Basis by Number of Years Lobbying

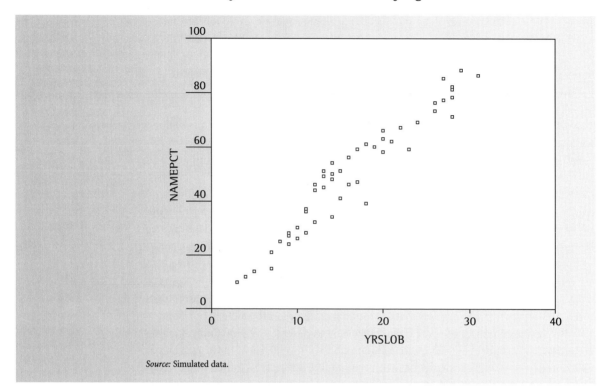

Source: Simulated data.

variable on the horizontal (X) axis and the dependent variable on the vertical (Y) axis.
The units of analysis appear as individual dots placed at the intersection of that unit's
values on the X- and Y-axes. The pattern of the plotted points on the graph is called a
scatterplot. The advantage of a scatterplot over a simple tabular presentation of two
columns of numbers is the graph allows you to see more clearly the relationship between
the variables.

Figure 15.1 is an example of a scatterplot. Using simulated data for fifty lobbyists
who work in a state capital, it shows the relationship between the lobbyists' level of experience and their familiarity with decision makers. The operational definition of the independent variable is the number of years that a lobbyist has worked at his or her profession,

while for the dependent variable it is the percentage of legislators each lobbyist knows on a first-name basis. Each of the fifty dots represents an individual lobbyist's position on the two variables.

The initial step in interpreting the scatterplot is to determine if the variables have a linear relationship—that is, if the relationship between the variables can be suitably described by a straight line. Figure 15.1 does approximate a linear relationship because as the values of the independent variable of years of experience go up, the values of the dependent variable of percentage of legislators known on a first-name basis go up in an essentially unswerving fashion. The scatterplot in this graph displays a positive, linear relationship between the variables: Among these fifty state lobbyists, as experience goes up, familiarity with decision makers also goes up.

Figures 15.2a through 15.2d show four possible scatterplot patterns. In Figures 15.2a and 15.2b, a straight line can be used to describe the relationship between X and Y, but in Figures 15.2c and 15.2d, a linear model to describe the relationship between the variables is inadequate. In rough terms, the scatterplot in Figure 15.2a shows a positive relationship between the variables. As the value of the independent variable goes up along the X-axis, the value of the dependent variable does the same on the Y-axis, and the pattern of the dots roughly approximates a straight line. In both respects, it is similar to the scatterplot in Figure 15.1. Figure 15.2b shows another linear relationship, but this one is negative. As the value of X goes up, the value of Y goes down—an inverse linear relationship.

On the other hand, the scatterplot in Figure 15.2c shows no visible pattern between the variables. The dots seem to be randomly placed, indicating that the two variables are unrelated. Figure 15.2d shows a relationship between the variables, but it is nonlinear. The variables instead are related in a curvilinear fashion. In the lower range of X values, as X goes up, so does Y, but at about the midpoint of the distribution of X, the relationship is reversed. As X continues to rise, the value of Y falls. Linear regression analysis is inappropriate to describe either the random dots in Figure 15.2c or the curvilinear relationship shown in Figure 15.2d and should not be used in these circumstances. Linear regression analysis is used when there is a constant change in Y relative to X.

■ Outliers

On occasion, you will find a situation where the dots form an identifiable linear pattern, with one or a very few exceptions that are well outside the range of the other cases. These individual exceptions are called **outliers.** An example of an outlier is shown in Figure 15.3, which is a graph of the vote for the Reform party candidate by county in Florida for the 2000 presidential election. [3] Along the X-axis is the number of registered

Figure 15.2
Four Possible Patterns of Scatterplots

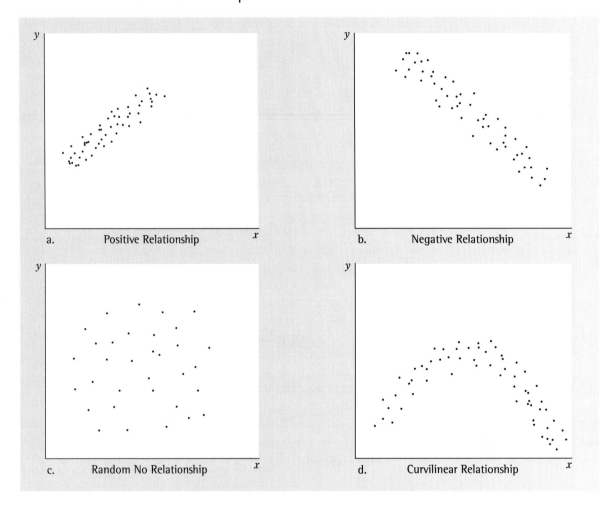

Reform party voters in each county, and along the Y-axis is the number of votes cast for the Reform party candidate for president, Patrick Buchanan, in the corresponding county. The dots each represent one of the sixty-seven Florida counties. With one exception, the dots representing the counties lie in a recognizable positive, linear pattern—for every one registered Reform party voter in the county, there are about two votes for Buchanan. The one obvious exception is Palm Beach County, where there are approximately 100

Figure 15.3
SPSS Scatterplot for Reform

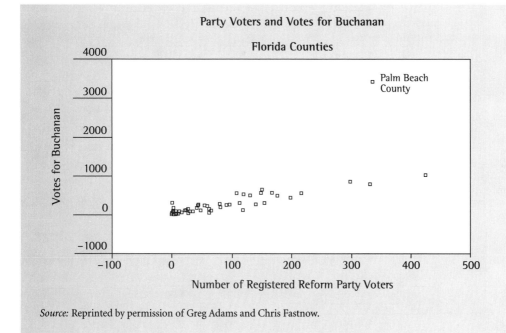

Source: Reprinted by permission of Greg Adams and Chris Fastnow.

To the Web

times as many votes for Buchanan as there are registered Reform party members.

If you have a large number of cases to analyze, a few outliers will make little difference in your overall analysis, but if you have just a few cases, a single outlier can be a problem. Oftentimes a single outlier reveals something unusual about that particular unit of analysis. In the instance of the Florida counties, the outlier is Palm Beach County, and some people attributed the large discrepancy between the number of Reform party members and the number of votes for Buchanan in that county compared to all the other counties to voting irregularities and ballot confusion in Palm Beach. The scatterplot, however, cannot tell us *why* there is an outlier, only that there is one.

Exercises 15.1 and 15.2   Creating Scatterplots by Hand and Computer

The logic underlying graphing two variables and displaying the results in a scatterplot is more easily grasped when it is done at least once by hand. We have prepared an exercise that will help you create a scatterplot by hand. Go to the **DEPR Web Page**, click on **Chapter 15**, then on **Creating Scatterplots by Hand**. It is much more convenient to use software for data analysis, including the construction of scatterplots. To learn how to create a scatterplot using SPSS, go to the **DEPR Web Page**, click on **Web Exercises, Chapter 15**, then on **Creating Scatterplots by Computer**.

Figure 15.4
Scatterplot with Regression Line for State Lobbyists: Percentage
of Lobbyists Known on First-Name Basis by Number of Years Lobbying

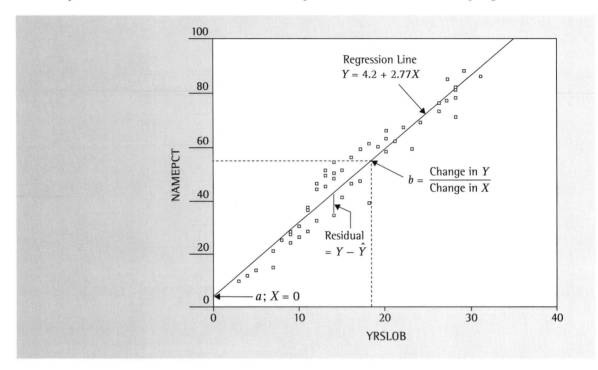

Interpreting a Scatterplot by Using a Regression Line

Once you have established that the scatterplot displays an approximately linear relationship between the two variables, you can construct a **regression line** that will more explicitly describe the association between the variables. The regression line for the scatterplot of lobbyist experience by legislator name familiarity is shown in Figure 15.4. In practice, researchers use statistical software to draw the regression line. It is drawn so as to minimize the total of the squared vertical distance from each dot in the scatterplot to the line. The resulting regression line is the best straight line description of the plotted points and is used to describe the association between the variables by writing the equation for that line. If the line can be drawn through each of the dots—that is, if all the dots fall exactly on the line—then the distance from the dots to the line is zero, and you have found a perfect relationship between the variables. That result, however, is extremely unlikely, and you generally will have a cluster of cases, some of which fall on the line and most of which do not.

In general terms, the equation for any straight line, including a regression line, is as follows.

$$Y = a + bX + e$$

where

> Y represents the predicted values of the dependent variable.
> X represents the observed values of the independent variable.
> b represents the **slope** of the line.
> a represents the **Y-intercept:** the value of X when $Y = 0$; the point at which the line crosses the Y-axis.
> e stands for error, the variation in Y that is not accounted for by the independent variable in the equation.

Let's consider each of these terms separately. Notice that what we are solving for is Y, which represents the dependent variable. Certainly we are on target here because the dependent variable is always the behavior we are trying to explain, and now we have a formula to estimate its value for each case as a function of the value of the independent variable X, the presumed cause in our hypothesis. The value for each case of both X and Y is recorded in our data set. b is the slope of the line, which can be either positive or negative, and it indicates how much change in the value of Y is associated with a change in the value of X. This is an important piece of information about any hypothesis you might test: You will know how much change in your dependent variable is associated with any change in your independent variable. The regression line enables you to predict the value of your dependent variable (the predicted value is represented by $\hat{Y}$) for each case by knowing the value of your independent variable for each case. Remember, however, that because not all cases lie on the line, there will be a discrepancy between $\hat{Y}$ and the actual value of Y contained in your data. The difference between $\hat{Y}$ and Y is called the **residual,** and it represents how much error there is in the prediction of the regression equation for the Y value of any individual case as a function of X.

In our example of the fifty state lobbyists shown in Figure 15.4, the equation for the regression line is $Y = 4.2 + 2.77X$, where Y is the percentage of legislators known on a first-name basis and X is the lobbyist's years of experience. The slope of the regression line is $+2.77$,

To the Web

Seeing the Effects of Adding Cases, Including Outliers, to a Regression Analysis

This Web site will show you the effect on the regression line of adding cases to a scatterplot. Cases added close to the line produce little change, but those added more distant from the line change the line more dramatically. Go to the **DEPR Web Page,** click on **Web Links, Chapter 15,** then on **Outlier Effect.**

indicating that for every additional year of experience, a lobbyist will know 2.77 percent more of the legislators on a first-name basis. The Y-intercept, the predicted value of Y when X is zero, is 4.2. This is the estimated percentage of legislators known on a first-name basis for someone just starting a lobbyist career. [4]

Some Concerns About Regression Analysis

You need to be cautious about regression equations. First, notice that we are talking about association between the variables, not causation. Association is a necessary prerequisite for inferring causation, but there are three other conditions (outlined in Chapter 6) required to establish a causal relationship as well: (1) the independent variable must precede the dependent variable in time, (2) the two variables must be plausibly linked by a theory, and (3) competing independent variables must be eliminated. The latter condition, eliminating competing explanations by adding new independent variables, will be covered in the next chapter when we discuss multivariate analysis. But you need to keep in mind the temporal and theoretical constraints in establishing causality whenever you test a hypothesis, including when you employ linear regression analysis.

The second concern we must note is the **units of measurement** on each axis. The **regression coefficient** is affected by how the two variables are represented quantitatively—that is, whether different units of measurement are used on the X- and Y-axes. In our example of state lobbyists, the independent variable of experience is measured in years along the X-axis, while the dependent variable of familiarity is measured as a percentage along the Y-axis. One way to circumvent this problem is to convert the values of both variables to z-scores, which, as you know from Chapter 13, are the original values of the variables expressed in standard deviation units. The slope of the regression line that is drawn after the variables have been normalized is called a **beta weight** rather than a regression coefficient. Virtually all data analysis and statistical software, including SPSS, provide in their output both a regression coefficient and a corresponding beta weight for a regression analysis. We will make more use of beta weights when we consider multivariate regression analysis in the next chapter.

A final caveat with which you need to concern yourself is that the regression coefficient is not a good indicator for the strength of the relationship because the same regression line might be drawn for scatterplots that are considerably different. The regression line is drawn to minimize the vertical difference from the dots (units of analysis) to the line. Unless you have a perfect relationship between your variables (the case in which all the dots are on the line) there will be a difference between the value of $\hat{Y}$ and the actual value of Y as shown in the scatterplot. (See Figure 15.4.) These residuals indicate how much your regression line underestimates or overestimates the actual value of the dependent variable for each case under study. Figure 15.5 shows two different scatterplots that produce identical regression lines, and we can see that the regression line in the

Figure 15.5
Identical Regression Lines from Different Scatterplots

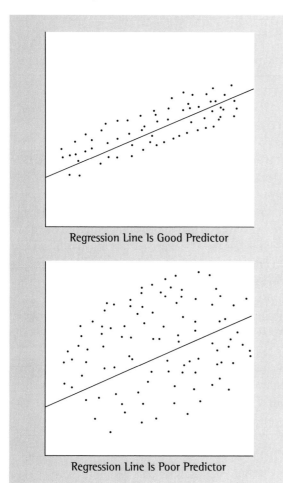

Regression Line Is Good Predictor

Regression Line Is Poor Predictor

upper scatterplot is a much better description of the data than the same regression line is of the data in the lower scatterplot. In the lower scatterplot, the residuals are much greater. The strength of the relationship is determined by how closely the dots are clustered around the line. The more tightly the cases are clustered around the line, the stronger the relationship, while the more distant from the line, the weaker the relationship. A statistical measure of that clustering is the Pearson Product Moment Correlation Coefficient, generally referred to by the letter "r."

Questions for Thought and Discussion

1. Name two variables measured at the interval or ratio level that you think would show a positive relationship on a scatterplot. Do you imagine in your example that the relationship would be "perfect"—that is, all the cases would lie directly on the regression line? Why or why not?
2. Think of two more variables, using American states as your unit of analysis, that you believe would show a negative relationship on a scatterplot.

■ Correlation—A Measure of Association

The Pearson correlation coefficient is a measure of how closely the cases in a regression analysis are clustered around the regression line. As such, it tells you how strong the relationship is between the variables. If you have many cases to analyze, it is often difficult to tell from looking at the scatterplot how strong the relationship between your variables actually is. The correlation coefficient will give you that information with a precise quantitative indicator. It ranges from -1 to $+1$, with -1 being a perfect negative linear relationship (all cases lying on a straight line with a negative slope) and $+1$ a perfect positive linear relationship (all cases lying on a straight line with a positive slope), while 0 means there is no linear relationship at all (the cases are arranged randomly around the line). So the closer to 1 the correlation coefficient is, either positive or negative, the stronger the relationship between the variables. A zero correlation tells you the knowledge of the value of one variable is useless in helping to predict the value of the other variable.

The correlation coefficient is another example of the proportionate reduction of error, discussed in Chapter 14 when we calculated values of lambda and gamma as measures of association used with nominal- and ordinal-level variables. You should perhaps review that section of material if you do not remember it clearly. With nominal-level data, we tried to guess the value of a variable and concluded the best estimate, knowing nothing else, would be to choose the modal value. Choosing the modal value would produce the fewest mistakes when guessing. With a normally distributed variable measured at the interval or ratio level, our best guess for the value of the variable for any individual case (lacking any other information) would be the mean. Our predictions for the values for individual cases of our dependent variable would hopefully become more accurate (that is, we would make fewer mistakes when guessing) if we added the information from an independent variable. In the case of nominally measured variables, we calculated a proportionate reduction in error achieved with the addition of an independent variable. The reduction was reflected in the value of lambda, an indicator of how much more we knew about the values of the dependent variable for all our units of analysis from our knowledge of the independent variable compared to simply always choosing the modal value.

With interval/ratio data, the "errors" are reflected in the unexplained variation of the dependent variable, which is the sum of the squared differences between the actual values of Y (from the data) and the expected values of Y (predicted from the regression line)—in other words, the square of the residuals. (Remember how a regression line is fitted to a scatterplot; the sum of the squares of the distances from each actual value of Y to the regression line is set to a minimum.) This variation is unexplained because it is the difference between what we would predict (guess) Y to be using the regression line based on our independent variable X and what it actually is in the data we collected and displayed in our scatterplot. This unexplained variation, or **error component,** in our dependent variable is then compared to the total variation in the dependent variable, which is the sum of the squared differences between the actual value of Y for each case and the mean of Y. Subtracting the unexplained variation from the total variation leaves the explained variation. If you then divide the explained variation by the total variation, you get the proportion of the total variation you have explained. It is a measure of the proportionate reduction in error, similar to the quantity when lambda is computed for nominal data, and an expression of how much of the variance in the dependent variable has been accounted for by the independent variable.

The result of this calculation is the correlation coefficient squared, r^2, also called the **coefficient of determination,** but we generally compute r instead in order to show the sign, indicating the direction of the relationship between the variables. If we instead calculated r^2 and took the square root, we would always have a positive sign. The correlation coefficient, or "r," is a quantitative expression of the ratio of the explained variation to the total variation in a regression analysis. In symbolic terms, the proportionate reduction in error is represented as follows.

$$r^2 = \frac{\text{total variance} - \text{unexplained variance}}{\text{total variance}} \quad \text{or} \quad \frac{1 - \Sigma(Y - \hat{Y})^2}{\Sigma(Y - \bar{Y})^2}$$

To calculate the correlation coefficient directly from the data and avoid losing the sign, use the following formula.

$$r = \frac{N\Sigma\,XY - (\Sigma X)(\Sigma Y)}{\sqrt{[N\Sigma X^2 - (\Sigma X)^2]\,[N\Sigma Y^2 - (\Sigma Y)^2]}}$$

Fortunately for all of us, SPSS calculates correlation coefficients as well as regression coefficients, so you need not memorize either of these calculation formulas or calculate a correlation coefficient with a calculator. On the other hand, you should take the time to look them over carefully, in conjunction with the discussion about proportionate reduction of error, in order to more fully

To the Web

Exercise 15.3   Interpreting a Correlation Coefficient

In order to make sure you understand what a correlation coefficient represents and how it is interpreted, we have designed a few short-answer questions to assess your level of comprehension. The more questions you can answer correctly, the better you understand the use of the correlation coefficient. Go to the DEPR Web Page, click on Web Exercises, Chapter 15, then on Interpreting a Correlation Coefficient.

understand the logic underlying the use of Pearson's correlation coefficient in the context of regression analysis.

Regression Analysis Results in SPSS

Figure 15.6 shows some of the SPSS output produced when doing the regression analysis demonstrated in Figure 15.4 that linked the number of years an individual has worked as a lobbyist to the percentage of legislators he or she knows on a first-name basis. In the top table titled "Variables Entered/Removed" is the independent variable entered

Figure 15.6
SPSS Regression Output for Lobbyists
Example Shown in Figure 15.4

Variables Entered/Removed[b]

Model	Variables Entered	Variables Removed	Method
1	YRSLOB[a]		Enter

a. All requested variables entered.
b. Dependent Variable: NAMEPCT

Model Summary

Model	R	R Square
1	.961[a]	.924

a. Predictors: (Constant), YRSLOB

Coefficients[a]

Model		Unstandardized Coefficients		Standardized Coefficients
		B	Std. Error	Beta
1	(Constant)	4.169	2.072	
	YRSLOB	2.765	.115	.961

a. Dependent Variable: NAMEPCT

Source: Simulated data.

into the equation; "yrslob" is the SPSS variable name for number of years an individual has worked as a lobbyist. The second table, titled "Model Summary," shows the correlation coefficient and its square-in this case, $r = .961$ and $r^2 = .924$. The final table, titled "Coefficients," gives the regression coefficient for the independent variable of "yrslob"—

To the Web

2.77—and for the "constant," which is the error term for the regression equation representing the combined effect of all other independent variables. This coefficient (4.169) is equivalent to the Y-intercept, the predicted value of Y when $X = 0$. Also shown in this table is the standardized regression coefficient, the beta weight, which is .961. Note that in a bivariate relationship the beta weight is the same as the correlation coefficient because r is the mean of the cross products of X and Y when both are formulated in standard units. [5]

> **Working with Scatterplots**
>
> These two sites display various scatterplots and ask you to try to draw the regression line that fits best or to guess the correlation coefficient. Both sites provide good practice for becoming more familiar with regression analysis. Go to the **DEPR Web Page**, click on **Web Links, Chapter 15**, then on **Drawing Regression Lines by Eye and Guessing Correlations**.

Conclusion

Both the regression coefficient and the correlation coefficient need to be employed to properly interpret a bivariate linear regression analysis. As pointed out, each provides entirely different information about the relationship you have hypothesized. The regression coefficient is the slope of the regression line and tells you what the nature of the relationship between the variables is, how much change in the independent variables is associated with how much change in the dependent variable. The larger the regression coefficient, the more change there is in the dependent variable associated with change in the independent variable. A minus sign preceding the regression coefficient indicates an inverse relationship between the variables. To account for different units of measurement along the X- and Y-axes, the beta weight, the slope of the line after the units of measurement for each axis have been standardized (expressed in z-scores), is employed to display the change in Y relative to the change in X.

The Pearson correlation coefficient, on the other hand, ranges between -1 and $+1$ and tells you how well the regression line fits the scatterplot—that is, it indicates the strength of the relationship. The closer the correlation coefficient is to 1, the stronger is the relationship between the variables. r^2 tells you, in proportion terms, how much of the variance in the dependent variable is accounted for by the independent variable. By subtracting that number from 1, you can tell what proportion of the variance is left to be explained by other independent variables beyond the one you have used.

Large regression coefficients, indicating substantial change in the dependent variable associated with changes in the independent variable, may be accompanied by a small correlation coefficient, an indication that the regression line does not describe the scatterplot very well and you have a weak relationship. On the other hand, a small regression coefficient accompanied by a large correlation coefficient indicates that while the change in the dependent variable associated with movement in the independent variable may be small, that independent variable can account for most of the change in the dependent variable that does occur. Ideally, your regression analysis will produce both a regression coefficient in the predicted direction and a correlation coefficient approaching 1, which would both confirm your hypothetical statement of the relationship between the variables and tell you that virtually all of the change in the behavior you are seeking to explain can be accounted for by your single independent variable. That ideal, however, is rarely achieved. You will generally need more than one independent variable to explain political behavior. How to analyze data when using more than one independent variable is the topic of the next chapter.

Summary of the Main Points

- Linear regression analysis is used with two variables operationalized at the interval or ratio level.
- The two variables are graphed, producing a scatterplot.
- If the scatterplot shows a roughly linear relationship, a regression line is drawn through the scatterplot and is used to describe the relationship between the two variables.
- The slope of the line, which can be either positive or negative, indicates how much change in the value of Y is associated with a one unit change in the value of X.
- The difference between the observed value of Y and the value predicted by the regression line is called the residual, and it represents how much error there is in the prediction of the regression equation.
- The slope of the regression line that is drawn after the variables have been normalized is called a beta weight.
- The Pearson correlation coefficient (r), which ranges from -1 to $+1$, is a measure of how closely the cases in a regression analysis are clustered around the regression line; it tells you how strong the relationship is between the variables.
- r^2, called the coefficient of determination, tells you, in percentage terms, how much of the variance in the dependent variable is accounted for by the independent variable.
- Linear regression analysis assesses the level of association between two variables, not causation.

Terms Introduced

beta weight
coefficient of determination
error component
linear regression analysis
outlier
Pearson correlation coefficient
regression coefficient

regression line
residual
scatterplot
slope
units of measurement
Y-intercept

Montgomery, Douglas C., Elizabeth A. Peck, and G. Geoffrey Vining. *Introduction to Linear Regression Analysis,* 3rd Ed. New York: John Wiley & Sons, 2001.

Pyrczak, Fred. *Making Sense of Statistics, A Conceptual Overview,* 2nd Ed. Los Angeles: Pyrczak Publishing, 2001.

Schroeder, Larry, David L. Sjoquist, and Paula E. Stephan. *Understanding Regression Analysis, An Introductory Guide.* Newbury Park, CA: Sage Publications, 1986.

Sirkin, R. Mark. *Statistics for the Social Sciences* Thousand Oaks, CA: Sage Publications, 1999.

Selected Readings

Activities

Activity 15.1
Drawing a Regression Line in SPSS

This activity will show you how to have SPSS draw a regression line for a scatterplot created in that program.

Create the scatterplot for the HIV/AIDS rate and death rate for the nations in the "COUNTRIESdepr" data set as described in Web Exercise 15.2. When the scatterplot is showing in the SPSS viewer, double-click within the framework of the chart. A new, small window will appear titled SPSS Chart Editor. Click on "Chart" in the status bar area and choose "Options" from the drop-down menu. A new window, titled "Scatterplot Options," will open. In the upper right-hand quarter of the window, titled "Fit Line," click on "Total." Click on the "OK" button. Close the "Scatterplot Options" window. When you return to the SPSS viewer, the chart you originally created will have the regression line drawn through the cases in the scatterplot. Print the scatterplot with the regression line showing.

What does the regression line tell you about the relationship between a country's HIV/AID infection rate and its death rate?

Activity 15.2
Calculating a Regression Coefficient, Beta Weight, and Correlation Coefficient in SPSS

This activity will show you how to have SPSS calculate a regression coefficient, beta weight, and Pearson correlation coefficient for the regression line created in Activity 15.1. Open the "COUNTRIESdepr" data set in the SPSS data editor. Click on "Analyze" at the top of the screen; choose "Regression" from the drop-down menu and "Linear" from the next drop-down menu. A new window, titled "Linear Regression," will appear. In the "Linear Regression" window, put the variable "death" in the box marked "Dependent," and put the variable "hivaids" in box marked "Independent." Then click on the "OK" button. Output similar to that shown in Figure 15.6 will appear in the viewer.

The two important tables are the "Coefficients" and "Model Summary." Look first at the "Coefficients" table; on the left is your independent variable, percent aged 15 to 49 living with HIV/AIDS, and something called "Constant." (Constant is what is left over to explain after you have exhausted the explanatory power of your independent variable; it is the value of the Y-intercept.) For your independent variable, find the unstandardized regression coefficient, *B,* which in this table equals +.487. Next find the standardized regression coefficient, Beta, for your independent variable, which in this table equals +.559.

What do the regression coefficient and beta weight tell you about the relationship between the HIV/AIDS rate and the death rate in these countries?

Return to the viewer. The other table is labeled "Model Summary." *r* (SPSS uses an uppercase *R*) is the Pearson correlation coefficient—in this case, .559, and r^2 is the correlation coefficient squared, which tells you what percentage of the variance in the dependent variable you have explained—in this case, .312 or 31.2 percent.

What does the Pearson correlation coefficient and its square tell you about the relationship between the HIV/AIDS rate and the death rate in these countries?

Chapter 16

Analyzing More Than Two Variables

Learning Objectives

After completion of this chapter, students should be able to do the following:

Understand the process of multivariate analysis and why it is important.

Describe what a control variable is and how it is used in testing a bivariate hypothesis.

Recognize and interpret the various effects of a control variable on a bivariate relationship and/or a dependent variable as shown in percentage tables.

Interpret the regression coefficients, beta weights, and multiple correlation coefficient that result from multiple linear regression.

Sorting Out Multiple Influences

A woman's right to an abortion has been a divisive issue in American politics, and many people hold strong opinions on both sides of the issue. What affects an individual's attitude toward abortion? Why do some people rigorously defend a woman's right to choose, whereas others feel just as strongly that abortion should be illegal? There are no simple answers, and it is improbable that one single explanation can account for the varied opinions held by Americans. Perhaps gender, religious beliefs, political views, education, and other factors all play a role in the formation of an individual's attitude toward abortion. In order to study attitudes toward abortion empirically, you would have to figure out the influence of more than one independent variable on a person's attitude. This is a research problem that requires multivariate analysis.

As you learned in Chapter 6, behavior is unlikely to be explained by employing only a single independent variable. Political behavior and attitudes are generally complex enough to have multiple rather than single causes. In order to explain such complex behavior or attitudes, then, you must be able to test for the *simultaneous* effects of more than one independent variable. In bivariate relationships, you are limited to testing for each cause separately, independent of each other. With analysis involving more than one independent variable, competing causes can be placed one against the other and their relative influence compared. Statistical analysis encompassing the simultaneous exploration of the relationship among more than two variables is called **multivariate analysis.** It can take a number of forms.

First, when you test to determine if a second (or third, or fourth) independent variable affects a relationship stated in a two-variable hypothesis, the alternative independent variables introduced into the research in this way are called "control variables." Testing a simple bivariate hypothesis requires subjecting it to continuous attempts at falsification or disproof by adding these control variables and considering that hypothesis confirmed only when it has withstood these efforts at falsification. This use of control variables allows you to see not only if the original relationship stands up to the control variable but also how that relationship might change under the varying conditions represented by the different values of the control variable. Control variables introduced in the testing of a bivariate hypothesis can have a wide variety of effects on the original relationship. These effects may be seen in only some or in all of the categories of the control variable. In general terms, the original relationship may completely disappear (indicating an original spurious relationship), weaken, strengthen, or be unchanged. The direction of the original relationship may also be reversed in some or all of the categories of the control variable. It is also possible that even when an original hypothesis is disconfirmed, the addition of a control variable may reveal a positive or negative relationship that had been previously hidden.

When control variables have some observable effect on the original relationship—strengthening, weakening, or changing its direction in some or all categories of the control variable—the original hypothesized relationship is more complex than first observed and must be sorted out by close examination of the data analysis results. This process of adding other independent variables as you work through your data analysis is called elaboration, initially discussed in Chapter 6. Elaboration consists of suggesting and testing alternate hypotheses as possible explanations of changes in your dependent variable and theorizing about how the results fit with the original hypothesis.

On the other hand, when starting a research project, you might initially hypothesize that more than one independent variable directly affects your dependent variable—that is, you have multiple independent variables—and that is also multivariate analysis. When you move beyond a simple bivariate hypothesis to hypotheses with two or more independent variables, multivariate statistical techniques will allow you to examine both the separate simultaneous effect of each independent variable *and* the combined effects of all the independent variables directly on the dependent variable at the same time. But regardless if you are initially employing these other variables as control variables or more independent variables, the choice of which additional explanatory variables to adopt is largely guided by the theory you are using to explain the behavior under consideration, as well as the existing literature in the particular substantive area of inquiry.

The purpose of this chapter is to demonstrate how data analysis employing more than one independent variable is actually conducted. Exactly how do you control for a second independent variable and interpret the results? How do you set up your data analysis to examine the simultaneous effects of more than one independent variable on your dependent variable? The answers depend on what level of measurement you have achieved with your operational definitions. With variables measured at the nominal or ordinal level, you will employ multivariate crosstabulation with the results shown in **multivariate percentage tables,** defined as tables with at least two independent variables. For variables operationalized at the interval or ratio level, you will use a technique called **multiple linear regression.**

Nominal- and Ordinal-Level Data

When analyzing nominal or ordinal data to test a hypothesis with more than one independent variable, you will have to construct percentage tables that show the results of your efforts at sifting through control variables or adding competing independent variables. [1] Initially, you might think using two separate tables, one for the independent variable and the other for the control variable, would make sense. In fact, that would entirely miss the point of using control variables and provide less information about the relationship among your variables than combining them in a single table because you could not examine the effects of both independent variables simultaneously on the dependent variable. You would end up missing the context of one variable or the other. The independent and control variables must both be displayed with the dependent variable in a multivariate table. Such tables yield much more information about the relationship among your variables than separate, bivariate tables can provide.

Adding a Control Variable to the Test of a Bivariate Relationship

Multivariate tables follow the same general principles as simple, bivariate tables, covered in Chapter 14. The one significant difference is that a multivariate table will have a second independent variable, the control variable, usually along the top. The values of the original independent variable will be nested within this second independent variable. **Nesting** is the construction of a table with the original relationship reproduced

Table 16.1
Relationship Between Level of Education and Attitude on Abortion

| | LEVEL OF EDUCATION | | |
| | Low | Intermediate | High |
Abortion Should Be	High School or Less	Some Education After High School	BA/BS or More
Not permitted at all	11.4%	7.5%	6.1%
Available with restrictions	62.9%	57.1%	50.8%
Generally available	25.7%	35.4%	43.1%
Total	727	545	606

Gamma = .243

Note: Both variables recoded to three categories; those answering "don't know" were excluded.

Source: Pew Center Religion and Politics Survey, 1996.

individually *within each of the separate categories of the control variable.* The original independent/dependent variable relationship can then be examined under each of these controlled conditions.

Tables 16.1 and 16.2 together provide an example of elaboration of a hypothesis using a control variable. Picking up on the example about attitude toward abortion at the start of this chapter, Table 16.1 displays the bivariate relationship between a person's attitude toward abortion and his or her level of education. Table 16.2 shows the same relationship while controlling for political ideology. The data for these tables come from a survey done by the Pew Center for The People and The Press in 1996 titled "Religion and Politics." [2] The conclusion that can be drawn from Table 16.1 is straightforward: The higher the level of education, the more likely a person is to support wider availability of abortions for women. Only 25.7 percent of those with a high school education or less support the position that abortions should be generally available. The percentage rises to 35.4 percent for those who have some education after high school, and it tops out at 43.1 percent among people with at least a four-year college degree. Conversely, those with the lowest level of education are most likely to indicate that abortion should not be permitted at all (11.4 percent), and those with the highest level are least likely to support this antiabortion position (6.1 percent). Gamma, the measure of association for ordinal-level data you learned about in Chapter 14, is .243, reflecting the positive relationship between the variables.

Variables other than a person's education, however, such as political ideology, may also influence his or her attitude toward abortion. To examine the effect of political ide-

Table 16.2
Relationship Among Education, Political Ideology, and Attitude on Abortion

Abortion Should Be	IDEOLOGY								
	CONSERVATIVE			MODERATE			LIBERAL		
	Low Education	Intermediate Education	High Education	Low Education	Intermediate Education	High Education	Low Education	Intermediate Education	High Education
Not permitted at all	15.3%	13.1%	12.2%	8.2%	4.4%	3.0%	9.0%	2.8%	2.9%
Available with restrictions	62.4%	64.0%	64.4%	65.7%	57.8%	49.4%	57.9%	41.5%	33.3%
Generally available	22.3%	22.9%	23.4%	26.1%	37.8%	47.5%	33.1%	55.7%	63.8%
Total	314	214	205	280	225	263	133	106	138
	Gamma = .045			Gamma = .305			Gamma = .398		

Note: All these variables recoded to three categories; those answering "don't know" were excluded.

Source: Pew Center Religion and Politics Survey, 1996.

ology, that variable was added as a control during crosstabulation. The actual question about ideology from the survey provided five categories that ranged from very liberal to very conservative, but for the purposes of this table the original five categories were collapsed into three. Table 16.2 displays the result of adding political ideology as a control variable in testing the relationship between the two original variables of education and abortion attitude. First, notice how Table 16.2 is constructed. The control variable, political ideology, is now at the top of the table, and the independent variable, level of education, is nested within the three categories of political ideology. Now we can examine the original independent/dependent relationship of level of education and attitude toward abortion within each category—conservative, moderate, liberal—of the control variable. In effect, we have reproduced the original bivariate table three times over, once for conservatives, once for moderates and once for liberals. [3] The original relationship can now be examined for each category of political ideology.

For conservatives, the original relationship between level of education and attitude toward abortion does *not* hold up: 22.3 percent of conservatives with low levels of education feel abortion should be generally available. The percentage goes up to only 22.9 percent for those with an intermediate level of education and to 23.4 percent for those at the highest level of education. The same very slight differences across levels of education show up for the conservatives' response that abortions should not be permitted at all. Among moderates and liberals, however, the original independent/dependent relationship between education and attitude toward abortion is largely unaffected. For those with a moderate political ideology, only 26.1 percent with a low education feel abortion should be generally available, but the percentages rise to 37.8 percent and 47.5 percent among the more educated groups. The same holds for liberals, with support for abortion being generally available rising from 33.1 percent to 55.7 percent to 63.8 percent as level of education rises. The substantive conclusion to be drawn from this multivariate analysis is that abortion attitudes among conservatives do not change based on level of education. For moderates and liberals, however, their attitudes toward abortion are affected by their level of education: the more education, the more support for abortion being generally available. In the original bivariate table, the relationship between education and attitude was strong enough among the sample as a whole to mask the lack of a relationship among conservatives. The actual lack of a relationship between level of education and attitude toward abortion for conservatives was only uncovered by employing a control variable and displaying the results in a multivariate percentage table.

Note the values of gamma at the bottom of Table 16.2. There is one for conservatives, one for moderates, and one for liberals. Each gamma shows the strength of the original independent/dependent relationship for each separate category of political ideology. The gamma showing the strength of the relationship between education and abortion attitude for conservatives is only .045, while for moderates it is .305 and for liberals .398. The gamma for Table 16.1 was .243. Measures of association provide a quick way to see any effect of a control variable. In this case, compared to the original relationship between education and attitude in Table 16.1, gamma drops for conservatives and rises somewhat for political moderates and liberals. Gamma thus reflects the lack of a relationship between the original variables for conservatives and a somewhat stronger relationship between the variables for moderates and liberals compared to the sample as a whole.

Effects of Control Variables on Original Relationships.

The substantive change in the relationship between education and attitude toward abortion that appeared in Table 16.2 as a result of adding the control variable of political ideology is called a **refining effect**. The original relationship was shown to hold only under certain circumstances, leading us to refine our hypothesis that more educated people are more supportive of abortion. The refinement is that the relationship holds for political moderates and liberals only, not for conservatives. Among conservatives, the relationship between education and abortion attitude disappears.

Other effects that might show up when a control variable is employed are **replicating, reducing, revealing,** and **reversal** effects, examples of which are shown in Table 16.3. [4]

A replicating effect, seen in Table 16.3a, occurs when the control variable has no effect on the initial independent/dependent relationship. The relationship between the two variables does not change within any category of the control variable. A reducing effect, shown in Table 16.3b, shows up when the original bivariate relationship is diminished or disappears completely. A revealing effect comes about when the original independent/dependent relationship is strengthened within one or more of the categories of the control variable and is displayed in Table 16.3c. Finally, a reversal effect, exhibited in Table 16.3d, means that the direction of the original relationship is reversed from positive to negative, or vice versa. This final effect, reversal, is sometimes difficult for people to grasp. How can a positive relationship between variables demonstrated for a group of people be reversed when examining subgroups of those very individuals? Paying attention to the number of people in each subgroup, as well as the percentages, will perhaps make such a reversal somewhat easier to understand.

To the Web

Exercise 16.1   Showing the Effects of a Control Variable

Exercise 16.1 displays a bivariate table about ideology and the death penalty, followed by two empty or "dummy" tables for you to show the effects of adding a control variable. Go to the **DEPR Web Page**, click on **Web Exercises, Chapter 16**, then on **Showing the Effects of a Control Variables**.

Key Points

Control variables can show the following effects on the original independent/dependent relationship:

- Refining—original relationship holds only under certain conditions.
- Replicating—control variable has no effect on original relationship.
- Reducing—original relationship diminishes or disappears.
- Revealing—original relationship is strengthened under certain conditions.
- Reversing—direction of original relationship changes from positive to negative.
- Control variables can also have a direct effect on the dependent variable and, together with the independent variable, a combined effect on the dependent variable.

Table 16.3
Examples of Effects of Control Variables on Bivariate Relationships

a. Replicating Effect: Candidate Choice and Sex, Controlling for Age

| | BIVARIATE TABLE | | | MULTIVARIATE TABLE | | | |
| | SEX | | | | OLDER | | YOUNGER | |
Choice	Male	Female	Choice	Male	Female	Male	Female
Smith	50%	50%	Smith	50%	50%	50%	50%
Jones	50%	50%	Jones	50%	50%	50%	50%
Total	400	400	Total	200	200	200	200

Source: Simulated.

b. Reducing Effect: Candidate Choice and Gun Ownership, Controlling for Residence

| | BIVARIATE TABLE | | | MULTIVARIATE TABLE | | | |
| | OWN GUN? | | | | RURAL | | URBAN | |
Choice	Yes	No	Choice	Yes	No	Yes	No
Smith	55%	50%	Smith	65%	65%	45%	45%
Jones	45%	50%	Jones	35%	35%	55%	55%
Total	400	400	Total	200	100	200	300

Source: Simulated.

Direct Effect of the Control Variable on the Dependent Variable. Well-constructed multivariate tables also allow you to see the direct effect of a control variable on the dependent variable. The focus is no longer on how the original independent/dependent relationship is affected by the control variable, but instead the control variable is considered as a separate independent variable with its own direct effect on the dependent variable. Table 16.2, for example, allows you to examine the effects of the control variable of political ideology directly on the dependent variable of attitude toward abortion. This can be done, in effect, by holding the original independent variable of education constant and searching for effects of ideology on abortion attitude within the

Table 16.3 (continued)
Examples of Effects of Control Variables on Bivariate Relationships

c. Revealing Effect: Candidate Choice and Sex, Controlling for Income

| BIVARIATE TABLE | | | MULTIVARIATE TABLE | | | | |
| | SEX | | | UPPER INCOME | | LOWER INCOME | |
Choice	Male	Female	Choice	Male	Female	Male	Female
Smith	50%	50%	Smith	33%	20%	100%	80%
Jones	50%	50%	Jones	67%	80%	0%	20%
Total	400	400	Total	300	200	100	200

Source: Simulated.

d. Reversal Effect: Candidate Choice and Education, Controlling for Country of Birth

| BIVARIATE TABLE | | | MULITVARIATE TABLE | | | | |
| | EDUCATION | | | U.S.A. | | NOT U.S.A. | |
Choice	Higher	Lower	Choice	Higher	Lower	Higher	Lower
Smith	45%	37%	Smith	20%	30%	50%	70%
Jones	55%	63%	Jones	80%	70%	50%	30%
Total	400	400	Total	66	334	334	66

Source: Simulated.

categories of education. To accomplish this, compare in Table 16.2 the percentages of those supporting a particular position on this policy within each of the three categories of education—low, intermediate, and high. If we look at those with low levels of education, we see 22.3 percent of conservatives, 26.1 percent of moderates, and 33.1 percent of liberals agree that abortions should be generally available. At least for those with low levels of education, support for abortion increases with rising levels of liberalism. The relationship holds as well for intermediate levels of education—22.9 percent for conservatives to 37.8 percent for political moderates to 55.7 percent of liberals, respectively, supporting the general availability of abortions. Finally, the pattern continues among those with a high level of education—23.4 percent for conservatives, 47.5 percent for political moderates, and 63.8 percent for liberals. Table 16.2 clearly shows that the more liberal a person, regardless of level of education, the more likely he or she is to agree that abortion should be widely available. We have determined the effect of the control variable directly on the dependent variable.

Combined Effect of Control and Independent Variables on the Dependent Variable.   The objective of data analysis is to explore as fully as possible the variation in the dependent variable. So in addition to assessing the separate effects of the independent and control variables, you should examine their combined effect on the dependent variable as well. In Table 16.2, we have seen that the independent variable of education and the control variable of political ideology were each individually related to abortion attitude: The more liberal respondents and the more educated respondents were more supportive of abortion. Given these separate effects of education and ideology, you would logically expect that highly educated liberals would be most supportive of abortion and the least-educated conservatives would be the least supportive of abortion. This is indeed the case, with only 22.3 percent of the least-educated conservatives supporting the position that abortions should be generally available and 63.8 percent of highly educated liberals supporting that position. So in addition to the separate effects of each variable, you can also see the combined effect of the control variable and independent variable on the dependent variable.

Condensing Tables to Simplify Interpretation.   Table 16.2 is not without problems. It is large and cumbersome, awkward to read, and most important, it has some cells with relatively few cases in them. For example, there are only four highly educated liberals who think abortion should not be permitted at all. When the number of cases in the cell of a table gets too small (sometimes reaching zero), and the number of cells with only a few or no cases in them increases, the relationship between the variables is hard to determine. These problems of size and empty, or nearly empty, cells are endemic to multivariate tables. When you add even one control variable, especially if it has more than three values, the percentage table becomes quite large and awkward to read. Trying to add a second control variable magnifies these problems, very often leaving some cells of the table empty. If your variables are operationalized at the interval or ratio level, you can avoid percentage tables altogether, but with exclusively nominal- and ordinal-level data, you will sometimes have difficulty constructing reasonably sized and readable multivariate percentage tables.

One option for at least reducing the physical size of a multivariate table is to construct a **condensed table.** The term *condensed* is used because the researcher chooses to display the results from only one value of the dependent variable, then rearranges the

Table 16.4
Percentages Who Said Abortion Should Be Generally Available by Education and Political Ideology

Ideology	LEVEL OF EDUCATION			
	Low High School or Less	Intermediate Some Education After High School	High BA/BS or More	
Conservative	22.3% (70)	22.9% (49)	23.4% (48)	gamma = .045
Moderate	26.1% (73)	37.8% (85)	47.5% (125)	gamma = .305
Liberal	33.1% (44)	55.7% (59)	63.8% (88)	gamma = .398

Note: Percentages are those responding that abortion should be "generally available." Other response categories were "available with restrictions" and "not permitted at all."

Source: Pew Center Religion and Politics Survey, 1996.

location of the control variable in order to condense the display of what is left in the table. For example, the dependent variable in Table 16.2 has three values (generally available, available with restrictions, not permitted at all), but the argument could be made that knowing the number and percentage of respondents to the survey who chose the response "generally available" would tell the reader all he or she needed to know about the relationship among education, political ideology, and attitude toward abortion. Consequently, we could remove from the table the results about who answered "available with restrictions" and "not permitted at all," saving considerable space. In cases where the dependent variable has only two values (such as agree/disagree or yes/no), showing only one value of the dependent variable makes even more sense. With a dichotomous dependent variable, the percentage of one value is by definition 100 percent minus the percentage of the other value of the dependent variable, so if you know one value, the other can be calculated as well, whether it is reported in the table or not.

Once the decision is made to show only one value of the dependent variable, the control variable is moved from the top to the left side of the table, and the labels for the dependent variable are removed entirely from the body of the table. The title should indicate exactly what categories of the dependent variable are included in the table, such as, "Percentage Who Said Abortion Should Be Generally Available. . . ." Sometimes a note under the table alerts the reader that the percentages in the table reflect only one value of the dependent variable. The result is a "condensed" table, as illustrated in Table 16.4, recognizable as condensed because the percentages that run down the columns (as well as across the rows) do not total 100 percent. The original independent variable—education—is at the top, while the control variable—political ideology—is on the left side.

The numbers in the cells, noted in the title and at the bottom of the table, are respondents who answered the question about availability of abortion with the response "generally available." The respondents in each cell share characteristics of the independent and control variables: 70 conservatives with low education, 125 highly educated moderates, 59 liberals with an intermediate level of education, and so on. The percentage in each cell of the tables is what proportion each of those numbers is of all people in those categories who responded to the question. Individual numbers and percentages in the table are read as follows: 48 or 23.4 percent of highly educated conservatives agree that abortions should be generally available, 44 or 33.1 percent of liberals with a low level of education agree that abortions should be generally available, 85 or 37.8 percent of political moderates with an intermediate level of education agree that abortions should be generally available, and so on.

Just as in Table 16.2, the individual effects of the independent and control variables, and their combined effect, can be observed in Table 16.4. First, by comparing across the rows, one can see the effects of the independent variable of education on attitude toward abortion, while controlling for ideology. With the data separated by political ideology, as well as education, we need to make three comparisons of education differences: one for conservatives (22.3 percent to 22.9 percent to 23.4 percent), one for moderates (26.1 percent to 37.8 percent to 47.5 percent), and one for liberals (33.1 percent to 55.7 percent to 63.8 percent). These comparisons show just what was revealed in Table 16.2. Among political moderates and liberals, the higher the level of education, the greater the support for making abortion generally available. Among conservatives, there is no relationship between education and abortion attitude.

Second, by comparing down the columns of a condensed table, we can see the effects of the control variable—political ideology—on the attitude. Again, because the data are separated by education, as well as ideology, we need to make three comparisons of ideological differences: one for those with low levels of education (22.3 percent to 26.1 percent to 33.1 percent), one for those with an intermediate level of education (22.9 percent to 37.8 percent to 55.7 percent), and one for those with a high level of education (23.4 percent to 47.5 percent to 63.8 percent). Just as in Table 16.2, all three comparisons show that, regardless of the level of education, the more liberal respondents are more supportive of abortion being generally available. Finally, the combined effects of the independent and control variables can be assessed by comparing the percentage differences in the extreme upper left and lower right corners of the table: 22.3 percent to 63.8 percent. This is the same comparison for combined effect made in Table 16.2.

To the Web

Exercise 16.2   Creating a Condensed Table from a Three-Variable Table

Starting with a full three-variable percentage table, you will be asked to condense the table. Then you will start with a condensed table and expand it into its initial, full format. Go to the **DEPR Web Page**, click on **Web Exercises, Chapter 16**, then on **Creating a Condensed Table from a Three-Variable Table**.

Questions for Thought and Discussion

How do you go about selecting a control variable for use in multivariate analysis? On what basis should you choose one control variable rather than another?

Why might you avoid using a condensed table with a dependent variable that had more than three values?

Interval- and Ratio-Level Data

Up to here, we have discussed ways to do multivariate analysis when you have nominal- or ordinal-level data. We now shift to data with variables operationalized at the interval and ratio levels, where hypotheses with two or more independent variables are tested using multiple linear regression. One of our cautions about bivariate regression was that we were attempting to determine the level of association between the variables, not causation. One of the necessary prerequisites for inferring causation in any type of analysis is that competing explanations for change in the dependent variable must be eliminated. Multiple regression, just as multivariate crosstabulation, tries to eliminate competing explanations by adding new independent variables as controls. And just as with crosstabulation, these control variables may have their own effect on the dependent variable, allowing elaboration of the original hypothesis. In fact, virtually all regression analyses start with more than one independent variable and are based upon a multi-causal model of behavior. The logic behind the analysis is the same as that for nominal and ordinal data. Additional independent variables are introduced that may account for changes in the dependent variable. Multiple linear regression is less cumbersome than constructing multivariate percentage tables because the controls are done mathematically, not by actually grouping together cases in the cells of a table.

Remember that linear regression analysis involves constructing a scatterplot and fitting a line that best describes the relationship between the independent and dependent variables. As you learned in the previous chapter, this is the equation for a regression line for two variables.

$$Y = a + bX + e$$

where Y represents the predicted values of the dependent variable, X represents the observed values of the independent variable, b represents the slope of the line (the regression coefficient), and a represents the Y-intercept, the value of Y when $X = 0$. e stands for error, the variation in Y that is not accounted for by the independent variables in the equation. Multiple regression simply adds more independent variables to the equation, so the general equation for linear multiple regression is an extension of the bivariate equation.

$$Y = a + b_1X_1 + b_2X_2 + b_3X_3 + \ldots b_nX_n + e$$

where

> Y represents the predicted values of the dependent variable.
> a is the Y-intercept, the value of Y when all independent variables are set to zero.
> $X_1, X_2, X_3, \ldots X_n$ represent the observed values of the independent variables.
> $b_1, b_2, b_3, \ldots b_n$ are the slopes (regression coefficients) for each independent variable respectively, while controlling for the effect of other independent variables in the equation.
> e stands for error, the variation in Y that is not accounted for by the independent variables in the equation.

Multiple regression reveals essentially the same information about the relationship between variables as does a bivariate analysis. The regression coefficient for each independent variable is more correctly called a **partial regression coefficient,** however, because the slope for each independent variable is calculated while controlling simultaneously for the effects of the other independent variables in the equation. Judging the importance of each partial regression coefficient relative to the others is not straightforward. The calculation of the coefficients, just as in bivariate regression, is sensitive to the units of measurement used with the independent variables. One partial regression coefficient may be larger than another because the former was measured in much smaller units than the latter, not because one is more strongly related to the dependent variable than the other. As pointed out in Chapter 15, one way to circumvent this problem is to convert the values of all variables to z-scores, which are the original values of the variables expressed in standard deviation units. The slopes after the values of the variables are standardized are referred to as standardized partial regression coefficients, or beta weights.

These standardized partial regression coefficients, beta weights, for each independent variable are employed by some researchers to assess the importance of the independent variables relative to one another in accounting for change in the dependent variable. These standardized coefficients indicate the direction of the controlled relationship between a particular independent variable and the dependent variable and are employed to determine the relative amount of change in the dependent variable accounted for by each of the independent variables. The larger the value of a beta weight for a particular independent variable, the greater the amount of change in the dependent variable associated with that independent variable when all other independent variables in the equation are held constant.

Calculation of the beta weight for an independent variable, however, involves multiplying the partial regression coefficient by the ratio of the standard deviation of the independent variable to the standard deviation of the dependent variable. [5] Because the standard deviation of any measure is in part dependent on its variability, two beta weights may have numerically different sizes, in part because of the differing variability of the two measures reflected in their respective standard deviations in the formula. Therefore, one must be cautious about interpreting the size of one beta weight relative to another. This is also why comparing beta weights across samples should be avoided; the different samples may have differing levels of variability. [6]

An Example of Multiple Linear Regression

An example from one of the data sets accompanying this book—the countries data—will help with your understanding of multiple regression analysis. For this example, we will try to explain political and social stability in nation states. Why are some countries more politically and socially stable than others? Why do some have less and others more political and social violence? Do economic conditions somehow affect level of stability? Does the political socialization of citizens through agents such as schools affect both political and social stability? In an attempt to answer these questions about stability, we first reasoned that economic conditions do indeed affect political and social stability, leading us to hypothesize that the better the economic conditions of a country, the more politically and socially stable it will be. The measure of political stability is an index provided by the World Bank Institute and includes a wide variety of incidents of political unrest. To operationalize the variable of social stability, we used another measure provided by the World Bank Institute called the Rule of Law, which includes over twenty-five indicators about crime, property rights, enforceability of contracts, intellectual property protection, and so on. We expect a positive relationship between economic conditions and both of these indexes. Our operational definition of economic strength is per capita Gross Domestic Product (the value of the goods and services produced domestically in a country divided by the population) expressed in U.S. dollars. This measure reflects how economically well off, on average, each person is in any country.

We further reasoned that not just the total wealth of a country but also the distribution of that wealth would affect its political and social stability. The less equitably distributed the wealth, the more unstable the country was the hypothesis we derived. Our measure of wealth distribution is the percentage of household income received or percentage of consumption by the richest 10 percent of the population; the higher this

Table 16.5
Regression Analysis: Political and Social Stability Regressed on Gross Domestic Product per Capita, Controlling for Wealth Distribution and Education Spending

Independent Variables	Political Stability b	Social Stability b
Per Capita GDP in U.S. Dollars, 1999	.007	.008
Controlling for		
Wealth Distribution	.005	.007
Education Spending	.006	.008
Wealth Distribution and Education Spending	.005	.007

Note: The indexes for political and social stability in the data set were multiplied by 100 for this analysis. The number of cases for this analysis ranges from 100 to 156 due to missing data.

Source: Doing Empirical Political Research, "COUNTRIESdepr" data set.

percentage, the less equitably distributed is the wealth. We expect this measure of wealth distribution to be negatively related to both our measure of political stability (more concentrated wealth, less politically stable) and our measure of social stability (more concentrated wealth, less socially stable). Finally, reasoning that schools are an important socialization agent in teaching citizens to respect the social norms and political institutions of a country, we added the variable of education expenditures as a percentage of the Gross National Product (the value of all goods and services produced by a country). The more spent on education, the more effective would be the socialization of citizens to the established political and social norms and practices of a country, leading to greater political and social stability. We could have added more independent variables to the analysis if we wanted to. For purposes of simplicity, however, we have limited the number of independent variables to three in this illustration. All of the variables are measured at the interval/ratio level.

The analysis could proceed in one of two directions. We could test our original hypothesis that countries with higher levels of per capita GDP will be more politically and socially stable than countries with lower levels of per capita GDP and then subject that relationship to individual controls with the other two independent variables. That is elaborating the original hypothesis, and those results are shown in Table 16.5. Alternatively, we could set up a single multivariate model and examine the effect of all three independent variables simultaneously on the level of political stability. The results of that model are shown in Table 16.6. Each type of analysis has its value, and both show in slightly different ways the results of multiple regression analysis using wealth of a coun-

Table 16.6
Regression Analysis: Political and Social Stability in Countries by Gross Domestic Product per Capita, Wealth Distribution, and Education Expenditures

Independent Variables	Political Stability		Social Stability	
	b	Beta	b	Beta
Per Capita GDP in U.S. Dollars, 1999	.005	.617	.007	.784
Wealth Distribution	−1.82	−.172	−.399	−.036
Education Spending	3.57	.080	6.73	.147
R^2		.559		.738
Number of Cases		100		105

Note: The indexes for political and social stability in the data set are multiplied by 100 for this analysis. Entries under *b* are partial regression coefficients.

Source: Doing Empirical Political Research, "COUNTRIESdepr" data set.

try, wealth distribution, and educational expenditures to account for differences in political and social stability.

Table 16.5 reports the findings of testing the original relationship between per capita GDP and political and social stability, the effect of controlling for each other independent variable individually on the original relationship, and finally the effect of controlling for the other independent variables simultaneously on that original relationship. The first column is made up of the two variables and partial regression coefficients for the dependent variable of political stability, while in the second column are the partial regression coefficients for social stability. You can compare the coefficients up and down each column because in each instance you are showing the relationship between GDP per capita and a single dependent variable, either political or social stability. The units of measurement on the X- and Y-axes do not change within each column. You cannot, however, compare coefficients across the rows because the two dependent variables are measured in different units along the Y-axis, and the differences in size between the coefficients may be due to the imbalance in the scales of those two Y-axes.

The original hypothesis about political and social stability is confirmed, Table 16.5 showing a positive relationship between per capita GDP and both measures of stability. For every unit increase in per capita GDP, there is a corresponding .007 unit increase in the index of political stability and a .008 increase in the index of social stability. The first control variable, wealth distribution, has a decreasing effect, because the regression coefficient for the original relationship drops slightly for each measure of stability. Part of the relationship between per capita GDP and stability has to do with the distribution of the wealth in the country as well as its overall level. When education spending is employed as a control, there is another, smaller effect on the original relationship between GDP and political stability because the regression coefficient drops to .006. There is no effect on the relationship between GDP and social stability when controlling for education because the partial regression coefficient stays the same:, .008. When wealth distribution and education spending are used as controls simultaneously, the regression value drops to .005 for political stability and .007 for social stability, showing the overall effect of both control variables.

Table 16.6 shows the effect of each independent variable controlling simultaneously for the other independent variables rather than elaborating with each independent variable separately. The beta weights, the standardized regression coefficients, are included in this table. When you consider the results relative to political stability, for per capita GDP the beta weight is .617, showing that for every standard deviation unit increase in per capita GDP there is a corresponding .617 standard deviation unit increase in political stability, controlling for both wealth distribution and education expenditures. The beta weight for this variable is clearly larger than that for the other two independent variables, indicating that GDP likely accounts for more change in political stability than either of the other two independent variables. The beta weight for percentage of the national income received by the richest 10 percent of the population is −.172, meaning that, while controlling for GDP and educational expenditures, as wealth is more concentrated (a larger percentage of the wealth is controlled by the richest group), the political stability index declines. This is consistent with our hypothesis. Finally, the beta weight for educational expenditures is .080, indicating a comparatively small relationship between this variable and level of political stability, while controlling for the other independent variables.

The results for social stability are also consistent with our hypothesis. For per capita GDP the beta weight is .784, showing that for every standard deviation unit increase in per capita GDP there is a corresponding .784 standard deviation unit increase in political stability, controlling for both wealth distribution and education expenditures. As with political stability, the beta weight for GDP is clearly larger than that for the other two independent variables, indicating this variable likely accounts for more change in social stability than either of the other two independent variables. The effect of wealth distribution on social stability is not as great as that of education expenditures as reflected in the comparison of the beta weights: −.036 to .147.

Why leave in variables that show little or no relationship to the dependent variable—in this case, educational expenditures for political stability and wealth distribution for social stability? Because it shows you and other readers that we initially considered these variables important for explaining stability, but that was not confirmed. If these variables are removed from the respective regression equations, the beta weights for the other two variables change very little, but it is helpful to a curious reader to know that these variables were considered and, at least as measured in our analysis, rejected as a partial explanation of stability.

Measure of Association— Multiple Correlation Coefficient

Just as with bivariate regression analysis, we need to supplement reporting of the regression coefficients and beta weights with a measure of association. We will use a multivariate version of the Pearson correlation coefficient to determine the strength of the relationship between the independent variables as a group and dependent variable in the equation. The multivariate Pearson correlation coefficient (R) ranges only from 0 to +1 because some independent variables, as in our preceding example, may be negatively related to the dependent variable and others positively related. The direction of the **multiple correlation coefficient** makes no sense in that situation. The closer to 1 the correlation coefficient is, the stronger the relationship among the variables. The square of the multivariate Pearson correlation coefficient (R^2), as in the bivariate case, is a quantitative expression of the ratio of the explained variation to the total variation in a multivariate regression analysis. It is also called the **coefficient of multiple determination,** and it tells you what proportion of the variance in the dependent variable is explained by all the independent variables in the equation. In our example of political and social stability in countries (see Table 16.6), the value of R^2 is .559 for political stability, meaning that 55.9 percent of the variance in the measure of political stability can be accounted for by the collective variance in our measures of GDP, concentration of wealth, and education expenditures. Those variables account for 73.8 percent ($R^2 = .738$) of the variance in social stability.

Most statistical software programs, including SPSS, will calculate and report, in addition to R^2, an "adjusted" R^2. The adjustment is a decrease in the value of R^2 as more independent variables are added to the equation. An adjusted R^2 will never be larger than the original R^2. You will generally see only small differences between R^2 and the adjusted R^2 for any multiple regression equation unless you have relatively few cases and many independent variables. You might be tempted when performing multiple regression analysis to aimlessly and indiscriminately add independent variables to the equation in order to increase the value of R^2 to ensure you have explained as much of the variance in the dependent variable as you can. Such an approach is not a good idea, even if each independent variable might add a percentage point or two to the value of your coefficient of determination. Parsimony is one your goals; you do not want your model to be cluttered with so many independent variables that its complexity makes it difficult to understand and apply to the political world in general.

Remember that the goal is to explain change in the dependent variable. Your findings from a regression analysis will make sense only to the extent that the reasoning on which you chose independent variables makes sense. If you enter independent variables into the regression equation with no theoretical basis, you will still be unable to explain why one variable is related to the dependent variable and another is not. Choice of independent variables must always have a theoretical, logical basis, or your findings will be a mystery to you. Second, you must be careful not to add too many independent variables. At the limit, you should never have more independent variables than cases to study because you will be custom-fitting a regression equation to that particular data and be unable to generalize to other circumstances.

To the Web

Explanations of Multivariate Regression

There are a number of online statistics textbooks that cover the topic of multiple regression. There are also applications of linear regression analysis as part of a strategy for investing in the stock market. Go to the **DEPR Web Page**, click on **Web Links, Chapter 16**, then on **Online Statistics Texts and Regression and the Stock Market.**

Conclusion

Multivariate data analysis techniques allow you to put into practice the concept of controlling and elaboration you learned about in Chapter 6. This type of analysis enables you to provide more complex and complete empirical explanations of political behavior and attitudes as well as better assess the causality of posited relationships. These objectives are accomplished with nominal and ordinal data by grouping together cases in multivariate percentage tables to observe directly the effect of control variables. For interval and ratio data, on the other hand, the controls are implemented mathematically through regression analysis, not by grouping. While there are certainly many other statistical techniques for analyzing empirical data that we have not covered in this text, an understanding of the concepts and techniques in this section of the book will permit you to test empirically your own hypotheses. You are now prepared to undertake your own scientific study of political behavior.

In Chapter 14 we said that whether relationships between variables found in samples also exist in the population cannot be determined by examining measures of association. We will discuss in the next chapter tests of statistical significance that aid in the process of drawing conclusions about whether relationships in a sample are strong enough to warrant rejection of the null hypothesis in the population. How to report the findings of your study, including clear and precise visual displays of your data analysis results, are covered in the final chapter.

Summary of the Main Points

- Multivariate data analysis employs two or more independent variables to account for changes in the dependent variable.
- Multivariate crosstabulation is used to analyze nominal- and ordinal-level data.

- Multiple linear regression is used to analyze interval and ratio data.
- Control variables in multivariate crosstabulation can have a reducing, refining, replicating, reversal, or no effect on the original independent/dependent relationship.
- Beta weights in multiple regression are standardized regression coefficients.
- The coefficient of determination, R^2, in multiple regression indicates what percentage of the variance in the dependent variable is accounted for by the independent variables as a whole.

		Terms Introduced
coefficient of multiple determination	partial regression coefficient	
condensed table	reducing effect	
multiple correlation coefficient	refining effect	
multiple linear regression	replicating effect	
multivariate analysis	revealing effect	
multivariate percentage table	reversal effect	
nesting		

Selected Readings

Berry, William D., and Mitchell S. Sanders, *Understanding Multivariate Research: A Primer for Beginning Social Scientists.* Boulder, CO: Westview Press, 2000.

Kerlinger, Fred N., and E. Pedhazer. *Multiple Regression in Behavioral Research.* New York: Holt, Rinehart, & Winston, 1973.

Schroeder, Larry D., David L. Sjoquist, and Paula E. Steven. *Understanding Regression Analysis: An Introductory Guide.* Newbury Park, CA: Sage Publications Series on Quantitative Applications in the Social Sciences, No. 57, 1986.

Tufte, Edward R. *Data Analysis for Politics and Policy.* Englewood Cliffs, NJ: Prentice Hall, 1974.

Activity 16.1
Reading a Multivariate Percentage Table

Activities

1. Name the independent and dependent variables in Table 16.7.
2. What are the values of the dependent variable?
3. In the upper left-hand corner of the table is the value 50.8 percent. What does that percentage represent?
4. Are 25.9 percent of those against less government regulation of business liberal women?
5. Is ideology related to attitude regarding regulation of business, regardless of sex?
6. Regardless of ideology, do males show greater opposition to regulation of business than females?
7. Write a paragraph describing the relationship among the variables in the table.

Table 16.7
Relationship Among Political Ideology, Sex, and Attitude on Business Regulation

Less Government Regulation of Business	MALE			FEMALE		
	Liberal	Moderate	Conservative	Liberal	Moderate	Conservative
Favor	66	109	166	60	113	112
	50.8%	54.8%	74.1%	34.5%	41.1%	50.0%
Neutral	37	57	32	69	121	66
	28.5%	28.6%	14.3%	39.7%	44.0%	29.5%
Against	27	33	26	45	41	46
	20.8%	16.6%	11.6%	25.9%	14.9%	20.5%
Total	130	199	224	174	275	224
	100%	100%	100%	100%	100%	100%

Source: General Social Survey, 1996, National Opinion Research Center.

Activity 16.2
Constructing a Condensed Table

Rearrange the information provided in Table 16.7 to create a condensed table.

Activity 16.3
Creating and Editing a Multivariate Percentage Table Using SPSS

The objective in this exercise is to create a multivariate percentage table using the software package SPSS. This exercise is a continuation of Activity 14.4, in which we created a bivariate percentage table from the General Social Survey for 2000 using SPSS, with the dependent variable of confidence in Congress and the independent variable of age. In this activity, we will add a control variable.

Click on "Analyze" near the top of the page. When the box appears under "Analyze," click on "Descriptive Statistics." When a box appears to the side, click on "Crosstabs." Now you are looking at a new window titled "Crosstabs." Scroll through variables on the left and highlight "conlegis." Use the arrow button to move "conlegis" into the box titled "Row(s)"; this will be your dependent variable.

Scroll through the variables on the left again and highlight "agequart." Use the arrow button to move "agequart" into the box titled "Column(s)"; this will be your independent variable. Click on the "Cells" button at the bottom of the window. Now you are looking at a new window titled "Crosstabs: Cell Display." In the small box titled "Percentages," click on "Column" so a check mark appears; this will ensure that percentages in the table are calculated down the columns. Click on the "Continue" button. Now you are back at the window titled "Crosstabs." Click on "OK." A window titled "Output—SPSS Viewer" appears; the results of your data analysis examining the relationship between age and confidence in Congress are in this window. Scroll through the results, noting differences among the age groupings in their confidence in Congress.

With the SPSS Viewer window still open and showing the bivariate table, click on "Analyze" near the top of the page. When the gray box appears under "Analyze," click on "Descriptive Statistics," and when the box appears to the side, click on "Crosstabs." You are now back to the bivariate "Crosstab" analysis you previously set up. Scroll through the variables on the left and highlight "sex." Then use the arrow button to move "sex" into the box titled "Layer 1 of 1." This will be your CONTROL variable.

Click on the "OK" button, and a window titled "Output—SPSS Viewer" will appear; results of your data analysis are in this window. The table compares, separately, the attitudes of MALES and FEMALES, with age as the independent variable and confidence in Congress as the dependent. SPSS does not create multivariate tables in the standard format shown in this chapter. The control variable will appear on the side, next to the dependent variable rather than at the top of the table. If using this table in a report or term paper, you will need to rearrange the table with the control variable at the top and the original independent variable nested under the values of the control variable.

Scroll through the results, noting any differences between males and females. What kind of effect, if any, did the control variable have on the original relationship? Write a one-paragraph summary of the effect of adding the control variable of sex on the relationship between age and confidence in Congress.

To print this table from SPSS, the output will run more than one page, so you may want to edit the table to reduce its size. To check how much paper will be used in printing, click on "File" and choose the "Print preview" option from the drop-down menu. After viewing the size of the table, close print preview. One choice is to reduce the size of the entire table. Double-click on the table. A squiggly line box will appear around the table, and a new status bar will appear at the top of the screen. Click on the icon labeled "Format" and from the drop-down menu click on "Table properties." A folder will appear that has a series of tabs; click on the tab labeled "Printing." A new window will appear, near the center of which will be two options from which you can choose: "Rescale wide table to fit page" and "Rescale long table to fit page." Choose either or both, depending on the size of your table, click on the "OK" button, and the window will close. The printed table will now fit on one page of paper.

The second option for reducing the size of the table is to remove specific parts. Double-click on the table so the squiggly line box appears around it. Then click on any section of the table, and a dark, heavy line will appear around that section of the table. Right-click within that part of the table, and a new window will appear; one of the options in the window is "Cut." Left-click on "Cut," and that section of the table will disappear. While the squiggly line is still around the table, you can also place the cursor on any vertical line in the table, wait for a small double-headed arrow to appear in place of the usual single-headed cursor arrow, and then hold down the left mouse button, and you can drag the line right or left to expand or reduce the size of the table.

Activity 16.4
Multiple Regression Using SPSS

Now we will do a multiple regression analysis in SPSS, trying to explain the difference in the dependent variable of income per capita in the fifty American states (perinccu) by two independent variables: (1) the level of education in the states (bachdegr), operationalized as the percentage of a state's population over 25 years old with a bachelor's degree; and (2) population density (popsqmi), measured by dividing the state's population by its area in square miles. The reasoning behind this analysis is that the income in a state is affected by these two independent variables. For the first independent variable, education, the argument is that a more educated populace will have higher-paying jobs, producing a higher level of per capita income in the state. The second independent variable is included because we expect to find better-paying jobs, and therefore more opportunity for state residents to obtain them, in urban rather than rural areas.

Open the "STATESdepr" data file in SPSS. Just as you did in Activity 15.2, click on "Analyze" at the top of the screen, and choose "Regression" from the drop-down menu and then "Linear" from the next drop-down menu. A new window will appear, titled "Linear Regression." In the "Linear Regression" window, move the variable "perinccu" into the box marked "Dependent," and move both "bachdegr" and "popsqmi" into the box marked "Independent." Then click on the "OK" button. As with a simple bivariate regression, look at the "Coefficients" box to ascertain both the unstandardized and standardized regression coefficients for each of your independent variables. Look at the "Model summary" box to determine R and R^2.

Write a brief description about what all this tells you about the relationship among level of education, population density, and per capita income in the United States.

Chapter 17

Determining the Statistical Significance of Results

Learning Objectives

After completion of this chapter, students should be able to do the following:

Explain the concept of statistical significance and how it differs from substantive significance.

Comprehend that statistical significance involves testing the null hypothesis.

Understand when it is appropriate to employ a chi square, a t-test, or an F-test.

Know how to interpret the benchmark levels of statistical significance.

Calculate a chi square value for a crosstabulation.

Sample Versus Population Relationships

The final topic to be discussed about data analysis is **statistical significance,** the likelihood that an observed relationship in a probability sample has occurred by chance and is not present in the population from which the sample was drawn. Tests of statistical significance are important because they help you to avoid falsely claiming, based on analysis of data in a sample, that there is a relationship between variables in the population when there actually is none. The idea of statistical significance can be a slippery concept, so we need to discuss this notion a bit more fully before demonstrating and applying the actual tests of significance. Statistical significance is conceptually different from determining the strength of a relationship between variables, although stronger relationships are indeed more likely to be statistically significant. Strength of a relationship has to do with how much more likely you are to know the value of a dependent variable by knowing the value of an independent variable. As discussed in previous chapters, lambda, gamma, and the Pearson correlation coefficient (used with nominal-, ordinal-, and interval/ratio-level data, respectively) all indicate the strength of a relationship between an independent and dependent variable by measuring the proportionate reduction in error. Each of theses measures of association tells you how much better off you are by using an independent variable to estimate the value of the dependent variable for any case compared to simply guessing the value of the dependent variable. Statistical significance, on the other hand, has to do with how likely the strength of the relationship you found in your sample exists in the population from which the sample was drawn. Tests of significance are generally used only with probability samples.

In Chapter 13, we talked about probability sampling, how close the value of a variable found in a sample was to the actual value in the population from which the sample was drawn. We explored, as an example, how confident we could be that the mean age of a sample was within a certain range of the mean age of the population from which the sample was drawn. The reasoning behind probability sampling is based on the normal distribution, which has known characteristics, such as what percentage of cases are contained within so many standard deviations around the mean. The answer to whether a sample statistic is representative of the population parameter can be provided only in probabilistic terms, based on the size and variability of the sample. In this sense, determining statistical significance is analogous to sampling, except that instead of inferring the value of a single variable in the population (for example, mean age, percentage support for a candidate) from the value in the sample, you are instead trying to determine how likely it is that a relationship between two or more variables found in the sample data also exists in the population data. The question is "How confident can I be inferring that a hypothesis I have confirmed using a sample of cases would also be confirmed in the population from which the sample was drawn?" As with trying to infer population parameters from sample statistics, the answer can be given only in probabilistic terms. Statistical significance is a function of both the strength of the relationship between the variables in your hypothesis as well as the homogeneity in the sample with which you are working. The stronger the relationship in the sample, and the more homogeneous the sample is, the more likely the same relationship will be found in the entire population.

The Framework of Statistical Significance

Before we examine some of the statistics that can help you figure out how confident you can be about applying your sample findings to the population as a whole, the conceptual framework surrounding the idea of statistical significance must be explored. The parts of this framework to be addressed are the distinction between **Type I** and **Type II errors,** the difference between statistical and **substantive significance,** and the **benchmarks of acceptable risk.**

Type I Versus Type II Errors

Two quite different types of errors might occur when testing hypotheses using sample data and inferring the results to a population. First, you could make a Type I error, the situation when there is actually no relationship between the variables in the population, but based on your analysis of the sample data, you erroneously conclude that there is. This is also called a false positive. A Type II error occurs when there is in fact a relationship between the variables in the population, but your analysis of the sample data leads you to say there is not. This second type of error is referred to as a false negative. [1] Tests of statistical significance focus on Type I errors, mistakenly claiming there is a relationship in the population when there is none. Unfortunately, the more one focuses on reducing the probability of making a Type I error—being more certain that you have not incorrectly claimed a relationship in the population when there is none—the more likely you are to commit a Type II error—failing to find in the sample data an actual relationship in the population.

Which error has more serious consequences depends on the empirical phenomenon under analysis. Type II errors—failing to discover an existing relationship in the population by examining your sample data—have serious negative consequences especially in areas of safety and disease. For example, government health professionals analyzing sample data to test for the presence of a relationship between some environmental condition and the presence of a dangerous infectious disease must be especially careful not to make a Type II error. Failure to detect the presence of such a relationship in the population could lead to serious illnesses or many deaths. On the other hand, committing a Type I error—claiming with their sample data that there is a relationship between the conditions and the disease in the population when there is none—might lead to a waste of limited health-care resources being devoted to a nonexistent problem. You should keep in mind that tests of statistical significance, the topic of this chapter, focus on Type I errors.

Statistical Significance Versus Substantive Significance

Notice that we are talking about statistical, not substantive, significance. The substance of your findings takes on importance only to the extent that it contributes information valuable for the understanding of political behavior. Often the hypothesis being tested will be derived from a theory, and the substantive finding might lend further credence to that theory, or suggest ways it might be modified, or seriously undermine the logic on which the theory is based. Other times your data analysis might reveal unexpected substantive changes in an attitude or behavior that alters previous research findings in that area. Statistical significance, in contrast, helps you determine how likely it is that your findings, whether substantively interesting or not, can be generalized to a population. It is possible to have findings that are statistically but not substantively significant.

Accepted Benchmarks for Statistical Significance

Specific benchmarks have been established in the social sciences to decide whether findings from a sample are worth talking about in terms of a population. Of course, the range of probabilities that a finding from the sample might exist in the population can range from 0 percent to 100 percent. Although some researchers will accept a 90 percent level, the most common standard used in empirical political science says that you must be at least 95 percent confident that the relationship you found in the sample exists in the population. That is, you can say that 95 times out of 100, with a sample of the size and homogeneity with which you are working, the strength of the relationship between variables found in the sample will also exist in the population from which the sample is drawn. If you can say that, your findings are statistically significant. If you cannot establish that level of certainly between the findings in the sample and what exists in the population, your findings are not statistically significant.

Two other standard benchmarks for statistical significance are recognized in political science: a 99 percent chance and a 99.9 percent chance that findings in the sample are present in the population. All of these benchmarks are reported not as percentages but as probabilities, expressed as p (for probability) $< .05$, $p < .01$, and $p < .001$. $p < .05$ indicates that you would make a mistake in concluding that there is a relationship in the population as strong as the one you found in the sample fewer than 5 times out of every 100 samples of similar size and homogeneity. $p < .01$ denotes that such an error would occur less than 1 time in 100 samples, and $p < .001$ means less than once in 1 time in 1,000 samples. The lower the p value, the more likely a relationship of the same strength is present in the population as what you found in the sample.

These values are reported as probabilities rather than percentages because you are not really establishing that a relationship exists in the population. Instead, you are only claiming that the null hypothesis stating there is no relationship between the variables in the population is being rejected. Because we can never prove in absolute terms that there is a relationship between variables, we instead posit the null hypothesis that there is no relationship between the variables in the population and then express in probabilistic terms how confident we are in rejecting that null hypothesis. Statistical significance is a probabilistic judgment of how confident you are in rejecting the null hypothesis about the population. A .05 level of statistical significance means that you will incorrectly reject the null hypothesis (claim there is a relationship between the variables in the population based on analysis of data in the sample when in fact there is not such a relationship in the population) 5 times in every 100 samples. You are 95 percent confident that with a sample of the size and variability from which you obtained your data that the relationship you found in the sample exists in the population.

Sometimes the level of acceptable statistical significance is established prior to the research being undertaken. The researcher decides in advance of the study what criterion he or she will employ: .05, .01, or .001. Findings that do not reach the preset criterion for significance will not be reported. More often, political scientists doing empirical work report all their findings, including those that are not statistically significant by any benchmark, so the reader can see the full scope of the study. How the findings are reported vary from one researcher to another, but all of them will indicate, in one manner or another, which findings are statistically significant and which are not. The most commonly found notation when reporting multiple findings in a single table is to mark those findings statistically significant at the .05 level with a single asterisk, those at the .01 level with two asterisks, and those at the .001 level with three asterisks. You can see an example of this method in Table 18.3.

Key Points

Statistical significance has the following features:

- It is the likelihood of finding a probability sample relationship in the population.
- It is related to the strength of the relationship between variables.
- It differs from substantive significance.
- It tests for Type I errors only.
- It usually is reported by benchmarks of .05, .01, and .001.
- It uses χ^2, t, and F distributions, depending on the situation.

Tests of Statistical Significance

We mentioned previously that inferring relationships to populations from samples was analogous to making inferences about the values of variables in a population from the values found in the sample. Instead of using the normal distribution and calculating standard deviations as we did with sampling, however, other distributions are employed for determining levels of statistical significance. They are the chi square, t, and F distributions.

For each of these distributions, the probability is known for getting any particular value in the distribution when there is no association between the variables in the population. By setting confidence intervals at the .05, .01, .001, or any level you decide, you can reject the null hypothesis in the population based on your sample findings at varying levels of certainty. You should note that, in general, statistical significance should be computed only for probability samples. Sometimes, however, researchers will report levels of statistical significance for regression coefficients calculated from nonsample data to show the strength of those relationships.

Chi Square

The **chi square** distribution is used to determine level of statistical significance for relationships between variables measured at the nominal and ordinal levels. After first computing an appropriate measure of association, such as lambda or gamma, and if support for the hypothesized relationship is found, you need to ask how likely it is that the relationship in the sample occurred by chance and there actually is no such relationship in the population from which the sample was drawn. The general principle on which the test is based is a comparison of the number of observations one would expect to find in the cells of a crosstabulation table and what the actual, observed numbers are in that table. Notice that you are comparing the **expected frequencies** with **observed frequencies,** not percentages, in the crosstabulation.

The observed numbers in a table are simply how many cases fall into each cell. The expected numbers in each cell are determined by looking at the frequency distribution for each of the two variables in the table, reflected in the totals of the columns and rows. These totals are called the **marginals** because they are found at the margins of the table. Look at Table 17.1, showing the results of a crosstabulation between ideology and attitude on confidence in the press based on a random sample of respondents from the 2000 General Social Survey. The gamma for the table is +.154, indicating a positive relationship between conservatism and lack of confidence in the press. The more conservative a respondent, the more likely he or she is to have hardly any confidence in the press. Conversely, the more liberal respondents are more likely to have only some or a great deal of confidence in the press compared to conservatives.

In Table 17.1, the independent variable, located appropriately at the top, has three values: liberal, moderate, and conservative. As seen at the bottom of the table in the column totals, there are 456 liberals, 675 moderates, and 605 conservatives. The dependent variable, level of confidence in the press, has three values: a great deal, only some, and hardly any. The number of respondents falling into each category of the dependent variable are the row totals at the right-hand margin of the table; 181 respondents had a great deal of confidence in the press, 829 had only some confidence, and 726 answered they had hardly any confidence in the press. These column and row totals are the marginals.

Table 17.1
Relationship Between Political Ideology and Confidence in the Press

| | POLITICAL IDEOLOGY | | | |
Confidence in Press	Liberal	Moderate	Conservative	Total
A Great Deal	11.2%	11.6%	8.6%	10.4%
	(51)	(78)	(52)	(181)
Only Some	53.5%	48.6%	42.5%	47.8%
	(244)	(328)	(257)	(829)
Hardly Any	35.3%	39.9%	48.8%	41.8%
	(161)	(269)	(296)	(726)
Total	100%	100%	100%	100%
	(456)	(675)	(605)	(1,736)

Gamma = +.154

Note: Ideology was recoded from seven categories ranging from extremely liberal to extremely conservative to the three shown in the table.

Source: General Social Survey, 2000, National Opinion Research Center.

Using these marginals, we can determine the expected frequencies, which is how many cases would fall into each cell of the table if there were no relationship between the variables—that is, if the null hypothesis were correct. To get these expected frequencies, you multiply the row total for the cell by the column total for the cell and divide by the total number of cases in the table. Calculations for the expected frequencies in Table 17.1 are as follows.

upper left cell	$(181 \times 456) \div 1{,}736 = 48$
upper center cell	$(181 \times 675) \div 1{,}736 = 70$
upper right cell	$(181 \times 605) \div 1{,}736 = 63$
middle left cell	$(829 \times 456) \div 1{,}736 = 218$
middle center cell	$(829 \times 675) \div 1{,}736 = 322$
middle right cell	$(829 \times 605) \div 1{,}736 = 289$
lower left cell	$(726 \times 456) \div 1{,}736 = 191$
lower center cell	$(726 \times 675) \div 1{,}736 = 282$
lower right cell	$(726 \times 605) \div 1{,}736 = 253$

If there were no relationship between political ideology and confidence in the press in the sample data, which is positing the null hypothesis, these are the expected frequencies for each cell in the table. Assuming a person's political ideology has no effect on confidence in the press, 48 liberals would have a great deal of confidence, 218 would have only some, and 191 would say they had hardly any confidence. For moderates, we would expect 70 to say a great deal, 322 would say only some, and 282 would say hardly any. The conservatives would have expected totals of 63 saying a great deal, 289 answering only some, and 253 responding hardly any. By comparing the observed number of cases falling into each cell to these expected frequencies we have computed, we can determine how likely it is that a person's ideology affects his or her level of confidence in the press. The greater the difference between the observed and expected frequencies, the more likely there is a relationship that will hold up in the population from which the sample was drawn.

The formula for computing the chi square value is

$$\chi^2 = \Sigma \left[\frac{(O - E)^2}{E} \right]$$

where O is the observed frequency, the actual value in each cell, and E is the expected value, calculated from the marginals. Consistent with other formulas you have seen, Σ means to add up all the values.

To the Web

Calculating and Learning More About Chi Square

For connection to a series of interactive links about chi square, go to the **DEPR Web Page** and click on **Links to Chi Square**. To calculate chi squares for a 2×2 table, allowing you to change any or all of the values in the table to see the effect, click on **2X2 Chi Squares**. To get to an interactive link to calculate chi square values for any size table, click on **Chi Square for Any Size Table**.

Let's return to Table 17.1 and calculate the chi square value for that crosstabulation. The gamma value, showing the strength of association between the variables, is +.154. The chi square, you remember, will tell us how likely it is that the strength of association we are reporting in this sample data also exists in the population. Or to say it another way, the chi square value will determine how likely it is we are making a mistake in rejecting the null hypothesis in the population based on our findings in the sample. We have already calculated the expected frequencies, and the remaining procedures described in the formula for chi square as applied to Table 17.1 can be found in Figure 17.1.

The chi square for Table 17.1 is 22.39, but you will need one more bit of information to make use of this chi square value: the degrees of freedom (noted as df) associated with the table. The degrees of freedom are calculated with the formula $(C - 1)(R - 1)$, where C is the number of columns in the table, and R is the number of rows. For Table 17.1, with three columns and three rows, the calculation is $(3 - 1)(3 - 1) = (2)(2) = 4$. Table 17.1 has four degrees of freedom, meaning that as soon as four of the nine cells in the table are filled, the values in the rest of the cells are not free to vary. This is because the marginals—the column and row totals—are already set and the numbers in remaining cells are delimited by these totals. Look back at Table 17.1. If you fill the top row of cells and one in the second row (or any other four cells), and in addition leave the marginals as they are, the numbers in the remaining cells are already predetermined. Only four cell values are free to vary in a 3×3 table.

Figure 17.1
Calculation of Chi Square Value for Table 17.1

$$\text{Chi Square} = \Sigma \left[\frac{(O - E)^2}{E} \right]$$

Cell	Expected Frequency	$(O - E)$	$(O - E)^2$	$(O - E)^2 \div E$
Upper left	48	3	9	.19
Upper center	70	8	64	.91
Upper right	63	−11	121	1.92
Middle left	218	26	676	3.10
Middle center	322	6	36	.11
Middle right	289	−32	1,024	3.54
Lower left	191	−30	900	4.71
Lower center	282	−13	169	.60
Lower right	253	43	1,849	7.31

Sum = 22.39 = Chi Square Value

Statisticians have prepared tables of chi square values that reveal what values are significant at differing degrees of freedom. In the table of Chi Square Values (see Table B in Appendix 2) you will find the χ^2 values for differing degrees of freedom at various levels of confidence, such as .05 and .01. Because our chi square value for Table 17.1 was 22.39, and we had four degrees of freedom, you can see from the table that our χ^2 is large enough so that the probability of mistakenly rejecting the null hypothesis based on the relationship we have found in the sample is less than 1 in 1,000. At the bottom of Table 17.1, next to the lambda value, you would put $\chi^2 = 22.39$, p < .001. Others reading Table 17.1, based on the reported chi square test of statistical significance, would understand that you were 99.9 percent confident that the relationship you found in Table 17.1 existed in the population, not just in the sample data.

In general, the larger the value of the chi square, the better off you are because you will be able to reject the null hypothesis in the population. As you can see from the formula, larger values of χ^2 are produced when the differences between the observed and expected frequencies get larger for more cells in the table. The size of the chi square value is also dependent on the size of the sample, however, and tables with the same level of association between the variables but based on different-sized samples may be statistically significant for the larger sample but not for the smaller. Larger sample sizes will mean a greater likelihood of detecting statistically significant relationships in the population— once again reminding us that sample size matters.

Q Questions for Thought and Discussion

If you want to demonstrate that a relationship between variables you have discovered in sample data is also present in the population from which it is drawn, explain why it is better to have a lower probability for your chi square value, such as .01, rather than a higher probability, such as .05.

Explain what degrees of freedom are for a crosstabulation.

▪ t-test and F-test

When you have an independent variable that is nominal or ordinal and a dependent variable that is interval or ratio, a comparison of means will often be the appropriate data analysis technique. When employing an experimental research design, for example, you would likely compare mean scores on some measure of a dependent variable for the experimental and control groups. Or you may organize sample data from a field study in a way that suggests comparing means across the categories of a nominal variable, such as comparing the mean yearly incomes of men and women in a survey sample. If the independent variable has two categories, then you would use a difference of means test, commonly called a **t-test,** to determine if any divergence in the mean values of the dependent variable between the two groups was statistically significant. You are testing the probability that the two group means represent different populations. For independent variables with more than two categories, **analysis of variance,** also called an F-ratio, is used. The analysis of variance procedure is frequently abbreviated as **ANOVA.** When there is only one independent variable—that is, cases are classified only in one way—the procedure is referred to as a one-way ANOVA. [2]

As with chi square, you are trying to determine with t- and **F-tests** how likely it is that the differences you find in the mean scores of the groups using sample data would also exist in the larger population. The logic underlying these two tests is similar. The cases under study are divided into groups based on the values of the independent variable, such as males and females as in the preceding example. Means for the interval/ratio-level dependent variable, such as yearly income, are calculated for each group. The question is whether these mean values diverge enough from one another *and* whether the cases within groups are more similar (have less variance) on the dependent variable than the cases as a whole. The greater the difference between the mean scores of the groups created by the independent variable, and the greater the homogeneity of scores on the dependent variable within the groups compared to the cases taken as a whole, the more likely the differences are to be statistically significant. In sum, the more similar the cases in the groups are to each other than to the cases as a whole, and the more the mean scores of the two groups are dissimilar, the more likely the differences in those mean scores are to be statistically significant. Both t- and F-tests are ratios that compare differences on the dependent variable between the groups to actual or estimated variances on that variable within the groups.

Again, like chi square, statisticians have computed tables showing which values in the distribution of t and F meet which criteria of statistical significance for differing degrees of freedom. When comparing means with a t-test, however, you must know if you are working with a **one-tailed** or **two-tailed test.** Tails refer to the two ends of the approximately bell-shaped t distribution. Are you willing to accept scores that are beyond the .05 level or .01 level at either the positive *or* negative tail of the t distribution or only at one tail? This has to do with how your hypothesis is stated. On the one hand, you could be testing the null hypothesis (no difference between the means in the population) and be willing to accept significant differences between the means in either a positive or negative direction to reject that null hypothesis. That involves a two-tailed test. You are, in effect, testing a nondirectional hypothesis, such as "There is a difference between the mean campaign contributions for male and female state legislative candidates." In this hypothesis, you are not stating which group has the higher mean, only that there is a difference. On the other hand, you might be testing a directional hypothesis: one stating a specific, directional difference between the means. For example, you might hypothesize that male candidates for state legislative offices receive higher mean campaign contributions than do female candidates. In this instance, you will only accept the hypothesis as confirmed if the difference between the mean contributions for the two groups shows women candidates having smaller mean contributions than men. The other way around, men having a smaller mean, would lead you to reject your hypothesis. The testing of a directional hypothesis such as this one involves a one-tailed test.

Figure 17.2 shows a diagram of one- and two-tailed tests for this hypothetical example of male and female state legislative candidates. If the mean contribution of the two groups is the same, the difference between the means would be zero. So to test the hypothesis, you would need to determine if the difference between the means departed significantly from zero. For the two-tailed test, the hypothesis is nondirectional: You will accept significant differences from zero in *either* direction. You would confirm the hypothesis that the means between the groups differed if the value was significantly above *or* below zero—that is, at either tail of the distribution. A one-tailed test is employed to test the directional hypothesis that the mean for men is greater than that for women. With this hypothesis, if you subtracted the mean of female candidate contributions from the mean of male candidate contributions, you would expect a positive difference. The hypothesis would be confirmed only for values in the critical area of the right, or positive, tail. Tables of the t distribution show t values needed for

To the Web

**Exercises 17.1, 17.2, and 17.3
Statistical Significance**

These exercises are designed to review some material about statistical significance by asking about applications of tests of significance. They will help you better understand when and how to apply the tests, as well as how to interpret the results. Go to the DEPR Web Page, click on Web Exercises, Chapter 17, and then on Exercises 17.1, 17.2, and 17.3. To see a *mistaken* interpretation of statistical significance, click on Chapter 17, then on Wrong Interpretation.

Figure 17.2
One- and Two-Tailed Tests

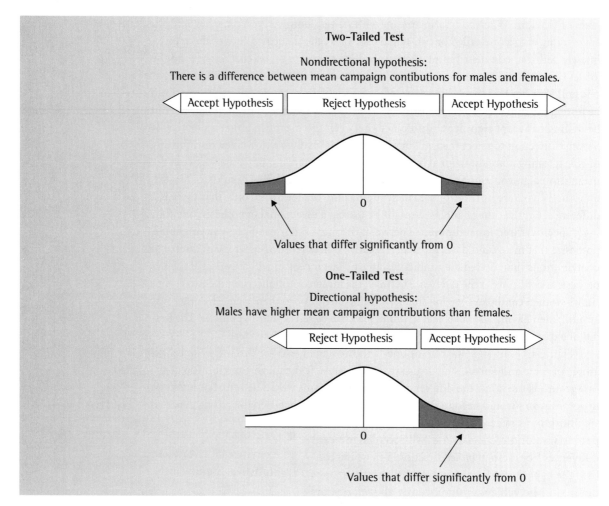

Two-Tailed Test

Nondirectional hypothesis:
There is a difference between mean campaign contibutions for males and females.

| Accept Hypothesis | Reject Hypothesis | Accept Hypothesis |

0

Values that differ significantly from 0

One-Tailed Test

Directional hypothesis:
Males have higher mean campaign contributions than females.

| Reject Hypothesis | Accept Hypothesis |

0

Values that differ significantly from 0

varying levels of statistical significance for both one- and two-tailed tests. As you might expect, higher t values are needed for the same level of statistical significance for two-tailed tests than for one-tailed tests. Also, you need to know how many degrees of freedom there are with your t-test, which is equal to the sample size minus 2 (df = N − 2).

We can use data from the 2000 General Social Survey accompanying this text for an example of a t-test. Let's hypothesize that men, on average, work more hours per week at their job than women. The independent variable is a nominally measured, two-value vari-

Figure 17.3
Partial SPSS Output for t-test

Group Statistics

	RESPONDENT'S SEX	N	Mean	Std. Deviation
NUMBER OF HOURS WORKED LAST WEEK	MALE	899	45.37	13.082
	FEMALE	919	38.50	12.820

Independent Samples Test

	t-test for Equality of Means		
	t	df	Sig. (2-tailed)
NUMBER OF HOURS WORKED LAST WEEK	11.316	1816	.000

able. The dependent variable is response to the question of how many hours the respondent worked in the week prior to the survey, which is an interval/ratio measurement. Comparing the mean hours worked by men in the previous week with the mean hours worked by women in the same period requires a t-test. It will be a one-tailed test because the hypothesis is directional: We are conjecturing that men work more hours than women.

The results of the analysis show that in the week prior to the survey, the 899 men who answered the question had a mean value of 45.37 hours worked, and the 919 women had a mean value of 38.5 hours worked. Our hypothesis is confirmed, but how likely is it that there is no difference between the mean hours worked in the population as a whole and that our sample finding is an aberration? The probability is very small. The t value for the difference between these means is 11.3. With 1,818 respondents in the sample, the degrees of freedom are equivalent to 1,816. By checking the table of Critical Values for the t Distribution (see Table C in Appendix 2) for the appropriate number of degrees of freedom, you can see that the level of significance is $p < .001$. The likelihood that we have incorrectly rejected the null hypothesis and there is no difference between the mean values in the population is less than 1 in 1,000. The results of t-tests are generally reported in the text of a report in the form $t = 11.3$, df $= 1,186$, $p < .001$. If the results are not statistically significant, the p term would be replaced with the letters "ns" for "not significant." Figure 17.3 shows what some of the SPSS output for this t-test analysis looks like.

With F-tests, used for comparing three or more groups, a comparison is made between the variance in the measure of the dependent variable *within* each group created by the values of the independent variable and the variance *between* these same groups. The more of the total variance in the dependent variable that can be accounted for by the groupings within the values of the independent variable, the more likely the findings are to be statistically significant. The F-test will reveal only if there are significant differences among all the means created by values of the independent variable. It does not indicate which of the specific differences led to the rejection of the null hypothesis. To determine if there are significant differences between any two of the means, a separate t-test must be run just for those two values. For tables of F values, degrees of freedom are expressed as two numbers: one for within groups and the other for between groups. The within-groups df is equal to the sample size minus the number of values of the independent variable (that is, the number of groups under comparison), while the between-groups df is equal to the number of values of the dependent variable—again, the number of groups—minus 1.

For an example of an F-test, let's return to the General Social Survey of 2000. In this instance, we want to know if there is any effect of education level on television viewing habits. More specifically, we hypothesize that the higher the level of education, the less likely a person is to watch television. The independent variable in this analysis has five values: less than high school, high school graduate, some college, college graduate, and postcollege. The dependent variable is operationalized by response to the question "On the average day, about how many hours do you personally watch television?" The independent variable is measured at the ordinal level, with five categories, and the dependent measured at the interval/ratio level, which is just the situation for comparing means with an F-test. The mean response for hours per day watching television for those with less than a high school education was 4.11. The mean value for high school graduates was 3.04, those with some college 2.44, college graduates 2.42, and those with at least some postcollege education 1.64. Our hypothesis, not surprisingly, is confirmed. Those in our sample with more education report watching less television, but we must ask whether our sample findings are reflective of the larger population.

The F ratio for this analysis is 29.2. The within-group degrees of freedom is equal to the sample size minus the number of groups: $1,819 - 5 = 1,814$. The between-groups df is the number of groups minus 1: in this case, $5 - 1 = 4$. The Critical Values of F table (Table D in Appendix 2) tells you that an F value of 29.2 with these two values for the between and within degrees of freedom is statistically significant. The likelihood that you would reject the null hypothesis in the population when it was accurate, therefore, is less than 1 in 1,000. With an F-test, remember, we are comparing all five means simultaneously. We do not know if each mean is statistically significantly different from any other individual mean, only that overall the five means can be described in this manner. The results of F-tests are ordinarily reported in the text of a report as $F = 29.2$, $df = 4, 1,814$, $p < .001$. As with a t-test, when the results are not statistically significant, the p term would be replaced with the letters "ns," for "not significant."

Figure 17.4
Partial SPSS Output for F-test

Descriptives
HOURS PER DAY WATCHING TV

	N	Mean	Std. Deviation
LT HIGH SCHOOL	290	4.11	3.314
HIGH SCHOOL	985	3.04	2.551
JUNIOR COLLEGE	133	2.44	1.554
BACHELOR	282	2.42	2.165
GRADUATE	129	1.64	1.274
Total	1819	2.97	2.586

ANOVA
HOURS PER DAY WATCHING TV

	Sum of Squares	df	F	Sig.
Between Groups	734.749	4	29.176	.000
Within Groups	11420.707	1814		
Total	12155.456	1818		

Figure 17.4 shows what some of the SPSS output for this F-test or analysis of variance looks like.

■ Statistical Significance for Regression Analysis

In addition to testing the difference between means, t-tests and F ratios are used to determine the level of statistical significance for regression analysis. t-tests can be used to check the statistical significance of individual regression coefficients in either a bivariate or multiple regression analysis. F ratios are employed in multiple regression for testing the statistical significance, as a whole, of an entire regression equation. This latter procedure is important if you believe that although no single individual regression coefficient reaches the level of rejecting the null hypothesis, the independent variables taken as a whole affect the dependent variable in the population as well as the sample.

For t values, you are testing the likelihood that the value of the regression coefficient you found in the sample data has a value of zero in the population from which the sample data was taken. As you remember from Chapter 15, the regression coefficient is the slope of the graphed line of the values of the independent and dependent variables. When that slope is zero, the variables are unrelated. Thus, using the t-test for regression coefficients is testing the null hypothesis that there is no relationship between the variables in the population. You are determining how likely it is that the value of the regression coefficient you found in the sample data is actually zero in the population. The greater the t value, the more confident you will be in rejecting the null hypothesis and concluding that your findings are statistically significant. For regression analysis, the degrees of freedom is equal to the size of the sample (number of cases being analyzed) minus the number of parameters (number of independent variables plus the intercept) being estimated. Most software for analyzing data, including SPSS, provides a t value and corresponding level of significance for each regression coefficient.

Many researchers determine statistical significance of regression coefficients using the **standard error of the estimate.** This is an estimate of the variation in $\hat{Y}$, the predicted value of Y. For all practical purposes, plus or minus twice the standard error of the estimate approximates the 95 percent confidence intervals. So if a regression coefficient is twice the size of its standard error, it can be considered to be statistically significant at the .05 level. SPSS reports the standard error of the estimate for each regression coefficient it calculates. Thus, you have two options for assessing the statistical significance of a regression coefficient: the t value and the standard error.

F-tests are used to assess the level of statistical significance for an entire multiple regression equation. As previously mentioned, this is especially important in the unlikely, but not unheard of, situation in which no individual regression coefficient reaches a .05 level of significance, but the regression model in its entirety might reach that criterion. On the other hand, failing to test the model as a whole may leave you in the opposite position of having some individual regression coefficients attaining statistical significance but with a model that does not. All high-quality data analysis software will calculate an F ratio for whatever model you test, so you should check to determine its value and associated level of significance.

Conclusion

Statistical significance is important for hypothesis testing. Inferring the confirmation or rejection of a hypothesis from a sample to the larger population from which it is drawn allows you to generalize your findings beyond the limited data that you have analyzed. Appropriate statistical procedures will permit you to state in explicit, probabilistic terms how confident you are in making those inferences. If the probability of incorrectly rejecting the null hypothesis in the population drops below .05, your findings are deemed statistically significant, but you must be wary of two hazards. First, the more certain you are about avoiding a Type I error, the more likely you are to commit a Type II error. Second, statistical significance does not equate to substantive significance.

Depending on the level of measurement achieved in the operational definition of your variables and the number of values for your dependent variable, you will employ a chi square, t, or F distribution to determine if your findings are statistically significant. When both variables are nominally or ordinally measured, you will use a chi square. When comparing means of interval- or ratio-level variables across categories of a nominal or ordinal independent variable, you will employ a test for two means and an F-test for more than two means. t-tests are used to determine level of statistical significance for individual regressions coefficients, while F-tests assess level of significance for a whole multiple regression equation. If a regression coefficient is more than twice the size of its standard error, you can assume it is statistically significant at the .05 level.

All that is now left to do is communicate the results of your research to others. This includes writing not only about your substantive findings but also precisely describing the procedures you employed in conducting the research. The final chapter will help you understand how best to summarize and report the original, empirical research you have completed.

Summary of the Main Points

- Statistical significance is the likelihood that an observed relationship in a sample has occurred by chance and is not present in the population from which the sample was drawn.
- A Type I error is made when there is no relationship between variables in a population and you erroneously conclude that there is.
- A Type II error occurs when there is a relationship between the variables in the population, but you wrongly conclude there is not.
- Substantive significance refers to the theoretical and informational worth of your findings and is different from statistical significance.
- Level of statistical significance is usually reported by the benchmarks of .05, .01, .001.
- For crosstabulations, the chi square distribution is used to establish level of statistical significance.
- For comparing means and for regression analysis, t-tests and F-tests (ANOVA) are applied to establish level of statistical significance.
- Degrees of freedom is how many parameters in a statistical analysis are free to vary. t and F values needed for statistical significance vary according to the number of degrees of freedom.

Terms Introduced

analysis of variance (ANOVA)
benchmarks of acceptable risk
chi square
expected frequencies

F-test
marginals
observed frequencies
one-tailed test

standard error of the estimate	two-tailed test
statistical significance	Type I error
substantive significance	Type II error
t-test	

Selected Readings

Chow, Siu L. *Statistical Significance: Rationale, Validity and Utility.* Thousand Oaks, CA: Sage Publications, 1996.

Henkel, Ramon E. *Tests of Significance.* Beverly Hills, CA: Sage Publications, 1976.

Mohr, Lawrence B. *Understanding Significance Testing.* Newbury Park, CA: Sage Publications, 1990.

Morrison, Denton E., and Ramon E. Henkel, Eds. *The Significance Test Controversy: A Reader.* Chicago: Aldine Publishing, 1970.

Activities

Activity 17.1
Computing and Interpreting a Chi Square

1. Calculate the chi square value for Table 17.2. When finished, check Table B, Critical Values of Chi Square, in Appendix 2 to see if the chi square value reaches statistical significance.

Table 17.2
Political Ideology and Attitude on Spending to Solve Problems of Big Cities

Spending on Solving Problems of Big Cities Is	POLITICAL IDEOLOGY		
	Liberal	Moderate	Conservative
Too Little	56.0%	54.9%	43.9%
	(178)	(252)	(166)
About Right	36.8%	35.3%	38.1%
	(117)	(162)	(144)
Too Much	7.2%	9.8%	18.0%
	(23)	(45)	(68)
Total	100%	100%	100%
	(318)	(459)	(378)

Gamma = +.177

Note: Ideology was recoded from seven categories ranging from extremely liberal to extremely conservative to the three shown in the table.

Source: General Social Survey, 2000, National Opinion Research Center.

Cell	Expected Frequency	$(O - E)$	$(O - E)^2$	$(O - E)^2 \div E$
Upper left				
Upper center				
Upper right				
Middle left				
Middle center				
Middle right				
Lower left				
Lower center				
Lower right				
	Sum =			= Chi Square Value

2. Are the findings in Table 17.2 statistically significant? How do you know that? Do you think they are substantively significant?

Activity 17.2
Computing Chi Square Using SPSS

SPSS will calculate a chi square value for every crosstabulation analysis *if you request it.* If needed, review Activities 14.3 and 14.4 to refresh your memory about how to do a crosstabulation and request measures of association using SPSS. When you click on the "Statistics" button that opens the window titled "Crosstabs: Statistics," one option (shown in the upper left-hand corner) with a box to check off is "Chi Square." When that box is checked, SPSS will calculate a chi square value for each crosstabulation you perform. To try this procedure, choose the 2000 General Social Survey data set (GSS2000depr) that accompanies this text. Do a crosstabulation for the independent variable "conbus" (level of confidence in major companies) and the dependent variable "class" (subjective class identification), requesting the appropriate measure of association and the chi square value. What is the chi square value for this crosstabulation? Describe what this value means for the relationship between level of confidence in major companies and class identification.

Activity 17.3
Using SPSS to Compare Two Means with a t-test

Go to SPSS and open the 2000 National Election Studies data set (NES2000depr) that accompanies this text. You are going to test the hypothesis that younger people are more likely to do volunteer work than older people by comparing the mean ages of those who say they do volunteer work with those who say they do not. Click on "Analyze" near the top of the page; when a box appears under "Analyze," click on "Compare Means"; when a box appears to the side, click on "Independent Samples T-test." You are now looking at a new window titled, "Independent Samples T-test." Scroll through the variables on the left and highlight "age." Use the arrow button to move "age" into the box titled "Test Variable(s)." Next use the arrow button to move the variable "voluntwk" into the box titled "Grouping Variable." Below this box is a button labeled "Define Groups," which allows you to tell SPSS which two groups you want to compare. After clicking on this button, you will be prompted to fill in the appropriate variable values for "voluntwk." In the data set, the variable "voluntwk" has two values: yes and no. Yes has been given the value label 1, and No is 5. Consequently, enter the value 1 for Group 1 and 5 for Group 2. Click on the "Continue" button, then on the "OK" button. SPSS will calculate the mean age for those who volunteered and those who did not, a t score for those two means, and the level of statistical significance. Describe the difference between the mean age of those who do volunteer work and those who do not. Explain how likely is it that there is no difference between these mean ages in the population from which this sample was drawn.

Activity 17.4
Using SPSS to Compare Three Means with an F-test (ANOVA)

Go to SPSS and open the 2000 General Social Survey data set (GSS2000depr) that accompanies this text. You are going to compare the mean hours of television watched by race (white, black, other). Click on "Analyze" near the top of the page; when a box appears under "Analyze," click on "Compare Means." When a box appears to the side, click on "One-Way ANOVA." You are now looking at a new window titled "One-Way ANOVA." Scroll through the variables on the left and highlight "tvhours." Use the arrow button to move "tvhours" into the box titled "Dependent List." Next, use the arrow button to move the variable "race" into the box titled "Factor." Below this box is a button labeled "Options." Click on this button and check off "Descriptive." If you do not choose this option, SPSS will not provide the mean values of the dependent variable by group in the output viewer. Click on the "Continue" button, then on the "OK" button. SPSS will calculate the mean hours of television watching for the three groups of whites, blacks, and others, an F score for those three means, and the level of statistical significance. Describe the difference between the mean hours of television watching of white, black, and other respondents. Explain how likely is it that there is no difference between these mean ages in the population from which this sample was drawn.

Chapter 18

Reporting the Results of Empirical Political Research: Pulling It All Together

Learning Objectives

After completion of this chapter, students should be able to do the following:

Outline and write a report of the findings of an empirical political research project.

Understand different ways in which the statistical results of empirical political research can be presented in tabular and graphical form.

Recognize ethical issues that might arise in the process of completing research reports.

The Work Is Not Finished Until You Communicate Your Results

Since the first chapter of this text we have focused on the processes of *doing* empirical political research. Now it is time to pull things together and give our attention to *reporting* the results of our research. Scientific knowledge about politics will advance only if you communicate your findings to others. Writing a research report is the final stage of the research process and is equally important and requires as much skill and expertise as any of the earlier stages. Some would argue that report writing is the most important stage of all because the care you give to developing hypotheses, defining and operationalizing variables, collecting and analyzing data will go for naught if you cannot effectively communicate the results of your efforts. A poorly prepared report might raise doubts about the validity of your research findings.

Most social scientists will tell you that writing research reports is hard work and is fraught with anxiety because so much is at stake. Sociologist Howard Becker, who teaches a course on writing for graduate students, says that many of his students approached report writing fearing that they "would not be able to organize their thoughts, that writing would be a big confusing chaos, that would drive them mad." [1] Most of us probably have those feelings when we sit down to write up our research. With that in mind, we want to emphasize that social scientific writing requires practice. We could never guarantee that the process will eventually become anxiety free, but like most experiences, familiarity tends to increase comfort.

Substantively, a high-quality research report is one that clearly communicates to an audience the specific questions that you seek to answer, the research process, the findings, and the relation of the findings to a general body of knowledge. It also offers a guide to future research. Achievement of this goal will depend on your knowledge of the general area of research, ability to organize information in logical and sequential order, and skill in writing clearly about complex information.

In this final chapter we focus on the basics of producing research reports. We begin with a brief consideration of the various forms that reports can take, with special attention given to the potential audience. Most of the chapter is devoted to the elements of effective report writing: organization, presentation of quantitative data, and the process of writing. We conclude with a brief discussion of the ethics of reporting empirical political research.

Forms of Reporting Empirical Political Research

We know that in all likelihood any research report you write will be in the form of a student paper aimed at fulfilling a requirement for a course. We think that it is important that you understand the various forms that the end products of social science research can take, however, because you are likely to be consumers of a number of different types of research reports. Before the process of writing begins, you must ask, "Who will read my research report?" A general distinction should be made between other social scientists, sponsors, and general readers. If the audience will be social scientists (like your professor), you can probably assume some knowledge of social science methodology and perhaps some familiarity with your research question. If you are writing for a more general audience, perhaps for readers of a popular magazine or a sponsor such as a government agency that has contracted for your research, you will have to make some decisions about how to describe your methodology and present your data. For example, mass-media organizations would likely not be interested in the intricate details of checks for reliability and validity, but a sponsor of your research might want them explained in a way that could be understood by those who are not social scientists. The structure of presentation might also vary somewhat, depending on your audience. We will focus for the most part on the forms of reporting that are aimed at those with some knowledge of social science methodology, but it is useful for you to know a bit about some other alternatives.

While you are likely to write a research report to fulfill the requirement of a course, social scientists usually write reports for presentation at professional meetings that may later be revised for submission for publication to a professional journal. The basic form and organization of a student paper and one written for presentation at a professional meeting are very similar. Since there are usually no page limitations on student papers or professional meeting papers, they can include a comprehensive review of previous research and a very detailed description of the methodology along with a discussion of methodological issues. Often findings are presented that are not central to the research problem but nevertheless might interest readers. Appendixes can be attached that contain extensive information concerning survey questions, additional findings, and so on. Still, it is important to remember that your paper is more likely to be carefully read the more concisely it is written. While papers prepared for professional meetings are often comprehensive, the oral presentations themselves will highlight findings and conclusions, with a very abbreviated discussion of previous research and details of methodology.

The most common form of reporting empirical research is an article in a professional journal such as the *American Political Science Review, Comparative Politics,* or *World Politics.* Professional journal articles often begin as professional meeting papers that have been revised and shortened. Professional journals are expensive to produce, so editors urge writers to report their research as concisely and parsimoniously as possible. A premium is placed on the presentation of results, and authors are often urged to shorten their reviews of previous research. *Research notes,* brief summaries of research, also appear in professional journals. They are tightly focused reports on a narrow range of research findings. There is seldom space for an extensive review of previous literature in research notes, and often discussions of methodology are abbreviated.

Books are the most ambitious forms for reporting social science research. Books, like papers presented at professional meetings and articles in professional journals, are designed to be read by professionals, although they may also be read by students and some members of the public. Similar to books in structure, but not purpose, are theses and dissertations. Like student papers, theses and dissertations are designed to be read by professors, although they may be of interest to other professionals and students as well. The lengths of books and theses provide an opportunity to be comprehensive in your approach, especially regarding the review and criticism of previous research. They usually contain more detail about methodological decisions than can be provided in articles or professional papers. The intended audience for a book will determine, at least to some extent, discussions of methodology. If a book is aimed at an audience that may not be familiar with social science methodology, it might be best to place the most technical information in appendixes. The most readable research reports that appear in book form are those that tell a compelling "story" about research findings and their political and social relevance.

You may need to prepare a report for a sponsor such as a government agency or some other organization that commissioned your research. Commissioned reports are usually read by sponsors who use them as a basis for policy decisions or generating publicity for their organizations. They should be crafted so that experts can evaluate methodology (to determine credibility) and nonexperts can clearly understand the findings and infer implications. Sponsors may request an explicit discussion of the implications of research findings and expect specific policy recommendations. The form of commissioned reports can vary but often begin with an executive summary of findings with a few charts and recommendations. Technical material is placed in the body of the report and in an appendix.

Reports of research findings to the mass media often follow the production of a report for professional colleagues or sponsors. For example, if you were hired by your city's Director of Parks and Recreation to survey residents about the use of city parks, you would first produce a full report with findings and recommendations that could be used for decision making. Part of your obligation might be to provide a summary of the report to the local media and perhaps answer questions at a press conference. The media are also interested in the results of research that have been prepared for a professional audience. If you wrote and presented a paper reporting the results of research that projected the outcome of a presidential election, for example, you might be asked to present a summary to the print and electronic media. Regardless of the original audience for your research, a report designed for the mass media should emphasize your basic findings and their possible implications.

To the Web

Effective Presentations

Our discussion has focused on written communication of research, but there are other means for communicating results. Oral reports of research at professional meetings, to the mass media, or in other forums can be enhanced by the use of computer projectors and presentation software, such as *PowerPoint*. Social scientists increasingly report their research during "poster sessions" at professional conferences where they are given space on a bulletin board to summarize their papers visually and stimulate one-on-one discussions with interested colleagues. Information about making effective presentations can be accessed by going to the DEPR Web Page. Click on Web Links, Chapter 18, then on Effective Presentations.

Organization and Presentation of the Elements of a Research Report

You should have a good idea of the basic elements and structure of a research report by now because they are identical to the "wheel of science" and the steps in the research process outlined in Chapter 2. Additionally, in Chapter 5 we dissected an article from a professional journal that is a good example of a research report. Like the research process itself, research reports have an "hourglass" shape. They begin with a discussion of a broad question that has been the subject of extensive research, then narrow the focus to descriptions of how variables are defined, hypotheses operationalized, and data collected. The findings are then described and compared with those of earlier research. Finally, the specific findings are generalized back to the original broad question, and suggestions are made for future research. [2]

We will outline the organization of elements as they should appear in a paper prepared for an upper-level political science course, presentation at a professional meeting, or publication in an academic journal. There is a general consensus about what should be included and the sequence of presentation. Some elements may be combined under one heading in some reports and considered separately in others. An introduction and review of previous research, for example, may be combined in some reports and separated in others. Likewise, a discussion of findings, summary, and conclusion may be combined or separated. The headings that appear in research reports reflect differences in style and the conventions of professional journals.

Title.   Too little attention is given to crafting titles for research reports. An effective title is very important and difficult to construct. When conducting a literature search using an index like the *Social Sciences Index,* the first piece of information about an article in a professional journal you encounter is the title. The less accurately the title represents the contents of a report, the more likely you are to skip reading the abstract and locating an article that might be helpful. If you want your research to be read and considered as part of the scholarly literature on your subject, you should construct a title that accurately describes your study. The title should be neither too general nor too specific. Scholars often joke about the large number of titles of scholarly reports that contain colons. The use of colons makes a lot of sense, however, because the general title of a research report can be followed by more specific information in a subtitle. The following titles of articles are concise, clear, and descriptive: "Democracy and Social Spending in Latin American, 1980–1992," "Unified Government, Divided Government, and Party Responsiveness," and "Do Negative Campaigns Mobilize or Suppress Turnout? Clarifying the Relationship Between Negativity and Participation." [3]

Abstract.   An abstract generally follows the title of an article in a professional journal. Like the title, the abstract is important in sparking the interest of scholars who are scanning the literature and might find value in your research. Abstracts run about 100 to 250 words, highlighting the major findings of the research and focusing on the hypotheses that were tested. Some attention is given to measurement of variables and data

To the Web

Exercise 18.1   Evaluating Titles and Abstracts of Research Reports

Summarizing research concisely and accurately is an important skill. On the DEPR Web site you will find some abstracts written to describe articles published in professional political science journals. This exercise requires you to read and evaluate these titles and abstracts. To access the exercise, go to the DEPR Web Page, click on Web Exercises, Chapter 18, then on Evaluating Titles and Abstracts of Research Reports.

collection. Abstracts should be written with care because they are the "hook" that will determine if your research report will be read. They have to be concise, but they also should adequately convey enough information to allow readers to understand your research. We think that the specifications for abstracts required by the *American Journal of Political Science* are particularly useful. (For a good example of an abstract, see the article "Gender and Citizen Participation" in Chapter 5.) The AJPS requires all authors in a uniform format to briefly describe *theory, hypotheses, methods,* and *results.*

Introduction.   The introduction outlines the purpose of the research in general terms. The general theme or problem should be stated explicitly and clearly, with the idea being to convince the reader that your study is important. You should provide a theoretical, and in some instances a practical, rationale for the research. Hypotheses or research questions can be stated in very general terms, and you may want to provide a brief preview of your findings. A good example can be found in the article on gender and citizen participation you read in Chapter 5. Toward the end of their introduction, the authors indicate that their research will seek to answer the question of "whether women and men differ as citizen activists—in the forms of their participation, in the rewards they seek, and in their issue concerns." [4]

Beginning a research report is difficult—what will your first sentence be? We think that it is a good idea to save the writing of the introduction until you have completed your report. At that point you will have a clear sense of what is most important to say at the outset to frame what comes later. Since we discuss the process of reviewing previous research next, we should mention now that integrating the review of previous research with the introduction, where a clear statement of the theoretical significance of the study appears, makes considerable sense. Discussing the general problem and theory that is addressed by your research is difficult without reference to previous research.

Review of Literature.   The review of literature places your study within the context of developed theory and knowledge. As we noted in Chapter 4, most empirical studies of politics have their roots in earlier research completed by others. The research you are reporting will likely test previously developed hypotheses with new data, take into account new variables or operationalizations, perhaps apply different methodological techniques, and attempt to resolve inconsistencies in the findings of earlier research. The review of previous research is necessary to show the reader where your research "fits."

You should review earlier studies based on their relevance to the problem under study. You can determine the relevance of previous research by initially choosing studies that test similar hypotheses and examine similar variables, and second, by giving more attention to the most recent research rather than to studies that were conducted some time ago. Third, if you are at all familiar with the professional literature in this area, look for studies that have received the most attention from other scholars and are most frequently cited. There are probably good reasons for the attention these studies have received, and you should try to discern those reasons. Fourth, take into account the reputation and prestige of authors and the status of publications where research reports appear. Finally, your research review should be selective. Do not review every study that is remotely related to your research because you will find that many studies are not particularly useful or have been replicated by more recent research.

Focus on a number of goals as you develop the literature review. Show that you are in command of the relevant research and bring the reader up to date regarding the most recent studies. Discuss the strengths and weaknesses of each study you review to provide a rationale for your research. Show how your research arises from previous work and will make a contribution to the professional literature. Make an effort to focus on the most significant findings of each study and, if appropriate, the methodology employed. Be critical and challenge research findings if warranted. Your literature review should be an orderly comparison of studies and is most effectively organized conceptually or by theme rather than by date of publication. Too often literature reviews are organized chronologically and read like a series of note cards.

Key Points

Literature reviews should do the following:

- Place your research in the context of other research on the same subject.
- Bring the reader up to date on the current findings regarding the subject.
- Critically assess the findings and methodology of relevant studies.
- Show how your research will contribute to the solution of problems or respond to weaknesses in previous research.

Statement of Hypotheses.   A clear statement of the hypotheses being tested should come after the review of literature but before a discussion of methodology. We believe that, consistent with the hourglass shape of the research process, a general hypothesis should be stated toward the end of an introduction to the problem (as in the example just cited) and more specific hypotheses after the literature review. The development of specific hypotheses should be shown to be informed by the research of others. Again, the article on gender and civic participation provides a fine example. After writing a clear and very focused review of the literature on the subject, the authors posited the following hypotheses for testing.

1. Men and women activists specialize in different forms of participation, with women more likely to engage in informal, grassroots, and organizationally based activities and to focus their energies at the local level.
2. Men and women derive different gratifications from taking part, with men more likely to emphasize material, as opposed to civic, rewards.
3. Men and women bring different clusters of policy concerns to their participation with women's activity more likely than men's to be inspired by issues involving children and families; broad public interests such as consumer or environmental concerns; the use of violence in the home, the streets, or the international arena; and the protection of human rights and the fulfillment of basic human needs. [5]

Method.   This section should be so clearly written and comprehensive that a reader experienced in social science methodology could replicate the study using the procedures described. You must describe your units of analysis and the process of sampling, the measurement of variables, and the procedures used for data collection. Research reports vary regarding the placement of the details of methodology. If the method is not very complex, a secondary analysis of data is undertaken, or well-known measures are used, a comprehensive description can appear in the body of the report. Technical details concerning such matters as the exact wording of survey questions, construction of indexes, and sampling procedures are more commonly placed in substantive footnotes, endnotes, or appendixes.

To the Web

Calculating Response Rates for Surveys

The American Association of Public Opinion Research has set the standard for calculating response rates for surveys. You can find a thorough description at its Web site. Go to the **DEPR Web Page**, click on **Web Links, Chapter 13**, then on **Calculating Response Rates for Surveys**.

Your description of the units of analysis should focus on how they were chosen. If a sample was selected, you should describe the population, sampling frame, and the process of selection. The key issue for sampling, you should recall, is representativeness. You should describe the sample size, tolerated error, and limitations. Providing a table that describes the demography of the sample, with comparisons to characteristics of the population if those figures are available, is helpful to the reader. Also, provide your readers with response rates and a description of how they were calculated, which can affect the representativeness of samples.

Description of the measurement of your variables must be precise. If you asked questions of individuals, provide the exact wording (as we noted previously, often this information is placed in an appendix). If you used measures collected from published sources, describe the source thoroughly enough that others can replicate your findings. For content analyses and classified media messages, clearly describe the construction of categories. Describe how items were selected for any indexes you constructed. Regardless of how variables are measured, provide the reader with information about validity and reliability.

Finally, you will need to describe the procedures used for data collection. This includes everything you did with respondents and subjects, mass-media messages, or any other units of analysis. For an experiment, describe your experimental design and the process of random assignment to groups, as well as experimental material and tasks. For a Q-sort, describe the instructions provided to subjects about the sorting process. When using a survey, you need to describe the process by which it was administered. Regardless of the procedures employed in the study, you should acknowledge any weaknesses of the process.

Findings.   The heart of the research report is the presentation of findings. As you present your findings, do not lose sight of the general hypothesis presented in your introduction. Keep the discussion of the findings orderly and focused on the primary hypotheses. You may be tempted to include all of your findings, but if you do, your readers will have difficulty distinguishing the more from the less important. Use tables, graphs, and figures to present quantitative findings, keeping in mind that the goal of tabular and graphical presentation is to clarify the presentation of results. (We will review the presentation of quantitative data following.) If you find it difficult to describe the contents of a table or a graph verbally, then your reader will certainly not be aided by its inclusion.

The best way to begin the presentation of your findings is with a summary table or graph showing relationships that test your primary hypothesis. A summary table of statistics should be organized so that the strongest relationships appear before the weakest. After an examination of your primary hypothesis, start a process of elaboration that examines the influence of other variables. Explain the results of testing your original hypotheses under a variety of conditions or with alternative measures of your independent and dependent variables. The presentation of findings many times involves the comparison of alternative theoretical models, and if that is the case with your research, highlight the distinctions you have found. Do not discuss every statistic in every table or graph. Instead, focus the text on the critical findings. Report negative and nonfindings, as well as those that support your hypotheses. Unexpected findings may be as important as those that support your hypothesis, and in any event, you have an obligation to report them to interested readers.

Discussion and Interpretation of Findings.

The methodology and findings sections of your report in all likelihood represent the narrow center of the hourglass-shaped report. You should begin this section of your report with a review of your research question and hypotheses. After your findings are described, you need to discuss and interpret them in light of your original expectations, theory, and earlier research. Your discussion will broaden as you inductively relate your specific findings to generalizations developed in the literature. If your general hypothesis was supported but mitigated by other variables, this is the section of the report where you speculate about the likely reasons for those findings. On the other hand, when your general hypothesis is not supported by the data, you will need to offer some alternative explanations for why that was the case.

Summary and Conclusions.

What did the research show that is of interest? Your interpretation of the findings should be followed by a brief summary and set of conclusions. At this point your discussion, like the bottom of an hourglass, should broaden as you outline the implications of your findings for general theories and perhaps policy. After recapping your research in light of previous findings and discussing their implications, you will be in a unique position for recommending future research. In the interest of continuing to develop knowledge about the subject of your study, the recommendations you make for future research should be as specific as possible.

Appendix and Substantive Notes.

As you are writing, you will find material that deserves inclusion but would be a distraction if it was in the body of your report. You can place such technical material in substantive notes and the appendix. An appendix, for example, might include the measurement of variables, such as the coding scheme in content analysis, construction of indexes, specific wording of survey questions, description of sampling, or tables that are not central to the findings. Substantive notes might be used to detail how calculations of certain statistics were undertaken or how values of variables were collapsed. As the author of the report, you are responsible for deciding what information is important enough to include in the main body and what should be placed elsewhere.

References.

At the end of the research report are the references. Include all of the references cited in the body of the report or in substantive footnotes. You need to be compulsive about the form that is used, and several publication manuals describe proper forms, but individual preferences vary. We will discuss this process of citation later.

Key Points

The elements of a research report include the following:

- Title
- Abstract
- Introduction
- Review of literature
- Statement of hypotheses
- Method
- Findings
- Discussion and interpretation of findings
- Summary and conclusions
- Appendix and substantive notes
- References

Writing: Style and Form

Social scientific writing is different from other forms of writing because of the required degree of precision and caution, but it still should be as readable as any other written communication. While your research report should not read like a novel or popular non-fiction, you can still write as if you have a story to tell or a case to make. The story to tell is how you conducted your research and the results of your efforts. Make the case to your readers that your findings are valid and are to be taken seriously. As you tell your story and make your case, focus on being concise and clear, while remembering the negative relationship between use of technical jargon and effectiveness of communication to a diverse audience.

There are many paths to an effective research report. While there is a general consensus among social scientists concerning the order of presentation, no such consensus exists on the process or style because no two people approach writing in the same way. Providing a comprehensive discussion of writing is beyond the scope of this book, but there are fortunately many sources to assist you. Most colleges and universities have writing centers on campus where you can receive one-on-one assistance. Recent years have seen the development of **online writing laboratories (OWLs),** where you can receive assistance with organizing the writing, grammar, punctuation, sentence structure, and all the other component parts of the writing process. In the Selected Readings section at the end of this chapter, we have listed some **writing handbooks** specifically developed for political science students. They are very useful tools for organizing research reports and recommending proper formats. We recommend you consult at least one of them. We also strongly urge that you read and reread (it is less than 100 pages long) *The Elements of Style* by Strunk and White. [6] Every writer should have a copy of the latest edition of this wonderful, useful book close at hand. It lays out the principles of writing in an easy-to-understand manner and concentrates attention on the rules of usage and principles of good writing most commonly violated. We also enthusiastically recommend a book we quoted at the outset of this chapter: *Writing for Social Scientists,* by Howard Becker. While Becker's book is filled with advice about good writing, it also provides comforting information about the anxieties associated with the process of writing. By recommending campus writing centers, OWLs, and writing manuals, we mean to emphasize that effective writing is something that can be learned and is improved through practice.

To the Web

Links to Help with Writing

The original version of *Elements of Style* written by William Strunk, Jr., and published in 1918 is available online. A directory of online writing laboratories can be found at the Web site for the Purdue University OWL. Both can be accessed from the **DEPR** Web Page. Click on **Web Links, Chapter 18,** then on **Effective Writing.**

While we recommend that you consult a couple of writing handbooks to improve your writing style, we have some suggestions to offer regarding the process of writing. Most writing handbooks propose that you develop an outline before you begin writing. This is a good idea for most people because it encourages planning and organization. In fact, as we have emphasized, the basic outline for a report is pretty much defined by the process of research. On the other hand, some authors think that outlines can be constraining. Becker argues that writers should begin not with an outline but by writing down *everything.* By "free writing," according to Becker, you get a sense of the fragments that need to be organized. [7] Becker's proposal may not work for everyone, but he makes an essential point that there is no "right way" to approach the process of writing. We recommend starting with an outline but consider writing the results section first. A completed results section should allow you to state clearly the nature of the problem and the rationale for the study in the introduction. Additionally, some of the anxiety of beginning a research report might be reduced by beginning in the middle.

Every manual stresses the basic rule of writing: reread, revise, rewrite, proofread. Your first draft of a research report should never be your final draft. In fact, a research report should go through more than a couple of drafts, with others reading and reviewing these evolving drafts. If possible, ask for a reading and editorial comments from one person familiar with your research and another who is not used to reading social science. Those versed in social science methodology can advise you on the precision and accuracy of your writing, while others can let you know how well you communicate with nonexperts. After completing a revision, let a few days go by before returning to it. A fresh reading will often reveal ambiguities and errors that were overlooked.

The form of a research report contributes to the effectiveness of communication. Form refers to how the report is formatted as to margins, spacing, headings, acknowledgment of sources, and table construction. The social sciences do not have a standard format or set of guidelines that all follow. Several **style manuals,** listed among the Selected Readings at the end of the chapter, are commonly used. When writing a term paper, your professor can recommend a particular format style. All professional journals provide information about their required format in every issue. The *American Political Science Review,* for example, recommends that authors consult an article in a recent issue and use it as a model for formatting. For unusual formatting issues, the *APSR* editor recommends that the *Chicago Manual of Style* be consulted. Professional political science journals (such as *American Politics Research, Comparative Political Studies, Political Communication*) are increasingly adopting the reference style outlined in the *Publication Manual for the American Psychological Association*. Regardless of the format you choose, be consistent in its use.

To the Web

Writing Style

Unfortunately, the *Style Manual for Political Science,* published by the American Political Science Association, is available only in hard-copy form. An abbreviated version is provided by the University of Wisconsin Writing Laboratory. You can access it and abbreviated versions of the Modern Language Association and American Psychological Association format from the **DEPR** Web Page. Click on **Web Links, Chapter 18,** then on **Online Style Manuals (Abbreviated).**

Presenting Quantitative Results

You have already been introduced to proper construction of statistical tables and graphs in the chapters that focused on data analysis. While we emphasized proper form in those earlier chapters, we were mostly concerned with one particular function of tables and graphs: aiding in the interpretation of data analyses. We have seen that a well-constructed table or graph can help us determine whether our hypotheses are supported. While the analysis and interpretation of data are important steps in the social scientific process, we are concerned here with another function of tables and graphs: the effective communication of our findings. Communication of quantitative findings is so important in the social sciences that we feel that it is worthwhile to review the practices of good table and graph construction.

Quantitative findings can be communicated in text, tables, and graphics, but effective communication requires more than one means of delivery. The goal of presenting findings efficiently, precisely, and clearly, so they are easily understood by the reader, is best accomplished with a table or a graph accompanied by a description of the contents in the text. Despite the need to offer verbal descriptions of tables and graphs, they should be able to stand alone. In other words, if a graph is somehow separated from the text, the variables included and the hypotheses tested should still be obvious.

By now you know that choice of statistics for analysis is based on the number of variables (univariate, bivariate, and multivariate) and levels of measurement (nominal, ordinal, and interval/ratio). The graphs constructed to report statistical findings can be two-dimensional or three-dimensional. Given the array of statistics and possible forms of presentation, there are many combinations of tables and graphs to choose from—certainly too many to consider in this book. Our limited purpose here is to review some guidelines to follow in displaying statistical findings. We also provide a few examples of tables and graphs, but be aware that within the guidelines there is room for creativity. In fact, statistical programs like SPSS and spreadsheets like Excel make it easy for the beginner to create effective tables and graphs that are pleasing to the eye.

Creating Effective Tables

Examining a sample of recent articles in social science journals will reveal that tables are the most common means for summarizing quantitative findings because they effectively present a lot of detailed information in a relatively small space. The most efficient tables present information in an easily readable form, so there is a concern with structural issues such as spacing and clearly labeled parts. Also, you want to provide as much information as possible in the limited space. The goal is to provide enough information about the content of tables so the reader can draw his or her own conclusions about your results. Clearly, one concern is to balance quantity of information with readability. We will discuss the anatomy of effective tables using three examples (see Tables 18.1, 18.2, and 18.3).

Title.   The title should state exactly what is contained in the table. For bivariate and multivariate tables, titles should begin with mentioning the dependent variable or variables. The words "and" or "by" are used to indicate that the variable names that follow are independent or control variables. In a bivariate table it is usually possible to provide specific descriptions of variables in the title. Sometimes, as in the cases of the titles for Table 18.1 and Table 18.2, a title can be a bit cumbersome when a variable is operationalized by a survey question. When the name of a variable cannot be summarized to clearly indicate its content, and it has not been defined clearly in the text of the report, a more extensive definition can be added in a footnote to the table. This is often necessary for multivariate tables. When writing a title for a table, ask, "Will the reader be able to determine what hypothesis or hypotheses are being tested by the contents?" In multivariate tables like Table 18.3, where there may be one or more dependent variables and many independent variables, provide variable names in the title without elaboration. Adding a headnote in parentheses that follows the title of the table can indicate limitations, such as the exclusion of some data, specific statistics that appear in the body of the table, or the total number of cases.

Structure and Identifiers.   A distinction can be made between information in a table that is inside or outside of the "box." Often the content of table is set off by a horizontal

Table 18.1
Opinion on Whether Women Are Not Suited for Politics by Political Ideology

	POLITICAL IDEOLOGY		
Women Are Not Suited for Politics	Liberal	Moderate	Conservative
Agree	18.2%	20.6%	28.5%
	(81)	(133)	(156)
Disagree	81.8%	79.4%	71.5%
	(365)	(512)	(391)
Total	100%	100%	100%
	(446)	(645)	(547)

Gamma = −.19

$X^2 = 15.77$, p < .001

Note: Those who were "not sure" were excluded.

Source: General Social Survey, 2000, National Opinion Research Center.

Table 18.2
Percentage Who Agree That Women Are Not Suited for Politics by Political Ideology and Sex

	POLITICAL IDEOLOGY			
Sex	Liberal	Moderate	Conservative	
Male	19.3%	22.7%	29.7%	Gamma = −.19, p < .01
	(33)	(58)	(80)	
Female	17.5%	19.3%	27.3%	Gamma = −.19, p < .01
	(48)	(75)	(76)	
Total	18.2%	20.6%	28.5%	Gamma = − .19, p < .001
	(81)	(133)	(156)	

Source: General Social Survey, 2000, National Opinion Research Center.

line below the title and another just below the reported figures (sometimes vertical lines are used to close in the box). Within the box are the labels identifying variables and values and the analyzed figures themselves. Statistical tables are described in general terms by their size and dimensions. Size is the number of rows and columns, and dimensions

Table 18.3
Regression Analysis: Representation of Women in Governments of Countries and Indicators of Social and Economic Development

Independent Variables	Percentage of Women Legislators (2001)	Percentage of Administrative Positions Held by Women (2000)
Percent of Population Living in Urban Areas, 2000	$-.105^{**}$	$-.004$
	(.036)	(.076)
Gross Domestic Product per Capita in Dollars, 1999	$.004^{***}$	$-.003^{***}$
	(.000)	(.000)
Daily Newspaper Circulation per 1,000 Persons, 1997	$.014^{*}$	$-.009$
	(.006)	(.012)
Human Development Index	2.50	54.14^{**}
	(6.21)	(19.14)
Constant	11.23	-8.49
F	15.64^{***}	2.41
Adjusted R^2	.299	.074
Number of Cases	137	69

Note: Entries are ordinary least-squares partial regression coefficients with standard errors in parentheses.
$^*p < .05, ^{**}p < .01, ^{***}p < .001.$

Source: Doing Empirical Political Research, "COUNTRIESdepr" data set.

refer to the number of variables contained in the table. Bivariate percentage tables, such as Table 18.1, are most effective when the independent variable is placed at the top, with the columns representing values or categories, and dependent variable at the side, with the rows representing values or categories. The identifiers for variables and values should be clearly labeled and abbreviations avoided, if possible. As you should recall from our discussion of the interpretation of bivariate tables in Chapter 14, tables are most easily read by beginning with labels on the outside and working inward. Figures themselves are most easily read from left to right. Thus, variables and values must be clearly distinguished so that readers can interpret the figures in the body of the table. If the variables included in the table are measured at the ordinal level or are collapsed interval/ratio-level variables, they should be displayed in the same direction across columns or rows (for example, from low to high or from weak to strong).

The structure of multidimensional (multivariate) tables differs from bivariate tables, but the principle of clearly identifying variables and values remains. Table 18.2 is a condensed three-variable table that adds a control (sex) to the relationship displayed in Table 18.1. Since the independent variable of interest is political ideology, it is placed at the top of the table to facilitate comparisons of percentages across values for each sex. The statistics (gamma and significance level) are placed in the body of the table to facilitate comparisons of the original relationship to situations where sex is controlled. Note that the dependent variable (opinion on the suitability of women for politics) appears only in the title, which should be the first part of the table examined by the reader.

Table 18.3 reports the results of a multiple regression analysis. Included are two dependent variables and four independent variables. In contrast to the percentage tables, it is much more efficient to place the dependent variable(s) at the top (column) and independent variables on the side (rows) when reporting regression analyses. In addition to variable identifiers, columns of statistics are clearly identified in tables reporting multivariate analyses.

Analyzed Data in the Body of the Table. The body of the table consists of summary percentage figures or statistics such as means, standard deviations, regression coefficients, and tests of significance. Remember that tables should be designed to ease interpretation of findings, so make sure there is enough space between figures to avoid confusion. Figures that are to be compared, however, should be in close proximity to each other. One way to reduce clutter is through rounding, which also helps avoid the unwarranted portrayal of precision. Percentages should never have more than one digit to the right of the decimal point. Means, standard deviations, and regression coefficients should usually be rounded to no more than two decimal places, depending on the range of values. Too many figures in a single table tend to obscure findings, and creating more tables with fewer figures (perhaps a table for each dependent variable) helps to reduce clutter. One advantage in using summary statistics like measures of association is that more information can be included in a single table. Note that Table 18.3 includes statistics that display relationships between four independent variables and a dependent variable, while Table 18.1 displays a single bivariate relationship.

Supplementary Information at the Bottom of the Table. Three types of information may appear at the bottom of a table in the form of notes. One is additional statistical information, such as tests of significance and measures of association. A second is additional information about the variables and figures in the table. This may include definitions of variables (perhaps the wording of questions), how values of variables have been collapsed or combined, how missing cases were handled, or the number of cases included in the table. A third type of information provided is the source of the data. When the data (or the entire table) were taken from another source, your reader should be informed with an acknowledgment. Sometimes data have been collected from a variety of sources, as is the case with Table 18.3. In that case, acknowledge sources in other parts of the research report, such as the methodology section or in an appendix.

■ Creating Effective Graphs and Visual Representations of Findings

As with tables, design graphs to present detailed information in a small space in a manner pleasing to the eye with easy interpretation. Edward Tufte, who has written a number of important books on the visual display of quantitative data, offers a useful set of goals for the design of graphs. According to Tufte, graphics should do the following: [8]

- Show the data
- Induce the viewer to think about the substance rather than about methodology, graphic design, technology of graphic production, or something else.
- Avoid distorting what the data have to say.
- Present many numbers in a small space.
- Make large data sets coherent.
- Encourage the eye to compare different pieces of data.
- Serve a reasonably clear purpose: description, exploration, tabulation, or decoration.
- Be closely integrated with the statistical and verbal description of the data set.

Most of the goals Tufte advances for graphs are also relevant for tables. So why design a graph or other form of visual display? This decision should be based entirely on an evaluation of the effectiveness of communication to the reader. Most findings that are displayed in a graph or visual display began as a table or could at least be contained in a table. You need to ask, "What can the reader learn about the findings from a graph that cannot be learned from a table?" Tufte provides some possible answers in his list of goals. You may decide that an attractive graph, as opposed to a table, would be more interesting to look at and more likely to attract the attention of the reader. A graph may highlight a key piece of information or relationship or draw the reader's attention to the substance of your presentation. Obviously, your decision will also be based on the nature of the variables and relationships you wish to display. Graphs can help clarify complex relationships, but on the other hand, they can sometimes make simple relationships seem complex.

The construction of graphs follows conventions that contribute to clarity. Generally, they are presented in relation to two axes: the horizontal (X-axis) and vertical (Y-axis). The scale for the independent variable is laid out along the X-axis, and the dependent variable is along the Y-axis. For describing a single variable, the scale is laid out along the X-axis, and the frequency or proportion of occurrence of each value is indicated on the Y-axis. Of course, as in the case of tables, you will find exceptions when the dependent variable is at the side and the independent variable is at the bottom of a graph. Like tables, graphs should have titles that clearly describe the variables and identifiers indicating the location of the variables and their values or categories. You must take care in deciding on the proportion and scale for each variable included in a graph. Tufte cautions against graphs distorting what the data have to say. Adjustments of the scale of one of the variables can exaggerate or diminish the perceived strength of a relationship. [9] The choice of a scale for each variable should be approximately the same. As we mentioned earlier, graphs and other forms of visual displays of data come in many varieties. We provide examples of the more common forms, but we urge you to consult the sources listed at the end of this chapter to get a sense how creative you can be in displaying statistical results.

Bar Charts and Histograms.   **Bar charts** are used for displaying variables that are measured at the nominal or ordinal level, whereas **histograms** display variables measured at the interval/ratio level and later collapsed into categories. Both types are used for description of the distribution of a single variable or for purposes of explaining bivariate and multivariate relationships. Figure 18.1 is an example of a two-dimensional bar chart. On the X-axis are the categories for the variable "Opinion on Highest Priority for America." On the Y-axis is the scale for the percentage of the sample who hold each opinion. Figure 18.2 is a three-dimensional bar chart that shows a relationship between two variables. The independent variable, the extent to which countries are categorized

Figure 18.1
Opinion on Highest Priority for America—Bar Chart

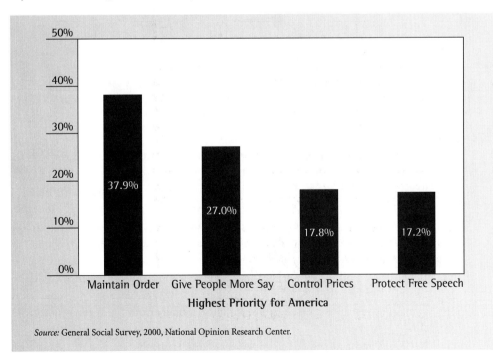

Source: General Social Survey, 2000, National Opinion Research Center.

Figure 18.2
Freedom Status and Women in Parliaments (*N* = 154 Countries)

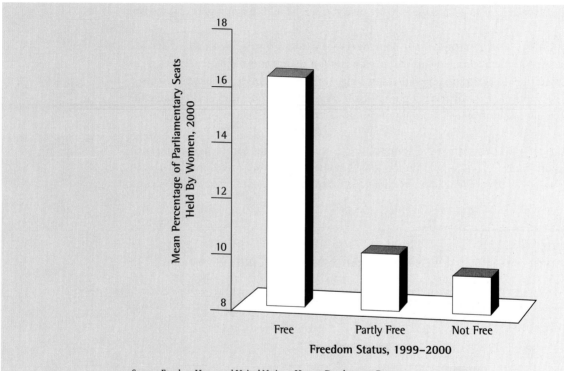

Sources: Freedom House and United Nations, Human Development Report.

as "free," is on the horizontal X-axis. On the vertical Y-axis is the dependent variable, the Mean Percentage of Parliamentary Seats Held by Women. Notice that the independent variable is measured at the ordinal level and the dependent at the interval/ratio level. The fact that "Freedom Status" is measured at the ordinal level is indicated by the space between each bar. Visually, the distinction between a bar chart and a histogram is a small one. If the variable on the X-axis were measured at the interval/ratio level, there would be no space between bars, indicating the continuous nature of the variable, a histogram. Bar charts and histograms can take a number of forms. Two or more independent variables can be displayed, along with a dependent variable. Some bar charts and histograms are constructed so the bars extend horizontally from the Y-axis.

Pie Charts.   **Pie charts** provide a simple way to display the distribution of a single variable. The 360 degrees in the circular "pie" are equivalent to 100 percent. The pie is "sliced"

Figure 18.3
Opinion on Highest Priority for America—Pie Chart

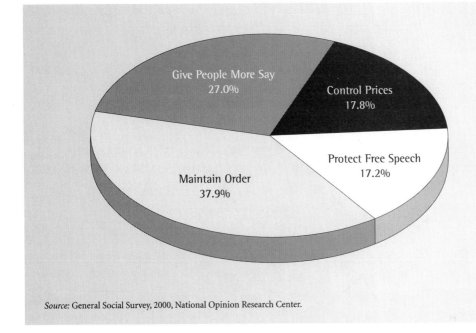

Source: General Social Survey, 2000, National Opinion Research Center.

into wedges in proportion to the magnitude of each value of the variable. Figure 18.3 is a three-dimensional pie chart that shows the distribution of opinions on the highest priority for America. The percentages are identical to those displayed in Figure 18.1. In the past, pie charts were difficult to draw to proportion by hand. Today many computer programs can be used to design two- and three-dimensional pie charts in an assortment of styles.

Line Graphs.   Data measured at the interval/ratio level can be displayed using a line chart. The most common are the **frequency polygon** and the **time series graph,** sometimes called a trend curve. Frequency polygons are univariate charts in which an interval/ratio variable is scaled on the X-axis and the frequency or proportion of each value is scaled on the Y-axis. For each value of the variable a dot is placed on the corresponding point of the Y-axis that represents the number or proportion of occurrences. A time series chart displays a bivariate relationship with dates, as the independent variable scaled on the X-axis and the scale for the dependent variable on the Y-axis. Figure 18.4 shows the percentage of respondents surveyed over time who support gun registration. Note that for each year (a value of the independent variable) the percentage who support

Figure 18.4
Percent Favoring Gun Registration

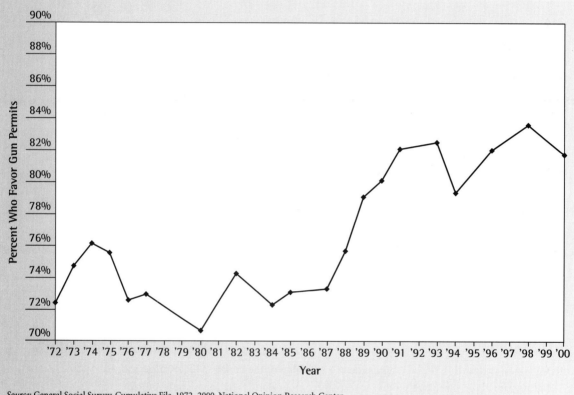

Source: General Social Survey, Cumulative File, 1972–2000, National Opinion Research Center.

gun registration is indicated by a dot on the appropriate point on the Y-axis. The dots are connected to show a trend (there is a positive relationship between time and the percentage favoring gun registration). Like bar charts and histograms, line charts can be used to examine the effects of two or more independent variables. For example, separate lines could have been plotted on Figure 18.4 for males and females or Republicans and Democrats and the pattern of the lines compared.

Mapping Data.   Using maps to show relationships between dependent variables and regions of the world, countries, states, counties, or even small units like voting precincts has a long history in political science. V. O. Key in his classic book *Southern Politics,* published in 1949, used maps productively to explain voting patterns and demographic char-

Figure 18.5
Percentage of State Legislators Who Are Women

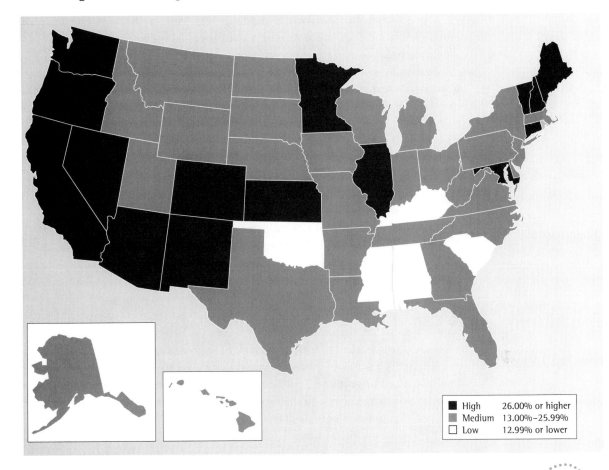

■ High	26.00% or higher
■ Medium	13.00%–25.99%
□ Low	12.99% or lower

acteristics of the southern states. [1] Mapping is a form of visually displaying findings that can be done by hand, but computer programs make it easy to color code or shade areas within geographical boundaries on a map. The results can often reveal striking regional differences and visually capture the strength of a relationship in a way that would not be possible with a table. Obviously maps are useful only in instances where variables are defined geographically and bivariate relationships need to be displayed. Figure 18.5 is an example of how a variable of interest to political scientists can be mapped effectively.

To the Web

Displaying Quantitative Findings

There is a plethora of Web sites that provide guidance and examples for creating visual displays of quantitative findings. To access some of these sites, go to the DEPR Web Page, click on Web Links, Chapter 18, then on Displaying Quantitative Findings.

Ethical Considerations in Reporting Research

We discussed ethical issues in social research in some depth in Chapter 3 and at relevant points in several other chapters. We need to raise the issue again because important ethical obligations arise when reporting research. When writing a research report, you have an obligation to protect respondents, organizations, and communities from harm. Your obligation also extends to those in the social scientific community who will read your report and on whose work you relied.

Should the identities of those who served as subjects or respondents in your research be revealed? The answer is "It depends." The norm of social science is full disclosure of the process of research so that others can evaluate and replicate what you have done. You need to ask, however, whether the revelation of your respondents' identities would serve any social scientific purpose. Remember, the goal of social scientific research is to develop generalizations, not to describe or analyze single individuals. There is usually no need to know the identities of respondents.

Clearly, if in the course of your research you guaranteed anonymity or confidentiality to your respondents, you cannot reveal their identities. This is usually the case in projects that employ survey research and intensive techniques such as experimentation, Q-technique, or focus groups. Personal information gathered from public records such as the Web page of the Clerk of the House of Representatives or mass-media reports of public acts by public figures may properly be revealed in your analysis. In fact, public figures are often chosen for analysis because of their visibility and public record. The issue becomes a bit trickier in cases where your data are based on intensive interviews of political elites or prominent members of political organizations. Journalists commonly reach an agreement with their sources concerning statements that are "on or off the record." This norm is not as well established among political scientists because many times the specific positions of elites who are interviewed are directly relevant to research conclusions. Masking identities using pseudonyms is common in reporting the results of interviews with elites. For well-known individuals, however, pseudonyms can be transparent. In his famous study of community power, Floyd Hunter went so far as to change some of the descriptive characteristics of his respondents. [11] Disguising the location of where data were collected to protect both respondents and communities from embarrassment or harm is also done. In general, a good principle to follow is that identities of individuals or communities not revealed cannot be harmed. But as with all good rules, there are exceptions.

In writing your research report you have as well an ethical responsibility to others in the social scientific community. The report should include a complete and accurate review of previous research, free of distortion. Misquotation of other authors is unusual and obviously wrong, but misrepresentation of the research of others does happen. Researchers want to frame previous work in a way that makes their own appear needed and valuable. Keeping this in mind, make sure your review is not deceptive. Social scientific knowledge is cumulative, and your readers will depend on your honest and accurate review of earlier research. You also owe earlier researchers the courtesy of that accurate review and only fair criticism of their work.

In your report, fully and accurately disclose the methods you used and all of your relevant findings. There are some famous cases where scholars have fabricated or falsified statistical findings. For example, the late British social psychologist Cyril Burt has been accused of fabricating statistical findings regarding heredity and intelligence. While there was other evidence of fraud, Burt's report of two extremely unlikely identical correlation coefficients from two different data sets tipped off his critics. He appeared to have inserted correlation coefficients from an earlier analysis into the later work. [12] We have no way of estimating how frequently data are deliberately fabricated or falsified, but questionable manipulation of data to produce desired results is probably a more common occurrence. Results can be influenced by decisions about whether or not to exclude cases from data analyses or by the choice of one statistic over another, such as with measures of association. There are often several defensible choices about which statistical procedure to employ, and it may seem natural to choose the statistical procedure that produces results that support your expectations. However, you should not let your choice be guided by anticipated results. No matter what criteria you choose for excluding cases or selecting statistics, you must clearly state your rationale if your choices are at all questionable.

Let your readers know about any weaknesses in your data or shortcomings in techniques. You should also report negative and unexpected findings. Readers who may depend on your research for the advancement of their own have a right to know if any of your data fail to support your hypotheses. Statistical analyses once in a while produce results opposite of what you expected (perhaps a negative relationship when you posited a positive one or a relationship that was enhanced instead of reduced when a control variable was taken into account). Writing up your findings as if you expected the surprising finding is tempting, but it is more honest and appropriate to let the reader know that you were surprised and offer a post hoc explanation.

All social scientists rely on what others have written before them. That is the nature of the enterprise of research, and we all have an obligation to give credit to others whose words or ideas we use. When incorporating someone else's words or ideas into your own research report without acknowledgment, you are committing **plagiarism.** Plagiarism is essentially theft. Most of us know that using someone else's exact words without quotation marks and proper reference is wrong. There is often confusion, however, about the use of ideas. For that reason we have added an extensive discussion of plagiarism with examples in Appendix 1. We advise you to read it carefully.

Questions for Thought and Discussion

You have conducted a study of social studies students at six high schools to explain why some students exhibit high levels of civic obligation. You find that the training of teachers and the emphasis given to civics by school principals make a big difference. The schools in which social studies teachers are active in the community and principals emphasize civics education have students who are likely to be engaged in community service. When you write up the results of your study, will you identify the schools by name, indicating which are most successful at producing "good" citizens? Why or why not?

Conclusion

In this final chapter we focused on writing research reports as the final stage of an empirical research project. We noted initially that a high-quality research effort will be diminished by a final product that is poorly organized and written. Our emphasis throughout the chapter has been on the development of research reports that are clear, concise, accurate, and ethical. We discussed the basic elements of a research report, indicating that there is a general consensus on their order of presentation. The outline of a research report is very similar to the steps in the process of research. We also discussed clarity as it relates to writing and the presentation of findings in tables and graphs. Effective social scientific writing, we emphasized, is the result of practice. There are plenty of resources at your disposal to help you improve your writing skills. We outlined a series of goals that should be considered in the presentation of numerical findings. Most of them boiled down to choosing tables and graphs that enhance clarity and accuracy of presentation. Finally, we emphasized the importance of maintaining ethical standards in report writing, with a special focus on protecting respondents from harm and obligations to members of the social scientific community.

Summary of the Main Points

- Research reports take the form of papers presented at professional meetings, articles in professional journals, books, theses, dissertations, and reports to sponsors or government agencies.
- The structure of a research report is like an hourglass, beginning with a broad discussion of theory and previous research, then narrowing the research problem through operationalization of variables and hypotheses, data collection, and analysis. In the discussion of findings, the focus is broadened as the implications of the research are related to theory and earlier research.
- Writing handbooks, campus writing centers, and online writing laboratories can help you improve your writing skills.
- Research reports should follow a consistent style of presentation and documentation. A style manual should be consulted to determine proper format for your report.

- The goal of presenting findings efficiently, precisely, and clearly is best accomplished with a table or a graph accompanied by a description of the contents in the text.
- The decision to use a table or a graph should be based entirely on whether it will enhance communication of results to the reader.
- Writers of research reports have ethical obligations to their respondents and to members of the social science community. Avoid revealing the identities of respondents, communities, or organizations if it is likely to produce harm. Research reports should fully disclose procedures and findings (even negative ones) and fully acknowledge the research of others whose work was consulted.

Terms Introduced

bar chart
frequency polygon
histogram
online writing laboratory (OWL)
pie chart

plagiarism
style manual
time series graphs
writing handbook

Selected Readings

American Psychological Association. *Publication Manual of the American Psychological Association,* 5th Ed. Washington, DC: American Psychological Association, 2001.

*Chicago Manual of Style,*14th Ed. Chicago: University of Chicago Press, 1993.

Cleveland, William S. *The Elements of Graphing Data.* Monterey, CA: CRC Press, 1994.

Gibaldi, Joseph. *MLA Style Manual and Guide to Scholarly Publishing,* 2nd Ed. New York: Modern Language Association, 1999.

Hart, Chris. *Doing a Literature Review.* Beverly Hills, CA: Sage Publications, 1999.

Kimmel, Alan J. *Ethics and Values in Applied Social Research.* Newbury Park, CA: Sage Publications, 1988.

Schmidt, Diane E. *Writing in Political Science: A Practical Guide,* 2nd Ed. New York: Addison Wesley Longman, 2000.

Scott, Gregory M., and Stephen M. Garrison. *The Political Science Student Writers Manual.* Englewood Cliffs, NJ: Prentice-Hall, 1995.

Strunk, William, Jr., E. B. White, Charles Osgood, and Roger Angell. *The Elements of Style,* 4th Ed. New York: Allyn and Bacon, 2000.

Turabian, Kate. *A Manual for Writers of Term Papers, Theses, and Dissertations,* 6th Ed. Chicago: University of Chicago Press, 1996.

Tufte, Edward R. *The Visual Display of Quantitative Information.* Cheshire, CT: Graphics Press, 1983.

Activities

Activity 18.1
Media Reports of Social Research

It is instructive to see how the results of political and social research are communicated to the public. This activity involves comparing a media report with an original research report. First, locate a media report of the results of a study of public policy or politics published in a national magazine (*Time, Newsweek, U.S. News and World Report*) or a national newspaper like the *New York Times* or *Washington Post*. Second, locate a copy of the original report (this should be cited in the media report). Finally, read both reports and provide a written evaluation of the media report that takes into account completeness and accuracy.

Activity 18.2
Writing Abstracts of Research Reports

Summarizing research concisely and accurately is an important skill. Carefully read and then write an abstract (no more than 250 words) of one of the following articles.

> Bertelsen, Judy. "Political Interest, Influence and Efficacy: Differences Between the Sexes and Among Marital Status Groups," *American Politics Quarterly*, 4 (October 1974), 412–425.
>
> Fiorina, Morris P. "Electoral Margins, Constituency Influence, and Policy Moderation: A Critical Assessment," *American Politics Quarterly*, 1 (October 1973), 479–498.
>
> Lamare, James W. "The Political World of the Rural Chicano Child." *American Politics Quarterly*, 5 (January 1977), 83–108.
>
> Long, Samuel. "Political Alienation Among Black and White Adolescents: A Test of the Social Deprivation and Political Reality Models," *American Politics Quarterly*, 4 (July, 1976), 267–297.

Activity 18.3
Creating a Simple Bar Chart Using SPSS

Go to SPSS and open the "GSS2000depr" data set that accompanies this text. You are going to create a bar graph for the sex of the respondents in the survey. Click on "Graphs" near the top of the page; when the gray box appears, click on "Bar." A small window titled "Bar Charts" will appear. Click on "Simple," check off "Summaries for groups of cases," and click on the "Define" button. Now you will see a new window titled "Define Simple Bar: Summaries for Groups of Cases." Under "Bars Represent" check off "% of cases," scroll through the variables on the left, and move "sex" into the box titled "Category Axis." Then click on "Titles" and type "Sex of 2000 GSS Respondents" in Line 1 under "Title." Click on the "Continue" button and then when the original chart window reappears, click on the button labeled "OK." A bar graph will appear in the SPSS Output Viewer. If you want to customize your bar graph, right-click anywhere in the graph and choose the option "SPSS Chart Object." A new window will open that allows you to customize your bar graph. Looking at the bar graph you constructed, what are the sex characteristics of the 2000 General Social Survey sample?

Activity 18.4
Creating a Simple Pie Chart Using SPSS

Go to SPSS and open the "GSS2000depr" data set that accompanies this text. You are going to create a pie chart for the race of the respondents in the survey. Click on "Graphs" near the top of the page; when the gray box appears, click on "Pie." A small window titled "Pie Charts" will appear. Check off "Summaries for groups of cases," and click on the "Define" button. You are now looking at a new window titled "Define Pie: Summaries for Groups of Cases." Under "Slices Represent" check off "% of cases," scroll through the variables on the left, and move "race" into the box titled "Define Slices by." Then click on "Titles" and type "Race of 2000 GSS Respondents" in Line 1 under "Title." Click on the "Continue" button, and then when original chart window reappears, click on the button labeled "OK." The pie chart will appear in SPSS Output Viewer. If you want to customize your pie chart, right-click anywhere in the chart and choose the option "SPSS Chart Object." A new window will open that allows you to customize your pie chart. Looking at your pie chart, what are the race characteristics of the 2000 General Social Survey sample?

Activity 18.5
Editing Tables in SPSS and Exporting Them to Word Processing Documents

The objective of this activity is to create a bivariate percentage table using SPSS, edit the table so that is in a form appropriate for a research report, and then export the table to a document created by word processing software.

Go to SPSS and open the data file containing General Social Survey for 2000; the file name is GSS2000depr. Create a bivariate percentage table in which the dependent variable is attitude on allowing incurable patients to die ("letdie1") and the independent variable is political views recoded to three values ("ideology"). As in Activity 14.3, remember to click on the "Cells" button and choose "Columns" to be sure you have the percentages running down the columns. When the Output Viewer appears, place the cursor within the table and double-click. A squiggly line will appear around the table. This mode is necessary for editing SPSS output.

You can begin by deleting unwanted or unnecessary parts of the table. Click on "Count," and you will see that all occurrences are highlighted. Touch your Delete key, and the labels are deleted. Now click on the part of the table titled "% within POLVIEWS RECODED TO THREE CATEGORIES." Touch Delete to eliminate that label. You probably are not interested in including the row totals and percentages in your final table, so place your cursor on the right border of the table. When the double arrow appears, click and drag the left border toward the column labeled "Conservative" until the two vertical lines merge. Lift your finger, and the Totals column will be deleted. Now place your cursor on the vertical line to the right of the variable labels "Yes" and "No." Drag the line to the left to eliminate space and reduce the size of the table.

You can also edit text. Double-click on the column heading title POLVIEWS RE-CODED TO THREE CATEGORIES, and it will be highlighted. Type "Political Views" to replace the original heading. Click within the table, and the new heading will be centered. Now double-click on the table's title. Replace the original title with "Table 1. Should Incurable Patients Be Allowed to Die by Political Views?" Click inside the table. Double-click outside the table to get an idea of how the table will look in a research report.

You can also choose from among a wide variety of table styles. Double-click on the table again and make sure that it is surrounded by a squiggly line. Click on "Format," then on "Table Looks." Click on "Academic 2," then on "OK." You can see that the style of the table has changed, but the substance and labels remain the same. Click on "Format" near the top of the page; then from the drop-down menu, click on "Table Looks." From the box titled "TableLook files," choose "Hot Dog," then click "OK." This colorful scheme illustrates the wide variety of table looks offered by SPSS. Return to "Table Looks" and change the style back to "Academic 2." This time click on "Save Look," then on "OK." There are many other ways tables can be edited. For example, you can change fonts, colors, labels from horizontal to vertical, and vice versa. Use the help menus to experiment.

Finally, it is important to learn how to export your table to a Word or WordPerfect document. Click only once on your table. This table will be boxed with a solid (not squiggly) line. Click on "Edit," then "Copy." Open Word or WordPerfect. Click on "Edit," then on "Paste Special." Choose "Picture," and click "OK." Your table will appear in your Word or WordPerfect document.

Now return to SPSS. Create a bivariate percentage table similar to the one constructed earlier, but replace "letdie1" with "fefam"—opinion about whether it is better for men to work and women to tend to the home. Edit the resulting table and export it to a Word or WordPerfect document. Write a short essay interpreting the table.

Appendix 1

Avoiding Plagiarism

The academic counterpart of the bank embezzler and of the manufacturer who mislabels his products is the plagiarist, the student or scholar who leads his reader to believe that what he is reading is the original work of the writer when it is not. If it could be assumed that the distinction between plagiarism and honest use of sources is perfectly clear in everyone's mind, there would be no need for the explanation that follows; merely the warning with which this definition concludes would be enough. But it is apparent that sometimes men of good will draw the suspicion of guilt upon themselves (and, indeed, are guilty) simply because they are not aware of the illegitimacy of certain kinds of "borrowing" and of the procedures for correct identification of materials other than those gained through independent research and reflection.

The spectrum is a wide one. At one end there is a word-for-word copying of another's writing without enclosing the copied passage in quotation marks and identifying it in a footnote, *both* of which are necessary. (This includes, of course, the copying of all or any part of another student's paper.) It hardly seems possible that anyone of college age or more could do that without clear intent to deceive. At the other end there is the almost casual slipping in of a particularly apt term which one has come across in reading and which so admirably expresses one's opinion that one is tempted to make it personal property. Between these poles there are degrees and degrees, but they may be roughly placed in two groups. Close to outright and blatant deceit—but more the result, perhaps, of laziness than of bad intent—is the patching together of random jottings made in the course of reading, generally without careful identification of their source, and then woven into the text, so that the result is a mosaic of other people's ideas and words, the writer's sole contribution being the cement to hold the pieces together. Indicative of more effort and, for that reason, somewhat closer to honesty, though still dishonest, is the paraphrase, an abbreviated (and often skillfully prepared) restatement of someone else's analysis or conclusion, without acknowledgment that another person's text has been the basis for the recapitulation.

The examples given below should make clear the dishonest and the proper use of source material. If instances occur which these examples do not seem to cover, conscience will in all likelihood be prepared to supply advice.

The Source

The importance of the *Second Treatise of Government* printed in this volume is such that without it we should miss some of the familiar features of our own government. It is safe to assert that the much criticized branch known as the Supreme Court obtained its being as a result of Locke's insistence upon the separation of powers; and that the combination of many powers in the hands of the executive under the New Deal has still to encounter opposition because it is contrary to the principles enunciated therein, the effect of which is not spent, though the relationship may not be consciously traced. Again we see the crystallizing force of Locke's writing. It renders explicit and adapts to the British politics of his day the trend and aim of writers from Languet and Bodin through Hooker and Grotius, to say nothing of the distant ancients, Aristotle and the Stoic school of natural law. It sums up magistrally the arguments used through the ages to attack authority vested in a single individual, but it does so from the particular point of view engendered by the Revolution of 1688 and is in harmony with the British scene and mental climate of the growing bourgeoisie of that age. Montesquieu and Rosseau, the framers of our own Declaration of Independence, and the statesmen (or should we say merchants and spectators?) who drew up the Constitution have re-echoed its claims for human liberty, for the separation of powers, for the sanctity of private property. In the hands of these it has been the quarry of liberal doctrines; and that it has served the Socialist theory of property based on labor is final proof of its breadth of view.

—CHARLES L. SHERMAN, "Introduction" to John Locke, *Treatise of Civil Government and A Letter Concerning Toleration.*

Word-for-Word Plagiarizing

It is not hard to see the importance of the *Second Treatise of Government* to our own democracy. Without it we should miss some of the most familiar features of our own government. It is safe to assert that the much criticized branch known as the Supreme Court obtained its being as a result of Locke's insistence upon the separation of powers; and that the combination of many powers in the hands of the executive under the New Deal has still to encounter opposition because it is contrary to the principles enunciated therein, the effect of which is not spent, though the relationship may not be consciously traced. The framers of our own Declaration of Independence and the statesmen who drew up the Constitution have re-echoed its claims for human liberty, for the separation of powers, for the sanctity of private property. All these are marks of the influence of Locke's *Second Treatise* on our own way of life.

In this example, after composing half of a first sentence, the writer copies exactly what is in the original text, leaving out the center section of the paragraph and omitting the names of Montesquieu and Rousseau where he takes up the text again. The last sentence is also the writer's own.

If the writer had enclosed all the copied text in quotation marks and had identified the source in a footnote, he would not have been liable to the charge of plagiarism; a reader might justifiably have felt, however, that the writer's personal contribution to the discussion was not very significant.

The Mosaic

The crystallizing force of Locke's writing may be seen in the effect his *Second Treatise of Government* had in shaping some of the familiar features of our own government. That much criticized branch known as the Supreme Court and the combination of many powers in the hands of the executive under the New Deal are modern examples. But even the foundations of our state—the Declaration of Independence and the Constitution—have re-echoed its claims for human liberty, for the separation of powers, for the sanctity of private property. True, the influence of others is also marked in our Constitution—from the trend and aim of writers like Languet and Bodin, Hooker and Grotius, to say nothing of Aristotle and the Stoic school of natural law; but the fundamental influence is Locke's *Treatise,* the very quarry of liberal doctrines.

Note how the following phrases have been lifted out of the original text and moved into new patterns:

crystallizing force of Locke's writing
some of the familiar features of our own government
much criticized branch known as the Supreme Court
combination of many powers in the hands of the executive under the New Deal
have re-echoed its claims for human liberty . . . property
from the trend and aim . . . Grotius
to say nothing of Aristotle and . . . natural law
quarry of liberal doctrines

As in the first example, there is really no way of legitimizing such a procedure. To put every stolen phrase within quotation marks would produce an almost unreadable, and quite worthless, text.

The Paraphrase

PARAPHRASE: Many fundamental aspects of our own government are
ORIGINAL: Many familiar features of our own government are

apparent in the *Second Treatise of Government.* One can safely
apparent in the *Second Treatise of Government.* It is safe to

say that the oft-censured Supreme Court really owes its exist-
assert that the much criticized . . . Court obtained its being as

ence to the Lockeian demand that powers in government be kept
a result of Locke's insistence upon the separation of powers;

separate; equally one can say that the allocation of varied
and that the combination of many powers

and widespread authority to the President during the era of
in the hands of the executive under the

the New Deal has still to encounter opposition because it is
New Deal has still to encounter opposition because it is

contrary to the principles enunciated therein . . . . Once more it
contrary to the principles enunciated therein . . . . Again we see

is possible to note the way in which Locke's writing clarified
the crystallizing force of Locke's writing.

existing opinion.

The foregoing interlinear presentation shows clearly how the writer has simply traveled along with the original text, substituting approximately equivalent terms except where his understanding fails him, as it does with "crystallizing," or where the ambiguity of the original is too great a tax on his ingenuity for him to proceed, as it is with "to encounter opposition . . . consciously traced" in the original.

Such a procedure as the one shown in this example has its uses; for one thing, it is valuable for the student's own understanding of the passage; and it may be valuable for the reader as well. How, then, may it be properly used? The procedure is simple. The writer might begin the second sentence with: "As Sherman notes in the introduction to his edition of the *Treatise,* one can safely say . . ." and conclude the paraphrased passage with a footnote giving the additional identification necessary. Or he might indicate directly the exact nature of what he is doing, in this fashion: "To paraphrase Sherman's comment . . ." and conclude that also with a footnote indicator.

In point of fact, this source does not particularly lend itself to honest paraphrase, with the exception of that one sentence which the paraphraser above copied without change except for abridgement. The purpose of paraphrase should be to simplify or to throw a new and significant light on a text; it requires much skill if it is to be honestly used and should rarely be resorted to by the student except for the purpose, as was suggested above, of his personal enlightenment.

■ The "Apt" Term

The *Second Treatise of Government* is a veritable quarry of liberal doctrines. In it the crystallizing force of Locke's writing is markedly apparent. The cause of human liberty, the principle of separation of powers, and the inviolability of private property—all three, major dogmas of American constitutionalism—owe their presence in our Constitution in large part to the remarkable *Treatise* which first appeared around 1685 and was destined to spark, within three years, a revolution in the land of its author's birth and, ninety years later, another revolution against that land.

Here the writer has not been able to resist the appropriation of two striking terms— "quarry of liberal doctrines" and "crystallizing force"; a perfectly proper use of the terms would have required only the addition of a phrase: *The Second Treatise of Government* is, to use Sherman's suggestive expression, a "quarry of liberal doctrines." In it the "crystallizing force"—the term again is Sherman's—of Locke's writing is markedly apparent....

Other phrases in the text above—"the cause of human liberty," "the principle of the separation of powers," "the inviolability of private property"—are clearly drawn directly from the original source but are so much matters in the public domain, so to speak, that no one could reasonably object to their re-use in this fashion.

Since one of the principal aims of a college education is the development of intellectual honesty, it is obvious that plagiarism is a particularly serious offense, and the punishment for it is commensurately severe. What a penalized student suffers can never really be known by anyone but himself; what the student who plagiarizes and "gets away with it" suffers is less public and probably less acute, but the corruptness of his act, the disloyalty and baseness it entails, must inevitably leave a mark on him as well as on the institution of which he is a member.

Source: From *The Logic and Rhetoric of Exposition,* 3rd Ed., by Harold C. Martin, Richard M. Ohman, and James H. Wheatley. © 1969. Reprinted with permission of Heinle, a division of Thomson Learning: www.thomsonrights.com. Fax 800 730-2215.

Appendix 2

Statistical Tables

Table A
Random Numbers

Line								
101	19223	95034	05756	28713	96409	12531	42544	82853
102	73676	47150	99400	01927	27754	42648	82425	36290
103	45467	71709	77558	00095	32863	29485	82226	90056
104	52711	38889	93074	60227	40011	85848	48767	52573
105	95592	94007	69971	91481	60779	53791	17297	59335
106	68417	35013	15529	72765	85089	57067	50211	47487
107	82739	57890	20807	47511	81676	55300	94383	14893
108	60940	72024	17868	24943	61790	90656	87964	18883
109	36009	19365	15412	39638	85453	46816	83485	41979
110	38448	48789	18338	24697	39364	42006	76688	08708
111	81486	69487	60513	09297	00412	71238	27649	39950
112	59636	88804	04634	71197	19352	73089	84898	45785
113	62568	70206	40325	03699	71080	22553	11486	11776
114	45149	32992	75730	66280	03819	56202	02938	70915
115	61041	77684	94322	24709	73698	14526	31893	32592
116	14459	26056	31424	80371	65103	62253	50490	61181
117	38167	98532	62183	70632	23417	26185	41448	75532
118	73190	32533	04470	29669	84407	90785	65956	86382
119	95857	07118	87664	92099	58806	66979	98624	84826
120	35476	55972	39421	65850	04266	35435	43742	11937
121	71487	09984	29077	14863	61683	47052	62224	51025
122	13873	81598	95052	90908	73592	75186	87136	95761
123	54580	81507	27102	56027	55892	33063	41842	81868
124	71035	09001	43367	49497	72719	96758	27611	91596
125	96746	12149	37823	71868	18442	35119	62103	39244

Table A (continued)
Random Numbers

Line								
126	96927	19931	36809	74192	77567	88741	48409	41903
127	43909	99477	25330	64359	40085	16925	85117	36071
128	15689	14227	06565	14374	13352	49367	81982	87209
129	36759	58984	68288	22913	18638	54303	00795	08727
130	69051	64817	87174	90517	84534	06489	87201	97245
131	05007	16632	81194	14873	04197	85576	45195	96565
132	68732	55259	84292	08796	43165	93739	31685	97150
133	45740	41807	65561	33302	07051	93623	18132	09547
134	27816	78416	18329	21337	35213	37741	04312	68508
135	66925	55658	39100	78458	11206	19876	87151	31260
136	08421	44753	77377	28744	75592	08563	79140	92454
137	53645	66812	61421	47836	12609	15373	98481	14592
138	66831	68908	40772	21558	47781	33586	79177	06928
139	55588	99404	70708	41098	43563	56934	48394	51719
140	12975	13258	13048	45144	72321	81940	00360	02428
141	96767	35964	23822	96012	94591	65194	50842	53372
142	72829	50232	97892	63408	77919	44575	24870	04178
143	88565	42628	17797	49376	61762	16953	88604	12724
144	62964	88145	83083	69453	46109	59505	69680	00900
145	19687	12633	57857	95806	09931	02150	43163	58636
146	37609	59057	66967	83401	60705	02384	90597	93600
147	54973	86278	88737	74351	47500	84552	19909	67181
148	00694	05977	19664	65441	20903	62371	22725	53340
149	71546	05233	53946	68743	72460	27601	45403	88692
150	07511	88915	41267	16853	84569	79367	32337	03316

Source: David S. Moore, *The Basic Practice of Statistics* (New York: W. H. Freeman and Co., 1995).

Table B
Critical Values of Chi Square

df	.99	.98	.95	.90	.80	.70	.50	.30	.20	.10	.05	.02	.01	.001
1	.00016	.00063	.0039	.016	.064	.15	.46	1.07	1.64	2.71	3.84	5.41	6.64	10.83
2	.02	.04	.10	.21	.45	.71	1.39	2.41	3.22	4.60	5.99	7.82	9.21	13.82
3	.12	.18	.35	.58	1.00	1.42	2.37	3.66	4.64	6.25	7.82	9.84	11.34	16.27
4	.30	.43	.71	1.06	1.65	2.20	3.36	4.88	5.99	7.78	9.49	11.67	13.28	18.46
5	.55	.75	1.14	1.61	2.34	3.00	4.35	6.06	7.29	9.24	11.07	13.39	15.09	20.52
6	.87	1.13	1.64	2.20	3.07	3.83	5.35	7.23	8.56	10.64	12.59	15.03	16.81	22.46
7	1.24	1.56	2.17	2.83	3.82	4.67	6.35	8.38	9.80	12.02	14.07	16.62	18.48	24.32
8	1.65	2.03	2.73	3.49	4.59	5.53	7.34	9.52	11.03	13.36	15.51	18.17	20.09	26.12
9	2.09	2.53	3.32	4.17	5.38	6.39	8.34	10.66	12.24	14.68	16.92	19.68	21.67	27.88
10	2.56	3.06	3.94	4.86	6.18	7.27	9.34	11.78	13.44	15.99	18.31	21.16	23.21	29.59
11	3.05	3.61	4.58	5.58	6.99	8.15	10.34	12.90	14.63	17.28	19.68	22.62	24.72	31.26
12	3.57	4.18	5.23	6.30	7.81	9.03	11.34	14.01	15.81	18.55	21.03	24.05	26.22	32.91
13	4.11	4.76	5.89	7.04	8.63	9.93	12.34	15.12	16.98	19.81	22.36	25.47	27.69	34.53
14	4.66	5.37	6.57	7.79	9.47	10.82	13.34	16.22	18.15	21.06	23.68	26.87	29.14	36.12
15	5.23	5.98	7.26	8.55	10.31	11.72	14.34	17.32	19.31	22.31	25.00	28.26	30.58	37.70
16	5.81	6.61	7.96	9.31	11.15	12.62	15.34	18.42	20.46	23.54	26.30	29.63	32.00	39.29
17	6.41	7.26	8.67	10.08	12.00	13.53	16.34	19.51	21.62	24.77	27.59	31.00	33.41	40.75
18	7.02	7.91	9.39	10.86	12.86	14.44	17.34	20.60	22.76	25.99	28.87	32.35	34.80	42.31
19	7.63	8.57	10.12	11.65	13.72	15.35	18.34	21.69	23.90	27.20	30.14	33.69	36.19	43.82
20	8.26	9.24	10.85	12.44	14.58	16.27	19.34	22.78	25.04	28.41	31.41	35.02	37.57	45.32
21	8.90	9.92	11.59	13.24	15.44	17.18	20.34	23.86	26.17	29.62	32.67	36.34	38.93	46.80
22	9.54	10.60	12.34	14.04	16.31	18.10	21.34	24.94	27.30	30.81	33.92	37.66	40.29	48.27
23	10.20	11.29	13.09	14.85	17.19	19.02	22.34	26.02	28.43	32.01	35.17	38.97	41.64	49.73
24	10.86	11.99	13.85	15.66	18.06	19.94	23.34	27.10	29.55	33.20	36.42	40.27	42.98	51.18
25	11.52	12.70	14.61	16.47	18.94	20.87	24.34	28.17	30.68	34.38	37.65	41.57	44.31	52.62
26	12.20	13.41	15.38	17.29	19.82	21.79	25.34	29.25	31.80	35.56	38.88	42.86	45.64	54.05
27	12.88	14.12	16.15	18.11	20.70	22.72	26.34	30.32	32.91	36.74	40.11	44.14	46.96	55.48
28	13.56	14.85	16.93	18.94	21.59	23.65	27.34	31.39	34.03	37.92	41.34	45.42	48.28	56.89
29	14.26	15.57	17.71	19.77	22.48	24.58	28.34	32.46	35.14	39.09	42.56	46.69	49.59	58.30
30	14.95	16.31	18.49	20.60	23.36	25.51	29.34	33.53	36.25	40.26	43.77	47.96	50.89	59.70

Source: George A. Ferguson, *Statistical Analysis in Psychology and Education,* 5th Ed. (New York: McGraw-Hill, 1981).

Table C
Critical Values of t

df	LEVEL OF SIGNIFICANCE FOR ONE-TAILED TEST					
	.10	.05	.025	.01	.005	.0005
	LEVEL OF SIGNIFICANCE FOR TWO-TAILED TEST					
	.20	.10	.05	.02	.01	.001
1	3.078	6.314	12.706	31.821	63.657	636.619
2	1.886	2.920	4.303	6.965	9.925	31.598
3	1.638	2.353	3.182	4.541	5.841	12.941
4	1.533	2.132	2.776	3.747	4.604	8.610
5	1.476	2.015	2.571	3.365	4.032	6.859
6	1.440	1.943	2.447	3.143	3.707	5.959
7	1.415	1.895	2.365	2.998	3.499	5.405
8	1.397	1.860	2.306	2.896	3.355	5.041
9	1.383	1.833	2.262	2.821	3.250	4.781
10	1.372	1.812	2.228	2.764	3.169	4.587
11	1.363	1.796	2.201	2.718	3.106	4.437
12	1.356	1.782	2.179	2.681	3.055	4.318
13	1.350	1.771	2.160	2.650	3.012	4.221
14	1.345	1.761	2.145	2.624	2.977	4.140
15	1.341	1.753	2.131	2.602	2.947	4.073
16	1.337	1.746	2.120	2.583	2.921	4.015
17	1.333	1.740	2.110	2.567	2.898	3.965
18	1.330	1.734	2.101	2.552	2.878	3.922
19	1.328	1.729	2.093	2.539	2.861	3.883
20	1.325	1.725	2.086	2.528	2.845	3.850
21	1.323	1.721	2.080	2.518	2.831	3.819
22	1.321	1.717	2.074	2.508	2.819	3.792
23	1.319	1.714	2.069	2.500	2.807	3.767
24	1.318	1.711	2.064	2.492	2.797	3.745
25	1.316	1.708	2.060	2.485	2.787	3.725
26	1.315	1.706	2.056	2.479	2.779	3.707
27	1.314	1.703	2.052	2.473	2.771	3.690
28	1.313	1.701	2.048	2.467	2.763	3.674
29	1.311	1.699	2.045	2.462	2.756	3.659
30	1.310	1.697	2.042	2.457	2.750	3.646
40	1.303	1.684	2.021	2.423	2.704	3.551
60	1.296	1.671	2.000	2.390	2.660	3.460
120	1.289	1.658	1.980	2.358	2.617	3.373
∞	1.282	1.645	1.960	2.326	2.576	3.291

Source: George A. Ferguson, *Statistical Analysis in Psychology and Education,* 5th Ed. (New York: McGraw-Hill, 1981).

Table D
Critical Values of F

5 percent (roman type) and 1 percent (bold-face type) points for the distribution of F

DEGREES OF FREEDOM FOR NUMERATOR

Degrees of Freedom for Denominator		1	2	3	4	5	6	7	8	9	10	11	12	14	16	20	24	30	40	50	75	100	200	500	∞
1	5%	161	200	216	225	230	234	237	239	241	242	243	244	245	246	248	249	250	251	252	253	253	254	254	254
	1%	**4052**	**4999**	**5403**	**5625**	**5764**	**5859**	**5928**	**5981**	**6022**	**6056**	**6082**	**6106**	**6142**	**6169**	**6208**	**6234**	**6258**	**6286**	**6302**	**6323**	**6334**	**6352**	**6361**	**6366**
2	5%	18.51	19.00	19.16	19.25	19.30	19.33	19.36	19.37	19.38	19.39	19.40	19.41	19.42	19.43	19.44	19.45	19.46	19.47	19.47	19.48	19.49	19.49	19.50	19.50
	1%	**98.49**	**99.01**	**99.17**	**99.25**	**99.30**	**99.33**	**99.34**	**99.36**	**99.38**	**99.40**	**99.41**	**99.42**	**99.43**	**99.44**	**99.45**	**99.46**	**99.47**	**99.48**	**99.48**	**99.49**	**99.49**	**99.49**	**99.50**	**99.50**
3	5%	10.13	9.55	9.28	9.12	9.01	8.94	8.88	8.84	8.81	8.78	8.76	8.74	8.71	8.69	8.66	8.64	8.62	8.60	8.58	8.57	8.56	8.54	8.54	8.53
	1%	**34.12**	**30.81**	**29.46**	**28.71**	**28.24**	**27.91**	**27.67**	**27.49**	**27.34**	**27.23**	**27.13**	**27.05**	**26.92**	**26.83**	**26.69**	**26.60**	**26.50**	**26.41**	**26.35**	**26.27**	**26.23**	**26.18**	**26.14**	**26.12**
4	5%	7.71	6.94	6.59	6.39	6.26	6.16	6.09	6.04	6.00	5.96	5.93	5.91	5.87	5.84	5.80	5.77	5.74	5.71	5.70	5.68	5.66	5.65	5.64	5.63
	1%	**21.20**	**18.00**	**16.69**	**15.98**	**15.52**	**15.21**	**14.98**	**14.80**	**14.66**	**14.54**	**14.45**	**14.37**	**14.24**	**14.15**	**14.02**	**13.93**	**13.83**	**13.74**	**13.69**	**13.61**	**13.57**	**13.52**	**13.48**	**13.46**
5	5%	6.61	5.79	5.41	5.19	5.05	4.95	4.88	4.82	4.78	4.74	4.70	4.68	4.64	4.60	4.56	4.53	4.50	4.46	4.44	4.42	4.40	4.38	4.37	4.36
	1%	**16.26**	**13.27**	**12.06**	**11.39**	**10.97**	**10.67**	**10.45**	**10.27**	**10.15**	**10.05**	**9.96**	**9.89**	**9.77**	**9.68**	**9.55**	**9.47**	**9.38**	**9.29**	**9.24**	**9.17**	**9.13**	**9.07**	**9.04**	**9.02**
6	5%	5.99	5.14	4.76	4.53	4.39	4.28	4.21	4.15	4.10	4.06	4.03	4.00	3.96	3.92	3.87	3.84	3.81	3.77	3.75	3.72	3.71	3.69	3.68	3.67
	1%	**13.74**	**10.92**	**9.78**	**9.15**	**8.75**	**8.47**	**8.26**	**8.10**	**7.98**	**7.87**	**7.79**	**7.72**	**7.60**	**7.52**	**7.39**	**7.31**	**7.23**	**7.14**	**7.09**	**7.02**	**6.99**	**6.94**	**6.90**	**6.88**
7	5%	5.59	4.74	4.35	4.12	3.97	3.87	3.79	3.73	3.68	3.63	3.60	3.57	3.52	3.49	3.44	3.41	3.38	3.34	3.32	3.29	3.28	3.25	3.24	3.23
	1%	**12.25**	**9.55**	**8.45**	**7.85**	**7.46**	**7.19**	**7.00**	**6.84**	**6.71**	**6.62**	**6.54**	**6.47**	**6.35**	**6.27**	**6.15**	**6.07**	**5.98**	**5.90**	**5.85**	**5.78**	**5.75**	**5.70**	**5.67**	**5.65**
8	5%	5.32	4.46	4.07	3.84	3.69	3.58	3.50	3.44	3.39	3.34	3.31	3.28	3.23	3.20	3.15	3.12	3.08	3.05	3.03	3.00	2.98	2.96	2.94	2.93
	1%	**11.26**	**8.65**	**7.59**	**7.01**	**6.63**	**6.37**	**6.19**	**6.03**	**5.91**	**5.82**	**5.74**	**5.67**	**5.56**	**5.48**	**5.36**	**5.28**	**5.20**	**5.11**	**5.06**	**5.00**	**4.96**	**4.91**	**4.88**	**4.86**
9	5%	5.12	4.26	3.86	3.63	3.48	3.37	3.29	3.23	3.18	3.13	3.10	3.07	3.02	2.98	2.93	2.90	2.86	2.82	2.80	2.77	2.76	2.73	2.72	2.71
	1%	**10.56**	**8.02**	**6.99**	**6.42**	**6.06**	**5.80**	**5.62**	**5.47**	**5.35**	**5.26**	**5.18**	**5.11**	**5.00**	**4.92**	**4.80**	**4.73**	**4.64**	**4.56**	**4.51**	**4.45**	**4.41**	**4.36**	**4.33**	**4.31**
10	5%	4.96	4.10	3.71	3.48	3.33	3.22	3.14	3.07	3.02	2.97	2.94	2.91	2.86	2.82	2.77	2.74	2.70	2.67	2.64	2.61	2.59	2.56	2.55	2.54
	1%	**10.04**	**7.56**	**6.55**	**5.99**	**5.64**	**5.39**	**5.21**	**5.06**	**4.95**	**4.85**	**4.78**	**4.71**	**4.60**	**4.52**	**4.41**	**4.33**	**4.25**	**4.17**	**4.12**	**4.05**	**4.01**	**3.96**	**3.93**	**3.91**
11	5%	4.84	3.98	3.59	3.36	3.20	3.09	3.01	2.95	2.90	2.86	2.82	2.79	2.74	2.70	2.65	2.61	2.57	2.53	2.50	2.47	2.45	2.42	2.41	2.40
	1%	**9.65**	**7.20**	**6.22**	**5.67**	**5.32**	**5.07**	**4.88**	**4.74**	**4.63**	**4.54**	**4.46**	**4.40**	**4.29**	**4.21**	**4.10**	**4.02**	**3.94**	**3.86**	**3.80**	**3.74**	**3.70**	**3.66**	**3.62**	**3.60**
12	5%	4.75	3.88	3.49	3.26	3.11	3.00	2.92	2.85	2.80	2.76	2.72	2.69	2.64	2.60	2.54	2.50	2.46	2.42	2.40	2.36	2.35	2.32	2.31	2.30
	1%	**9.33**	**6.93**	**5.95**	**5.41**	**5.06**	**4.82**	**4.65**	**4.50**	**4.39**	**4.30**	**4.22**	**4.16**	**4.05**	**3.98**	**3.86**	**3.78**	**3.70**	**3.61**	**3.56**	**3.49**	**3.46**	**3.41**	**3.38**	**3.36**
13	5%	4.67	3.80	3.41	3.18	3.02	2.92	2.84	2.77	2.72	2.67	2.63	2.60	2.55	2.51	2.46	2.42	2.38	2.34	2.32	2.28	2.26	2.24	2.22	2.21
	1%	**9.07**	**6.70**	**5.74**	**5.20**	**4.86**	**4.62**	**4.44**	**4.30**	**4.19**	**4.10**	**4.02**	**3.96**	**3.85**	**3.78**	**3.67**	**3.59**	**3.51**	**3.42**	**3.37**	**3.30**	**3.27**	**3.21**	**3.18**	**3.16**

Table D (continued)
Critical Values of F

5 percent (roman type) and 1 percent (bold-face type) points for the distribution of F

Degrees of Freedom for Denominator (left), DEGREES OF FREEDOM FOR NUMERATOR (columns)

Denominator	1	2	3	4	5	6	7	8	9	10	11	12	14	16	20	24	30	40	50	75	100	200	500	∞
14	4.60	3.74	3.34	3.11	2.96	2.85	2.77	2.70	2.65	2.60	2.56	2.53	2.48	2.44	2.39	2.35	2.31	2.27	2.24	2.21	2.19	2.16	2.14	2.13
	8.86	**6.51**	**5.56**	**5.03**	**4.69**	**4.46**	**4.28**	**4.14**	**4.03**	**3.94**	**3.86**	**3.80**	**3.70**	**3.62**	**3.51**	**3.43**	**3.34**	**3.26**	**3.21**	**3.14**	**3.11**	**3.06**	**3.02**	**3.00**
15	4.54	3.68	3.29	3.06	2.90	2.79	2.70	2.64	2.59	2.55	2.51	2.48	2.43	2.39	2.33	2.29	2.25	2.21	2.18	2.15	2.12	2.10	2.08	2.07
	8.68	**6.36**	**5.42**	**4.89**	**4.56**	**4.32**	**4.14**	**4.00**	**3.89**	**3.80**	**3.73**	**3.67**	**3.56**	**3.48**	**3.36**	**3.29**	**3.20**	**3.12**	**3.07**	**3.00**	**2.97**	**2.92**	**2.89**	**2.87**
16	4.49	3.63	3.24	3.01	2.85	2.74	2.66	2.59	2.54	2.49	2.45	2.42	2.37	2.33	2.28	2.24	2.20	2.16	2.13	2.09	2.07	2.04	2.02	2.01
	8.53	**6.23**	**5.29**	**4.77**	**4.44**	**4.20**	**4.03**	**3.89**	**3.78**	**3.69**	**3.61**	**3.55**	**3.45**	**3.37**	**3.25**	**3.18**	**3.10**	**3.01**	**2.96**	**2.89**	**2.86**	**2.80**	**2.77**	**2.75**
17	4.45	3.59	3.20	2.96	2.81	2.70	2.62	2.55	2.50	2.45	2.41	2.38	2.33	2.29	2.23	2.19	2.15	2.11	2.08	2.04	2.02	1.99	1.97	1.96
	8.40	**6.11**	**5.18**	**4.67**	**4.34**	**4.10**	**3.93**	**3.79**	**3.68**	**3.59**	**3.52**	**3.45**	**3.35**	**3.27**	**3.16**	**3.08**	**3.00**	**2.92**	**2.86**	**2.79**	**2.76**	**2.70**	**2.67**	**2.65**
18	4.41	3.55	3.16	2.93	2.77	2.66	2.58	2.51	2.46	2.41	2.37	2.34	2.29	2.25	2.19	2.15	2.11	2.07	2.04	2.00	1.98	1.95	1.93	1.92
	8.28	**6.01**	**5.09**	**4.58**	**4.25**	**4.01**	**3.85**	**3.71**	**3.60**	**3.51**	**3.44**	**3.37**	**3.27**	**3.19**	**3.07**	**3.00**	**2.91**	**2.83**	**2.78**	**2.71**	**2.68**	**2.62**	**2.59**	**2.57**
19	4.38	3.52	3.13	2.90	2.74	2.63	2.55	2.48	2.43	2.38	2.34	2.31	2.26	2.21	2.15	2.11	2.07	2.02	2.00	1.96	1.94	1.91	1.90	1.88
	8.18	**5.93**	**5.01**	**4.50**	**4.17**	**3.94**	**3.77**	**3.63**	**3.52**	**3.43**	**3.36**	**3.30**	**3.19**	**3.12**	**3.00**	**2.92**	**2.84**	**2.76**	**2.70**	**2.63**	**2.60**	**2.54**	**2.51**	**2.49**
20	4.35	3.49	3.10	2.87	2.71	2.60	2.52	2.45	2.40	2.35	2.31	2.28	2.23	2.18	2.12	2.08	2.04	1.99	1.96	1.92	1.90	1.87	1.85	1.84
	8.10	**5.85**	**4.94**	**4.43**	**4.10**	**3.87**	**3.71**	**3.56**	**3.45**	**3.37**	**3.30**	**3.23**	**3.13**	**3.05**	**2.94**	**2.86**	**2.77**	**2.69**	**2.63**	**2.56**	**2.53**	**2.47**	**2.44**	**2.42**
21	4.32	3.47	3.07	2.84	2.68	2.57	2.49	2.42	2.37	2.32	2.28	2.25	2.20	2.15	2.09	2.05	2.00	1.96	1.93	1.89	1.87	1.84	1.82	1.81
	8.02	**5.78**	**4.87**	**4.37**	**4.04**	**3.81**	**3.65**	**3.51**	**3.40**	**3.31**	**3.24**	**3.17**	**3.07**	**2.99**	**2.88**	**2.80**	**2.72**	**2.63**	**2.58**	**2.51**	**2.47**	**2.42**	**2.38**	**2.36**
22	4.30	3.44	3.05	2.82	2.66	2.55	2.47	2.40	2.35	2.30	2.26	2.23	2.18	2.13	2.07	2.03	1.98	1.93	1.91	1.87	1.84	1.81	1.80	1.78
	7.94	**5.72**	**4.82**	**4.31**	**3.99**	**3.76**	**3.59**	**3.45**	**3.35**	**3.26**	**3.18**	**3.12**	**3.02**	**2.94**	**2.83**	**2.75**	**2.67**	**2.58**	**2.53**	**2.46**	**2.42**	**2.37**	**2.33**	**2.31**
23	4.28	3.42	3.03	2.80	2.64	2.53	2.45	2.38	2.32	2.28	2.24	2.20	2.14	2.10	2.04	2.00	1.96	1.91	1.88	1.84	1.82	1.79	1.77	1.76
	7.88	**5.66**	**4.76**	**4.26**	**3.94**	**3.71**	**3.54**	**3.41**	**3.30**	**3.21**	**3.14**	**3.07**	**2.97**	**2.89**	**2.78**	**2.70**	**2.62**	**2.53**	**2.48**	**2.41**	**2.37**	**2.32**	**2.28**	**2.26**
24	4.26	3.40	3.01	2.78	2.62	2.51	2.43	2.36	2.30	2.26	2.22	2.18	2.13	2.09	2.02	1.98	1.94	1.89	1.86	1.82	1.80	1.76	1.74	1.73
	7.82	**5.61**	**4.72**	**4.22**	**3.90**	**3.67**	**3.50**	**3.36**	**3.25**	**3.17**	**3.09**	**3.03**	**2.93**	**2.85**	**2.74**	**2.66**	**2.58**	**2.49**	**2.44**	**2.36**	**2.33**	**2.27**	**2.23**	**2.21**
25	4.24	3.38	2.99	2.76	2.60	2.49	2.41	2.34	2.28	2.24	2.20	2.16	2.11	2.06	2.00	1.96	1.92	1.87	1.84	1.80	1.77	1.74	1.72	1.71
	7.77	**5.57**	**4.68**	**4.18**	**3.86**	**3.63**	**3.46**	**3.32**	**3.21**	**3.13**	**3.05**	**2.99**	**2.89**	**2.81**	**2.70**	**2.62**	**2.54**	**2.45**	**2.40**	**2.32**	**2.29**	**2.23**	**2.19**	**2.17**
26	4.22	3.37	2.98	2.74	2.59	2.47	2.39	2.32	2.27	2.22	2.18	2.15	2.10	2.05	1.99	1.95	1.90	1.85	1.82	1.78	1.76	1.72	1.70	1.69
	7.72	**5.53**	**4.64**	**4.14**	**3.82**	**3.59**	**3.42**	**3.29**	**3.17**	**3.09**	**3.02**	**2.96**	**2.86**	**2.77**	**2.66**	**2.53**	**2.50**	**2.41**	**2.36**	**2.28**	**2.25**	**2.19**	**2.15**	**2.13**

Table D (continued)
Critical Values of F

5 percent (roman type) and 1 percent (bold-face type) points for the distribution of F

Degrees of Freedom for Denominator	DEGREES OF FREEDOM FOR NUMERATOR																							
	1	2	3	4	5	6	7	8	9	10	11	12	14	16	20	24	30	40	50	75	100	200	500	∞
27	4.21	3.35	2.96	2.73	2.57	2.46	2.37	2.30	2.25	2.20	2.16	2.13	2.08	2.03	1.97	1.93	1.88	1.84	1.80	1.76	1.74	1.71	1.68	1.67
	7.68	**5.49**	**4.60**	**4.11**	**3.79**	**3.56**	**3.39**	**3.26**	**3.14**	**3.06**	**2.98**	**2.93**	**2.83**	**2.74**	**2.63**	**2.55**	**2.47**	**2.38**	**2.33**	**2.25**	**2.21**	**2.16**	**2.12**	**2.10**
28	4.20	3.34	2.95	2.71	2.56	2.44	2.36	2.29	2.24	2.19	2.15	2.12	2.06	2.02	1.96	1.91	1.87	1.81	1.78	1.75	1.72	1.69	1.67	1.65
	7.64	**5.45**	**4.57**	**4.07**	**3.76**	**3.53**	**3.36**	**3.23**	**3.11**	**3.03**	**2.95**	**2.90**	**2.80**	**2.71**	**2.60**	**2.52**	**2.44**	**2.35**	**2.30**	**2.22**	**2.18**	**2.13**	**2.09**	**2.06**
29	4.18	3.33	2.93	2.70	2.54	2.43	2.35	2.28	2.22	2.18	2.14	2.10	2.05	2.00	1.94	1.90	1.85	1.80	1.77	1.73	1.71	1.68	1.65	1.64
	7.60	**5.42**	**4.54**	**4.04**	**3.73**	**3.50**	**3.33**	**3.20**	**3.08**	**3.00**	**2.92**	**2.87**	**2.77**	**2.68**	**2.57**	**2.49**	**2.41**	**2.32**	**2.27**	**2.19**	**2.15**	**2.10**	**2.06**	**2.03**
30	4.17	3.32	2.92	2.69	2.53	2.42	2.34	2.27	2.21	2.16	2.12	2.09	2.04	1.99	1.93	1.89	1.84	1.79	1.76	1.72	1.69	1.66	1.64	1.62
	7.56	**5.39**	**4.51**	**4.02**	**3.70**	**3.47**	**3.30**	**3.17**	**3.06**	**2.98**	**2.90**	**2.84**	**2.74**	**2.66**	**2.55**	**2.47**	**2.38**	**2.29**	**2.24**	**2.16**	**2.13**	**2.07**	**2.03**	**2.01**
32	4.15	3.30	2.90	2.67	2.51	2.40	2.32	2.25	2.19	2.14	2.10	2.07	2.02	1.97	1.91	1.86	1.82	1.76	1.74	1.69	1.67	1.64	1.61	1.59
	7.50	**5.34**	**4.46**	**3.97**	**3.66**	**3.42**	**3.25**	**3.12**	**3.01**	**2.94**	**2.86**	**2.80**	**2.70**	**2.62**	**2.51**	**2.42**	**2.34**	**2.25**	**2.20**	**2.12**	**2.08**	**2.02**	**1.98**	**1.96**
34	4.13	3.28	2.88	2.65	2.49	2.38	2.30	2.23	2.17	2.12	2.08	2.05	2.00	1.95	1.89	1.84	1.80	1.74	1.71	1.67	1.64	1.61	1.59	1.57
	7.44	**5.29**	**4.42**	**3.93**	**3.61**	**3.38**	**3.21**	**3.08**	**2.97**	**2.89**	**2.82**	**2.76**	**2.66**	**2.58**	**2.47**	**2.38**	**2.30**	**2.21**	**2.15**	**2.03**	**2.04**	**1.98**	**1.94**	**1.91**
36	4.11	3.26	2.86	2.63	2.48	2.36	2.28	2.21	2.15	2.10	2.06	2.03	1.98	1.93	1.87	1.82	1.78	1.72	1.69	1.65	1.62	1.59	1.56	1.55
	7.39	**5.25**	**4.38**	**3.89**	**3.58**	**3.35**	**3.18**	**3.04**	**2.94**	**2.86**	**2.78**	**2.72**	**2.62**	**2.54**	**2.43**	**2.35**	**2.26**	**2.17**	**2.12**	**2.04**	**2.00**	**1.94**	**1.90**	**1.87**
38	4.10	3.25	2.85	2.62	2.46	2.35	2.26	2.19	2.14	2.09	2.05	2.02	1.96	1.92	1.85	1.80	1.76	1.71	1.67	1.63	1.60	1.57	1.54	1.53
	7.35	**5.21**	**4.34**	**3.86**	**3.54**	**3.32**	**3.15**	**3.02**	**2.91**	**2.82**	**2.75**	**2.69**	**2.59**	**2.51**	**2.40**	**2.32**	**2.22**	**2.14**	**2.08**	**2.00**	**1.97**	**1.90**	**1.86**	**1.84**
40	4.08	3.23	2.84	2.61	2.45	2.34	2.25	2.18	2.12	2.07	2.04	2.00	1.95	1.90	1.84	1.79	1.74	1.69	1.66	1.61	1.59	1.55	1.53	1.51
	7.31	**5.18**	**4.31**	**3.83**	**3.51**	**3.29**	**3.12**	**2.99**	**2.88**	**2.80**	**2.73**	**2.66**	**2.56**	**2.49**	**2.37**	**2.29**	**2.20**	**2.11**	**2.05**	**1.97**	**1.94**	**1.88**	**1.84**	**1.81**
42	4.07	3.22	2.83	2.59	2.44	2.32	2.24	2.17	2.11	2.06	2.02	1.99	1.94	1.89	1.82	1.78	1.73	1.68	1.64	1.60	1.57	1.54	1.51	1.49
	7.27	**5.15**	**4.29**	**3.80**	**3.49**	**3.26**	**3.10**	**2.96**	**2.86**	**2.77**	**2.70**	**2.64**	**2.54**	**2.46**	**2.35**	**2.26**	**2.17**	**2.08**	**2.02**	**1.94**	**1.91**	**1.85**	**1.80**	**1.78**
44	4.06	3.21	2.82	2.58	2.43	2.31	2.23	2.16	2.10	2.05	2.01	1.98	1.92	1.88	1.81	1.76	1.72	1.66	1.63	1.58	1.56	1.52	1.50	1.48
	7.24	**5.12**	**4.26**	**3.78**	**3.46**	**3.24**	**3.07**	**2.94**	**2.84**	**2.75**	**2.68**	**2.62**	**2.52**	**2.44**	**2.32**	**2.24**	**2.15**	**2.06**	**2.00**	**1.92**	**1.88**	**1.82**	**1.78**	**1.75**
46	4.05	3.20	2.81	2.57	2.42	2.30	2.22	2.14	2.09	2.04	2.00	1.97	1.91	1.87	1.80	1.75	1.71	1.65	1.62	1.57	1.54	1.51	1.48	1.46
	7.21	**5.10**	**4.24**	**3.76**	**3.44**	**3.22**	**3.05**	**2.92**	**2.82**	**2.73**	**2.66**	**2.60**	**2.50**	**2.42**	**2.30**	**2.22**	**2.13**	**2.04**	**1.98**	**1.90**	**1.86**	**1.80**	**1.76**	**1.72**
48	4.04	3.19	2.80	2.56	2.41	2.30	2.21	2.14	2.08	2.03	1.99	1.96	1.90	1.86	1.79	1.74	1.70	1.64	1.61	1.56	1.53	1.50	1.47	1.45
	7.19	**5.08**	**4.22**	**3.74**	**3.42**	**3.20**	**3.04**	**2.90**	**2.80**	**2.71**	**2.64**	**2.58**	**2.48**	**2.40**	**2.28**	**2.20**	**2.11**	**2.02**	**1.96**	**1.88**	**1.84**	**1.78**	**1.73**	**1.70**

Table D (continued)
Critical Values of F

5 percent (roman type) and 1 percent (bold-face type) points for the distribution of F

Degrees of Freedom for Denominator	DEGREES OF FREEDOM FOR NUMERATOR																							
	1	2	3	4	5	6	7	8	9	10	11	12	14	16	20	24	30	40	50	75	100	200	500	∞
50	4.03	3.18	2.79	2.56	2.40	2.29	2.20	2.13	2.07	2.02	1.98	1.95	1.90	1.85	1.78	1.74	1.69	1.63	1.60	1.55	1.52	1.48	1.46	1.44
	7.17	**5.06**	**4.20**	**3.72**	**3.41**	**3.18**	**3.02**	**2.88**	**2.78**	**2.70**	**2.62**	**2.56**	**2.46**	**2.39**	**2.26**	**2.18**	**2.10**	**2.00**	**1.94**	**1.86**	**1.82**	**1.76**	**1.71**	**1.68**
55	4.02	3.17	2.78	2.54	2.38	2.27	2.18	2.11	2.05	2.00	1.97	1.93	1.88	1.83	1.76	1.72	1.67	1.61	1.58	1.52	1.50	1.46	1.43	1.41
	7.12	**5.01**	**4.16**	**3.68**	**3.37**	**3.15**	**2.98**	**2.85**	**2.75**	**2.66**	**2.59**	**2.53**	**2.43**	**2.35**	**2.23**	**2.15**	**2.06**	**1.96**	**1.90**	**1.82**	**1.78**	**1.71**	**1.66**	**1.64**
60	4.00	3.15	2.76	2.52	2.37	2.25	2.17	2.10	2.04	1.99	1.95	1.92	1.86	1.81	1.75	1.70	1.65	1.59	1.56	1.50	1.48	1.44	1.41	1.39
	7.08	**4.98**	**4.13**	**3.65**	**3.34**	**3.12**	**2.95**	**2.82**	**2.72**	**2.63**	**2.56**	**2.50**	**2.40**	**2.32**	**2.20**	**2.12**	**2.03**	**1.93**	**1.87**	**1.79**	**1.74**	**1.68**	**1.63**	**1.60**
65	3.99	3.14	2.75	2.51	2.36	2.24	2.15	2.08	2.02	1.98	1.94	1.90	1.85	1.80	1.73	1.68	1.63	1.57	1.54	1.49	1.46	1.42	1.39	1.37
	7.04	**4.95**	**4.10**	**3.62**	**3.31**	**3.09**	**2.93**	**2.79**	**2.70**	**2.61**	**2.54**	**2.47**	**2.37**	**2.30**	**2.18**	**2.09**	**2.00**	**1.90**	**1.84**	**1.76**	**1.71**	**1.64**	**1.60**	**1.56**
70	3.98	3.13	2.74	2.50	2.35	2.23	2.14	2.07	2.01	1.97	1.93	1.89	1.84	1.79	1.72	1.67	1.62	1.56	1.53	1.47	1.45	1.40	1.37	1.35
	7.01	**4.92**	**4.08**	**3.60**	**3.29**	**3.07**	**2.91**	**2.77**	**2.67**	**2.59**	**2.51**	**2.45**	**2.35**	**2.28**	**2.15**	**2.07**	**1.98**	**1.88**	**1.82**	**1.74**	**1.69**	**1.62**	**1.56**	**1.53**
80	3.96	3.11	2.72	2.48	2.33	2.21	2.12	2.05	1.99	1.95	1.91	1.88	1.82	1.77	1.70	1.65	1.60	1.54	1.51	1.45	1.42	1.38	1.35	1.32
	6.96	**4.88**	**4.04**	**3.56**	**3.25**	**3.04**	**2.87**	**2.74**	**2.64**	**2.55**	**2.48**	**2.41**	**2.32**	**2.24**	**2.11**	**2.03**	**1.94**	**1.84**	**1.78**	**1.70**	**1.65**	**1.57**	**1.52**	**1.49**
100	3.94	3.09	2.70	2.46	2.30	2.19	2.10	2.03	1.97	1.92	1.88	1.85	1.79	1.75	1.68	1.63	1.57	1.51	1.48	1.42	1.39	1.34	1.30	1.28
	6.90	**4.82**	**3.98**	**3.51**	**3.20**	**2.99**	**2.82**	**2.69**	**2.59**	**2.51**	**2.43**	**2.36**	**2.26**	**2.19**	**2.06**	**1.98**	**1.89**	**1.79**	**1.73**	**1.64**	**1.59**	**1.51**	**1.46**	**1.43**
125	3.92	3.07	2.68	2.44	2.29	2.17	2.08	2.01	1.95	1.90	1.86	1.83	1.77	1.72	1.65	1.60	1.55	1.49	1.45	1.39	1.36	1.31	1.27	1.25
	6.84	**4.78**	**3.94**	**3.47**	**3.17**	**2.95**	**2.79**	**2.65**	**2.56**	**2.47**	**2.40**	**2.33**	**2.23**	**2.15**	**2.03**	**1.94**	**1.85**	**1.75**	**1.68**	**1.59**	**1.54**	**1.46**	**1.40**	**1.37**
150	3.91	3.06	2.67	2.43	2.27	2.16	2.07	2.00	1.94	1.89	1.85	1.82	1.76	1.71	1.64	1.59	1.54	1.47	1.44	1.37	1.34	1.29	1.25	1.22
	6.81	**4.75**	**3.91**	**3.44**	**3.14**	**2.92**	**2.76**	**2.62**	**2.53**	**2.44**	**2.37**	**2.30**	**2.20**	**2.12**	**2.00**	**1.91**	**1.83**	**1.72**	**1.66**	**1.56**	**1.51**	**1.43**	**1.37**	**1.33**
200	3.89	3.04	2.65	2.41	2.26	2.14	2.05	1.98	1.92	1.87	1.83	1.80	1.74	1.69	1.62	1.57	1.52	1.45	1.42	1.35	1.32	1.26	1.22	1.19
	6.76	**4.71**	**3.88**	**3.41**	**3.11**	**2.90**	**2.73**	**2.60**	**2.50**	**2.41**	**2.34**	**2.28**	**2.17**	**2.09**	**1.97**	**1.88**	**1.79**	**1.69**	**1.62**	**1.53**	**1.48**	**1.39**	**1.33**	**1.28**
400	3.86	3.02	2.62	2.39	2.23	2.12	2.03	1.96	1.90	1.85	1.81	1.78	1.72	1.67	1.60	1.54	1.49	1.42	1.38	1.32	1.28	1.22	1.16	1.13
	6.70	**4.66**	**3.83**	**3.36**	**3.06**	**2.85**	**2.69**	**2.55**	**2.46**	**2.37**	**2.29**	**2.23**	**2.12**	**2.04**	**1.92**	**1.84**	**1.74**	**1.64**	**1.57**	**1.47**	**1.42**	**1.32**	**1.24**	**1.19**
1000	3.85	3.00	2.61	2.38	2.22	2.10	2.02	1.95	1.89	1.84	1.80	1.76	1.70	1.65	1.58	1.53	1.47	1.41	1.36	1.30	1.26	1.19	1.13	1.08
	6.66	**4.62**	**3.80**	**3.34**	**3.04**	**2.82**	**2.66**	**2.53**	**2.43**	**2.34**	**3.26**	**2.20**	**2.09**	**2.01**	**1.89**	**1.81**	**1.71**	**1.61**	**1.54**	**1.44**	**1.38**	**1.28**	**1.19**	**1.11**
∞	3.84	2.99	2.60	2.37	2.21	2.09	2.01	1.94	1.88	1.83	1.79	1.75	1.69	1.64	1.57	1.52	1.46	1.40	1.35	1.28	1.24	1.17	1.11	1.00
	6.64	**4.60**	**3.78**	**3.32**	**3.02**	**2.80**	**2.64**	**2.51**	**2.41**	**2.32**	**2.24**	**2.18**	**2.07**	**1.99**	**1.87**	**1.79**	**1.69**	**1.59**	**1.52**	**1.41**	**1.36**	**1.25**	**1.15**	**1.00**

Source: G. W. Snedcor and William G. Cochran, Statistical Methods, 6/e. © 1967 Iowa State University Press.

Notes

Chapter 1

1. Three of these categories (logic, authority, science) are provided by Fred N. Kerlinger, *Foundations of Behavioral Research* (New York: Holt, Rinehart and Winston, Inc., 1967), pp. 6–8. We have changed the title of his category *tenacity* to *investment* and added the category of *faith*.
2. Leon Festinger, Henry Riechen, and Stanley Schachter, *When Prophecy Fails* (Minneapolis: University of Minnesota Press, 1956).
3. Kenneth Arrow, *Social Choice and Individual Values* (New York: Wiley, 1963), pp. 2–3.
4. Kerlinger, *Foundations of Behavioral Research*, p. 9.
5. Earl Babbie, *Observing Ourselves, Essays in Social Research* (Belmont, CA: Wadsworth, 1986), p. 13.
6. Ibid., p. 28.
7. Paul H. Rubin, "Study: Death Penalty Deters Scores of Killings," *Atlanta Journal-Constitution* (March 14, 2002), Home Ed., p. 22A.

Chapter 2

1. Earl Babbie, *The Practice of Social Research*, 7th Ed. (Belmont, CA: Wadsworth, 1995), pp. 20–26.
2. Center for Media and Public Affairs, "Murder News and Murder Rates," *http://www.cmpa.com/factoid/crime.htm#real.*
3. Arnold Brecht, *Political Theory: The Foundations of Twentieth Century Political Thought* (Princeton, NJ: Princeton University Press, 1959), p. 114.
4. Alan S. Isaak, *Scope and Methods of Political Science*, 4th Ed. (Homewood, IL: Dorsey, 1984), p. 103.
5. This list is taken from Dickinson McGaw and George Watson, *Political and Social Inquiry* (New York: Wiley, 1976), pp. 12–13. For an earlier discussion of these assumptions, see Carlo Lastrucci, *The Scientific Approach, Basic Principles of the Scientific Method* (Cambridge, MA: Schenkman, 1967), pp. 37–47.
6. Earl Babbie, *Observing Ourselves: Essays in Social Research* (Belmont, CA: Wadsworth, 1986), Chapter 4.
7. Ernest Gellner, *Relativism and the Social Sciences* (New York: Cambridge University Press, 1985), p. 89.
8. Sociologist Robert K. Merton coined the term "theories of the middle range" for those theories that are broadly abstract but narrow enough so that specific propositions can easily be developed and tested. See Robert K. Merton, *On Theoretical Sociology* (New York: Free Press, 1967), Chapter 2.
9. Robert Putnam, "Tuning In, Tuning Out: The Strange Disappearance of Social Capital in America," *PS: Political Science and Politics*, 28 (December 1995): 664–683.

Chapter 3

1. Dickinson McGaw and George Watson, *Political and Social Inquiry* (New York: Wiley, 1976), p. 85.
2. C. Wright Mills, *The Sociological Imagination* (New York: Oxford University Press, 1959).
3. A discussion of how the project was chosen and developed can be found in S. M. Lipset, "The Biography of a Research Project: Union Democracy," in *Sociologists at Work*, ed. Phillip Hammond (Garden City, NY: Doubleday, 1964). The research was reported in S. M. Lipset, Martin Trow, and James S. Coleman, *Union Democracy* (Glencoe, IL: The Free Press, 1956).
4. Sullivan's account of the research project can be found in W. Phillips Shively, Ed., *The Research Process in Political*

Science (Itasca, IL: Peacock Publishers, 1984), pp. 36–46. The research report can be found in John L. Sullivan, James Pierson, and Stanley Feldman, "An Alternative Conceptualization of Political Tolerance: Illusory Increases, 1950s–1970s," *American Political Science Review,* 73 (September 1979): 781–794.

5. James M. Carlson, Mark S. Hyde, and Gladys Ganiel, "Scandal and Candidate Image," *Southeastern Political Review,* 28 (December 2000): 747–758.

6. David Easton, *The Political System* (New York: Knopf, 1959). A very clear and brief summary of definitions can be found in William A. Welsh, *Studying Politics* (New York: Praeger Publishers, 1973), pp. 4–8.

7. Kenneth Wald and Corwin E. Smidt, "Measurement Strategies in the Study of Religion and Politics," in *Rediscovering the Religious Factor in American Politics,* ed. David C. Ledge and Layman A. Kellstedt (New York: M. E. Sharpe, 1993), 26–52.

8. For students it is a worthwhile exercise to reexamine well-established research findings using new data. For example, researchers who are interested in explaining voting participation have repeatedly established a link between education and voting in presidential elections. Students can replicate these findings by examining the most recent data available that are provided with this book.

9. Robert J. Lifton, *Nazi Doctors* (New York: Basic Books, 1967).

10. National Commission for the Protection of Human Subjects of Biomedical and Behavioral Research, *The Belmont Report: Ethical Principles and Guidelines for the Protection of Human Subjects of Research* (April 18, 1979). *http://ohsr.od.nih.gov/mpa/belmont.php3.*

11. Ibid.

12. For examples of ethical abuses, see Edward Diener and Rick Crandall, *Ethics in Social and Behavioral Research* (Chicago: University of Chicago Press, 1978).

13. See C. Haney, C. Banks, and Philip G. Zimbardo, "Interpersonal Dynamics in a Simulated Prison," *International Journal of Criminology and Penology,* 1 (1973): 69–97, and Philip G. Zimbardo, "On the Ethics of Intervention in Human Psychological Research," *Cognition,* 2 (1973): 243–256.

14. George Kelling, Tony Pate, Duane Dieckman, and Charles Brown, *The Kansas City Preventive Patrol Experiment: A Summary Report* (Washington, DC: Police Foundation, 1974).

15. Scott G. McNall, *Career of a Radical Rightist: A Study in Failure* (Port Washington, NY: Kennikat Press, 1975).

16. See Carlson, Hyde, and Ganiel (2000).

17. Kai T. Erickson, "A Comment on Disguised Observation in Sociology," *Social Problems,* 12 (1967): 373.

18. Herbert C. Kelman, "Human Use of Human Subjects: The Problem of Deception in Social Psychological Experiments," *Psychological Bulletin,* 71 (1967): 1–11.

19. The social scientific approach to developing generalizations through a process of falsification comes from philosopher Karl Popper, who argues that no statement could ever be found to be true with finality but could be found false with finality. See Karl R. Popper, *The Logic of Scientific Discovery* (New York: Wiley, 1961).

20. Ernest Gellner, *Relativism and the Social Sciences* (New York: Cambridge University Press, 1985), p. 159.

21. Fred N. Kerlinger, *Behavioral Research—A Conceptual Approach* (Sydney: Holt, Rinehart and Winston, 1979), p. 36.

22. The distinctions between types of value statements and means of reformulation were outlined in Herbert Jacob and Robert Weisberg, *Elementary Political Analysis* (New York: McGraw-Hill, 1975).

23. Deane E. Neubauer, "Some Conditions of Democracy," *American Political Science Review,* 61 (December 1967): 1002–1009.

24. Fred N. Kerlinger, *Foundations of Behavioral Research,* 3rd Ed. (New York: Holt, Rinehart and Winston, 1986), p. 27.

Chapter 6

1. Ronald Hrebenar, *Interest Groups Politics in America* (New York: M. E. Sharpe, 1997).

2. Ted Robert Gurr, *Why Men Rebel* (Princeton, NJ: Princeton University Press, 1970).

3. Warren E. Miller and Donald E. Stokes, "Constituency Influence in Congress," *American Political Science Review,* 57 (March 1963): 45–56.

Chapter 7

1. See, for example, Lewis Feuer, "What Is Alienation?: The Career of a Concept," *New Politics,* 1 (Spring 1962): 116–134, and Frank Johnson, Ed., *Alienation: Concept, Term and Meaning* (New York: Seminar Press, 1973).

2. Ada W. Finifter, "Dimensions of Political Alienation," *American Political Science Review,* 64 (June 1970): 389–410.

3. Robert S. Gilmour and Robert B. Lamb, *Political Alienation in Contemporary America* (New York: St. Martins, 1975), p. 14.

4. W. Phillips Shively, *The Craft of Political Research,* 5th Ed. (New York: Prentice-Hall, 2002).

5. Abraham Kaplan, *The Conduct of Inquiry* (San Francisco: Chandler Publishing, 1964), p. 55.

6. Edward G. Carmines and Richard A. Zeller, *Reliability and Validity Assessment* (Beverly Hills, CA: Sage Publications, 1979), p. 10.

7. Shively, *The Craft of Political Research,* p. 60.

8. Much of our discussion of the methods for establishing validity and reliability relies on Carmines and Zeller, *Reliability and Validity Assessment,* and Gene F. Summers (Ed.), *Attitude Measurement* (Skokie, IL: Rand McNally, 1970).

9. Carmines and Zeller, *Reliability and Validity Assessment,* p. 20.

10. Ibid., p. 23.

11. J. Miller McPherson, Susan Welch, and Cal Clark, "The Stability and Reliability of Political Efficacy: Using Path Analysis to Test Alternative Models," *American Political Science Review,* 71 (June 1977): 509–521.

12. A book full of interesting and useful approaches to unobtrusive measures is Eugene F. Webb, Donald T. Campbell, Richard D. Schwartz, and Lee Sechrest, *Unobtrusive Measures* (Chicago: Rand McNally, 1966).

Chapter 8

1. SPSS has an excellent on-screen help system as part of its program that should be reviewed when trying *any* new procedure. The company also produces a series of written users' and applications guides that can be ordered from their Web site. Two introductory guides to SPSS are listed in the selected readings for this chapter.

Chapter 9

1. James L. Gibson and Raymond M. Duch, "Political Tolerance in the USSR: The Distribution and Etiology of Mass Opinion," *Comparative Political Studies,* 26 (1993): 286–329.

2. Charles L. Davis and John G. Speer, "The Psychological Bases of Regime Support Among Urban Workers in Venezuela and Mexico: Instrumental or Expressive?" *Comparative Political Studies,* 24 (1991): 319–343.

3. A description of weighting for disproportionate stratified samples can be found in Leslie Kish, *Survey Sampling* (New York: John Wiley, 1965), pp. 390–393.

4. A description of the multistage sampling process and an example of a respondent selection card can be found in the *Interviewer's Manual: Survey Research Center* (Ann Arbor: Institute for Social Research, University of Michigan, 1976).

5. See Gary T. Henry, *Practical Sampling* (Newbury Park, CA: Sage Publications, 1990), pp. 111–115.

6. "Scientists Solve Mystery of Sex-Survey Numbers," *Providence Journal* (October 10, 2000), p. A9.

7. Paul J. Lavrakas, *Telephone Survey Methods: Sampling, Selection, and Supervision* (Newbury Park, CA: Sage Publications, 1987), pp. 14–15.

8. Herbert Asher, *Polling and the Public: What Every Citizen Should Know,* 4th Ed. (Washington, DC: Congressional Quarterly Press, 1998), p. 66.

9. Robert E. Lane, *Political Ideology* (New York: Free Press, 1962).

10. The formula for estimating standard error (equivalent to sampling error) for averages or means will be considered in a later chapter. Sampling error is most frequently considered by social scientists for proportions, so we provide more detail for it in this chapter.

Chapter 10

1. An interesting history of survey research in the United States is Jean M. Converse, *Survey Research in the United States: Roots and Emergence, 1890–1960* (Berkeley: University of California Press, 1987).

2. For a very useful definition of public opinion, see Robert E. Lane and David O. Sears, *Public Opinion* (Englewood Cliffs, NJ: Prentice-Hall, 1964), Chapter 2.

3. See Rensis Likert, "Technique for the Measurement of Attitudes," *Archives of Psychology,* 22, no. 140 (1932): 1–55.

4. See Charles E. Osgood, George J. Suci, and Percy H. Tannenbaum, *The Measurement of Meaning* (Urbana, IL: University of Illinois Press, 1957).

5. For a discussion of measuring "nonattitudes" and some solutions to the problem, see Herbert Asher, *Polling and the Public: What Every Citizen Should Know,* 4th Ed. (Washington, DC: Congressional Quarterly Press, 1998), Chapter 2.

6. Herbert F. Weisberg, Jon. A. Krosnick, and Bruce D. Bowen, *An Introduction to Survey Research and Data Analysis,* 2nd Ed. (Glenview, IL: Scott, Foresman, 1989), pp. 72–73.

7. See Howard Schulman and Stanley Presser, *Questions and Answers in Attitude Surveys* (New York: New York Academic Press, 1981).

8. For an extensive discussion with examples of common problems with question wording, see Charles H. Backstrom and Gerald Hursh-Cesar, *Survey Research*, 2nd Ed. (New York: Wiley, 1981), pp. 140–153.

9. Ibid., p. 154.

10. For a checklist of important factors to consider in formatting a survey instrument, see Seymour Sudman and Norman M Bradburn, *Asking Questions: A Practical Guide to Questionnaire Design* (San Francisco: Jossey-Bass, 1982), p. 230.

11. For a discussion of criteria to be used in deciding how to administer a survey instrument, see Floyd J. Fowler Jr., *Survey Research Methods*, Rev. Ed. (Newbury Park, CA: Sage Publications, 1988), Chapter 4.

12. A useful example of a guide to interviewer training is the *Interviewers' Manual*, Rev. Ed. (Ann Arbor: Institute for Social Research, 1976). See also Pamela J. Guenzel, Tracy R. Beckmans, and Charles F. Cannell, *General Interviewing Techniques* (Ann Arbor: Institute for Social Research, 1983).

13. A thorough description of administration of surveys over the telephone can be found in James H. Frey, *Survey Research by Telephone*, 2nd Ed. (Newbury Park, CA: Sage Publications, 1989), Chapter 5.

14. The most comprehensive discussion of CATI is found at the Web site for the University of California's Computer-Assisted Survey Methods Program. In addition to computer-assisted telephone interviewing, the site provides information on sampling, questionnaire design, and analysis. You can reach the Web site at *http://socrates.berkeley.edu:7500/CSM/csmmission.html.*

15. See the table listing the effectiveness of techniques for increasing returns of mail questionnaires in Delbert Miller, *Handbook of Research Design and Social Measurement*, 5th Ed. (Newbury Park, CA: Sage Publications, 1991), pp. 77–78.

Chapter 11

1. Ted Robert Gurr, *Politimetrics: An Introduction to Quantitative Macropolitics* (Englewood Cliffs, NJ: Prentice-Hall, 1972), p. 53.

2. See Richard Merritt, *Systematic Approaches to Comparative Politics* (Chicago: Rand McNally, 1970), p. 27.

3. Ibid., pp. 28–36.

4. For a full description see *http://europa.eu.int/comm/dg10/epo/eb.html.*

5. Robert S. Erikson, Gerald C. Wright, and John P. McIver, *Statehouse Democracy: Public Opinion and Policy in the American States* (New York: Cambridge University Press, 1993).

6. Cornelius P. Cotter, et al., *Party Organizations in American Politics* (New York: Praeger, 1984).

7. David C. McClelland, *The Achieving Society* (Princeton, NJ: Van Nostrand, 1961).

8. Pippa Norris, *Digital Divide? Civic Engagement, Information Poverty and the Internet in Democratic Societies* (New York: Cambridge University Press, 2001).

9. Gurr, *Politimetrics,* pp. 92–111.

10. Seymour Martin Lipset, *Political Man: The Social Basis of Politics* (Garden City, NY: Doubleday, 1960).

11. Tatu Vanhanen, *The Process of Democratization: A Comparative Study of 147 States, 1980–1988* (New York: Crane Restock, 1990).

12. James Q. Wilson and Edward C. Banfield, "Public-Regardingness as a Value Premise in Voting Behavior," *American Political Science Review,* 58 (1964): 876–887.

13. Harold D. Lasswell, Daniel Lerner, and Ithiel de Sola Pool, *The Comparative Study of Symbols* (Palo Alto, CA: Stanford University Press, 1952), p. 12.

14. Ole R. Holsti, *Content Analysis for the Social Sciences and Humanities* (Reading, MA: Addison-Wesley, 1969), p. 1.

15. Jisuk Woo, "Television News Discourse in Political Transition: Framing the 1987 and 1992 Korean Presidential Elections," *Political Communication,* 13 (1996): 63–80.

16. Darrell West, *Air Wars: Television Advertising in Election Campaigns, 1952–1996*, 3rd Ed. (Washington, DC: Congressional Quarterly Press, 2001), Chapter 3.

17. Thomas E. Patterson, *Out of Order* (New York: Alfred A. Knopf, 1993), p. 23.

18. David S. Meyer, "Framing National Security: Elite Public Discourse on Nuclear Weapons During the Cold War," *Political Communication,* 12 (1995): 173–192.

19. Mary Beth Oliver, "Portrayals of Crime, Race, and Aggression in 'Reality-Based' Police Shows: A Content Analysis," *Journal of Broadcasting and Electronic Media* (1994): 179–192.

20. Norris, *Digital Divide?* Chapter 5.

Chapter 12

1. Harold Lasswell, "Intensive and Extensive Methods of Observing the Personality—Culture Manifold," *Yenching Journal of Social Studies*, 1 (1938): 72–86.
2. Robert K. Yin, *Case Study Research: Design and Methods*, Rev. Ed. (Beverly Hills, CA: Sage Publications, 1989), pp. 17–19.
3. Steven R. Brown, "Intensive Analysis in Political Research," *Political Methodology*, 1 (1974): 3.
4. Ibid., 5.
5. Harry M. Scoble, *Ideology and Electoral Action, A Comparative Case Study of the National Committee for an Effective Congress* (San Francisco: Chandler Publishing, 1967); Jo Freeman, *The Politics of Women's Liberation, A Case Study of an Emerging Social Movement and Its Relation to the Policy Process* (New York: David McKay Company, 1975).
6. Seymour Martin Lipset, Martin A. Trow, and James S. Coleman, *Union Democracy: The Internal Politics of the International Typographical Union* (Garden City, NY: Doubleday, 1956).
7. Robert Dahl, *Who Governs? Democracy and Power in an American City* (New Haven: Yale University Press, 1967).
8. Marion Orr, "Black Political Recall and Black Politics: A Case Study," in Hanes Walton, Jr., Ed., *Black Politics and Black Political Behavior: A Linkage Analysis* (Westport, CT: Praeger, 1994).
9. Yin, *Case Study Research*, p. 21. Yin's work is relied upon heavily for our discussion of case studies.
10. Ibid., p. 23.
11. Theda Skocpol, *Boomerang: Clinton's Health Security Effort and the Turn Against Government in U.S. Politics* (New York: W. W. Norton, 1996).
12. Donald T. Campbell and Julian C. Stanley, *Experimental and Quasi-Experimental Designs for Research* (Chicago: Rand McNally, 1966).
13. Nehemia Geva and D. Christopher Hanson, "Cultural Similarity, Foreign Policy Actions, and Regime Perception: An Experimental Study of International Cues and Democratic Peace," *Political Psychology*, 20, no. 4 (1999): 812.
14. Alan S. Gerber, "The Effects of Canvassing, Telephone Calls, and Direct Mail on Voter Turnout: A Field Experiment," *The American Political Science Review*, 94 (September 2000): 653–664.
15. Jeanne B. Grossman and Joseph P. Tierney, "Does Mentoring Work? An Impact Study of the Big Brothers and Big Sisters Program," *Evaluation Review*, 22 (June 1998): 403–426.
16. Thomas D. Cook and Donald T. Campbell, *Quasi-Experimentation: Design and Analysis Issues for Field Settings* (Chicago: Rand McNally, 1979).
17. Diana Burgess et al., "Rocking the Vote: Using Personalized Messages to Motivate Voting Among Young Adults," *Public Opinion Quarterly*, 64 (Spring 2000): 29–52.
18. James Simon and Bruce D. Merrill, "Political Socialization in the Classroom Revisited: The Kids Voting Program," *Social Science Journal*, 35, no. 1 (1998), 29–42.
19. Our discussion of Q-technique relies on Bruce McKeown and Dan Thomas, *Q Methodology* (Newbury Park, CA: Sage Publications, 1988).
20. For a description of factor analysis, see Jae-On Kim and Charles W. Mueller, *Introduction to Factor Analysis* (Newbury Park, CA: Sage Publications, 1978).
21. The research described in this section can be found in James M. Carlson and Richard M. Martin, "Conceptions of Representation: A Study of Delegates to the 1984 National Party Conventions," *American Politics Quarterly*, 15 (July 1987): 355–372.
22. The most comprehensive and definitive discussion of the application of Q-technique to problems of interest to political scientists can be found in Steven R. Brown, *Political Subjectivity: Applications of Q Methodology in Political Science* (New Haven: Yale University Press, 1980).
23. David L. Morgan, *Focus Groups as Qualitative Research* (Newbury Park, CA: Sage Publications, 1988).
24. Cindy Simon Rosenthal, *When Women Lead: Integrative Leadership in State Legislatures* (New York: Oxford University Press, 1998), p. 171.
25. Marion R. Just et al., *Crosstalk: Citizens, Candidates, and the Media in a Presidential Campaign* (Chicago: University of Chicago Press, 1996), p. 28.
26. Jarol B. Mannheim and Richard C. Rich, *Empirical Political Analysis* (White Plains, NY: Longman Publishers, 1995).

Chapter 13

1. For the sense of excitement that comes with developing new knowledge, read James D. Watson, *The Double Helix: A Personal Account of the Discovery of the Structure of DNA* (New York: Atheneum, 1968).

2. For a discussion of political culture in the American states, see Daniel J. Elezar, *American Federalism: A View from the States,* 3rd Ed. (New York: Harper and Row, 1984).

3. Edward R. Tufte, *The Visual Display of Quantitative Information* (Cheshire, CT: Graphics Press, 1983).

4. If one were to employ the absolute values of the deviation scores rather than the square of them, the statistic obtained with the formula is called the "average" or mean deviation. It is discussed here for help with understanding the logic behind the standard deviation, which is the preferred statistic.

5. The standard deviation formula shown is for a population. For samples, N is replaced with (N–1).

Chapter 14

1. We chose gamma for the measure of association with ordinal variables because it is intuitively obvious and thus appropriate, we feel, for an introduction to this material.

2. See John Mueller, Karl Schuessler, and Herbert Costner, *Statistical Reasoning in Sociology,* 3rd Ed. (Boston: Houghton Mifflin, 1977), pp. 186–194.

Chapter 15

1. Bivariate linear regression analysis can be employed with a dichotomous, nominally measured variable as either the independent or dependent variable. The dichotomous variable is referred to as a "dummy variable." See K. J. Meier and J. L. Brudney, *Applied Statistics for Public Administration,* 4th Ed. (Fort Worth, TX: Harcourt Brace College Publishers, 1997), pp. 327–330, for examples of both of these procedures.

2. For a discussion of regression to the mean and examples, see "How Regression Got Its Name," at *http://www.stat.wmich.edu/s160/book/node70.html,* and "Regression to the Mean" at *http://trochim.human.cornell.edu/kb/regrmean.htm.*

3. Both the idea and data for this example were provided by Greg Adams of Carnegie Mellon University and Chris Fastnow of Chatham College. See *http://madison.hss.cmu.edu/.*

4. You should note that sometimes the regression line intercepts the Y-axis below zero, producing a negative Y-intercept, which in an example as the one here, makes no substantive sense. One cannot know a negative percentage of legislators.

5. See John L. Philips, Jr., *How to Think About Statistics,* 5th Ed. (New York: W. H. Freeman and Co., 1996), pp. 70–73.

Chapter 16

1. The explanation of control variables relies on both Morris Rosenberg, *The Logic of Survey Analysis* (New York: Basic Books, 1968), and Herbert Hyman, *Survey Design and Analysis* (Glencoe, IL: The Free Press, 1955). Although published almost fifty years ago, Hyman's discussion of control variables and elaboration are still appropriate for an introduction to analyzing survey data.

2. The survey data for this exercise can be found at the American Religion Data Archive: *http://www.arda.tm/datafiles_ix.html.*

3. When using SPSS, the results of a crosstabulation that employs a control variable will in fact produce as many tables as there are values of the control variable. In this example, SPSS produced three bivariate percentage tables with relevant statistics showing the relationship between level of education and abortion attitude. One table had only respondents self-identified as liberals, a second only political moderates, and the third only conservative respondents.

4. The terms *refining, replicating, reducing, revealing,* and *reversal* come from Dickinson McGaw and George Watson, *Political and Social Inquiry* (New York: Wiley, 1976), pp. 437–438.

5. For a clear discussion of calculating beta weights, see R. Mark Sirkin, *Statistics for the Social Sciences,* 2nd Ed. (Thousand Oaks, CA: Sage Publications, 1999), pp. 508–509.

6. For a discussion of this and other problems with using beta weights, see Gary King, "How Not to Lie with Statistics: Avoiding Common Mistakes in Quantitative Political Science," *American Journal of Political Science,* 30, no. 3 (August 1986), 666–687. See also H. M. Blalock, "Causal Inferences, Closed Populations, and Measures of Association," *American Political Science Review,* 61, no. 1 (March 1967): 130–136.

Chapter 17

1. George Ferguson, *Statistical Analysis in Psychology and Education,* 2nd Ed. (New York: McGraw-Hill, 1966), pp. 163–165.

2. With two or more independent variables, multivariate analysis of variance (MANOVA) would be employed. This

procedure groups cases to compare means not only by the values of each independent variable separately but also by all possible combinations of the values of all the independent variables.

Chapter 18

1. Howard S. Becker, *Writing for Social Scientists: How to Start and Finish Your Thesis, Book, or Article* (Chicago: University of Chicago Press, 1986), p. 4.
2. See Louise H. Kidder, *Research Methods for Social Relations,* 4th Ed. (New York: Holt, Rinehart and Winston, 1981), Chapter 14.
3. These articles appeared in the December 1999 issue of the *American Political Science Review.*
4. Kay Lehman Schlozman, Nancy Burns, Sidney Verba, and Jesse Donahue, "Gender and Citizen Participation: Is There a Different Voice?" *American Journal of Political Science,* 39 (May 1995): 268.
5. Ibid., 271.
6. William Strunk, Jr., E. B. White, Charles Osgood, and Roger Angell, *The Elements of Style,* 4th Ed. (New York: Allyn and Bacon, 2000).
7. Becker, *Writing for Social Scientists,* 60.
8. Edward R. Tufte, *The Visual Display of Quantitative Information* (Cheshire, CT: Graphics Press, 1983), p. 13.
9. For a good example of graphic distortion, see Darrell Huff, *How to Lie with Statistics* (New York: W. W. Norton, 1954), pp. 62–63.
10. V. O. Key, *Southern Politics in State and Nation* (New York: Vintage Books, 1949).
11. Floyd Hunter, *Community Power Structure* (Chapel Hill: University of North Carolina Press, 1953).
12. Nicolas Wade, "I.Q. and Heredity: Suspicion of Fraud Beclouds Classic Experiment," *Science,* 194 (1976): 916–919.

Glossary

aggregate data. Data based on aggregation of smaller units of analysis (usually people) that describe groups or collectivities such as countries, cities, schools, or political parties. (11)

alternative forms method. A method for establishing reliability by measuring the same variable more than once using two different but equivalent forms applied to the same units of analysis at different times. (7)

analysis of variance (ANOVA). A statistical procedure that compares the variance in the dependent variable in each of three or more analysis groups with the total variance in the dependent variable. (17)

anonymity. Assurance given to subjects of research that their identity cannot be linked to the information they provide about themselves. (3)

antecedent variable. An independent variable that logically precedes other independent variables in multivariate analyses. (6)

arithmetic mean. (See **mean.**)

association. When the values of two variables covary. A change in the value of one variable is accompanied by a change in another variable. (6)

authority (as a source of knowledge). Authoritative knowledge is acquired from individuals or institutions that are perceived to be credible. Such knowledge is accepted as factual because of the characteristics of the authority. (1)

bar chart. Used for displaying the frequency distribution of variables measured at the nominal or ordinal level. The length or height of a bar represents the number or proportion of cases within each value of the variable. (18)

benchmarks of acceptable risk. Specific levels of risk generally accepted by researchers for making inferences from a probability sample to a population. (17)

beta weight (also standardized regression coefficient). The slope of a regression line after the variables have been standardized. (15)

bivariate analysis. The analysis of two variables simultaneously to determine quantitatively if there is a statistical relationship between them. (13)

Boolean connectors. Used in electronic searches of databases or the Web, these are words such as *and, or,* and *not* that can be used to link or omit concepts in order to narrow or broaden a search. (4)

call numbers. The numbers that are used to organize the holdings of libraries according to subject matter. Most libraries use a call number system established by the Library of Congress. (4)

case study. Examining, usually in considerable detail, a single case on only one occasion. (12)

causal chain. A sequence of variables logically interconnected that purports to explain a dependent variable. (6)

causal hypothesis. A statement that an independent variable causes changes in another variable without exception. (3)

causation. Causation occurs when the change in the dependent variable is a direct result of changes in the independent variable. The variables not only change together, but the change in the dependent variable is *due* to the change in the independent variable. (6)

census. Gathering data from every member of a population, as opposed to a sample or subset of a population. (9)

census data. Information collected by governments about an entire population. (11)

chi square. A statistical measure used with crosstabulation to determine the level of statistical significance. (17)

classic experimental design. An experiment where, at the minimum, the researcher manipulates the independent variable and a pretest and posttest are given to both experimental and control groups in which subjects are randomly assigned. (12)

cleaning data. The process of checking for and correcting errors that might have occurred when information was organized into a data file. (8)

closed-ended questions (also forced-choice questions). Survey questions that provide respondents with a limited number of alternative answers from which they must choose. (10)

cluster sampling. A sampling process in which population elements are divided into a large number of groups often based on geographical boundaries, called clusters. From the comprehensive list of clusters a probability sample is selected. (9)

codebook. A document used for the organization of data that indicates where variables are found in the data file, their names, and the meaning of codes that represent their values. (8)

coefficient of determination. The proportion of variation in a dependent variable that is accounted for or explained by an independent variable, symbolized by r^2. (15)

coefficient of multiple determination. The proportion of variation in a dependent variable that is accounted for or explained by all of the independent variables in a multivariate analysis, symbolized by R^2. (16)

collapse a variable. Combine values of a variable to simplify analysis.

comparative value statement. A statement that compares the relative worth of objects or ideas in terms of an individual's values. (3)

comparison group. Any control group in an experimental research design that has members not randomly assigned. (12)

compound hypothesis. A hypothesis that states a relationship between more than two variables. (3)

concept. An abstract term that represents and organizes characteristics of objects, phenomena, and ideas. (3)

conceptualization. Defining concepts so that their meanings are precise and closely related to theory. Definitions of concepts should be acceptable to scholars in the field to facilitate communication. (7)

concurrent validity. One of two forms of criterion-related validity. Validity is demonstrated by measuring the predictor and criterion at the same time. (7)

condensed table. A multivariate table in which only one value of the dependent variable is shown. (16)

confidentiality. A promise offered by a researcher to a subject that information provided by the subject will not be revealed to anyone but those who are working on the research project. (3)

confounding factors. Additional independent variables that may be affecting dependent variables of interest. (12)

consistency bias. A problem encountered in survey research when respondents are motivated to answer questions in a way that makes them sound logical and consistent. (10)

construct validity. The extent to which a measured variable relates to other variables in ways predicted by a specific theory. (7)

content analysis. A research technique that is used to collect and analyze the recorded content of written and electronic communications. (11)

content validity. The extent to which a measure covers the full domain of the meaning of a concept. (7)

contingency questions. Questions in a survey that are asked only of some respondents who answered a previous question in a specified way. Used in conjunction with *filter questions*. (10)

control group. A group in an experiment that is identical to experimental groups but whose members are not exposed to experimental treatment. (See **experimental group.**) (12)

control variable. An alternative independent variable that is introduced and held constant in an analysis to determine its effect on the relationship between two other variables. (6)

convenience sampling. A type of nonprobability sampling for which the most available elements in a population are selected. Sometimes called *accidental* or *haphazard* samples. (9)

criterion-related validity (sometimes called predictive validity). The extent to which a measure is actually correlated to another distinct measure to which it should be logically related. (7)

crosstabulation. A joint frequency distribution of variables in which one variable is classified in terms of another. A technique for analyzing the relationship between variables measured at the nominal or ordinal level. (14)

cumulative percentage. Associated with frequency distributions of variables. It is the additive percentage of cases when each additional category, or value, of the variable is displayed. (13)

data archives. Libraries that maintain large numbers of data sets collected in previous research. The leading archive of political data in the United States is the Inter-University

Consortium of Political and Social Research at the University of Michigan. (10)

data file.   A computer file used to store data in a specified format. (8)

data matrix.   A template used to organize quantitative data and prepare it for analysis. The basic format lists cases by rows and variables by columns to form a grid. Values of variables for cases are placed within the matrix. (8)

debriefing.   A session with research subjects conducted by a researcher after an experimental study to explain the purpose of the study and the nature of any deception that was employed.

deductive reasoning.   A logical process through which generalizations about the world are used to generate specific statements about distinct events or behaviors. (See also **inductive reasoning.**) (2)

dependent variable.   The variable that is affected by or *depends* on other (*independent*) variables. It is usually the variable that research is designed to explain. (6)

description.   Information about a single variable or a single case. (2)

descriptive question.   A question asking about the characteristics of reality rather than seeking an explanation. (1)

descriptive statistics.   Summary of values of a single variable commonly using measurements of central tendency and dispersion. (13)

deviation score.   The difference between a score or value of a variable and the mean score for the distribution of that variable. Deviation scores will always add up to zero. (13)

dichotomous variable.   A nominal-level variable with only two possible categories or values. (13)

direction of a relationship.   How the values of two variables are associated. (See **positive** and **negative relationships.**) (6, 14)

directional hypothesis.   A hypothesis that specifically states how the values of two variables are related, not simply that they are associated. (3)

disproportionate stratified sample.   A stratified sample in which sample elements of selected groups (or strata) are overrepresented or underrepresented with respect to the entire population. This sampling method may be used to ensure that individuals from specified groups (usually because of their small numbers in the population) are included in the sample. (9)

ecological fallacy.   An ecological fallacy occurs when the analysis of collectivities is used to make inferences about individuals. (11)

elaboration.   The process of examining the effects of control variables on the relationship between two variables included in an original hypothesis. (6)

element.   The entity about which a survey researcher collects information. (9)

empirical political analysis.   Using the scientific method to test one's ideas about politics by collecting and analyzing information. (1)

empirical (fact-based) question.   A question that can be answered by gathering information through a combination of the use of senses and reasoning. (1)

error component.   Unexplained variation of the dependent variable in a regression equation. (15)

evaluative statement.   The expression of a judgment about an object or idea that is based on personal values or preferences. (3)

event statistics.   A type of data used to describe collectivities such as countries or cities. Events, such as demonstrations and resignations of government officials, are recorded for a specific time period, summarized, and used as variables to describe the units of analysis. (11)

expected frequencies.   The number of cases anticipated in each cell of a crosstabulation if the two variables being analyzed are unrelated. (17)

experimental group.   Groups of subjects in experiments that are exposed to experimental treatment. (See **control group.**) (12)

experimental mortality.   The loss of subjects from experimental and control groups over time. Experimental mortality can be a threat to internal validity. (12)

explanation.   Statement that makes clear the cause or reason for a phenomenon. (2)

explanatory question.   A question about why a particular state of affairs exists or the cause of some behavior. (1)

extensive approach.   Answering research questions by collecting a relatively small amount of information from a large number of units of analysis. (See **intensive approach.**) (12)

external validity.   The extent to which the results of an experiment can be generalized to other populations and situations. (12)

F-test.   A procedure to determine the level of statistical significance among means from three or more analysis groups. (17)

face validity.   Similar to content validity; asserted but not demonstrated empirically that a measurement makes sense and is consistent with a common and accepted definition of a concept. (7)

face-to-face interviews.   A method of administering a survey involving a direct social interaction between interviewer and respondent; the interviewer asks questions and the respondent provides answers. (10)

factorial design.   An experimental design in which more than one independent variable is employed. (12)

faith (as a source of knowledge).   Knowledge or belief that is not based on empirical proof. (1)

field experiment.   An experiment that is conducted in a real-world setting, as opposed to a laboratory. It is more difficult to impose controls in field experiments, but they tend to have greater external validity. (12)

filter questions (also screening questions).   Survey questions that are designed to separate respondents into groups based on background characteristics, opinions, or behaviors so they can be asked relevant contingency questions. (See **contingency question.**) (10)

focus group.   Small groups brought together by a researcher for the purpose of directed discussion in order to learn how people think about a specific topic. (12)

frequency distribution.   A way of arranging the number of cases for each value (category) of a variable, usually presented in numbers and percentages. (8)

frequency polygon.   Univariate line graphs on which an interval/ratio level variable is scaled on the X-axis and the frequency or proportion of each value is scaled on the Y-axis, indicating the shape of the distribution. (18)

gamma.   A statistic that indicates the strength and direction of an association between two variables measured at the ordinal level. (14)

histogram.   Similar to bar charts, histograms display variables that have been measured at the interval/ratio level and then collapsed into categories. The width of each bar indicates the interval, and each bar in a histogram touches the next bar, indicating the continuous nature of the variable. (18)

history (and validity).   Events occurring in the lives of subjects during an experiment that might affect individual scores on a dependent variable and threaten internal validity. (12)

hypothesis.   A conjectural statement of a relationship, association, or connection between two or more concepts that can be tested empirically. (2)

hypothetical-deductive system.   Describes the logic and procedures of scientific investigation and the ways in which observation and the application of reasoning result in generalizations about the nature of the world. (2)

independent variable.   The variable that is the presumed cause of the variable that researchers are attempting to explain. (See **dependent variable.**) (6)

index.   A measurement device employing a set of combined indicators to produce a summary measure of a concept. (7)

indicator.   Observable evidence that is used to describe a dimension of a variable. (7)

inductive reasoning.   A logical process through which specific observations of phenomena are used to arrive at generalizations. (See also **deductive reasoning.**) (2)

informed consent.   The ethical principle that research subjects must be informed of the purposes of research as well as the risks and benefits that might result from participating. Furthermore, subjects must understand the objectives of the research and freely give their consent before they participate. (3)

institutional review board (IRB).   A committee found in those institutions receiving federal funds for research on human subjects. The purpose of the committee is to review research proposals and ensure that the safety and rights of subjects are protected. (3)

instrumentation.   The process of developing measurement devices. (7)

intensive approach.   Answering research questions by obtaining a wide variety of information from a relatively small number of units of analysis over an extended period of time. (See **extensive approach.**) (12)

interactive effect.   The simultaneous effect of two or more independent variables on a dependent variable. (12)

intercoder reliability.   The level of consensus achieved about how messages will be categorized by multiple coders when doing content analysis. (11)

internal validity.   The extent to which an experiment demonstrates that manipulation of an independent variable causes a change in a dependent variable. (12)

interquartile range.   The range of values in which the middle 50 percent of observations are found. (13)

intersubjective agreement.   The level of common perception between two or more observers about how a phenomenon should be described. (1)

interval level of measurement.   A scale of measurement that not only rank-orders values of a variable but also displays equal intervals between values. (See **nominal level, ordinal level,** and **ratio level.**) (7)

intervening variable.   A control variable that is logically placed between the independent and dependent variables in an original hypothesis. (6)

investment (as a source of knowledge). Persistently holding fast to knowledge or belief based on one's stake in that position. (1)

judgmental data. Measures that are based on the opinions of experts in categorizing units of analysis (usually collectivities) on the values of a particular variable. (11)

judgmental sample (or purposive samples). Nonprobability sample; the researcher selects the sample units of analysis believed to be representative of a population. (9)

keywords and phrases. Used in bibliographical searches of Internet or library databases, these are words or phrases that are related to the topic or concept of interest. (4)

lambda. A statistic that indicates the strength and direction of an association between two variables measured at the nominal level. (14)

latent content. Deeper meanings of media messages that may be categorized using content analysis. (See **content analysis** and **manifest content.**) (11)

levels of measurement. The amount of information and degree of precision that a measurement provides. (7)

linear regression analysis. A statistical analysis that involves determining the best-fit straight line between two variables measured at the interval/ratio level. (15)

logic (as a source of knowledge). A means of acquiring knowledge through mental reflection. (1)

macro level of analysis. Research that involves the analysis of units that are defined geographically such as countries, states, provinces, or cities. (11)

main effect. The direct effect of independent variables on dependent variables in an experiment. (12)

manifest content. Visible surface content of media messages that easily lends itself to the development of categories and counting for purposes of content analysis. (See also **latent content.**) (11)

marginals. The totals of the columns and rows in a cross-tabulation, so called because they are found at the margins of the table. (17)

maturation. The change in subjects due to maturity and experience between a pretest and posttest in an experiment, a potential threat to internal validity. (12)

mean (arithmetic mean). A measure of central tendency for variables measured at the interval/ratio level. Calculated by adding up the values for all cases and then dividing by the number of cases. (13)

measurement. The process by which numbers are assigned to units of analysis based on specific rules and procedures. (7)

measurement error. The difference between a concept and its operational definition and measurement. This is a general problem because the process of observation always leads to some error. (7)

measure of association. A statistic that summarizes the strength and direction of a relationship between variables. (14)

measures of central tendency. Summaries of frequency distributions that indicate the most frequent, middle, or central value. (See **mode, median,** and **mean.**) (13)

measures of dispersion. Measures that summarize the distribution of values around a measure of central tendency, such as a mean. (13)

median. The middle point in an ordered distribution of values. Divides the values of the distribution into equal halves; mostly used for variables measured at the ordinal level. (13)

median group. Whichever category of an ordinally measured variable that contains the middle score. (13)

micro level of analysis. A focus on people or traits of people as units of analysis. (See **macro level of analysis.**) (11)

modal category. The category of a variable that contains the greatest number of cases. (13)

mode. A measure of central tendency. The most frequently occurring value or category of a variable. (13)

multigroup design. An experimental design in which the independent variable has more than two values; an additional experimental group is added for each value of the independent variable beyond two. (12)

multigroup time series design. Experimental designs with multiple pretests and posttests. (12)

multiple correlation coefficient. A measure of association between a dependent variable and two or more independent variables measured at the interval/ratio level. (16)

multiple linear regression. A technique for measuring the relationship between a dependent variable and two or more independent variables. The influence of each independent variable on the dependent variable can be determined by holding other independent variables constant. (16)

multistage cluster sampling. A form of probability sampling that proceeds through a series of stages where defined clusters or groups are sampled in the early stages and people are sampled at the last stage. (9)

multivariate analysis.   Analysis involving the simultaneous exploration of the relationship among more than two variables. (13, 16)

multivariate percentage table.   Percentage table that presents relationships between three or more variables measured at the nominal or ordinal levels. (16)

natural experiment.   An experiment during which experimental and control groups occur naturally in the real world and are not selected randomly by the researcher. (12)

necessity.   A criterion used to infer a causal relationship. Changes in an independent variable must be necessary for producing changes in a dependent variable. (6)

negative relationship.   Relationship between two variables that vary in the opposite direction; as the values of one variable increase, the values of another decrease. (See **positive relationship.**) (14)

nesting.   A technique used for multivariate analysis of relationships between variables measured at the nominal or ordinal level. Bivariate tables showing the relationship between an independent and dependent variable are reproduced for each value of a control variable. (16)

nominal definition.   A definition using words that is assigned to a concept by a researcher during the process of narrowing the concept to several variables. (7)

nominal level of measurement.   Classifies units of analysis without rank ordering. Categories or values are mutually exclusive and collectively exhaustive. (See ordinal, interval, and ratio levels). (7)

nonprobability sample.   Samples that are selected at the researcher's discretion and offer no guarantees against selection bias. Each sampling element has an unknown probability of being selected. (9)

nonrandom measurement error.   Measurement error that is the result of the measurement process itself. (7)

normal curve (or normal distribution).   A frequency curve with a bell-shaped distribution and an identical mean, mode, and median. A fixed proportion of cases are found between the mean and any distance from the mean. (13)

normative (value-based) question.   A question that is value-laden and concerned with prescription or evaluation. (1)

null hypothesis.   States that there is no relationship between variables. This hypothesis is confirmed or rejected by tests of significance. (6)

observed frequencies.   The number of cases found in each cell of a crosstabulation. (17)

one-tailed test.   The testing of a directional hypothesis by comparing two means. (17)

online writing laboratory (OWL).   Laboratories on college and university campuses where students and others submit their written work online to receive advice and assistance. (18)

open-ended questions.   Survey questions that allow respondents to structure their own answers using their own words. (See **closed-ended questions.**) (10)

operationalization.   The process of defining concepts, allowing them to be measured using empirical evidence. (7)

ordinal level of measurement.   Classifies units of analysis into categories or dimensions that have an inherent hierarchical order, but the size of the differences between categories is unknown. (7)

outlier.   Value (or data point) plotted on a graph that deviates from the trends in the data. (15)

P-sample.   The sample of persons analyzed in a study using Q-technique. (12)

parameter.   The actual characteristics of populations of units of analysis, which are often inferred using samples. (9)

partial regression coefficient.   A statistic that indicates how much change occurs in a dependent variable if an independent variable changes one unit and other variables in the regression equation were simultaneously held constant. (16)

Pearson correlation coefficient.   A statistic that indicates the strength and direction of a relationship between two variables measured at the interval/ratio level. (15)

percentage table.   Displays the proportion (as opposed to the raw numbers) of units of analysis for categories of variables. (14)

percentile.   A value or rank below which a certain percentage of cases are found. (13)

pie chart.   A circular graph indicating the frequency distribution of a variable. The circle (pie) represents the whole amount, and each part (slice) represents proportional segments. (18)

plagiarism.   Incorporation of someone else's words or ideas into a research report without proper acknowledgment of the source. (18)

population (or universe).   The total set of units of analysis about which researchers wish to generalize. (9)

population element.   A single member of a population about which the researcher collects information. (9)

positive relationship.   Relationship between two variables that vary in the same direction. As the values of one variable increase, the values of another increase. (See **negative relationship**.) (14)

posttest. Measurement of the dependent variable in an experiment after subjects have been exposed to the independent variable. This measurement is compared to the pretest. (12)

prediction. Use of explanation to foretell the outcome of future events. (2)

predictive validity. A type of criterion-related validity, established when used successfully to predict a future event or behavior. (7)

prescriptive value statement. A value (normative) statement characterized by the imperative terms such as "should" or "ought." (3)

pretest. Measurement of the dependent variable in an experiment before the subjects have been exposed to the independent variable. Compared to the posttest. (12)

pretesting (survey instruments). Presenting a survey instrument to a few respondents prior to exposure to a full sample in order to identify such potential problems as question wording and time required for administration. (10)

probability sample. A sample selected in a manner consistent with probability theory in which every population element has a known probability of being selected. (9)

program evaluation. A component of the study of public administration; attempts to measure the effects of public programs on intended clients using experimental designs. (12)

proportionate reduction of error. Used in the prediction of the strength of association between variables. A ratio of the number of errors in predicting a dependent variable that occur if there is no information about the independent variable to the errors that occur when information about the independent variable is available. (14)

proportionate stratified sampling. A form of probability sampling in which populations are stratified and samples selected based on known characteristics of population elements. Care is taken to ensure that samples of subgroups (strata) are proportionate to their representation in the population. (9)

Q-sample. A deliberate sample of statements or stimuli chosen from a population of communications. Used for Q-sorts when Q-technique is used for data collection. (12)

Q-sort. Respondents indicate their viewpoints by sorting statements or stimuli along a continuum (often ranging from strong agreement to strong disagreement) according to specific instructions. Used in studies that employ Q-technique for data collection. (12)

Q-technique. An intensive approach to data collection aimed at the study of human subjectivity. (12)

qualitative research methods. Used to describe a situation, phenomenon, or event within a natural setting. Analysis focuses on subtleties generally not amenable to a quantitative comparison of representative cases.

quasi-experiment. A research design that approximates an experiment but lacks some important elements of control (such as random assignment of subjects to groups); is often employed in applied research. (12)

quota sampling. A form of nonprobability sampling in which units are selected in proportion to their representation in the population. (9)

random assignment. Assigning subjects to groups in experiments so that membership is determined completely by chance, resulting in groups that can be considered equivalent. (12)

random digit dialing. A method of selecting a probability sample of telephone numbers (usually by computer) for a survey conducted by telephone. (9)

random measurement error. Error that occurs in measuring variables that is randomly distributed across units of analysis. Over repeated applications of measurement of the same variable, an equivalent number of results will be greater than and less than the actual value. (7)

range. A measure of dispersion indicating the difference between the highest and lowest values or scores of a variable in a set of observations. (13)

ratio level of measurement. A level of measurement that has all of the characteristics of lower levels of measurement (see **nominal, ordinal,** and **interval levels**) as well as a true zero point. (7)

recode a variable. Combining values of a variable for purposes of simplifying analysis. (8)

recording units. Units of data collected in content analyses. Examples are sentences or paragraphs in written communications, people, and characters portrayed in television news or entertainment broadcasts. (11)

reducing effect. When controlling for the effects of a third variable, the strength of the original relationship between two variables is diminished. (16)

refining effect. When controlling for the effects of a third variable, the original relationship survives only under specific conditions. (16)

regression coefficient. The slope of a regression line between two variables measured at the interval/ratio level; represented as b. (15)

regression line. The straight line that best fits the data points on a scatterplot and describes the association between two variables measured at the interval/ratio level. (15)

reliability. The stability and consistency of a measurement. A measure is reliable to the extent that it produces the same results over repeated applications. (7)

replicating effect. When controlling for the effects of a third variable, the original relationship is unchanged. (16)

replication. Retesting tests of hypotheses to see if the same results are produced at different points in time and/or under different conditions. Important for confirming research results. (3)

research design. A plan to show how research questions under study will be answered. Especially important for explanatory research to plan how extraneous independent variables will be controlled for. (6)

residual. The difference between a value for a dependent variable predicted by a regression line and the actual value of the variable for a specific unit of analysis. (15)

response set bias. Respondents to a survey, through acquiescence, provide the same answers to a series of items with identical response categories without paying careful attention to each question. (10)

revealing effect. When controlling for the effects of a third variable, a relationship between two variables is revealed that was not apparent in a bivariate analysis. (16)

reversal effect. When controlling for the effects of a third variable, the direction of the original relationship between two variables is reversed (from positive to negative or vice versa) under specific conditions. (16)

saliency bias. Respondent's attention to a particular issue or behavior in a survey is aroused by a question. Depending on the order of questions in the survey instrument, responses to later questions on the same topic may be biased. (10)

sample. A subgroup chosen for analysis to represent a population. (9)

sampling element. Individual units of analysis included in a sample. (9)

sampling error. The difference between a sample statistic and a population parameter. (See **parameter.**) (9)

sampling frame. The enumerated list of elements in a study population from which a sample is drawn. (9)

sampling interval. Used for a systematic sample; determined by dividing the total number of the sample frame by the desired sample size. (9)

sampling ratio. The proportion of a population that is sampled. (9)

scale. A multi-indicator measure of a concept that can identify patterns of intensity or structure. (7)

scatterplot. A technique for displaying the relationship between two variables measured at the interval/ratio level; the independent variable is plotted on the horizontal (X-axis) and the dependent variable on the vertical (Y-axis). (15)

science. A method of research using empirical data to develop generalizations about phenomena. (1)

search engine. A computer program that can be used to search databases, like those maintained by libraries and the Internet. (4)

secondary analysis. The analysis of data collected by others in an earlier study. (10)

self-administered questionnaires. Survey questionnaires that are completed by respondents themselves as opposed to being administered by an interviewer. (10)

simple posttest design. An experimental design with severe shortcomings where subjects in experimental and control groups are not given a pretest but are administered a posttest. (12)

simple random sample. Probability sample in which each element, and every possible combination of elements, in a sampling frame have an equal likelihood of being selected. (9).

slope. In linear regression analysis, indicates how much change in the value of the dependent variable is associated with a change in the value of the independent variable. (15)

snowball sampling. A nonprobability sample in which the researcher selects a few respondents who possess the qualities being studied (for example, membership in an elite group) and asks them to identify others with similar characteristics or interests. (9)

Solomon four group design. A comprehensive experimental design that takes into account the possible confounding effects of a pretest and treatment. Two groups are added to the classic experimental design. (12)

split-halves method. A means of establishing the reliability of a multi-item index; involves splitting the items into two equal halves, administering them to the same group of subjects, and comparing the results. (7)

SPSS. Statistical Package for the Social Sciences. Statistical computer software that is used extensively by social scientists. (8)

spurious relationship. A relationship between two variables that appears to be causal, but actually is the result of the effects of a third variable. (6)

standard deviation. A measure of dispersion of values around the mean for variables measured at the interval/ratio level. (13)

standard error. The standard deviation of the distribution of sample means. A statistic that indicates the degree of sampling error. (13)

standard error of the estimate. Square root of the average squared error of the regression estimates. (17)

standard score. Scores in a distributions that have been converted to standard deviation units. (13)

statistic. A characteristic of a sample and an *estimate* of a population parameter. (9)

statistical significance. The likelihood that a relationship found in a probability sample exists in the population from which the sample was drawn. (17)

stratified sampling. A form of probability sampling where a population is divided into groups, called strata, and then a probability sample is chosen from elements in each stratified group. (9)

strength of a relationship. The extent to which the values of two or more variables consistently vary together. (6, 14)

study population. The group of elements (sampling elements) from which a sample is actually selected. (9)

style manual. A reference book that provides information and examples regarding the written format of research reports; includes information on such matters as formatting headings, footnotes, bibliographies, and statistical tables. (18)

subsample method. A method for establishing the reliability of measurements by comparing results based on subsamples of a larger sample. (7)

substantive significance. The extent to which research findings are theoretically worthwhile or provide new or different knowledge. (17)

sufficiency. A criterion used to infer a causal relationship. Changes in an independent variable must be sufficient for producing changes in a dependent variable. (6)

summation variables. A measure of group characteristics created by combining individual characteristics of members of the group. (11)

survey research. A method of collecting data by directly asking people questions concerning their background characteristics, opinions, knowledge, and behavior. (10)

syntality variables. Variables that describe the qualities of a region or group as a whole, such as American cities being described as having city manager forms of government. (11)

systematic sampling. Sampling by selecting for inclusion every *n*th element on a list. (9)

t-test. A statistical procedure to determine the level of statistical significance between means from two analysis groups. (17)

tautology. A statement or hypothesis that is true by definition and cannot be confirmed or falsified. (3)

telephone survey. Surveys in which respondents are questioned by interviewers over the telephone. (10)

temporal order. A criterion for inferring causality; change in an independent variable must precede the change in the dependent variable in time. (6)

test-retest method. A technique for establishing the reliability of measurements that involves applying the measurement to the same subjects at two different points in time and comparing the results. (7)

theoretical population. The population about which a researcher wishes to develop generalizations. (9)

theories of the middle range. Theories offering reasonably accurate explanations of a limited number of social behaviors. (2)

theory. A unified set of propositions used to explain phenomena. (2)

time series graphs. A line chart that displays a bivariate relationship with dates as the independent variable scaled on the X-axis and the scale for the dependent variable on the Y-axis. (18)

two-tailed test. Testing the null hypothesis by comparing two means. (17)

Type I error. The situation when there is actually no relationship between variables in the population, but based on analysis of sample data, a researcher erroneously concludes that there is; a false positive. (17)

Type II error. The situation when there is in fact a relationship between variables in the population, but based on analysis of sample data, a researcher erroneously concludes that there is not; a false negative. (17)

unit of analysis. The objects (such as the people, countries, political parties, media messages) that a hypothesis describes or explains and are the focus of study. (3)

units of measurement. The distance between units on the axes of a graph. (15)

units of observation. A term used in content analyses to refer to units that may be the basis for data collection but are not the recording units that are described or explained by hypotheses. For example, television newscasts might be sampled units of observation, but news stories contained in the newscast would serve as recording units of interest to the researcher. (11)

univariate statistics.   Statistics that describe a single variable for purposes of description. (13)

unobtrusive measures.   Measurements that do not involve the direct interaction between the researcher and the objects of research (usually people). The goal is to reduce the impact of the observer on measurement in order to reduce error. (7)

validity.   The extent to which a measurement reflects the concept it is intended to measure. (7)

value.   The characteristic of a variable for a particular unit of analysis. (3)

value label.   Descriptive labels given to values of a variable for purposes of analysis and communication. (8)

variable.   Characteristics of units of analysis that take on more than one value. (3)

variable name.   The assigned names of variables designed to facilitate analysis and communication. (8)

variance.   A measure of dispersion of units of analysis around a mean for variables measured at the interval/ratio level. (13)

World Wide Web gateways.   Web sites that contain many linkages to other Web sites that contain information about specific topics. For example, there are Web pages constructed by political scientists that contain numerous linkages to sites containing information about such subjects as the presidential elections. (4)

writing handbook.   Documents that cover such matters as the process of writing, proper grammar, word usage, punctuation, and sentence structure. (18)

Y-intercept.   The point at which a line crosses the Y-axis. (15)

z-score.   A standard score that indicates the number of standard deviation units that a score differs from the mean. (13)

Index

abbreviated bivariate tables, 340–41
abstracts
    for political science articles, 98, 101
    reading, 99
    for research reports, 411–12
    for scholarly articles, 89
accuracy
    in measurement, 151, 155–58
    in observations, 19
    in sampling, 193
"add a digit" approach, 205
additive properties, 153
aggregate data, 255, 459
Almanac of American Politics, 256
AltaVista, 86
alternative forms method, 161, 459
ambiguous questions, 232
American Journal of Political Science, 100, 412
American Political Science Association, 100
American Political Science Review, 45, 89, 90–91,
    419
American Psychological Association (APA) style,
    90–91, 419
America Votes, 259
analysis of variance (ANOVA), 396, 459
annotated bibliographies, 77–78
anonymity, 55–56, 459
antecedent variables, 133–34, 135, 459
arithmetic mean, 315, 317. *See also* mean
Arrow, Kenneth, 6
Arrow's Paradox, 6–7
Ask Jeeves, 77, 87
association of variables
    causation *vs.,* 128, 354
    defined, 128, 459
    temporal order and, 129, 131

audience, for research reports, 408–10
authority
    defined, 10, 459
    scientific literature as, 9
    types of, 5
    as way of knowing, 5–6
averages, 313

Babbie, Earl, 12, 15, 19
background characteristics, 223
bandwagon effect, 12
Banfield, Edward C., 261
bar charts, 311, 425–26, 459
Beck, Susan E., 90
Becker, Howard, 408, 418
bell curve, 320–21
Belmont Report, 50
benchmarks of acceptable risk, 388, 390–91, 459
beneficence, 51
beta weight
    defined, 459
    in linear regression, 354–55
    in multiple regression, 376–77, 380
Beyond Freedom and Dignity (Skinner), 25–26
bias
    consistency, 237
    in disproportionate stratified sampling, 202
    of interviewers, 208–9
    in open-ended questions, 225
    in questions, 231
    response set, 237–38
    saliency, 237
    sampling, 211
    social class, in telephone sampling, 205
    in systematic sampling, 200
bibliographical references, 87–88